The German War Machine in World War II

The German War Machine in World War II

AN ENCYCLOPEDIA

David T. Zabecki, Editor

Foreword by Professor Williamson Murray

ABC-CLIO®

An Imprint of ABC-CLIO, LLC
Santa Barbara, California • Denver, Colorado

Library of Congress Cataloging-in-Publication Data

Names: Zabecki, David T., editor.
Title: The German war machine in World War II : an encyclopedia / David T. Zabecki, editor ; foreword by Professor Williamson Murray.
Description: Santa Barbara : ABC-CLIO, 2020. | Includes bibliographical references and index.
Identifiers: LCCN 2019030626 (print) | LCCN 2019030627 (ebook) | ISBN 9781440869174 (hardcopy) alk. paper | ISBN 9781440869181 (ebook)
Subjects: LCSH: World War, 1939–1945—Germany—Encyclopedias. | Germany—Armed Forces—Encyclopedias. | World War, 1939–1945—Encyclopedias.
Classification: LCC D757 .G44 2020 (print) | LCC D757 (ebook) | DDC 940.54/094303—dc23
LC record available at https://lccn.loc.gov/2019030626
LC ebook record available at https://lccn.loc.gov/2019030627

ISBN: 978-1-4408-6917-4 (print)
978-1-4408-6918-1 (ebook)

24 23 22 21 20 1 2 3 4 5

This book is also available as an eBook.

ABC-CLIO
An Imprint of ABC-CLIO, LLC

ABC-CLIO, LLC
147 Castilian Drive
Santa Barbara, California 93117
www.abc-clio.com

This book is printed on acid-free paper ∞

Manufactured in the United States of America

For my distinguished colleague Professor Spencer C. Tucker,
the creative force behind the
ABC-CLIO Military History Encyclopedias.

Contents

List of Entries, ix

Guide to Related Topics, xiii

List of Documents, xvii

Foreword Professor Williamson Murray, xix

Introduction: Germany in World War II (1939–1945), xxi

A–Z Entries, 1

Epilogue: Why Germany Lost World War II, 301

Primary Source Documents, 309

Appendix A: German Aces (1936–1945), 327

Appendix B: Chiefs of the General and Admiralty Staffs (1919–1945), 333

Appendix C: Field Marshals and Grand Admirals (1933–1945), 337

Appendix D: German Military Ranks (1919–1945), 339

Appendix E: German Military Medals and Decorations (1933–1945), 345

Appendix F: Wehrmacht Officers in the Bundeswehr (1955–1990), 349

Chronology of the Wehrmacht, 353

Selected Bibliography, 377

List of Contributors, 383

About the Editor, 389

Index, 391

List of Entries

Abwehr
Afrika Korps
Aircraft, Military
American Military Tribunals
Anglo-German Naval Agreement
Antwerp, Allied Liberation of
Anzio, Battle of
Ardennes Offensive (Battle of the Bulge)
Artillery
Atlantic, Battle of the
Atlantic Wall
Austria, Annexation of (*Anschluss*)
Avranches Counteroffensive
Babi Yar Massacre
Bach-Zelewski, Erich von dem
Balck, Hermann
Barents Sea, Battle of
Barkhorn, Gerhard
Bastogne, Battle for
Bayerlein, Fritz
Beck, Ludwig
Belgium and Flanders Campaign
Belorussia Offensive, Soviet
Berlin, Land Battle for
Berlin Air Campaign, Allied
Bey, Eric
"Big Week" Allied Air Campaign
Bismarck, Sortie and Sinking of
Bittrich, Willi
Black May, Allied Anti-U-Boat Campaign
Blaskowitz, Johannes Albrecht
Blitz, Air Campaign
Blitzkrieg
Blomberg, Werner von
Blomberg-Fritsch Crisis
Blumentritt, Günther
Bock, Fedor von
BODENPLATTE, Air Operation
Bohemia and Moravia, Annexation of
Brandenberger, Erich
Brauchitsch, Walther von
Braun, Wernher von
Britain, Battle of
Budapest, Soviet Siege of
Busch, Ernst
Canaris, Wilhelm
Cassino/Rapido River, Battles of
Caucasus Campaign
Channel Dash
Channel Islands Campaign
Chir River, Battle of
Choltitz, Dietrich von
Ciliax, Otto
COBRA, Allied Breakout Operation
Colmar Pocket, Battle for the
Cologne, Allied Air Raid on
Combined Bomber Offensive, Allied (Operation POINTBLANK)
Commando Order
Commissar Order
Convoy PQ 17, Battle of
Convoys SC 122 and HX 229, Battle of

Crete, German Invasion of
Crimea Campaign, Soviet
Crimean Campaign
CROSSBOW, Anglo-American Air Operation
Denmark Campaign
Dieppe, British Raid on
Dietl, Eduard
Dietrich, Josef "Sepp"
Dönitz, Karl
Dornberger, Walter
Dresden, Allied Air Attack on
DRUMBEAT, U-Boat Operation
Einsatzgruppen
Enigma Machine
Falaise-Argentan Pocket
Fallschirmjäger (Airborne Troops)
FORTITUDE, Allied Deception Operation
France, Allied Liberation of
France, Battle of
Freikorps (Free Corps)
Friedeburg, Hans Georg von
Fritsch, Werner von
Fromm, Friedrich
Führer Directives
Galland, Adolf
German General Staff of World War II
German-Soviet Nonaggression Pact
Germany, Collapse and Surrender of
GOODWOOD, British Operation
Göring, Hermann
Greece Campaign
Greim, Robert Ritter von
Guderian, Heinz
Halder, Franz
Hamburg, Allied Air Raids (Operation GOMORRAH)
Hartmann, Erich Alfred
Hausser, Paul
Heinrici, Gotthard
Heisenberg, Werner
Hermann, Hans-Joachim "Hajo"
Heusinger, Adolf
Himmler, Heinrich
Hindenburg, Paul von
Hitler, Adolf
Hitler Youth
Hoepner, Erich
Holocaust, German Military Complicity in
Hossbach, Friedrich
Hoth, Hermann
Hürtgen Forest Campaign, Allied
Infantry Weapons
International Military Tribunal: The Nuremberg Trials
Italy Campaign, Allied
Jeschonnek, Hans
Jodl, Alfred
Kammhuber, Josef
Kammhuber Line
Keitel, Wilhelm
Kesselring, Albert
Kharkov, Battles of
Kleist, Paul Ewald von
Kluge, Günther von
Kondor Legion
Krebs, Hans
Kretschmer, Otto
Kriegsakademie (War Academy)
Kriegsmarine (German Navy)
Krupp, Alfried Felix
Krupp, Gustav
Küchler, Georg von
Kursk, Battle of
Laconia Order
Landwehr
Langsdorff, Hans Wilhelm
Leeb, Wilhelm Ritter von
Leningrad, Siege of
Lidice Massacre
List, Siegmund Wilhelm Walter
Löhr, Alexander
Lorraine Campaign, Allied
Loyalty Oath to Hitler
Ludendorff, Erich
Luftwaffe (German Air Force)
Lütjens, Günther
Mackensen, Eberhard von

Malmédy Massacre
Malta Air and Naval Campaign
Manstein, Erich von
Manteuffel, Hasso Eccard von
MARKET-GARDEN, Allied Operation
Marschall, Wilhelm
Marseille, Hans-Joachim
Mellenthin, Friedrich-Wilhelm von
Messerschmitt, Wilhelm
Metz, Battle of
Milch, Erhard
Model, Walther
Mölders, Werner
Moscow, Battle of
Munich Conference and Agreement
Netherlands Campaign
NEULAND, U-Boat Operation
Night of the Long Knives
NORDWIND, Operation
Normandy Invasion and Campaign
North Africa Campaign
North Cape, Battle of
Norway Campaign
Oberkommando der Luftwaffe (OKL)
Oberkommando der Marine (OKM)
Oberkommando der Wehrmacht (OKW)
Oberkommando des Heeres (OKH)
Opposition to Hitler, German Military
Oradour-sur-Glane Massacre
Organization Todt (OT)
Palatinate Campaign, Allied
Panzer Division
Panzergrenadier
Paris, Allied Liberation of
Paulus, Friedrich
PEDESTAL, Convoy Battle
Peiper, Joachim
Plan Z
Plate River, Battle of
Ploesti Air Raids, Allied
Poland Campaign
Poland-East Prussia Campaign, Soviet
Prien, Günther
Raeder, Erich
Rall, Günther
Reichenau, Walther von
Reichsarbeitsdienst (Reich Labor Service)
Reichsheer (German Army)
Reichssicherheitshauptamt (Reich Main Security Office)
Reichswald, Battle of the
Reitsch, Hanna
Remagen Bridge, U.S. Capture of
Rhine Crossings, Allied
Rhineland, Remilitarization of
Rhineland Offensive, Allied
Richthofen, Wolfram von
Rockets, Guided Bombs, and Guided Missiles
Rogge, Bernhard
Röhm, Ernst
Romania Campaign, Soviet
Rommel, Erwin
Rostov, Battle of
Rudel, Hans-Ulrich
Ruge, Friedrich
Ruhr Air Campaign, Allied
Ruhr Ground Campaign, Allied
Rundstedt, Karl Rudolf Gerd von
Saarland, French Invasion of the
Saint-Lô, Battle for
Salerno Landings, Allied
Scheldt Estuary, Battles for
Schörner, Ferdinand
Schweinfurt and Regensburg Air Raids, Allied
Seeckt, Hans von
Seelow Heights, Battle of
SEELÖWE (SEA LION), Operation
Senger und Etterlin, Fridolin Rudolf von
Sicily, Allied Invasion of
Siegfried Line Campaign, Allied
Skorzeny, Otto
Southern France, Allied Invasion and Campaign (Operation DRAGOON)
Soviet Union, Invasion of (Operation BARBAROSSA)
Spanish Civil War

Speer, Albert
Speidel, Hans
Sperrle, Hugo
Stab-in-the-Back Legend (*Dolchstosslegende*)
Stalingrad, Battle of
Stauffenberg, Claus Schenk von
Steinhoff, Johannes
STRANGLE, Allied Air Operation
Stroop, Jürgen
Student, Kurt
Stülpnagel, Joachim von
Stülpnagel, Karl von
Stülpnagel, Otto von
Sturmabteilungen (SA)
Submarines
Tanks and Self-Propelled Guns
Thoma, Wilhelm von
Tirpitz, Allied Attacks on
Todt, Fritz
Tresckow, Henning von
Udet, Ernst
Ukraine Campaign, Soviet
Undeclared Naval War with the United States
Vietinghoff genannt Scheel, Heinrich von
Volksgrenadier
Volkssturm
Waffen-SS
Warlimont, Walter
Warsaw Ghetto Uprising
Warsaw Rising
Warships, Surface
Wehrmacht (German Armed Forces)
Weichs zur Glon, Maximilian von
Westphal, Siegfried
Westwall
Westwall, Allied Advance to
Wever, Walther
Wilhelm Gustloff Sinking
Witzleben, Erwin von
Wolf Pack Tactics (*Rudeltaktik*)
Wolff, Karl
Yugoslavia Campaign
Zeitzler, Kurt

Guide to Related Topics

Battles

Antwerp, Allied Liberation of
Anzio, Battle of
Avranches Counteroffensive
Babi Yar Massacre
Barents Sea, Battle of
Bastogne, Battle for
Berlin, Land Battle for
Bismarck, Sortie and Sinking of
BODENPLATTE, Air Operation
Budapest, Soviet Siege of
Cassino/Rapido River, Battles of
Channel Dash
Chir River, Battle of
Colmar Pocket, Battle for the
Cologne, Allied Air Raid on
Convoy PQ 17, Battle of
Convoys SC-122 and HX-229, Battle of
Crete, German Invasion of
Dieppe, British Raid on
Dresden, Allied Air Attack on
Falaise-Argentan Pocket
Kharkov, Battles of
Kursk, Battle of
Lidice Massacre
Malmédy Massacre
Metz, Battle of
North Cape, Battle of
Oradour-sur-Glane Massacre
Paris, Allied Liberation of
PEDESTAL Convoy Battle
Plate River, Battle of
Reichswald, Battle of the
Remagen Bridge, U.S. Capture of
Rostov, Battle of
Saint-Lô, Battle for
Salerno Landings, Allied
Scheldt Estuary, Battles for
Seelow Heights, Battle of
Warsaw Ghetto Uprising
Warsaw Rising
Wilhelm Gustloff Sinking

Campaigns

Ardennes Offensive (Battle of the Bulge)
Atlantic, Battle of the
Austria, Annexation of (*Anschluss*)
Belgium and Flanders Campaign
Belorussia Offensive, Soviet
Berlin Air Campaign, Allied
"Big Week" Allied Air Campaign
Black May, Allied Anti-U-Boat Campaign
Blitz, Air Campaign
Bohemia and Moravia, Annexation of
Britain, Battle of
Caucasus Campaign
Channel Islands Campaign
COBRA, Allied Breakout Operation
Combined Bomber Offensive, Allied
(Operation POINTBLANK)
Crimea Campaign, Soviet

Crimean Campaign
CROSSBOW, Anglo-American Air Operation
Denmark Campaign
DRUMBEAT, U-Boat Operation
FORTITUDE, Allied Deception Operation
France, Allied Liberation of
France, Battle of
Germany, Collapse and Surrender of
GOODWOOD, British Operation
Greece Campaign
Hamburg, Allied Air Raids (Operation GOMORRAH)
Hürtgen Forest Campaign, Allied
Italy Campaign, Allied
Leningrad, Siege of
Lorraine Campaign, Allied
Malta Air and Naval Campaign
MARKET-GARDEN, Allied Operation
Moscow, Battle of
Netherlands Campaign
NEULAND, U-Boat Operation
NORDWIND, Operation
Normandy Invasion and Campaign
North Africa Campaign
Norway Campaign
Palatinate Campaign, Allied
Ploesti Air Raids, Allied
Poland Campaign
Poland-East Prussia Campaign, Soviet
Rhine Crossings, Allied
Rhineland, Remilitarization of
Rhineland Offensive, Allied
Romania Campaign, Soviet
Ruhr Air Campaign, Allied
Ruhr Ground Campaign, Allied
Saarland, French Invasion of the
Schweinfurt and Regensburg Air Raids, Allied
Sicily, Allied Invasion of
Siegfried Line Campaign, Allied
Southern France, Allied Invasion and Campaign (Operation DRAGOON)
Soviet Union, Invasion of (Operation BARBAROSSA)
Spanish Civil War
Stalingrad, Battle of
STRANGLE, Allied Air Operation
Tirpitz, Allied Attacks on
Ukraine Campaign, Soviet
Undeclared Naval War with the United States
West Wall, Allied Advance to
Yugoslavia Campaign

Individuals

Bach-Zelewski, Erich von der
Balck, Hermann
Barkhorn, Gerhard
Bayerlein, Fritz
Beck, Ludwig
Bey, Eric
Bittrich, Willi
Blaskowitz, Johannes Albrecht
Blomberg, Werner von
Blumentritt, Günther
Bock, Fedor von
Brandenburger, Erich
Brauchitsch, Walther von
Braun, Wernher von
Busch, Ernst
Canaris, Wilhelm
Choltitz, Dietrich von
Ciliax, Otto
Dietl, Eduard
Dietrich, Josef "Sepp"
Dönitz, Karl
Dornberger, Walter
Friedeburg, Hans Georg von
Fritsch, Werner von
Fromm, Friedrich
Galland, Adolf
Göring, Hermann
Greim, Robert Ritter von
Guderian, Heinz

Halder, Franz
Hartmann, Erich Alfred
Hausser, Paul
Heinrici, Gotthard
Heisenberg, Werner
Hermann, Hans-Joachim "Hajo"
Heusinger, Adolf
Himmler, Heinrich
Hindenburg, Paul von
Hitler, Adolf
Hoepner, Erich
Hossbach, Friedrich
Hoth, Hermann
Jeschonnek, Hans
Jodl, Alfred
Kammhuber, Josef
Keitel, Wilhelm
Kesselring, Albert
Kleist, Paul Ewald von
Kluge, Günther von
Krebs, Hans
Kretschmer, Otto
Krupp, Alfried Felix
Krupp, Gustav
Küchler, Georg von
Langsdorff, Hans Wilhelm
Leeb, Wilhelm Ritter von
List, Siegmund Wilhelm Walter
Löhr, Alexander
Ludendorff, Erich
Lütjens, Günther
Mackensen, Eberhard von
Manstein, Erich von
Manteuffel, Hasso Eccard von
Marschall, Wilhelm
Marseille, Hans-Joachim
Mellenthin, Friedrich-Wilhelm von
Messerschmitt, Wilhelm
Milch, Erhard
Model, Walther
Mölders, Werner
Paulus, Friedrich
Peiper, Joachim
Prien, Günther
Raeder, Erich
Rall, Günther
Reichenau, Walther von
Reitsch, Hanna
Richthofen, Wolfram von
Rogge, Bernhard
Röhm, Ernst
Rommel, Erwin
Rudel, Hans-Ulrich
Ruge, Friedrich
Rundstedt, Karl Rudolf Gerd von
Schörner, Ferdinand
Seeckt, Hans von
Senger und Etterlin, Fridolin Rudolf von
Skorzeny, Otto
Speer, Albert
Speidel, Hans
Sperrle, Hugo
Stauffenberg, Claus Schenk von
Steinhoff, Johannes
Stroop, Jürgen
Student, Kurt
Stülpnagel, Joachim von
Stülpnagel, Karl von
Stülpnagel, Otto von
Thoma, Wilhelm von
Todt, Fritz
Tresckow, Henning von
Udet, Ernst
Vietinghoff genannt Scheel, Heinrich von
Warlimont, Walter
Weichs zur Glon, Maximilian von
Westphal, Siegfried
Wever, Walter
Witzleben, Erwin von
Wolff, Karl
Zeitzler, Kurt

Organizations

Abwehr
Afrika Korps
Einsatzgruppen

Fallschirmjäger (Airborne Troops)
Freikorps (Free Corps)
German General Staff of World War II
Hitler Youth
Kondor Legion
Kriegsakademie (War Academy)
Kriegsmarine (German Navy)
Landwehr
Luftwaffe (German Air Force)
Oberkommando der Luftwaffe (OKL)
Oberkommando der Marine (OKM)
Oberkommando der Wehrmacht (OKW)
Oberkommando des Heeres (OKH)
Organization Todt (OT)
Panzer Division
Panzergrenadier
Reichsarbeitsdienst (Reich Labor Service)
Reichsheer (German Army)
Reichssicherheitshauptamt (Reich Main Security Office)
Sturmabteilungen (SA)
Volksgrenadier
Volkssturm
Waffen-SS
Wehrmacht (German Armed Forces)

Social/Political

American Military Tribunals
Anglo-German Naval Agreement
Blomberg-Fritsch Crisis
Commando Order
Commissar Order
German-Soviet Nonaggression Pact
Holocaust, German Military Complicity in
International Military Tribunal: The Nuremberg Trials
Laconia Order
Loyalty Oath to Hitler
Munich Conference and Agreement
Night of the Long Knives
Opposition to Hitler, German Military
Stab-in-the-Back Legend (Dolchstosslegende)

Strategy and Tactics

Atlantic Wall
Blitzkrieg
Führer Directives
Kammhuber Line
Plan Z
SEELÖWE (SEA LION), Operation
Westwall
Wolf Pack Tactics (*Rudeltaktik*)

Weapons and Equipment

Aircraft, Military
Artillery
Enigma
Infantry Weapons
Rockets, Guided Bombs, and Guided Missiles
Submarines
Tanks and Self-Propelled Guns
Warships, Surface

List of Documents

1. Wehrmacht Principal Operations Manual, HDv 300 *Truppenführung*: Introduction
2. Hitler's Directive for Fall Weiss, the Attack on Poland
3. Declaration of the Government of the German Reich and the Government of the U.S.S.R.
4. Three-Power (Tripartite) Pact between Germany, Italy, and Japan, Signed in Berlin
5. Wehrmacht Compliance with the Commissar Order
   a. Daily Intelligence Report from I Army Corps to Eighteenth Army Headquarters, June 27, 1941
   b. Evening Report from V Army Corps to Ninth Army Headquarters, June 30, 1941
   c. Daily Intelligence Report from I Army Corps to Fourth Panzer Group Headquarters, July 20, 1941
6. Radio Message to Hitler from Sixth Army Commander General Friedrich Paulus, Requesting Permission to Break Out from Stalingrad
7. Adolf Hitler, Secret "Night-and-Fog Decree" on the Punishment of Offenders in Occupied Territory
8. Luftwaffe Report of the Effects of Operation GOMORRAH, the Allied Fire Bombing of Hamburg
9. Field Marshal Erwin Rommel, Normandy Situation Report to Hitler
10. Final Coordinating Order from Hitler to Field Marshal Walther Model for the Ardennes Offensive
11. Message from Reichsführer-SS Heinrich Himmler to the Officers of Army Group Vistula for the Defense of Berlin
12. German Army Group Vistula Intelligence Assessment of the Soviet 1st Belorussian Front, Battle of Seelow Heights
13. Grand Admiral Karl Dönitz, Broadcast Informing the German People of Their Unconditional Surrender
14. German Surrender at Reims, France
15. German Surrender at Berlin

Foreword

David T. Zabecki has done God's work in editing this wonderful encyclopedia of the German military during World War II. Given the immense changes that have taken place in our historical understanding of the Wehrmacht's culture, military effectiveness, and contribution to the Third Reich's criminal behavior over the past thirty years, this work provides an up-to-date reference for students as well as academics who are interested in the period from 1933 through 1945. In effect, this work represents the starting point for the serious examination of the German military in World War II.

Ironically, brilliant grand strategy in the mid-nineteenth century had provided the framework within which the elder Helmuth con Moltke and his generals could wage the three wars that created the modern German state. Only Bismarck's sophisticated strategy and foreign policy prevented the widening of those conflicts in a fashion that might have robbed Prussia of the fruits of its victories. However, all that understanding disappeared from the consciousness of the German officer corps and even the General Staff in the period after the Franco-Prussian War. They showed little interest in Clausewitz's sharp warning that war is a continuation of politics by other means. To them, something they termed "military necessity" was of far greater importance than political and strategic concerns. The experience of World War I should have warned the German military that Clausewitz was right: politics and strategy really do matter. Tactical genius alone cannot repair the damage that mistakes at the political and strategic level will cause. Yet, in the next great war caused by German hubris, the Wehrmacht's senior leaders, and not just Adolf Hitler, managed to repeat every strategic mistake that the Reich's leaders had made in World War I.

At the beginning of that world war, the German Army's brilliant tactics, compounded by gross Allied strategic incompetence, allowed its panzer divisions to overthrow the Western powers on the Continent in 1940, but brilliant tactics could not trump incompetence at the operational and strategic levels. Moreover, as the Germans soon discovered, victory over Allied armies on the Continent did not mean the end of the war. The Battle of Britain should have served as a wakeup call. It did not.

Even before Hitler expressed an interest in attacking Russia, the senior army leaders were already thinking along those lines. At the end of July 1940, Generals Franz Halder and Walter von Brauchitsch met with the Führer, and the strategic line the three took was to invade the Soviet Union in the near future. But through the entire planning process, from late July 1940 to June 22, 1941, neither Hitler nor his generals recognized the extraordinary challenges that such a military operation would involve. But perhaps the saddest comment on the Wehrmacht's leadership was the enthusiastic acceptance of the criminal nature of the coming invasion, a reality that Hitler never made any effort to hide from the onset of discussions.

Thus, Operation BARBAROSSA began with extraordinary weaknesses in both logistics and intelligence, two of the three crucial elements on which success at the operational level depend. With intelligence estimates that forecast the Soviets would last no more than a few months, and logistics incapable of dealing with Russian distances, the Germans had little chance. Thus, once military operations began, the deeper that panzer spearheads proceeded to drive into the seemingly endless spaces of the Soviet Union, the more difficult became the difficulties of supplying German troops engaged against a far-more tenacious enemy than intelligence estimates had calculated.

The war crimes that occurred from the beginning of BARBAROSSA in unbelievable numbers were not just the result of the efforts of SS and Nazi Party functionaries. The army cooperated enthusiastically with the murderous actions of the SS Einsatzgruppen in the killing of hundreds of thousands of Jews. And the army committed its own war crimes. Of the three million plus Soviet prisoners of war captured in the first five months of the war, barely one hundred thousand would survive.

While BARBAROSSA was unwinding in the summer of 1941, the Kriegsmarine's leaders, Admirals Erich Raeder and Karl Dönitz, pushed Hitler heavily to declare war on the United States in order to give the U-boat campaign greater room to attack British commerce. Obviously, the lesson of the last world war had made no imprint on their strategic vision of the world. Thus, on December 11, 1941, having involved the Reich in a massive campaign in the east from a weak economic base, Hitler, with the enthusiastic support of his generals and admirals, declared war on the United States, the economic potential of which most German leaders remained ignorant. This time, there was to be no stab in the back legend, because the massive Allies juggernaut would grind the Reich, quite literally, into dust over the next three and a half years.

The Wehrmacht would fight on from 1942 through May 1945, but its tactical versatility and skill counted for little against the strategic and economic weight of the coalition ranged against the Reich. In the east, the massive production of Soviet weaponry, buttressed by the U.S. Lend-Lease, provided the Red Army with the means to destroy the Wehrmacht by attrition. In addition, Soviet *maskirovka* (deception) ensured that every major Soviet offensive would catch the Germans by surprise. In the west, by May 1943, the overwhelming power of Anglo-American industry had broken the back of the U-boat offensive in the Atlantic. That same spring, the impact of the Combined Bomber Offensive ended the rapid upsurge of German military production. In the early months of 1944, the daylight bombing offensive by the U.S. Eighth Air Force quite literally destroyed the Luftwaffe in the skies over Germany in a massive battle of attrition.

However frightful the legacy left by the German military, its history provides crucial insights into how the modern world was made. Thus, this wonderful volume represents an important contribution. It also provides warning about the future that ignorance of the past will most probably result in a catastrophic smashup.

Professor Williamson Murray
Fairfax, Virginia

Introduction: Germany in World War II (1939–1945)

World War II was the most destructive enterprise in human history, and Germany was the foremost aggressor of that war. Yet, in the end, Germany was more devastated than it had been by any war since the Thirty Years War. Out of a 1939 population of 69,850,000, Germany, by 1945, suffered 4,450,000 military deaths and an estimated 2,500,000 civilian deaths. It is sobering to consider that worldwide, more resources, material, and human lives (approximately fifty million total dead) were expended on the war than on any other human activity. Indeed, this conflict was so all-encompassing that very few "side" wars took place simultaneously, the 1939–1940 Finnish-Soviet War (the Winter War) being one of the few exceptions.

The debate over the origins of World War I had become something of a cottage industry among historians in the 1920s and 1930s. Yet the question of origins rarely arises over World War II, except on the narrow issue of whether U.S. President Franklin D. Roosevelt had advance knowledge of the Japanese attack on Pearl Harbor. Whatever their grievances (certainly minor in comparison to the misery they inflicted on their victims), Germany and Japan are still considered the aggressors of World War II.

World War II is historically unique; in that, it represents, if not necessarily a "crusade" of good against evil, at least a struggle against almost pure evil by less evil forces. Three-quarters of a century after the end of this war, no mainstream or serious historians defend any significant aspect of Nazi Germany. Perhaps more surprisingly, there are also few, if any, such historians who would do likewise for militaristic Japan. In practically all previous conflicts, historians have found sufficient blame to give all belligerents a share. For example, no prominent historian takes seriously the Treaty of Versailles clause that Germany was somehow completely responsible for the outbreak of World War I. German Führer Adolf Hitler and his followers have thus retained mythic status as personifications of pure evil, something not seen since the Wars of Religion of seventeenth-century Europe.

The starting date of World War II, however, can be disputed. Some scholars have gone as far back as the Japanese seizure of Manchuria in 1931. Others date its outbreak to the opening of the full-scale Sino-Japanese War in 1937. But these were conflicts between two Asian powers, hardly global war. The more traditional and more widely accepted date for the start of World War II is September 1, 1939, with the quick but not quite blitzkrieg (lightning war) German invasion of Poland. This action brought

France and Great Britain into the conflict two days later, in accordance with their guarantees to Poland. (The Soviet Union's invasion of eastern Poland on September 17 provoked no similar reaction.)

The Germans learned from their Poland Campaign and mounted a true blitzkrieg offensive against the Low Countries and France, commencing on May 10, 1940. In this blitzkrieg warfare, the tactical airpower of the German Luftwaffe (Air Force) knocked out command and communications posts as integrated armor division pincers drove deeply into enemy territory, bypassing opposition strong points. When all went well, the pincers encircled the slow-moving enemy. Contrary to legend, the panzer (armored) forces were simply the spearheads; the bulk of the German Army was composed of foot soldiers and horses. Further, the French Army and the British Expeditionary Force combined had more and usually better tanks than the Germans, and they were not too seriously inferior in the air. The sluggish Allies were simply outmaneuvered, losing France in six weeks, much to the astonishment of the so-called experts. France remains the only major industrial democracy ever to be conquered—and, also uniquely, after a single campaign. It was also the only more-or-less motorized nation to suffer such a fate; many French refugees fled the rapidly advancing Germans in their private cars. The Germans found that the French *Routes Nationales* (National Routes), designed to enable French forces to reach the frontiers, could also be used in the opposite direction by an invader. The Germans themselves relearned this military truth on their autobahns in 1945.

Germany suffered its first defeat of the war when its air offensive against Great Britain, the world's first great air campaign, was thwarted in the Battle of Britain. The margin of victory was small, for there was little to choose between the Hurricane and Spitfire fighters of the Royal Air Force (RAF) and the Luftwaffe's Bf 109 or between the contenders' pilots. The main advantages of the RAF in this battle were radar and the geographic fact that its pilots and their warplanes were shot down over Britain itself; German pilots and aircraft in a similar predicament were out of action for the duration, and they also had farther to fly from their bases. But Great Britain's greatest advantage throughout this stage of the war was its prime minister, Winston S. Churchill, who gave stirring voice and substance to the Allied defiance of Hitler.

Nonetheless, by the spring of 1941, Nazi Germany had conquered or dominated all of the European continent, with the exception of Switzerland, Sweden, and Vatican City. Greece, which had held off and beaten back an inept Italian offensive, finally capitulated to the German Balkan Blitzkrieg in spring 1941. Nazi Germany then turned on its erstwhile ally, the Soviet Union, on June 22, 1941, in Operation BARBAROSSA, the greatest military campaign of all time, in order to fulfill Hitler's enduring vision of crushing "Judeo-Bolshevism." (How far Hitler's ambitions of conquest ranged beyond the Soviet east is still disputed by historians.) If he had any introspective moments then, Soviet dictator Josef Stalin must have wished that he still had the legions of first-rate officers he had shot or slowly destroyed in the gulags in the wake of his bloody purge of the military in 1937. Stalin's own inept generalship played a major role in the early Soviet defeats, and German forces drove almost to within sight of the Kremlin's towers in December 1941 before being beaten back.

Early that same month, war erupted in the Pacific, and the conflict then became truly a world war, with Japan's coordinated combined attacks on the U.S. naval base at Pearl Harbor and on British, Dutch, and U.S. imperial possessions. With the Soviet Union holding out precariously and the United States now a belligerent, the Axis had lost the war, even though few recognized that fact at the time. The United States' "great debate" as to whether to aid Britain and to what extent to aid was silenced in a national outpouring of collective wrath against the enemy.

Three days after the Pearl Harbor attack, Hitler decided to declare war on the United States, a blunder fully as deadly as his invasion of the Soviet Union and even less explicable. But the Nazi dictator, on the basis of his customary "insights," had dismissed the U.S. soldier as worthless, and he considered U.S. industrial power vastly overrated. His decision meant that the United States could not focus exclusively on Japan.

Although considered a sideshow by the Soviets, the North African Campaign was of the utmost strategic importance, and until mid-1943, it was the only continental land campaign that the Western Allies were strong enough to mount. Had North Africa, including Egypt, fallen to the Axis powers (as almost occurred several times), the Suez Canal could not have been held, and German forces could have gone through the Middle East, mobilizing Arab nationalism, threatening the area's vast oil fields, and even menacing the embattled Soviet Union itself. Not until the British commander in North Africa, General Sir Bernard Montgomery, amassed a massive superiority in armor was German Field Marshal Erwin Rommel defeated at El Alamein in October 1942 and slowly pushed back toward Tunisia. U.S. and British landings to the rear of Rommel's forces, in Algeria and Morocco, were successful, but the raw U.S. troops received a bloody nose at Kasserine Pass. The vastly outnumbered North African Axis forces did not capitulate until May 1943. Four months earlier, the German Sixth Army had surrendered at Stalingrad, marking the resurgence of the Soviet armies. One should, nonetheless, remember that the distance between Casablanca, Morocco, and Cape Bon, Tunisia, is much the same as that from Brest-Litovsk to Stalingrad, and more Axis troops surrendered at "Tunisgrad" than at Stalingrad. (One major difference was that almost all Axis prisoners of the Western Allies survived their imprisonment, whereas fewer than one in ten of those taken at Stalingrad returned.)

By this time, U.S. production was supplying not only U.S. military needs but also those of most of the Allies—on a scale, moreover, that was simply lavish by comparison to all other armed forces. Everything from the canned-meat product Spam to Sherman tanks, and from aluminum ingots to finished aircraft crossed the oceans to the British Isles, the Soviet Union, the Free French, the Nationalist Chinese, the Fighting Poles, and others. Moreover, quantity was not produced at the cost of quality. The army trucks, the boots, the small arms, and the uniforms provided by the United States were unsurpassed. The very ships that transported the bulk of this war material—the famous, mass-produced Liberty ships, could still be found on the world's oceanic trade routes decades after they were originally scheduled to be scrapped.

After the North African Campaign ended in 1943, the Allies drove the Axis forces from Sicily, and then, in September 1943, they began the interminable Italian Campaign. It is perhaps indicative of the frustrating nature of the war in Italy that the lethargic Allies allowed the campaign to begin with the escape of most Axis forces from Sicily to the Italian peninsula. The Germans were still better at this sort of thing. For Winston Churchill, to the contrary, Italy was no "soft underbelly." The Germans conducted well-organized withdrawals from one mountainous fortified line to the next. The Italian Campaign was occasionally justified for tying down many German troops, but the truth is that it tied down far more Allied forces—British, Americans, Free French, Free Poles, Brazilians, Canadians, Indians, and British and French African colonials among them. German forces in Italy ultimately surrendered in late April 1945, only about a week before Germany itself capitulated.

The military forces of World War II's belligerents, as might be expected in so historically widespread a conflict, varied wildly. The French Army in 1939, considered by "experts" the world's best, was actually a slow-moving mass that was often supplied with very good equipment and was led by aged commanders who had learned the lessons of World War I. No other such powerful army was so completely defeated in so short a period of time. The French air force and navy, likewise, had some excellent equipment, as well as more progressive commanders than the army, but France fell before they could have any great impact on the course of battle.

It is generally agreed that the German Army was superb—so superb, in fact, that some authorities would venture that the Germans traditionally have had "a genius for war." (Then again, it was hardly a sign of genius to provoke the United States into entering World War I or to invade the Soviet Union in World War II while the British Empire still fought on, before declaring war on the United States six months later.) Obviously, Germany's greatest and traditional military failing has been the denigration of the fighting ability of its opponents. But on the ground, at the operational and tactical levels, the combination of realistic training, strict discipline, and flexible command made the German Army probably World War II's most formidable foe. One need only look at a map of Europe from 1939 to 1945 and calculate Germany's enemies compared to its own resources. The Luftwaffe had superbly trained pilots, although their quality fell off drastically as the war turned against their nation. German fighters were easily the equal of any in the world, but, surprisingly, given that Hitler's earlier ambitions seemingly demanded a "Ural bomber," the Luftwaffe never put a heavy, four-engine bomber into production. Germany led the world in aerodynamics, putting into squadron service the world's first jet fighter (the Me 262), with swept wings, and even a jet reconnaissance bomber (although German jet engines lagged somewhat behind those of the British). The Luftwaffe also fielded a rocket-powered interceptor, but this craft was as great a menace to its own pilots as to the enemy.

The German Navy had some outstanding surface vessels, such as the battleship *Bismarck*, but Hitler found the sea alien, and he largely neglected Germany's surface fleet. Submarines were an entirely different matter. U-boat wolf packs decimated Allied North Atlantic shipping, and the Battle of the Atlantic was the only campaign the eupeptic Churchill claimed cost him sleep. German U-boats ravaged the Atlantic coast of the United States, even ranging into Chesapeake Bay in the first months of 1942 to take advantage of inexcusable U.S. naval unpreparedness. As in World War I, convoying was the answer to the German U-boat, a lesson that had to be learned the hard way in both conflicts.

The British Army, on the whole, put in a mediocre performance in World War II. As with the French, although to a lesser degree, the British feared a repetition of the slaughter experienced on the World War I western front, and, except for the elite units, they rarely showed much dash or initiative. Montgomery, the war's most famous British general, consistently refused to advance until he had great superiority in men and material over his enemy. The British Expeditionary Force fought well and hard in France in 1940 but moved sluggishly thereafter.

The Royal Navy suffered from a preponderance of battleship admirals at the opening of the war. The Royal Navy was also handicapped by the fact that it did not win control of the Fleet Air Arm (FAA) from the RAF until 1937. The RAF had little use for naval aviation and had starved the FAA of funds and attention through the years between the world wars. Although the Royal Navy's carriers were fine ships, and their armored flight decks gave them a protection that the U.S. Navy envied, albeit at the cost of smaller aircraft capacity, Fleet Air Arm aircraft were so obsolete that the service had to turn to U.S. models. Even so, the FAA made history on November 11, 1940 when its obsolete Fairy Swordfish torpedo bombers sank three Italian battleships in Taranto harbor, a feat that the Japanese observed carefully, but the Americans did not. British battleships and carriers kept the vital lifeline through the Mediterranean and the Suez Canal open through the darkest days of the war, and, together with the Americans and Canadians, they defeated the perilous German submarine menace in the North Atlantic. Significant surface actions of the Royal Navy included the sinking of the German battleship *Bismarck* in May 1941 by an armada of British battleships, cruisers, carriers, and warplanes and the December 1943 Battle of North Cape, which culminated in the destruction of the pocket battleship *Scharnhorst* by the modern battleship *Duke of York*.

The Soviet Army almost received its deathblow in the first months of the German invasion. Caught off-balance and shorn by Stalin's maniacal purges of its best commanders (whose successors were the dictator's obedient creatures), the Soviet Army suffered heavier losses than any other army in history. Yet, spurred by the bestiality of the German war of enslavement and racial extermination and by Stalin's newfound pragmatism, the Red Army was able to spring back and, at enormous cost at the hands of the more professional Germans, fight its way to Berlin.

The Red Air Force developed into one of the most effective tactical air powers of the war. (The Soviets constructed very few heavy bombers.) The Shturmovik was certainly one of the best ground-attack aircraft of the time. The Red Navy, by contrast, apparently did little to affect the course of the war; its main triumph may have been in early 1945 when its submarines sank several large German passenger ships crammed with refugees from the east in the frigid Baltic, the worst maritime disasters in history.

The United States emerged from World War II as the only nation since the time of the Romans to be a dominant power on both land and sea, not to mention in the air. In 1945, the U.S. Air Force and Navy could have defeated any combination of enemies, and only the Soviet Army could have seriously challenged the Americans on land. In 1939, the U.S. Army was about the size of that of Romania; by 1945, it had grown to some twelve million men and women.

The aftermath of World War II proved considerably different from that of World War I, with its prevailing spirit of disillusionment.

Amazingly, all of World War II's belligerents, winners and losers alike, could soon look back and realize that the destruction of the murderous, archaic, racialist Axis regimes had genuinely cleared the way to a better world. All enjoyed peace and the absence of major war. Even for the Soviets, the postwar decades were infinitely better than the prewar years, although much of this measure of good fortune might be attributed simply to the death of Josef Stalin. Except for Great Britain, the British Commonwealth nations and, even more so, the United States emerged from the war far stronger than when they entered it after enduring a decade of the Great Depression. By the 1950s, both war-shattered Western Europe and Japan were well on their way to becoming major competitors of the United States.

The uniquely sagacious and foresighted Western Allied military occupations of Germany, Japan, and Austria, in many ways, laid the foundations for the postwar prosperity of these former enemy nations. Indeed, seventy-five years after the end of the war, the once-divided and now reunited Germany is one of the strongest economies and most vibrant democracies in the world. Within a few years of World War II's end, former belligerents on both sides could agree that, despite its appalling casualties and destruction, World War II had been, if not perhaps "the Good War," at least something in the nature of a worthwhile war.

Stanley Sandler

See also: Atlantic, Battle of the; Belgium and Flanders Campaign; Berlin, Land Battle for; *Bismarck*, Sortie and Sinking of; Blitzkrieg; Britain, Battle of; France, Battle of; Greece Campaign; Hitler, Adolf; Italy Campaign, Allied; Moscow, Battle of; Netherlands Campaign; North Africa Campaign; North Cape, Battle of; Rommel, Erwin; Sicily, Allied Invasion of; Soviet Union, Invasion of (Operation BARBAROSSA); Stalingrad, Battle of; *Wilhelm Gustloff* Sinking

Additional Reading

Dziewanowski, M. K. *War at Any Price: World War II in Europe, 1939–1945.* New York: Prentice-Hall, 1991.

German Armed Forces Military History Research Office. *Germany and the Second World War* (English translation of *Das Deutsche Reich und der Zweite Weltkrieg*). Vols. I–VII, IX. Oxford: Clarendon Press, 1990–2010.

Tucker, Spencer C., ed. *The Encyclopedia of World War II: A Political, Social, and Military History.* 5 vols. Santa Barbara, CA: ABC-CLIO, 2005.

Zabecki, David T., ed. *Germany at War: 400 Years of Military History*, 4 vols. Santa Barbara, CA: ABC-CLIO, 2014.

A

Aachen, Battle of (October 2–22, 1944). *See* Siegfried Line Campaign, Allied

Abwehr (1921–1944)

Abwehr was the designation for German military intelligence from 1921 until 1944. After the Nazis took power in 1933, the Abwehr was in a period of transition until Captain (later Admiral) Wilhelm Canaris took control in January 1935. The Abwehr was subordinated to the Armed Forces High Command (*Oberkommando der Wehrmacht*—OKW) in February 1938, although Heinrich Himmler and Reinhard Heydrich both tried to bring the Abwehr and all intelligence gathering organs under the control of the Schutzstaffel (SS). Canaris and Heydrich eventually worked out an agreement, and the Abwehr and the SS's Security Service (Sicherheitsdienst—SD) shared redundant domestic and foreign intelligence and espionage missions. Although the activities of the Abwehr proved effective and useful during the early years of the war, the fact that it was led by Canaris and his small coterie of hand-picked and loyal subordinates gradually diminished its importance. They were distrusted by the Nazi leadership, especially Himmler and Heydrich, who maintained their own far-reaching intelligence operations through the Reich Security Main Office (Reichssicherheitshauptamt—RSHA) and the SD.

As a result of the growing dissatisfaction with the Hitler regime and Nazi dominance over military intelligence, Canaris and several other high-ranking Abwehr officers began to cooperate actively with Allied intelligence and with members of the German resistance. Many of them came under investigation by the Gestapo. Hitler finally fired Canaris on February 18, 1944, and abolished the Abwehr. Himmler took control of the remnant Abwehr bureaucracy, which was absorbed into the RSHA, now led by Ernst Kaltenbrunner. This move strengthened Himmler's control over the military. Following the July 1944 assassination attempt against Hitler, Canaris and other former Abwehr leaders were arrested and charged with complicity in the failed coup and were eventually executed.

Steven B. Rogers

See also: Canaris, Wilhelm; Himmler, Heinrich; Opposition to Hitler, German Military; Reichssicherheitshauptamt (Reich Main Security Office)

Additional Reading

Paine, Lauran. *German Military Intelligence in World War Two: The Abwehr*. New York: Military Heritage Press, 1988.

Afrika Korps (1941–1943)

The German Africa Corps (Deutsches Afrika Korps—DAK) was the designation given to the initial two German panzer divisions sent to Libya in 1941 as part of Operation SONNENBLUME (SUNFLOWER). Commanded by Major General Erwin Rommel, the Afrika Korps grew and changed in character, as Rommel received promotions, and as other commanders took over. The DAK's 5th Light Division began to arrive in Libya in February 1941 (in August it was officially reconstituted as the 21st Panzer Division). Elements of the 15th Panzer Division arrived in April. At various times, other units were added to, or subtracted from, the Afrika Korps. At the time of the Battle of El Alamein in November 1942, the DAK consisted of the 15th and 21st Panzer Divisions, the 90th and 164th Light Motorized Infantry Divisions, the Ramcke Parachute Brigade, the Italian Giovanni Fascisti Regiment, and assorted supporting units. During the Tunisia Campaign, the 10th Panzer Division was added.

The DAK ended the war serving under Italy's best general, Marshal Giovanni Messe, who commanded the First Italian Army. The DAK's last commander, General Hans Cramer, surrendered with the DAK on May 13, 1943. More than one million Axis soldiers served in Africa, and 260,000 of them were German. The majority of German forces arrived during the Tunisia Campaign, and only a small percentage of them belonged to the DAK.

Jack Greene

See also: North Africa Campaign; Rommel, Erwin

Additional Reading

Gudmundsson, Bruce L., ed. *Inside the Afrika Korps.* London: Greenhill, 1999.

Aircraft, Military (1933–1945)

The harsh terms of the Treaty of Versailles that ended World War I imposed strict limits on German military aircraft. The Germans nonetheless spent the interwar years in clandestine aviation development until 1935, when Adolf Hitler renounced the terms of the Treaty of Versailles and openly resumed a military buildup, including a resurgent Luftwaffe. When the Civil War broke out in Spain in July 1936, German-supplied Junkers Ju 52/3m trimotor transports played a critical role in airlifting Moroccan troops into Spain to reinforce the Nationalists. Joining fascist Italy in equipping and assisting the Nationalists—while the Soviet Union similarly assisted the Republicans—Germany sent an aerial contingent called the Kondor Legion, largely to take advantage of a golden opportunity to test its aircraft and tactical doctrine under real wartime conditions.

Among the Kondor Legion's first arrivals was Nazi Germany's first production fighter, the Heinkel He 51. It was a conventional biplane with an open cockpit and fixed landing gear whose shortcomings were swiftly exposed against the Republicans' Soviet-supplied Polikarpov I-15 biplanes and groundbreaking I-16 monoplanes. Another biplane was the Henschel Hs 123, a sturdy, single-seater used as a dive bomber in Spain and as a ground strafer in World War II. More advanced planes were soon on the way, however, including the Heinkel He 111, a twin-engine bomber derived from the aerodynamically clean He 70 single-engine transport; the Dornier Do 17, a sleek and slender twin-engine bomber popularly known as the "flying pencil"; and the Junkers Ju 87 "Stuka," a two-seat monoplane dive bomber with inverted gull wings, fixed landing gear, and a siren to enhance the psychological effect of its swooping bird of prey appearance.

Also making its fighting debut over Spain was the Messerschmitt Bf 109B, a clean monoplane fighter that turned the tables on the I-16. Just as significantly, the Kondor Legion's most successful fighter ace,

German Military Aircraft of World War II

Model	Junker Ju 52/3m g7e	Fieseler Fi 152
Type	Transport	Liaison Aircraft
Years in Service	1932–1945	1936–1945
Crew Number	3	1
Number Engines	3	1
Max. Range	540 miles	240 miles
Max. Ceiling	18,000 feet	15,090 feet
Max. Speed	132 mpg	109 mph

Model	Heinkel He 51B-1	Heinkel He 111H-6	Henschel Hs 123A-1
Type	Fighter	Bomber	Close Support
Years in Service	1934–1938	1935–1945	1936–1944
Crew Number	1	5	1
Number Engines	1	2	1
Max. Range	354 miles	1,429 miles	530 miles
Max. Ceiling	25,256 feet	21,330 feet	29,530
Max. Speed	205 mph	273 mph	214 mph

Model	Junkers Ju 87B-2	Messerschmitt Me 109E-3
Type	Dive Bomber	Fighter
Years in Service	1936–1945	1937–1945
Crew Number	2	1
Number Engines	1	1
Max. Range	311 miles	410 miles
Max. Ceiling	26,903 feet	34,450 feet
Max. Speed	242 mph	348 mph

Model	Arado Ar 196	Blohm und Voss BV 138B-1
Type	Floatplane Scout	Maritime Reconnaissance
Years in service	1938–1945	1940–1945
Crew number	2	6
Number Engines	1	3
Max. Range	690 miles	3,105 miles
Max. Ceiling	23,000 feet	16,400 feet
Max. Speed	193 mph	171 mph

(*continued*)

German Military Aircraft of World War II (continued)

Model	Junkers Ju 88A-4	Dornier Do 217E-2	Focke-Wulf Fw 189A-1
Type	Bomber	Bomber	Army Cooperation
Years in Service	1939–1945	1941–1945	1941–1945
Crew Number	4	4	3
Number Engines	2	2	2
Max. Range	1,429 miles	1,429 miles	476 miles
Max. Ceiling	29,500 feet	29,527 feet	27,550 feet
Max. Speed	317 mph	320 mph	222 mph

Model	Focke-Wulf Fw 190A-8
Type	Fighter
Years in Service	1941–1945
Crew Number	1
Number Engines	1
Max. Range	500 miles
Max. Ceiling	37,430 feet
Max. Speed	408 mph

Model	Henschel Hs 129B-2	Messerschmitt Me 110G-2
Type	Close Support	Night Fighter
Years in Service	1942–1945	1943–1945
Crew Number	1	3
Number Engines	2	2
Max. Range	428 miles	807 miles
Max. Ceiling	29,530 feet	36,000 feet
Max. Speed	253 mph	370 mph

Model	Messerschmitt Me 163B-1	Messerschmitt Me 262A-1
Type	Interceptor	Fighter
Years in Service	1944–1945	1944–1945
Crew Number	1	1
Number Engines	1	2
Max. Range	25 miles	652 miles
Max. Ceiling	39,700 feet	37,730 feet
Max. Speed	56 mph	541 mph

German Military Aircraft of World War II (continued)

Model	Arado Ar 234B-2
Type	Bomber
Years in Service	1944–1945
Crew Number	2
Number Engines	2
Max. Range	967 miles
Max. Ceiling	32,808 feet
Max. Speed	459 mph

Werner Mölders, also developed new tactics for the Bf 109, abandoning large, tight formations and breaking into single combats in favor of two sets of two-man teams, called the *Vierfinger* (finger-four) formation, flying in a relatively loose but mutually supporting element that provided greater flexibility in a dogfight. This, as much as the fighter itself, was the key to German air superiority in the first year of World War II.

Amid the drive to mobilize an air arm that was second to none, three unhealthy trends arose in the Luftwaffe. When Major General Walther Wever died in an air crash on June 3, 1936, the cause of building a strategic air arm of long-range, multiengine bombers died with him, never to be effectively revived. In that same year, second-ranking World War I ace and Luftwaffe technical procurement chief Ernst Udet was so impressed with a U.S. Curtiss F11C-2 Goshawk he flew that he became an obsessive advocate of the dive bomber, to the extent of demanding that dive-bombing capability be incorporated into all warplane designs—including, for example, the twin-engine Junkers Ju 88 and even the four-engine Heinkel He 177. But that resulted in unnecessarily heavy, overengineered aircraft. A third error was Luftwaffe commander Hermann Göring's advocacy of a heavily armed twin-engine "general purpose fighter," capable of escorting bombers, carrying out hit-and-run bombing strikes, or high-speed reconnaissance missions, in the form of the Messerschmitt Bf 110 Zerstörer (Destroyer).

In 1938, Willy Messerschmitt gained a controlling share of the Bayerische Flugzeugwerke, resulting in his later designs having an "Me" designator, though the older one still applied to the Bf 108 Taifun four-seat monoplane transport, the Bf 109B through D, and the Bf 110A and B. When Hitler invaded Poland in 1939, the spearhead of the Luftwaffe's fighter arm was the Me 109E and the Me 110C, both lent much-improved performance by fuel-injected 1,085-horsepower Daimler-Benz DB 601 inverted V-12 engines.

It was in the Battle of Britain, fought between July and October 1940, that the Luftwaffe ran afoul of the Royal Air Force's formidable fighter force and its own limitations. British radar allowed the RAF to counter Luftwaffe incursions with economic efficiency, and attempts to dive-bomb the British radar installations resulted in a slaughter that showed the Ju 87 Stuka's vulnerability in the face of serious aerial opposition. Although capable of 370 miles per hour, the Me 110Cs lacked the maneuverability to engage British Hawker Hurricanes and Supermarine Spitfires, and soon

German Junkers Ju 87B-2 Stuka dive bombers of the Luftwaffe's Staffel 5, Stukageschwader 2 fly in formation over France during the Battle of France on May 30, 1940. (Hulton Archive/Getty Images)

Me 109Es were required to escort the escorts. Although the Spitfire and Me 109E were classically matched adversaries, the latter's inadequate range limited loiter time over England to no more than thirty minutes, a serious handicap. Even so, the Luftwaffe almost succeeded in inflicting more attrition on Britain's fighters and their airfields than its industry could make up—until mid-September, when Hitler and Göring shifted their emphasis to bombing London and other cities. That strategy failed to terrorize the British into capitulation, but it gave the RAF a much-needed reprieve.

After overrunning Yugoslavia and Greece in April 1941, German paratroopers landed on Crete on May 20, suffering heavy losses before securing Maleme Airfield on April 21, allowing Ju 52s to airlift reinforcements of the 5th Mountain Division to clinch victory by June 1. Although Crete was the first island in history to be conquered entirely from the air, its high cost—6,698 casualties and 284 aircraft destroyed or written off—led Hitler to prohibit comparable airborne operations thereafter.

Hilter's invasion of the Soviet Union on June 22, 1941, was attended by spectacular thrusts and massive victories, on land and in the air, the latter spearheaded by the redesigned Me 109F, soon to be joined that fall by the 1,455-horsepower DB 605-engine Me 109G and a formidable new fighter, the Focke-Wulf Fw 190A, powered by a 1,539-horsepower BMW 801 engine and capable of outperforming the British Spitfire Mark V.

German naval efforts against Britain and the United States centered on submarines against supply convoys, but the Luftwaffe tried to support the U-boats with long-range maritime reconnaissance planes, such as the Focke-Wulf Fw 200C Condor, modified from a prewar airliner; the bizarre trimotor, twin-boom Blohm und Voss BV 138 flying boat; the twin-engine Heinkel He 115 floatplane torpedo bomber; and the gigantic, six-engine BV 222 Wiking. Originally built for the Dutch in 1934, 279 trimotor Dornier Do 24 flying boats were built by German, Dutch, and French manufacturers, most of them serving the Luftwaffe on maritime reconnaissance and search-and-rescue duties. Operating from German warships and from coastal bases, the Arado Ar 196A was a formidable floatplane with outstanding handling characteristics on air and water that was heavily armed with two 20mm-cannons, as well as two machine guns and two 110-pound bombs. Allied patrol bombers' menacing U-boats in the Bay of Biscay frequently came under attack by Ju 88Cs, cannon-armed fighter versions of Junkers' versatile dive bomber. In 1943, German naval convoys in the Mediterranean and Aegean seas were afforded surveillance and protection by twenty of the world's first production helicopter, Anton Flettner's Fl 282 Kolibri (Hummingbird), which had twin intermeshing rotors. None of these aircraft, however, were in adequate supply to offset the greater numbers of their Allied opponents.

German transport needs on all fronts also outstripped supplies of the ubiquitous but aging Ju 52, but most of its supplemental aircraft were modifications of airliners, such as the Junkers Ju 90. History's largest glider, the ill-conceived Messerschmitt Me 321 Gigant, ultimately required two He 111s grafted together with a fifth engine, as the He 111Z Zwilling ("Twin") to tow it to and from Russia, but the ultimate solution was to give it six radial engines of its own as the Me 323. Even in that form, the Gigant could barely keep out of its own way, and it fell easy prey even to Allied medium bombers, let alone fighters, that intercepted Me 323s over the Mediterranean.

The requirements of the sweeping land battles on the Russian steppes dictated new requirements of the Luftwaffe. The Henschel Hs 129 was a twin-engine cannon-armed, armored antitank plane that proved to be underpowered, overweight, and numerically inadequate in comparison to its Soviet opponent, the Ilyushin Il-2 Shturmovik. Stukas also were pressed into successful tank-busting service, with two underwing-mounted 37mm cannon, as the Ju 87G.

Eclipsing the Henschel Hs 126 parasol monoplane in battlefield reconnaissance was the twin-boom, twin-engine Focke-Wulf Fw 189, whose glazed nacelle earned it the sobriquet "Flying Eye" from the troops it supported. Ably serving in the roles of liaison, observation, and medical evacuation was the Fieseler Fi 156C Storch (Stork), a single-engine plane designed in 1935 by Reinhold Mewes and Erich Bachem to incorporate forward wing slats with hinged, slotted flaps to achieve remarkable short takeoff and landing performance.

Starting in June 1943, the Allies' Combined Bomber Offensive compelled the Luftwaffe to devote a growing amount of its fighter force to defending the Reich. RAF Bomber Command's thousand-plane raids brought on an escalating competition in radar technology, which took to the air in the form of night fighters equipped with radar and obliquely mounted dorsal 20mm cannons called *Schräge Muzik* (Jazz Music). The Ju 88, in its C and G models, was pressed into such service, as well as the Do 17, Do 215, and Do 217 bombers and the new Heinkel He 219 twin-engine fighter. Most successful of all, however, was the Me 110G, a radar-equipped version of the general-purpose fighter that had failed by day but got a new lease on life at night. Supplementing that defense were single-seat Me 109Gs and Fw 190As, following searchlights and radio references to seek out their nocturnal prey without radar, in what were called *Wilde Sau* (Wild Pig) missions to distinguish them from the radar-guided *Zahme Sau* (Tame Pig) tactics.

Although the strategic scales were tipping against Germany, Luftwaffe fighters continued to take a grisly toll of Allied aircraft, including bombers of the U.S. Eighth Air Force, but that would change early in 1944, as the Rolls-Royce Merlin-powered North American P-51B Mustang entered combat, offering the war's best combination of performance, maneuverability, and range. Improved Allied fighters, such as the Spitfire Mark IX, Yakovlev Yak 9, and Lavochkin La 5FN, were also taking the measure of Germany's best, while German engineers strove to regain a decisive edge. The Me 109G's engine received a succession of improved fuel-injection systems, raising its output to 1,973 horsepower in the DB 605D, powering the definitive Me 109K to a maximum speed of 470 miles per hour. Focke-Wulf's chief engineer, Kurt Tank, revised the Fw 190 around a 2,240-horsepower Junkers Jumo 213A-1 inverted V-12 engine with MW50 methanol-water injection, as the Fw 190D, capable of 438 miles per hour—later joined by the elongated, Ta 152H-1 high-altitude fighter with a similarly boosted Juno 213E engine that gave it a top speed of 472 miles per hour. All of these fighters came out too late to turn the tide, however. Worse, the steady loss of experienced Luftwaffe pilots was being replaced by a new generation of pilots with far less airtime, who fell easy prey to their steadily improving Allied opponents.

July 1944 saw the introduction of a radical new design, the Messerschmitt Me 262A, powered by twin Junkers Jumo 004 jet engines that gave it a maximum speed of 540 miles per hour. At Hitler's insistence, these potential game changers were committed as Me 262A-2a fighter-bombers carrying two 550-pound bombs, as well as Me 262A-1a interceptors armed with four 30mm cannons. Shocking though they were to Allied pilots, the Me 262s soon displayed an Achilles' heel in the form of unreliable engines that needed replacement after twenty-five hours and a low acceleration rate that made them vulnerable when taking off or landing—a weakness that Mustang pilots, especially, exploited by attacking their airfields on the return legs of their bombing missions. A larger twin-jet design, the Arado Ar 234B, had a speed of 461 miles per hour, and its 967-mile range made it a superb photoreconnaissance plane as well as the world's first purpose-built jet bomber. In 1945, the Heinkel He 162 entered service with a single jet engine mounted above the largely wooden fuselage and wings. Intended for hastily trained pilots, it was, in fact, difficult to fly and flew only a few combat missions in the Reich's final month.

Alongside such groundbreaking jet aircraft, Germany's growing desperation bred some fascinating oddities. The He 177 was a four-engine bomber with two pairs of coupled engines and dive-bombing capability that was handicapped by a chronic tendency to overheat and catch fire. August 1944 saw the debut of the Me 163B Komet (Comet), a rocket-powered point interceptor powered by a binary mixture of two unstable fuels that thrust it along at up to 596 miles per hour for about four minutes, while also rendering it more dangerous to its own pilots than to the Allied aircraft it only occasionally shot down. Too late to see service was the Dornier Do 335 Pfeil (Arrow), a large fighter with twin-piston engines, mounted fore and aft, to drive a tractor and pusher propeller. The Blohm und Voss BV 40, in contrast, did away with engines altogether, being intended to be towed over Allied bombers and released to glide through the formation, two 30mm cannons blazing.

Hitler's "Thousand Year Reich" collapsed in ruins on May 8, 1945, 988 years ahead of schedule. It left behind spoils of war at which the victorious Allies could marvel and a wealth of engineers and aeronautical data that helped both sides advance their own technology in the Cold War years to follow.

Jon Guttman

See also: Barkhorn, Gerhard; Britain, Battle of; Combined Bomber Offensive, Allied (Operation POINTBLANK); Crete, German Invasion of; Göring, Hermann; Hartmann, Erich Alfred; Kondor Legion; Messerschmitt, Wilhelm; Mölders, Werner; Rall, Günther; Spanish Civil War; Udet, Ernst; Wever, Walther

Additional Reading

Green, William. *Warplanes of the Third Reich*. New York: Galahad Books, 1986.

Alam Halfa, Battle of (August 30–September 5, 1942). *See* North Africa Campaign

American Military Tribunals (November 1946–April 1949)

The American Military Tribunals were a series of war crimes trials conducted by the United States following the Trial of the Major War Criminals before the International Military Tribunal at Nuremberg. The British conducted similar military courts in Hamburg, Wuppertal, and other locations in the north of Germany. The American trials were conducted at Nuremberg.

Starting in November 1946 and lasting to April 1949, U.S. authorities conducted twelve separate trials. The Judges Trial, which started on March 5, 1947, was the inspiration for the fictional 1961 Stanley Kraemer film *Judgment at Nuremberg*. Of the 185 individuals indicted, 177 were brought to trial. Four committed suicide before their trials, and another four were declared unfit to stand trial. Twenty-four of those tried were condemned to death. Twelve of those were executed; one was extradited to Belgium, where he later died; and eleven later had their sentences commuted to life. Twenty of the defendants were sentenced to life in prison, and ninety-eight received prison sentences ranging from eighteen months to twenty-five years. Many of those sentenced had their sentences reduced or commuted on January 31, 1951. Thirty-five defendants were acquitted. Some of those acquitted and many of those who were sentenced and released later faced German denazification courts.

The High Command Trial, which started on December 30, 1947, prosecuted twelve generals, one admiral, and one senior judge-advocate general officer for war crimes and crimes against humanity. Among those convicted were Field Marshal Wilhelm von Leeb, Field Marshal Georg von Küchler, Colonel General Hermann Hoth, Colonel General Georg-Hans Reinhardt, General of Artillery Walter Warlimont, and General of Infantry Otto Wöhler. Field Marshal Hugo Sperrle and Colonel General Johannes Blaskowitz were acquitted on all counts, although Blaskowitz committed suicide during the trial. The German General Staff itself had been tried at the International Military Tribunal and was acquitted of being a criminal organization.

David T. Zabecki

See also: Blaskowitz, Johannes Albrecht; Hoth, Hermann; International Military Tribunal: The Nuremberg Trials; Küchler, Georg von; Leeb, Wilhelm Ritter von; Sperrle, Hugo; Warlimont, Walter

Additional Reading

Buscher, Frank M. *The U.S. War Crimes Trial Program in Germany, 1946–1955*. New York: Greenwood Press, 1989.

Anglo-German Naval Agreement (1935)

The Anglo-German Naval Agreement was signed between Germany and Great Britain on June 18, 1935. The British hoped the agreement would be the first step in limiting German rearmament. The agreement limited the German Navy to 35 percent the size of that of the Royal Navy. This restriction applied to each category of warship except submarines, where the Germans were allowed to build up to 45 percent of Britain's tonnage. The Treaty of Versailles of 1919 had limited the German Navy to a much smaller total size of 108,000 tons, and it prohibited submarines. Hitler, however, had already proclaimed that Germany would no longer abide by the disarmament provisions of the Treaty of Versailles. The German government signed it because it gave Germany the green light to begin naval building within the limits of an international agreement, proving Germany's good intentions. Hitler, however, denounced the Anglo-German Naval Agreement in 1939 when he approved the Plan Z naval construction program.

The Anglo-German Naval Agreement is sometimes seen as an example of the error of Britain's appeasement policy, because it openly condoned a violation of the Treaty of Versailles. But Hitler had already embarked on rebuilding the German military. The agreement's weakness lay largely in Britain's inability to verify German compliance. The agreement resulted from strong antiwar feeling in Britain and the need to cope with not one, but three potential enemies (Germany, Japan, and Italy) in the mid-1930s.

Paul W. Doerr

See also: Plan Z; Submarines; Warships, Surface

Additional Reading

Maiolo, Joseph. *The Royal Navy and Nazi Germany, 1933–39: A Study in Appeasement and the Origins of the Second World War*. London: Macmillan, 1998.

Antwerp, Allied Liberation of (September 4–October 2, 1944)

Antwerp's port facilities made it an important strategic objective for the invading Allied armies in 1944. Antwerp is about fifty-four miles from the open sea, connected by the Scheldt River, which is fairly narrow below the city and then broadens into a wide estuary. The southern bank of the estuary is formed by the European mainland. The northern side is formed by the South Beveland Peninsula and Walcheren Island, which is connected to the peninsula by a narrow causeway. In 1944, the port had six hundred hydraulic and electric cranes, as well as numerous floating cranes, loading bridges, and floating grain elevators. It was essential for the Anglo-American forces to secure Antwerp as a supply port in order to sustain their offensive into the heart of Germany.

The British Second Army took Brussels on September 3, and then managed to cover the sixty miles to Antwerp on September 4. The British 11th Armoured Division entered the city to find that the port was relatively intact, largely because of activities of the Belgian Resistance. But then the 11th Armoured Division paused for two days and neglected to secure the bridges over the Albert Canal on the northern edge of the city. Had the bridges been secured on September 4, the way would have been open to the eastern base of the South Beveland Peninsula, some seventeen miles distant. That would have trapped the remaining units of Colonel General Gustav von Zagen's Fifteenth Army, totaling some one hundred thousand men in the pocket. By September 6, however, German resistance had rallied to permit the British only a small bridgehead, which was subsequently destroyed.

The German Fifteenth Army was sealed off in the Calais-Flanders region in what was known as the "Breskens Pocket." On September 4, Zagen ordered an evacuation across the estuary to Walcheren. By the time the evacuation was completed on September 23, the Germans had managed to extract some 86,000 men, 616 guns, 6,200 vehicles, and 6,000 horses.

British Field Marshal Sir Bernard Montgomery did not bring the full force of his 21st Army Group to bear on clearing the surrounding countryside to allow traffic on the Scheldt River. Indeed, he did not even order the Canadian First Army to clear the Scheldt estuary until late September, even while that force was still tasked with clearing the channel ports. Not until October 16 did Montgomery order that the Scheldt be cleared with the utmost vigor, irrespective of casualties. The port itself did not open for traffic until November 26. By the time the Scheldt was cleared, the Germans had taken some 10,000 casualties and lost another 41,000 as prisoners. British and Canadian total casualties were around 12,800. The Battle of Antwerp and the failure to immediately clear the Scheldt estuary was a lost opportunity for the Allies to open a major port early, trap a large German force, and potentially end the war sooner.

Britton W. MacDonald

See also: Scheldt Estuary, Battles for

Additional Reading

Ludwig, Joachim. *Rückzug: The German Retreat from France, 1944.* Lexington: University Press of Kentucky, 2012.

Anzio, Battle of (January 22–May 25, 1944)

The Allies conducted an amphibious landing at Anzio, Italy, in January 1944 but could not break out and exploit until May 1944. Following the British and U.S. landings on the Italian peninsula in September 1943, German forces under Field Marshal Albert Kesselring established the Gustav Line defenses north of Naples. This formidable position took advantage of the Apennine Mountains as well as the Garigliano and Rapido Rivers. The line's western end, closer to Rome, was anchored by the impressive mountain abbey of Monte Cassino. Kesselring's forces repulsed four separate Allied attempts to break through the line. The failure of frontal assaults on the Gustav Line led to Allied plans for an amphibious flanking operation near the town of Anzio on the Tyrrhenian Sea, approximately halfway between the Gustav Line and Rome.

Designated Operation SHINGLE, the Allied landing on January 22, 1944, initially caught the Germans by surprise. The Allies soon established a beachhead, but because of hurried and muddled planning, Allied leaders had only prepared for a fight on the beaches. Once troops were ashore, confusion reigned. The Americans made no effort to seize the Alban Hills overlooking Anzio. The delay allowed Kesselring to move reserves from Rome to the Alban Hills and pin the Americans down without weakening the defenses of the Gustav Line.

The Germans soon had one hundred and twenty-five thousand men against the one hundred thousand Americans and British on the Anzio beachhead. The Allied forces in the beachhead were under U.S. VI Corps, commanded by Major General John P. Lucas. The German forces containing the beachhead were under the operational control of the Fourteenth Army, commanded by Colonel General Eberhard von Mackensen.

On May 17, Polish and Free French units south of Anzio broke the Gustav Line with a costly direct attack on Monte Cassino, which the Anzio operation was supposed to have rendered unnecessary. The German troops at Anzio were forced to redeploy to the Caesar Line north of Rome. On May 25, Allied forces from Anzio linked up with those from the Gustav Line. They entered Rome on June 4. The fighting and breakout from the Anzio beachhead cost the Allies some forty-three thousand casualties and the Germans forty thousand.

Michael S. Neiberg

See also: Italy Campaign, Allied; Kesselring, Albert; Mackensen, Eberhard von

Additional Reading

D'Este, Carlo. *Fatal Decision: Anzio and the Battle for Rome.* London: HarperCollins, 1991.

Ardennes Offensive (Battle of the Bulge) (December 16, 1944–January 25, 1945)

Hitler's second-to-last major counteroffensive in Western Europe was meant to drive a wedge between the Anglo-American alliance and capture the port city of Antwerp, thus denying that vital supply center to the Allies and rupturing the Western Alliance. The main effort in the north of the offensive was led by the Sixth Panzer Army, commanded by Oberstgruppenführer Josef "Sepp" Dietrich. In the center, the supporting attack of the Fifth Panzer Army was commanded by General of Panzer Troops Hasso von Manteuffel. On the southern flank, the Seventh Army of General of Infantry Erich Brandenburger conducted a screening attack to block Allied reinforcements from moving up.

The Ardennes Offensive of December 16, 1944, was a gamble. Hitler chose an offensive in the west in order to protect the industrial areas in western Germany, to try to split the often tension-filled Western Alliance and to use the Westwall as the perfect staging ground for such a counteroffensive. The Ardennes were chosen by Hitler for a number of reasons. The Allied front in that sector was poorly manned; the distance from there to the final objective of Antwerp was not too great; it was a constricted area, requiring fewer attacking troops; the terrain was wooded and offered cover against Allied observation; and, perhaps, Hitler was trying to restage the glory of the very successful German 1940 invasion through the Ardennes.

There was no debating with Hitler. The senior military leaders did try to persuade him to scale back the objectives and magnitude of the operation. Colonel General Alfred Jodl, Chief of the Wehrmacht Operations Staff, was responsible for developing the operational plan. The commander in chief west, Field Marshal Gerd von Rundstedt, was not even informed of the operation until very late in the planning stage. Jodl and his staff developed a two-pronged attack, attempting a double envelopment of the Allies. But the final objective of Antwerp was overly ambitious and came to be known among the German general staff as the "Big

BATTLE OF THE BULGE, 1944

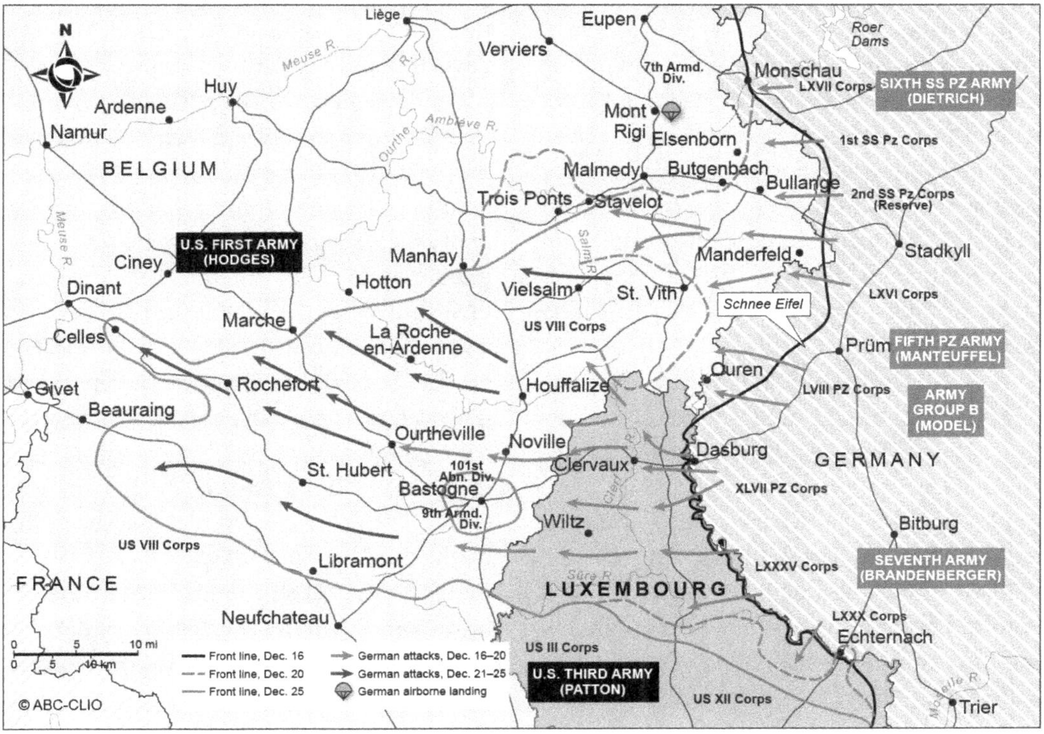

Solution." As other officers became aware of the plan and were sworn to secrecy, some of them realized at once that the Führer's plan was too ambitious and the time frame for preparation too short. General of the Cavalry Siegfried Westphal and General of Infantry Hans Krebs, upon learning of the counteroffensive, thought they could work with Jodl and Rundstedt to persuade Hitler to follow a different course of action. Rundstedt's commander of Army Group B, Field Marshal Walter Model, who retained the good favor of Hitler, also supported the alternative plan. These officers recognized immediately that the planned counteroffensive lacked the manpower and equipment necessary to reach Antwerp; that the flanks of such an attack would be dangerously exposed; and that the attack was unlikely to penetrate the Allied line but would, instead, create a salient or a bulge. They ultimately developed a plan for the envelopment and destruction of the Allies of the Meuse River, a plan called the "Small Solution." Hitler rejected it as nothing more than a half measure.

In the end, the final plan for the counteroffensive code named Wacht am Rhein (Watch on the Rhine). If Hitler was hoping to recreate the breakthrough in the Ardennes of 1940, he was trying to do it with far fewer resources. The 1940 breakthrough and race to the English Channel was done with forty-four divisions; in 1944, only twenty-eight divisions were available. In addition, the Germans only had about one-quarter of the fuel they thought they would need, and the Allies were in a far better position than they had been in 1940. Last, this offensive through the Ardennes was coming at the worst time of the year. Waist-deep snow and narrow, winding roads covered in ice or mud were not ideal conditions for tanks or troops. Hitler counted on the weather being a major factor in the success of this operation. The main thrust to Antwerp would come from Sixth Panzer Army on the right. Its spearhead element would be Kampfgruppe Peiper (Battle Group Peiper).

At 0530 hours on December 16, 1944, the Germans achieved total operational surprise. Initially more than two hundred thousand German troops, supported by 340 tanks and 1,600 artillery pieces, attacked against the positions thinly held by the 83,000 U.S. troops, with 242 medium tanks and 394 artillery pieces under the command of Lieutenant General Courtney Hodges's U.S. First Army. In the confusion of the first hours and days of the attack, the Americans were pushed back. However, stiffer than expected resistance on the north shoulder by the U.S. 99th, 2nd, and 26th Infantry Divisions, disrupted the German timetable almost from the start.

Kampfgruppe Peiper, however, penetrated only about fifty miles into Allied lines by the third day of the offensive. Peiper's mission was to race to the Meuse River without regard for his flanks and seize the key Meuse crossing at Huy. Peiper's force was making progress until it reached the Stavelot and Trois-Ponts region. Largely because U.S. combat engineers kept blowing up the bridges to his front and because his fuel ran low, Peiper came to a stop just short of Stavelot on the night of December 17 to 18, forty-two miles from the Meuse. On December 17, some of Peiper's units summarily executed a number of U.S. POWs at Malmédy. By the night of the December 18, Peiper's entire group was exposed, the element of surprise was gone, and the U.S. 30th Infantry Division and the 82nd Airborne Division were on their way to block Peiper.

On December 24, Peiper was given permission to break out. Leaving vehicles and the wounded, Peiper led about eight hundred of his men out on foot. With the German north shoulder now jammed, German morale sunk. The focus of the operation then shifted south to the Fifth Panzer Army and the standoff at Bastogne from December 19 to 26. By that point in the operation, however, only the most ardent supporters of the counteroffensive believed anything positive could still be achieved. After the war, even Dietrich said the attack had been lost by the third or fourth day.

British and U.S. commanders rushed to move forces into the Bulge to block the German advance. The U.S. 101st Airborne Division, supported by elements of the 10th Armored Division, moved to Bastogne and assumed defensive positions around the vital road junction city, which the Germans surrounded on December 21. Meanwhile, the U.S. Third Army of Lieutenant General George S. Patton, operating south of the Bulge, disengaged three divisions under its III Corps, turned the force to the north, and, on December 22, started attacking into the German southern flank, through the screen of the German Seventh Army. The U.S. Third Army finally broke through to Bastogne on December 26, but fought for several more days to lift the siege.

On December 23, the weather also started to clear, allowing the Allied air forces to attack the Germans from the air with little opposition from what was left of the Luftwaffe. The U.S. Third Army attack from the south and the U.S. First Army coming from the north finally linked up at the town of

Houffalize on January 16. The last German units were pushed back to their starting points by January 25. By the time the battle was over, the Germans had committed more than three hundred thousand troops and almost eight hundred tanks. The Allies had committed four hundred thousand troops and eleven hundred tanks. German casualties were seventeen thousand: two hundred killed, thirty-four thousand wounded, and some fifty thousand captured. The Americans suffered 10,276 killed, 47,493 wounded, and 23,218 missing. British casualties were about fourteen hundred.

Paul Frazier and David T. Zabecki

See also: Bastogne, Battle for; Brandenberger, Erich; Dietrich, Josef "Sepp"; Jodl, Alfred; Malmédy Massacre; Manteuffel, Hasso Eccard von; Model, Walther; Peiper, Joachim; Rundstedt, Karl Rudolf Gerd von; Westphal, Siegfried

Additional Reading

MacDonald, Charles B. *A Time for Trumpets: The Untold Story of the Battle of the Bulge.* New York: William Morrow, 1985.

Parker, Danny S., ed. *Hitler's Ardennes Offensive: The German View of the Battle of the Bulge.* London: Greenhill Books, 2006.

Artillery (1933–1945)

Through World War I, all German field artillery was horse-drawn. In the interwar years, the horse gave way to the truck as the prime artillery mover in the British and U.S. armies. But, along with many other armies, including Japan, Italy, and the Soviet Union, German artillery relied heavily on horses until the very end of World War II. Self-propelled (SP) artillery—guns mounted on a wheeled or tracked carriage—appeared shortly after the end of World War I. By the end of World War II, almost all armies had SP guns and howitzers.

During World War II, the three primary calibers of German field artillery were 7.5 cm, 10.5 cm, and 15 cm. Almost from the start of the war, the Germans recognized that 7.5 cm guns were ineffective for modern warfare. Those guns, including ones captured from the French, were issued only to low-priority units. The towed 10.5 cm leichte Feldhaubitze 18 (le FH18) was the principal German close-support gun. Designed at the end of World War I, it remained a capable weapon throughout World War II. The main problems were that the Germans never had enough of them, and, in almost all units, right up until the end of the war, they were drawn by horses. On the eastern front, the le FH18 was an effective antitank weapon when armed with the proper ammunition. A self-propelled version for the panzer divisions called the Wespe (Wasp) was mounted on a Pz.Kpfw.II tank chassis.

The heavier artillery at the divisional level included the 10 cm schwere Kanone 18 (sK 18) heavy gun and the 15 cm schwere Feldhaubitze 18 (s FH18) heavy howitzer. The SP version of the s FH18, called the Hummel (Bumblebee), was mounted on a Pz.Kpfw.IV tank chassis. At the corps and field army echelons, the most common heavy-support guns were the 17 cm Kanone 18 (K 18) gun and the 21 cm Mörser 18 (Mrs 18) heavy howitzer. Both weapons had a common carriage.

In most World War II armies, the organic fire support for infantry units came from infantry mortars. The Germans did have effective mortars at both company and battalion levels, but, on the basis of their experiences from World War I, they also fielded infantry guns right up until the end of the war. The two basic types were the 7.5 cm

World War II German Artillery

Model	Type	Caliber	HE Shell Weight (kilograms)	Gun Weight (kilograms)	Maximum Range (meters)	Year in Service
le IG18	Light Infantry Gun	7.5 cm	5.5	400	3,795	1927
Stu. K40	SP Assault Gun	7.5 cm	5.8	22,000	5,000	1940
Flak 35	Air Defense Gun	8.8 cm	9.4	4,985	14,800	1934
s K18	Heavy Field Gun	10 cm	15.1	5,640	19,075	1934
le FH18	Light Field Howitzer	10.5 cm	14.8	1,985	10,675	1935
Sd.Kfz. 124 Wespe	SP Howitzer	10.5 cm	14.8	11,700	10,675	1943
Stu. H42	SP Assault Howitzer	10.5 cm	14.8	23,950	7,700	1942
s FH18	Heavy Field Howitzer	15 cm	43.5	5,512	13,250	1934
Sd.Kfz. 165 Hummel	SP Howitzer		43.5	24,050	13,250	1942
Stu. H43 Brummbär	SP Assault Howitzer	15 cm	43.5		4,500	1943
K18	Field Gun	17 cm	62.8	17,520	29,600	1941
Mrs 18	Heavy Howitzer	21 cm	133	16,700	16,700	1939

leichtes Infantriegeschütz 18 (le IG18), designed late in World War I, and the heavier 15 cm schweres Infantriegeschütz 33 (s IG33). The latter was actually too heavy for an infantry gun.

The Germans did produce several SP versions of their field and antitank guns, and they also produced a self-propelled weapon called an assault gun that was more like a turretless tank. Whereas the SP field and antitank guns consisted mostly of standard towed guns mounted on various tank chassis, many of the SP assault guns had no towed equivalent. The 7.5 cm Sturmkanone 40 (StuK 40) fired a 15-pound shell approximately three miles; the 10.5 cm Sturmhaubitze 42 (StuH 42) fired a 33-pound projectile 4.8 miles; and the 15 cm Sturmhaubitze 43 (StuH 43) Brummbär (Growling Bear) fired a 95-pound shell only 2.8 miles from a barrel that was only about six feet long.

The most famous artillery piece of World War II, the "German 88," was not a field artillery gun but, rather, an antiaircraft gun. Designed by Krupp in the mid-1920s and designated a *Flugzeugabwehrkanone* (air-defense gun), the 88 cm Flak 18 proved to be a remarkably versatile and devastatingly effective weapon that was a superb antitank gun, and it could also be used in a field artillery role. Mounted on a wide variety of

A German 15 cm s FH18 heavy field howitzer firing in North Africa in 1941 or 1942. (Scheffler/PhotoQuest/Getty Images)

towed and self-propelled carriages, the "88" required different ammunition and different fire control equipment for its various missions. Upgraded throughout the war as the Flak 36, Flak 37, and Flak 41, more than twenty-five thousand of all types were produced.

German artillerymen were tactically skilled, and their guns were generally technically advanced. The main problems were that the Germans did not have nearly enough of them, and the mobility of the guns they did have was generally poor. Initially, the Luftwaffe provided the close fire support for the fast-moving panzer divisions on the eastern front. But when the Germans found that the Luftwaffe could not be everywhere at once across the vast expanses of the east, especially in bad weather, they found themselves woefully outgunned by the Soviets.

Ironically, Germany, in the interwar years all but abandoned most of the artillery lessons it had taught the rest of the world during World War I. German artillery had been so devastating that the Treaty of Versailles only allowed the postwar German Army 284 artillery pieces, none larger than 10.5 cm. As late as 1936, three years after Adolf Hitler came to power, the German Army still had only 284 guns. An army not allowed any significant amount of artillery, then, focused on developing alternative tactics centered on the tank, which, in theory, was supposed to provide its own close fire support. This, in turn, led the Germans to conclude that even if they had adequate artillery, the guns and especially their ammunition supply would not be able to keep pace with the tanks.

The Germans did recognize that even a massive tank force would sometimes encounter stiff opposition that would slow the momentum of the advance. In such situations, the additional required fire support would come from the air. By 1940, the Germans had developed an impressively sophisticated air-to-ground coordination system that was capable of concentrating as many as twenty-seven hundred aircraft over a critical sector. As successful as this system was in France, the Germans did recognize that their panzer forces would still benefit by the addition of highly mobile, organic fire-support assets. At that point, they started to develop and field a limited number of self-propelled assault, antitank, and field guns.

The German system of relying primarily on airpower for fire support worked fairly well in France. As the war progressed, though, the Germans came to realize that their approach was subject to flaws in three critical areas: mass, weather, and air superiority. When the German Army invaded the Soviet Union, the operational theater was so vast and Soviet ground forces were spread so widely that the Luftwaffe could not be overhead everywhere it was needed at any one time. The weather in the Soviet Union also severely restricted Luftwaffe operations. But conventional field artillery is practically impervious to weather conditions, and the massively gunned Red Army almost always had adequate fire support. Finally, as the war progressed and attrition sharply affected the Luftwaffe, the Germans lost air superiority.

Abandoning lessons it had taught the world in 1918, the German Army of World War II rarely emphasized the massing of artillery above the divisional level. It failed to provide artillery concentrations at the corps, army, or army group levels. The Soviets, though, considered artillery at those levels to be decisive. By 1944, the Germans had come to recognize fully their critical error with respect to artillery, and they desperately tried to recreate the fire-support structure and assets that had served them so well in 1918. By then, however, it was too little, too late.

David T. Zabecki

See also: Rockets, Guided Bombs, and Guided Missiles; Tanks and Self-Propelled Guns

Additional Reading

Bailey, Jonathan B. A. *Field Artillery and Fire Power*. 2nd ed. Annapolis, MD: Naval Institute Press, 2003.

Hogg, Ian V. *German Artillery of World War Two*. Mechanicsburg, PA: Stackpole Books, 1997.

Atlantic, Battle of the (September 1939–May 1945)

The Battle of the Atlantic was the longest campaign of World War II. The German Navy tried to sever the Allied sea lines of communication, along which supplies necessary to fight the war were sent to Great Britain. The Germans employed a few surface raiders, but principally they used U-boats. At the beginning of the war, the German Navy had, not the three hundred U-boats deemed necessary by Commodore Karl Dönitz, but fifty-seven boats, of which only twenty-seven were of types that could reach the Atlantic from their home bases. Although an extensive building program was immediately

The Battle of the Atlantic

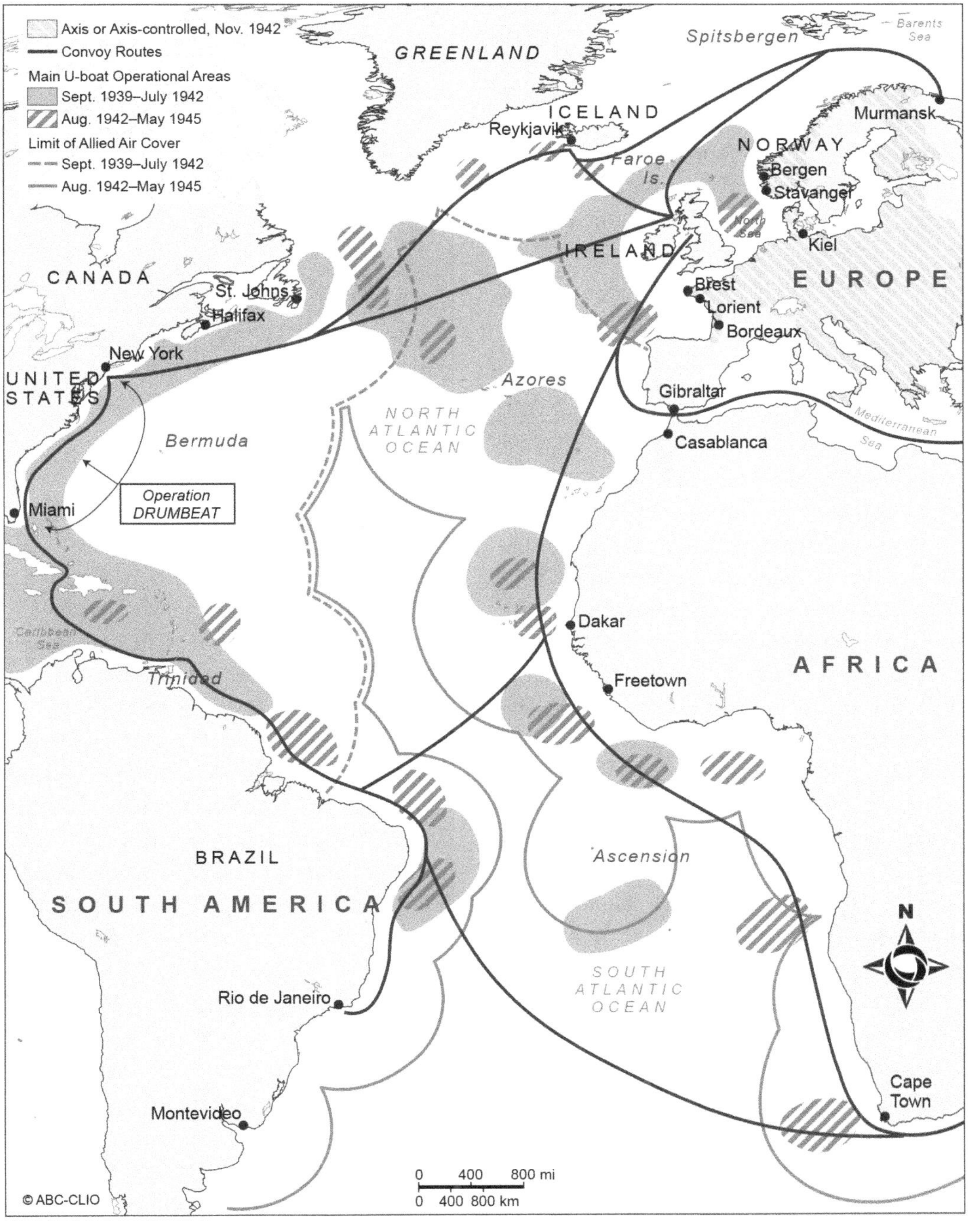

begun, only in the second half of 1941 did U-boat numbers begin to rise.

On the Allied side, British Navy leaders were at first confident that their ASDIC (for Allied Submarine Detection Investigating Committee) location device—later called Sonar—would enable their escort vessels to defend the supply convoys against the submerged attackers, so that shipping losses might be limited until the building of new merchant ships by Britain, Canada, and the United States might settle the balance. However, Dönitz planned to concentrate groups of U-boats (called "wolf packs" by the Allies) against the convoys and to attack them jointly on the surface at night. It took time, however, before the battles of the convoys really began. The Battle of the Atlantic became a running match between numbers of German U-boats and the development of their weapons against the Allied merchant ships, their sea and air escorts (with improving detection equipment), and new weapons.

The Battle of the Atlantic lasted without interruption for sixty-nine months, during which time German U-boats sank 2,850 Allied and neutral merchant ships, 2,520 of them in the Atlantic and Indian Oceans. The U-boats also sank many warships, from aircraft carriers to destroyers, frigates, corvettes, and other antisubmarine vessels. The Germans lost, in turn, one large battleship, one pocket battleship, some armed merchant raiders, and 650 U-boats, 522 of them in the Atlantic and Indian Oceans. The Allied victory in the Battle of the Atlantic resulted from the vastly superior resources on the Allied side in shipbuilding and aircraft production (the ability to replace lost ships and aircraft) and from superior antisubmarine detection equipment and weapons. Allied signals intelligence was critical to the victory.

Jürgen Rohwer

See also: Dönitz, Karl; Kriegsmarine (German Navy); Submarines; Wolf Pack Tactics (*Rudeltaktik*)

Additional Reading

Blair, Clay. *Hitler's U-Boat War.* Vol. 1, The Hunters, 1939–1942; vol. 2, The Hunted, 1942–1945. New York: Random House, 1996, 1998.

Gardner, W. J. R. *Decoding History: The Battle of the Atlantic and Ultra.* Annapolis, MD: Naval Institute Press, 1999.

Rohwer, Jürgen. *Chronology of the War at Sea, 1939–1945.* Annapolis: Naval Institute Press, 2005.

Atlantic Wall (1941–1944)

German defensive system.

After conquering France in June 1940, the Germans fortified the main harbors, fuel installations, and railway yards, particularly after the British retaliated with artillery and aircraft. In October 1941, Hitler ordered fortification of the Channel Islands. In December 1941, Hitler required a "new Western wall" (*neue Westwall*), concentrated on the Norwegian, French, Dutch, Danish, and German coasts. In March 1942, Hitler directed a more continuous "coastal defense" (*Küstenverteidigung*). Centralized planning began in May 1942 and construction in June. Before the end of 1942, propagandists had designated the *Atlantikwall* ("Atlantic Wall"), although the fortifications were discontinuous and concentrated in north-eastern France, which became known as the "Iron Coast."

The *Atlantikwall* absorbed perhaps eleven million cubic meters of reinforced concrete and boasted more than twenty thousand covered structures, tens of thousands of uncovered structures, and more than one thousand coastal batteries, including 114 guns of 280 mm to 406 mm caliber. Deliveries surged in 1940, fell in 1941, increased more than thirty-three times in 1942, and more than doubled again in 1943. Deliveries peaked in April 1943, and then fell in deference to other requirements. In the first half of 1944, deliveries approached the previous year's rate. The Germans were months, if not years, short of completion, particularly in Normandy, where the western Allies landed that June.

The *Atlantikwall* encouraged the western Allies to conduct costly invasions of North Africa and Italy in 1942, 1943, and 1944, and then land in Normandy, still far from Germany. They then fought for three months to reach the Pas de Calais. In August and September 1944, the Allies were short of port facilities and were forced to assault most of the defensive areas in northern France and Belgium. Five fortresses in France survived until after Germany surrendered.

Antwerp should have been upgraded to a fortress, although it was protected by other fortresses. On November 1, 1944, the British invaded the island of Walcheren, after which they finally captured Antwerp. The Allies spent the rest of 1944 restoring Antwerp. Short of supplies and good weather, the Western Allies faced several reversals before invading Germany in spring 1945. The *Atlantikwall* was not effective in defending the German Reich, but that does not mean that it was inefficient.

Bruce Newsome

See also: Antwerp, Allied Liberation of; Westwall

Additional Reading

Forty, George. *Fortress Europe: Hitler's Atlantic Wall.* Hersham, England: Ian Allan, 2002.

Austria, Annexation of (*Anschluss*) (March 11–13, 1938)

The *Anschluss* (or joining) of Germany and Austria was an event long in the making. Austrian Pan-Germanist politicians and proponents in the latter decades of the nineteenth century sought union between Germany and Austria. As Hitler and the Nazis gained popular support and ascended to power in Germany, the Austrian Nazi Party also enjoyed a surge, gaining credibility and traction against the proindependence administration of Chancellor Engelbert Dollfuss. Austrian Nazis, realizing that Dollfuss was not going to be intimidated, killed him in a botched coup attempt on July 25, 1934. In July 1936, Dollfuss's successor, Kurt von Schuschnigg, signed an agreement with the German ambassador to Vienna, Franz von Papen, which ensured Austria's domestic independence, forfeiting its independence in the realm of foreign policy.

By the summer of 1937, as Germany struggled to procure the raw materials necessary for rearmament, Hitler came to see Austria as a source of currency, labor, and desperately needed natural resources. Furthermore, annexing Austria would shore up its borders and provide an additional pool of conscripts for the Wehrmacht. On March 11, 1938, Austrian chancellor von Schuschnigg received an ultimatum from Hitler, demanding his resignation and the installation of Arthur Seyss-Inquart as chancellor, or suffer invasion. On the morning of March 12, 1938, the one-hundred-thousand-strong German Eighth Army, under the command of General Fedor von Bock, crossed the Austrian border just hours after Miklas finally relented and accepted Schuschnigg's resignation and Seyss-Inquart's chancellorship. Simultaneously, Austrian Nazis seized control of government buildings and railroad stations in cities throughout Austria. On March 13, 1938, Hitler entered Austria, signing into law in Linz the incorporation of Austria into Germany as Ostmark—a reference to Austrian kingdom of the medieval Holy Roman Empire. A doctored plebiscite, in which over 99 percent of Austrians supposedly voted in the affirmative for Austria's incorporation into Germany, later finalized the annexation.

Jason C. Engle

See also: Bock, Fedor von

Additional Reading

Low, Alfred D. *The Anschluss Movement: 1931–1938 and the Great Powers.* New York: Columbia University Press, 1985.

Avranches Counteroffensive (August 7–12, 1944)

After the Allies broke out of the Normandy lodgment with their Operation COBRA south of Saint-Lô, they started they started expanding deeper into France. Determined to restore the situation, Hitler, on August 2, 1944, ordered German forces to launch a strong counterattack toward Avranches on the coast, to cut off the Allied penetration. Field Marshal Günther von Kluge, commander of German Army Group B, was ordered to commit eight of his nine available panzer divisions to the operation. If this armored force could drive to the sea, Hitler expected it to isolate the forces of General George S. Patton's newly activated U.S. Third Army in the Brittany peninsula. Because Kluge thought it would take too long to assemble and prepare all eight panzer divisions, he planned an immediate attack with only four.

Shortly after midnight on August 7, the panzers started moving forward without artillery preparation. General Hans von Funck, commander of XLVII Panzer Corps, was in overall tactical command, but with only about two hundred tanks in total. The 116th Panzer Division was on the right, the 2nd Panzer Division was in the center, and the 2nd SS Panzer Division was on the left. The 1st SS Panzer Division came close behind, preparing to exploit the breakthrough. Operation LÜTTICH struck squarely on the boundary between U.S. VII Corps and XV Corps, which also was the boundary between the U.S. First and Third Armies. The U.S. 30th Infantry Division was in the main path of the attack.

The 2nd SS Panzer Division quickly took Mortain, about twenty miles east of Avranches, and then started moving toward the coast. The panzers ran into trouble, however, when they tried to go past the high ground outside the city, where Americans of the 30th Infantry Division held Hill 317. Forward observer Lieutenant Robert Weiss called in air strikes and artillery fire on the Germans. By the evening of August 7, Allied air forces had knocked out forty of the seventy German tanks that penetrated the American lines. Hitler insisted on continuing the attack, although Kluge recommended breaking it off. A renewal of the offensive was scheduled for August 9 but never launched, as the Germans began to realize what was happening to them around Falaise. Kluge met with the Seventh Army commander SS-Oberstgruppenführer Paul Hausser on August 11, and they jointly concluded that they had no alternative but to withdraw the panzers from the Mortain-Avranches area for recommitment against the Allied thrust toward Falaise. Hitler finally agreed, but when the panzers started pulling back on the night of August 11, they were already too late to help the encircled Seventh Army at Falaise. By the time Operation LÜTTICH ended, the Germans had lost some 150 almost irreplaceable tanks. The Avranches Offensive turned out to be just another in a long line of Hitler's half-baked military schemes that did more than anything else to assure German defeat.

David T. Zabecki

See also: COBRA, Allied Breakout Operation; Falaise-Argentan Pocket; Hausser, Paul; Kluge, Günther von

Additional Reading

Ludwig, Joachim. *Rückzug: The German Retreat from France, 1944.* Lexington: University Press of Kentucky, 2012.

Reardon, Mark J. *Victory at Mortain: Stopping Hitler's Counteroffensive.* Lawrence: University Press of Kansas, 2002.

B

Babi Yar Massacre (September 29–30, 1941)

The Germans conducted a mass shooting of Soviet Jews at Babi Yar, outside Kiev, Ukraine. Following the German Army's invasion of the Soviet Union on June 22, 1941, four Einsatzgruppen (SS mobile killing squads) entered Soviet territory, their task the physical annihilation of Communist Party functionaries, Red Army commissars, the physically and mentally handicapped, partisans, and Jews.

Among the numerous Einsatzgruppen crimes, the slaughter of Jews at Babi Yar in late September 1941—perpetrated by Standartenführer Paul Blobel's Sonderkommando 4a, a subunit of Brigadeführer Otto Rasch's Einsatzgruppe C—was arguably the most notorious. On September 19, 1941, units of the German Army Group South occupied Kiev, the capital of Soviet Ukraine. In the days immediately following, a series of explosions rocked the city, destroying German field headquarters, burning more than one-third of a square mile of the Kiev city center, and leaving some ten thousand residents homeless. Although these explosions were likely the work of the Soviet political police, or NKVD, the Germans saw in them a convenient justification to massacre the city's Jews, a task Blobel's Sonderkommando would have carried out regardless.

The city's Jews were ordered to assemble with their possessions—including money, valuables, and warm clothing—near the Jewish cemetery no later than 0700 on Monday, September 29. Once assembled, they were marched to Babi Yar, a partially wooded ravine just outside the city. There, the Germans, following the procedure used by Einsatzgruppen since the mass shootings of Soviet Jews began in late June, forced the Jews to strip, dispossessed them of their belongings, and shot them to death in groups of thirty to forty people. In the course of two gruesome days, Blobel's men, relying exclusively on firearms, murdered 33,771 innocent men, women, and children. Subsequently, they reported that the Jews had offered no resistance and, until the last minute, had believed they were to be resettled.

Bruce J. DeHart

See also: Einsatzgruppen; Holocaust, German Military Complicity in; Waffen-SS

Additional Reading

Rhodes, Richard. *Masters of Death: The S.S. Einsatzgruppen and the Invention of the Holocaust.* New York: Vintage, 2002.

Bach-Zelewski, Erich von dem (1899–1973)

Schutzstaffel (SS) Obergruppenführer and commander of antipartisan units on the eastern front.

Born to a Junker family in Lauenburg, Pomerania, on March 1, 1899, Bach-Zelewski served in the German Army during World War I. After the armistice, he served in the Freikorps and as a Reichswehr officer until 1924. In 1930, Bach-Zelewski joined the National Socialist Party and the SS. In 1941, he was assigned to Army Group Center on the eastern front, where he was largely responsible for masterminding and carrying out the massacre of ethnic and political enemies of the Reich. In the late summer of 1944, he commanded the German units that crushed the Warsaw Rising. Bach-Zelewski testified for the prosecution at the Nuremberg war crimes trials. He was never prosecuted for his role in the anti-Jewish massacres. Instead, he was tried in 1961 for his participation in the 1934 Night of the Long Knives blood purge and sentenced to four and a half years in prison. Indicted again in 1962 for the murder of six communists in 1933, Bach-Zelewski died in a prison hospital in Munich on March 8, 1973.

Martin Moll

See also: Freikorps (Free Corps); Holocaust, German Military Complicity in; Night of the Long Knives; Waffen-SS; Warsaw Rising

Additional Reading

Reitlinger, Gerald. *The SS: Alibi of a Nation, 1922–1945.* New York: Viking, 1957.

Balck, Hermann (1893–1984)

Wehrmacht general of panzer troops.

Born in Danzig-Langfuhr, Prussia, on December 7, 1893, Hermann Balck served as a mountain infantry officer on the western, eastern, Italian, and Balkan fronts during World War I. He was wounded seven times and was recommended for the *Pour le Mérite* but never received the award. Balck remained in the postwar Reichswehr and became an early exponent of mechanization. On May 13, 1940, Balck commanded the 1st Rifle Regiment, 1st Panzer Division of the XIX Panzer Corps, crossing the Meuse River and spearheading General Heinz Guderian's breakthrough at Sedan.

General of Panzer Troops Hermann Balck, ca. 1940. Balck is considered by many military historians as Germany's finest battlefield commander of World War II. (ullstein bild via Getty Images)

In May 1942, Balck assumed command of the 11th Panzer Division in the Soviet Union. That December, during the Soviet offensive along the Chir River north of Stalingrad, the 11th Panzer Division crushed an assault by the Soviet Fifth Tank Army with a series of stunning counterattacks, in what was perhaps the most brilliantly fought divisional-level battle of World War II. In November 1943, Balck assumed command of the XLVIII Panzer Corps, leading it during the fierce battles at Kiev, Radomyshl, and Tarnopol in 1944. During those battles, his corps destroyed three Soviet armies. In August 1944, Balck and his chief of staff, Colonel Friedrich-Wilhelm von Mellenthin took over the Fourth Panzer Army. Counterattacking near Baranov, they halted the Soviet offensive in the great bend of the Vistula. For that action, Balck became the nineteenth recipient of the Knight's Cross of the Iron Cross with Oak Leaves, Swords, and Diamonds.

In September 1944, Balck assumed command of Army Group G in the west. His mission was to stop Lieutenant General George S. Patton's Third Army and prevent Patton from interfering in the Ardennes Offensive, planned for that December. Late in December, however, Balck was relieved of his command, the victim of political intrigues by Schutzstaffel (SS) chief Heinrich Himmler. Thanks to the intervention of Heinz Guderian, his old mentor, Balck was reassigned as commander of the reconstituted German Sixth Army on the eastern front. When the war ended, Balck kept his troops out of Soviet hands by surrendering them to the U.S. XX Corps in Austria. In his widely regarded 1956 book, *Panzer Battles*, Mellenthin called Balck Germany's finest field commander. Balck died in Erbenbach-Rockenau, Germany, on November 29, 1982.

David T. Zabecki

See also: Ardennes Offensive (Battle of the Bulge); Chir River, Battle of; France, Battle of; Guderian, Heinz; Himmler, Heinrich; Hitler, Adolf; Lorraine Campaign, Allied; Mellenthin, Friedrich-Wilhelm von

Additional Reading

Balck, Hermann. *Order in Chaos: The Memoirs of General of Panzer Troops Hermann Balck.* Translated and Edited by David T. Zabecki and Dieter Biedekarken. Lexington: University Press of Kentucky, 2015.

Barents Sea, Battle of (December 30–31, 1942)

The battle of the Barents Sea was fought between German surface warships and British warships escorting convoy JW 51B to Kola Inlet in the Soviet Union. Following the high losses sustained during the battles of convoys PQ 17 and PQ 18 during the summer of 1942, the British temporarily suspended the Arctic convoys to the Soviet Union. The convoys were later resumed with the onset of winter and the long Arctic nights, which offered greater security.

In late 1942, the German naval forces based in Alta Fjord, near Norway's North Cape, under the command of Vice Admiral Oskar Kummetz, included the pocket battleship *Lützow*; the heavy cruiser *Admiral Hipper*; and six fleet destroyers. The Germans also had twenty-three U-boats operating in Arctic waters. Convoy JW 51B consisted of fourteen merchant ships, escorted six British destroyers and two corvettes. The distant cover was provided by the Royal Navy's Force R, under the command of Rear Admiral Robert L. Burnett, and consisting of the cruisers HMS *Sheffield* and *Jamaica*, and two destroyers. Convoy JW 51B sailed from Scotland on December 22, 1942 and linked up with its escort on December 25. The day prior, German aircraft spotted and started tracking the convoy.

Kummetz launched Operation REGENBOGEN (RAINBOW) shortly after noon on December 30. Proceeding cautiously, Kummetz, at 0240 hours on December 31, divided his force into two sections in an attempt to close a pincer on the convoy. By late that morning, however, the second arm of the pincer missed the convoy completely. With the German force now split, Force R attacked Kummetz's element and opened fire on the *Hipper*, scoring several hits.

Convoy JW 51B continued its voyage and successfully delivered 202 tanks, 2,046 other vehicles, 87 fighters, 33 bombers, 11,500 tons of fuel, and 12,650 tons of aviation fuel to Murmansk. The battle had been a tactical draw that cost the Germans one destroyer, and 330 seamen were killed. The British lost one destroyer and one minesweeper, and 250 were killed. Operation REGENBOGEN, however, was a major operational and strategic failure for the Germans. The supplies made it through to the Soviets, bolstering Allied confidence, sustaining the Soviet war effort and severely damaging German morale. The failure at the Barents Sea contributed directly to Grand Admiral Raeder's downfall three weeks later. He was replaced as commander of the German Navy by Grand Admiral Karl Dönitz. Hitler also ordered that German naval strategy would now focus on U-boat operations, at the expense of the surface warships.

David T. Zabecki

See also: Convoy PQ 17, Battle of; Dönitz, Karl; Raeder, Erich

Additional Reading

Pope, Dudley. *73 North: The Defeat of Hitler's Navy.* New York: Berkley Books, 1959.

Barkhorn, Gerhard (1919–1983)

Luftwaffe major and ace, Bundesluftwaffe major general

Born in Königsberg, East Prussia, on March 20, 1919, Gerhard Barkhorn joined the Luftwaffe in March 1938. Barkhorn was the second-highest-scoring fighter ace of World War II, with 301 victories. He flew more than eleven hundred combat missions, was shot down nine times, bailed out once, and was wounded twice. Barkhorn ended the war flying the Me 262 jet fighter in JV-44, Major General Adolf Galland's "Squadron of Experts." At the end of the war, he surrendered to the Americans and was held prisoner until September 1945. Barkhorn later served in the Federal Republic of Germany's *Bundesluftwaffe* from 1956 until his retirement as a major general in 1976. On January 6, 1983, he was involved in a serious automobile accident near Cologne and died in the hospital there two days later.

Marlyn R. Pierce

See also: Galland, Adolf; Luftwaffe (German Air Force)

Additional Reading

Spick, Mike. *Luftwaffe Fighter Aces: The Jagdflieger and Their Combat Tactics and Techniques.* Mechanicsburg, PA: Stackpole Books, 1996.

Bastogne, Battle for (December 19, 1944–January 9, 1945)

Bastogne was a key battle within the German Ardennes Offensive (Battle of the Bulge). Bastogne, Belgium, was an important communications hub; seven main roads, a railroad line, and several minor roads met there. Elements of the U.S. First Army had liberated Bastogne and the Ardennes area in September 1944. Operation WACHT AM RHEIN was a counteroffensive intended to destroy Allied units and recapture the port of Antwerp. Operation WACHT AM RHEIN depended on surprise and a rapid capture of bridges across the Meuse River and the Allied fuel depots and communications routes on the way to Saint Vith.

The German attack, which opened early on December 16, caught the Americans completely by surprise. General of Panzer Troops Heinrich von Lüttwitz's XLVII Panzer Corps, the spearhead of the southern German thrust, made for Bastogne, some twenty miles from the German line of departure. The Germans expected to occupy Bastogne no later than December 18, but the poor state of the roads and misinformation provided by Belgians delayed them.

Meanwhile, Supreme Allied Commander General Dwight D. Eisenhower correctly concluded that this was a major German offensive rather than a spoiling attack and ordered up reinforcements. Elements of the U.S. 10th Armored Division arrived at Bastogne in the evening of December 18, and the U.S. 101st Airborne Division closed shortly before midnight.

Lieutenant General Fritz Bayerlein's Panzer Lehr Division reached Bastogne just after midnight on December 19 and attacked immediately. The Americans beat back the German assault but were under constant German pressure and were completely encircled in a six-mile-diameter pocket by the evening of December 21. On December 22, the Germans sent a message demanding surrender to the Americans. The response of Brigadier General Anthony McAuliffe, the acting commander of the 101st, was, "To the German Commander: Nuts! The American Commander."

On December 23, the weather cleared, freezing the ground and making it passable for armor. Allied planes filled the skies, and transports dropped supplies to the Bastogne defenders, then extremely short of ammunition. On Christmas Day, the U.S. 2nd Armored Division destroyed the 2nd Panzer Division at Celles, near the Meuse, destroying eighty-two German tanks. On December 26, Lieutenant Colonel Creighton Abrams's 37th Tank Battalion of the 4th Armored Division of Patton's Third Army broke through the German lines to Bastogne.

The battle now expanded as both sides poured in reinforcements. General of Panzer Troops Hasso von Manteuffel, commanding the Fifth Panzer Army, made Bastogne its principal effort, as the now defunct German drive on Antwerp turned into a struggle for Bastogne. Meanwhile, the Americans brought up significant amounts of artillery and armor. Allied aircraft also attacked the German armor without letup, destroying large numbers of tanks. The last major German attack on the city occurred on January 4. Other smaller attacks took place until January 8, with the battle ending the next day. The fight for the city had claimed about 3,000 German and 2,700 American casualties; 782 Belgian civilians also died.

William P. Head and Spencer C. Tucker

See also: Ardennes Offensive (Battle of the Bulge); Bayerlein, Fritz; Manteuffel, Hasso Eccard von

Additional Reading

Marshall, S. L. A. *Bastogne: The Story of the First Eight Days*. Washington, DC: Infantry Journal Press, 1946.

Parker, Danny S., ed. *Hitler's Ardennes Offensive: The German View of the Battle of the Bulge*. London: Greenhill Books, 2006.

Bayerlein, Fritz (1899–1970)

Wehrmacht lieutenant general.

Born in Würzburg, Germany, on January 14, 1899, Fritz Bayerlein joined the German Army in 1915 and fought on the western front in World War I. He joined the Reichswehr in 1921 and was commissioned a second lieutenant the following year.

During the Battle for France in 1940, Bayerlein was the operations officer in General Heinz Guderian's XIX Panzer Corps. He continued to serve with Guderian as the operations officer of Guderian's 2nd Panzer Group in the first three months of the invasion of the Soviet Union.

In October 1941, Bayerlein transferred to North Africa as chief of staff to General Erwin Rommel's Afrika Korps (Africa Corps). On August 30, when General Walther Nehring was wounded at the start of the Battle of Alam Halfa, Bayerlein took command of the Afrika Korps. He again led a decimated Afrika Korps during its long retreat after the Battle of El Alamein. Wounded during the last days of the fighting in North Africa, he was evacuated prior to the Axis surrender on May 13, 1943.

Bayerlein commanded the newly formed Panzer Lehr Division, which he led from its creation in early 1944 until February 1945. The division fought in Normandy and helped slow the British advance on Caen. He also commanded the Panzer Lehr as part of General Hasso von Manteuffel's Fifth Panzer Army in the attack on Bastogne in December 1944. Bayerlein took command of LIII Corps in February 1945 and defended the Ruhr Pocket until its surrender on April 15, 1945. Bayerlein died in Würzburg on January 30, 1970.

Jon D. Berlin

See also: Afrika Korps; Bastogne, Battle for; Guderian, Heinz; Manteuffel, Hasso Eccard von; North Africa Campaign; Rommel, Erwin; Ruhr Ground Campaign, Allied

Additional Reading

Menzoff, Julius. "Fritz Bayerlein." In *Chief of Staff: The Principal Officers Behind History's Great Commanders, vol. 2, World War II to Korea and Vietnam*, edited by David T. Zabecki. Annapolis, MD: U.S. Naval Institute Press, 2008.

Beck, Ludwig (1880–1944)

Wehrmacht colonel general and one of the key opponents of Adolf Hitler.

Born in Biebrich, Germany, on June 29, 1880, Ludwig Beck joined the army in 1898. In 1913, he qualified as a General Staff officer and served in a variety of staff and command positions during World War I on the western front. Beck continued in the postwar Reichswehr. In October 1933, he became chief of the Truppenamt (Troop Office), the thinly disguised covert General Staff prohibited to the Germans under the Treaty of Versailles. In 1932 to 1933, Beck was the primary author of *Truppenführung* (*Unit Command*), which remained the principal war-fighting manual of the German Army until 1945.

In March 1935, the Truppenamt was redesignated as the General Staff of the army. Beck presided over the expansion of the revived General Staff and the development of war plans based on a defensive strategy. His peers considered him a master military planner. He clearly understood that any future war would necessarily become a multifront conflict, which Germany could not win. As late as 1935, however, Beck continued to believe the German officer corps could keep the National Socialists under control, and he attempted to mobilize other generals to oppose Hitler's policies. In August 1938, Beck retired from the army. He then organized a covert opposition group of active and retired officers and became one of the key leaders in the failed attempt to assassinate Hitler in July 1944. Arrested in Berlin, Beck was executed on the night of July 20 to 21, 1944.

Colonel General Ludwig Beck, chief of the German General Staff, 1935–1938. He was a key leader of the unsuccessful plot to kill Adolf Hitler on July 20, 1944. Had the plot succeeded, Beck most probably would have become the German head of state. Arrested when the plot failed, he unsuccessfully attempted suicide and was later shot and killed by an army sergeant. (Popperfoto via Getty Images)

Despite being unfairly and inaccurately painted by Heinz Guderian as a rigid and unimaginative opponent of armored warfare, Beck helped rebuild the German military into an efficient war-fighting machine. Ludwig Beck also proved that during the Third Reich, true German patriotism was incompatible with Nazism.

David T. Zabecki

See also: German General Staff of World War II; Guderian, Heinz; Opposition to Hitler, German Military; Document 1: Wehrmacht Principal Operations Manual, HDv 300 *Truppenführung:* Introduction

Additional Reading

Hoffmann, Peter. *The History of the German Resistance, 1933–1945.* Cambridge, MA: MIT Press, 1977.

Belgium and Flanders Campaign (May 10–28, 1940)

The German overrun of Belgium and the Flanders section of the Netherlands was a supporting action to the German attack on France at the start of World War II. Belgium had proclaimed its neutrality and sought to avoid involvement in World War II, but to invade and defeat France swiftly, the Germans needed to secure Belgium. When Germany invaded Poland in September 1939, thereby initiating World War II, Belgium declared a state of armed neutrality. Prime Minister Hubert Pierlot resolved to defend the country against all invaders and deployed the army along both the French and the German borders.

In May 1940, Belgium fielded an army of more than six hundred thousand men organized into twenty-two divisions. Unfortunately for Belgium, this sizable force was hardly equipped to defeat a German invasion. The Belgians had few antiaircraft guns and had only forty-two light and twelve medium tanks. Their air service had only 184 operational aircraft. Thus, Belgium had no hope of winning a prolonged land campaign with Germany without outside support.

Colonel General Fedor von Bock's German Army Group B operated against Belgium and the Netherlands. The Germans committed Colonel General Walther von Reichenau's Sixth Army, with seventeen infantry and two panzer divisions, to the initial invasion of Belgium. It was to drive southwest. Meanwhile, General of Artillery Georg von Küchler's Eighteenth Army of eleven divisions, including one cavalry and one panzer division, was expected to subdue the Netherlands quickly, and then drive south to join the fighting in Belgium.

Fort Eben Emael, the lynchpin of the Belgian defenses, was a series of concrete and steel emplacements north of Liège that guarded bridges over the Albert Canal at Briedgen, Veldwezelt, and Vroenhoven. Garrisoned by more than seven hundred men, the fortress's only hope of slowing the German panzers lay in keeping them east of the canal. At 0525 hours on May 10, 1940, the Germans sent seventy-eight specially trained men of Assault Detachment Kock in gliders to land on top of the fortress. The attackers used hollow charges to destroy the key gun turrets and bunkers. At the same time, German paratroopers captured the major bridges in the sector. Troops of the 223rd Infantry Division followed close behind and took the rest of the Belgian position the next day. In less than twenty-four hours, the Germans had breached the key Belgian defensive line on the Albert Canal.

Fighting bravely, the Belgians fell back to the line of the Dyle River east of Brussels, with King Leopold III in personal command. The British and French had planned to send their own forces into Belgium in the event of a German invasion, but there had been little prior coordination between Britain, France, and neutral Belgium. On May 12, however, elements of the British Expeditionary Force (BEF) and General Georges Blanchard's French First Army began joining the Belgian defenders, and, by May 15, the Allies had some thirty-five divisions in the Namur-Antwerp area.

As Reichenau's Sixth Army probed the Dyle Line, Küchler's Eighteenth Army turned south from the Netherlands after the surrender of that country on May 15. That move threatened the Allied left flank. At the same time and to the south, the hammer blow of Colonel General Gerd von Rundstedt's Army Group A, heavy in tanks, was driving west, and then north through the Ardennes Forest. The overall German plan, Operation SICHELSCHNITT (SICKEL CUT), worked to perfection.

With the situation hopeless, King Leopold II surrendered the Belgian armed forces on May 28. That, in turn, exposed the left flank of the British-French line and ended any Allied hopes of holding part of Flanders. British Prime Minister Winston Churchill then ordered the British Navy to evacuate British forces from Dunkirk.

The eighteen days of the Belgian Campaign cost the nation some 7,500 troops killed in action and 15,850 wounded. The country remained under German occupation for the next four years. The German records did not report specific casualty counts for operations in Belgium or the Netherlands. German casualties for "operations in the west" in May and June 1940 totaled 10,232 dead, 8,463 missing, and 42,523 wounded, and 432 aircraft lost.

Lance Janda and Spencer C. Tucker

See also: Bock, Fedor von; Küchler, Georg von; Reichenau, Walther von; Rundstedt, Karl Rudolf Gerd von

Additional Reading

Mrazek, James E. *The Fall of Eben Emael.* Reprint ed. New York: Presidio Press, 1999.

Belorussia Offensive, Soviet (June 22–August 29, 1944)

The massive Soviet offensive against Field Marshal Ernst Busch's German Army Group Center in Belorussia was code-named Operation BAGRATION. It was timed to meet Soviet leader Josef Stalin's pledge at the Allied Tehran Conference for an operation to prevent the transfer of German forces to the west to meet the Allied invasion of Normandy. The Soviets deployed four fronts (army groups) for the operation. From north to south were the 1st Baltic Front and the 3rd, 2nd, and 1st Belorussian Fronts, commanded by Generals Ivan Bagramyan, Ivan Chernyakhovsky, Georgy Zakharov, and Konstantin Rokossovsky, respectively. The Soviet forces included 168 divisions, with a total strength of 2,411,000 troops (including 80,000 Poles), 2,715 tanks, 1,355 assault guns, 24,363 artillery pieces, and 5,327 aircraft.

Army Group Center consisted of the Third Panzer Army, commanded by Colonel General Georg-Hans Reinhardt; the Fourth Army, commanded by General Kurt von Tippelskirch; the Ninth Army, commanded by General Hans Jordan; and the Second Army, commanded by Colonel General Walter Weiss. Army Group Center had only 54 divisions, with a total strength of 886,000 troops, 118 tanks, 377 assault guns, 2,589 artillery pieces, and 602 aircraft.

Operation BAGRATION started on June 22. Over the next six days, the Red Army broke through German lines in six places and encircled large German forces at Vitebsk and Bobruisk, taking twenty thousand prisoners. On July 28, Field Marshal Walther Model replaced Busch as commander of Army Group Center. On July 3, the Soviets entered Minsk, the Belorussian capital, capturing nearly one hundred thousand Germans east of the city.

Between June 23 and August 20, 1944, the Red Army had advanced almost 360 miles along a more than 600-mile-wide front, effectively destroying Army Group Center. The Soviets destroyed seventeen German divisions. The German Army High Command's official loss figure was about three hundred thousand men. Soviet losses were also high, with more than one hundred and seventy-eight thousand dead and missing, and more than five hundred and eighty-seven thousand wounded.

The advance into Belorussia led to advances in other sectors of the front, the Ukraine, and Estonia and Latvia, where Army Group North's link to other German forces was cut temporarily. Operation BAGRATION was one of the greatest Soviet victories of the war and one from which German forces could never recover.

Arthur T. Frame and David T. Zabecki

See also: Busch, Ernst; Model, Walther

Additional Reading

Adair, Paul. *Hitler's Greatest Defeat: The Collapse of Army Group Centre, June 1944.* London: Weidenfeld Military, 1994.

Glantz, David M., and Harold S. Orenstein, eds. *Belorussia, 1944: The Soviet General Staff Study.* London: Cass, 2001.

Berlin, Land Battle for (March 31–May 2, 1945)

Berlin had been attacked by Royal Air Force Bomber Command in August 1940, after the German bombing of London, but this had inflicted little damage. The real air

DESTRUCTION OF ARMY GROUP CENTER, 1944

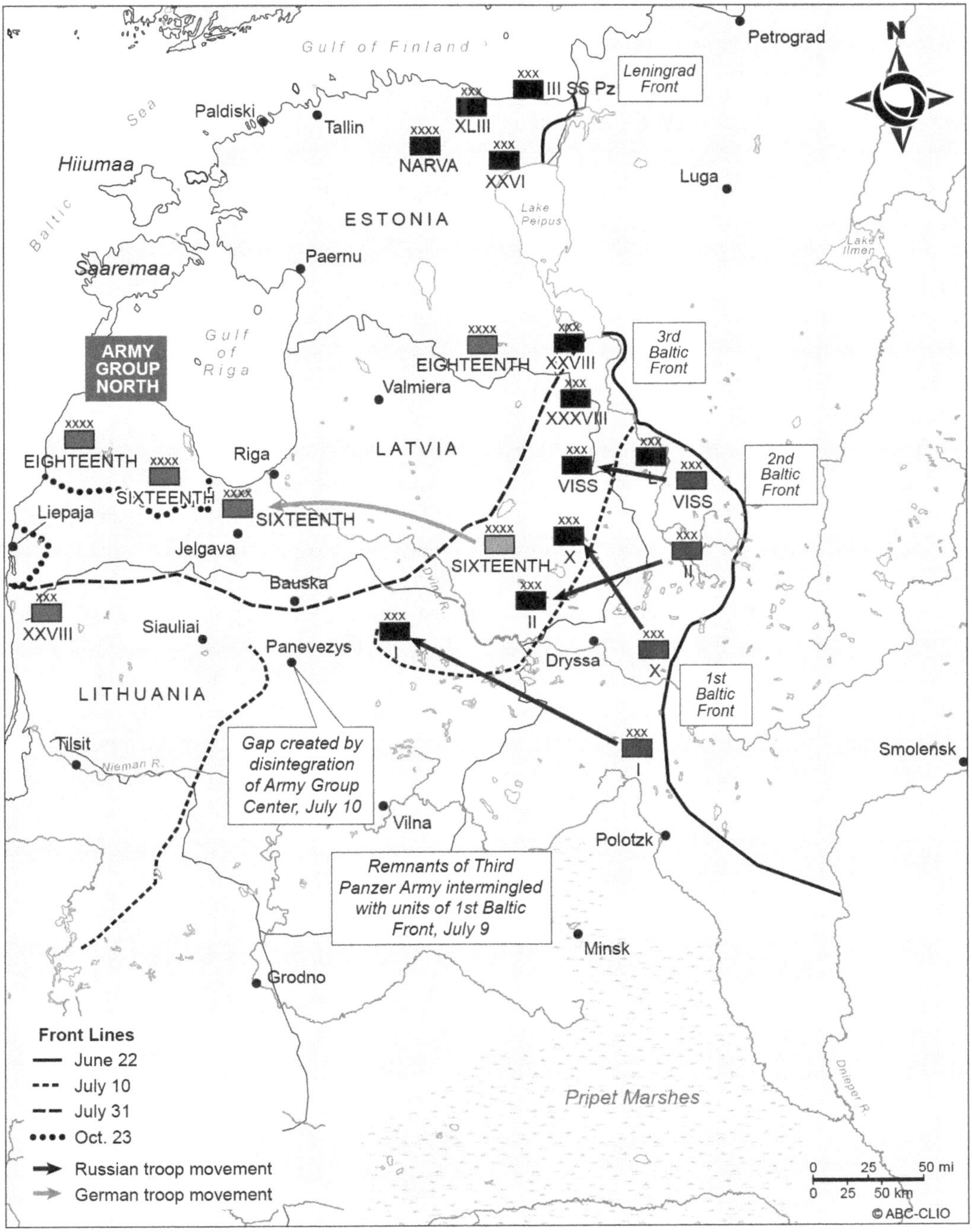

campaign for the city began in earnest in November 1943, with the first in a long series of punishing Allied air raids. Berliners managed to carry on amid the ruins. As the war in Europe drew to a close, the city became the ultimate prize, at least for the Soviets. Soviet dictator Josef Stalin wanted it desperately. By early February 1945, Marshal Georgy Zhukov's 1st Belorussian Front and Marshal Ivan Konev's 1st Ukrainian Front had completed the initial phase of their advance into Germany. Zhukov's troops were across the Oder River, one hundred miles from Berlin. The Soviets had surrounded large German troop concentrations at Breslau and Posen.

To defend Berlin, Hitler had only Army Group Vistula, formed on January 24, 1945, with the severely depleted Third Panzer and Ninth Armies, as well as a number of new ad-hoc formations. Hitler initially wanted Field Marshal Maximilian von Weichs to command the new army group but, given SS chief Heinrich Himmler's desire for military command, appointed him instead. When Himmler proved totally inadequate to the task, Hitler replaced him on March 20 with General Gotthard Heinrici. Hitler, meanwhile, ordered that the German capital be held "to the last man and the last shot."

On March 31, Stalin ordered the offensive to begin. Zhukov made the principal drive on Berlin, while Konev supported him on the left flank and Marshal Konstantin Rokossovsky's 2nd Belorussian Front on the lower Oder moved on Zhukov's right flank. Altogether, the three fronts had some 1.5 million troops, 6,250 armored vehicles, and 7,500 aircraft. Opposing them, the German Ninth Army and Third Panzer Army had only twenty-four under-strength divisions, with 754 tanks and few aircraft. Zhukov's frontal assaults on Berlin's defenses stalled at Seelow Heights. On April 18, Stalin ordered him to go around Berlin from the north, while Konev encircled the city from the south. The Soviets completed the encirclement of the city on April 25. Also, on that day, Soviet and U.S. forces met on the Elbe River.

On April 30, with the defenders' ammunition nearly depleted and the defenses fast crumbling, and as Soviet troops took the Reichstag building, Hitler committed suicide. On May 2, General of Infantry Hans Krebs, chief of the German General Staff, surrendered Berlin. According to one source, the "Berlin Strategic Offensive" from April 16 to May 8, involving the 1st Belorussian, 2nd Belorussian, and 1st Ukrainian Fronts, produced a staggering total of 352,475 Soviet casualties (including 78,291 dead)—an average of 15,325 a day. Exact German casualties will never be known. One estimate is ninety-two thousand to one hundred thousand killed, two hundred and twenty thousand wounded, and four hundred and eighty thousand prisoners. Within Berlin itself, the total may have been about twenty-two thousand military personnel and an equal number of civilians dead.

Spencer C. Tucker

See also: Heinrici, Gotthard; Himmler, Heinrich; Krebs, Hans; Seelow Heights, Battle of

Additional Reading

Beevor, Antony. *The Fall of Berlin, 1945*. New York: Viking Penguin, 2002.

Berlin Air Campaign, Allied (August 25, 1940–April 21, 1945)

Berlin was a major target for the Allies. As well as being the seat of government, it was a major industrial centre and accounted for 14 percent of Germany's economic output.

Berlin was responsible for 100 percent of all U-boat electric motor production. One quarter of all German tanks and half of German field artillery were produced in greater Berlin.

The defense of Berlin was the task of the Luftwaffe. Typically, a *Jagdflieger* (Fighter) Division was tasked with aerial defense, but other specialist units controlled night fighters and other forces. The Kammhuber Line was a key element of defense against night attacks, which, for the most part, were carried out by the British Royal Air Force. In 1944, Luftflotte Reich was established to provide command and control of the daylight forces that defended against the attacks of the U.S. Army Air Forces. High attrition effectively destroyed the daytime force by the end of 1944. Berlin was also defended by flak (antiaircraft) units, controlled by the Luftwaffe. Three large flak towers, mounting 128 mm flak guns, were built in the Berlin Zoo area. By January 1, 1944, Berlin was heavily defended by 104 heavy and 25 medium and light flak batteries.

The first raid against Berlin took place on August 25, 1940, when ninety-five aircraft of RAF Bomber Command attacked Tempelhof Airport in response to the German attacks on the United Kingdom during the Battle of Britain. The raid had little material effect, but its psychological impact on Hitler was one factor in his decision to shift Luftwaffe attacks to the British cities. On November 7, 1941, RAF Bomber Command sent out 160 bombers to attack Berlin, suffering 12.5 percent losses in the process. That failure led to the appointment of Air Marshal Arthur Harris to command Bomber Command in early 1942.

Harris was not able to muster the resources to attack Berlin in force until 1943. From November 18, 1943, to the end of March 1944, RAF Bomber Command carried out thirty-five major raids against key industrial targets around Berlin, with sixteen raids directed at the city itself. Improved Luftwaffe defensive night-fighter tactics using *Wilde Sau* (Wild Sow) and *Zahme Sau* (Tame Sow) fighters caused heavy RAF losses. Until the introduction of very long-range fighters, the U.S. Army Air Force was reluctant to attack Berlin. The first major USAAF attack on Berlin came on March 4, 1944. On February 3, 1945, USAAF launched its largest raid against Berlin with approximately sixteen hundred aircraft attacking the city. The last Allied air mission against Berlin was flown on April 21, 1945, just as the Soviet Army was about to fight its way into the city.

During the course of the war, Berlin was attacked from the air 314 times, including several raids by the Soviet Air Force. Casualty estimates vary between twenty thousand and fifty thousand deaths. A significant number of key buildings were destroyed, including the Reich Chancellery, the Nazi Party Chancellery, Gestapo headquarters, and the People's Court. The campaign successfully de-housed the population of Berlin. By the time it was over, there was an estimated thirty-nine cubic yards of rubble for every inhabitant of Berlin.

Ross Mahoney

See also: Kammhuber Line

Additional Reading

Middlebrook, Martin. *The Berlin Raids: RAF Bomber Command Winter 1943–44.* London: Cassell, 2007.

Bey, Eric (1898–1943)

Kriegamarine rear admiral.

Born in Hamburg on March 23, 1898, Eric Bey joined the Imperial German Navy in

1916 and served in destroyers during World War I. During the naval battles at Narvik on April 10 and 13, 1940, Bey commanded a destroyer force against a superior British navy force. Despite the annihilation of his command, his performance earned him the Knights Cross of the Iron Cross. In February 1943, Bey commanded the destroyer screen, protecting the battle cruisers *Scharnhorst* and *Gneisenau* and the heavy cruiser *Prinz Eugen* during Operation CERBERUS, the Channel Dash.

On December 25, 1943, Bey commanded the task force consisting of the battle cruiser *Scharnhorst* and five destroyers that sortied from Altafjord, Norway, against the Allied Murmansk convoys. He encountered a superior British force, led by the battleship HMS *Duke of York*. The ensuing battle of the North Cape on December 26 was fought in conditions of poor visibility, with the British having significant radar superiority. It was the last classic single-ship duel between battleships. Bey died when the *Scharnhorst* went down.

Spencer C. Tucker

See also: Channel Dash; North Cape, Battle of

Additional Reading

Bekker, Cajus. *Hitler's Naval War.* Translated and Edited by Frank Ziegler. Garden City, NY: Doubleday, 1974.

"Big Week" Allied Air Campaign (February 20–25, 1944)

"Big Week" was the popular name later given by the press to Operation ARGUMENT, a series of intensive Allied air strikes at the end of February 1944 against the German aircraft industry's final-assembly plants, ball-bearing factories, and facilities producing aircraft components. The Western Allies initiated the operation in order to reduce the numbers of Luftwaffe fighters contesting the presence of Allied bombers over Germany and to prepare for the invasion of Normandy.

A period of clear weather allowed the Allies to begin the campaign. Bomber Command of the Royal Air Force (RAF) joined in for nighttime raids, but the bulk of the attacks were carried out by the U.S. Army Air Forces (USAAF) in daylight operations. Between February 20 and 25, 1944, some one thousand bombers and nine hundred fighters of the U.S. Eighth Air Force carried out thirteen major attacks against fifteen centers of the German aviation industry, such as the Messerschmitt Bf 109 factory at Leipzig. In the last four days of the offensive, U.S. Fifteenth Air Force, headquartered at Foggia, Italy, joined in. During February 20 to 25, the Eighth and Fifteenth Air Forces flew a combined total of thirty-eight hundred sorties (thirty-three hundred from Britain and five hundred from Italy) and dropped almost ten thousand tons of bombs. German fighters contested the raids, and USAAF losses were heavy, with 226 bombers shot down, amounting to 6 percent of the force committed.

Clearly, the days of the Luftwaffe were now numbered. "Big Week" was a major defeat for the Luftwaffe. German aircraft production levels fell off in the following weeks, although they would rise again later in the spring. By that time, Allied fighters were more than a match for anything the Germans could send aloft. Particularly grievous from the German standpoint was the number of trained fighter pilots lost. This reduction in German air strength was an essential prelude to the successful Normandy Invasion in June 1944.

Spencer C. Tucker

See also: Normandy Invasion and Campaign

Additional Reading

Neillands, Robin. *The Bomber War: The Allied Air Offensive against Nazi Germany.* New York: Overlook Press, 2001.

Bismarck, Sortie and Sinking of (May 18–27, 1941)

The sinking of the *Bismarck* occurred at the height of German battleship operations in the Atlantic Ocean. The commander of the German Navy, Grand Admiral Erich Raeder, expected the new battleship *Bismarck*, which was to be operational in the spring of 1941, to provide an opportunity to test the navy's "battle group" strategy in support of a war on commerce. Repairs to the battleships *Gneisenau* and *Scharnhorst* forced delays, and the naval command decided to send the *Bismarck* and the heavy cruiser *Prinz Eugen* to sea as soon as possible to attack shipping in the North Atlantic in Operation RHEINÜBUNG (RHINE EXERCISE). Raeder was determined to demonstrate the value of the battleships to the war effort, and the *Bismarck* was rushed into action with an incomplete antiaircraft control system and equipment scavenged from other ships. Vice Admiral Günther Lütjens, the task force commander, opposed the "piecemeal approach" and advocated delaying the mission until the other battleships were available.

Off Iceland at 0555 hours on May 24, in the Battle of the Denmark Strait, British Rear Admiral Lancelot E. Holland's battle cruiser HMS *Hood* and battleship *Prince of Wales* engaged the *Bismarck*. The *Hood* was hit in its magazines by the German battleship's fourth salvo and blew up. Only three of the 1,419 crewmen survived. The *Prince of Wales* took seven hits and was damaged. Although the *Bismarck* had received only three hits, the ship was leaking oil, and its speed was also reduced from flooding in the forward compartments. In the early morning of May 25, the *Bismarck* managed to elude its pursuers. On May 26, Swordfish torpedo bombers from the MHS *Ark Royal* regained contact with the *Bismarck*. Late in the day, Swordfish from the *Ark Royal* attacked, and a lucky torpedo hit jammed the German battleship's twin rudder system, making it incapable of maneuvering.

At 0845 hours on May 27, the British battleships HMS *King George V* and *Rodney* opened fire. As the heavy cruiser HMS *Dorsetshire* closed to fire torpedoes, three torpedoes struck, and the *Bismarck* went down. Only 110 of the crew of 2,300 survived. Lütjens was not among them. A furious Hitler regarded the sinking of the *Bismarck* as a major loss of prestige and ordered that no more battleship operations be undertaken without his permission. The major German surface warships were now relegated to the defense of Norway, leaving the brunt of Germany's naval war to the U-boats.

Keith W. Bird

See also: Lütjens, Günther; Raeder, Erich

Additional Reading

Bercuson, David J., and Holger H. Herwig. *The Destruction of the "Bismarck."* Woodstock, NY and New York: Overlook Press, 2001.

Bismarck Battleship See Warships, Surface

Bittrich, Willi (1894–1979)

SS-Gruppenführer and Waffen-SS lieutenant general.

Born in Wernigerode, Germany on February 26, 1894, Willi Bittrich was a fighter pilot in the German Air Service during World War I. Following the war, he served in the Freikorps. He joined the Schutzstaffel (SS) in 1932. Bittrich served in Waffen-SS units during the Poland Campaign of 1939, the France Campaign of 1940, and the invasion of the Soviet Union in 1941. In 1944, he commanded the 9th SS Panzer Division (*Hohenstaufen*) in Russia. In July 1944, Bittrich transferred to the Normandy front in France and assumed command of II SS Panzer Corps. In September 1944, his corps played a key role in defeating British forces at Arnhem during Operation MARKET-GARDEN.

Bittrich's II SS Panzer Corps participated in the December 1944 Ardennes Offensive (Battle of the Bulge). In January 1945, the corps was transferred to the eastern front but fought its way back to the west to surrender to the Americans. Bittrich was turned over to the French, who convicted him of war crimes and imprisoned him until 1954. Bittrich died in Wolfratshausen, Germany, on April 19, 1979.

Dana Lombardy

See also: Ardennes Offensive (Battle of the Bulge); Freikorps (Free Corps); Market-Garden, Allied Operation; Waffen-SS

Additional Reading

Kershaw, Robert. *"It Never Snows in September": The German View of MARKET-GARDEN and the Battle of Arnhem, September 1944.* Hersham, Surrey, UK: Ian Allen, 1990.

Black May, Allied Anti-U-Boat Campaign (May 1943)

The Allied anti-U-boat campaign of May 1943 resulted in the decisive defeat of German submarine operations in the North Atlantic. The climactic convoy battles of March 1943 had given a first hint that Allied antisubmarine forces were finally gaining the upper hand in the battle for the North Atlantic sea lines of communication. By early 1943, the fully mobilized U.S. shipyards were producing vast numbers of escort vessels, in addition to building more merchant ships than were being sunk by U-boats. Long-range naval patrol aircraft, such as the B-24 Liberator, and escort carrier–based aircraft were closing the dreaded "Atlantic Gap," the wolf packs' last refuge from Allied airpower in the North Atlantic. At the same time, Allied signals intelligence was reading the German U-boat cipher Triton almost continuously and with minimal delay. On April 26, the Allies suffered a rare blackout in their ability to read the German cipher, just as fifty-three U-boats regrouped for an assault on the convoy routes. During the next forty-eight hours, the U-boats sank twelve ships but at an unacceptable cost: escort vessels sank six U-boats, and long-range air patrols claimed three more. Starting the second week in May, the survivors of the North Atlantic wolf packs regrouped, but by May 23, not a single U-boat had managed to close with a convoy. During the month to that point, thirty-three U-boats had been sunk, and almost the same number had been damaged. The month went down in German naval annals as "Black May." On May 24, Grand Admiral Karl Dönitz cancelled U-boat operations in the Atlantic.

Dirk Steffen

See also: Atlantic, Battle of the; Dönitz, Karl

Additional Reading

Gannon, Michael. *Black May: The Epic Story of the Allies' Defeat of the German U-Boats in May 1943.* New York: HarperCollins, 1998.

Blaskowitz, Johannes Albrecht (1883–1948)

Wehrmacht colonel general.

Born on July 10, 1883 at Peterswalde, East Prussia, Johannes Blaskowitz served on both fronts during World War I. On October 23, 1939, Blaskowitz assumed command of German forces occupying Poland. An officer of the old school, he was shocked by the brutal actions of the Schutzstaffel (SS) against the local population. Blaskowitz went so far as to draw up a memorandum protesting these actions, which earned him Adolf Hitler's distrust.

In May 1944, Blaskowitz assumed command of Army Task Group G in southern France. During Operation DRAGOON in August 1944, the Allies landed on the French Riviera and easily pushed back Blaskowitz's thinly spread forces. Relieved of his command in September 1944, he returned to command Army Group H in the Netherlands in January 1945, where he permitting the Dutch to receive medical supplies and food during the Allied advance. Captured on May 8, 1945, by Canadian forces, Blaskowitz was charged with war crimes for passing along Hitler's orders to execute summarily enemy commandos. Rather than face trial, he committed suicide on February 5, 1948, in Nuremberg, Germany.

Harold Wise

See also: Commando Order; France, Battle of; Poland Campaign; Southern France, Allied Invasion and Campaign (Operation DRAGOON)

Additional Reading

Giziowski, Richard. *The Enigma of General Blaskowitz.* New York: Hippocrene Books, 1997.

Blitz, Air Campaign (September 7, 1940–May 12, 1941)

The Blitz, derived from the German word *Blitzkrieg* (Lightning War), was the German strategic air campaign against Britain from September 7, 1940 to May 12, 1941. While it started during the course of the Battle of Britain, it continued after that battle ended. Indeed, the start of the Blitz coincided with a distinct shift in German strategy that coincides with the final phase of the Battle of Britain. However, the *Blitz* campaign continued after the indefinite cancellation of Operation SEELÖWE (SEA LION), Germany's planned invasion of Britain.

The Blitz campaign itself can be split into three distinct phases with different target sets. During the first phase, September 7 to November 14, the Luftwaffe attacked London. Launching Operations LOGE (LODGE) and SEESCHLANGE (SEA SERPENT) on September 9, the Luftwaffe High Command (*Oberkommando der Luftwaffe*—OKL), ordered round the clock bombing of London with Luftflotte 2 (Second Air Fleet) attacking by day and Luftflotte 3 (Third Air Fleet) attacking by night. On September 15, Luftflotte 2 launched its largest raids against London, with twelve hundred aircraft involved. The Germans, however, suffered the significant loss of eighty aircraft. Two days later SEELÖWE was cancelled, and the air attacks were expanded to other British cities, including Birmingham and Coventry.

The second phase—November 14 to February 20, 1941—began with the attack on Coventry, Operation MONDSCHEIN-SONATE (MOONLIGHT SONATA). The German bombers carried mixed loads of high explosives and incendiaries, which caused a firestorm in the city. There was no follow-up attack, and OKL underestimated the British ability to withstand the strains of strategic bombing. This phase of the campaign saw the increasing use of incendiaries against British cities. With eleven hundred available aircraft, the Luftwaffe typically sent out raids of two hundred aircraft. On November 10, for example, 369 aircraft attacked Birmingham. Besides the attack on Coventry, the attack on the City of London on December 20 was the worst raid of the Blitz with over ten thousand incendiaries dropped, damaging wide areas of the city.

During the third phase, February 20 to May 12, the attacks moved to the port cities of Britain. The Luftwaffe attacked Liverpool, Plymouth, Portsmouth, and most of the major port cities, causing massive damage. Liverpool suffered more casualties than many of the inland cities. By the end of this phase, however, German strategic focus had begun to shift to the east in preparation for the invasion of the Soviet Union.

During the course of the Blitz, the Luftwaffe lost 2,265 aircraft. Britain suffered about forty-three thousand deaths. The air campaign's impact on British morale and production are questionable. Production increased, and Home Intelligence Reports noted that while morale fluctuated, it did not break under the pressure of bombing, with social cohesion remaining strong, despite the need to evacuate parts of Britain's major cities.

Ross Mahoney

See also: Britain, Battle of; SEELÖWE (SEA LION), Operation

Additional Reading

Gardiner, Juliet. *The Blitz: The British under Attack.* London: Harper Press, 2010.

Murray, Williamson. *Strategy for Defeat: The Luftwaffe 1933–45.* Maxwell, AL: Air University Press, 1983.

Blitzkrieg

The so-called Blitzkrieg (lightning war) doctrine is one of the most enduring myths of World War II. In the early years of the war, however, the swift and stunning German successes in Poland in 1939 and France in 1940 came to be interpreted in the West as the result of some sort of revolutionary new military doctrine that relied on combined-arms operations, with ground and air forces working together as a well-oiled military machine.

Military doctrine has been defined as the fundamental principles by which military forces guide their actions in support of national objectives. But what became known popularly as Blitzkrieg was not a set of fundamental principles, nor was it written down as an authoritative document. Rather, the term *Blitzkrieg* was created for public consumption. The term did appear occasionally in the military literature between 1936 and 1940, but the German writers generally used it in reference to a short war, as opposed to the drawn-out trench warfare of World War I. The term became fixed in the public mind after articles appeared in *Time* magazine, one on September 25, 1939 about Germany's invasion of Poland, and another on May 27, 1940 about the fall of France.

Immediately following World War I, the leaders of the much reduced German Army studied the causes of the defeat in 1918 and concluded that a lack of traditional mobile, maneuverable forces and tactics had resulted in the war of attrition that eventually doomed Imperial Germany on the battlefield. Unlike the French, who determined that better defenses would be the key to winning the next war and hence built the Maginot Line, the Germans concluded that the next war would be of short duration and won by maneuver warfare in the classical sense.

The German field service regulations of 1921, *Führung und Gefecht der verbundenen Waffen* (Command and Combat of the Combined Arms), together with the updated version of 1934, *Truppenführung* (Unit Command), were infantry-oriented documents that cast tank and air assets strictly in an infantry-support role. Although *Truppenführung,* which remained the official doctrine for the German Army through 1945, emphasized traditional German thinking on mobility, it did allow for decentralization of control, and it provided considerable latitude for force structure changes. It was also not tied rigidly to specific operational concepts, to the exclusion of all others. Rather than an inflexible tactical cookbook, the manual was a philosophical treatment of the conduct of operations and leadership.

During the interwar years, the German mobility advocates enthusiastically read the works of the leading mobile warfare theorists of the time, J. F. C. Fuller, Charles de Gaulle, and Basil Liddell Hart. Younger German officers aggressively advanced the argument that a tank force could alter the outcome of battles. Many of the older officers resisted the notion that the tank could be a decisive combat arm, remembering the grave difficulties armored units experienced in World War I.

After Hitler came to power in Germany in 1933, he quickly made it clear that he intended to rearm the nation, and he was interested in the iconoclastic ideas of the younger officers. In June 1934, Colonel Heinz Guderian became the chief of staff of the newly formed Motorized Troop Command. A little more than a year later, the Germans fielded an experimental panzer division. In October 1935, while still only a colonel, Guderian assumed command of one of the three new panzer divisions. He immediately set out to convince the traditionally infantry-oriented German General Staff to accept the concepts of armored warfare. Although Guderian received only limited support from some of his superiors, Hitler encouraged him and his aggressive concepts.

Meanwhile, the fledgling German Air Force also underwent important changes. Prior to the German intervention in the Spanish Civil War, most Luftwaffe officers saw airpower in the same terms as their peers in most other air forces of the period. The two most essential missions were conducting long-range strategic bombing and achieving air superiority over the battlefield; the ground-support mission was largely ignored. But the successes of German air-ground operations during the Spanish Civil War convinced a number of high-ranking Luftwaffe officers to reconsider ground support. General Ernst Udet, in charge of Luftwaffe development after 1936, pushed through the development of a dive bomber, the Ju 87 Stuka. The aircraft was extremely accurate, very mobile, and designed specifically to support ground forces. It became the plane that added the critical air dimension to mobile operations.

The Polish Campaign of 1939 was executed in very short order and had all the outward appearances of a dazzling success of German arms. But the so-called Blitzkrieg doctrine was never used in that campaign. Rather than being committed in mass, the panzer units were allocated to the

Germany invades Poland, September 25, 1939. German soldiers advancing behind a Pz.Kpfw.II light tank on the outskirts of Warsaw. (Popperfoto via Getty Images)

various field armies. The Luftwaffe was primarily concerned with establishing air superiority and striking deep at Polish lines of communications. Tank maintenance was a severe problem, and too often, the German system of resupply was unequal to the required tasks. But, in the end, Germany crushed Poland very quickly, and that success obscured the serious operational, tactical, and technical problems the Wehrmacht experienced.

Between the end of the Polish Campaign and the start of the attack in the west against France and Britain in May 1940, the German Army made some significant changes. The panzer divisions were organized into corps. The number of tanks in the German Army increased only slightly, but the number of tanks per division decreased, and thus, the number of panzer divisions grew. Out of necessity rather than doctrinal design, the panzer divisions became combined-arms units, with a balance between tanks, infantry, artillery, engineers, and other arms. Tactical air, especially the Stuka, became an important element in the combined-arms mix because Germany was woefully short of field artillery. In France, the Germans achieved a rapid and overwhelming victory because of a combination of luck; better leadership and training; superior concentration of forces; and correspondingly poor French leadership, training, and tactics. At first, the Germans were stunned by their success, but they soon fell victim to their own propaganda and began to believe in the myth of Blitzkrieg.

In June 1941, the Germans invaded the Soviet Union, this time anticipating a rapid campaign. They did not mobilize their economy for the invasion, nor did they accumulate the necessary stockpiles or provide adequately for the long lines of communications or winter conditions. Drawing the wrong lessons from the French Campaign, they believed that their use of tactical airpower had been so successful that it more than compensated for their severe shortage of artillery. That approach may have worked against the poorly deployed French and British, but against the artillery-oriented Soviets, it was a recipe for failure. The Germans learned quickly that the Luftwaffe could not be everywhere at the same time over the vast expanses of the eastern battlefields, especially with the onset of poor weather. The Soviets, with their abundant conventional field artillery, seldom lacked direct-fire support.

The term *Blitzkrieg* described a set of results, unique to a specific place and a specific time. The coordinated use of mobility, communications, and combined arms was not a revolution in military affairs, as it has often been portrayed, but rather a natural evolution of military doctrine that was clearly identifiable in the closing months of World War I. The myth of Blitzkrieg, however, did obscure serious flaws in the German war machine, including supply, transport, maintenance, artillery, and intelligence. That circumstance proved progressively costly to the Germans as the war advanced and the Allies grew stronger, and as the mechanized battlefield became increasingly lethal.

David T. Zabecki

See also: Guderian, Heinz; Udet, Ernst

Additional Reading

Citino, Robert M. *The Path to Blitzkrieg: Doctrine and Training in the German Army, 920–1939.* Boulder, CO: Lynne Rienner, 1999.

Frieser, Karl-Heinz. *The Blitzkrieg Legend: The 1940 Campaign in the West.* Annapolis, MD: U.S. Naval Institute Press, 2005.

Zabecki, David T., and Bruce Condell, eds. *On the German Art of War: "Truppenführung."* Boulder, CO: Lynne Rienner, 2001.

Blomberg, Werner von (1878–1946)

Wehrmacht field marshal, minister of war, and commander in chief of the Wehrmacht.

Born in Stargard, Germany, on September 2, 1878, Werner von Blomberg served during World War I, earning the *Pour le Mérite.* From 1927 to 1929, he headed the Truppenamt, the clandestine general staff organization outlawed under the Treaty of Versailles. At the end of January 1933, he became defense minister in Hitler's first cabinet. In April, Blomberg was made commander in chief of the German armed forces.

An enthusiastic Nazi supporter, Blomberg was a key figure in Hitler's consolidation of power. He pressured the Führer to remove the Sturmabteilungen (SA) as a possible threat to the army and supported Hitler in the subsequent June 1934 Night of the Long Knives purge. On the death of German president Paul von Hindenburg, Hitler called on Blomberg to swear an oath of allegiance to him personally, which Blomberg, in turn, imposed on his fellow officers, thereby consolidating Hitler's control of the Wehrmacht. As a reward for his support, the Führer promoted Blomberg in April 1936, making him the first field marshal of the Third Reich.

After Hitler revealed his expansionist plans in November 1937, Blomberg and Army

Commander General Werner von Fritsch objected, and Hitler determined to remove both men from their posts. The chance to get rid of Blomberg came in January 1938, after he remarried, and his new wife was exposed as a former prostitute. After Blomberg was dismissed, he took no part in the war, but as a prominent German official, he was detained and testified at the war crimes trials in Nuremberg. He died there while still in detention on March 14, 1946.

Robert T. Kaczowka

See also: Blomberg-Fritsch Crisis; Fritsch, Werner von; Hindenburg, Paul von; Night of the Long Knives; Sturmabteilungen (SA)

Additional Reading

Görlitz, Walter. "Blomberg." In *Hitler's Generals*, edited by Correlli Barnett, 129–137. New York: Grove Weidenfeld, 1989.

Blomberg-Fritsch Crisis (1938)

The Blomberg-Fritsch Crisis resulted in the removal of Minister of War Field Marshal Werner von Blomberg, Army Commander in Chief Colonel General Werner von Fritsch, and Foreign Minister Konstantin von Neurath, and resulted in Hitler's consolidation of personal power over the German military. All three had been opposed to Adolf Hitler's policy of *Lebensraum*, the establishment of "living space" at the expense of nations in the east. The first scandal centered on Blomberg's marriage to his twenty-four-year-old secretary, rumored to have been a prostitute. After forcing Blomberg into retirement, Hitler named himself commander in chief of the armed forces. The army commander in chief, Colonel General Werner von Fritsch, was next to be sidelined. Fritsch never hid his contempt for the Nazi party or the Schutzstaffel (SS). In early 1938, he was accused of committing a homosexual act by an inept thief and blackmailer named Otto Schmidt. Despite the flimsy evidence, Hitler suspended Fritsch. On March 18, a military court exonerated Fritsch, but Hitler refused to reinstate him as army commander in chief. The final act came in February 1938, when Hitler dismissed Neurath and replaced him with Joachim von Ribbentrop. This final transition happened without the dramatic flair that characterized the Blomberg and Fritsch removals. Hitler had cleaned house and eliminated those key players who refused to come on board to his plans.

William H. Van Husen

See also: Blomberg, Werner von; Fritsch, Werner von; *Oberkommando der Wehrmacht* (OKW)

Additional Reading

Taylor, Telford. *Sword and Swastika: Generals and Nazis in the Third Reich.* New York: Simon and Schuster, 1952.

Blumentritt, Günther (1892–1967)

Wehrmacht general of infantry.

Born in Munich on February 10, 1892, Günther Blumentritt entered the German Army in 1911, serving on the eastern front during World War I. He served briefly in the Freikorps in 1919, before joining the Reichswehr. After qualifying as a General Staff officer, Blumentritt served as Colonel General Gerd von Rundstedt's operations chief for the invasion of Poland and then as Colonel General Günther von Kluge's chief of staff for the invasions of France and the Soviet Union.

Blumentritt's association with Kluge and others involved in efforts to overthrow Adolf Hitler led to his temporary suspension in early September 1944. Later that same month, he was promoted to general of infantry and given command of SS XII Corps on the western front. In March 1945, he assumed command of the First Parachute Army, ending the war in Schleswig-Holstein. He was held prisoner by the Allies until January 1948. Blumentritt had a brief postwar career as a commentator on Western Allied strategy, and he wrote extensively. Blumentritt died in Munich on October 12, 1967.

Carl O. Schuster

See also: France, Battle of; Freikorps (Free Corps); Kluge, Günther von; Poland Campaign; Rundstedt, Karl Rudolf Gerd von

Additional Reading

Barnett, Correlli. *Hitler's Generals.* London: Orion, 1995.

Bock, Fedor von (1880–1945)

Wehrmacht field marshal.

Born into an old noble Prussian family at Küstrin, Germany, on December 3, 1880, Fedor von Bock joined the army in 1898. During World War I, he earned the *Pour le Mérite.* After the war, Bock remained in the Reichswehr. Upon coming to power, Adolf Hitler did not purge him despite Bock's being a well-known monarchist. Bock participated in the German invasions of Poland and France as commander of Army Groups North and B, respectively. He was shocked by the Schutzstaffel (SS) treatment of Jews in Poland, but he registered no official protest. In July 1940, he was one of twelve new field marshals promoted by Hitler.

During the invasion of the Soviet Union, Bock's Army Group Center had the task of capturing Moscow. When bad weather brought the drive to a halt in December 1941, Hitler sacked him, but just a month later, Bock returned to the eastern front as the commander of Army Group South. Hitler again sacked him in July 1942. Bock never returned to command. In 1944, his nephew, Henning von Tresckow, approached him about joining the July plot against Hitler, but Bock refused. Bock and his wife were killed during an Allied air raid in Schleswig-Holstein on May 3, 1945. Bock died the following day.

Martin Moll

See also: France, Battle of; Opposition to Hitler, German Military; Poland Campaign; Soviet Union, Invasion of (Operation BARBAROSSA); Tresckow, Henning von

Additional Reading

Mitcham, Samuel W., Jr. *Hitler's Field Marshals and Their Battles.* Chelsea, MI: Scarborough House, 1988.

BODENPLATTE, Air Operation (January 1, 1945)

Operation BODENPLATTE (BASEPLATE) was the last major effort by the Luftwaffe to check Allied airpower in the west. The Germans hoped to force the Allies to remove their fighters from the continent, allowing the Luftwaffe an opportunity to regain control of the skies over the front and achieve some advantage against the Allied bombers. The plan envisioned hurling all available aircraft in an early-morning, low-level attack against sixteen Allied fighter fields in Belgium. Weather analysts determined that the conditions would be right on January 1, 1945, and orders were issued accordingly on December 31.

Early on January 1, eight hundred aircraft under the command of Major General Dietrich Peltz, commander of II Jagdkorps

(Fighter Corps), lifted off from fields behind the front. An unexpected ground mist delayed some takeoffs, and confused German antiaircraft gunners opened fire on late-arriving aircraft, shooting down a number of them. In the final analysis, Operation BODENPLATTE achieved some tactical success but at an unacceptable cost. The Germans destroyed a total of 134 Allied aircraft and damaged an additional 62. The Allies could easily absorb these losses, however, and there was no thought of relocating air operations to Britain. The Luftwaffe lost some three hundred aircraft to all causes. More important, 214 Luftwaffe pilots were killed, missing, or captured. This operation marked the end of the road for the German Air Force, which was largely ineffective for the remainder of the war.

Marlyn R. Pierce

See also: Luftwaffe (German Air Force)

Additional Reading

Gerbig, Werner. *Six Months to Oblivion: The Eclipse of the Luftwaffe Fighter Force.* New York: Hippocrene Books, 1975.

Bohemia and Moravia, Annexation of (1939–1945)

As part of the Munich Agreement in September 1938, the Western Allies compromised the independence of Czechoslovakia by allowing Germany to seize those areas in which greater than 50 percent of the population was ethnically German. On October 10, 1938, Germany annexed the Sudetenland and incorporated it into the German Reich. On March 15, 1939, at the Prague castle, German Chancellor Adolf Hitler established an independent Slovak Republic and forced President Emile Hacha to sign over the remaining areas of the Czech region. The Protectorate of Bohemia and Moravia was established, thus ending the state of Czechoslovakia until the end of World War II. The protectorate was composed of two *Lander*, Böhmen (Bohemia) and Mähren (Moravia). *Reichsprotektorat Böhmen und Mähren* was placed under the supervision of Reichsprotektor Konstantin von Neurath. Serving alongside the Reichsprotektor was the political office of state secretary, later state minister to the Reichsprotektor, led by SS-Gruppenführer Karl Hermann Frank. The six years of German occupation were excessively brutal. Three hundred and fifty thousand Czechs were sent to concentration camps, of which two hundred and thirty-five thousand died. One hundred and forty thousand Czech Jews also perished. The extermination of Bohemian Romani was so complete that their language became extinct; most were gassed at Auschwitz-Birkenau. Nazi occupation of Bohemia and Moravia ended on May 5, 1945.

William H. Van Husen and Donna Sinclair

See also: Munich Conference and Agreement

Additional Reading

Mastny, Vojtech. *The Czechs under Nazi Rule: The Failure of National Resistance, 1939–1942.* New York: Columbia University Press, 1971.

Brandenberger, Erich (1892–1955)

Wehrmacht general of panzer troops.

Born on July 15, 1892, in Augsburg, Germany, Erich Brandenberger joined the German Army in 1911 and served during World War I. In 1941, he commanded the 8th Panzer Division at the start of Operation BARBAROSSA, the invasion of the Soviet Union. He later commanded the XVII and XXIX Corps in

Russia. Brandenberger assumed command of the Seventh Army on the western front in August 1944. During the Ardennes Offensive in December 1944, his army had the mission of screening the southern flank to protect the Fifth and Sixth Panzer Armies. He had some initial success, but, in the end, he was forced back by the counterattacks of Lieutenant General George S. Patton's U.S. Third Army. As the Allies advanced to the east in 1945, Brandenberger fought skillful delaying actions until he was relieved of his command by Field Marshal Walther Model on February 20, 1945. Brandenberger assumed command of the Nineteenth Army on March 25, 1945, facing the French First Army in the Black Forest area. His army surrendered on May 5, 1945, near Innsbruck, Austria. Brandenberger died in Bonn on June 21, 1955.

Jon D. Berlin

See also: Ardennes Offensive (Battle of the Bulge); Model, Walther; Soviet Union, Invasion of (Operation BARBAROSSA)

Additional Reading

Cole, Hugh. *The Ardennes: The Battle of the Bulge.* Washington, DC: Center of Military History, U.S. Army, 1965.

Brauchitsch, Walther von (1881–1948)

Wehrmacht field marshal.

Born in Berlin on October 4, 1881, Heinrich von Brauchitsch entered the 3rd Guards Field Artillery Regiment in 1901 and served as a General Staff officer during World War I. In 1930, he was assigned as a major general to the Truppenamt, the covert General Staff. In 1932, as inspector of artillery, Brauchitsch was instrumental in modernizing the 88 mm gun, one of the most effective antitank and antiaircraft weapons of World War II.

In 1938, when General Werner von Fritsch resigned as commander of the German Army, Hitler promoted Brauchitsch to colonel general and appointed him to succeed Fritsch. Brauchitsch was an enthusiastic National Socialist, but he opposed Hitler's plans for territorial expansion. Brauchitsch also believed strongly that the military should remain neutral in politics, but he felt bound by his soldier's oath to obey Hitler. Hitler promoted Brauchitsch to field marshal in July 1940, but the German invasion of the Soviet Union, Operation BARBAROSSA, increased tensions between the two. Ultimately, Hitler blamed Brauchitsch for the failure of the offensive and relieved him on December 9, 1941. At the end of the war, Brauchitsch was classified as a major war criminal. Although in poor health, he testified at the International War Crimes Tribunal at Nuremberg. He died in a British military hospital at Hamburg-Barmbeck while awaiting trial, on October 18, 1948.

Gene Mueller and
Spencer C. Tucker

See also: Fritsch, Werner von; International Military Tribunal: The Nuremberg Trials

Additional Reading

Bond, Brian. "Brauchitsch: Field Marshal Walter von Brauchitsch." In *Hitler's Generals*, edited by Corelli Barnett, 75–99. New York: Grove Weidenfeld, 1989.

Braun, Wernher von (1912–1977)

German physicist who developed the V-2 missile and, after the war, led in establishing the foundations of the U.S. Space Program.

Born in Wirsitz, Posen, on March 23, 1912, Wernher von Braun earned a doctorate in physics from the University of Berlin, concentrating on developing liquid-fueled rocket engines. In 1932, the German military began funding von Braun's work, and he headed a team of engineers building and testing rockets, first at Kummersdorf and then at Peenemünde on the Baltic. The first operational V-2 ("Vengeance-2") rocket was launched in September 1944.

Fearing for his group's personal safety, in early 1945, von Braun led his research team to surrender to the U.S. military in western Germany. Von Braun's efforts were instrumental in the establishment of the National Aeronautics and Space Administration in 1958 and the Apollo space program during the 1960s. Von Braun retired in 1972 and died in Alexandria, Virginia, on June 16, 1977.

Priscilla Roberts

See also: CROSSBOW, Anglo-American Air Operation

Additional Reading

Bergaust, Erik. *Wernher von Braun: The Authoritative and Definitive Biographical Profile of the Father of Modern Space Flight.* Washington, DC: National Space Institute, 1976.

Britain, Battle of (July 10–October 31, 1940)

The German air campaign now known as the Battle of Britain was a series of engagements between the German Luftwaffe and the British Royal Air Force (RAF) in the summer and fall of 1940. The battle was given its name by Prime Minister Winston Churchill during a speech in the British Parliament on June 18, 1940.

Adolf Hitler assigned the Luftwaffe the task of eliminating the RAF and winning control of the skies over Britain, an essential precondition to the German invasion of England, Operation SEELÖWE (SEA LION). German plans called for the Luftwaffe to establish air superiority over southern England between August 8 and September 15. To accomplish this, it had to achieve a highly favorable kill ratio in the air or destroy RAF Fighter Command's infrastructure on the ground, while keeping a sufficiently large fighter force intact to protect the German invasion fleet. Reich Marshal Hermann Göring had three *Luftflotten* (air fleets) available to prosecute the battle. Luftflotte 2, based in Belgium and commanded by Field Marshal Albert Kesselring, was the largest, with 1,206 aircraft, over half of them fighters. Field Marshal Hugo Sperrle commanded Luftflotte 3, with 1,042 aircraft, was based in France, and Colonel General Hans-Jürgen Stumpff commanded Luftflotte 5, based in Norway, with only 155 offensive aircraft.

RAF Fighter Command, headed by Air Chief Marshal Hugh Dowding, was organized into four fighter groups, with a total of 754 single-seat aircraft. Air Vice Marshal Sir Quintin Brand commanded Number 10 Group, covering the southwestern United Kingdom. It bordered Number 11 Group, commanded by Air Vice Marshal Keith Park, which was in the southeast and thus likely to bear the brunt of the German attack. Air Vice Marshal Trafford Leigh-Mallory commanded Number 12 Group in the Midlands, and Air Vice Marshal Richard Saul commanded Number 13 Group, covering northern England and Scotland.

A significant advantage held by Dowding was that his force had the world's only integrated air defense system. Based on the telephone and teleprinter network, it was very resilient, merging inputs from radar stations and observer corps, filtering

Battle of Britain, 1940

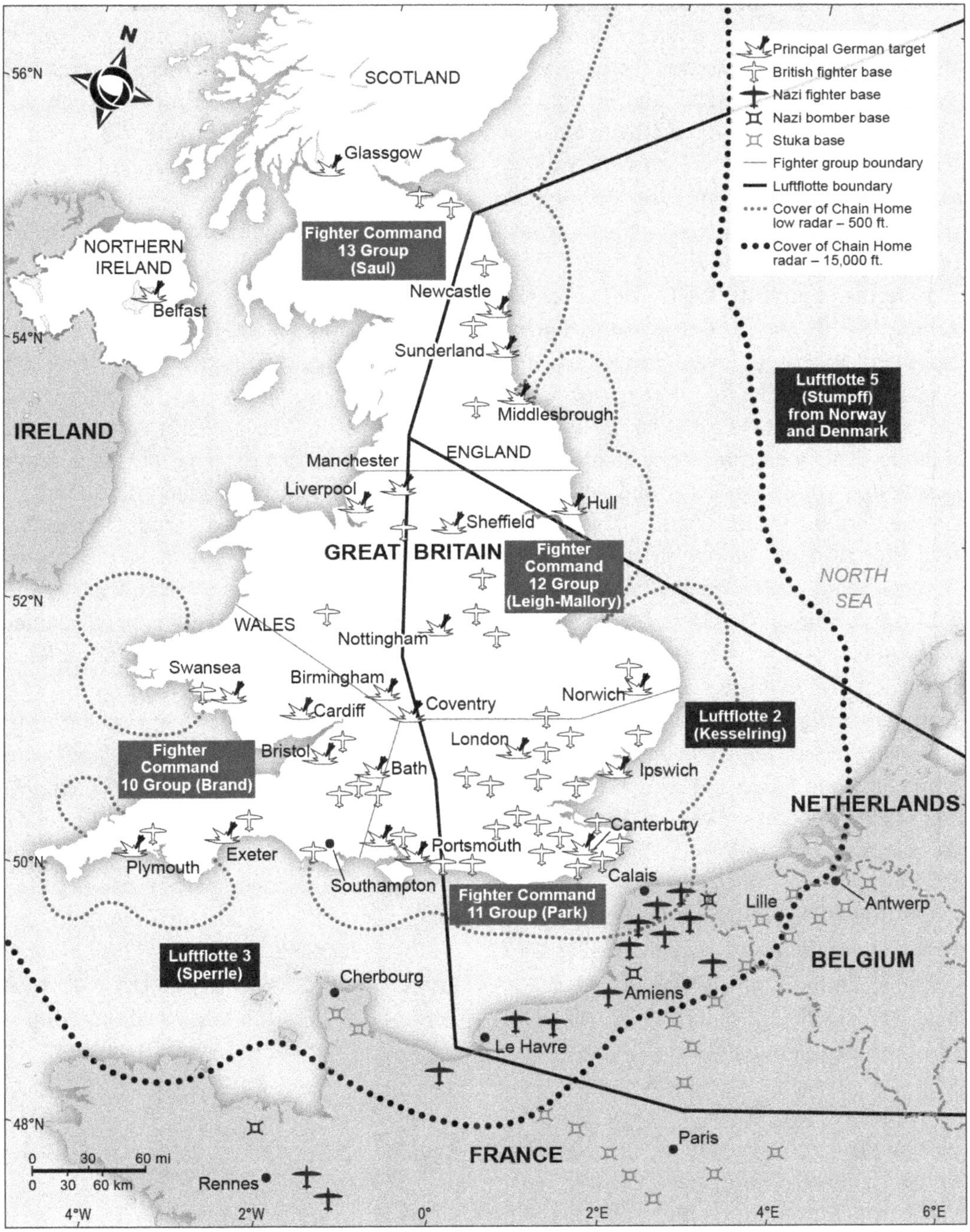

friendly or "doubtful" contacts, and devolving responsibility to group and sector levels. Group headquarters allocated raids to sectors, which then scrambled fighters and guided them by radio to intercept the attacking aircraft. The system was the product of years of careful thought, and it enabled Dowding to make the most effective use of his scarce resources. The Luftwaffe was, of course, aware that some sort of fighter-direction system was in use but had no idea of its scope or capabilities.

In terms of aircraft, the German Messerschmitt Bf 109 and the British Supermarine Spitfire were quite evenly matched; the British Hurricane had a lower performance but was more maneuverable. Both RAF fighters benefited from the introduction of constant-speed propellers and hundred-octane fuel during the battle. The Bf 110 was shown to be inferior to single-engine fighters, and the German Junkers Ju 87 Stuka dive bomber was so vulnerable that it was withdrawn partway through the Battle of Britain. The RAF, however, had much to learn about fighter tactics. The Luftwaffe was using flexible, open formations that had worked well in Spain and earlier in the war. Many RAF squadrons were still using close formations that allowed little tactical flexibility.

On July 10, the Germans began the battle by mounting their first bombing raid against a convoy in the English Channel. Over the next few weeks, the Luftwaffe mounted repeated raids on convoys and coastal targets and attempted to engage British fighters en masse with fighter sweeps, but RAF controllers carefully avoided fighter-versus-fighter combat. On August 12, the Luftwaffe attacked and temporarily disabled radar stations at Dover, Pevensey, and Rye, and the Ventnor station was out of action for three days, although a dummy signal was sent out while repairs were made. The following day was designated *Alder Tag* (Eagle Day) and marked the beginning of the German direct attack on Fighter Command. There was very heavy fighting on August 15, with the Luftwaffe flying more than two thousand sorties against airfields and aircraft factories. The Luftwaffe lost a total of seventy-five aircraft in exchange for thirty-four RAF fighters.

Following the inadvertent jettisoning of German bombs over London on August 15 and subsequent night raids by the RAF on Berlin starting on August 25, the Luftwaffe shifted its focus to London on September 7. With hindsight, this decision can be seen as a mistake, but the prevailing view in the Luftwaffe was that the RAF had taken heavy damage and had few fighters left. German daylight raids continued during October but tailed off through November, as the emphasis gradually shifted to night attacks.

The Luftwaffe had effectively blunted itself on the most sophisticated air-defense system in the world and was never again to be as strong relative to its opponents. During the Battle of Britain, the Luftwaffe suffered 2,698 experienced aircrew killed, 967 captured, and 638 missing, resulting in a shortfall that the German training machine was poorly equipped to make up. The Germans also lost 1,887 aircraft. The RAF lost 544 fighter pilots, more than 1,100 bomber aircrew, and 1,547 aircraft, but it learned several important lessons and built up a cadre of experienced fighter units.

Andy Blackburn

See also: SEELÖWE (SEA LION), Operation

Additional Reading

Bungay, Stephen. *The Most Dangerous Enemy: A History of the Battle of Britain.* London: Aurum, 2000.

Deighton, Len. *Fighter: The True Story of the Battle of Britain.* London: Random House, 1996.

Brody-Lwów, Battle of (July 13–27, 1944). *See* Ukraine Campaign, Soviet

Budapest, Soviet Siege of (November 3, 1944–February 13, 1945)

The liberation of the Hungarian capital was a long siege that ended with the expulsion of German troops from Budapest by the Soviet army. The siege of Budapest lasted 108 days, and for 52 of those days, the defending Germans were completely surrounded. SS-Obergruppenführer Karl Pfeffer-Wildenbruch commanded the German defense of Budapest. The Soviet 2nd Ukrainian Front (army group), commanded by General Rodion Y. Malinovsky, and the 3rd Ukrainian Front, commanded by Marshal of the Soviet Union Fedor I. Tolbukhin, converged on the Hungarian capital. In all, the Soviets committed some one hundred and fifty-seven thousand men. Red Army troops first reached the east bank of the city on November 3, 1944, but operations then halted. Following several unsuccessful attempts, Soviet forces completed the encirclement of the city on December 25.

The German Sixth Army, under the command of General of Panzer Troops Hermann Balck, made three unsuccessful attempts to break through to Budapest. Operation KONRAD I was conducted between January 1 and 5, 1945, by SS-Obergruppenführer Herbert Gille's IV SS Panzer Corps. KONRAD II was conducted between January 7 and 11. The final push, KONRAD III, was fought between January 18 and 27. On February 11, 1945, Pfeffer-Wildenbruch and his remaining troops attempted to break out of the city westward through the Buda Hills to join up with other German forces just outside the Soviet encirclement. Only some eight hundred succeeded. The Soviets declared Buda secure on February 13. The fighting is estimated to have claimed the lives of sixty thousand German troops. The Soviets lost seventy-two thousand confirmed dead, with another eighty thousand missing. Some one hundred and five thousand Hungarians, mostly civilians, were also killed.

Anna Boros-McGee, Spencer C. Tucker, and David T. Zabecki

See also: Balck, Hermann; Romania Campaign, Soviet

Additional Reading

Balck, Hermann. *Order in Chaos: The Memoirs of General of Panzer Troops Hermann Balck.* Edited and Translated by David T. Zabecki and Dieter J. Biedekarken. Lexington: University Press of Kentucky, 2015.

Busch, Ernst (1885–1945)

Wehrmacht field marshal and commander of Army Group Center in Russia.

Born in Essen-Steele in the Ruhr on July 6, 1885, Ernst Busch was commissioned in the German Army in 1908. During World War I, he was awarded the *Pour le Mérite*. Busch became an enthusiastic follower of Adolf Hitler, and he was rewarded for his support of Hitler during the 1938 Blomberg-Fritsch crisis, with promotion to general of infantry and assignment as commander of VIII Army Corps, which he commanded during the invasion of Poland in 1939. He commanded the Sixteenth Army during the 1940 invasion of France and during the 1941 invasion of the Soviet Union. Promoted to field marshal in February 1943, Busch assumed command of Army Group Center in October. Eight months later, during the Soviet's Operation BAGRATION, Army Group Center was effectively destroyed. Relieved of command on June 28, 1944, Busch was retired but was then brought back to command Army Group Northwest in March 1945, to oppose the Allied western advance into Germany. Busch died in British captivity at Aldershot, England, on July 17, 1945.

Dana Lombardy and T. P. Schweider

See also: Belorussia Offensive, Soviet; Blomberg-Fritsch Crisis; France, Battle of; Poland Campaign; Soviet Union, Invasion of (Operation BARBAROSSA)

Additional Reading

Mitcham, Samuel W. *Hitler's Field Marshals and Their Battles.* Chelsea, MI: Scarborough House, 1988.

C

Canaris, Wilhelm (1887–1945)

Kriegsmarine admiral and head of the Abwehr.

Born in Aplerbeck, Westphalia, Germany, on January 1, 1887, Wilhelm Canaris entered the German Navy in 1905. During World War I, he served as a U-boat commander and an intelligence officer. In 1932, he assumed command of the battleship *Schlesien*, and, in January 1935, he was named to head military intelligence—the Abwehrabteilung (Abwehr). The Blomberg-Fritsch Crisis in 1938 disillusioned Canaris. Shortly thereafter, the Abwehr became associated with anti-Nazi elements in Germany. Canaris opposed Hitler's policies, predicting they would lead to war and inevitable defeat. Despite Canaris's reticence, Hitler personally liked him, and the Abwehr did provide much useful information, all of which gave Canaris some protection as he aided a limited number of Jews. Canaris resisted Reinhard Heydrich's efforts to take over the *Abwehr*, but his position was threatened when Heydrich uncovered evidence of his anti-Nazi activities. In February 1944, Hitler removed Canaris from his post. Implicated in the July 1944 bomb plot against Hitler—though he did not take an active role—Canaris was arrested and later hanged at Flossenbürg Prison on April 9, 1945.

Rodney Madison

See also: Abwehr; Blomberg-Fritsch Crisis; Fritsch, Werner von; Opposition to Hitler, German Military

Additional Reading

Hohne, Heinz. *Canaris: Hitler's Master Spy.* Translated by J. Maxwell Brownjohn. Garden City, NY: Doubleday, 1979.

Cassino/Rapido River, Battles of (January 17–May 18, 1944)

The battle for Monte Cassino pitted the defending German Tenth Army, under Colonel General Heinrich von Vietinghoff genannt Scheel against the U.S. Fifth and British Eighth Armies as they advanced toward Rome. Monte Cassino was a massif, strategically located at the entrance of the Liri Valley. The site of a Benedictine abbey established in 529 CE, Monte Cassino was a key sector of the German Gustav Line, a set of defensive positions stretching across the Italian peninsula and blocking the Allied approach to Rome. Following the British and U.S. landings on the Italian peninsula in September 1943, German forces under Field Marshal Albert Kesselring established defenses north of Naples, known as the Gustav Line. This formidable defensive position took advantage of the Apennine Mountains, as well as the Garigliano and Rapido Rivers. The line's western end, closer to Rome, was anchored by Monte Cassino.

After Kesselring's forces repulsed four separate Allied attempts to break through the line, the Allies tried to outflank the line by making an amphibious landing at Anzio in January 1944. To prepare for the Anzio landings, U.S. Fifth Army commander

General Mark Clark ordered supporting attacks by the British X Corps and the U.S. II Corps. Lieutenant General Richard McCreery's British X Corps failed to cross the Garigliano River on January 17, 1944. Three days later, Major General Geoffrey Keyes's U.S. II Corps attacked across the Rapido River and into the Liri Valley. By February 11, the II Corps attack was spent, stalled in front of Monte Cassino, at the entrance to the Liri Valley.

The task of opening the Liri Valley fell to Lieutenant General Sir Bernard Freyberg's New Zealand II Corps. Believing that the only way to capture Cassino was to eliminate the abbey from the commanding heights above the town, Freyberg received permission to bomb it, and, on February 15, waves of Allied bombers dropped 435 tons of high explosives, reducing the abbey to ruins. The loss, however, was not as great as it might have been. In October 1943, Colonel Julius Schlegel of the Herman Göring Panzer Division had persuaded Abbot Diamare to move the abbey's treasures, including the reliquary of St. Benedict and the famous library. Schlegel also convinced Diamare to evacuate most of the monks and civilian refugees from the abbey. Although the Germans had not previously garrisoned the abbey, its destruction allowed them to position troops amid the rubble and to strengthen their lines. By March 24, the attacks of the New Zealand II Corps had halted, with the Germans still in possession of portions of Cassino and the abbey's ruins. The Allies resumed attacking on May 11, and, seven days later, the Polish II Corps, commanded by Lieutenant General Władysław Anders, finally occupied Monte Cassino, completing a four-month battle for the heights. Allied casualties for the entire campaign totaled some one hundred and twenty thousand; the Germans suffered almost one hundred and thirty thousand.

David M. Toczek

See also: Anzio, Battle of; Kesselring, Albert; Salerno Landings, Allied

Additional Reading

Blumenson, Martin. *Bloody River: The Real Tragedy of the Rapido.* Boston, MA: Houghton Mifflin, 1970.

Böhmler, Rudolf. *Monte Cassino: A German View.* London: Cassell, 1964.

Caucasus Campaign (July 22, 1942–October 9, 1943)

Operation EDELWEISS was a German campaign to capture the rich Caspian oil fields. Although the offensive was unsuccessful, the territory taken represented the farthest points to the east and south reached by the German Army during the war. The great German summer offensive, Operation BLAU (BLUE), opened on June 28. The main effort was supposed to be south against the Caucasus oil fields, located near the cities of Baku, Maikop, and Grozny.

Hitler's original plan was for Army Groups A and B to cooperate in a great effort to secure the Don and Donets valleys and capture the cities of Rostov and Stalingrad. On July 13, Hitler ordered a change of plans, now demanding that Stalingrad and the Caucasus be captured simultaneously. This demand placed further strains on already inadequate German resources, especially logistical support. The twin objectives also meant that a gap would inevitably appear between the two German army groups, enabling most Soviet troops caught in the Don River bend to escape eastward.

German troops conducting a river-crossing operation during the Caucasus Campaign (July 22, 1942–October 9, 1943). (ullstein bild via Getty Images)

In late July, the First Panzer and Seventeenth Armies of Field Marshal Siegmund List's Army Group A established a bridgehead across the Don River at Bataysk. Hitler then issued Führer Directive 45, initiating EDELWEISS. He believed that the Red Army was close to defeat and that the advance into the Caucasus should proceed without waiting until the Don was cleared and Stalingrad had fallen. But List had only ten infantry divisions, three panzer, and two motorized divisions with which to conquer an area the size of France.

On July 28, the Soviets established the north Caucasus front, commanded by Marshal Semen Budenny. By August 9, the 5th SS Panzer Division had taken the first of the Caucasus oil fields at Maykop. To the west, infantry and mountain formations of the Seventeenth Army had made slower progress, but, on August 9, they took Krasnodar, capital of the rich agricultural Kuban region. Soviet forces, meanwhile, continued to fall back into the Caucasus, sabotaging the oil fields, removing much of the equipment and destroying the wellheads.

By the end of August, the German advance had slowed to a crawl. The problems there were largely logistical, with a serious shortage of fuel. Displeased with the progress, Hitler sacked List on September 10 and assumed personal control of Army Group A. Weather and logistical problems continued, however, and, on October 14, the Germans suspended offensive operations in the Caucasus.

Events at Stalingrad took precedence when the Soviets encircled the German

Sixth Army at the end of November. Then, on November 29, the newly organized Soviet Transcaucasus front went on the offensive. At the end of December, with the situation to the north growing more precarious daily, Hitler reluctantly ordered Army Group A to withdraw. This movement began in early January, with Soviet forces unable to seriously disrupt it. By October 9, 1943, Soviet forces had retaken all of the Caucasus. The campaign had been a costly and unsuccessful gamble. Ultimately, by splitting his resources between Stalingrad and the Caucasus, Hitler got neither.

Michael Share and Spencer C. Tucker

See also: List, Siegmund Wilhelm Walter; Stalingrad, Battle of

Additional Reading

Erickson, John. *The Road to Stalingrad.* London: Weidenfeld and Nicolson, 1975.

Glantz, David M., and Jonathan M. House. *When Titans Clashed: How the Red Army Stopped Hitler.* Lawrence: University Press of Kansas, 1995.

Channel Dash (February 11–13, 1942)

The Channel Dash was the passage of the German battleships *Scharnhorst* and *Gneisenau* and the heavy cruiser *Prinz Eugen* through the English Channel from Brest, France, to Wilhelmshaven, Germany, in February 1942. In March 1941, the *Scharnhorst* and *Gneisenau* had arrived at Brest, on the French Atlantic coast, after a commerce-raiding voyage, and they were joined by the *Prinz Eugen* in June 1941. Though vulnerable to British bombing, the ships constituted a standing threat to Allied convoys in the Atlantic. However, by late 1941, Hitler was convinced that the British were planning to invade Norway, and, against the advice of his naval commanders, he demanded that the ships return to Germany for deployment in Norwegian waters.

In early 1942, when British intelligence strongly suggested a possible German breakout and passage through the Straits of Dover, preparations for aerial and naval attacks, already under way for nearly a year, were accelerated. The British assumed that the German ships would transit the narrowest part of the channel at night, but the Germans planned Operation CERBERUS to conceal the ships' departure from Brest and to run the straits in daylight, counting on surprise to prevent a timely British concentration. At 2245 hours on February 11, the three big ships and an escort of six destroyers, with Vice Admiral Otto Ciliax commanding, cleared Brest Harbor. The British were caught completely by surprise. Although the *Gneisenau* struck one mine, and the *Scharnhorst* hit two (the second one seriously slowing her and separating her from the rest of the flotilla), all the German ships were safely in the Elbe estuary by 1030 hours on February 13.

John A. Hutcheson Jr.

See also: Kriegsmarine (German Navy); Warships, Surface

Additional Reading

Kemp, Peter. *The Escape of the "Scharnhorst" and "Gneisenau."* Annapolis, MD: Naval Institute Press, 1975.

Channel Islands Campaign (June 30, 1940–May 1945)

The Channel Islands, situated in the south-central portion of the English Channel and closer to France than mainland Britain, were the only British territory occupied by Germany during World War II. The Germans occupied the Bailiwicks of Jersey and Guernsey on June 30, 1940 and fortified and equipped them with powerful coastal artillery emplacements as part of the Atlantic Wall. After the Allies invaded Normandy on June 6, 1944, the 26,100-man German garrison—which included the 319th Infantry Division, commanded in 1945 by Major General Rudolf Wulf, and assorted coastal artillery, air force, navy, construction and supply personnel—remained in place. The decision to hold the islands rather than evacuate them led to a miniature naval war far behind the front lines that lasted nearly a year, until the defeat of the Nazi regime in May 1945.

After the Allied landed in Normandy on June 6, 1944, the U.S. Army largely cleared the Brittany Peninsula by that October, the Channel Islands were largely cut off by the Allied navies. As autumn passed into winter, supplies began to run low in the Channel Islands, and the civilian population faced starvation. The German naval commander, Admiral Friedrich Hüffmeier, decided to raid the mainland to obtain food and coal. By coincidence, the Allies were shipping coal to the nearby port of Granville on the Cotentin Peninsula, which had good rail connections to Paris.

On the night of March 8, 1945, German naval vessels sailed from St. Hélier. They encountered and badly damaged the U.S. submarine-chaser *PC-564* outside of Granville. The Germans then stormed ashore. At 0300 hours, the Germans retired with one collier loaded with coal and returned to St. Hélier. It was the last German attack in France during World War II.

On May 9, 1945, following the collapse of the Nazi regime, the German garrison surrendered to the Royal Navy. The defenders of the Channel Islands believed they had never been defeated.

Vincent P. O'Hara

See also: Normandy Invasion and Campaign

Additional Reading

Cruickshank, Charles. *The German Occupation of the Channel Islands.* London: Oxford University Press, 1975.

Chir River, Battle of (December 7–22, 1942)

Part of the Stalingrad Campaign, the Battle of the Chir River is one of the most skillful divisional-level battles of modern times. Under the command of General Hermann Balck, the 11th Panzer Division fought a fifteen-day running series of battles along the Chir River north of Stalingrad that resulted in the destruction of the Soviet Fifth Tank Army. The commander of Army Group Don, Field Marshal Eric von Manstein, had planned to relieve the Sixth Army with General Hermann Hoth's Fourth Panzer Army, attacking from the north of Stalingrad and supported by the XLVIII Panzer Corps, which included Balck's 11th Panzer Division. On December 7, before the XLVIII Panzer Corps could link up with the Fourth Panzer Army, elements of the Soviet Fifth Tank Army launched heavy attacks at various points along the Chir River.

By December 22, the series of defensive battles along the Chir were over, with the Germans the clear tactical victors. That same day, however, the XLVIII Panzer Corps received immediate orders to move ninety miles to the west to form blocking positions in front of Rostov. Despite their tactical success, the Germans were outmaneuvered by the Soviets at the operational level. Nonetheless, the battles the 11th Panzer Division along the Chir River were some of military history's most outstanding examples of maneuver warfare and mobile defense.

David T. Zabecki

See also: Balck, Hermann; Hoth, Hermann; Manstein, Erich von; Stalingrad, Battle of

Additional Reading

Balck, Hermann. *Order in Chaos: The Memoirs of General of Panzer Troops Hermann Balck*. Translated and Edited by David T. Zabecki and Dieter Biedekerken. Lexington: University Press of Kentucky, 2015.

Mellenthin, Friedrich-Wilhelm von. *Panzer Battles*. Norman: University of Oklahoma Press, 1956.

Choltitz, Dietrich von (1894–1966)

Wehrmacht general of infantry and military governor of Paris.

Born on November 9, 1894, in Wiesegräflich, Germany, Dietrich von Choltitz served as an infantry company commander in World War I. He commanded a battalion during the 1939 Poland Campaign and a regiment during the early stages of the invasion of the Soviet Union. During the Crimea Campaign in the autumn of 1941, his regiment sustained heavy losses during the siege of Sevastopol. In August 1942, Choltitz assumed command of the 260th Infantry Division in Russia, and, in 1942 and 1943, he was the deputy commander, and then acting commander, of the XLVIII Panzer Corps.

On June 15, 1944, Choltitz assumed command of the LXXXIV Corps in France. Much of his command was destroyed during the carpet bombing prior to the Allied breakout at Saint-Lô, and Choltitz was relieved of his command on July 28. Hitler, however, reassigned Choltitz as commander of the Greater Paris area on August 7, 1944. Choltitz had few available resources to stop the advance of the Western Allies. Receiving orders from Hitler on 23 August to begin demolishing parts of the city, he refused and ensured a relatively orderly turnover of the city, with little damage to its public buildings and monuments, via negotiations with the French Resistance. Choltitz formally surrendered on August 25, 1944 and became a prisoner of war. Following his release in April 1947, he retired in Baden-Baden, where he died on November 5, 1966, probably better remembered in France than in Germany.

Jon D. Berlin

See also: Paris, Allied Liberation of; Saint-Lô, Battle for

Additional Reading

Collins, Larry, and Dominique Lapierre. *Is Paris Burning*? New York: Simon & Schuster, 1965.

Ciliax, Otto (1891–1964)

Kriegsmarine admiral.

Otto Ciliax was born in Gotha-Neudietendorf, Germany, on October 30, 1891. He entered the German Navy in 1910 and served in submarines during World War I. During the 1936 to 1939 Spanish Civil War, he commanded the pocket battleship *Admiral Scheer*. At the outbreak of World War II, Ciliax commanded the battleship *Scharnhorst*. In February 1942, Ciliax, flying his flag in the *Scharnhorst*, commanded Operation CERBERUS, more widely known as the Channel Dash, during which the battleships *Scharnhorst* and *Gneisenau* and the heavy cruiser *Prinz Eugen*, escaped from an Allied blockade at Brest and returned to Wilhelmshaven, Germany. From March 1943 to April 1945, Ciliax commanded German naval forces in Norway. Ciliax died at Lübeck-Travemünde on December 12, 1964.

Spencer C. Tucker

See also: Channel Dash

Additional Reading

Bekker, Cajus. *Hitler's Naval War.* New York: Doubleday, 1975.

COBRA, Allied Breakout Operation (July 25–31, 1944)

COBRA was the code name for the Allied operation that broke through the German positions and out of the Normandy beachhead in July 1944. While British General Sir Bernard Montgomery—facing the right of the German lines—garnered moderate success with the capture of Caen, his attempt at a breakout during Operation GOODWOOD was a failure. The Allied high command still needed a decisive breakthrough that would extricate their forces from the Cotentin Peninsula and allow a drive into Brittany. Montgomery's operation, however, did convince Field Marshal Günther von Kluge, who was both OB West and commander of Army Group B, that the major Allied breakout effort would occur on his right.

On Kluge's left, however, American General Omar Bradley planned to break the German defensive line on the Saint-Lô–Perier Road. Before the operation could go into effect, the crossroads town of Saint-Lô had to be secured as a jump-off point. Despite a dogged defense by II Parachute Corps, commanded by General Eugen Meindl, and the 352nd Infantry Division, the German forces could not hold the town, and it fell to the Allies on July 18.

In the path of the planned U.S. advance from Saint-Lô was the German Seventh Army, commanded by SS-Oberstgruppenführer Paul Hausser. Under Hausser were Meindl's II Parachute Corps and the LXXXIV Corps commanded by General Dietrich von Choltitz. The thirty-five thousand German troops under Hausser were outnumbered five-to-one. Hitler ordered Kluge to hold the line in northern France at all cost. Because he was a suspect in the failed attempt on Hitler's life during the July 20 Assassination Plot, Kluge was determined to prove his loyalty to the Führer.

Operation COBRA began on the morning of July 25 with a massive Allied carpet-bombing and artillery barrage of Choltitz's section of the German lines, occupied by Lieutenant General Fritz Bayerlein's Panzer Lehr Division, which suffered devastating casualties. But even with the destruction wrought by the bombing, artillery, and the initial assaults, the U.S. spearhead advanced only three miles on the operation's first day. Hausser's efforts at a counterattack were thwarted by U.S. air superiority.

On the second day, however, American Major General J. Lawton Collins—commanding the spearhead—committed the 2nd Armored Division to the assault. This attack, combined with another by the U.S. 1st Infantry Division and elements of the 3rd Armored Division farther west, made significant advances. Handicapping the Seventh Army was Hausser's failure to establish a sufficient reserve force and Kluge's preoccupation with the British and Canadians on the Caen front. By the end of COBRA's second day, there was an irreparable gap in the German lines, and portions of the U.S.

forces were seven miles south of the Saint-Lô—Perier Road.

Desperate fighting occurred all over the base of the Cotentin Peninsula, as German units struggled to avoid encirclement, while Kluge struggled in vain to reform a German line. Meanwhile, the U.S. VIII Corps turned the German Army's left flank and captured Avranches, the gateway into Brittany. The Normandy breakout was complete. Operation COBRA was a decisive defeat for Germany. It opened the way for U.S. General George Patton's Third Army thrust into Brittany, cost the German Army sixty thousand casualties, and marked a shift in combat in Western Europe from a plodding war of attrition to a war of rapid maneuver.

Robert L. Glaze

See also: Bayerlein, Fritz; Choltitz, Dietrich von; Hausser, Paul; Kluge, Günther von; Normandy Invasion and Campaign

Additional Reading

Carafano, James Jay. *After D-Day: Operation Cobra and the Normandy Breakout.* Boulder, CO: Lynne Rienner Publishers, 2000.

Isby, David C. *Fighting the Breakout: The German Army in Normandy from Cobra to the Falaise Gap.* London: Greenhill, 2004.

Colmar Pocket, Battle for the (January 20–February 9, 1945)

The Colmar Pocket was the German bridgehead west of the Rhine River and south of the city of Strasbourg, held by General of Infantry Siegfried Rasp's Nineteenth Army of eight divisions, totaling some fifty thousand men. On January 7, 1945, the Germans launched a major attack out of the Colmar Pocket, in support of Operation NORDWIND (NORTHWIND). The attack gained very little ground, but the Allies wanted to eliminate the pocket. The task was assigned to General Jean de Lattre de Tassigny's French First Army of the Allied 6th Army Group.

On January 20, de Lattre's troops attacked the Colmar Pocket. The objective was to envelop the pocket by converging on Neuf-Brisach and the Rhine Bridge at Breisach. Deep snow along with German mines, machine guns, tanks, and artillery kept the attacks from gaining much ground. The U.S. 3rd Infantry Division, which was attached to the French, then crossed the Fecht and Ill Rivers. The Germans counterattacked, but the 3rd Infantry Division held them off and reinforced its bridgehead. Severe shortages of French troops led to the eventual attachment to the operation of the entire U.S. XXI Corps, commanded by Major General Frank Milburn. U.S. XXI Corps then enveloped the Colmar Pocket from the north, with the French II Corps screened its left flank.

French forces finished off the pocket on February 9. For the entire operation, the Allies had sustained about eighteen thousand casualties, and the Germans between twenty-two thousand and thirty-six thousand. Only the 708th Volksgrenadier Division, evacuating the pocket on February 3, escaped reasonably intact. The German 2nd Mountain Division had one thousand battle casualties and forty-seven hundred men taken as prisoners. Only five hundred members of the German 198th Infantry Division and four hundred men of the German 338th Infantry Division managed to escape. The Germans also abandoned fifty-five armored vehicles and sixty-six field pieces.

Uzal W. Ent

See also: NORDWIND, Operation

Additional Reading

Clarke, Jeffrey J., and Robert Ross Smith. *Riviera to the Rhine. United States Army in World War II.* Washington, DC: Center of Military History, 1993.

Cologne, Allied Air Raid on (May 30–31, 1942)

The German city of Cologne (Köln) was bombed in 262 separate air raids during World War II. The first Allied thousand-plane raid of the war was carried out against Cologne on the night of May 30 to 31, 1942. With the assignment of Air Marshal Sir Arthur Harris as commander of Royal Air Force Bomber Command in February 1942, the British began a deliberate program of targeting built-up areas instead of industries. Cologne and Hamburg were the two possible targets for the RAF's first thousand-plane raid. They were selected over the more valuable Essen because each was located on a large body of water and could be readily identified by Gee (for G or grid), a new British navigational system. On the day of the raid, bad weather ruled Hamburg, but Cologne was clear. Known as Operation MILLENNIUM, the raid was conducted on the night of May 30 to 31, 1942. Harris got 1,046 bombers aloft, and his objective was to pass all aircraft over Cologne in only ninety minutes.

The British bombers dropped more than 1,455 tons of bombs on the city, two-thirds of them incendiaries. The bombing resulted in the destruction of an estimated thirteen thousand homes and the razing of almost six hundred acres of the city. Casualties amounted to 469 dead and more than five thousand wounded on the German side, with another forty-six thousand left homeless. The British lost more than three hundred crewmen in the forty-one bombers that failed to return, a loss of 3.8 percent. The large number of bombers overwhelmed the German fighter defenses and the Kammhuber Line. The Cologne raid shattered German illusions about who was winning the war and caused Hitler to lose confidence in the Luftwaffe. But instead of accepting the need to strengthen Germany's air defenses, Hitler ordered retaliatory German air attacks.

C. J. Horn

See also: Combined Bomber Offensive, Allied (Operation POINTBLANK); Kammhuber Line

Additional Reading

Neillands, Robin. *The Bomber War: The Allied Air Offensive against Nazi Germany.* Woodstock, NY and New York: Overlook Press, 2001.

Combined Bomber Offensive, Allied (Operation POINTBLANK) (June 10, 1943–April 12, 1945)

The Anglo-American Combined Bomber Offensive (CBO) was the principle Allied air campaign against the Third Reich. The initial top priority for CBO targets from June 1943 to 1944 was the Luftwaffe itself. As the Allies prepared to launch Operation OVERLORD, their invasion of the continent of Europe, CBO targeting priority shifted to destroying the ability of the Germans to defeat the invasion. Transportation infrastructure in France was an especially high priority. Subsequent highest priority campaigns included the V-weapon installations and Germany's petroleum, oil, and lubricants (POL) capabilities. The British prosecuted their half of the campaign primarily through nighttime bombing, which they believed resulted in lower friendly losses. The Americans operated primarily through daylight "precision" bombing, which was anything but precise. In theory, the combined campaign resulted in round-the-clock pressure from the air on Germany. When World War II began, only two nations had a coherent and committed strategic bombing program: Great Britain and the United States. Despite having the world's most powerful air force in 1939, Germany's essentially tactical air force was designed to support ground operations.

At the Casablanca Conference in January 1943, Allied leaders agreed to a combined bomber offensive (CBO) of round-the-clock attacks. The campaign started on June 10, 1943, although the Allied combined chiefs of staff did not issue the formal directive for what was designated Operation POINTBLANK until June 14. Elements of the U.S. Eighth Air Force had started bombing the European continent from England in August 1942, although they did not fly deep penetration raids into central and eastern Germany until a year later. Losses among unescorted B-17 and B-24 bombers were horrendous, especially during attacks against ball-bearing plants at Schweinfurt in August and October 1943. By the end of the year, such deep attacks on Germany were suspended, and it appeared that the Luftwaffe was on the verge of winning the strategic air war in Europe.

Everything changed with the advent of the Allied long-range escort fighter, most notably the P-51 Mustang. In mid-February 1944, the U.S. Strategic Air Forces (USSTAF) began their Operation ARGUMENT ("Big Week") attacks against German aircraft factories. The air battles that ensued decimated the Luftwaffe, and, by the time of the D-Day landings in June, the Allies achieved air supremacy over France and air superiority over Germany. The escort fighters began by sticking close to their bombers, but they proved most effective when they were released to sweep against enemy aircraft in the air and on the ground. Although the strategic bombers had an initial priority to operations in support of the coming invasion, Allied airpower had built up to the point that USSTAF commander General Carl Spaatz could begin sustained attacks against oil targets in May. By the fall of 1944, Luftwaffe and Wehrmacht operations were severely crippled by fuel shortages, and concentrated attacks against transportation networks further limited German mobility and economic activity.

In Europe, U.S. air leaders remained committed to attacks aimed primarily at economic and military targets instead of at civilian morale, a policy that sometimes caused friction with their British allies. The differing national approaches also played a role as the war in Europe approached its end, and both air forces sought an aerial death blow to finish the war. The British plan, code-named THUNDERCLAP, was based on shattering morale by destroying Berlin. That major assault was conducted by the U.S. Eighth Air Force on February 3, 1945. Allied concerns about supporting the Soviet advance led to the raid that produced the firestorm that devastated Dresden ten days later. The corresponding American plan, code-named CLARION, aimed to awe the German populace with widespread attacks on targets in every village. It was eventually changed into primarily a transportation-system attack because of concerns for efficiency, public image, and even morality. The controversy in Great Britain over the Dresden attack was one factor in the suspension of the strategic air war against Germany in April 1945, although it was not as important as the simple fact that Allied bombing forces were running out of suitable targets.

Both the British and Americans conducted postwar assessments of the strategic bombing campaign. The massive U.S. Strategic Bombing Survey compiled an impressive collection of data, although differing personalities and agendas within the survey committees produced several conflicting conclusions. They agreed, however, that the U.S. approach to targeting was superior to RAF area bombing. In retrospect, the most important contribution Allied strategic bombing made in Europe was to defeat the Luftwaffe and ensure that when Allied troops driving across northwestern Europe saw aircraft, they could be certain that the planes were friendly. The CBO did not prevent the late-mobilizing German economy from peaking in 1944, but the oil and transportation campaigns had a major impact on degrading it thereafter. Civilian morale did not break, but some British observers have noted that the city bombing motivated German industry to disperse, thus making it more vulnerable to transportation interdiction. More than seven hundred thousand German civilians died from Allied bombing, about the same number who succumbed to the effects of the British naval blockade in World War I. The cost of the CBO was also high for the air forces involved. The USSTAF lost 9,949 bombers, 8,500 fighters, and 64,000 airmen killed. RAF Bomber Command lost fifty-seven thousand killed or missing from all causes.

Conrad C. Crane and David T. Zabecki

See also: Berlin Air Campaign, Allied; "Big Week" Allied Air Campaign; Cologne, Allied Air Raid on; Dresden, Allied Air Attack on; Hamburg, Allied Air Raids (Operation GOMORRAH); Schweinfurt and Regensburg Air Raids, Allied

Additional Reading

Crane, Conrad C. *Bombs, Cities, and Civilians: American Airpower Strategy in World War II.* Lawrence: University Press of Kansas, 1993.

MacIsaac, David, general ed. *The United States Strategic Bombing Survey.* 10 vols. New York: Garland, 1976.

Commando Order (October 18, 1942)

The Commando Order was issued by Hitler to counter British commando raids. Two months after the British commando raid on Dieppe, Hitler issued the order on October 18, 1942. It was issued in twelve copies only, and headquarters required that in no circumstances was it to fall into Allied hands. Hitler claimed that the Allied commando raids were a violation of the Geneva Convention, and, he ordered, "From now on all enemies on so-called commando missions in Europe or Africa challenged by German troops, even if they are in uniform, whether armed or unarmed, in battle or in flight, are to be slaughtered to the last man." For their complicity in the Commando Order, various German commanders were tried at the International Military Tribunal at Nuremberg or at the follow-up American Military Tribunals.

Berryman E. Woodruff IV

See also: American Military Tribunals; Dieppe, British Raid on; International Military Tribunal: The Nuremberg Trials

Additional Reading

Davidson, Eugene. *The Trial of the Germans.* New York: Collier, 1966.

Commissar Order (June 6, 1941)

The Commissar Order was issued to the German Army by Hitler on June 6, 1941, two weeks before the start of Operation BARBAROSSA, the German invasion of the Soviet Union. The order required the German military to execute any captured Soviet commissars, the Communist Party political officers assigned to military units. This order contravened all international conventions governing the treatment of prisoners of war. Hitler specifically stipulated that German soldiers guilty of breaking international law would be "excused." Although some German generals took an ambivalent approach to the order, it was widely carried out.

Craig S. Hamilton

See also: Commando Order; International Military Tribunal: The Nuremberg Trials

Additional Reading

Bartov, Omer. *The Eastern Front, 1941–1945: German Troops and the Barbarisation of Warfare.* New York: St. Martin's Press, 1986.

Convoy PQ 17, Battle of (June 27–July 7, 1942)

PQ 17 was a disastrous Allied Arctic convoy to Murmansk in the Soviet Union. From August 1941 through May 1945, the Western Allies sent some four million tons of supplies to the northern Soviet Union via the Arctic. Convoy PQ 17 sailed from Iceland on June 27, 1942, with thirty-six merchantmen protected by four corvettes, two antiaircraft ships, and four antisubmarine trawlers. At the same time, eastbound Convoy QP 13, made up of thirty-five merchantmen, sailed from Kola Inlet. British rear admiral L. H. K. Hamilton commanded a covering force to protect both convoys, consisting of two British and two U.S. heavy cruisers, plus one British and two U.S. destroyers. En route, British commander J.E. Broome joined them with six destroyers to provide additional protection. Distant cover was provided by the British Home Fleet under Admiral Sir John Tovey. He commanded a mixed British and U.S. force, consisting of two battleships, one aircraft carrier, two cruisers, and fourteen destroyers.

Tovey was under strict orders to steer clear of the German airfields in northern Norway, where Luftwaffe forces, under the command of Colonel General Hans-Jürgen Stumpff, had massed 103 bombers, 42 torpedo-bombers, 20 dive bombers, and 89 reconnaissance aircraft to block any convoy's passage. The Germans also had ten U-boats on station. Their tactical reconnaissance advantage was formidable. Political pressure from Washington and Moscow compelled leaders to insist that the convoy proceed, and it sailed blindly into a German trap. The convoy was attacked by at least nine U-boats, thirty-three torpedo aircraft, and six bombers. Of the thirty-four merchant ships still with the convoy when the order to scatter was given, only thirteen reached Murmansk. The Allies suffered one of their worst maritime defeats of the war. Convoys to Murmansk were then suspended for the summer, as perpetual Arctic daylight and German naval and air strength made them untenable.

James Levy

See also: Atlantic, Battle of the

Additional Reading

Woodman, Richard. *Arctic Convoys.* London: Pen & Sword, 2007.

Convoys SC 122 and HX 229, Battle of (March 16–20, 1943)

The battle for Convoys SC 122 and HX 229 was the largest convoy battle in the Battle of the Atlantic. March 1943 was the high-water mark of the German U-boat campaign against Allied convoys in the North Atlantic. Between March 10 and 20, Allied signals intelligence suffered a temporary blackout in its operations against the German U-boat cipher Triton. At the same time, the German signals intelligence service was able to decipher the rerouting instructions for two eastbound convoys: SC 122 and HX 229. Wolfpacks *Raubgraf* (eight boats) and *Stürmer* (eighteen boats) were to operate against SC 122, and group *Dränger* (eleven boats) was deployed against HX 229.

Both convoys were sailing close to each other, and HX 229 was closing in on the slower SC 122. On March 16, the first U-boat made contact with HX 229, which suffered a heavy mauling during the night of March 16 to 17. By the time Grand Admiral Karl Dönitz called off the operation on March 20, twenty-one Allied ships had been sunk, totaling one hundred and forty-one thousand tons of shipping, as well as one destroyer lost. Two U-boats were damaged, and the *U-384* was sunk. Those results had been achieved primarily because the sheer numbers of U-boats had saturated the convoys' defenses. Nevertheless, only sixteen of the forty U-boats deployed against both convoys had actually been able to make contact, and, due to the diligence of the convoys' hard-pressed air and sea escorts, only nine succeeded in torpedoing ships. Of the thirty-nine U-boats that survived the battle, sixteen subsequently required more than forty days of maintenance for damage sustained during the battle. The Allies were about to turn the corner in the Battle of the Atlantic.

Dirk Steffen

See also: Atlantic, Battle of the

Additional Reading

Middlebrook, Martin. *Convoy: The Battle for Convoys SC.122 and HX.229.* New York: William Morrow, 1976.

Crete, German Invasion of (May 20–June 1, 1944)

On April 23, the Greek government evacuated to Crete, before Allied forces completed their evacuation. On April 15, Lieutenant General Alexander Löhr, commander Luftflotte 4, submitted a plan for the aerial conquest of Crete. Operation MERCURY had the objective of using Crete as an air base against British and Allied forces in the eastern Mediterranean. German intelligence forecast five thousand defenders, but they actually faced 42,640 Allied ground troops, including 27,500 British and Commonwealth troops and 9,000 Greek troops who had arrived from Greece or Egypt by April 30. The invasion was the largest airborne assault to date, but the Axis lacked capacity, with almost disastrous consequences. Crete was easy to defend and difficult to invade.

The Luftwaffe high command ordered the paratroops to assault four drop zones in two waves. Two drops of seventy-five hundred paratroops each were planned, eight hours apart, on the first day. Overnight, ships would land sixty-three hundred mountain and airborne support troops, one tank company, and one motorcycle battalion at two of the objective towns. On the second day, transport aircraft were supposed to land five thousand mountain troops on captured airfields. In the event, the first wave dropped on May 20 and was left decimated on the edge of the Maleme Airfield. The second wave, around Heraklion and Rethymnon, was pushed back by aggressive Allied counterattacks, and the invasion fleets were delayed and intercepted by the Royal Navy. The paratroop forces on the ground were separated by up to seventy-five miles. German parachute forces commander General Kurt Student was forced to choose between abandoning Crete or landing reinforcements on the contested airfield at Maleme.

German paratroopers landing in Crete, May 20–21, 1941. This is probably a composite propaganda photo. (ullstein bild via Getty Images)

During the second day, combat aircraft attacked the airfield's defenders, before transports dropped the remaining paratroop reserve of 550 men in two waves. Combining with previously landed troops, they overran the airfield in the late afternoon. The Germans diverted the second invasion fleet from Heraklion to Maleme, but it was intercepted at sea.

The paratroops were saved on May 22, when transport aircraft landed about eleven thousand mountain troops on Maleme airfield, despite direct enemy fire. On May 23, motorcyclists, artillery, and the rest of the mountain troops landed. They helped push Allied ground forces eastward, out of sight of the airfield. The landings on Maleme Airfield had cost the Germans about 230 transport aircraft but restarted the offensive. Only 8,060 paratroops ever dropped by parachute; aircraft landed 13,980 troops at Maleme. The remaining four thousand or so ground troops arrived belatedly by ship.

German troops moved inland across the mountains, outflanking Allied troops on the coast. By the end of May 30, the Germans had secured the entire north coast. The retreating Allied troops withdrew slowly and exhaustingly to the south shore, leaving most of their equipment along the way. They then evacuated some fifteen thousand ground troops from the small fishing village of Sfakia. When the last rearguard surrendered on June 1, the Allied forces had lost altogether 11,835 soldiers captured, 1,742 killed, and 1,737 wounded, Some additional two thousand soldiers and sailors were lost at sea. Axis aircraft sank three cruisers and six destroyers and damaged one carrier, three battleships, six cruisers, and nine destroyers.

The Germans lost 6,580 casualties, including 3,352 dead—2,521 of them paratroops, most within the first two days—506 mountain troops lost at sea, and 325 mountain troops lost on land. That summer Hitler should have authorized further airborne operations in coordination with the Axis thrust into Egypt, but he misattributed the high paratroop losses and forbade such operations.

Bruce Newsome

See also: Greece Campaign; Löhr, Alexander; Student, Kurt

Additional Reading

Sadler, John. *Operation Mercury: The Fall of Crete, 1941.* Barnsley, England: Pen & Sword, 2007.

Crimea Campaign, Soviet (April 8–May 12, 1944)

The Crimea fell to German forces when General Erich von Manstein's Eleventh Army captured the port of Sevastopol after an eight-month siege on July 4, 1942. By the spring of 1944, the German situation in Russia had been reversed, and Soviet forces were pushing back to reclaim their lost territories. The German Seventeenth Army held the Crimea but had been isolated from other Wehrmacht units north of it since October 1943. Meanwhile, General Rodion Malinovsky Malinovsky's 3rd Ukrainian Front recaptured Nikolaiev on March 28 and then drove toward Odessa, which it retook on April 10. General Fedor I. Tolbukhin's 4th Ukrainian Front was assigned the task of destroying Colonel General Erwin Jänecke's Seventeenth Army, a mixed force of eleven German and Romanian divisions, totaling some one hundred and fifty thousand men.

On April 8, Tolbukhin's artillery opened the attack at Perekop. On April 12, Jänecke ordered his divisions to retreat toward Sevastopol from two prepared lines of defense, stretching some twenty miles. By April 13, Tolbukhin's troops had captured Simferopol. At the end of April, Hitler ordered that Sevastopol had to be held, but its defenses were much weaker than they had been in 1941, when the Germans had attacked there. Jänecke had only five weak divisions and little equipment, and because of his repeated requests that his forces be evacuated, Hitler replaced him on May 2 with General of Infantry Karl Allmendinger.

The main Soviet attack started on May 7, separating Sevastopol from the Inkerman Valley. The Soviets then broke through the German lines at Sevastopol, forcing the defenders to retreat to the Chersonese subpeninsula. On May 9, with both the city and harbor in Soviet hands, Hitler finally authorized an evacuation, but Soviet air and naval forces made that impossible. On May 13, the remaining Axis troops in the Crimea surrendered. The Soviets put total German losses in the Crimea Campaign at fifty thousand killed and sixty-one thousand taken prisoner; the Germans admitted losing sixty thousand.

Neville Panthaki

See also: Crimean Campaign; Manstein, Erich von

Additional Reading

Erickson, John. *The Road to Berlin.* New Haven, CT: Yale University Press, 1984.

Crimean Campaign (September 29, 1941–July 4, 1942)

The Wehrmacht's Army Group South, including the German Eleventh Army, supported by elements of the Romanian Third and Fourth Armies, was deployed along the southern sector of the eastern front at the beginning of Operation BARBAROSSA, the invasion of the Soviet Union, in June 1941. The Eleventh Army, under the command of General Erich von Manstein, pursued the retreating Red Army across the Ukraine in the opening months of the German offensive before launching its Crimean campaign in September 1941. The German invasion of the Crimea was spearheaded by the LIV Corps. The plan was to occupy the Crimea quickly before launching a major offensive against Rostov-on-Don.

LIV Corps advanced from Jasy, Romania, to Kishinev, on the Dniester, before securing the Perekop Isthmus and advancing toward the Crimean Peninsula. The 46th Infantry Division secured the eastern approaches to the Crimea on the Kerch Peninsula, while the 50th and the 73rd Infantry Divisions and elements of the Romanian Army breached the thinly defended Perekop Isthmus in late September, occupied much of the Crimea, and then headed southwest toward the strategic seaport city of Sevastopol. Standing in their way was the Red Army's Fifty-first Independent Army and its nine divisions and support units, under the command of Colonel General F. I. Kuznetsov.

The Germans surrounded the entire city on October 30, 1941, launching an initial assault, which was turned back after much bloody fighting. The Germans then laid siege to the city, but additional assaults in November and December were likewise repulsed. In late December, Soviet reinforcements landed on the Kerch peninsula in the eastern Crimea to relieve the besieged city by distracting the German invaders. The situation remained static until early April 1942, when the Germans launched an offensive against the Red Army positions at Kerch, successfully dislodging them the following month. The Germans assaulted Sevastopol, finally managing to penetrate the Soviet defensive lines. The 248-day siege came to an end on July 4, 1942 as the Germans took more than one hundred thousand Soviet prisoners. With the fall of Sevastopol and the complete occupation of the Crimea, Manstein recommended that his Eleventh Army cross the Kerch straits and push into the Kuban area to capture Rostov. Instead, Manstein and elements of the Eleventh Army were transferred to Army Group North and the Leningrad front.

Steven B. Rogers

See also: Manstein, Erich von; Soviet Union, Invasion of (Operation BARBAROSSA)

Additional Reading

Glantz, David, and Jonathan M. House. *When Titans Clashed: How the Red Army Stopped Hitler.* Lawrence: University Press of Kansas, 1995.

Melvin, Mungo. *Manstein: Hitler's Greatest General.* London: Weidenfeld & Nicolson, 2010.

CROSSBOW, Anglo-American Air Operation (December 5, 1943–March 28, 1945)

CROSSBOW was the code name for the Anglo-American air operation against the German long-range weapons. Approximately 40 percent of all Allied reconnaissance flights from Britain between May 1, 1943 and March 31, 1944 sought intelligence on Germany's V programs. Two main types of V weapons were developed by Germany. First was the V-1, an unmanned flying bomb powered by a pulse-jet engine. The second was the V-2, a missile that reached the edge of the earth's atmosphere and flew at supersonic speeds. The V-2 was much more difficult for the Allies to attack because it used a mobile launching platform mounted on a truck. On the night of August 17 to 18, 1943, 597 RAF bombers left Britain to strike Peenemünde, the center of German rocket research on the Baltic coast. More than seven hundred people died in the attack; most were forced laborers.

In November 1943, the CROSSBOW Committee was established to coordinate all information on Germany's missile program as well as the direction of appropriate countermeasures. On June 12, 1944, the first V-1s struck Britain. Initially, Allied commanders did not divert resources from Operation OVERLORD, the invasion of France, to attack the V-1 launch sites, but, within two weeks, the number of V-1s reaching Britain forced a response. As a result, the supreme commander of the Allied Expeditionary Forces, General Dwight Eisenhower, gave priority to Crossbow sites above all other targets, except for "the urgent requirements of the battle." During the next two months, operations against these sites consumed half the energies of Royal Air Force Bomber Command, and some three thousand Allied aircrew were lost in Operation CROSSBOW. At its peak, the defense of the British Isles against the V-1s included an antiaircraft belt along the coast of one thousand guns using the new proximity fuze, more than two thousand barrage balloons, and twenty-one fighter squadrons.

By September 1944, the Allied advance in France had pushed the Germans beyond the range from which V-1s could reach Britain. After a brief respite, attacks continued from the Netherlands, either launched in midair by obsolescent bombers or from newly constructed launch rails. By July 15, 2,579 V-1s had struck Britain, 1,280 of which fell within the London area. Meanwhile, the first operational V-2 strike occurred against Paris on September 8, 1944. The last V-1 reached Britain on March 28, 1945. One day earlier, the last 1,402 V-2s struck Britain. Casualties from the V-1 amounted to 6,139 killed and 17,239 seriously wounded; the V-2 accounted for 2,885 deaths and 6,268 seriously wounded.

Rodney Madison

See also: Combined Bomber Offensive, Allied (Operation POINTBLANK); Rockets, Guided Bombs, and Guided Missiles

Additional Reading

Collier, Basil. *The Battle of the V-Weapons, 1944–1945*. Yorkshire: Emfield Press, 1964.

CRUSADER, British Operation. See North Africa Campaign

D

Denmark Campaign (April 9, 1940)

Code-named Operation WESSERÜBUNG SUD (WESER EXERCISE SOUTH), the German invasion of Denmark began at approximately 0415 hours on April 9, 1940. It formed an integral part of the much larger German assault on Norway (Operation WESSERÜBUNG) that began on the same day. German units under the command of General of Aviation Leonhard Kaupisch quickly overran the Danish Peninsula, abrogating a nonaggression pact signed between Germany and Denmark in May 1939.

German troops march into the city of Aalborg on the first day of the German occupation of Denmark, April 9, 1940. (Corbis via Getty Images)

The poorly trained and inadequately equipped Danish Army numbered only some fourteen thousand men, eight thousand of whom had enlisted within eight weeks of the German attack. The Danish Navy consisted of just two small vessels and approximately three thousand men. The navy surrendered without going on alert, allowing a German troopship to arrive at Copenhagen. The air force had only fifty obsolete planes and a handful of pilots, no match for the Luftwaffe.

On April 9, German seaborne forces moved into the capital of Copenhagen and secured the city by 0600 hours. Meanwhile, German paratroopers conducted the first airborne operation of the war when they seized the undefended fortress of Masnedø and, shortly thereafter, the airport at Aalborg in north Jutland. At the same time, German Army units raced across the Jutland Peninsula in motorized columns. Although Danish Army units briefly contested the Germans in north Schleswig, the outcome was never in doubt. King Frederik IX and Premier Thorvald Stauning believed that they had no choice but to order surrender at 0720 hours. Danish casualties amounted to twenty-six dead and twenty-three wounded; the Germans lost twenty dead and wounded.

The German invasion provided the excuse for the Allied occupation of Iceland, which belonged to Denmark. Allied possession of strategically located Iceland proved vital in the Battle of the Atlantic. German forces occupied Denmark until the end of the war in May 1945.

Lance Janda

See also: Atlantic, Battle of the; Norway Campaign

Additional Reading

Deighton, Len. *Blitzkrieg: From the Rise of Hitler to the Fall of Dunkirk.* New York: Alfred A. Knopf, 1980.

Dieppe, British Raid on (August 19, 1942)

The first serious test of Germany's Atlantic Wall coastal defenses on the English Channel came on August 19, 1942, when a landing force of five thousand Canadian and one thousand British troops, plus a token force of sixty U.S. Army Rangers raided the German-held French port of Dieppe. The raid, which was undertaken at the instigation of the chief of combined operations, Lord Louis Mountbatten, was launched as a demonstration to the Soviet Union of Western Allied resolve and as a rehearsal for a subsequent major cross-Channel invasion.

Dieppe had been selected because it was within range of fighter support from Britain, and its wide beaches adjacent to the town provided good prospects for landing troops. The main German defending force was the 302nd (Static) Infantry Division, commanded by Lieutenant General Konrad Haase. Other German defenses included two naval coastal artillery batteries; an offshore minefield; and nearby airfields, which had nearly three hundred Luftwaffe fighters and bombers.

Operation JUBILEE, as the raid was called, began before dawn on August 19 and ran into trouble early. The assault boats were discovered as they approached the landing site, and they were then fired on by five German Navy coastal patrol craft. By 0900 hours, the situation was so dire that the British commanders decided to abandon the operation and withdraw the surviving troops. By early afternoon, the rescue boats were headed back to Britain with the remnants of the Dieppe raiders, leaving twenty-four officers and 3,164 men behind, who had been either killed or captured. The overall Allied personnel casualty rate was more than 40 percent, the highest of the war for any major offensive involving all three services. The Canadians suffered the worst; with 4,963 men, they made up 80 percent of the attackers, and 3,367 were casualties (907 killed). The German defenders had denied the raiders all of their objectives and drove the Allied force back into the sea with a loss of fewer than 600 casualties, 311 of which had been killed. After a slow start, the Luftwaffe had also done a measure of damage to the Royal Air Force and the assaulting ground troops. The British lost 106 aircraft shot down (mostly fighters); the Germans lost only forty-eight (mostly bombers).

The lessons of the failed operation, however bitter, were very important—both on the general points of how difficult it is to capture a defended port and how crucial a preliminary bombardment is, to the more detailed lessons relating to equipment for beach landings. The Dieppe raid was more than a political setback. Its most telling consequence was to dissuade Prime Minister Winston L. S. Churchill and the British chiefs of staff from any immediate commitment to cross-Channel operations. It convinced Hitler that he still had at least one more summer campaign season in Russia without a significant threat from the west.

James H. Willbanks and John A. Suprin

See also: Atlantic Wall

Additional Reading

Atkin, Ronald. *Dieppe 1942: The Jubilee Disaster.* London: Book Club Associates, 1980.

Dietl, Eduard (1890–1944)

Wehrmacht colonel general.

Born on July 21, 1890, at Bad Aibling, Bavaria, Eduard Dietl served as a lieutenant in the German Army during World War I and joined Freikorps Epp in 1919. During the invasion of Norway in April 1940, Dietl's 3rd Mountain Division captured Narvik. He was forced out by an Allied counterattack but then reoccupied the town when the Allies withdrew from Norway. During the opening stages of Operation BARBAROSSA, the invasion of the Soviet Union, Dietl's division failed to take Murmansk. In June 1942, Dietl assumed command of the Twentieth Mountain Army in Finland. On June 23, 1944, Dietl died when his airplane crashed near Hochwedel, Austria. Hitler personally delivered the funeral oration for one of his most devoted followers in the Wehrmacht.

Martin Moll

See also: Norway Campaign

Additional Reading

Ziemke, Earl. *The German Northern Theater of Operations, 1940–1945.* Washington, DC: U.S. Government Printing Office, 1960.

Dietrich, Josef "Sepp" (1892–1966)

Schutzstaffel (SS) Oberstgruppenführer and Waffen-SS colonel general.

Born on May 28, 1892, in Hawangen, Bavaria, Josef Dietrich served as an enlisted soldier in World War I. After the war, Dietrich was active in the Freikorps before joining the Nazi Party and the SS in 1928. One of Adolf Hitler's bodyguards, Dietrich, during the Night of the Long Knives Blood Purge of July 1934, led an execution squad against the leadership of the Sturmabteilung (SA). In early 1940, Dietrich assumed command of the Leibstandarte SS Adolf Hitler (LSSAH), which became a panzergrenadier division in 1942. With that unit, he took part in the invasions of France, Greece, and the Soviet Union. When the Western Allies landed in Normandy in June 1944, Dietrich commanded the I SS Panzer Corps. In September, he assumed command of the Sixth Panzer Army, which was the main effort of the failed Ardennes Offensive that December. After the war, Dietrich was found guilty in the execution of U.S. prisoners of war at Malmédy and was sentenced to twenty-five years' imprisonment. Dietrich served only ten years, but he was later arrested and charged for murders committed in 1934. He was sentenced to only eighteen months in prison. Dietrich died at Ludwigsburg on April 21, 1966.

Martin Moll

See also: Ardennes Offensive (Battle of the Bulge); Freikorps (Free Corps); Malmédy Massacre; Night of the Long Knives; Sturmabteilungen (SA); Waffen-SS

Additional Reading

Messenger, Charles. *Hitler's Gladiator: The Life and Times of Oberstgruppenführer and Panzergeneraloberst der Waffen-SS Sepp Dietrich.* London: Brassey's Defence Publishers, 1988.

Dönitz, Karl (1891–1980)

Kriegsmarine grand admiral, chief of U-boat command, and successor of Adolf Hitler as president of the Third Reich.

Born in Gruenau-bei-Berlin on September 16, 1891, Karl Dönitz served during World War I on the cruiser *Breslau.* He transferred to U-boats in 1916, commanding several submarines in the Mediterranean. In October 1918, his *U-68* attacked an Allied convoy, sinking one of the ships. His submarine was forced to the surface when it developed mechanical problems, and Dönitz was taken prisoner.

During the interwar years, Dönitz commanded a torpedo-boat flotilla, during which time he experimented with tactics he would later develop into the *Rudeltaktik* (Wolf Pack) concept. German Chancellor Adolf Hitler named Dönitz commander of the fledgling German submarine force in 1935. Dönitz's passionate advocacy of submarines led to friction between him and the commander of the navy, Grand Admiral Erich Raeder, who preferred conventional large surface ships.

Grand Admiral Karl Dönitz, commander of the German U-boat fleet, 1939–1943; commander in chief of the German Navy, 1943–1945; and last president of the Third Reich, April–June 1945. (Heinrich Hoffmann/The LIFE Picture Collection/Getty Images)

During World War II, Dönitz's wolf-pack tactics centralized the control of U-boat groups that struck Allied convoys at night in surface attacks. In January 1943, Hitler, frustrated by the performance of his surface navy, removed Raeder and replaced him with Dönitz as head of the *Kriegsmarine.* Dönitz tried to continue the U-boat war, but during "Black May" in 1943, his U-boats were essentially defeated through newly developed Allied antisubmarine countermeasures.

Unlike virtually all other senior German military officers, Dönitz managed to retain Hitler's confidence and favor. On April 15, 1945, Hitler appointed Dönitz as commander of all forces in northern Germany. On April 30, the day that Hitler committed suicide, Dönitz was informed that Hitler had appointed him president of the Reich and supreme commander of the Wehrmacht. Dönitz tried to delay the Soviet advances to allow millions of German troops and civilians to flee westward to British and U.S. lines. Dönitz surrendered Germany unconditionally to Allied representatives on May 7, 1945.

The British arrested Dönitz on May 23. Tried by the International Military Tribunal at Nuremberg, Dönitz was found guilty of crimes against peace and violation of the rules of war, particularly the Laconia Order. He was sentenced to ten years in Spandau Prison. He was released in 1956. Unrepentant about his role in the war, Dönitz, died in Aumuhle, Federal Republic of Germany, on December 24, 1980.

Steven J. Rauch

See also: Atlantic, Battle of the; International Military Tribunal: The Nuremberg Trials; Kriegsmarine (German Navy); Laconia Order; Raeder, Erich; Submarines; Wolf Pack Tactics (*Rudeltaktik*)

Additional Reading

Edwards, Bernard. *Dönitz and the Wolf Packs.* London: Cassell, 1999.

Padfield, Peter. *Dönitz, the Last Führer: Portrait of a Nazi War Leader.* New York: Harper and Row, 1984.

Dornberger, Walter (1895–1980)

Wehrmacht major general.

Born in Giessen, Germany, on September 6, 1895, Walter Dornberger served as an artillery officer during World War I. As a Reichswehr officer between the wars, he studied mechanical engineering at the Technical University in Berlin. In July 1936, he became a department chief in the Army Weapons Office, with responsibility for special experiments at the Army Experimental Station at Peenemünde. Work on the A-series of missiles resulted in the V-2 (A-4), which made its first successful test flight on October 3, 1942. Dornberger's key associate at Peenemünde was Wernher von Braun. A British air raid on the night of August 17 to 18, 1943, destroyed part the Peenemünde facility.

Captured by the British, Dornberger was charged as a war criminal for launching the V-2s against London, but he was never brought to trial. Following his release in 1947, he emigrated to the United States, became a U.S. citizen, and worked for the Air Force Air Material Command as a consultant on rocket programs. Dornberger became vice-president of Bell Aircraft in 1959. He retired in 1965. Dornberger died in Obersasbach, West Germany, on June 27, 1980.

Jon D. Berlin

See also: Braun, Wernher von; Rockets, Guided Bombs, and Guided Missiles

Additional Reading

Neufeld, Michael J. *The Rocket and the Reich: Peenemünde and the Coming of the Ballistic Missile Era.* New York: Free Press, 1995.

Dresden, Allied Air Attack on (February 13–15, 1945)

The Allied bombing of the German city of Dresden remains one of the most controversial air raids of World War II. The operation, conducted between February 13 and 15, 1945, has become commonly evoked to illustrate the excesses and horror of conventional bombing of cities. The immediate controversy about the raid contributed to the suspension of the Allied Strategic Bombing Campaign.

At the Allied Yalta Conference on February 4, 1945, the Soviets asked for air attacks on communication centers to prevent the shifting of German troops to the eastern front. On February 8, Supreme Headquarters, Allied Expeditionary Forces (SHAEF) instructed RAF Bomber Command and the U.S. Strategic Air Forces to prepare an attack on Dresden because of its importance in relation to movements of military forces to the eastern front. Contrary to later popular reports, Dresden did contain many important industrial and transportation targets, and it was defended.

The operation opened on the night of February 13, with two separate British raids. The first blow was delivered by 244 Lancaster bombers, dropping more than eight hundred tons of bombs. A second attack came three hours later by 529 Lancasters delivering a further eighteen hundred tons of bombs. The resulting terrible conflagration made aiming very difficult the next day for the more than three hundred U.S. B-17 bombers attempting to drop another seven hundred tons of bombs on the city's marshaling yards. Obscuration of the target area was even worse for a similar attack on February 15.

When news of the attacks reached Britain, there was considerable public outcry over the destruction of such a beautiful city when the war seemed to be virtually won. The casualty figures reported by German fire and police services ranged between twenty-five thousand and thirty-five thousand dead. However, thousands more were missing, and there were many unidentified refugees in the city. It is probable that the death total approached the forty-five thousand killed in the bombing of Hamburg in July to August 1943.

Conrad C. Crane

See also: Combined Bomber Offensive, Allied (Operation POINTBLANK)

Additional Reading

Taylor, Frederick. *Dresden: Tuesday, February 13, 1945.* New York: HarperCollins, 2004.

DRUMBEAT, U-Boat Operation (January 13–July 19, 1942)

German U-boat offensive conducted off the U.S. East Coast, in the Caribbean, in the Gulf of Mexico, and off Brazil.

Commander of German U-boats Vice Admiral Karl Dönitz welcomed the entry of the United States into the war in December 1941 as an opportunity to widen the U-boat offensive in the Atlantic. In planning Operation PAUKENSCHLAG (DRUMBEAT), Dönitz intended to operate against the United States and into the Caribbean with the larger Type IX U-boats, which had greater operational range. He committed the shorter-range Type VII U-boats off Newfoundland and Nova Scotia.

DRUMBEAT never involved more than a dozen German submarines at any one time. To keep the Americans off balance, a month after DRUMBEAT was launched, Dönitz switched its focus to the Caribbean, where several Italian submarines joined operations. The United States was totally unprepared for the U-boat attacks. Coastal cities were ablaze with lights at night, silhouetting the merchant ships plying the coast and making them easy targets. There were also few escort vessels available, and merchant ships sailed independently in the hundreds because commander of the U.S. Atlantic Fleet, Admiral Royal Ingersoll refused to institute a convoy system, believing that an inadequately protected convoy system was worse than none.

In July 1942, U.S. chief of naval operations Admiral Ernest King ordered Ingersoll to initiate coastal convoys. On July 19, 1942, Dönitz withdrew his last two U-boats from the East Coast of the United States, relocating his submarine assets back to the mid-Atlantic and signaling an end to the campaign. U.S. unpreparedness had come at a high price. Operation DRUMBEAT was arguably Germany's most successful submarine operation of the entire war, resulting in the sinking of some three million tons of shipping.

Berryman E. Woodruff IV and Spencer C. Tucker

See also: Atlantic, Battle of the; Dönitz, Karl

Additional Reading

Gannon, Michael. *Operation Drumbeat: The Dramatic True Story of Germany's First U-Boat Attacks along the American Coast in World War II.* New York: Harper and Row, 1990.

Dunkirk, Evacuation of (May 26–June 4, 1940). See France, Battle of

E

Eben Emael, Battle of (May 10–11, 1940). *See* Belgium and Flanders Campaign

Einsatzgruppen (1941–1945)

German SS special extermination units deployed on the eastern front during World War II.

In June 1941, the German Army invaded the Soviet Union in Operation BARBAROSSA. Following closely behind the main fighting force were four small SS units called the Einsatzgruppen (Special Task Groups). Their job was the extermination of Jews, communists, gypsies, and anyone else designated racially or politically undesirable. The Einsatzgruppen were divided into four units (A, B, C, and D) that were attached to the army groups involved in the invasion (except for D, which operated independently of all army groups). Each group had between six hundred and one thousand men drawn from the Waffen-SS, Gestapo, Sicherheitsdienst, and the regular police. The Einsatzgruppen were established by and subordinated to Reinhard Heydrich. After World War II, the leadership of the Einsatzgruppen was tried for murder and crimes against humanity. Of twenty-four defendants, fourteen were sentenced to death, and eight were sentenced to prison.

Lee Baker

See also: Holocaust, German Military Complicity in; Reichssicherheitshauptamt (Reich Main Security Office); Waffen-SS

Additional Reading

Dawidowicz, Lucy. *The War against the Jews, 1933–1945*. New York: Henry Holt, 1975.

El Alamein, Battle of (October 23–November 11, 1942). *See* North Africa Campaign

Enigma Machine (1923–1945)

The Enigma was an encoding machine invented by Dr. Arthur Scherbius. He demonstrated it at the 1923 International Postal Congress as a commercial encoding device. The Enigma resembled a typewriter in appearance and had a series of rotors or wheels, the settings of which could be changed. Early versions of the device enabled the operator to encode a plain text in any of 150 million possible ways. An operator with a second Enigma machine set identically to the sending machine read the encoded radio message and decoded it. Settings were changed regularly according to a prearranged schedule in order to confound any interception and decoding. As with all the major military powers, the Germans sought a secure means of military communications, and they assumed that messages encoded by Enigma were unbreakable. By 1928, the German military was using the Enigma machine.

The Poles, concerned about a resurgent Germany as a threat to their own security, in 1928 formed a special cryptography group at the University of Poznan. They also purchased the commercial model of Enigma, and, by 1935, they had broken the German radio ciphers, information that they largely shared with the British and French in 1938. Late that same year, however, the Germans added a sixth rotor, which helped to convince the Poles that the Germans were about to make an aggressive military move. The Poles modified their own machines to keep up with the German advances and continued to break into the German codes, but the defeat of their country in September 1939 came too quickly for Enigma to be of use to them.

On the defeat of Poland, the Polish code breakers and their machines were spirited out to France and to England. At Bletchley Park outside of Buckingham, the British assembled a mixed group of experts to continue the work begun by the Poles, and, over time, they developed additional devices that could sort through the possible variations of an encoded text, although the Enigma's changeable settings meant that most messages could not be read in real time. Intelligence gathered from Enigma traffic was given the code name of Ultra.

Secure in their belief that its messages could not be read, the Germans continued to rely on Enigma throughout the war. Obviously, land-line communication was even more secure, and Adolf Hitler's proscription on radio communication concerning the German Ardennes Offensive (Battle of the Bulge), launched on December 16, 1944, combined with Allied complacency, led the offensive's concealment from the Allies until the attack began.

Ultra intelligence proved invaluable in the Allied military effort on a variety of fronts and undoubtedly shortened the war. Information on Ultra was not made public until 1974, when Royal Air Force Group Captain F. W. Winterbotham published *The Ultra Secret.* Its revelations forced the rewriting of most earlier histories of the war.

Spencer C. Tucker

Additional Reading

Kahn, David. *Seizing the Enigma: The Race to Break the German U-Boats Codes, 1939–1943.* New York: Houghton Mifflin, 1991.

Lewin, Ronald. *Ultra Goes to War.* New York: McGraw-Hill, 1978.

F

Falaise-Argentan Pocket (August 12–21, 1944)

In July 1944, U.S. Operation COBRA shattered the German defensive lines, ending what had been a month-long stalemate in Normandy and opening a war of movement. Hitler ordered Field Marshal Günther von Kluge, who was simultaneously commander of Army Group B and commander in chief west (OB West), to counterattack the Allied armies. Kluge scrapped together elements of four panzer divisions and, in Operation LÜTTICH, these attacked the Allies at Mortain near Avranches. The resulting attack was insufficient to have the desired effect and, as Kluge feared, merely drove the Germans deeper into the Allied lines, making them all the more vulnerable to encirclement.

At this point, however, Allied planning began to break down. Patton suggested a deeper envelopment that would net all the Germans west of the Seine. His superior, Lieutenant General Omar N. Bradley, commander of U.S. 12th Army Group, rejected this and insisted on a shorter hook. On August 10, Patton turned units north from Le Mans, and, by August 12, he had taken Alençon. The speed of Patton's movements surprised all concerned. The opportunity to close the Falaise Pocket seemed in the offing. Excluding forces in the Brittany peninsula, there were then some three hundred and fifty thousand German troops west of the Seine. About half were caught in the Falaise Pocket, their only route of escape the fifteen-mile-wide gap between Falaise and Argentan. If the Allied forces could close this gap, the envelopment would be complete.

At that point, with success apparently in hand, the cautious Bradley ordered Patton to hold at Argentan. Officially, this was to avoid a chance head-on meeting between the two converging Allied armies. Meanwhile, continued slow movement by British and Canadian forces from the north left the pocket open. Allied ineptness, more than German skill, was the primary reason the trap was not closed in time. By the time the Allies finally closed the Falaise Pocket, the German Seventh Army had lost approximately two hundred tanks, three hundred heavy guns, seven artillery pieces, five thousand vehicles, and a great many carts and horses. But the German personnel losses were considerably less than the Allies had hoped for—no more than ten thousand Germans killed and fifty thousand captured. Some one hundred and fifteen thousand German troops escaped the pocket. Most importantly, almost all of the German headquarters' elements managed to escape from the pocket, and those highly trained and skilled staff officers would be the vital element in the Wehrmacht's ability to reconstitute an effective defensive line along the German border. In all, two hundred and forty thousand German soldiers crossed the Seine in the last week of August. In September, the Allied Operation MARKET-GARDEN, a combined-arms assault to cross the lower Rhine River into Germany, was stymied by German units that had escaped from Normandy.

Fred R. van Hartesveldt and Spencer C. Tucker

See also: Avranches Counteroffensive; Kluge, Günther von; MARKET-GARDEN, Allied Operation; Saint-Lô, Battle for

Additional Reading

Blumenson, Martin. *The Battle of the Generals: The Untold Story of the Falaise Pocket: The Campaign that Should Have Won World War II.* New York: William Morrow, 1993.

Ludewig, Joachim. *Rückzug: The German Retreat from France, 1944.* Lexington: University Press of Kentucky, 2012.

Fallschirmjäger (Airborne Troops) (1935–Present)

The German paratroop forces were first established in 1936 as a special battalion of the Luftwaffe. The newly formed paratroop battalion was used in the 1936 Wehrmacht joint maneuvers in a successful experiment to take key objectives and defend them until the motorized forces could link up with them on the ground. The Wehrmacht soon established an entire paratroop division, the 7th Air Division, which would be supported by the army's 22nd Infantry Division, trained to go to battle in gliders. The Wehrmacht employed paratroops with great success in the first part of World War II. The first combat use of paratroops came in April 1940 at the opening of the invasion of Denmark and Norway. Luftwaffe paratroops seized key airfields at Aalborg in Denmark and Stavanger in Norway, allowing follow-on forces to arrive by air transport. In May 1940, the Germans used paratroops to seize the key Belgian border fortress at Eben Emael at the opening of the Western offensive.

The month of May 1941 saw the largest and most dramatic use of paratroops by Germany during the course of the war. Because the Allies held naval superiority in the Mediterranean, the Germans decided to use their air superiority to take Crete from the air. On May 20, ten thousand paratroops of the 7th Parachute Division were dropped in three dispersed areas to seize the main British airfields so that follow-on troops and supplies could be flown in. The operation was a costly success. Appalled by the heavy losses at Crete, Hitler forbade any major airborne operations again. Still, in the course of the war, the Luftwaffe established thirteen parachute divisions that were committed as infantry divisions with the army on every front. The German airborne divisions earned a reputation as elite units and exceptionally tough fighters—much like the Allied airborne units.

James S. Corum

See also: Belgium and Flanders Campaign; Crete, German Invasion of

Additional Reading

Ailsby, Christopher. *Hitler's Sky Warriors: German Paratroopers in Action, 1939–1945.* Staplehurst, UK: Spellmount Limited, 2000.

Flak 18 88 mm Gun. *See* Artillery

FORTITUDE, Allied Deception Operation (1944)

FORTITUDE was a set of deception operations in support of Operation OVERLORD, the Allied invasion of Normandy in June 1944. FORTITUDE was designed to mislead the German defenders as to the timing and location of the Allied invasion. The deception narratives were built around preconceptions the Allies knew the Germans already had. As German military intelligence and counterintelligence organizations and operations were far less sophisticated than those of the Allies (especially the British), FORTITUDE was very successful.

Operation FORTITUDE had two components: FORTITUDE North and FORTITUDE South. Operation FORTITUDE North was designed to convince the Germans that the Allies planned to invade Norway in coordination with a Soviet offensive designed to drive Finland from the war. As the time for OVERLORD approached, the second component of the deception plan, FORTITUDE South, became critical. Knowing that the Allied buildup in southern England could not be kept hidden, the British and Americans planned to persuade the Germans that the primary Allied assault would fall in the Pas de Calais (across the English Channel from Dover), rather than in Normandy. The Pas de Calais was the most obvious choice for a major amphibious operation. It was the closest point on the French coast to Britain and would minimize the length of Allied supply lines, as well as offer an extensive road network that could be exploited in follow-on attacks through the Low Countries toward Germany, once the beaches were taken.

To build the desired perception on the part of German intelligence, a fictitious First U.S. Army Group (FUSAG) was portrayed directly across from Calais in Kent and Sussex. Lieutenant General George S. Patton, whose reputation as a hard-driving army leader was very well known by the Germans, was repeatedly identified as FUSAG's commander. Special Allied signal units were used to transmit false radio transmissions from FUSAG and to simulate division, corps, and other army-level communications; these were transmitted in easily breakable ciphers so the Germans could decode the messages.

German intelligence arrived at the desired conclusion. German Army maps captured following the Normandy invasion indicated the presence of FUSAG in southeast England. However, Hitler was only partly deceived. On March 4 and 20 and April 6, he alluded to the likelihood of a Normandy landing in messages to his senior commanders. Still, apart from allocating the Panzer Lehr and 116th Panzer Divisions to Normandy in the early spring, he made no decisive alteration of German defensive dispositions. Indeed, until he allowed divisions to cross the Seine into Normandy from the Pas de Calais at the very end of July, he remained prisoner to the misbelief in a second main invasion in the Calais area throughout the critical weeks following the initial landings at Normandy.

James H. Willbanks and
John A. Suprin

See also: Normandy Invasion and Campaign

Additional Reading

Brown, Anthony Cave. *Bodyguard of Lies.* New York: Harper and Row, 1975.

Cruickshank, Charles. *Deception in World War II.* New York: Oxford University Press, 1980.

France, Allied Liberation of (June 6–September 29, 1944)

In June 1944, Field Marshal Gerd von Rundstedt was Oberbefehlshaber West (commander in chief, west or OB West). Rather than being a joint commander, Rundstedt commanded only the German Army forces in western Europe. The Luftwaffe forces came under Field Marshal Hugo Sperrle's Luftflotte 3 (Third Air Fleet). Field Marshal Erwin Rommel's Army Group B was responsible for northern France, from the Loire River north, including Belgium to the Netherlands border. Colonel General Hans von Salmuth's Fifteenth Army covered Army Group B's northern sector, including the Pas-de-Calais region, where many German leaders thought the Allied invasion would actually come. The southern half of the Army Group B sector, including Brittany and Normandy, where the Allies actually landed was covered by Colonel General Friedrich Dollman's Seventh Army. South of the Loire River France was garrisoned by Colonel General Johannes Blaskowitz's Army Task Group G. The northernmost sector of southern France was held by General of Infantry Kurt von der Chevallerie's First Army. Southernmost France, down to the Mediterranean coast, was held by General of Infantry Friedrich Wiese's Nineteenth Army.

The Allied campaign to drive Germans out of France began with the June 6, 1944, Allied landing in Normandy. U.S. General Dwight D. Eisenhower had overall command; General Sir Bernard L. Montgomery commanded the landing force of 21st Army Group, which consisted of Lieutenant General Sir Miles Dempsey's British Second Army and Lieutenant General Omar N. Bradley's U.S. First Army.

Even with stiff resistance by German defenders, especially the 352nd Division at Omaha Beach, Allied forces expanded the beachhead from five to twenty miles inland and joined all five beaches into a single continuous front by June 12. French Resistance forces supported the Allied effort by providing intelligence, sabotaging bridges and railways, and conducting harassment operations. Dempsey's Second Army began the drive toward Caen but met heavy resistance from German forces, including two panzer divisions. Meanwhile, Bradley's First Army moved up the Cotentin Peninsula toward the important port city of Cherbourg. By June 27, Cherbourg was secure, but the Germans had heavily damaged the port facilities, which were unusable for more than a month.

By the beginning of July, Allied progress in Normandy had been slowed by the hedgerows of the *bocage* (hedgerow) country, strong German positions at Caen, and the logistical challenges of supplying the Allied forces over the beaches. Having the advantage of overwhelming air superiority, the eight corps of 21st Army Group pushed south, seizing Caen on July 10, and Saint-Lô on July 18. The capture of these two important cities set the stage for the Allied breakout west into the Brittany peninsula and east toward Paris.

Bradley believed that the weak link in the German army defenses was SS Oberstgruppenführer Paul Hausser's Seventh Army, south of Saint-Lô. Bradley's breakout plan, code-named Operation COBRA, was temporarily put on hold so that vital supplies could be sent to support the British Second Army's Operation GOODWOOD, an attempt to penetrate German lines outside of Caen. Although GOODWOOD did not achieve a breakout, it assisted COBRA by holding two German panzer divisions in place and preventing their redeployment to the Saint-Lô area.

Heavy saturation bombing along a four-mile-wide corridor preceded COBRA, as elements of Major General J. Lawton Collins's

U.S. VII Corps attacked west of Saint-Lô on July 25. Sensing that the breakthrough was decisive, Bradley ordered Collins to continue the drive south toward the strategic city of Avranches. By the end of July, it too was in Allied hands, and the German Seventh Army was in a precarious position, with its left flank exposed. The capture of Avranches opened the Brittany peninsula to the Allies. Meanwhile, Lieutenant General George S. Patton's U.S. Third Army became operational on August 1. The Third Army immediately exploited the opening at Avranches: Patton sent his VIII Corps to clear the Brittany peninsula, the XX and XII Corps south to the Loire River, and the XV Corps east toward Le Mans. These objectives were secured by August 13.

While the U.S. Third Army moved against limited opposition, the German Seventh Army hastily reorganized to launch a counterattack toward Avranches, hoping to cut off the Third Army. Not only did this spoiling attack fail, but it also put the Seventh Army in a position in which it might be surrounded by the Allies. To accomplish this, Montgomery, who was still overall Allied ground commander, ordered the Canadian II Corps to attack south as Patton's XV Corps drove north. The objective for both corps was the town of Argentan. U.S. XV Corps reached Argentan on August 13, but the Canadian II Corps progressed slowly and was more than twenty miles from the objective. Even though the gap between the towns of Falaise and Argentan was not closed until August 19, the area was turned into a killing ground by constant Allied air attack, artillery bombardment, and direct ground fire from armored and infantry units. Although the German Seventh Army was savaged in these attacks, a great many German soldiers escaped. More importantly, most of the senior command staffs escaped, which later allowed the Germans to reconstitute the Seventh Army. Failure to close the gap was one of the major Allied mistakes of the war. Had the gap been sealed and the Seventh Army completely annihilated, the Western Allies would have faced far less resistance as they pushed east toward Germany. Operations following COBRA were so successful that most German forces in northwest France had to retreat to the Seine River. Paris was liberated on August 25.

The Western Allies addressed the concern about the exposed southern flank of their armies, the need to secure a large functioning port, and interest in cutting off what German forces remained in southern France in Operation DRAGOON, the invasion of southern France. DRAGOON commenced on August 15. Lieutenant General Alexander Patch's U.S. Seventh Army landed in southern France, just east of Toulon. U.S. VI Corps spearheaded the landing and, by August 17, had established a twenty-mile-deep beachhead. The French II Corps followed with the task of driving west to secure Toulon and Marseille, which it accomplished by August 28. VI Corps moved rapidly west, and then north, up the east side of the Rhône River—except for an armored group, Task Force Butler, that moved east of the Rhône River Valley in an effort to envelop German forces assembling at Montelimar. By this time, the German Nineteenth Army was evacuating southern France. However, VI Corps inflicted severe material damage on the retreating Germans, capturing fifty-seven thousand and liberating Montelimar by August 28.

By September 3, the Seventh Army had driven north almost 250 miles up the Rhône River. On September 14, Patch's Seventh Army linked up with Patton's Third Army, sealing the open southern flank. On September 15, the 6th Army Group was formed, with Lieutenant General Jacob Devers commanding. By the middle of September 1944, France had been liberated, and German forces had withdrawn into the Netherlands and to the West Wall along the western German border. Although it had been severely bloodied, the German army in the west was not annihilated and was reorganizing and entrenching itself for a long fight. Unfortunately, the Allied drive east was so fast that lines of communication and supply could not keep up with the tactical advance. With insufficient supplies to advance all his army groups at once, Eisenhower decided to support Montgomery's plan to cross the lower Rhine into Germany, Operation MARKET-GARDEN.

After MARKET-GARDEN failed, the rapid Allied advance came to a halt. By September 29, Eisenhower admitted to the Allied Combined Chiefs of Staff that the Germans had managed to form a "relatively stable front." But there were now fifty-three Allied divisions along the line from the Netherlands to Switzerland. They faced the four field armies of Field Marshal Walther Models's Army Group B, deployed north of the French-Luxembourg border, and the three field armies of General Hermann Balck's Army Group B, extending down to the Swiss border. The long and bitter winter campaign of 1944 to 1945 lay ahead.

Robert W. Duvall and David T. Zabecki

See also: Avranches Counteroffensive; Blaskowitz, Johannes Albrecht; COBRA, Allied Breakout Operation; Falaise-Argentan Pocket; GOODWOOD, British Operation; Hausser, Paul; Normandy Invasion and Campaign; Paris, Allied Liberation of; Rommel, Erwin; Rundstedt, Karl Rudolf Gerd von; Saint-Lô, Battle for; Southern France, Allied Invasion and Campaign (Operation DRAGOON); Sperrle, Hugo

Additional Reading

Clarke, Jeffrey J., and Robert Ross Smith. *Riviera to the Rhine. United States Army in World War II.* Washington, DC: Center of Military History, 1993.

Ludewig, Joachim. *Rückzug: The German Retreat from France, 1944.* Lexington: University Press of Kentucky, 2012.

France, Battle of (May 10–July 25, 1940)

Germany's sudden strike west in May 1940 through neutral Belgium and the Netherlands caught the Allies by surprise, leading to military defeat and the collapse of the French government. Despite Germany's successful April 1940 invasions of Norway and Denmark, France remained committed to the defensive posture it had assumed on mobilization. The French and the four-hundred-thousand-strong British Expeditionary Force (BEF) could not occupy their intended defensive positions in neutral Belgium until events forced that nation into the war.

The Germans did not have numerical or technological superiority over their opponents. Against Adolf Hitler's 136 divisions (2.5 million men), the French, British, Belgians, and Dutch could field 135 divisions (more than two million men). The Allies and neutral powers had more tanks (perhaps thirty-six hundred, compared with twenty-five hundred for the Germans). The Allies were sadly deficient, however, in numbers of antiaircraft guns and aircraft. Against 1,444 German bombers, the Allies could send up only 830 fighters. These would have to cope with 1,264 German fighter aircraft, more than one thousand of

German Conquest of France, 1940

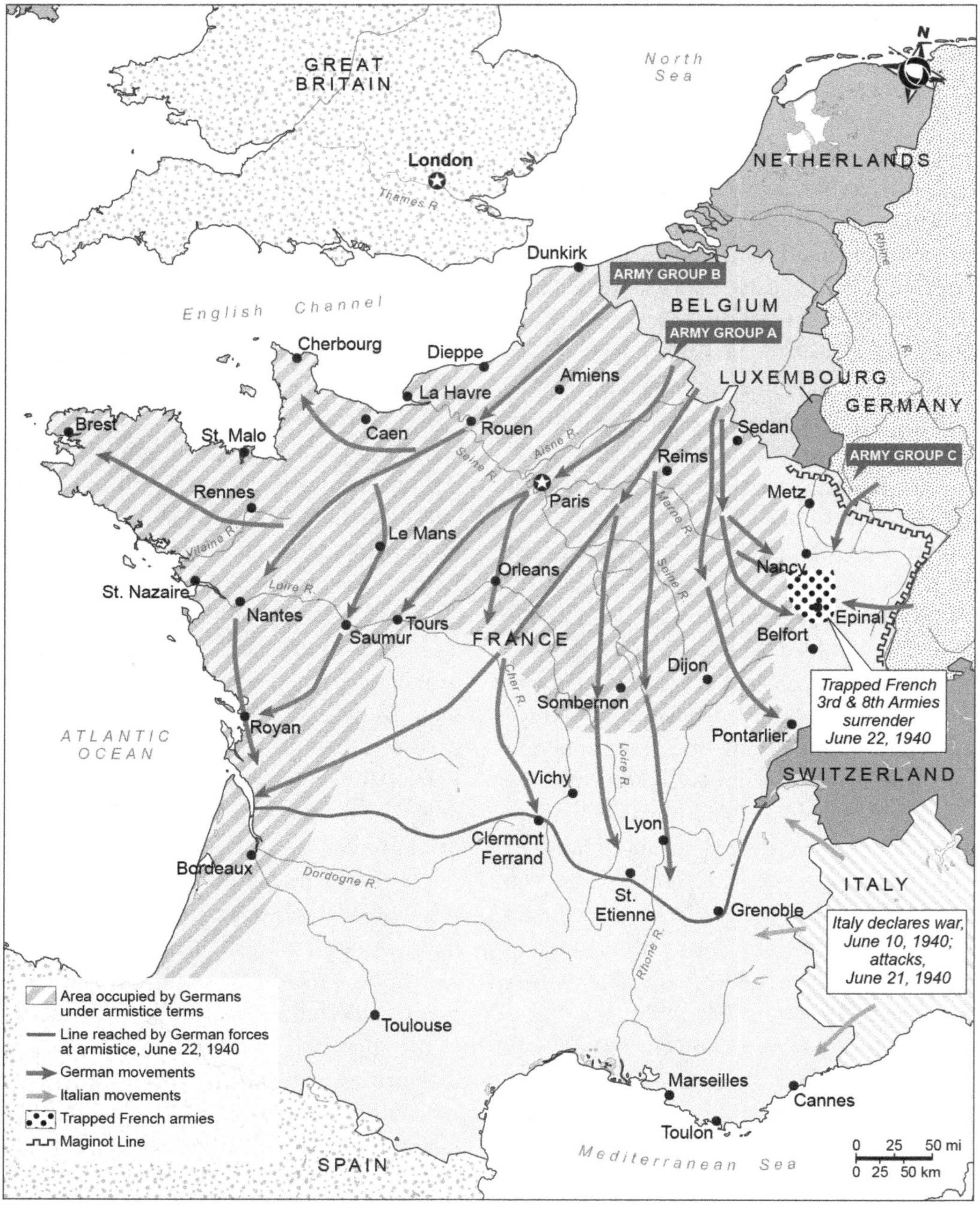

which were Bf 109s. Overall, the German air fleets deployed in the west numbered 3,226 combat aircraft, whereas the British and French had half that number. The first three French tank divisions did not assemble until January 1940, and they lacked radios. Most of France's tanks were parceled out in small packets along the front to act in support of infantry.

On January 10, 1940, the original plan for Fall GELB (Case YELLOW) fell into Allied hands when a German officer carrying the plans crash-landed in Mechelen, Belgium. The original version of Fall GELB had been somewhat similar to the Schlieffen Plan of 1914 and would have followed Allied staff predictions. Its axis of advance would have encountered the best Franco-British forces and, thus, might have ended in failure. Generals Erich von Manstein and Heinz Guderian convinced Hitler to abandon this approach in favor of concentrating the bulk of the resources on a more southern axis. Under the new *Sichelschnitt* (Sickel Cut) plan, while other units extended the line to the sea, the main German force would drive through the Ardennes forest, south of Liège to cut off the French Army, as it moved to defend Belgium.

General Feodor von Bock's Army Group B, charged with invading Belgium and the Netherlands, was downgraded from thirty-seven divisions in the original plan to only twenty-eight in the Manstein plan, and three, rather than eight, panzer divisions. General Gerd von Rundstedt's Army Group A, which was to move through the Ardennes, was upgraded from seventeen to forty-four divisions, including seven, rather than a single, panzer division. Thus, at the point of the breakthrough, the Germans would outnumber the French forty-four divisions to nine. On the German left flank, a tertiary holding attack against France's Maginot Line would be conducted by General Wilhelm von Leeb's Army Group C of eighteen divisions.

The operation began on May 10, with an attack into the Netherlands by von Bock's Army Group B. The French Seventh Army raced across Belgium to the rescue, arriving on May 12, only to join the retreat. Quickly overrunning Luxembourg, Rundstedt's Army Group A advanced through the Ardennes to reach the main French line along the Meuse River on May 12. French Army commander General Maurice Gamelin's belated efforts to stem the tide with reinforcements came too late to prevent German forces from crossing the Meuse. The Germans took Sedan and punched a fifty-mile-wide gap in France's defenses. By May 16, they were on the Aisne River in open country.

The speed of the German advance caught even Rundstedt by surprise, as his armored commanders subverted instructions to slow down, slipped around areas of heavy resistance, and reached the English Channel by May 21. Germany's spectacular success broke General Gamelin's ability to respond. Convinced of France's inevitable defeat, Gamelin ceased to exercise effective command. Premier Reynaud dismissed him on May 19 and replaced him with General Maxime Weygand. The BEF was trapped in the north, and cooperation between it and the French First Army broke down. Forced to choose between supporting an increasingly unlikely French breakout (which both Weygand and British Prime Minister Winston Churchill ordered) or maintaining his line of retreat to the sea, on May 24, BEF commander General Sir John Gort ordered the BEF to withdraw to the north and the port of Dunkirk.

This proved to be one of the important decisions of the war, for it saved the BEF to fight another day. Hitler now committed his first major military mistake of the war, which allowed the BEF to escape. On May 26, Rundstedt, worried about the speed of the advance, halted the panzer divisions when they were within striking range of the last Channel ports that were open to the British. Hitler then converted this temporary halt into a firm order. He wanted to allow time for the infantry to come up and was convinced by Luftwaffe commander General Hermann Göring that the Luftwaffe could destroy the British on the beaches, preventing their escape. Not until May 29 did Hitler release the panzers again, and by that time the BEF was in place, protected in large part by the French First Army. While the RAF fought the Luftwaffe to a standstill during the weeklong battle, the Royal Navy's Operation DYNAMO evacuated some three hundred and sixty-five thousand men from France, of whom nearly two hundred and twenty-five thousand were British.

By June 5, the Germans had repositioned the bulk of their forces in preparation for the final conquest of France. On June 8, von Bock's Army Group B reached the Seine. On June 12, Rundstedt's forces broke through the French line at Châlons. Open ground and the retreating French Army stretched before his tanks. That same day, the French government abandoned Paris for Bordeaux in the southwest. On June 13, the government declared Paris an open city to spare it the fate of Warsaw and Rotterdam, and the next day German troops took peaceful possession of the capital.

On June 10, Italy entered the war on Germany's side, although Italian forces did not attack France in the southeast until June 20. Late on the evening of June 16, with the Germans having taken Verdun and beginning to cut off the Maginot Line from the rear, Reynaud resigned. Retired marshal of France Phillippe Pétain succeeded him as premier, proclaiming in a radio address to the French people the next day that the country had lost the war and "the fighting must stop." Many army commanders interpreted this as an order, and the German advance continued largely without resistance. Brigadier General de Gaulle and a few other Frenchmen escaped to Britain.

France and Germany signed a cease-fire on June 22, 1940, but operations continued at Hitler's insistence until the Italians agreed to the armistice on June 25. Signed at Compiègne—at the same site and in the same railway carriage where the Germans had signed the armistice in 1918—the 1940 armistice allowed Germany to occupy northern France and the Atlantic coastal regions to the Spanish border, with France to pay for the German costs of administration. French prisoners of war remained under German control. The French fleet, much of which had escaped to North Africa, would remain under French control but was to be demobilized. The French government, having fled Paris, continued to rule the unoccupied zone from Vichy, under the leadership of Pétain. The Campaign in the West, as the Germans called it, cost the Allies three hundred and sixty thousand casualties dead or wounded, 1.9 million captured, and 2,233 aircraft destroyed. German forces suffered 157,621 casualties, more than 1,250 aircraft destroyed, and 795 tanks destroyed.

Jeffrey A. Charlston

See also: Blitzkrieg; Bock, Fedor von; Göring, Hermann; Guderian, Heinz; Leeb, Wilhelm Ritter von; Manstein, Erich von; Netherlands Campaign; Rundstedt, Karl Rudolf Gerd von

Additional Reading

Frieser, Karl-Heinz. *The Blitzkrieg Legend: The 1940 Campaign in the West.* Annapolis, MD: Naval Institute Press, 2005.

Horne, Alistair. *To Lose a Battle: France 1940*. Boston, MA: Little, Brown, 1969.

Freikorps (Free Corps) (1918–1923)

Paramilitary German forces following World War I.

In accordance with the November 11, 1918 armistice, German Army units withdrew from the western and eastern fronts. The Germany to which they returned seethed with revolutionary turbulence. Violence erupted in January 1919 in Berlin, as the Spartacus League tried to seize power. Defense Minister Gustav Noske commanded soldiers to restore order, only to have the first quartermaster general of the German Army, Lieutenant General Wilhelm Groener, advise him that the army could not be certain of the troops' loyalty and, in any case, could not provide sufficient units. Convinced the new regime could not survive a defeat, Noske wasted no time and called for volunteers to restore order. The units that responded received the name Freikorps. No standardized Freikorps organization existed. Units ranged in size from squads to brigades. The ranks were filled with veterans who were uncomfortable with a return to civilian life. There were also those who had pursued a military career all along and wished to continue it, even if on an unofficial basis.

In 1920, disaffected Freikorps units marched against the Ebert government in the so-called Kapp-Lüttwitz Putsch, a largely bloodless farce that led to Noske's ousting. The government used the Kapp-Lüttwitz Putsch as a pretext to disband most of the Freikorps units slowly. Many future members and leaders of the Nazi Party served in the Freikorps, including Ernst Röhm, future head of the Sturmabteilung (SA), and Heinrich Himmler, future head of the Schutzstaffel (SS). Although the Freikorps were extreme rightists, Hitler generally regarded them with suspicion, as potential competitors to his Nazi movement. On November 9, 1933, during a staged ceremony, most of the surviving Freikorps leaders surrendered their old battle standards to the SA as a demonstration of allegiance to the Nazi regime.

Michael B. Barrett

See also: Himmler, Heinrich; Röhm, Ernst; Sturmabteilungen (SA); Waffen-SS

Additional Reading

Waite, R. G. L. *Vanguard of Nazism: The Free Corps Movement in Postwar Germany, 1918–1923*. Cambridge, MA: Harvard University Press, 1969.

Friedeburg, Hans Georg von (1895–1945)

Kriegsmarine general admiral.

Born on July 15, 1895 in Strassburg (then Germany; now Strasbourg, France), Hans Georg von Friedeburg served as a submariner in World War I. In 1939, he was an assistant to commander of German submarines Admiral Karl Dönitz. From 1939 to 1941, Friedeburg was in the operations and organization department of the German submarine force. In February 1943, he succeeded Dönitz as commander of all German submarine forces. Friedeburg was appointed commander of all German naval forces on May 1, 1945. On May 7, he signed the instrument of surrender in northern Germany. Friedeburg committed suicide in Flensburg, Germany, on May 23, 1945.

Kyle D. Haire

See also: Dönitz, Karl

Additional Reading

Steinert, Marlis G. *23 Days: The Final Collapse of Nazi Germany*. New York: Walker, 1969.

Fritsch, Werner von (1880–1939)

Wehrmacht colonel general.

Born on August 4, 1880 at Benrath, near Düsseldorf, Werner von Fritsch served as a General Staff officer during World War I. In 1935, Fritsch was assigned as commander in chief of the army. He was not Adolf Hitler's choice; aging President Paul von Hindenburg selected him. Fritsch strengthened and expanded the army, but being far more cautious than Hitler, he sought to avoid conflict with Britain and France. He made no effort to conceal his disdain for the Nazis, the Schutzstaffel (SS), and even Hitler. When, in November 1937, Hitler laid out his plans for further territorial expansion, Fritsch expressed his opposition. In 1938, SS chief Heinrich Himmler trumped up charges of homosexuality against Fritsch, who did not help his case by remaining indignantly silent. Fritsch chose to resign and demanded a court-martial. Fritsch was acquitted on March 18, 1938, after witnesses confirmed that he had been framed. Formal rehabilitation came on August 18, 1938, with reinstatement of his rank of colonel general and an appointment as honorary colonel-in-chief of his old unit, the 12th Artillery Regiment. Fritsch accompanied his old regiment during the Poland campaign. He was killed in action on September 22, 1939 as his unit was approaching Praga, a suburb of Warsaw. Rumors that he deliberately sought death or was murdered by the SS have since been discounted.

Jon D. Berlin and Spencer C. Tucker

See also: Blomberg-Fritsch Crisis; Himmler, Heinrich; Hindenburg, Paul von

Additional Reading

Wheeler-Bennett, John W. *The Nemesis of Power: The German Army in Politics, 1918–1945*. London: St. Martin's Press, 1953.

Fromm, Friedrich (1888–1945)

Wehrmacht colonel general.

Born in Berlin on October 8, 1888, Friedrich Fromm served as a lieutenant during World War I. In 1939, Fromm was named commander of the Replacement Army (*Erstazheer*) and chief of army equipment. Fromm worked closely with Albert Speer, promoting research into new weapons. Late in the war, Fromm joined Colonel Klaus von Stauffenberg's conspiracy to assassinate Hitler. But when the Führer survived the bomb blast of July 20, Fromm lost his nerve and promptly ordered the arrest and execution of Stauffenberg and other conspirators. This action, designed to conceal his own participation, failed to save Fromm. Arrested the next day, he was executed by firing squad in Berlin on March 12, 1945.

Joseph C. Greaney

See also: Opposition to Hitler, German Military; Speer, Albert; Stauffenberg, Claus Schenk von

Additional Reading

Gill, Anton. *An Honourable Defeat: A History of German Resistance to Hitler, 1933–1945*. New York: Henry Holt, 1994.

Führer Directives (1939–1943)

Führerweisungen (Führer Directives) were a special category of military orders signed by Hitler and issued through the Wehrmachtführungsamt (Armed Forces Command Office), also known as the "Führer's Headquarters." The first of the numbered

Führer Directives 1939–1943

1.	Attack on Poland (Case WHITE)	Aug. 31, 1939
2.	Hostilities in the West	Sept. 3, 1939
3.	Transfer of Forces from Poland to the West	Sept. 9, 1939
4.	Conclusion of the War in Poland	Sept. 25, 1939
5.	The Partition of Poland	Sept. 30, 1939
6.	Plans for Offensive in the West	Oct. 9, 1939
7.	Preparations for Attack in the West	Oct. 18, 1939
8.	Additional Preparations for attack in the West	Nov. 20, 1939
9.	Instructions for Warfare Against the Enemy's Economy	Nov. 29, 1939
10.	Concentration of Forces for Case YELLOW	Jan. 19, 1940
10a.	Invasion of Denmark and Norway, Case WESSER EXERCISE	Mar. 1, 1940
11.	The Offensive in the West	May 14, 1940
12.	Prosecution of the Attack in the West	May 18, 1940
13.	The Next Objective in the West	May 24, 1940
14.	Continuation of the Offensive in France	June 8, 1940
15.	Advance on the Loire River	June 14, 1940
16.	Preparations for Invading Britain, Operation SEA LION	July 16, 1940
17.	The Conduct of Air and Sea Warfare Against Britain	Aug. 1, 1940
18.	Plans to take Gibraltar Through Spain	Nov. 12, 1940
19.	The Occupation of Vichy France	Dec. 10, 1940
20.	Invasion of the Balkans and Greece, Operation MARTIA	Dec. 13, 1940
21.	Operation BARBAROSSA: Attack on the Soviet Union	Dec. 18, 1940
22.	German Support to Mediterranean Campaign	Jan. 11, 1941
23.	Operations Against the British War Economy	Feb., 1941
24.	Coordination with Japan	Mar. 5, 1941
25.	Plans for Invading Yugoslavia	Mar. 27, 1941
26.	Cooperation with Balkan Allies	Apr. 3, 1941
27.	Operations in the Balkans	Apr. 4, 1941
28.	Operation MERCURY: The Invasion of Crete	Apr. 25, 1941
29.	Military Government of Greece	May 17, 1941
30.	German Intervention in Iraq	May 23, 1941
31.	German Military Organization in the Balkans	June 9, 1941
32.	Plans Following the Victory in the Soviet Union	June 11, 1941
32a.	Supplement to Directive 32: Reduction of the Army after the Victory over Soviet Union	July 14, 1941
33.	Continuation of the War in the East	July 19, 1941
33a.	Supplemental Instructions to Directive 33	July 23, 1941
34.	Change of Strategy in the Soviet Union	July 30, 1941
34a.	Supplemental Instructions to Directive 34	Aug. 12, 1941

Führer Directives 1939–1943 (continued)

35.	The Attack on Moscow	Sept. 6, 1941
36.	Objectives in the Arctic Theater	Sept. 22, 1941
37.	Reorganization of Forces in the Arctic Theater	Oct. 10, 1941
38.	The Air War in the Mediterranean	Dec. 2, 1941
39.	Defense on the Eastern Front	Dec. 8, 1941
40.	Operational Instructions for Coastal Defense	Mar. 23, 1942
41.	The Spring Offensive in the Soviet Union, Case BLUE	Apr. 5, 1942
42.	Occupation of Vichy France and the Iberian Peninsula	May 29, 1942
43.	Continuation of Operations in the Crimean Peninsula	July 11, 1942
44.	Operations in Northern Finland	July 21, 1942
45.	Continuation of the Caucasus Offensive, Operation BRUNSWICK	July 23, 1942
46.	Intensification of Anti-Partisan Operations in the Soviet Union	Aug. 18, 1942
47.	Command System and Defenses in the Balkans	Dec. 28, 1942
48.	Command Arrangements and Defenses in the Balkans	July 26, 1943
49.	Takeover of Italy and Italian Forces in the Balkans and the Soviet Union	July 31, 1943
50.	Withdrawal of the Twentieth Mountain Army from Norway and Northern Finland	Sept. 28, 1943
51.	The Danger of a Second Front in the West	Nov. 3, 1943

series was issued for the invasion of Poland. These numbered directives continued for four years and reached number fifty-one by November 1943. By this time, the directives ceased to be half political and half stategical. As the war progressed, Hitler became disillusioned with his commanders in the field. Directives became more than political statements, and Hitler involved himself in the smallest details of each unit on all fronts. He interfered with commanders on their ability to direct their own units down to the battalion level. In the last eighteen months of the war, the unnumbered edicts were addressed to the immediate crisis.

The study of the Führer Directives and subsequent orders issued later in the war is an essential outline, in Hitler's own words, of the aspiration and conduct of World War II. His interference and his insistence that the generals in the field submit all orders for his timely review led to the destruction of the concepts of the traditional historic General Staff and the German art of war.

Raymond D. Limbach

See also: *Oberkommando der Wehrmacht* (OKW)

Additional Reading

Trevor-Roper, Hugh R., ed. *Blitzkrieg to Defeat: Hitler's War Directives 1939–1945.* New York: Holt, Rinehart and Winston, 1965.

G

Galland, Adolf (1912–1996)

Luftwaffe ace and lieutenant general.

Born on March 19, 1912 in Westerholt, Westphalia, Adolf Galland completed pilot training at the Deutsches Verkehasflieger Schule (German Commercial Flyers' School). As a squadron leader, Galland flew three hundred ground-support missions with the Kondor Legion during the Spanish Civil War. Galland commanded a ground-attack squadron during the invasion of Poland but transferred to fighters in the spring of 1940. Galland commanded III.JG -26 (3rd Group, 26th Fighter Wing) during the Battle of Britain. Following the death of Galland's friend and rival Werner Mölders in November 1941, Galland was named to replace him as general of fighters (an office, not a rank). Promoted to major general in 1942, he was the youngest general in the Wehrmacht.

Galland was often at odds with Luftwaffe commander Hermann Göring and Führer Adolf Hitler on how to prosecute the air war. Galland was relieved of his command in January 1945 for his complicity in the "Fighter Pilots Revolt," during which a group of the Luftwaffe's most senior and decorated combat pilots confronted Göring with a list of demands on the prosecution of the air war. The following month, however, Galland was allowed to form his own Jagdverband 44 (JV-44), known as the "squadron of experts." Shot down and seriously wounded, Galland ended the war in a hospital. His official tally was 104 kills. Released from captivity in 1947, Galland served as adviser to Argentina's air force but returned to Germany in 1955 to run an aerospace consulting firm. He died at Oberwinter, Germany, on February 9, 1996.

Marlyn R. Pierce

See also: Britain, Battle of; Göring, Hermann; Kondor Legion; Mölders, Werner; Spanish Civil War

Additional Reading

Toliver, Raymond F., and Trevor J. Constable. *Fighter General: The Life of Adolf Galland.* Zephyr Cove, NV: AmPress Publishing, 1990.

Gazala, Battle of (May 26–June 21, 1942). *See* North Africa Campaign

German General Staff of World War II

The German General Staff of the World War II era reflected its predecessor organizations in many ways, and, in many ways, it did not. The differences reflected the philosophy and goals of dictator Adolf Hitler. While traditionally, the General Staff had provided planning, staff work, and advice to the political and military leadership in the Prussian and German states, Hitler wanted the planning and staff work but did not want the advice. Additionally, the Führer's method of rule was to create rival organizations with similar functions, with him being the final arbiter for all decisions.

In another break from the past, Hitler and the Nazis believed in the "Leader Principle" (*Führerprinzip*), which posited that leaders at all levels had absolute responsibility in their own areas and required absolute obedience from subordinates. This conflicted with the General Staff principle of directive control (*Auftragstaktik*), the use of issuing general directives to subordinates, rather than detailed instructions. As the war progressed and Hitler centralized more power into his own hands, his desire to direct even the smallest details of military operations gradually transformed the General Staff into a shadow of its traditional role.

The Treaty of Versailles that ended World War I forced Germany to disband its General Staff. During the interwar years, however, Reichswehr reestablished a clandestine General Staff in the form of the Truppenamt (Troop Office). On July 1, 1935, it was formally redesignated the Generalstab des Heeres, to complement the *Oberkommando des Heeres* (OKH), established that May. The OKH had, as its head, the commander in chief of the army, Colonel General Werner von Fritsch in 1936. The newly revived post of chief of the General Staff also served as the OKH chief of staff. In 1936, this post was held by Colonel General Ludwig Beck. Upon Beck's resignation in 1938, he was replaced by Colonel General Franz Halder.

After the 1938 Blomberg-Fritsch Crisis, in which Hitler replaced War Minister Field Marshal Werner von Blomberg with himself and dismissed the army commander in chief Fritsch, the Führer converted the war ministry into the *Oberkommando der Wehrmacht* (OKW). As chief of the OKW, he placed Field Marshal Wilhelm Keitel. Despite his title, Keitel's role was reduced essentially to forwarding Hitler's instructions to field commanders. Under the OKW was an operations staff (*Wehrmachtsführungsstab* or WFSt), headed by Colonel General Alfred Jodl, whose staff provided a competing planning agency to that found in the OKH. Most key OKW positions were filled by army General Staff officers, including Keitel and Jodl.

While the dichotomy between the OKW and OKH should have been senior to subordinate, there were many factors that made them competing agencies instead. The overall relative importance of the army to the German war effort; Hitler's personal assumption of command of the army after the dismissal of Brauchitsch in December 1941, making him direct head of both the OKW and the OKH; and his policy of using the OKW to plan various operations, starting with the invasion of Norway in 1940, made these agencies virtually parallel staffs. With the invasion of the Soviet Union in June 1941, the OKH became virtually exclusively devoted to operations in the East, along with general army administration, with the OKW directly responsible for all the other theaters of war. The OKH's status was further reduced by the establishment of the Luftwaffe as a separate service, under Hitler's political deputy Hermann Göring, the reestablishment of the navy (Kriegsmarine), and the enlargement of the Waffen-SS during the course of the war.

With Hitler occupying the three highest positions in the army chain of command, and Keitel and Jodl being relegated to virtual clerk status at OKW, the OKH chief of the General Staff became the only independent voice at Hitler's headquarters. Halder was at the post at the start of the war but was relieved by Hitler over disputes concerning operations on the eastern front in September 1942. Halder ended the war in a concentration camp. As his replacement, Hitler selected Lieutenant General Kurt Zeitzler, a relatively junior officer he expected to be pliable. With the Stalingrad crisis as a backdrop, Zeitzler proved not to be pliable and left the post in July 1944. In the wake of the July 20, 1944 assassination attempt, Hitler appointed panzer commander Colonel General Heinz Guderian as the next chief. While he knew Guderian was not pliable, he also knew he was loyal and adept organizationally. Despite many rows, Guderian lasted almost to the end of the war, going on sick leave at the end, in March 1945. His successor, General of Infantry Hans Krebs, died in the fighting in Berlin at the end of the war.

Of the qualified General Staff officers at the start of the war, half had become casualties or had been retired by 1945. The postwar International Military Tribunal at Nuremberg found the OKW and General Staff to not be inherently criminal organizations, but both Keitel and Jodl were executed for being accessories to the war-crime orders issued by Hitler.

John J. McGrath

See also: Beck, Ludwig; Blomberg-Fritsch Crisis; Fritsch, Werner von; Göring, Hermann; Guderian, Heinz; Halder, Franz; International Military Tribunal: The Nuremberg Trials; Jodl, Alfred; Keitel, Wilhelm; Krebs, Hans; Zeitzler, Kurt

Additional Reading

Citino, Robert M. *The German Way of War: From the Thirty Years War to the Third Reich*. Lawrence: University Press of Kansas, 2005.

Goerlitz, Walter. *History of the German General Staff 1657–1945.* Translated by Brian Battershaw. New York: Praeger, 1957.

German-Soviet Nonaggression Pact (August 23, 1939)

The treaty between Germany and the Soviet Union (often called the Nazi-Soviet Nonaggression Pact) facilitated Germany's September 1, 1939 invasion of Poland and its war effort before 1941. On August 21, 1939, Soviet leader Josef Stalin telegraphed Berlin and asked that Foreign Minister Joachim von Ribbentrop come to Moscow. Ribbentrop arrived on August 23 and met personally with Stalin. The pact was signed that same night, stunning the world. The pact had three major provisions, two of them secret and not revealed until the Nuremberg Tribunal after World War II had ended. The open provision consisted of a ten-year nonaggression pact between the Soviet Union and Germany.

The first of the two secret sections divided the Baltic States and Poland between the Soviet Union and Germany. The Soviet sphere of influence was to include eastern Poland, Bessarabia (a province of Romania), Estonia, Latvia, and Finland. The Germans secured western Poland and Lithuania. A month after the pact was signed, Hitler traded Lithuania to the Soviet Union in exchange for further German concessions in Poland. The second secret clause stipulated that the Soviet Union would provide Germany with massive amounts of raw materials and act as its purchasing agent abroad for items it could not furnish itself. In return, Germany agreed to provide finished goods and weapons technology from Germany. This was particularly helpful to Germany, nullifying the effects of the British naval blockade of Germany.

Stalin understood the danger of the alliance, yet he continued to trust his ally, until the German invasion of the Soviet Union, Operation BARBAROSSA, in June 1941. With the signing of the pact, Hitler freed himself of the threat of Soviet military intervention and a two-front war. He was now free to launch his invasion of Poland. On September 1, 1939, German forces crossed the border. Two days later, Great Britain and France honored their pledge to Poland and declared war on Germany. The Soviet Union denied the secret provisions of the pact until 1990.

Eric W. Osborne

See also: Poland Campaign

Additional Reading

Read, Anthony, and David Fisher. *The Deadly Embrace: Hitler, Stalin, and the Nazi-Soviet Pact, 1939–1941.* New York: W. W. Norton, 1988.

Roberts, Geoffrey. *The Unholy Alliance: Stalin's Pact with Hitler.* Bloomington: Indiana University Press, 1989.

Germany, Collapse and Surrender of (March–May 1945)

Germany's failed Ardennes Offensive during December 1944 to January 1945, far from stalling the western Allies, as Hitler had hoped, actually hastened the German military collapse. By March 1, 1945, Allied supreme commander in the west, General Dwight D. Eisenhower, had assembled sufficient forces for a full frontal assault. By April, it would be the largest coalition army ever assembled in war. Several hundred miles to the east, Soviet leader Josef Stalin amassed three fronts (army groups) for the final drive on Berlin. Supporting these huge Allied armies were their air forces, which now had complete control of the skies. Large numbers of British and U.S. aircraft continued the strategic bombing campaign against the German heartland. During the period from March 1 to 21, more than ten thousand U.S. and British bombers dropped in excess of thirty-one thousand tons of bombs on the Ruhr area alone.

Conducting operations from the troglodyte atmosphere of his Berlin bunker and surrounded primarily by sycophants, the Hitler relied on his so-called V (for "vengeance") weapons—the V-1 buzz bomb and V-2 missile—as well as new jet aircraft. He also hoped for some miracle, such as Allied dissension, to turn the tide. The only military realist in headquarters was army chief of staff General Heinz Guderian. His clashes with Hitler, however, led to his firing at the end of March.

The onslaught from the west began with a drive to the Rhine River, with Field Marshal Sir Bernard Montgomery's 21st Army Group in the north, Lieutenant General Omar Bradley's 12th Army Group in the center, and Lieutenant General Jacob Devers 6th Army Group in the south. Soon after, the U.S. First Army captured intact the bridge over the Rhine at Remagen on March 7, Hitler replaced his commander in the west, Field Marshal Gerd von Rundstedt, with Field Marshal Albert Kesselring. The western Allies then launched Operation UNDERTONE, an assault on the Saar-Palatinate region, wherein the U.S. Third and Seventh Armies broke through the German Siegfried Line and destroyed SS Oberstgruppenführer Paul Hausser's German First Army. On March 22 to 23, Montgomery launched Operation PLUNDER, a large-scale attack on the lower Rhine. On April 1, the U.S. First and Ninth Armies encircled all the German forces defending the Ruhr. Farther to the south, Nuremberg fell to the U.S. Third Army on April 20.

On March 31, on the eastern front, Marshal Ivan Konev's 2nd Ukrainian Front, Marshal Georgii Zhukov's 1st Belorussian Front, and Marshal Konstantin Rokossovski's 2nd Belorussian Front opened the attack to take the German capital. As the Soviets steadily drove Army Group Vistula back

COLLAPSE OF GERMANY, 1945

near Berlin, Hitler insisted on a scorched-earth policy; he also called on German citizens to act as "Werewolves," and he dared to hope that the miracle of the House of Brandenburg of the Seven Years' War—in which the coalition against Prussian King Friedrich II came undone on the death of Russian czarina Elizabeth—might be repeated. He even seized on the death of U.S. President Franklin D. Roosevelt on April 12, 1945 as an omen that Germany would yet survive. As propaganda minister Josef Goebbels exhorted the people of Berlin to defend their city, Hitler called up Volkstrum troops (the largely untrained older civilian militia) and the Hitler Youth to defend his dying Third Reich.

At the same time, millions of German refugees were fleeing west to avoid falling into the hands of the Soviets. The German Navy evacuated hundreds of thousands of Germans from the Baltics. Many others made their way west on foot. Ultimately, perhaps sixteen million Germans were displaced from their homelands in Poland, Czechoslovakia, and elsewhere. More than two million may have been killed in the exodus that followed. Those who escaped or were forced to leave added yet another burden on already strained German social services.

On Hitler's birthday, April 20, 1945, Zhukov's troops pierced through three German defensive belts defending Berlin. On April 22, Soviet troops were fighting in the city itself, and, three days later, they had surrounded Berlin. That same day, April 25, elements of Bradley's 12th Army Group linked up with Soviet troops of Konev's 1st Ukrainian Front at Torgau on the Elbe River.

On April 25 to 26, SS-Obergruppenführer Felix Steiner's Eleventh Army struck at Soviet forces driving on Berlin near Oranienburg, to no avail. Almost five hundred thousand Soviet troops were now battling for Berlin. Hitler, defiant to the last, refused to leave his capital and committed suicide on April 30. To the end, he refused to accept responsibility and blamed others for Germany's defeat. Hitler's designated successor as chief of state, Grand Admiral Karl Dönitz, then took over what remained of the German forces. Meanwhile, the Allies had overrun northern Italy. Remaining German forces there surrendered on May 2.

In the west, U.S. Third Army reached the Austrian border opposite Braunau on May 2. That same day, Lieutenant General Helmuth Weidling, commander of the Berlin garrison, surrendered to Soviet Colonel General Vassili Chuikov. On May 3, elements of Montgomery's 21st Army Group linked up with Rokossovsky's 2nd Belorussian Front at Wismar. Marshal Rodion Malinovsky's 2nd Ukrainian Front moved from Hungary into Austria and Czechoslovakia and prepared to link up with Patton's Third Army, which was advancing down the Danube near Linz.

Remaining German forces under Dönitz still controlled Norway; Denmark; the Western Netherlands; and portions of Germany, Yugoslavia, Austria, and Czechoslovakia. Although Dönitz realized defeat was certain, he briefly stalled for time to rescue additional German refugees fleeing westward. On May 7, Dönitz surrendered all German forces unconditionally to the victorious Allies; a formal ceremony was held the next day. The guns fell silent. Germany lay prostrate and in ruins, its social services a shambles, and its cities great wastelands of twisted girders and rubble.

Gene Mueller and Spencer C. Tucker

See also: Berlin, Land Battle for; Berlin Air Campaign, Allied; Dönitz, Karl; Guderian,

Heinz; Hausser, Paul; Kesselring, Albert; Palatinate Campaign, Allied; Remagen Bridge, U.S. Capture of; Rundstedt, Karl Rudolf Gerd von

Additional Reading

Beevor, Antony. *The Fall of Berlin, 1945*. New York: Viking, 2002.

Ryan, Cornelius. *The Last Battle*. New York: Simon and Schuster, 1966.

GOODWOOD, British Operation (July 18–20, 1944)

Operation GOODWOOD was a British Second Army attack in an attempt to break out of the Normandy beachhead near Caen. The city had been a D-Day (June 6) objective of the British 3rd Infantry Division. GOODWOOD was a follow-up to two previous efforts to take Caen: the failed Operation EPSOM on June 26 to 30, and Operation CHARNWOOD on July 8 to 9, which finally took Caen. But the Germans still held in force the strategic Bourguébus Ridge south of the city, preventing any Allied breakout in that sector. Operation GOODWOOD committed three corps: three armored divisions of the British VIII Corps in the east provided the main effort to gain the rolling plain southeast of Caen rising toward Falaise, the Canadian II Corps was to secure the southern half of Caen, and the British XII Corps would conduct diversionary attacks on the right several days before the July 18, 1944 kickoff. The British and Canadians had some twelve hundred tanks.

Caen was held by German forces under Field Marshal Günther von Kluge's Army Group B. Most of the German panzers were in the Caen area, under General of Panzer Troops Heinrich Eberbach's Panzer Group West. The XLVII Panzer Corps was southwest of the city, and the I SS and II SS Panzer Corps were to the south. The area directly east of Caen was held by the LXXXVI Corps. In all, the Germans had three panzer divisions, two separate heavy panzer battalions, four infantry divisions, and a total of 377 tanks directly opposing Operation GOODWOOD.

The air and ground bombardment began at 0530 hours on July 18, and the ground attack started on schedule at 0730 hours, advancing more than three miles in slightly more than three hours. VIII Corps was nearing a clean breakthrough when it encountered the final German defensive line of antitank and flak guns. In an oversight, this defensive line had not been targeted for air bombardment, and it, combined with dogged German defense, ground the advance to a halt. Limited local attacks continued on July 19 and 20, but a heavy thunderstorm on July 20 turned the landscape into a quagmire, and GOODWOOD came to a halt.

During the four-day operation, the Canadian II Corps captured the rest of Caen and part of the plain to the southeast, and the British VIII Corps secured nearly thirty-five square miles of terrain. However, the operation cost VIII Corps more than four thousand casualties and the loss of five hundred tanks—36 percent of all British armor on the Continent at that time. German casualties were approximately two thousand, with another twenty-five hundred captured, and some one hundred tanks destroyed.

Arthur T. Frame and David T. Zabecki

See also: COBRA, Allied Breakout Operation; Kluge, Günther von; Saint-Lô, Battle for

Additional Reading

Isby, David C., ed. *Fighting in Normandy: The German Army from D-Day to Villers-Boccage*. London: Greenhill Books, 2001.

Göring, Hermann (1893–1946)

Reich marshal and commander of the Luftwaffe.

Born on January 12, 1893 in Rosenheim, Bavaria, Hermann Göring served as a pilot in World War I. He scored twenty-two aerial victories and was awarded the *Pour le Mérite*. An early supporter Adolf Hitler, Göring was seriously wounded in the 1923 Beer Hall Putsch. He fled Germany but returned in 1927. In 1928, Göring was elected to the Reichstag, and, in 1932, he was its president. Among his many offices in the Third Reich were minister of the interior for the state of Prussia and minister of the air force (Luftwaffe). In April 1933, Göring established the Geheime Staatspolizei (Gestapo—Secret State Police). In 1936, Göring was appointed to oversee the Four-Year Plan, which gave him virtual control over the economy.

Hermann Göring in the uniform of a Luftwaffe field marshal. He is also wearing the Grand Cross of the Iron Cross, the only one awarded during World War II. Photograph taken at the time of his greatest power as air minister of Germany and Prussian minister of the interior. (Library of Congress)

As the new Luftwaffe developed, Göring supported the concept of a tactical as opposed to a strategic air force. In 1938, Göring was promoted to the rank of field marshal. In 1940, Hitler made Göring the Third Reich's only Reich marshal and designated him as his heir. Göring was also instrumental in the development of the concentration camps and the formulation of the *Endlösung* or "final solution" to the "Jewish Question." Göring amassed a large personal fortune through corruption.

Göring's Luftwaffe was influential in the early Nazi victories in Poland in 1939 and France in 1940. His interventions in the Battle of Britain in 1940, however, negatively affected the German effort and led to a loss of his influence with Hitler. Popular opinion also turned against him as Allied air raids on the Reich became increasingly effective. Increasingly marginalized, Göring spent more time at his estate of Karinhall, where he indulged his interests in hunting and collecting looted art. Göring surrendered to units of the U.S. 9th Infantry Division on May 9, 1945 and was tried at the International Military Tribunal at Nuremberg. Unrepentant, he was found guilty and sentenced to death. Göring committed suicide by swallowing poison on October 15, 1946, only hours before his scheduled execution by hanging.

Wendy A. Maier

See also: Holocaust, German Military Complicity in; International Military Tribunal: The Nuremberg Trials; Luftwaffe (German Air Force); Sturmabteilungen (SA)

Additional Reading

Mosley, Leonard. *The Reich Marshal: A Biography of Hermann Goering.* Garden City, NY: Doubleday, 1974.

Greece Campaign (April 6–30, 1941)

In the spring of 1941, Hitler launched Operation MARITA, sending his forces into Greece on the same day that Germany also invaded Yugoslavia. His decision was prompted by his intent to eject the British from the Aegean and eastern Mediterranean; to protect his southern flank—especially the Romanian oil fields at Ploesti—before launching Operation BARBAROSSA, the invasion of the Soviet Union; and to support Italy, his faltering ally. Greece was already at war, having been invaded by Italy on October 28, 1940. The Greeks had not only repelled that invasion, but they had launched a counterinvasion of Albania. In support of Greece, the British deployed Force W to Greece. Altogether, slightly more than sixty thousand British Empire troops were in Greece in April 1941.

The German invasion of Greece from Bulgaria began on April 6, 1941. Field Marshal Wilhelm List, commanding the German Twelfth Army, intended to smash through the Metaxas Line and drive on Athens. Within three days, German forces seized the port city of Salonika and breached the Metaxas Line. On April 23, the same day that the Greek Army was forced to surrender, Greek King George II fled to Egypt and established a government-in-exile. The following day, the British abandoned Thermopylae and began withdrawing into the Peloponnesus. Royal Navy ships, meanwhile, braved Luftwaffe attacks to carry out night evacuations of British troops from ports in eastern Greece. More

German infantry during Operation MARITA, the invasion of Greece by Germany and Italy in April 1941. (SeM/Universal Images Group via Getty Images)

than fifty thousand British Empire troops were evacuated, although most of their equipment had to be abandoned. The last formal evacuation took place on April 30. Many of the troops were then sent to Crete. British naval losses were two destroyers and four merchant ships. The Greeks lost three destroyers, a torpedo boat, and forty-three merchant ships totaling 63,975 tons.

In the entirety of the Greek Campaign, the Germans lost 2,559 killed (including 200 aircrew) and 5,820 wounded. The Greek army sustained 13,408 killed, 42,485 wounded, and 270,000 prisoners. Italian losses during April were 13,775 dead, 54,874 wounded, and 25,067 missing. The British suffered fifty-one hundred dead, wounded, and missing and some seven thousand taken prisoner. Some historians have suggested that Germany's invasion of Greece and Yugoslavia delayed Operation BARBAROSSA. However, other factors, especially the need to wait for dry weather for the panzers, were more important. Nonetheless, the panzer divisions that had served in Greece had to refit and were thus not immediately available for BARBAROSSA. The campaign also exacted a toll in equipment and in precious stocks of fuel.

Jack Greene

See also: Crete, German Invasion of; List, Siegmund Wilhelm Walter; Yugoslavia Campaign

Additional Reading

Papagos, Alexandros. *The German Attack on Greece.* Madison: University of Wisconsin Press, 1946.

Greim, Robert Ritter von (1892–1945)

Luftwaffe field marshal.

Born on June 22, 1892 in Bayreuth, Robert von Greim was a pilot during World War I. He had twenty-eight aerial victories and was awarded the *Pour le Mérite.* Greim joined the fledgling Luftwaffe in 1934. From 1943 to 1945, Greim commanded Luftflotte 6 (Air Fleet 6) on the eastern front. On April 26, 1945, Greim flew into the besieged city of Berlin with test pilot Hanna Reitsch. Hitler promoted him to field marshal (the last so appointed) and head of the Luftwaffe, replacing the dismissed Hermann Göring. Greim and Reitsch, on Hitler's orders, flew out of Berlin two days later. Following capture by the Americans, Greim, a fervent Nazi, who feared he would be handed over to the Soviets for trial, committed suicide on May 24, 1945 in Salzburg, Austria.

Spencer E. Robbins III

See also: Göring, Hermann; Reitsch, Hanna

Additional Reading

Mitcham, Samuel W., Jr. *Men of the Luftwaffe.* Novato, CA: Presidio Press, 1988.

Guderian, Heinz (1888–1953)

Wehrmacht colonel general.

Born in Kulm, Germany, on January 17, 1888, Heinz Guderian served during World War I as a communications officer and a General Staff officer. He was an early advocate of mechanization, based on British and French theorists. In October 1935, he assumed command of the 2nd Panzer Division, one of only three being formed. In 1937, Guderian published his treatise on armored warfare, *Achtung-Panzer!* In October 1938, Guderian was appointed chief of mobile troops, with direct access to Adolf Hitler. As commander of the XIX Panzer Corps, Guderian achieved the pinnacle of operational maneuvers during the invasion of France in May 1940, when he led his panzer corps across the Meuse River at Sedan and raced to the English Channel to cut Allied forces off in Belgium.

During Operation BARBAROSSA, the June 1941 invasion of the Soviet Union, Guderian commanded the Second Panzer Group in Army Group Center. That December, however, Guderian's short temper and mercurial disposition toward superiors led to his relief from command over tactical disputes. Guderian was recalled by Hitler as inspector general of armored troops in March 1943. After the assassination attempt against Hitler in July 1944, Guderian was appointed chief of the General Staff. He stood up to Hitler on numerous occasions, leading to his dismissal on March 28, 1945. Taken prisoner by U.S. forces at the end of the war, Guderian was not prosecuted for war crimes, although he remained a prisoner until June 1948. Guderian died at Schwengen, Bavaria, on May 14, 1953.

Steven J. Rauch

See also: France, Battle of; Soviet Union, Invasion of (Operation BARBAROSSA)

Additional Reading

Macksey, Kenneth. *Guderian: Creator of the Blitzkrieg.* New York: Stein and Day, 1976.

Guernica Air Raid (April 26, 1937). *See* Spanish Civil War

H

Halder, Franz (1884–1972)

Wehrmacht colonel general.

Born on August 30, 1884 in Würzburg, Germany, Franz Halder served in World War I as a General Staff officer. In October 1938, Halder was appointed chief of the army General Staff. Halder played a crucial role in the planning and execution of Germany's campaigns before World War II and during its first years. After the fall of France in 1940, Halder established a planning group that summer to develop a campaign plan against the Soviet Union. His unwillingness to encourage innovation among his subordinates, however, resulted in a plan that did not fully address the Red Army's capabilities or clearly identify the campaign's objectives. Hitler relieved Halder on September 24, 1942. He was marginally implicated in the July 20, 1944 assassination attempt against Hitler and imprisoned in the Flossenbürg concentration camp. Following the war, Halder spent fourteen years with the U.S. Army Historical Division working on the *Foreign Military Studies* series. For that work, he received the U.S. Army's Meritorious Civilian Service Medal in 1961. Halder died on April 2, 1972 in Aschau, West Germany.

David M. Toczek

See also: France, Battle of; Soviet Union, Invasion of (Operation BARBAROSSA)

Additional Reading

Halder, Franz. *The Halder Diaries: The Private War Journals of Colonel General Franz Halder.* Boulder, CO: Westview Press, 1976.

Hamburg, Allied Air Raids (Operation GOMORRAH) (July 24–August 3, 1943)

The port city of Hamburg was attacked by Allied aircraft many times during World War II. The city had a population of 1.5 million, and it was an important industrial center, with U-Boat production at its core—408 out of total of 1,131 U-boats built were produced in Hamburg. In late July 1943, Hamburg was the target for a Royal Air Force thousand-bomber raid, Operation GOMORRAH.

The first raid was launched on July 24, with 791 bombers. They carried a twenty-five-hundred-ton mix of high explosive and incendiary bombs. During that raid, the German flak defenses of Hamburg brought down only three bombers after firing more than fifty thousand shells. The first raid killed 10,289 civilians. The following day, the U.S. Eighth Air Force attacked the Blohm and Voss U-boat factory and an aero-engine factory. The Americans returned to those targets on July 26. The RAF's largest raid came on the night of July 27, when 729 aircraft equipped with blockbuster bombs attacked the city. The resulting firestorm caused more than eighteen thousand deaths. Additional raids occurring on the nights of July 29 and August 3 caused a total of more than ten thousand deaths. More than fifty-eight thousand buildings in Hamburg were damaged, and forty-two thousand civilians died, which equaled 80 percent of the total British civilian casualties for the entire war. Despite the devastation, however, German national morale was not significantly affected by Operation GOMORRAH.

Ross Mahoney

See also: Combined Bomber Offensive, Allied (Operation POINTBLANK)

Additional Reading

Middlebrook, Martin. *The Battle of Hamburg: The Firestorm Raid.* London: Cassell, 1980.

Hartmann, Erich Alfred (1922–1993)

Luftwaffe major and ace, Bundesluftwaffe colonel.

Erich Hartmann was the highest-scoring aerial ace of all time. Born in Weissach, Germany, on April 19, 1922, Hartmann joined the Luftwaffe in October 1940. In October 1942, he reported to *Staffel* (squadron) 7, III *Gruppe* (group), *Jagdgeschwader* (fighter wing) 52 (7.III/JG52) on the eastern front. Hartmann spent the next two and one-half years in various units of JG52. By the end of the war, he has been awarded the Knight's Cross of the Iron Cross with Oak Leaves, Swords and Diamonds, one of only twenty-seven German soldiers so honored. Hartmann scored his 352nd and last victory on May 8, 1945. He surrendered his fighter group to a U.S. Army unit but was handed over to the Soviets. Tried and convicted as a war criminal, Hartmann was imprisoned until his repatriation in late 1955. Hartmann joined the Federal Republic of Germany's new *Bundesluftwaffe*. He retired in 1970 as a colonel. Hartmann died on September 19, 1993 at Weil im Schönbuch.

Marlyn R. Pierce

See also: Luftwaffe (German Air Force)

Additional Reading

Hartmann, Ursula. *German Fighter Ace Erich Hartmann: The Life Story of the World's Highest Scoring Ace.* West Chester, PA: Schiffer Military History, 1992.

Hausser, Paul (1880–1972)

Schutzstaffel (SS) Oberstgruppenführer and colonel general of the Waffen-SS.

Born on October 7, 1880 at Brandenburg, Paul Hausser served during World War I as a General Staff officer. Retiring in 1932 as lieutenant general, Hausser joined the SS in 1934 and helped train the nucleus units of what became the Waffen-SS. In October 1939, Hausser assumed command one of the two new SS combat divisions, leading the 2nd SS Division "Das Reich" during in campaigns in France in 1940, in Yugoslavia in 1941, and on the eastern front in the invasion of the Soviet Union. From June 1942 to June 1944, he commanded the first SS corps-level unit, the I SS Panzer Corps. In June 1944, Hausser took command of the Seventh Army, which defended against the Allied invasion of Normandy. Generally regarded as the most militarily competent of the Waffen-SS generals, Hausser was imprisoned in May 1945 and not released until 1948. He was the author of the defensive claim that the Waffen-SS troops had been "soldiers as any others." Hausser died at Ludwigsburg, Germany, on December 21, 1972.

Martin Moll

See also: Soviet Union, Invasion of (Operation BARBAROSSA); Waffen-SS

Additional Reading

Stein, George H. *The Waffen SS: Hitler's Elite Guard at War, 1939–1945.* Ithaca, NY: Cornell University Press, 1966.

Heinrici, Gotthard (1886–1971)

Wehrmacht colonel general.

Born in Gumbinnen, East Prussia on December 25, 1886, Gotthard Heinrici served in World War I in both line and staff assignments. He commanded the 16th Infantry Division in the invasion of Poland in September 1939; the XII Army Corps during the invasion of France in 1940; and the XLIII Army Corps during Operation BARBAROSSA, the invasion of the Soviet Union. In January 1942, Heinrici assumed command of the Fourth Army in Russia. In August 1944, he assumed command of the First Panzer Army. Heinrici replaced Heinrich Himmler as commander of Army Group Vistula on March 20, 1945, following Himmler's brief but disastrous command tenure. With the decimated Third Panzer Army and Ninth Army, Heinrici held the Oder River line and masterfully defended Seelow Heights, just east of Berlin, against overwhelming odds, but he was unable to stem the Soviet tide. He disagreed with Adolf Hitler over the Führer's order to hold at all costs, and he was dismissed on April 29, 1945. Heinrici surrendered to British forces after the war and was released from imprisonment in May 1948. Widely regarded as one of the most capable German generals of the war, Heinrici died in Waiblingen, Germany, on December 13, 1971.

Jon D. Berlin

See also: Berlin, Land Battle for; Himmler, Heinrich; Soviet Union, Invasion of (Operation BARBAROSSA)

Additional Reading

Toland, John. *The Last 100 Days.* New York: Random House, 1965.

Heisenberg, Werner (1901–1976)

Nuclear physicist.

Born in Würzburg, Germany, on December 5, 1901, Werner Heisenberg graduated in 1923 from the University of Munich with a doctorate in physics. One of his greatest accomplishments was his theory of quantum mechanics, for which he won the Nobel Prize in physics in 1932. By the late 1930s, despite being an opponent of the Nazi regime, Heisenberg was the leader of the German project to develop an atomic weapon. The *Uranverein* project was not successful, but the cause of its failure is still a matter of debate. Heisenberg claimed after the war that he had tried to impede the project as best he could to deny the Nazis an atomic bomb, a claim that some scholars contest. Following the defeat of Germany, Heisenberg was among those German physicists imprisoned in Britain until 1946. Heisenberg remained active in the field of physics in subsequent years. He died in Munich on February 1, 1976.

Eric W. Osborne

Additional Reading

Powers, Thomas. *Heisenberg's War: The Secret History of the German Bomb.* Cambridge, MA: Da Capo Press, 2000.

Hermann, Hans-Joachim "Hajo" (1918–2010)

Luftwaffe colonel.

Born in Kiel on August 1, 1918, Hans-Joachim Hermann joined the newly formed Luftwaffe in 1935. He flew in combat during the Spanish Civil War and during the Battle of Britain. By the summer of 1943, RAF Bomber Command had discovered how to jam German radar, and, as a consequence, it gained the upper hand in the night skies over Germany. Hermann formed a unit called *Wilde Sau* (Wild Boar), flying single-engine fighters, without benefit of radar, to attack the bombers over the cities, while illuminated by ground searchlights. The tactics were successful but could not turn the tide of the air war. Taken prisoner by the Soviets at the end of the war, Hermann was held until 1955. He earned a law degree in 1965 and became a prominent lawyer in Düsseldorf. In 1993, he defended David Irving during the historian's trial in Munich for denying the Holocaust. Hermann died in Düsseldorf on November 5, 2010. He was the last living holder of the Knight's Cross of the Iron Cross with Oak Leaves and Swords.

Marlyn R. Pierce

See also: Berlin Air Campaign, Allied; Britain, Battle of

Additional Reading

Spick, Mike. *Luftwaffe Fighter Aces: The Jagdflieger and Their Combat Tactics and Techniques.* Mechanicsburg, PA: Stackpole Books, 1996.

Heusinger, Adolf (1897–1982)

Wehrmacht lieutenant general, Bundeswehr general.

Adolf Heusinger was born on August 4, 1897 in Holzminden, Germany. During World War I, he served as an infantry officer and was taken prisoner by the British in 1917. In 1940, Heusinger became the chief of operations Staff (*Operationsabteilung*) of the Army High Command (*Oberkommando des Heeres*—OKH), making him the third-most senior officer in the army planning hierarchy. He oversaw the planning for operations in Poland, Denmark, Norway, France, the Netherlands, and the Soviet Union. In 1944, Heusinger temporarily assumed office as chief of the General Staff of the Army. In this capacity, he attended the planning meeting on July 20, 1944, and was standing next to Adolf Hitler when the bomb planted by Colonel Claus von Stauffenberg exploded. Although there was evidence that Heusinger had contact with the conspirators, the prosecutors could not directly connect him to the plot. Nonetheless, he was placed into the Führer-Reserve for the duration of the war. Heusinger was taken prisoner by the western Allies in May 1945.

A prisoner of war until 1947, Heusinger testified during the Nuremberg Trials. With the establishment of the Bundeswehr in 1955, Heusinger returned to military service. As lieutenant general, he became the highest-ranking officer of the Bundeswehr. In June 1957, Heusinger was promoted to full general and named the first general inspector of the Bundeswehr (*Generalinspekteur*). Heusinger was appointed chairman of the NATO Military Committee in April 1961. Retiring in 1964, Heusinger died in Cologne on November 30, 1982.

Dieter H. Kollmer

See also: *Oberkommando des Heeres* (OKH); Stauffenberg, Claus Schenk von

Additional Reading

Gross, Gerhard. *The Myth and Reality of German Warfare: Operational Thinking from Moltke the Elder to Heusinger.* Lexington: University Press of Kentucky, 2016.

Himmler, Heinrich (1900–1945)

Reichsführer of the Schutzstaffel (SS) and commander of the Waffen-SS.

Born on October 7, 1900 in Munich, Heinrich Himmler was an officer candidate

Reichsführer-SS Heinrich Himmler (wearing glasses) inspects a prisoner-of-war camp in Russia, ca. 1941. When World War II broke out in 1939, the Schutzstaffel launched a genocidal campaign to liquidate Germany's "enemies" in the occupied territories. (National Archives)

during World War I. Shortly after the war, Himmler joined the National Socialist German Worker's Party (Nazi Party) and played a small role in the November 1923 Munich Beer Hall Putsch. In January 1929, Adolf Hitler appointed Himmler as head of the SS, which, at the time, was an elite bodyguard unit of the much larger Sturmabteilung (SA), the Nazi Party's paramilitary force. Within a few years, Himmler built the SS from a force of two hundred men into an organization fifty-thousand strong, with its own distinctive black uniform, personal devotion to Hitler, and ethos. In 1934, Reichsführer of the SS Himmler gained control of the Gestapo (Secret State Police). Hitler rewarded him for his active role in the 1934 Night of the Long Knives Blood Purge against the leadership of the SA by making the SS an independent organization, subject only to his immediate authority. In June 1936, Himmler also gained control of all the police forces of Germany.

Despite the promise Hitler made to the German Army when he suppressed the SA, he allowed Himmler to establish armed SS formations, known as the SS *Verfügungstruppen* (emergency troops), which evolved into the divisions of the Waffen-SS during World War II. The SS also came to have considerable economic interests, including armaments factories. By 1939, Himmler's influence overshadowed the Nazi Party, and many high-ranking officials, even in the military, found it prudent to hold SS ranks. Himmler was one of the most important figures in Germany, and perhaps the most dreaded. Although he was physically far removed from the ideal Aryan type, Himmler was a fanatical adherent of Nazi racial theories. Controlling Germany's racial policies, Himmler directed the *Endlossung* (Final Solution)—the extermination of the Jews as well as the incurably ill, the disabled, gypsies, and homosexuals. The SS already ran the concentration camps. It now established and ran the death camps as well.

After the July 1944 bomb plot against Hitler, Himmler took command of the Wehrmacht's Replacement Army. In November 1944, Hitler gave Himmler command of Army Group Upper Rhine, and during January to April 1945, he commanded Army Group Vistula—two positions for which he was utterly unqualified. In April 1945, Himmler attempted to negotiate surrender to the Western Allies. A furious Hitler stripped him of his posts. Himmler attempted to flee but was captured by British troops. Identified on May 23, 1945, Himmler committed suicide by means of a hidden cyanide capsule.

Annette E. Richardson

See also: Holocaust, German Military Complicity in; Night of the Long Knives; *Sturmabteilungen* (SA); Waffen-SS

Additional Reading

Breitman, Richard. *The Architect of Genocide: Himmler and the Final Solution.* New York: Knopf, 1991.

Hindenburg, Paul von (1847–1934)

Kaiserheer field marshal, president of the Weimar Republic.

Born on October 2, 1847 in Posen (now Poznań, Poland), into a Junker family, Paul Ludwig von Beneckendorff und von Hindenburg served in the Austro-Prussian War in 1866 and the Franco-Prussian War of 1870–1871. He retired in 1911, but on August 22, 1914, Hindenburg was recalled to active duty to command the Eighth Army in East Prussia. With Lieutenant General Eric Ludendorff as his chief of staff, Hindenburg became a national hero when he crushed the Russians at the Battle of Tannenberg on August 25 to 31, 1914. In 1916, Hindenburg and Ludendorff were transferred to the western front, where Hindenburg assumed command of all the German armies in the field. Strongly influenced by Ludendorff, Hindenburg took steps that went far beyond the scope of his authority, establishing what amounted to a virtual military dictatorship. The results were disastrous for Germany. Militarily they could not overcome the Allies' superior manpower and economic resources. Germany was finally defeated in November 1918; Kaiser Wilhelm abdicated; and Germany became a republic, but a very shaky one.

Hindenburg retired from the army in January 1919. Possessed of an imperturbable demeanor, Hindenburg is often portrayed as a slow, superannuated figurehead, manipulated by the brilliant but wily Ludendorff. Such an image is incorrect, as the field marshal was quite cunning and made decisions with considerable thought given to his reputation and place in history. Consequently, he adroitly escaped blame for Germany's defeat. The public venerated him, and, in the search for a scapegoat for the defeat and collapse, Hindenburg remained untouched. Hindenburg subsequently returned to political activity to run for president of the Weimar Republic, although he hardly bothered to campaign. Winning the election on April 26, 1925, Hindenburg presided over the death throes of the republic. In January 1933, verging on senility, he was maneuvered by those around him into appointing Adolf Hitler as chancellor. Hindenburg remained in office until his death at his estate in Neudeck, East Prussia, on August 2, 1934. As soon as Hindenburg died, Hitler announced the combination of the offices of president and chancellor, and his assumption of that office as *der Führer.*

Michael B. Barrett

See also: Hitler, Adolf

Additional Reading

Wheeler-Bennett, John W. *Hindenburg: The Wooden Titan.* New York: St. Martin's Press, 1967.

Hitler, Adolf (1889–1945)

Führer (leader) of Nazi Germany and commander in chief of the Wehrmacht.

Born on April 20, 1889 in Braunau am Inn, Austria, Adolf Hitler spent his early years in Vienna as an unsuccessful street artist. Probably to avoid compulsory military service, Hitler left Austria in May 1913 and settled in the south German state of Bavaria. On the outbreak of World War I, he enlisted in the Bavarian army. He saw extensive action, was wounded, and served in the dangerous position of *Meldegänger* (runner). Temporarily blinded in a British gas attack, Hitler ended the war in a military hospital. He had risen to the rank of *Gefreiter* and was awarded the Iron Cross Second Class and Iron Cross First Class, a significant distinction for someone of his low rank.

After the war, Hitler returned to Munich and remained in the Reichswehr as a counterintelligence agent, reporting on political groups. With the full support of the German Army he became involved full time in extremist politics. In the summer of 1919, Hitler joined the *Deutsche Arbeiterpartei* (German Worker's Party), later known as the National Socialist German Worker's Party or Nazi party (*Nationalsozialistische Deutsche Arbeiterpartei*—NSDAP). On November 8, 1923, Hitler and his followers attempted to seize power in Bavaria. The "Beer Hall Putsch" was put down by the authorities with some bloodshed. Hitler was arrested, tried, and sentenced to prison. He served only nine months, and, while at the Landsberg Fortress, he dictated his stream-of-consciousness memoir, *Mein Kampf (My Struggle).*

Hitler restructured the NSDAP, and, by 1928, the party had emerged as a political force in Germany, winning representation in the Reichstag. In April 1932, Hitler ran unsuccessfully against Field Marshal Paul von Hindenburg for the presidency of Germany. By June 1932, however, the Nazis were the largest political party in the Reichstag. On January 30, 1933, Hindenburg appointed Hitler chancellor. The Enabling Act of March 1933 gave Hitler dictatorial powers. On the death of Hindenburg in August 1934, Hitler amalgamated the offices of president and chancellor and took control of the armed forces. In the Night of the Long Knives of July 1934, Hitler purged the party and removed several of his political opponents and especially of leadership of the *Sturmabteilungen* (SA), the Nazi Party's paramilitary street thugs who had helped put him in power in the first place. Hitler also reorganized Germany administratively, dissolving political parties and labor unions and making Germany a one-party state. Nazi Germany became a totalitarian state that Hitler, now known as the Führer, ruled alone. Almost on assuming political power, Hitler initiated actions against the Jews. The Nuremberg Laws of 1935 defined as Jewish anyone with one Jewish grandparent. That a terrible fate would be their lot was clear in Hitler's remarks that war in Europe would lead to the "extinction of the Jewish race in Europe."

On August 2, 1934, Hitler required all German military personnel to swear an oath of loyalty to him personally. Although he was legally the commander in chief of all the German armed forces as the German head of state, Hitler assumed direct command of the Wehrmacht as its supreme commander in 1938. In 1941, Hitler went one step further by assuming direct operational command of the German Army. Hitler's most daring gamble was in March 1936, when he marched German troops into the Rhineland. In November 1937, he announced plans to his top advisers and generals for an aggressive foreign policy and war, and, in March 1938, he began his march of conquest with the *Anschluss* (annexation) of Austria. That fall, he secured the Sudetenland of Czechoslovakia, and, in March 1939, he took over the remainder of Czechoslovakia. Poland was the next pressure point. To secure Germany's eastern flank, Hitler in August 1939 concluded a nonaggression pact with the Soviet Union. On September 1, 1939, German forces invaded Poland, touching off World War II. Germany took Norway and Denmark in April 1940, and France and the Benelux countries in June. Hitler's first setback came in the July to October 1940 Battle of Britain, when the Luftwaffe failed to drive the Royal Air Force from the skies, a necessary precursor to a sea invasion. After next securing his southern flank in the Balkans by invading and conquering Greece and Yugoslavia in April 1941, Hitler invaded the Soviet Union that June. When the United States entered the war against Japan in December 1941, Hitler declared war on the United States.

Increasingly, Germany suffered the consequences of strategic overreach: German troops not only had to garrison much of Europe, but they were also sent to North Africa. Hitler's constant meddling in military matters, his changes of plans, and his divide-and-rule concept of administration all worked to the detriment of Germany's cause. On Hitler's express orders, millions of people, especially Jews, were rounded up and systematically slaughtered. With Germany crumbling around him, Hitler took up residence in Berlin in mid-January 1945. He refused negotiation to the end, preferring to see Germany destroyed. Hitler committed suicide in the bunker of the Chancellery on April 30, 1945.

Wendy A. Maier-Sarti

Austria-born Adolf Hitler became the constitutionally elected chancellor of Germany in January 1933. When President Paul von Hindenburg died in office in 1934, Hitler seized complete power by combining the offices of president and chancellor, and restyling himself as Germany's Führer. (Photos.com)

See also: Britain, Battle of; Hindenburg, Paul von; Night of the Long Knives; Rhineland, Remilitarization of; Soviet Union, Invasion of

(OPERATION BARBAROSSA); *Sturmabteilungen* (SA)

Additional Reading

Fest, Joachim C. *Hitler.* Translated by Richard and Clara Winston. New York: Harcourt Brace Jovanovich, 1974.

Kershaw, Ian. *Hitler.* 2 vols. New York: W. W. Norton, 1999–2000.

Hitler Youth (1922–1945)

The Hitler Youth was an organization established to indoctrinate German children into the ideology of the Nazi Party. The first Nazi youth organization was the *Jugendbund der Nationalsozialistische Deutsche Arbeiterpartei* (Youth League of the National Socialist German Workers' Party), established on March 8, 1922. In 1926, it was renamed the *Hitler-Jugend* (Hitler Youth) and officially made a part of the *Sturmabteilung* (SA), the Nazi Party's paramilitary organization. Although the public schools all taught the principles of Nazism, the Hitler Youth took care of children's spare time. The organization was later run by Baldur von Schirach, who managed all the country's youth programs. By 1935, about 60 percent of all German boys were members of the Hitler Youth. Membership became compulsory for all "Aryan" German boys on July 1, 1936, when the organization became an official agency of the state.

During World War II, members of the Hitler Youth served in local German fire brigades and assisted during recovery efforts after Allied bombing attacks against German cities. As the Allied air campaign increased, Hitler Youth also started serving as *Flakhelfer* (Flak Helpers) on air-defense artillery crews. By 1943, the Third Reich was forced to draw increasingly on the Hitler Youth to make up the military manpower shortages resulting from the huge casualty rates of the war. In 1943, the Waffen-SS formed the 12th SS-Panzer-Division (Hitlerjugend). The majority of the division's enlisted cadre was made up of Hitler Youth members between the ages of sixteen and eighteen. The division fought against British and Canadian forces to the north of Caen during the 1944 Normandy Campaign. The 12th SS-Panzer-Division established a reputation for ferocity and fanaticism. By 1945, Germany was routinely drafting Hitler Youth members as young as twelve into the Volkssturm. During the 1945 battle for Berlin, the Hitler Youth were among the fiercest defenders of the city, but they were almost completely annihilated by the attacking Soviet forces. The Hitler Youth was dissolved by the Allied occupation authorities after World War II.

Kellie Searle and David T. Zabecki

See also: Sturmabteilungen (SA); Volkssturm; Waffen-SS

Additional Reading

Rempel, Gerhard. *Hitler's Children: The Hitler Youth and the SS.* Chapel Hill: University of North Carolina Press, 1989.

Hoepner, Erich (1886–1944)

Wehrmacht colonel general.

Born in Frankfurt an der Oder on September 14, 1886, Erich Hoepner served in World War I as a company commander and as a General Staff officer. During the 1938 Czechoslovakian crisis, Hoepner supported an abortive plot by the German military opposition to remove Hitler from power. He commanded a corps during the 1939 invasion of Poland and the 1940 invasion of France. Hoepner commanded the Fourth

Panzer Group in Operation BARBAROSSA, the invasion of the Soviet Union. Following the Soviet counterattack in December 1941, Hoepner put his career in jeopardy when, in early January, he began withdrawing some of his units to save them from certain annihilation by Soviet forces. Hitler removed several of his generals on the eastern front, but he made a special example of Hoepner, who was court-martialed and cashiered. Publicly humiliated, Hoepner was denied the right to wear a uniform or his decorations. This treatment turned him into an active conspirator against the Nazi regime. He was deeply involved in the July 20, 1944 plot against Hitler, and he was designated to take command of the Replacement Army should General Friedrich Fromm prove unreliable. With the failure of the plot, Hoepner rejected an opportunity to commit suicide, preferring to go on trial. Tried by the People's Court, under Judge Roland Freisler, Hoepner was found guilty and executed by being hanged by wire suspended from meat hooks at Plotzensee Prison in Berlin on August 8, 1944.

Joseph C. Greaney and
Spencer C. Tucker

See also: Fromm, Friedrich; Opposition to Hitler, German Military; Soviet Union, Invasion of (Operation BARBAROSSA)

Additional Reading

Clark, Alan. *Barbarossa: The Russian-German Conflict, 1941–1945.* New York: Quill, 1965.

Holocaust, German Military Complicity in

Following the Trial of the Major War Criminals before the International Military Tribunal at Nuremberg, the German General Staff and the *Oberkommando der Wehrmacht* (OKW) were put on trial before the American Military Tribunal, also held in Nuremberg. The trial began on January 4, 1946. As the leading witness for the defense, Field Marshal Erich von Manstein argued vigorously that the German armed services had conducted themselves correctly throughout World War II, but not the Waffen-SS. On September 30, 1946, the trial of the General Staff and OKW as a body concluded with a finding of "no declaration of criminality should be made in respect of the General Staff and High Command." The Tribunal did condemn many of the individual generals "for planning and waging an aggressive war which resulted in war crimes against humanity." For many years after the war, through various published memoirs, and histories, the concept of a "clean *Wehrmacht*" perpetuated, especially by Manstein. Time has since proved that this was not at all the case.

With the invasion of Poland on September 1, 1939, Reinhard Heydrich, as the SS chief of the Reich Main Security Office (*Reichssicherheitshauptamt*), formed a number of *Einsatzgruppen*, which were subordinate to local Wehrmacht commanders. Those units went into action immediately behind the Wehrmacht, and many German military commanders worked closely with these special groups in securing the rear areas. It was a common perception among the Wehrmacht that the Poles were inferior and dangerous, which led the officers and troops to cooperate with the SS. The Wehrmacht was instrumental in a brutal campaign of mass murder and repression, such as in the city of Bydgoszcz. By the end of the Polish campaign in October, the brutality employed by German officers and Wehrmacht firing squads accounted for no fewer than sixteen thousand Polish deaths, without the need for Heydrich's *Einsatzgruppen*.

Prior to the invasion of the Soviet Union in June 1941, many preliminary orders were discussed and issued concerning the treatment of the civilian population, Jews, and POWs, especially Soviet commissars attached to military units. On May 19, the OKW issued "Guidelines for the Behavior of Troops in Russia," which demanded, "ruthless and energetic action against Bolshevism agitators, saboteurs, and Jews, and the total elimination of all active or passive resistance." Subordinate headquarters added their own endorsements to such directives. As the invasion of the Soviet Union began on June 22, 1941, the Wehrmacht and the Nazis achieved a symbiosis of ideology on the conduct of the war. The headquarters of all three army groups, North, South, and Center, had liaison officers attached from the Einsatzgruppen. The Wehrmacht coordinated the special missions of the Einsatzgruppen and provided the unit members with special logistics and documents that explicitly stated, "as a member of the *Sonderkommando* of the *Sipo*, the bearer of this document is obliged to carry out special police-security operations. Army officers and all other relevant personnel are asked to assist him in his mission." Einsatzgruppen reports on numerous occasions in all areas of operations documented "extremely gratifying" Wehrmacht assistance with the actions against the Jews. And, "In the course of some larger operations carried out by us, army units have been placed under our command . . . our requests have been granted every time."

The Wehrmacht also failed in its responsibilities toward captives. In the Soviet Union alone, 5.7 million prisoners were captured. While the German military was responsible for the POW camps and the treatment of prisoners, it failed to provide sufficient food, shelter, sanitation facilities, and medical aid. The German Army's quartermaster general, Eduard Wagner, ordered on November 13, 1941 that all "non-working prisoners of war in the camps are to starve." Of these 5.7 million prisoners, 3.3 million died. The survivors were taken to Germany for slave labor.

In 1997, Daniel Goldhagen's controversial book, *Hitler's Willing Executioners: Ordinary Germans and the Holocaust*, seriously challenged the assertion that most Germans had not known about the Holocaust. Between 2001 and 2004, the *Wehrmachtsausstellung* traveling exhibition in Germany examined the German military's complicity in the crimes of the Third Reich and helped pretty well demolish the myth of the "clean Wehrmacht."

Raymond D. Limbach

See also: American Military Tribunals; *Einsatzgruppen*; International Military Tribunal: The Nuremberg Trials; Manstein, Erich von; *Oberkommando der Wehrmacht* (OKW)

Additional Reading

Goldhagen, Daniel. *Hitler's Willing Executioners: Ordinary Germans and the Holocaust.* New York: Vintage Press, 1997.

Megargee, Geoffrey P. *War of Annihilation: Combat and Genocide on the Eastern Front 1941.* New York: Rowman & Littlefield Publishers, Inc., 2006.

Hossbach, Friedrich (1894–1980)

Wehrmacht general of infantry.

Born at Unna in Westphalia on November 21, 1894, Friedrich Hossbach served on the eastern front during World War I. He became adjutant to Adolf Hitler in August 1934 and is chiefly remembered for his notes—what became known as the

"Hossbach Memorandum"—during a key meeting between Hitler and his military chiefs in Berlin on November 5, 1937, in which the Führer spelled out his plans for an aggressive foreign policy leading to war. This became important evidence at the postwar Nuremberg trials. Hossbach was dismissed from his adjutant post in February 1938 and later served in various command positions throughout the war on both the eastern and western fronts. He died in Göttingen on September 10, 1980.

Spencer C. Tucker

See also: Hitler, Adolf; International Military Tribunal: The Nuremberg Trials

Additional Reading

Shirer, William L. *The Rise and Fall of the Third Reich: A History of Nazi Germany.* New York: Simon and Schuster, 1960.

Hoth, Hermann (1885–1971)

Wehrmacht colonel general.

Born in Neuruppin near Berlin on April 12, 1885, Hermann Hoth served during World War I as a General Staff officer. He commanded the XV Motorized Corps during the invasions of Poland in 1939 and France in 1940. He commanded the Third Panzer Group during the invasion of the Soviet Union in June 1941. He commanded the Seventeenth Army in Ukraine from October 1941 to June 1942, when he took command of Fourth Panzer Army, which he commanded during the Battle of Kursk in July 1943. That November, Adolf Hitler dismissed the capable and well-liked Hoth for his defeatist attitude. Tried by a U.S. military court after the war for crimes against humanity committed by subordinates, Hoth was found guilty and sentenced at Nuremberg in October 1948 to fifteen years in prison. Hoth died at Goslar/Harz on January 25, 1971.

Spencer C. Tucker

See also: France, Battle of; Kursk, Battle of; Poland Campaign; Soviet Union, Invasion of (Operation BARBAROSSA)

Additional Reading

Brett-Smith, Richard. *Hitler's Generals.* San Rafael, CA: Presidio Press, 1976.

Hürtgen Forest Campaign, Allied (September 12–December 16, 1944)

The Hürtgen Forest campaign was a brilliantly executed economy-of-force operation by the Germans. Although it is little remembered today, the battle for the Hürtgen Forest was one of the worst defeats ever suffered by the U.S. Army. In three months of combat operations, the Americans sustained almost thirty-three thousand casualties, but accomplished almost nothing tactically or operationally in the process.

By late August 1944, the apparently defeated German Army had been pushed out of France and back to the borders of the Reich. Many U.S. GIs began to believe that the war would be over by Christmas. But the situation changed as the Allies reached German territory and the defenses of the German Westwall (called the Siegfried Line by the Americans but never by the Germans). In the central sector of the Westwall defensive line lay the dark and almost impenetrable Hürtgen Forest. Early in September, the U.S. First Army, commanded by Lieutenant General Courtney H. Hodges, breached the Westwall in two places and attacked the city of Aachen, immediately north of the

Hürtgen Forest. After taking Aachen, Hodges planned to attack around the north end of the Hürtgen Forest across the flat, open Rhine plain, toward the city of Cologne. But Hodges also believed that he had to first secure the Hürtgen Forest to avoid dangerously exposing his southern flank.

Although the German army had a reputation as the master of mobile, offensive warfare, it was also tenacious and resourceful in the defense, and the Hürtgen Forest was classic defender's terrain. The Hürtgen Forest was in the sector of the German Seventh Army, commanded by General of Panzer Troops Erich Brandenburger. The higher echelon German Army Group B was commanded by Field Marshal Walter Model, a master defensive tactician.

The Hürtgen Forest campaign started on September 12, when the veteran U.S. 9th Infantry Division attacked the southern end of the forest in an attempt to move through a passage known as the Monschau Corridor. Most of the sector was defended by the thinly stretched German 275th Infantry Division, commanded by Lieutenant General Hans Schmidt. The 9th Infantry Division took the town of Lammersdorf in the south, but it was stopped just short of Germeter in the center of the forest. In late October, the 9th Infantry Division was withdrawn from the line after suffering forty-five hundred casualties. The U.S. 28th Infantry Division replaced it.

The U.S. First Army planned another attack, this time with VII Corps, commanded by Major General J. Lawton Collins. It was to move through the northern passage, called the Stolberg Corridor. As a diversionary effort to draw off German forces, Major Leonard Gerow's V Corps to the south would attack with one division against Schmidt on the far side of the Kall River gorge. The supporting attack was scheduled for November 2, and the main attack was to follow on November 5. However, VII Corps could not get ready in time, and the main attack was postponed—first until November 10, and then until November 16. For some reason, the timing for the supporting attack never changed.

V Corps' 28th Infantry Division launched the attack toward Schmidt, with all three of its infantry regiments attacking in diverging directions, which dissipated rather than concentrated its combat power. As always, the Germans reacted quickly. Ironically, when the U.S. attack started, most of Model's senior commanders were at his headquarters near Cologne—conducting a map exercise based on the scenario of an U.S. attack toward Schmidt. As soon as he learned of the attack, he ordered the exercise to continue, substituting real-world tactical data for the hypothetical exercise data. Model also ordered 116th Panzer Division, commanded by Major General Siegfried von Waldenburg, to start moving toward Schmidt from the north, and 89th Infantry Division, commanded by Lieutenant General Walter Bruns to start moving up from the south. The U.S. 112th Infantry Regiment took Schmidt on November 3. The Germans counterattacked immediately, supported by Pz.Kpfw.V Panther tanks. By November 8, the 28th Infantry Division was pushed back almost to its starting positions, having sustained 6,184 casualties in only seven days of fighting.

The 28th Infantry Division was relieved in the line by the U.S. 8th Infantry Division on November 13. Three days later, the Americans launched the postponed main assault, with three divisions of U.S. VII Corps attacking through the north of the forest. Once again, the Americans ran into a determined and skillful German defense. The attackers suffered heavy casualties in exchange for mere yards of ground. The GIs fought under terrible conditions of snow, rain, mud, cold, and almost impenetrable woods in fierce infantry combat reminiscent of World War I.

The Americans were still trying to punch their way through the Hürtgen Forest and making almost no progress when, on December 16, the Germans launched their Ardennes Offensive to the south. The almost complete tactical and operational surprise the Germans achieved brought the Hürtgen Forest campaign to a halt, as all Allied forces focused on containing the Germans in the Battle of the Bulge.

Most of the German records from that period did not survive, but Germany probably suffered twenty-eight thousand casualties. Nonetheless, the Germans held the vastly better-supplied and better-equipped attackers to a dead standstill for three months, while just a few miles to the south, three German field armies assembled in almost complete secrecy for the Ardennes Offensive. In doing so, the Seventh Army simultaneously had to shift itself far to the south, on the left flank of the Fifth Panzer Army, to become the southern-most of the three attacking armies in the Ardennes Offensive, which started on December 16.

David T. Zabecki

See also: Ardennes Offensive (Battle of the Bulge); Brandenberger, Erich; Model, Walther

Additional Reading

MacDonald, Charles B. *The Battle of the Huertgen Forest.* New York: Jove, 1983.

Miller, Edward G. *A Dark and Bloody Ground: The Hürtgen Forest and the Roer River Dams, 1944–1945.* College Station: Texas A&M University Press, 1995.

I

Infantry Weapons (1933–1945)

Rifles and Carbines

In 1898, the German Army adopted one of the finest military rifles ever invented, the Mauser G98. A bolt-action rifle firing a 7.92 mm bullet out to a maximum effective range of five hundred meters, the G98 had a five-round internal box magazine that was reloaded rapidly from a stripper clip. A trained solder could deliver up to fifteen well-aimed rounds per minute. When later fitted with optical telescopic sights, the G98 could hit man-sized targets out to one thousand meters. The shortened carbine version for cavalry troops was the K98. The G98 was the mainstay of the German Army in both world wars. Modernized and shortened slightly in the 1930s, the K98k (Karabiner 98 kurz) was carried by most German soldiers during World War II.

Semi-automatic and Automatic Weapons

As excellent as the K98k was, the Germans did not have the best infantry rifle of World War II. That was the U.S. M1 Garand, a semi-automatic rifle that used the gas of the fired round to extract and eject the expended shell casing and feed and chamber the next round. The cycle works automatically each time the soldier pulls the trigger, as long as rounds remain in the weapon's magazine. The German Army's first effort to field such a weapon was the Mauser-designed G41. The Walther-designed G43 was a much more successful design. Fed from a detachable ten-round box magazine, the G43 was capable of up to forty-five aimed rounds per minute. The G43, however, arrived too late in the war to have much of an impact.

A fully automatic weapon is one that continues firing as long as the soldier holds the trigger down. Machine guns, which are crew-served weapons, were the first such weapons, introduced in the late nineteenth century. By World War II, there were two basic types of fully automatic individual infantry weapons. Automatic rifles fired standard rifle ammunition and could generally be fired in either automatic or semi-automatic mode. Submachine guns were smaller, fired pistol ammunition, and generally only fired in fully automatic mode. The Germans designated submachine guns *Maschinenpistolen* (Machine Pistols). Introduced during the closing days of World War I, the MP 18 fired the 9 mm Parabellum pistol round. The World War II MP 40, popularly but incorrectly called the "Schmeisser" by the Allies, had a cyclic rate of fire of about five hundred rounds per minute. Firing 9 mm pistol rounds, its maximum effective range was only about 150 meters at best. It was, however, a deadly weapon at close ranges.

The modern assault rifle is a light and compact weapon that fires intermediate-sized rifle ammunition in either automatic or semi-automatic mode. The world's first true assault rifle was Germany's Sturmgewehr 44. Firing a shortened 7.92 mm rifle cartridge, the StG 44 had a cyclic rate of fire equal to the MP 40, but a maximum effective range of 350 meters. After World War II, the Soviets patterned their famous

Infantry Weapons

Weapon Type	Model	Year	Caliber	Weight (pounds)	Effective Range (meters)	Maximum Rate of Fire (rounds per minute)
Bolt-Action Rifle	Mauser G98	1898	7.92 mm	8.8	500	15
Semiautomatic Pistol	Mauser C96	1899	7.63 mm	2.5	50	30
Semiautomatic Pistol	Luger P08	1908	9 mm	1.9	50	32
Light Machine Gun	MG 34	1934	7.92 mm	26.5	1200	900
Bolt-Action Carbine	Mauser K98k	1935	7.92 mm	8.6	450	20
Semiautomatic Pistol	Walther P38	1938	9 mm	2.1	50	32
Submachine Gun	MP 40	1940	9 mm	8.9	150	500
Light Machine Gun	MG 42	1942	7.92 mm	25.5	1250	1200
Antitank Rocket Launcher	*Panzerfaust*	1942	149 mm	11	60	single-shot
Semiautomatic Rifle	Walther G43	1943	7.92 mm	9.5	450	45
Antitank Rocket Launcher	RPzB 43 *Panzerschreck*	1943	88 mm	20.5	150	8
Assault Rifle	StG 44	1944	7.92 mm	11.5	350	500

Kalashnikov AK 47 assault rifle on the German StG 44.

Pistols

The semiautomatic pistol was developed in the late nineteenth century. While semiautomatic rifles almost always use a gas operating system, the lighter weights and smaller sizes of pistols make recoil operating systems more practical. Recoil operating systems are also much simpler and almost never malfunction. Instead of a revolving cylinder, semi-automatic pistols are fed from a box magazine. The German Army's first semi-automatic pistol was the Mauser C96, which could fire up to thirty rounds per minute. Because of its unique shape and its extended wooden grip, the C96 is universally known as the "Broomhandle Mauser" which was still used during World War II.

Accepted by the German Navy in 1904 and by the German Army in 1908, the P-08 was a 9 mm, toggle-locked, recoil-operated, semiautomatic pistol. Designed by Georg Luger in 1898 and produced by Deutsche Waffen und Munitionsfabriken (DWM), the Luger is one of the world's most iconic and instantly recognizable pistol designs. The standard model had a 3.74-inch barrel. Just before World War II, the Wehrmacht adopted the Walther P38 pistol, which was significantly less expensive to manufacture. Although the Luger was supposed to be phased out, it remained in service through 1945.

Machine Guns

The 7.92 mm MG 34 and the improved MG 42 were the best light machine guns of World War II. The MG 42 weighed only 22.5 pounds and had a cyclic rate of fire of twelve hundred rounds per minute. Fired from its bipod, the MG 42 had a maximum effective range of 1,250 meters. When mounted onto a tripod and converted to a heavy machine gun, its effective range increased to twenty-two hundred meters. The MG 42 design greatly influenced the U.S. M 60 machine gun, the U.S. mainstay of the Vietnam War.

Antitank Rocket Launchers

As soon as the tank appeared during in the middle years of World War I, a wide range of antitank weapons evolved to counter it. By World War II, the primary antitank weapons were heavy artillery pieces and other tanks. In 1942, the Germans introduced a shoulder-fired antitank weapon for the infantry. The *Panzerfaust* (Panzer Fist) was a disposable, recoilless rocket launcher that fired an antitank rocket from a 44 mm launch tube. The main body of the rocket fit inside the launch tube, while the oversized 149 mm warhead sat outside the launch tube's muzzle. With an effective range of only about sixty meters, the *Panzerfaust*'s shaped charge warhead could defeat up to 200 mm of armor. The *Panzerfaust* was the forerunner of all modern rocket-propelled grenade (RPG) weapons.

Introduced in 1943, the *Raketenpanzerbüchse* was a German copy of the U.S. Bazooka. Called the *Panzerschreck* (Panzer Terror), the RPzB 43 was reloadable, and it fired a completely internal 88 mm antitank rocket from a 5.4-foot long aluminum launcher. The *Panzerschreck* was capable of defeating up to 200 mm of armor out to ranges of 150 meters.

Hand Grenades

A hand grenade is a small incendiary or explosive device designed to be thrown by an individual soldier. Hand grenades were widely used during the trench-warfare fighting of World War I. By the middle of the war, most grenades were mechanically activated prior to throwing and then detonated by an internal time fuze of five to seven seconds' duration. The two basic types of German hand grenades of World War I were the Model 1917 *Eierhandgranate* (Egg Grenade) and the Model 1915 *Stielhandgrenate* (Stick Grenade). Called the "Potato Masher" by the Allies, the *Stielhandgrenate* became a widely recognized symbol of the German soldier. Updated in 1924, and again in 1943, the World War II versions of the Potato Masher had a 6- to 7-ounce bursting charge of TNT. The overall length, including the wooden handle and explosive head, was fifteen inches.

Infantry Mortars

Called *Minenwerfer* (mine launchers) and used by combat engineers during World War I, mortars were redesignated *Granatenwerfer* (grenade launchers) in the 1930s and reclassified as infantry weapons. Adopted before the start of World War II, the 81 mm GrW 34 had a range of only twenty-three hundred meters and a rate of fire of twelve rounds per minute. The lighter GrW 36 fired a 50 mm round to a range of only five hundred meters. Both mortars had three-man crews. The 120 mm GrW 42 heavy mortar had a range of fifty-nine hundred meters and a rate of fire of eight rounds per minute. It had a six-man crew.

An invading German soldier, part of Operation BARBAROSSA, hurls a *Stielhandgranate* ("Potato Masher") hand grenade, while his comrade covers him with a K98k carbine in Russia, 1941. (National Archives)

Infantry Fighting Vehicles

The Germans pioneered the concept of mechanized or armored infantry. Such units were called Panzergrenadier in the Wehrmacht. Tanks operating without infantry support are very vulnerable. Just prior to World War II, several countries developed armored personnel carriers (APCs) to give infantry units the mobility to keep pace with the tanks and also provide additional firepower and a degree of protection. The standard vehicle of the Wehrmacht Panzergrenadier units was the half-tracked *Sonderkraftfahrzeug* 251 (Special Motor Vehicle 251). The Sd.Kfz. 251 mounted a MG 34 or MG 42 machine gun and carried a ten-man squad and a crew of two. The bed of the vehicle had good side protection, with up to 14.5 mm of armor. The top, however, was open.

David T. Zabecki

See also: Tanks and Self-Propelled Guns

Additional Reading

U.S. War Department. *TM-E 30-451 Handbook on German Military Forces*. Washington, DC: Government Printing Office, 1945. (Reprint Batton Rouge, LA: Louisiana State University, 1990.)

International Military Tribunal: The Nuremberg Trials (October 16, 1945–November 20, 1946)

The Allies were determined to hold German leaders, both civilian and military, accountable for the war and the mass killings that had taken place in German-occupied Europe. Broadly speaking, the Nuremberg proceedings fell into two categories. The first set took place between November 1945 and October 1946 and involved the trial of twenty-four defendants and seven organizations before an International

Military Tribunal (IMT), established by Britain, France, the Soviet Union, and the United States. Subsequently, a series of other trials, known as the American Military Tribunals, were held in the U.S. zone of occupation at Nuremberg until the spring of 1949, involving 185 other defendants. The Nuremberg IMT opened on October 8, 1945. The prosecution presented indictments against twenty-four individuals and seven organizations. The individuals were:

- Martin Bormann, deputy Führer after 1941 (tried in absentia)
- Karl Dönitz, grand admiral and commander of the navy from 1943 to 1945
- Hans Frank, governor-general of Poland
- Wilhelm Frick, minister for internal affairs
- Hans Fritzsche, head of the radio division of the Ministry of Propaganda
- Walther Funk, minister of economic affairs
- Hermann Göring, Reich marshal and commander of the Luftwaffe
- Rudolf Hess, deputy Führer until May 1941
- Alfred Jodl, colonel general and head of the Operations Staff, *Oberkommando der Wehrmacht* (OKW)
- Ernst Kaltenbrunner, head of the Reichssicherheitshauptamt (Reich Main Security Office)
- Wilhelm Keitel, field marshal and chief of staff of OKW
- Gustav Krupp von Bohlen und Halbach, industrialist and head of Krupp armaments
- Robert Ley, head of the Labor Front (he committed suicide on October 26, 1945)
- Konstantin Neurath, Reich protector of Bohemia and Moravia from 1939 to 1943
- Franz von Papen, former vice chancellor and ambassador to Turkey
- Erich Raeder, grand admiral and commander of the navy until 1943
- Joachim von Ribbentrop, foreign minister
- Alfred Rosenberg, minister for the Occupied Territories in the East until 1941
- Fritz Saukel, plenipotentiary for the mobilization of labor
- Hjalmar Schacht, president of the Reichsbank from 1933 to 1939 and minister of economics from 1934 to 1937
- Baldur von Shirach, leader of the Hitler Youth and *Gauleiter* (regional Nazi Party leader) of Vienna
- Arthur Seyss-Inquart, commissioner for the Netherlands from 1940 to 1945
- Albert Speer, minister of armaments from 1942 to 1945
- Julius Streicher, publisher of the newspaper *Der Stürmer*

The indicted organizations were the leadership of the Nazi Party (NSDAP); the Schutzstaffel (SS); the *S*icherheitsdienst (Security Service, SD); the Gestapo (Secret State Police); the Strumabteilungen (SA, the Nazi Party's paramilitary force); the German General Staff; and the Reich Cabinet.

The IMT trial itself lasted 218 days, and some 360 witnesses gave either written or oral testimony. The proceedings at Nuremberg laid bare before the world the horrific crimes committed by the Third Reich. Most revealing were testimonies regarding the brutalities of the death camps. One aspect of the trial that caused debate at the time was the legality of trying military officers. Some suggested it was the role of military officers to carry out orders, but this defense was disallowed at Nuremberg. The prevailing view held that German military leaders had knowingly approved and planned aggressive war and had sanctioned war crimes.

On October 1, 1946, the verdicts were read. Twelve defendants were found guilty and sentenced to death by hanging: Hans Frank, Wilhelm Frick, Hermann Göring, Alfred Jodl, Ernst Kaltenbrunner, Wilhelm Keitel, Robert Ley, Joachim von Ribbentrop, Alfred Rosenberg, Fritz Saukel, Arthur Seyss-Inquart, and Julius Streicher. Göring escaped the hangman's noose by committing suicide with poison smuggled into the prison. Franz von Papen, Hans Fritzsche, and Hjalmar Schacht were the only defendants to be acquitted. Charges against Gustav Krupp von Bohlen und Halbach were dropped on the grounds that he was physically unable to stand trial. The remaining defendants received various terms, ranging up to life in prison: Karl Dönitz (ten years), Walter Funk (life imprisonment), Rudolf Hess (life imprisonment), Konstantin Neurath (fifteen years), Erich Raeder (life imprisonment), Baldur von Schirach (twenty years), and Albert Speer (twenty years). Of those imprisoned, Rudolf Hess lived the longest. He died in Spandau Prison in 1987 at the age of ninety-three. Four of the seven tried organizations were found to be criminal. The acquitted organizations were the Reich Cabinet, the SA, and the General Staff. Former Field Marshal Erich von Manstein was among the most important members of the General Staff's defense team.

Even before the trial ended in 1946, debate began on the validity of the tribunal. Although some have argued that the IMT was merely a case of the victor trying the vanquished, it nonetheless exposed the horrors of the Third Reich, most especially the Holocaust, the use of slave labor, and the heinous war crimes.

Gene Mueller

See also: American Military Tribunals; Dönitz, Karl; Göring, Hermann; Holocaust, German Military Complicity in; Jodl, Alfred; Keitel, Wilhelm; Krupp, Gustav; Raeder, Erich; Speer, Albert

Additional Reading

Davidson, Eugene. *The Trial of the Germans.* London: Macmillan, 1966.

Taylor, Telford. *The Anatomy of the Nuremberg Trials: A Personal Memoir.* New York: Alfred A. Knopf, 1992.

Italy Campaign, Allied (1943–1945)

The German defensive campaign in Italy was one of the most effective economy-of-force operations of World War II. At the American-British Casablanca Conference in January 1943, with a cross-Channel invasion of France no longer an option for that year, British Prime Minister Winston S. Churchill and U.S. President Franklin D. Roosevelt agreed to follow the Axis defeat in North Africa with an invasion of Sicily. Several weeks later, the Americans also agreed to a subsequent invasion of the Italian peninsula.

In a month-long campaign commencing on July 10, 1943, in their largest amphibious assault in the war to date, Allied troops defeated Axis forces in Sicily. Meanwhile, Hitler used the interlude to move another sixteen German divisions to Italy, including the veteran 1st SS Panzer Division from the Soviet Union. After Italy capitulated on September 8, the Germans occupied Rome and the entire country on September 10 and took control of most of the Italian Army. On September 12, 1943, German commandos led by SS *Standartenführer* Otto Skorzeny rescued Mussolini from captivity in the mountains at Grand Sasso in a daring airborne raid. Hitler then installed Mussolini

ITALIAN CAMPAIGN, 1943–1945

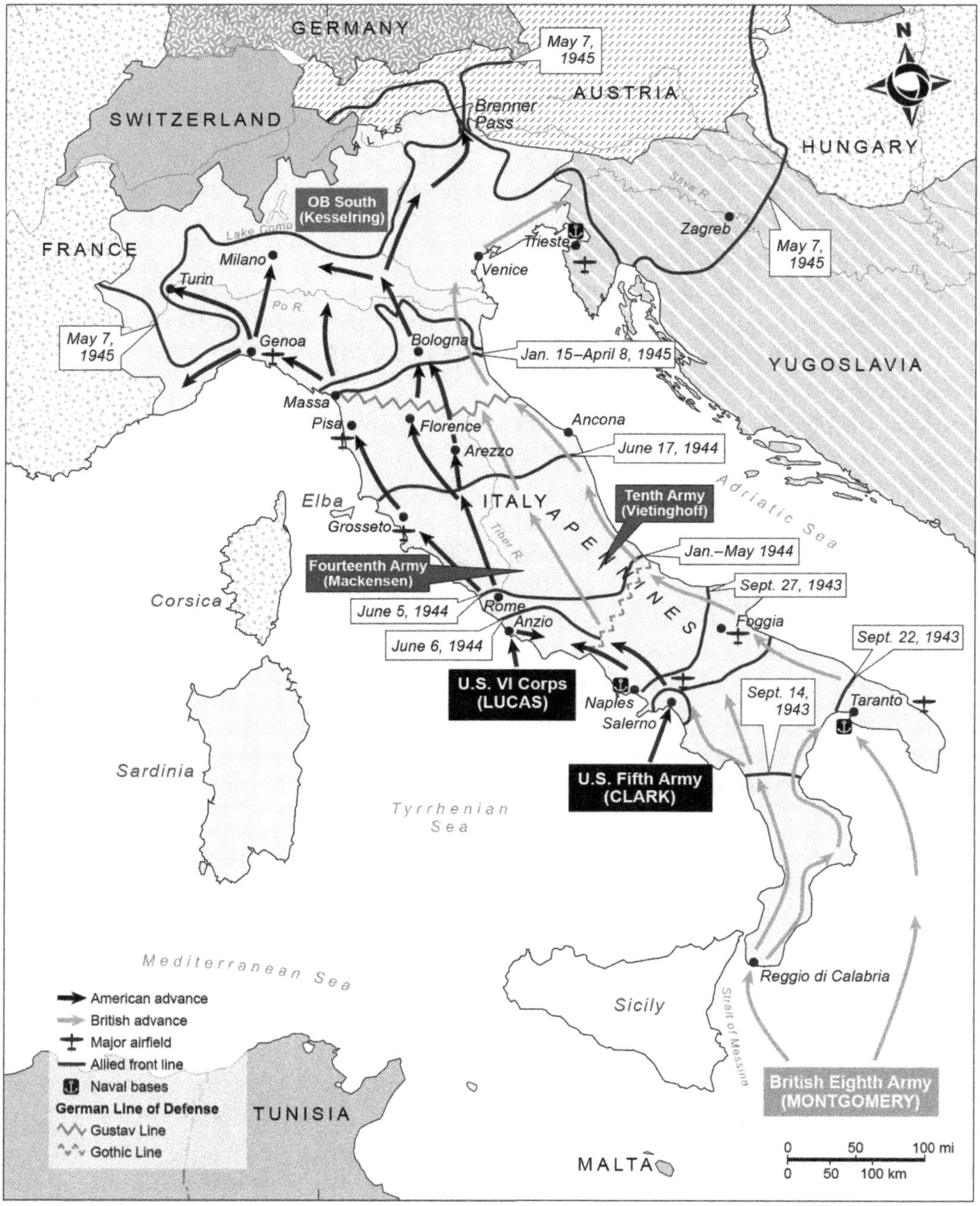

as head of the Italian Social Republic (RSI) in northern Italy.

The initial objective of the British General Sir Harold Alexander's 15th Army Group, was the vital southern port of Naples. In Operation BAYTOWN, General Sir Bernard Montgomery's British Eighth Army attacked across the Straits of Messina from Sicily to Reggio di Calabria on September 3, followed by the British 1st Airborne Division, which landed by sea at Taranto six days later. On September 9, the one hundred and sixty-five thousand troops of the Anglo-U.S. Fifth Army, under Lieutenant General Mark W. Clark, went ashore at Salerno in Operation AVALANCHE, thirty-five miles south of Naples.

German Field Marshal Albert Kesselring formed the six German divisions in the south of Italy into the Tenth Army, under General Heinrich von Vietinghoff, but he had anticipated a landing at Salerno and stationed the 16th Panzer Division in the area. After the Allies secured Salerno on September 15, after a tough fight, Kesselring ordered a fighting withdrawal to the first of the series of mountainous, fortified defensive lines, from which the Germans planned to defend the approaches to Rome. On October 1, the Fifth Army captured Naples, while the Eighth Army advanced up the Adriatic coast and captured the airfields at Foggia. By early October, the two Allied armies formed a continuous, 120-mile line across the peninsula, running along the Volturno and Biferno Rivers. Henceforth, the campaign in Italy became a slow, remorseless, and grinding battle of attrition. Kesselring had fortified a series of defensive lines, known collectively as the Winter Line, between Gaeta and Pescara. The western end based on the Garigliano and Rapido Rivers, known as the Gustav Line, was particularly strong and hinged on the great fortress of the Benedictine abbey at Monte Cassino.

On October 12, the Allies began the Volturno River Campaign, with the objective of seizing the approaches to Rome. Their plan was too ambitious, given the Germans' skill at defending the mountainous terrain. The failed Winter Line Campaign lasted from November 15, 1943 to January 15, 1944. By mid-December 1943, it was clear that the efforts to break through the German defenses were futile. Meanwhile, the Fifth Army was stopped at the Rapido River. One of the key points on the Gustav Line was the town of Cassino on the Rapido. Four successive attacks by Fifth Army failed to make any significant headway. The winter campaign had degenerated into a situation in which two separate Allied field armies were attempting to penetrate the Gustav Line.

Kesselring, who was appointed commander of Army Group C on November 21, now had fifteen (albeit weakened) divisions in the Tenth Army vigorously holding the Gustav Line. On January 22, 1944, in an attempt to unhinge this force, the Allies launched another amphibious landing, Operation SHINGLE, at Anzio, thirty miles south of Rome. The U.S. VI Corps, under Major General John Lucas, achieved complete surprise and safely landed seventy thousand troops within a week, but it failed to exploit the advantage.

Kesselring rapidly improvised eight divisions into the Fourteenth Army, commanded by General Eberhard von Mackensen, whose force counterattacked at Anzio. The beachhead was saved only by the excellent tactical use of intelligence in one of ULTRA's most important triumphs. Major General Lucian K. Truscott replaced Lucas, but for three months, he could do no more than hold the defensive ring.

Meanwhile, Allied forces to the south were unable to break through the Gustav Line. A stalemate persisted until spring.

On January 17, British V Corps launched an attack on the Gustav Line but was forced to call it off within a month, after the badly exhausted troops had advanced just seven miles, at a cost of seventeen thousand casualties. The New Zealand Corps then attempted a direct assault on Monte Cassino, preceded by the questionable bombing by 145 B-17 Flying Fortresses that destroyed the famous monastery. The 1st Parachute Division troops defending the heights were some of the German Army's best. They took up positions in the ruined monastery. A third attack by New Zealand and Indian infantry, using even heavier air and artillery bombardments, also failed. On May 11, the Allies launched Operation DAIDEM, in which General Alexander coordinated the Fifth and Eighth Armies as an army group for the first time. The objective was to destroy the German armies. In an astonishing feat of arms, Polish and Free French troops seized Monte Cassino, and British XIII Corps broke the Gustav Line in a set-piece battle.

Alexander ordered the Anzio breakout on May 23. He planned for the U.S. VI Corps to strike directly inland to encircle the German Tenth Army. Rome would thus be ripe for the taking. However, Clark was enticed by the glory of capturing Rome and altered the direction of his thrust directly toward the city. Fifth Army linked up with VI Corps on May 25 and took Rome on June 4. Clark's change of objective from Alexander's intent enabled most of Kesselring's forces to withdraw to the Pisa-Rimini Line, 150 miles north of Rome. This line was the first of the next series of defense lines across the peninsula that were known collectively as the Gothic Line.

A prolonged Allied tactical air-interdiction program during the autumn and winter of 1944 effectively closed the Brenner Pass and caused an acute German fuel shortage that drastically reduced the mobility of Army Group C in northern Italy. Army Group C was now commanded by Vietinghoff after Kesselring was severely injured in a road accident in October. The Germans still had more than half a million men in the field in Italy. On April 8, after the ground had dried, Alexander launched his spring offensive, with British Eighth Army attacking through the Argenta gap. U.S. Fifth Army struck on April 15, and just ten days later, both Allied armies met at Finale nell'Emilia, after having surrounded and eliminated the last German forces. The Allies then advanced rapidly northward, the Americans entering Milan on April 29, and the British reaching Trieste on May 2. Fifth Army continued to advance into Austria, linking with the U.S. Seventh Army in the Brenner Pass on May 6. German forces in Italy officially surrendered on May 2, 1945, six days before the German surrender in the west. Allied casualties came to 188,746 for Fifth Army and 123,254 for Eighth Army, whereas German casualties were about 434,646 men.

Philip L. Bolté and Paul H. Collier

See also: Anzio, Battle of; Cassino/Rapido River, Battles of; Kesselring, Albert; Mackensen, Eberhard von; Sicily, Allied Invasion of; Vietinghoff genannt Scheel, Heinrich von

Additional Reading

Carver, Michael. *The War in Italy, 1939–1945.* London: Macmillan, 2001.

D'Este, Carlo. *World War II in the Mediterranean, 1942–1945.* Chapel Hill, NC: Algonquin Press, 1990.

J

Jeschonnek, Hans (1899–1943)

Luftwaffe colonel general.

Born in Hohensala, Prussia, on April 9, 1899, Hans Jeschonnek served as a pilot during World War I. In September 1933, he became adjutant to Aviation Minister Erhard Milch and played an important role in the secret building of the Luftwaffe. He was assigned as Luftwaffe chief of operations in 1937, and, in February 1939, he was appointed chief of staff of the Luftwaffe. Jeschonnek was totally dedicated to Hitler and National Socialism. He never questioned policies and took Hitler at his word. Informed by the Führer that he intended to wage a short war, Jeschonnek never prepared the Luftwaffe for a protracted campaign, nor did he mobilize the production assets to ensure an adequate number of replacement aircraft. Made a scapegoat by Göring for the Luftwaffe's failure to stop the Allied bombing of Germany and to supply the Sixth Army at Stalingrad, Jeschonnek committed suicide on August 18, 1943, at Hitler's headquarters at Rastenburg, Germany.

Marlyn R. Pierce

See also: Göring, Hermann; Milch, Erhard

Additional Reading

Murray, Williamson. *Luftwaffe.* Baltimore, MD: Nautical and Aviation Publishing Company, 1985.

Jodl, Alfred (1890–1946)

Wehrmacht colonel general.

Born on May 10, 1890, in Würzburg, Germany, Alfred Jodl served as an artillery officer and a General Staff officer during World War I. Jodl was assigned in 1939 to the newly established Armed Forces High Command, the *Oberkommando der Wehrmacht* (OKW), as chief of the *Wehrmachtführungsamt* (Armed Forces Operations Office), which, in 1939, was renamed the *Wehrmachtführungsstab* (Armed Forces Operations Staff). Despite his position as Adolf Hitler's chief of operations, Jodl had little direct influence on the planning and execution of Germany's military campaigns, a result of Hitler's unwillingness to delegate authority to the OKW. Over time, Jodl became disillusioned with Hitler and the conduct of the war, but he held true to his belief in obedience and duty and remained at his post for the remainder of the war. Brought before the International Military Tribunal at Nuremberg after the war, Jodl was tried as a war criminal for crimes against peace, war crimes, and crimes against humanity. Found guilty on all counts, he was condemned to death and hanged on October 16, 1946.

David M. Toczek

See also: International Military Tribunal: The Nuremberg Trials; *Oberkommando der Wehrmacht* (OKW)

Additional Reading

Megargee, Geoffrey P. *Inside Hitler's High Command*. Lawrence: University of Kansas Press, 2000.

July 1944 Bomb Plot against Hitler. *See* Opposition to Hitler, German Military

K

Kammhuber, Josef (1896–1986)

Luftwaffe general of aviation, Bundesluftwaffe general.

Josef Kammhuber was the architect of the German night defenses against the Royal Air Force (RAF) Bomber Command. Born at Burgkirchen, Germany, on August 19, 1896, Kammhuber served on the western front in World War I. Although he qualified as a pilot in 1919, Kammhuber served mostly in the engineer assignments, until he took command of the clandestine Luftwaffe training facility in the Soviet Union at Lipetsk in 1930. During the 1940 Battle for France, he commanded *Kampfgeschwader* 51 (51st Bomber Wing) and was shot down and taken prisoner. Following his release, Kammhuber was ordered to organize the German aerial night defenses. He developed a highly efficient system that came to be known as the "Kammhuber Line." Following the war, Kammhuber passed on his night-fighting experiences to the U.S. Air Force. In 1956, he was named the inspector of the new *Bundesluftwaffe*, a post he held until his retirement as a full general in 1962. Kammhuber died in Munich, Germany, on January 25, 1986.

Marlyn R. Pierce

See also: Kammhuber Line

Additional Reading

Mitcham, Samuel W. *Eagles of the Third Reich: The Men Who Made the Luftwaffe.* Novato, CA: Presidio, 1997.

Kammhuber Line (1940–1945)

The Kammhuber Line was an initially successful ground-controlled night air-defense and night-fighter interception system created by Luftwaffe Colonel Josef Kammhuber. In July 1940, Kammhuber was placed in command of radar, searchlight and antiaircraft batteries and units linked to night-fighter interceptor squadrons. Until then, these units all operated independently of one another and without any unified or coordinated chain of command. Kammhuber's new integrated system was first deployed in the summer of 1940 from Denmark, through Holland and Belgium to central France, and was later supported by the XII Air Corps (night fighters), which was established in 1941 and commanded by now Lieutenant General Kammhuber. Initially, the system was devastatingly effective. But by 1942, British military intelligence had gathered valuable information on the operation of the German nighttime aerial defense system. During the summer of 1943, RAF and U.S. Army Air Forces bomber streams were attacking German cities as antiradar chaff countermeasures known as "Window" confounded the radar and forced ground-directed night fighters to false coordinates, rendering the Kammhuber Line defenses virtually useless.

Steven B. Rogers

See also: Kammhuber, Josef

Additional Reading

Bekker, Cajus. *The Luftwaffe War Diaries.* New York: Da Capo Press, 1994.

Field Marshal Wilhelm Keitel, chief of the *Oberkommando der Wehrmacht*, signs the instrument of surrender at Soviet Army headquarters in Berlin on May 7, 1945. (National Archives)

Kasserine Pass, Battle of (February 19–24, 1943). *See* North Africa Campaign

Keitel, Wilhelm (1882–1946)

Wehrmacht field marshal.

Born on September 22, 1882 in Helmscherode, Germany, Wilhelm Keitel served as an artillery officer and General Staff officer during World War I. In 1935, he was chosen chief of the Wehrmachtamt (Armed Forces Office). When Adolf Hitler assumed personal command of the Wehrmacht in 1938, Keitel remained with the title of chief of the *Oberkommando der Wehrmacht* (OKW). Keitel maintained his position throughout the war through his personal loyalty to Hitler and not because of his abilities. German commanders consistently bypassed him and OKW. Privately, they called Keitel "*Lakeitel*" (Lackey). On May 8, 1945 in Berlin, Keitel signed the formal instrument of unconditional surrender to Soviet forces. More than for any other act, his involvement in issuing the Commissar Order of 1941 led to his incitement as a war criminal. Tried before the International Military Tribunal at Nuremberg, Keitel pleaded not guilty on the basis of superior orders. Convicted and condemned to death, Keitel was hanged on October 16, 1946.

David M. Toczek

See also: Commissar Order; International Military Tribunal: The Nuremberg Trials; *Oberkommando der Wehrmacht* (OKW)

Additional Reading

Megargee, Geoffrey P. *Inside Hitler's High Command.* Lawrence: University of Kansas Press, 2000.

Kesselring, Albert (1885–1960)

Luftwaffe field marshal.

Born in Marksheft, Bavaria, on November 20, 1885, Albert Kesselring served as an artillery officer and balloon observer during World War I. In 1933, he transferred to the still-clandestine Luftwaffe as chief of administration and military assistant to State Secretary for Air Erhard Milch. Kesselring also learned to fly that year, at the age of forty-eight. In June 1936, following the death of Lieutenant General Walther Wever, Kesselring became the Luftwaffe chief of staff as a lieutenant general. He commanded Luftflotte 1 (First Air Fleet) during the invasion of Poland in September 1939. He then commanded Luftflotte 2 in the invasion of France in May 1940 and during the Battle of Britain later that year. He advised Hitler to concentrate on London in order to bring up the Royal Air Force (RAF), so that it could be destroyed. He also commanded Luftflotte 2 in the invasion of the Soviet Union in June 1941.

In December 1941, Kesselring went to Italy as Wehrmacht commander in chief, south (*Oberbefehlshaber-Süd*), a position he held until March 1945. Kesselring correctly believed that the key to the supply situation in North Africa was control of Malta, and he ardently urged Hitler to take the island by airborne assault. Hitler promised to but changed his mind after Kesselring's difficult subordinate, Field Marshal Erwin Rommel, argued that neutralizing Malta was not necessary. Kesselring showed himself to be one of the war's master defensive tacticians for the conduct of his delaying defense up the boot of Italy during 1944 to 1945.

On March 8, 1945, Kesselring succeeded Field Marshal Karl Gerd von Rundstedt as commander in chief, west (*Oberbefehlshaber-West*). On April 15, Hitler divided the remaining Reich into two defensive zones. Grand Admiral Karl Dönitz took command of the north, and Kesselring received command of the south. Kesselring surrendered his forces to the Western Allies on May 7, 1945. Tried after the war for his role in the Ardeatine Caves Massacre, Kesselring was sentenced to death in 1947, but his sentence was remitted to life in prison. He was released in October 1952 as "an act of clemency," when he developed throat cancer. He died in Bad Nauheim on July 20, 1960.

Spencer C. Tucker and John P. Vanzo

See also: Britain, Battle of; Italy Campaign, Allied; Milch, Erhard; Rommel, Erwin

Additional Reading

Macksey, Kenneth. *Kesselring: German Master Strategist of the Second World War.* Mechanicsburg, PA: Stackpole Books, 1996.

Kharkov, Battles of (1941, 1942, 1943)

Three separate battles were fought over the key Ukrainian city of Kharkov during World War II. Kharkov was an important rail and manufacturing hub, producing aircraft, tanks, and small arms. During

Operation BARBAROSSA, the initial German invasion of the Soviet Union, Kharkov lay in the path of Army Group South's Sixth Army, commanded by Field Marshal Walther von Reichenau. Kharkov was defended by Major General Aleksei Maslov's Thirty-Eighth Army. The Germans took the city between October 20 and 24, 1941.

During the Red Army's Winter Offensive from December 6, 1941 to May 7, 1942, the Ninth and Fifty-Seventh Armies pushed across the Izium River and drove a salient deep into the sector of Colonel General Hermann Hoth's Seventeenth Army, threatening to envelop Kharkov from the south. The second battle of Kharkov started on May 12, when units of Marshal Semyon Timoshenko's Southwest Front tried to break out of the Izium Bridgehead and continue the offensive against the German Sixth Army, now under the command of Colonel General Friedrich Paulus. On May 17, the German First Panzer Army, commanded by Field Marshal Ewald von Kleist, and the Seventeenth Army, commanded by Colonel General Hans von Salmuth, broke into the Soviet southern flank. When the battle ended on May 22, German forces had suffered some twenty thousand casualties and lost thirty-eight aircraft. The Soviets suffered 277,000 total casualties and lost 1,250 tanks, 2,080 artillery pieces, and 540 aircraft.

The third battle of Kharkov was fought between February 19 and March 15, 1943. Following their victory at Stalingrad in early February 1943, the Soviet Voronezh and Southwestern Fronts under Generals Filipp Golikov and Nikolai Vatutin drove to the Donets River in February and recaptured Kursk, Rostov, and Kharkov. Field Marshal Eric von Manstein's Army Group South stuck back at the Soviet flank with an attack from the south by the Fourth Panzer Army, commanded by Hoth, and the First Panzer Army, commanded by Colonel General Eberhard von Mackensen. Army Group South had only 350 operational tanks at that point.

Manstein thrust toward the rear of the Soviet forces west of Kharkov. A five-day battle around the city raged, with the Fourth Panzer Army getting the better of Lieutenant General Pavel S. Rybalko's Third Tank Army. Manstein then attacked north on March 7 and made steady progress, driving a wedge between the Soviet Third Tank and Sixty-Ninth Armies. Kharkov finally fell on March 14 to the SS Panzer Corps, commanded by SS-Obergruppenführer Paul Hauser. The capture of Kharkov marked the end of the German counteroffensive that reestablished the Donets-Mius Line. Total German casualties were approximately eleven thousand, five hundred. The Soviets suffered a total of eighty-six thousand casualties and lost more than twelve hundred tanks and nine hundred artillery pieces. The Soviets finally retook Kharkov on August 23, 1943, following their victory at the battle of Kursk.

Claude R. Sasso and David T. Zabecki

See also: Hausser, Paul; Hoth, Hermann; Kleist, Paul Ewald von; Kursk, Battle of; Mackensen, Eberhard von; Manstein, Erich von; Paulus, Friedrich; Reichenau, Walther von

Additional Reading

Glantz, David M. *Kharkov 1942: Anatomy of a Military Disaster*. New York: Aarpedon, 1998.

Glantz, David M., and Jonathan House. *When Titans Clashed: How the Red Army Stopped Hitler*. Lawrence: University Press of Kansas, 1995.

Kiev Pocket, Battle of (August 23–September 26, 1941). *See* Soviet Union, Invasion of (Operation BARBAROSSA)

Kleist, Paul Ewald von (1881–1954)

Wehrmacht field marshal.

Born at Braunfels an der Lahn, Germany, on August 8, 1881, Paul Ewald von Kleist served on both the eastern and western fronts during World War I. He retired as a lieutenant general in February 1938 during Adolf Hitler's purge of the army. Recalled to active duty in August 1939, Kleist commanded XXII Panzer Corps during the invasion of Poland, and then the army-sized Panzer Group, in the May 1940 invasion of France. During the latter battle, Kleist attempted to relieve General Heinz Guderian of his command of XIX Panzer Corps, after Guderian disobeyed orders to halt his advance toward the English Channel. General Gerd von Rundstedt, the commander of Army Group A, declined to confirm Guderian's relief. Kleist then commanded the First Panzer Group during Operation BARBAROSSA, the invasion of the Soviet Union. By March 1944, Hitler had lost confidence in Kleist and relieved him of command of Army Group South Ukraine. Captured by the Americans at the end of the war, Kleist was turned over to the Soviet Union. He died at Vladimir Prison Camp on October 15, 1954.

Roy B. Perry III

See also: Guderian, Heinz; Soviet Union, Invasion of (Operation BARBAROSSA)

Additional Reading

Mitcham, Samuel W., Jr. "Field Marshal Ewald von Kleist." In *Hitler's Generals*, edited by Corelli Barnett, 249–263. New York: Grove Weidenfeld, 1989.

Kluge, Günther von (1882–1944)

Wehrmacht field marshal.

Born at Posen, Prussia (now Poznan, Poland), into a Junker family on October 30, 1882, Günther von Kluge served on the General Staff in World War I. In 1938, Hitler purged Kluge, along with other German generals, for supporting General Werner von Fritsch, who was retired on trumped-up charges of homosexuality for his opposition to Hitler. With war looming, Hitler needed experienced commanders, and he recalled Kluge from retirement in October 1938. Kluge commanded the Fourth Army during the invasion of Poland in September 1939 and during the invasion of France in May 1940. From December 1941 to October 1943, Kluge commanded Army Group Center in the Soviet Union. In July 1944, he replaced Field Marshal Karl Gerd von Rundstedt as commander in chief, west, and simultaneously commanded Army Group B in Normandy. Kluge commanded the German counterattack at Avranches in August, but, on its failure, he was relieved of command on August 17, 1944 and replaced by Field Marshal Walther Model. Under suspicion for his marginal association with the assassination plot against Hitler, Kluge committed suicide at Valmy, France, on August 19, 1944.

Spencer C. Tucker

See also: Avranches Counteroffensive; Blomberg-Fritsch Crisis; Fritsch, Werner von; Model, Walther; Opposition to Hitler, German Military; Rundstedt, Karl Rudolf Gerd von

Additional Reading

Lamb, Richard. "Field-Marshal Günther von Kluge." In *Hitler's Generals*, edited by Correlli Barnett, 395–409. New York: Grove Weidenfeld, 1989.

Kondor Legion (1936–1938)

German Luftwaffe unit that fought on the Nationalist side in the Spanish Civil War.

The Kondor (Condor) Legion was instrumental in the eventual Nationalist victory over the Republicans. It also served as a laboratory for the tactics, technology, and organization that the Luftwaffe would use in World War II.

The beginning of the Spanish Civil War in July 1936 caught the Nationalist side unprepared, with many of its troops stationed in Spanish Morocco, and the Republican side controlling the sea via the Spanish Navy. The Nationalists sought German support, and, on July 26, 1936, Hitler began to provide clandestine military aid by airlifting troops to Spain from North Africa. In October 1936, Hitler decided to increase the Luftwaffe presence in Spain, resulting in the official formation of the Kondor Legion. A total of nineteen thousand men and three hundred to four hundred planes served in the Legion over the course of the war.

The Legion operated the most advanced German aircraft as they became available, including the Heinkel He 111 bomber and the Messerschmitt Bf 109 fighter. The Legion also field-tested new aircraft, such as the first Junkers Ju 87 Stuka dive bomber, and it experimented with new combat techniques. The Legion became notorious in 1937 for its bombing of the Basque city of Guernica. Some of the Luftwaffe's leading fighter aces, such as Adolf Galland, received their baptism of fire with the Legion. The Luftwaffe adopted much of the Legion's organization and tactics for World War II.

Jeffrey W. Stamp

See also: Galland, Adolf; Luftwaffe (German Air Force); Spanish Civil War

Additional Reading

Ries, Karl, and Hans Ring. *The Legion Kondor.* Translated by David Johnston. West Chester, PA: Schiffer Publishing, 1992.

Krebs, Hans (1898–1945)

Wehrmacht general of infantry.

Born in Helmstedt, Germany, on March 4, 1898, Krebs served as a regimental adjutant during World War I. He was an assistant military attaché in Moscow in 1933 and 1934, and again in 1939. He was the chief of staff of Army Group Center under Field Marshal Günther von Kluge in March 1943, and of Army Group B under Field Marshal Walther Model in September 1944. In March 1945, Hitler assigned Krebs to succeed Colonel General Heinz Guderian as German army chief of staff, following the latter's dismissal. With Hitler's suicide on April 30, 1945, Krebs's final duty was to act as the liaison with the Soviets for the surrender of the Berlin garrison. When the Soviets demanded an unconditional surrender, Krebs presumably committed suicide in Hitler's Bunker in Berlin on May 1 or 2, 1945. His body was never found.

Jon D. Berlin

See also: Berlin, Land Battle for; Guderian, Heinz; Kluge, Günther von; Model, Walther

Additional Reading

Brett-Smith, Richard. *Hitler's Generals.* San Rafael, CA: Presidio, 1977.

Kretschmer, Otto (1912–1998)

Kriegsmarine frigate captain, Bundesmarine flotilla admiral.

Otto Kretschmer was the most successful German U-Boat commander of World War II. Born at Liegnitz, Germany on May 1, 1912,

Kretschmer joined the German Navy in April 1930 and assumed command of the *U–23* in September 1937. In April 1940, he assumed command of the *U–99*, a Type VII U-boat. He began the first of eight patrols into the Atlantic in June 1940 and became the first German submarine commander to sink two hundred and fifty thousand tons of Allied shipping. From September 1939 to March 1941, he sank forty-seven merchant ships, totaling 273,503 tons, earning the Knight's Cross of the Iron Cross with Oak Leaves and Swords. On March 17, 1941, he successfully attacked the ten-ship HX-112 convoy south of Iceland. After expending his torpedoes, he was returning to base in France, when two British destroyers attacked and sank his boat. He and forty of his forty-three-man crew were rescued. Kretschmer spent the remainder of the war as a prisoner of war in Canada. In 1955, he joined the postwar navy of the Federal Republic of Germany, the *Bundesmarine.* He retired in 1970 with the rank of flotilla admiral. Kretschmer died at Straubing, Germany, on August 5, 1998.

C. J. Horn

See also: Atlantic, Battle of the

Additional Reading

Blair, Clay. *Hitler's U-Boat War.* Vol. 1, *The Hunters, 1939–1942.* New York: Random House, 1996.

Kriegsakademie (War Academy) (1810–1945)

The Kriegsakademie (War Academy) was the principal institution for training German General Staff officers. In 1810, Prussian military reformer David Gerhard von Scharnhorst established the Allgemeine Kriegsschule (General War School) to train staff officers for the Prussian Army. In 1859, it was renamed the Kriegsakademie. Following World War I, Article 160 of the Treaty of Versailles abolished the German General Staff and, by implication, the Kriegsakademie. Although the postwar Reichswehr was limited to a total officer corps of only four thousand, General Hans von Seeckt clandestinely reinstituted a three-year general staff-officer training course, starting with about seventy officers and producing between eight and ten General Staff officers at the end of each course. After Hitler came to power and repudiated the Treaty of Versailles and its restrictions, General Ludwig Beck formally reestablished the German Army General Staff and reopened the Kriegsakademie in 1935. Due to the rapid expansion of the Wehrmacht and the increased needs for trained General Staff officers, the size of the yearly classes increased, and the length of the course of instruction decreased progressively through 1945.

After the reestablishment of the German Army in 1956, the successor to the Kriegsakademie was established as the Führungsakademie (Leadership Academy) of the Federal Republic of Germany's Bundeswehr. Although the modern Führungsakademie is structured and organized to train General Staff officers for the army of a Western democracy, the tactical and operational methods and the staff procedures taught are the direct descendents of those taught at the Kriegsakademie during the first half of the twentieth century.

David T. Zabecki

See also: Beck, Ludwig; German General Staff of World War II; Seeckt, Hans von

Additional Reading

Muth, Jörg. *Command Culture: Officer Education in the U.S. Army and the German Armed Forces, 1901–1940, and the*

Table 1: Naval Order of Battle 1932, 1935, 1938, and 1939

Ship Type	Reichsmarine October 1, 1932	Kriegsmarine August 1935	Kriegsmarine August 1, 1938	Kriegsmarine August 31, 1939
Battleships	0	0	0	0*
Battle Cruisers	0	0	1	2
Armored Ships	0	2	3	3
Coastal Battleships	3	2	2	2
Heavy Cruisers	0	0	0	0*
Light Cruisers	3	4	5	5
Destroyers	0	0	10	21
Torpedo Boats	16	17	14	12
Schnellboote	4	6	12	22
Minesweepers	8	12	18	22
U-Boats	0	3	22	55

Notes: Numbers refer only to ships in commission. Does not include units under construction or undergoing sea trials.
***Battleships:** *Bismarck* did not start sea trails until January 1940. *Tirpitz* followed six months later. Both battleships were commissioned in 1941.
***Heavy Cruisers:** Germany had two heavy cruisers undergoing sea trials or precommission training at war's start (*Blücher* and *Hipper*).
Ship Types: The German Navy used some ship designations that were unique to Germany. The **"Pocket Battleships"** were designated as "armored ships" *Admiral Scheer* was commissioned in January 1936
The **Predreadnought Battleships** were designated as coastal battleships. They were to be decommissioned by 1944, but wartime exigencies led to their remaining in service.
Torpedo Boats were a uniquely German designation for small destroyers that sacrificed gun armament to carry two banks of torpedoes.
***Schnellboote*:** Patrol torpedo boats employed in a fashion similar to U.S. PT boats.
U-Boats *(Unterseeboote):* Submarines. Nine were undergoing sea trials in August 1935 and were commissioned by year's end. Six were undergoing sea trials in August 1939 and were fully operational by October 1939.

Consequences for World War II. Denton: University of North Texas Press, 2011.

Zabecki, David T., ed. *Chief of Staff: The Principal Officers Behind History's Great Commanders.* 2 vols. Annapolis, MD: U.S. Naval Institute Press, 2008.

Kriegsmarine (German Navy) (1935–1945)

Germany officially renamed its navy from Reichsmarine to Kriegsmarine in the spring of 1935, when Hitler abrogated the Treaty of Versailles, and he signed the Anglo-German Naval Agreement that authorized a German surface fleet that was 37 percent the size of Britain's and a submarine fleet that was 45 percent its size. With his dreams of recreating the High Seas Fleet of World War I dashed by that agreement, Admiral Erich Raeder chose to pursue a two-pole strategy, based on a fleet with a component that protected Germany's coastal waters and regional trade and one that conducted operations against enemy commerce (*Handelskrieg*) on the world's most distant oceans.

Table 2: Admiral Raeder's Z-Plan of January 1939

Ship Type	Class or Type	1940	1941	1942	1943	1944	1945	1946	1947	1948
Battleships	**H-Class**	0	0	0	2	6	6	6	6	6
Battleships	**Bismarck**	1	2	2	2	2	2	2	2	2
Battle Cruiser	**Scharnhorst**	2	2	2	2	2	2	2	2	2
Battle Cruisers	**Type O**	0	0	0	3	3	3	3	3	3
Armored Ships	**Type P**	0	0	0	3	3	8	8	10	10
Armored Ships	**Deutschland**	3	3	3	3	3	3	3	3	3
Aircraft Carriers	**Graf Zeppelin**	1	1	1	2	2	2	2	2	4
Aircraft Carriers	**Type B**	0	1	1	1	1	1	2	2	4
Heavy Cruisers	**Hipper**	2	2	2	2	2	2	2	2	2
Heavy Cruisers	**Prinz Eugen**	1	3	3	3	3	3	3	3	3
Light Cruisers	**M-Class**	0	0	3	3	4	4	4	4	4
Light Cruisers	**Improved M-Class**	0	0	0	0	1	1	4	8	12
Scout Cruisers	**S-Class**	0	0	2	3	5	6	9	12	15
Destroyers	**1934 and Later**	36	41	44	47	50	53	56	58	58*
Torpedo Boats	**1937 and Later**	18	27	35	44	54	64	74	78	78*
U-Boats	**All Classes**	84	111	130	161	194	229	240	241*	241*

Notes: Table contains number of units planned to be in commission during that year.

The H-Type Battleship was intended to be the centerpiece of the German raiding squadrons.

Type O Battlecruisers and Type P Armored Ships: Essentially expanded variants of the original classes of this type. More powerful and, in the case of the former, had greater range.

Scout Cruisers: A ship designation unique to the Kriegsmarine in World War II but used to describe unarmored cruisers built during the nineteenth century's final decade. In the Kriegsmariene, it refers to a class of unarmored light cruisers intended to scout ahead of the raiding group. Its main battery was concentrated aft, suggesting it was intended to withdraw in the face of armed opposition.

*These numbers incorporate the planned decommissioning of old and obsolete units.

But while Raeder saw battleship-centric surface battle groups as the primary striking arm, Germany's submarine commander, Captain (later Grand Admiral) Karl Dönitz saw massed U-boats in that role. Fortunately for the Allies, Raeder's battleship-centric view of naval operations precluded the Kriegsmarine from making the most of its expertise, research, and development in U-boats until Dönitz replaced Raeder on January 30, 1943.

Nonbelligerence with Britain marked official policy, so Raeder's planners focused on two enemies, France and Russia. Initial plans called for powerful heavy cruisers and destroyers, supported by air power, to block French entry into the North Sea and contain Soviet naval power in the Baltic. Battle cruisers and battleships, of which there were two of each under construction in 1935 and 1937, were to prey on French shipping in the Atlantic, supported by long-range destroyers, an aircraft carrier, and U-boats. In Raeder's concept, the U-boats and aircraft carriers were to play strictly supporting roles, driving the enemy to concentrate their shipping in convoys, where they could be attacked more efficiently.

Believing he had until 1943 to 1944 to build his fleet, Raeder thought he could convince Hitler to build a major force of super battleships, but he settled for a fleet that adhered to the Anglo-German Naval Agreement's limitations until 1943. Events quickly overcame Raeder's plans. Hitler's aggressive foreign policy incited Britain and France to rearm. Raeder initially saw the latter as an opportunity. His Plan Z, introduced in January 1939, was intended as a vital first step toward matching British naval power, but economic realities forced imposed serious constraints.

The start of the war in September 1939 caught the Kriegsmarine ill-prepared. Only twenty-six of its fifty-seven U-boats were capable of operations beyond the North Sea. Mine and torpedo stocks were incomplete, and the construction program was less than 20 percent complete. The battleships *Bismarck* and *Tirpitz* were not yet completed. Thus, Raeder had to deploy his long-range warships and U-boats to operate independently, while Hitler urged him to complete as many warships as possible. In response, Raeder gave first priority to the two battleships under construction, followed by U-boats and destroyers.

To expand the Kriegsmarine's access to the Atlantic, Raeder convinced Hitler to invade Demark and Norway. The resulting campaign cost the Kriegsmarine more than a third of its destroyers and the heavy cruiser *Blücher* and light cruiser *Königsberg* in the battle off Narvik. Raeder lamented the losses, but felt the expanded access to the Atlantic almost made them acceptable. Attacking the Allies' maritime sea-lanes became the Kriegsmarine's primary focus for the remainder of the war. The U-boats constituted the most successful component of that effort, sinking 14,687,321 Gross Registered Tons of Allied shipping before war's end. The greatest U-Boat successes came in the first six months of 1942 with Operation PAUKENSCHLAG (DRUMBEAT) off the U.S. Atlantic Coast. They also achieved significant success up to May 1943, as snorkels, radar, acoustic countermeasures equipment, and new guided torpedoes improved U-boat capabilities, but losses grew more rapidly than successes that year, finally forcing the U-boats to withdraw from Atlantic operations that summer. The surface fleet's contribution to *Handelskrieg* diminished more rapidly. The *Bismarck*'s sinking on May 27, 1941 all but ended the surface fleet's participation in *Handelskrieg*, particularly after the 1942 "Channel Dash," which saw the last of the major combatants withdraw to German home waters before redeploying to Norway, where they served primarily as a fleet-in-being.

When Dönitz replaced Raeder as navy commander on January 30, 1943, He immediately launched investigations into the security of Kriegsmarine communications and means of improving U-boat capabilities, both actions that Raeder had blocked or limited. But Dönitz's efforts came too late to affect the war. In one final irony, the Kriegsmarine conducted more than a dozen amphibious operations despite Admiral Raeder's aversion to working with the army. The Kriegsmarine had no doctrine for such operations, conducting all of them almost as ad hoc affairs. The Kriegsmarine planning for Operation SEELÖWE (SEA LION), the abortive assault on Great Britain, was desultory at best. The planning intended to support the assault on Crete was a dismal and costly failure. Nonetheless, the Kriegsmarine successfully evacuated German troops from Sicily in 1943 and the Aegean Islands in 1944, despite Allied naval superiority. More importantly, the

Kriegsmarine successfully conducted history's largest-ever maritime operation, evacuating more than 2,043,000 civilian and military personnel from the Baltic states and East Prussia during the war's final months.

The Kriegsmarine's record in the war remains controversial. It was never as apolitical as Raeder tried to present it during the postwar era, but neither was it the Nazi war machine depicted by Allied propaganda during the war. Its losses were heavy, with more than 95 percent of all U-boat personnel being captured or killed during the war. On the other hand, the Kriegsmarine never consumed more than 15 percent of Germany's wartime resources, yet tied down Allied forces far in excess of its strength. Viewed in the context of an economy-of-force operation, the Kriegsmarine was a costly but painful success.

Carl O. Schuster

See also: Anglo-German Naval Agreement; *Bismarck*, Sortie and Sinking of; Channel Dash; Crete, German Invasion of; Dönitz, Karl; DRUMBEAT, U-Boat Operation; Norway Campaign; Plan Z; Raeder, Erich; SEELÖWE (SEA LION), Operation; Submarines; Warships, Surface

Additional Reading

Mallmann-Showell, Jak P. *The German Navy in World War Two: A Reference Guide to the Kriegsmarine 1935–1945*. Annapolis, MD: U.S. Naval Institute Press, 1979.

Ruge, Friedrich. *Der Seekrieg: The German Navy's Story 1939–1945*. Annapolis, MD: U.S. Naval Institute Press, 1957.

Krupp, Alfried Felix (1907–1967)

Industrialist and arms manufacturer.

Alfried Felix Krupp was born near Essen, Germany on August 13, 1907. His mother was Bertha Krupp, and his father was Gustav von Bohlen und Halbach, who added the Krupp name after he married Alfried's mother. The Krupp *Aktiengesellschaft* (AG) company had been founded in 1810 by Friedrich Krupp and was expanded by his son, Alfred Krupp, who came to be known as the "Cannon King." Although Alfried Krupp did not join the full National Socialist party until 1938, he joined a supporting branch of the Schutzstaffel (SS) as early as 1931. During World War II, he served in the paramilitary National Socialist Flying Corps (Nationalsozialistisches Fliegerkorps), reaching the rank of *NSFK-Standartenfüher* (colonel). In 1943, Hitler appointed Krupp as minister of the war economy. At about the same time, Krupp took over the chairmanship of the company from his ailing father. By that point, the company's factories employed one hundred and sixty thousand workers, including slave laborers who were prisoners. Krupp's dedication to keeping his factories productive, even as procuring supplies became more difficult, unquestionably contributed to the efficacy of Hitler's huge war machine.

When World War II ended in 1945, Alfried Krupp and ten other company directors were arrested and tried by an American Military Tribunal on charges of plundering Nazi-occupied territory and employing slave labor in inhumane, concentration-camp-like conditions. During what became known as the Krupp Trial, the prosecution argued that Krupp had not only used slave labor but also actively sought concentration camp prisoners as laborers, even building new factories in close proximity to the Marlestadt and Auschwitz camps. The Krupp firm reportedly used as many as fifteen thousand foreign workers and twenty thousand prisoners of war, maintaining them under horrid conditions. Krupp was convicted in 1947 and sentenced to twelve years in prison. In 1951, however, his sentence was reduced to the six years he had already served, and he was released. When Krupp died on July 30, 1967 in Essen, he was a prosperous businessman, and his family's company was strong and geared toward producing for West Germany's robust peacetime economy.

Ilisa Horowitz

See also: American Military Tribunals; Krupp, Gustav

Additional Reading

Manchester, William. *The Arms of Krupp: The Rise and Fall of the Industrial Dynasty that Armed Germany at War.* New York: Back Bay Books, 2003.

Krupp, Gustav (1870–1950)

Industrialist and arms manufacturer.

Gustav von Bohlen und Halbach was born in The Hague on August 7, 1870. In 1906, he married Bertha Krupp, the elder daughter of Friedrich Alfred Krupp. After the death of her father in 1902, she had become the owner of the company. After their marriage, Bohlen und Halbach was granted the right by royal Prussian decree to bear the name Krupp as a prefix to his own family surname. He was the chairman of the board of Friedrich Krupp AG from 1909 to the end of 1943.

Following World War I, the Treaty of Versailles prohibited the company from producing armaments, but, nonetheless, it secretly continued artillery production through subsidiaries in the Netherlands and Sweden. In the early 1930s, Krupp AG started the manufacture of tanks and submarines. As chairman of the Association of German Industrialists, Krupp played a major role in encouraging other business leaders to contribute to the Nazi Party's coffers. Hitler later appointed him as the Economics Ministry's chief administrator of mines, with responsibility for the production of coal and iron.

After the outbreak of war, Krupp AG built factories in German-occupied countries and used the labor of over one hundred thousand concentration camps inmates. At the end of 1943, Krupp resigned as chairman of the supervisory board of Friedrich Krupp AG, whereupon he was succeeded by his oldest son Alfried. In 1945, Gustav Krupp was indicted by the International Military Tribunal in Nuremberg. He was never brought to trial because of his health, but he remained technically under indictment for the remainder of his life. Gustav Krupp died in Blühnbach, Austria, on January 16, 1950.

Peter Overlack

See also: International Military Tribunal: The Nuremberg Trials; Krupp, Alfried Felix

Additional Reading

Manchester, William. *The Arms of Krupp: The Rise and Fall of the Industrial Dynasty that Armed Germany at War.* New York: Back Bay Books, 2003.

Küchler, Georg von (1881–1968)

Wehrmacht field marshal.

Born near Hanau, Germany, on May 30, 1881, Georg von Küchler served in World War I as an artillery officer and a General Staff officer. During the German invasion of Poland, Küchler commanded the Third Army. Although seen as a favorite of Adolf Hitler, Küchler defied Schutzstaffel (SS) leader Heinrich Himmler and ordered the courts-martial of German soldiers guilty of committing atrocities against Poles. Küchler commanded the Eighteenth Army during the invasion of France in May 1940, and during Operation BARBAROSSA, the invasion of the Soviet Union in 1941. In January 1942, Küchler took command of Army Group North. When the Soviets launched their great counteroffensive at Leningrad on January 28, 1944, Küchler was forced to withdraw to the Luga River. Hitler made him the scapegoat for the reverse and sacked him. After the war, Küchler was tried at the American Military Tribunals and convicted of war crimes for his involvement in enforcing the Commissar Order. Freed in February 1955, he died in Garmisch-Partenkirchen, Germany, on May 25, 1968.

Spencer C. Tucker

See also: American Military Tribunals; Leningrad, Siege of

Additional Reading

Mitcham, Samuel W., Jr. *Hitler's Field Marshals and Their Battles.* Chelsea, MI: Scarborough House, 1990.

Kursk, Battle of (July 5–August 23, 1943)

The battle of Kursk was the largest tank engagement to that point in history. The 1942 to 1943 winter campaign had left a 120-mile-wide bulge around Kursk, an important rail junction north of Belgorod and Kharkov. By early May 1943, German plans to blast the Soviets from Kursk solidified into Operation ZITADELLE (CITADEL). The plan was to reduce the salient with two panzer-led pincer attacks from the northern and southern shoulders. From the north, near Orel, Field Marshal Günther von Kluge's Army Group Center would launch General Walther Model's Ninth Army, led by two panzer corps. The main thrust would come from the south by Field Marshal Eric von Manstein's Army Group South, with Colonel General Hermann Hoth's Fourth Panzer Army moving north from near Belgorod. Hitler, however, kept delaying the execution to allow his troops to build up their forces of the newly developed heavy Pz.Kpfw.V Panther and Pz.Kpfw.VI Tiger tanks.

Marshal Georgy Zhukov convinced Stalin that within the Kursk salient, the defenses of the central front, under General Konstantin Rokossovsky, and General Nikolai Vatutin's Voronezh Front would be able to absorb the initial German blows. Then General I. S. Konev's Steppe Front could counterattack from the rear. The Germans massed nine hundred thousand men in fifty divisions, of which nineteen were panzer and panzergrenadier, with twenty-seven hundred tanks and assault guns, ten thousand artillery pieces, and two thousand aircraft. The Soviets assembled 1.3 million men, 3,600 tanks, 20,000 artillery pieces, and 2,400 aircraft.

The German attack started on July 5. In the north, the Ninth Army assaulted on a narrow, thirty-mile front but managed to penetrate only six or seven miles in seven days of fierce fighting. The Fourth Panzer Army in the south did only slightly better. The critical stage came between July 11 and 12, when Hoth turned his panzer spearhead northwest to envelope the Soviet First Tank Army. As Hoth's four hundred tanks reached Prokhorovka Station, Zhukov counterattacked with five tank armies. This engagement was a cauldron embroiling more than twelve hundred tanks from both sides (three-quarters of them Soviet).

At that point, Hitler, on July 13, called off the offensive in order to withdraw panzer forces to reinforce units in Sicily, where the

BATTLE OF KURSK, JULY–AUGUST 1943

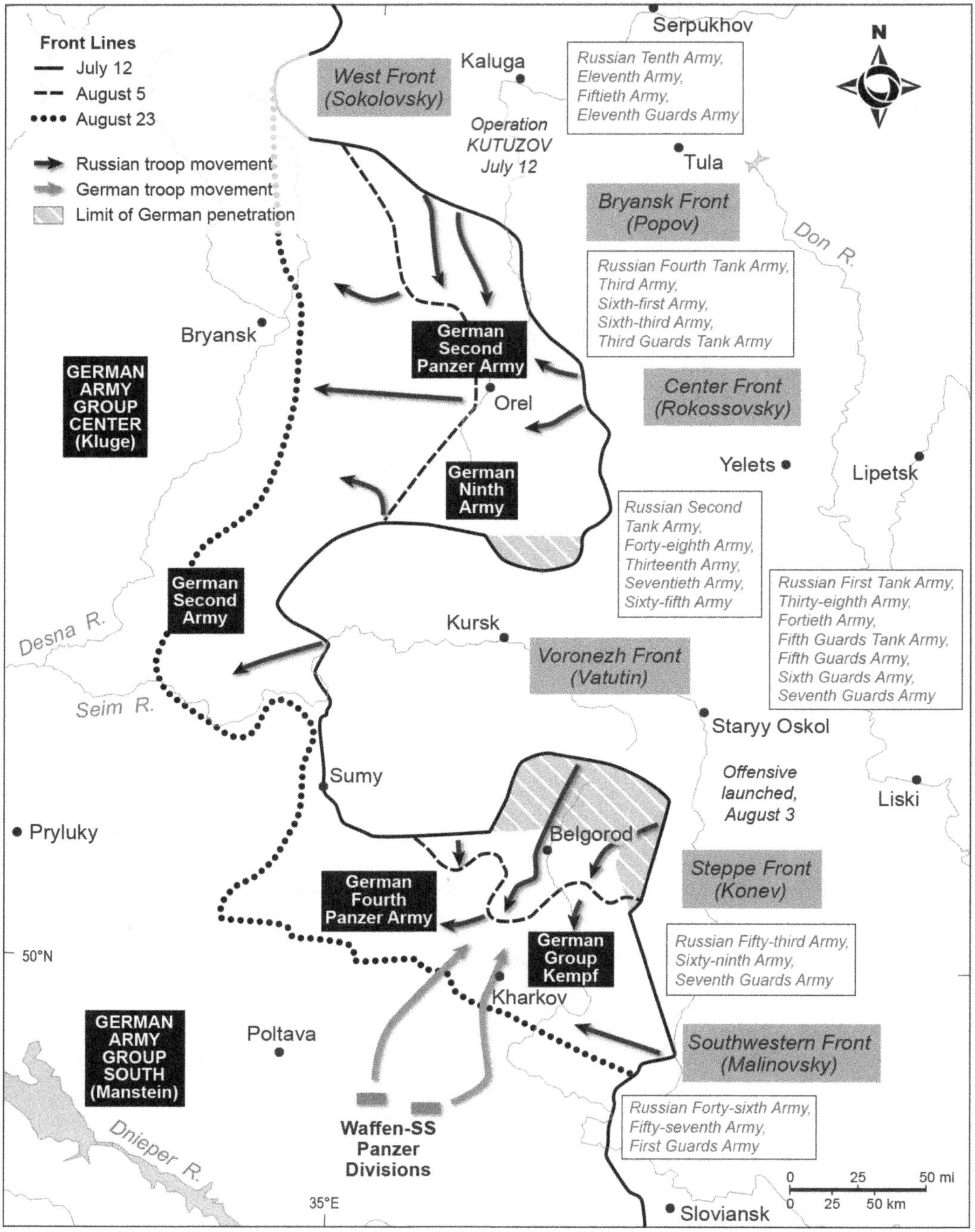

Allies had landed three days earlier. The German commanders had no choice but to conduct a fighting retreat in the face of a Soviet counteroffensive that began on July 12. By the time the battle ended on August 23, the Red Army had lost more than 1,040,000 casualties and 7,500 tanks and assault guns. The Germans suffered somewhere around five hundred thousand casualties and lost an estimated twenty-nine hundred tanks and assault guns. The battle marked the end of German dominance on the eastern front.

Arthur T. Frame

Additional Reading

Glantz, David M., and Jonathan M. House. *When Titans Clashed: How the Red Army Stopped Hitler.* Lawrence: University Press of Kansas, 1995.

Newton, Stephen H. *Kursk: The German View.* Cambridge, MA: Westview Press, 2003.

L

Laconia Order (September 17, 1942)

The Laconia Order was issued in the aftermath of the attack on U-boats by a U.S. B-24 Liberator operating out of Ascension Island. Having sunk the troopship *Laconia* on September 12, 1942, the *U-156* commanded by Captain Lieutenant Erich Hartenstein started to rescue survivors that included Italian POWs and civilians, until it was attacked from the air. In the aftermath of the attack, the order was given to abandon the survivors, who were picked up by Vichy French ships. There were only 1,120 survivors out of 2,700 on the *Laconia*. Dönitz had been in a dilemma over the operation: should he save civilian lives or concentrate on strategic operations in the South Atlantic? In response to the attack, he issued the so-called Laconia Order, which stated:

> No attempt of any kind must be made at rescuing members of ships sunk. . . .Rescue runs counter to the most primitive demands of warfare for the destruction of enemy ships and crews.

The Laconia order was the basis of the charges against Dönitz on Count Three, crimes against the laws of war, at the International Military Tribunal at Nuremburg after the war. One of Dönitz's defenders was U.S. Navy Admiral Chester Nimitz, who testified that the U.S. had used similar tactics in the Pacific. Dönitz was found guilty of Count Three at Nuremburg and sentenced to ten years' imprisonment.

Ross Mahoney

See also: Dönitz, Karl; International Military Tribunal: The Nuremberg Trials

Additional Reading

Duffy, James. *The Sinking of the Laconia and the U-Boat War: Disaster in the Mid-Atlantic*. Greenwood, CT: Praeger, 2009.

Landwehr (1813–1945)

German militia and reserve, intended to augment the regular army in times of war.

First organized in March 1813 when Prussian King Friedrich Wilhelm III decreed universal military service and called upon Prussia to defeat Napoleonic France, the Landwehr originated as a result of the military reforms following the defeats of 1806 to 1807. In 1819, the Landwehr was formally incorporated into the regular army, transforming it from a militia parallel to the regular army into a second-line reserve. After service in the regular army, recruits were then transferred to the Landwehr. Following defeat in World War I, the manpower of the German military was severely restricted by the Treaty of Versailles, and the Landwehr was disbanded. During the rearmament under Adolf Hitler in the 1930s, the Landwehr was revived. Following the German defeat in World War II in 1945, the Landwehr was permanently disbanded.

Stephen T. Satkiewicz

See also: Wehrmacht (German Armed Forces)

Additional Reading

Simpson, Keith. *History of the German Army.* Greenwich, CT: Bison Books Corp., 1985.

Langsdorff, Hans Wilhelm (1890–1939)

Reichsmarine captain.

Born March 20, 1890 in Bergen, Germany, Hans Wilhelm Langsdorff served in the Kaiserlichen Marine during World War I and fought at the 1916 Battle of Jutland. In November 1938, he assumed command of the *Panzerschiff* (pocket battleship) *Admiral Graf Spee.* On the outbreak of World War II, Langsdorff and his ship were already at sea, with orders to operate against Allied commerce in the South Atlantic and Indian Oceans. He sunk ten merchant ships for a total of fifty thousand tons by December. In response, the British dispatched a number of ships to intercept the *Admiral Graf Spee* off South America. The Battle of the River Plate on December 13, 1939 resulted in damage to the *Graf Spee.* Langsdorff took refuge in the port city of Montevideo, Uruguay being a neutral country. Believing that a greatly superior British force was waiting for him outside the harbor, Langsdorff ordered his ship out of port and scuttled her at the mouth of the River Plate. Langsdorff then took a hotel room ashore and, on December 20, 1939, shot himself.

Nicholas W. Barcheski

See also: Plate River, Battle of

Additional Reading

Gilbey, Joseph. *Langsdorff of the* Graf Spee*: Prince of Honor.* Hillsburgh, ON: J. Gilbey, 1999.

Leeb, Wilhelm Ritter von (1876–1956)

Wehrmacht field marshal.

Born in Landsberg-am-Lech, Bavaria, on September 5, 1876, Wilhelm von Leeb served as an artillery officer during the 1900 Boxer Rebellion and as a General Staff officer during World War I. An internationally recognized expert on defensive warfare, Leeb published the book *Die Abwehr* (*The Defense*) in 1938. The Soviets incorporated many of the principles he espoused in his various prewar publications into their 1936 field regulations. Ironically, Leeb indirectly contributed to the Soviet tactics and operational art that cost the Germans so heavily in World War II. Leeb stressed that in any new war, Germany initially should maintain the strategic defensive, force the numerically superior enemy to attack, and reduce his forces through attritional warfare, only then going over to offensive operations centered on armor.

Leeb was not fooled by Adolf Hitler, who branded him an "incorrigible anti-Nazi." He retired in 1938 in the wake of the Blomberg-Fritsch Crisis but was almost immediately recalled to active duty during the crisis over Czechoslovakia. After the occupation of the Sudetenland, Leeb again retired but was again recalled to active duty to command Army Group C to defend against a possible Allied attack in the west, while the Wehrmacht invaded Poland. Army Group C played only a minor role in the 1940 campaign for France, but Leeb's feints against the French Maginot Line were so successful that the French held many units there until it was too late to commit them to meet the main German thrust to the north.

Leeb commanded Army Group North in the invasion of the Soviet Union. Frustrated with Hitler's micromanagement of the forces in the field, Leeb asked to be relieved of his command on January 16, 1942 and retired for a third time. At the end of the war, he was tried and sentenced to three years of imprisonment as a minor war criminal, a severe sentence given his military record. Leeb died in Hohenschwangau in Bavaria on April 29, 1956.

Carl O. Schuster and Spencer C. Tucker

See also: Blomberg-Fritsch Crisis; Saarland, French Invasion of the

Additional Reading

Barnett, Correlli, ed. *Hitler's Generals.* New York: Grove Weidenfeld, 1989.

Leningrad, Siege of (July 10, 1941–January 27, 1944)

The battle for Leningrad was the longest and most devastating siege of a major urban center in the history of modern warfare. The Germans invaded the Soviet Union on June 22, 1941. The capture of Leningrad was one of the major strategic goals of Operation BARBAROSSA. Field Marshal Wilhelm von Leeb commanded Army Group North, consisting of the Fourth Panzer Group, commanded by General Erich Hoepner; the Eighteenth Army, commanded by Colonel General Georg von Küchler; and the Sixteenth Army, commanded by Colonel General Ernst Busch. Army Group North advanced northeast toward the city. Leeb believed that his troops would soon take the city in cooperation with the Finns, who had reentered the war against the Soviet Union. Finnish forces, meanwhile, drove south, both to the east and the west of Lake Ladoga, toward the Svir River and Leningrad.

On July 8, the German Fourth Panzer Group reached the old fortress of Shlisselburg east of Leningrad, guarding the point at which the Neva River flows out of nearby Lake Ladoga. The siege of the city officially began on July 10. Leeb's hopes for a quick victory were dashed, however, when the Finns merely reoccupied the territory taken by the Soviets during the 1939–1940 Finnish-Soviet War, thus halting some twenty-six miles north of Leningrad. The refusal of the Finns to push beyond the Svir or their pre-1940 borders was a major factor in the city's survival. Leeb also lost much of his Fourth Panzer Group, which Hitler diverted to the drive on Moscow.

Hitler ordered Leningrad to be obliterated through artillery fire, air attack, and blockade; moreover, he prohibited any acceptance of surrender. In mid-October, he ordered Leeb to make a wide sweep of some 150 miles around Lake Ladoga to link up with the Finns on the Svir River. On November 8, the Germans took the vital rail center of Tikhvin, about halfway to the Svir. Soviet leader Josef Stalin then shifted major reinforcements north, and, in mid-December, Hitler authorized Leeb to withdraw. Soviet troops reoccupied Tikhvin on December 18. By November, rations in the city had been cut to the starvation level. Lake Ladoga was the only means of accessing the rest of the Soviet Union. In winter, trucks were able to travel on a "road" across the ice, and, in summer, some boats got through. But this route was insufficient to keep the city supplied.

Hitler's plans for the summer 1942 campaign called for the destruction of Leningrad and the occupation of the area between Lake Ladoga and the Baltic in order to free up the Finns for operations against Murmansk. Field Marshal Eric von Manstein, sent with elements of his Eleventh Army to Leningrad by Hitler, attacked in September, cutting off two Soviet armies but failing to take Leningrad.

On January 14, 1944, the Soviets struck the German positions, with their forces outnumbering the Germans by a ratio of two-to-one in men and four-to-one in tanks and aircraft. Hitler refused to authorize a withdrawal, and bitter fighting ensued. Ultimately, the Soviets drove the Germans back. On January 27, 1944, with the Leningrad-to-Moscow railroad line reopened, Stalin declared the "nine-hundred-day" blockade at an end. The Germans and Finns sustained more than two hundred thousand combined casualties trying to take Leningrad. Red Army casualties totaled more the a million killed, and some 2.4 million wounded and sick.

Eva-Maria Stolberg and Spencer C. Tucker

See also: Busch, Ernst; Hoepner, Erich; Küchler, Georg von; Leeb, Wilhelm Ritter von; Manstein, Erich von

Additional Reading

Glantz, David. *The Siege of Leningrad 1941–44: 900 Days of Terror.* Osceola, WI: Zenith Press, 2001.

Salisbury, Harrison. *The 900 Days: The Siege of Leningrad.* New York: Harper and Row, 1969.

Lidice Massacre (June 9–10, 1942)

On June 4, 1942, SS-Obergruppenführer Reinhard Heydrich, chief of the German Sicherheitsdienst (SD) and acting *Reichsprotektor* (administrator) of Bohemia and Moravia, died of wounds suffered when his car was attacked with grenades in Prague on May 27, 1942. The attack was carried out by two agents of the London-based Czech government-in-exile, Jan Kubis and Jozef Gabcik. German reprisals for the attack on Heydrich were swift and deadly. Ultimately, the Germans raided five thousand towns and villages; in the process, some 3,180 persons were arrested, and 1,344 were sentenced to death. The mining village of Lidice near Kladno, eleven miles northwest of Prague, was chosen for a conspicuous reprisal. The German operation against Lidice was carried out on June 9 to 10 by Wehrmacht field police and SD personnel, led by SS-Hauptsturmführer Max Rostock. The execution squads killed 198 men and 71 women; 184 Lidice women were transported to Ravensbrück concentration camp; and 98 children in the village were transported to a camp at Gneisenau. The village of Lidice itself was burned to the ground. The site was then dynamited and bulldozed, and the ground was sowed with grain.

Charles R. Schrader

See also: Holocaust, German Military Complicity in

Additional Reading

Bradley, J. F. N. *Lidice: Sacrificial Village.* New York: Ballantine Books, 1972.

List, Siegmund Wilhelm Walter (1880–1971)

Wehrmacht field marshal.

Born on May 14, 1880 in Oberkirch, Germany, Siegmund List served in World War I as a General Staff officer. Although he was anti-Nazi, List failed to speak out against Adolf Hitler's dishonorable treatment of Generals Werner von Blomberg and Werner von Fritsch and thereby avoided the generals' purge of 1938. List commanded the Fourteenth Army during the 1939 invasion of Poland and the Twelfth Army during the 1940 invasion of France. After serving in the Balkans, List assumed command of

Army Group A in the Soviet Union in July 1942. Hitler removed him from command that September, after he failed to take the oil fields of Baku, Tiflis, and Batum. In February 1948, List was tried at Nuremberg on war crime charges, found guilty, and sentenced to life in prison. He was released in December 1952. List died in Garmish, Germany, on August 17, 1971.

M. David Yaman

See also: American Military Tribunals; Blomberg-Fritsch Crisis; Caucasus Campaign

Additional Reading

Mitcham, Samuel. *Hitler's Field Marshals and Their Battles.* London: Cooper, 1988.

Löhr, Alexander (1885–1947)

Luftwaffe colonel general.

Born at Turnu-Severin (in today's Romania) on May 20, 1885, Alexander Löhr served in the Austro-Hungarian air service during World War I. After Germany's annexation of Austria in March 1938, Löhr joined the Luftwaffe. In 1939, he commanded Luftflotte 4 (Fourth Air Fleet) during the invasion of Poland. In 1941, Löhr was assigned a similar mission against Yugoslavia. On the morning of April 6, 1941, without a declaration of war, Löhr's bombers attacked Belgrade. They destroyed the Yugoslav command structure, but also killed fifteen hundred civilians. Löhr was overall commander of the bloody German airborne assault of Crete, beginning on May 20, 1941. After the invasion of the Soviet Union on June 22, 1941, he commanded Luftflotte 4 in the southern part of the front. In July 1942, Adolf Hitler appointed him to command Twelfth Army in the Balkans (renamed Army Group E in January 1943). A prisoner of war of the Yugoslav government from May 11, 1945, Löhr was tried for war crimes by a Yugoslav military court, sentenced to death, and executed in Belgrade on February 26, 1947.

Martin Moll

See also: Crete, German Invasion of

Additional Reading

Orlow, Dietrich. *The Nazis in the Balkans. A Case Study of Totalitarian Politics.* Pittsburgh, PA: University of Pittsburgh Press, 1968.

Lorraine Campaign, Allied (September 1–December 18, 1944)

The Lorraine Campaign is the name given by U.S. Army historians to the operations of Lieutenant General George S. Patton's U.S. Third Army against German Army Group G, initially commanded by Colonel General Johannes Blaskowitz, and then by General of Panzer Troops Hermann Balck. At the start of the campaign, General of Infantry Kurt von der Chevallerie's First Army was deployed in the northern sector around Metz. General of Panzer Troops Hasso von Manteuffel's Fifth Panzer Army was deployed in the center, east of Nancy, until Fifth Pander Army was deployed north to the Luxembourg area to participate in the Ardennes Offensive. General of Infantry Friedrich Weise's Nineteenth Army was deployed in the south, west of Colmar, and facing the U.S. Seventh Army.

The Lorraine campaign in the fall of 1944 followed the successful Allied breakout from the Normandy beachhead and the rapid pursuit of the retreating German forces across France to the Meuse River between July and September 1944. After a brief pause at the Meuse to allow their supply lines to catch up, the Allies resumed their advance to the Rhine River in early September. The main effort was an attack through Belgium and Holland, toward the Rhine and the Ruhr industrial area by Field Marshal Sir Bernard Law Montgomery's British-Canadian 21st Army Group, supported to the south by the U. S. First Army of Lieutenant General Omar Bradley's 12th Army Group. Patton's U.S. Third Army, also a part of 12th Army Group, was assigned the mission of conducting a secondary offensive through Lorraine and across the Moselle River to occupy the Westwall sector covering the Saar, and then to seize Frankfurt. In 1944, two high-speed highways led from Lorraine into Germany: the first from Metz via Saarbrücken to Mannheim, and the second from Nancy through the Saverne gap in the Vosges Mountains to Strasbourg.

At the start of the campaign, Patton's Third Army had only two available corps, and his combat power was limited by the fact that his forces were at the far end of a fragile logistical line. Priority for logistical support had been assigned to Montgomery's 21st Army Group, and the French ports had not yet been fully cleared. Moreover, the U.S. Army was already beginning to run short of infantry replacements.

German forces were in even worse shape, having been badly battered on the eastern front and in Normandy. The principal German units facing Third Army were the First Army's LXXXII Corps, under General of Infantry Walter Hoernslein, and Fifth Panzer Army's XLVII Panzer Corps, under Lieutenant General Heinrich von Lüttwitz. Many of the German combat units were seriously understrength in both men and horses, their primary means of mobility. Many of the German defenders were in newly formed *Volksgrenadier* divisions, manned by poorly equipped troops of low quality. Although German lines of communications were shorter, Allied air interdiction made it difficult to move men and supplies to the front. On September 6, General of Panzer Troops Otto von Knobelsdorff replaced Chevallerie as the commander of First Army.

The campaign opened in early September with limited success. On September 13, the Americans conducted a double envelopment around Arracourt, twenty miles beyond the Moselle, and forced the German First Army to evacuate the city of Nancy on September 14. A German counterattack from the south, designed to destroy Third Army before it could link up with the Allied 6th Army Group advancing from southern France, failed. On September 20, Balck replaced Blaskowitz as commander of Army Group G. On September 22, Supreme Allied Commander General Dwight D. Eisenhower reaffirmed the logistical priority of Montgomery's 21st Army Group and ordered Patton to restrict his offensive operations. Despite serious shortages of gasoline and other supplies, the always aggressive Patton continued local attacks during October, the most important of which was a vain effort to capture Fort Driant on the west bank of the Moselle, facing Metz. The October pause was also costly for the Germans. Balck had to transfer two divisions and several of his higher headquarters, including that of the Fifth Panzer Army, north for the planned Ardennes Offensive. This situation left the German First Army with approximately eighty-seven thousand men and 130 tanks to oppose the two hundred and fifty thousand men and seven hundred tanks of Third Army.

The Allied logistical situation improved at the end of October. U.S. XX Corps finally took Metz through a double envelopment between November 8 and 19. The U.S. XII Corps attacks east of Nancy, however, did not go as smoothly. The slow advance of U.S. Third Army in November was mainly the result of poor weather and a lack of mass: its nine understrength divisions were spread along a sixty-two-mile front. Nevertheless, by December 2, the Third Army had reached the Westwall along the Upper Saar. Under cover of fog, a U.S. battalion crossed the river on the morning of December 3 and seized the bridge at Saarlautern intact. But just as Patton's infantry began to make progress, the German Sixth Panzer Army, Fifth Panzer Army, and Seventh Army launched the Ardennes counteroffensive, just north of Patton's sector.

Balck's mission had been one of economy of force, to fix Patton's Third Army and buy time for the German forces to the north to deploy into position for the Ardennes Offensive. Balck, however, ran afoul of SS chief Heinrich Himmler, and, on December 24, he was relieved of his command and transferred to the eastern front. He was replaced at Army Group G by his predecessor, Blaskowitz. During the Lorraine Campaign, U.S. Third Army sustained a total of 55,182 casualties. Exact German casualty figures are unknown, but they were at least as high. Third Army also took some seventy-five thousand German prisoners.

Charles R. Schrader and
David T. Zabecki

See also: Ardennes Offensive (Battle of the Bulge); Balck, Hermann; Blaskowitz, Johannes Albrecht; Manteuffel, Hasso Eccard von; Metz, Battle of

Additional Reading

Balck, Hermann. *Ordnung im Chaos: Erinnerungen, 1983–1948.* Osnabrück, Germany: Biblio Verlag, 1981.

Cole, Hugh M. *The United States Army in World War II: The European Theater of Operations—The Lorraine Campaign.* Washington, DC: Historical Division, U.S. Army, 1950.

Loyalty Oath to Hitler (August 2, 1934)

For the Prussian Officer Corps, taking an oath expressed a physical identity, and to break an oath was unthinkable for most of them. With the death of the Reich president and supreme commander, Field Marshal Paul von Hindenburg, Hitler had the offices of Reich president and Reich chancellor combined, and he was now to be addressed as Führer and Reich chancellor. Hitler also made himself the supreme commander of the armed forces on August 1, 1934. In anticipation of Hindenburg's death, Generals Werner von Blomberg and Walther von Reichenau rewrote the military oath of allegiance and assembled the armed forces on August 2, 1934 to take the new oath: "I swear by God this holy oath, that I want to offer unconditional obedience to the Führer of the German Reich, and people, Adolf Hitler, the commander in chief of the Wehrmacht, and be prepared as a brave soldier to risk my life for this oath at any time." The oath was made into law on August 20, 1934. From that day forward, "Herr Hitler" was now addressed "Mein Führer" by the military.

Raymond D. Limbach

See also: Blomberg, Werner von; Hindenburg, Paul von; Reichenau, Walther von

Additional Reading

Cooper, Matthew. *The German Army 1933–1945: Its Political and Military Failure.* London: Macdonald and Jane's, 1978.

Ludendorff, Erich (1865–1937)

Kaiserheer general of infantry.

Born on April 9, 1865 in Kruszczewina, Prussia, Erich Ludendorff was the most significant German military officer of World War I. As first quartermaster general (vice chief of staff) to Field Marshal Paul von Hindenburg from 1916 to almost the end of the war, the two formed the "Silent Dictatorship" that controlled almost every aspect of German political, economic, and military life. Ludendorff's postwar career tarnished whatever military reputation he had. Fearing Allied revenge, he fled temporarily to Sweden. He wrote his memoirs, blaming Germany's defeat on his foes and their lack of will. He railed at the new German republic and his new enemies, the Jews, Jesuits, Freemasons, and Communists, whom he blamed for "stabbing Germany in the back." He became the darling of the extreme right, marching with Adolf Hitler during the November 1923 Beer Hall Putsch. His views and demons grew more extreme, and he fell to bickering with Hitler and even his former wartime comrades. Successively, he publicly broke relations with each of them. In 1935, he published *The Total War*, arguing exactly the opposite of Clausewitz's famous dictum that war was an extension of politics. Ludendorff died on December 22, 1937 in Tutzing, Bavaria, two years after declining Hitler's offer of promotion to field marshal on the occasion of his seventieth birthday.

Michael B. Barrett and David T. Zabecki

See also: Hindenburg, Paul von; Stab-in-the-Back Legend (*Dolchstosslegende*)

Additional Reading

Brownell, Will, and Denise Drace-Brownell. *The First Nazi: Erich Ludendorff, the Man Who Made Hitler Possible.* Berkeley, CA: Counterpoint, 2016.

Luftwaffe (German Air Force) (1935–1945)

The air force of the Third Reich, the Luftwaffe, was the world's most powerful air force in 1939, with more than thirty-six hundred frontline aircraft. The Luftwaffe, however, was basically a tactical force, and it came apart under the strain of the German invasion of the Soviet Union. The Treaty of Versailles after World War I had denied Germany an air force, but in the 1920s, the Germans established clandestine air facilities in, ironically, the Soviet Union to build and test aircraft and train personnel. In 1935, Hitler openly began building an air force. He selected Hermann Göring, a World War I fighter ace, as minister of aviation and commander in chief of the Luftwaffe.

As with so many other agencies in the Reich, the Luftwaffe suffered from organizational weaknesses and overlap at the top. Göring was Hitler's designated successor, and the Führer allowed him to run the Luftwaffe without any interference. The Reich Air Ministry consisted of the office of state secretary for air Erhard Milch; it supervised aviation matters apart from operations. Milch was also general inspector of the Luftwaffe. The Luftwaffe chief of staff was General Hans Jeschonnek, who, until his suicide in 1943, was in charge of the organization, operations, intelligence, training, quartermaster, and signal branches. Milch and Jeschonnek did not get along. Jeschonnek only had access to Göring on operational matters and had no control over personnel, which Göring made his own province. Ernst Udet, chief of the Technical

Office and a World War I ace, proved an incompetent administrator. Udet reported to Milch, who took over Udet's office after the latter's 1941 suicide. Too late, in May 1944, the administrative structure was streamlined with the establishment of the *Oberkommando der Luftwaffe* (Air Force High Command, OKL). Also, in 1944, Albert Speer's Armaments Ministry gained control of all German aircraft production, and Milch's ministry was abolished.

The Luftwaffe controlled all air services but had little interest in naval aviation. Airborne troops were Luftwaffe personnel, and the air force also controlled antiaircraft artillery. Eventually, the Luftwaffe even fielded twenty-two ground divisions, including the Hermann Göring Panzer Division. The Luftwaffe itself was organized into seven *Luftflotten* (air fleets), constituted to execute a variety of roles and consisting of a wide variety of aircraft types. The next operational echelon was the *Fleigerkorps* (aviation corps), and below that was the *Fleigerdivision* (aviation division). These last two each consisted of several *Geschwader* (wings) that were organized by aircraft type—bombers, day fighters, night fighters, transports, and so forth. Each division controlled three to four *Gruppen* (groups) consisting of three or four *Staffeln* (squadrons). In September 1939, the Luftwaffe operated 302 *Staffeln.*

The Luftwaffe, essentially, was organized and equipped to support ground combat operations. The Luftwaffe's limitations first became evident during the Battle of Britain, when Göring attempted to wage a strategic bombing campaign with a tactical air force. Germany's defeat in that battle was its first setback of the war. The Luftwaffe was also impressive in the early fighting against the Soviet, but, by the fall of 1941, Germany was overextended, and the

Luftwaffe guard beside a Ju 87 Stuka dive bomber, ca. 1941. (Library of Congress)

Luftwaffe's small airlift capacity of Junkers Ju 52 trimotor transports was unable to fulfill all the missions required. Although Germany increased its aircraft production during the war, as the conflict continued and under relentless Allied bombing, it suffered from lack of aviation fuel. This was the key factor in the defeat of the Luftwaffe, rather than inferior or too few aircraft.

By 1944, the Luftwaffe was feeling the effects of the Operation POINTBLANK, the Allied Combined Bomber Offensive. During the first half of that year, pilot losses were averaging 20 percent a month, and the scarcity of fuel forced the routine grounding of aircraft, not only for operations but also for training. By the time of the Allies' June 1944 Normandy invasion, the much-vaunted Luftwaffe had been largely neutralized.

Pamela Feltus and Spencer C. Tucker

See also: Aircraft, Military; Britain, Battle of; Combined Bomber Offensive, Allied (Operation POINTBLANK); Göring, Hermann; Jeschonnek, Hans; Milch, Erhard; Speer, Albert; Udet, Ernst

Additional Reading

Corum, James S. *The Luftwaffe: Creating the Operational Air War, 1918–1940.* Lawrence: University Press of Kansas, 1997.

Murray, Williamson. *Luftwaffe.* Mount Pleasant, SC: Nautical and Aviation Publishing Company, 1985.

Lütjens, Günther (1889–1941)

Kriegsmarine admiral.

Born in Wiesbaden, Germany, on May 25, 1889, Günther Lütjens served on torpedo boats during World War I. At the start of World War II, German Navy commander, Grand Admiral Erich Raeder, was determined to send battleships into the North Atlantic to prove their value as surface raiders. In May 1941, he took the gamble of deploying the new battleship *Bismarck*, when only the new heavy cruiser *Prinz Eugen* was available as an escort. Lütjens, the commander of the task force, objected to Raeder's "piecemeal approach" to battleship operations, recommending waiting until the other battleships were ready for action.

Lütjens's halfhearted leadership and pessimism, along with his rigid adherence to his orders to avoid risks, hindered his ability to analyze objectively either his options or his opportunities. He declined to exploit his victory over the British battle cruiser HMS *Hood* and finish off the battleship HMS *Prince of Wales.* Influenced by his belief that the British were employing new radar, he gave his position away by radioing for instructions from Berlin, and he failed to recognize that he had actually eluded his pursuers. His decision to steam directly for Saint-Nazaire instead of withdrawing to a more remote area or even returning to Norway exposed the *Bismarck* to the British Force H from Gibraltar and the carrier HMS *Ark Royal.* Following damage by a lucky torpedo strike that jammed the *Bismarck*'s twin rudders, Lütjens resigned himself to carrying out Raeder's instructions to fight "to the last shell." He died when the *Bismarck* went down on May 27, 1941.

Keith W. Bird

See also: *Bismarck*, Sortie and Sinking of; Raeder, Erich

Additional Reading

Bercuson, David J., and Holger H. Herwig. *The Destruction of the* Bismarck. Woodstock, NY and New York: Overlook Press, 2001.

M

Mackensen, Eberhard von (1889–1969)

Wehrmacht colonel general.

Eberhard von Mackensen was born in Bromberg (in today's Poland) on September 24, 1889 into a distinguished military family. His father was Field Marshal August von Mackensen. The younger Mackensen served as a cavalry officer during World War I. During the invasion of France in May 1940, he was the chief of staff of the Twelfth Army. In Russia, Mackensen commanded the III Panzer Corps, and then the First Panzer Army. In November 1943, Mackensen assumed command of the Fourteenth Army in Italy. His forces opposed the Allied landing at Anzio on January 22, 1944 and contained the Allies there for several months. Hitler ultimately blamed Mackensen for the loss of Rome and relieved him of command in June 1944. Following the war, Mackensen was tried for his complicity in the Ardeatine Caves Massacre and was sentenced to death on November 30, 1945. The sentence later was commuted to life imprisonment. He was released from prison in October 1952. Mackensen died in Altmühlendorf, Germany, on May 19, 1969.

Jon D. Berlin

See also: Italy Campaign, Allied

Additional Reading

Brett-Smith, Richard. *Hitler's Generals.* San Rafael, CA: Presidio, 1977.

Malmédy Massacre (December 17, 1944)

The Malmédy Massacre was an incident involving the murder of unarmed U.S. POWs during the German Ardennes Offensive (Battle of the Bulge). During that offensive, the I SS Panzer Corps had the task of breaking through Allied lines in the Monschau-Losheim sector and advancing to the Meuse. The 1st SS Panzer Division was on the left wing of the corps, and SS-Obersturmbannführer Joachim Peiper commanded the division's spearhead, known as *Kampfgruppe* Peiper.

On December 17, the second day of the offensive, the 1st SS Panzer Division broke through the Allied lines between the Belgian towns of Malmédy and Saint Vith. At the village of Baugnez, Peiper's unit encountered a small group of trucks and jeeps belonging to Battery B, 285th Field Artillery Observation Battalion. In the ensuing fight, some twenty U.S. soldiers were killed, and Peiper's force took 125 prisoners. Peiper left behind some troops to guard the prisoners before moving on to his next objective. A few hours later, another 1st SS Panzer Division column arrived at Baugnez, adding some additional prisoners.

The Germans herded the Americans into a snowy field, where they were held under guard. Meanwhile, another group of separated Americans, who had previously escaped from the Germans, moved toward the crossroads, and a firefight broke out, in which more Americans were killed. This engagement led the guards in the field to fire on their prisoners, perhaps believing they would try to escape. The Germans then moved among the wounded, executing them with bullets to their heads. Most of those shot were unarmed. At least seventy-two men were killed, although some thirty others feigned death and later escaped to U.S. lines.

In May 1946, Peiper and seventy-three members of the 1st SS Panzer Division, a number of them selected randomly, were brought to trial by a U.S. military court for the Malmédy killings and the murder of soldiers and civilians elsewhere during the offensive. The court convicted all the defendants. Peiper and forty-two others were sentenced to death, and the rest were given lengthy prison sentences. Questions about the trial results were raised almost immediately, and review boards cited errors in the court's procedural rulings. The army reduced the death sentences to long prison terms, but ultimately, all the defendants, including Peiper, were released from prison within a few years.

Terry Shoptaugh

See also: Ardennes Offensive (Battle of the Bulge); Peiper, Joachim; Waffen-SS

Additional Reading

Bauserman, John M. *The Malmédy Massacre.* Shippensburg, PA: White Mane Press, 1995.

Malta Air and Naval Campaign (June 11, 1940–December 31, 1942)

The Axis air and naval campaign against Malta began on June 11, 1940 when Italian aircraft attacked the Mediterranean island.

MEDITERRANEAN MARITIME BATTLES, 1940–1943

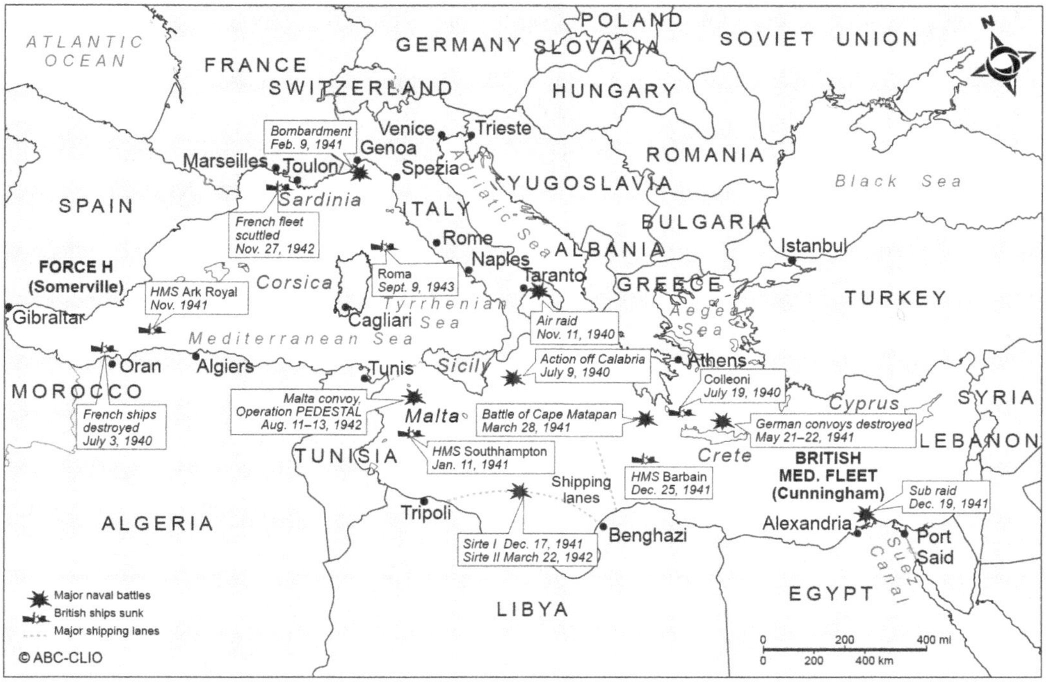

German Junkers Ju 88 bombers attacking the port of Vallette, while overhead a defending British Spitfire fighter dogfights with an escorting Italian Macchi MC-202 fighter during the Battle of Malta, June 11, 1940–December 31, 1942. (Roger Viollet Collection/Getty Images)

Over the course of the next thirty-one months, Malta became one of the most heavily bombed areas of World War II. Malta's position in the central Mediterranean made it strategically vital to both Britain and the Axis powers, as it sat astride the sea lines of communication to North Africa.

Between June and December 1940, the Italian Regia Aeronautica attempted to subdue the island in preparation for an invasion. After the Italians failed, the Luftwaffe deployed the *Fliegerkorps X* to Sicily to subdue Malta and clear the sea lines of communications. The Germans quickly established air superiority, and British convoys to the island suffered heavy losses. During February and March, the Luftwaffe conducted 112 raids against Malta. Later in 1941, when the Germans launched the invasion of the Soviet Union, Operation BARBAROSSA, the air offensive against Malta slackened because of the number of Luftwaffe units redeployed to the east.

In December 1941, the Luftwaffe resumed the offensive with *Fliegerkorps* II. Field Marshal Albert Kesselring, *Oberbefehlshaber Süd* (OB-Süd), ordered the neutralization of the island in coordination with the German Navy. In February 1942, the Luftwaffe flew 2,299 sorties against Malta. With Malta continuing to sit astride of and threaten the Axis' line of communications to North Africa, Germany and Italy again started planning the invasion of Malta. Designated Operation HERKULES, the plan was based on a simultaneous operation against the North African port of Tobruk and Malta, with the island to be seized by coup de main by *Fallschrimjagerkorps XI*, commanded by General Kurt Student. However, Hitler's concerns about airborne operations, following the near disaster on Crete and coordination problems with the Italian commando supreme, led to the operation's indefinite postponement.

In August 1942, Allied convoy PEDESTAL was attacked by a combined force of 505 Luftwaffe fighters and bombers, but enough of the convoy managed to get through to deliver fifty-three thousand tons of supplies. The arrival in Malta of RAF Air Vice-Marshal Sir Keith Park on July 14, 1942 was an important turning point. Park introduced a forward interception plan that attacked incoming Axis aircraft while still out at sea. Increasing German casualties forced Kesselring to call off the attacks after a series of large-scale raids between October 10 and 20. Thereafter, Luftwaffe assets were transferred to North Africa and the Malta raids diminished accordingly. On November 20, convoy Operation STONEAGE delivered another thirty-five thousand tons of supplies, and another fifty-five thousand tons were delivered in December. The Malta campaign officially ended on December 31, 1942.

Ross Mahoney

See also: Kesselring, Albert; Student, Kurt

Additional Reading

Douglas-Hamilton, James. *The Air Battle for Malta*. Shrewsbury, UK: Airlife, 2000.

Manstein, Erich von (1887–1973)

Wehrmacht field marshal.

Erich von Manstein remains a controversial figure in German military history. Born von Lewinski in Berlin on November 24, 1887, he was adopted by his mother's childless sister, who had married a von Manstein. During World War I, he served as a General Staff officer. At first glance, his record during World War II appears second to none. Famous for his ambitious SICKLE CUT plan for the 1940 invasion of France and the Low Countries (Fall GELB); his capture of the Crimea in 1941 to 1942, which earned him his field-marshal's baton; his brilliant "backhand" counterattack at Kharkov in February to March 1943; and, not least, his defensive battles against a superior Red Army in Ukraine until his dismissal by Hitler at the end of March 1944. Against this background, it is unsurprising that British military historian Basil Liddell Hart declared him, "The ablest of all German generals." Manstein's final year of service in command of Army Group South had its high at Kharkov and its low at Kursk in July 1943. As he was forced progressively to yield ground, while he strove to maintain the integrity of his overextended front, relations with Hitler became ever tenser.

There is another, darker, side to Manstein: he was a convicted war criminal. Tried at a British war crimes tribunal at Hamburg in 1949, he was found guilty on nine out of seventeen charges and was sentenced to eighteen years' imprisonment. Crucially, the court found him *not guilty* of the most serious charges that related to the mass murder of Jews, gypsies, and Communists by German forces within his area of responsibility, such as the Crimea. On three occasions, Manstein rejected overtures to join the military opposition to Hitler. In

May 1945, the British Army interned him. His leading role as a defense witness before the International Military Tribunal at Nuremberg incriminated him for his subsequent trial. He gained early release from prison in 1953 through a secret agreement between Chancellor Konrad Adenauer of the new Federal Republic of Germany and British Prime Minister Winston Churchill. Manstein then served as an expert adviser on the raising of the new *Bundeswehr.* A quiet and long retirement then ensued. He died in Irschenhausen, West Germany, on June 9, 1973 (1973-06-09). His military funeral was attended by thousands of his former soldiers.

Mungo Melvin

See also: Crimea Campaign, Soviet; France, Battle of; International Military Tribunal: The Nuremberg Trials; Kharkov, Battles of; Kursk, Battle of; Ukraine Campaign, Soviet

Additional Reading

Melvin, Mungo. *Manstein: Hitler's Greatest General.* New York: Thomas Dunne, 2011.

Manteuffel, Hasso Eccard von (1897–1978)

Wehrmacht general of panzer troops.

Born on January 14, 1897 in Potsdam, Germany, into a Prussian military family, Hasso von Manteuffel saw action on the western front during World War I as a cavalry officer. He did not serve in either the invasions of Poland or France. During the opening stages of Operation BARBAROSSA, the invasion of the Soviet Union, Manteuffel commanded a battalion of the 7th Infantry Regiment in the 7th Panzer Division. Ordered to North Africa in early 1943, Manteuffel commanded a collection of units known as Division Manteuffel. In August 1943, he returned to Russia to command the 7th Panzer Division. In September 1944, he assumed command of the Fifth Panzer Army, which was engaged against U.S. forces in eastern France and Lorraine. The Fifth Panzer Army was assigned to support Josef "Sepp" Dietrich's Sixth Panzer Army in the Ardennes Offensive of December 1944. Manteuffel agreed with Field Marshal Walther Model that Hitler's plan was too ambitious for the forces available and, instead, advocated unsuccessfully for Model's proposed "small solution." Despite the failure of the offensive, Manteuffel retained Hitler's confidence and was awarded the Diamonds to the Knight's Cross of the Iron Cross. In March 1945, Manteuffel took command of the battered Third Panzer Army, which was assigned the defense of the Oder River below Stettin. Although continually pushed back by superior Soviet forces, Manteuffel maintained unit cohesion and was able to retreat and surrender to the Western Allies on May 3. Manteuffel spent two years as a prisoner of war. After being released in December 1947, he engaged in business and joined the Free Democratic Party (FDP) in 1949. From 1953 to 1957, he was an FDP deputy in the Bundestag from Neuss (North Rhine Westphalia). Manteuffel retired in Diessen am Ammersee, Germany, where he died on September 28, 1978.

Jon D. Berlin

See also: Ardennes Offensive (Battle of the Bulge)

Additional Reading

Brownlow, Donald Grey. *Panzer Baron: The Military Exploits of General Hasso von*

Manteuffel. North Quincy, MA: Christopher Publishing House, 1975.

Mareth Line, Battle of (March 16–31, 1943). *See* North Africa Campaign

MARKET-GARDEN, Allied Operation (September 17–26, 1944)

The German Army Group B intelligence assessment in mid-September 1944 reported that the next Allied offensive, probably from southern Holland, would be preceded by airborne forces. Nobody foresaw the threat to the rear combat zone of Army Group B, which an Allied airborne assault, code named MARKET, would bisect, laying a carpet of three airborne divisions. The U.S. 101st Airborne Division would center on Eindhoven, the U.S. 82nd Airborne Division between Grave and Nijmegen, and the British 1st Airborne Division at Arnhem. The British XXX Corps ground thrust, code named GARDEN, would sweep up the airborne corridor to Arnhem and then exploit into the Ruhr.

The hastily assembled and scratch-built First Parachute Army, under General Kurt Student, held a thin thirty-two-battalion front, seventy-five miles long, between Antwerp on the North Sea coast and Maastricht. Badly mauled at Falaise, the II SS Panzer Corps had begun refitting in the Arnhem area prior to entraining for the Reich. Its two divisions, the 9th SS *Hohenstaufen* and 10th SS Frundsberg were at 20 percent to 30 percent strength, with only two dozen tanks, but within easy striking distance of the proposed British drop zones. East of Nijmegen, the skeleton headquarters of the Corps "Feldt" was collecting units retreating from France in the area of *Wehrkreis* VI (Military District VI), near the Reichswald Forest.

On September 17, 1944, 1,545 aircraft delivered nineteen thousand U.S. and British airborne troops in one afternoon. Their mission, miles behind the German front line on the Meuse-Escaut canal, was to secure seven crossings across five major waterways. The textbook landings were the first time in the war that the Allied airborne divisions had been accurately and cohesively delivered. Three of five major bridges were captured, including the bridge at Arnhem, but not the canal bridge at Son or the huge bridge spanning the Waal River at Nijmegen. The landings split Student's First Parachute Army completely in two.

General Walther Model, the Commander of Army Group B, immediately directed SS-Obergruppenführer Willi Bittrich's II SS Panzer Corps to take the swift countermeasures that were to blunt the impact of MARKET-GARDEN. Many of the 9th SS Panzer Division's quick-reaction units were only a thirty-minute drive from the British drop zones. SS Battalion "Krafft," fortuitously exercising in the woods next to the British landing zones, prevented two parachute battalions from reaching the bridge, but the 2nd Parachute Battalion commanded by Lieutenant Colonel John Frost slipped through to the south, moving along the Lower Rhine, taking the bridge at Arnhem. Despite chaos reigning in Arnhem, the 9th SS Panzer Division's *Kampfgruppe* (Battle Group) "Spindler" set up a blocking position in the western suburbs. No more British soldiers reached the bridge. Over the next three days, all German attempts to recapture the Arnhem Bridge were beaten back by Frost's gradually diminishing battalion.

The 10th SS Panzer Division's *Kampfgruppe* "Euling," meanwhile, successfully occupied the citadel at Nijmegen, covering the Waal Bridge, and *Kampfgruppe* "Rheinhold" held the north bank at Lent. A mixed bag of units forming *Kampfgruppe* "Henke" secured the approaches to the rail bridge. SS-Brigadeführer Heinz Harmel, commanding the 10th SS Panzer Division, was tasked to fight the Arnhem Bridge clear to reinforce his units at Nijmegen. Meanwhile, reinforcements had to be sent on a forty-kilometer round trip to cross the Waal further east, at the Pannerden ferry, a slow and laborious process. Holding the bridge at Nijmegen was clearly recognized as the German center of gravity, which would decide the outcome of Operation MARKET-GARDEN.

In the east, Spindler's battle group, aided by the arrival of Self-Propelled Gun Brigade 280 and other hastily assembled infantry and tank units, had blocked and defeated all British airborne attempts to reach Frost at the bridge. Decimated by superior firepower in street fighting between September 19 and 20, the British streamed back toward Oosterbeek. *SS-Standartenführer* Walther Harzer, commanding the 9th SS Division's battle groups, advanced west out of Arnhem and from the north, pinning the remnants of the British 1st Airborne Division into a tightly constricted perimeter at Oosterbeek. The British were down to twenty-five hundred from eight thousand men inserted, trapped on three sides and with their backs to the Lower Rhine.

British XXX Corps, spearheading the Allied ground advance coming up from the south, was already far behind schedule. After breaking through the defensive crust formed by the Regiment "von Hoffman" on the Meuse-Escaut Canal, the way to Eindhoven was virtually open. Tank ambushes and determined blocking actions by the SS *Kampfgruppe* "Roestel" and another force led by Major Kerutt impeded progress so that Eindhoven was not reached until 1900 hours on September 18. By the time the British Guards Armoured Division reached Grave at 0820 hours the next day, delayed by the blown bridge at Son, the airborne corridor was under enormous pressure. Two regiments from the German 59th Division of the retreating Fifteenth Army and *Fallschirmjäger* training battalions from S'Hertogenbosch began attacking the U.S. 101st Airborne Division sector between Eindhoven and Grave from the west. On September 19, Panzer Brigade 107 assaulted the U.S.-held bridge at Son, coming from the east. Further along the corridor, the U.S. 82nd Airborne Division was battling against four to five battalions that Corps "Feldt" was directing from the east against the Groesbeek Heights to secure access to Nijmegen.

A surprise assault river crossing by the U.S. 3rd Battalion, 504th Parachute Infantry Regiment on September 20, in concert with a British tank rush on the Nijmegen road bridge, unhinged the defense. German demolition charges failed to ignite, and both bridges were secured by 1900 hours. At the moment the Germans lost the Nijmegen Bridge, they recaptured the Arnhem Bridge. Pyrrhic victories on both sides cancelled out the other's gain.

At Arnhem, the remnants of the British 1st Airborne Division were hemmed in by up to fifteen German battalions. A final shock was administered by the Polish Parachute Brigade landings at Driel, south of the Lower Rhine on September 21, jumping behind German positions at Arnhem and outside Nijmegen. This unexpected move obliged the Germans to relocate five battalions, totaling twenty-five hundred men from the British perimeter, poised for a final assault. The life of the beleaguered perimeter was extended with the infusion of some Polish reinforcements for several days. By September 24, the British perimeter, measuring one by two kilometers, was ringed by 110 artillery pieces, ranging from 20 mm to 150 mm in caliber. Fifteen Pz.Kpfw.VIB Tiger tanks arrived from Heavy Tank Battalion 506 but soon bogged down in Oosterbeek, where the shattered buildings impeded the traverse of their long 88 mm guns.

Elements of the British XXX Corps vanguard reached the opposite side of the river at Oosterbeek on September 24, but they were too weak to establish a bridgehead. During the night of September 25 to 26, the survivors of the British 1st Airborne Division withdrew across the Lower Rhine. They had lost 7,212 men. The Germans hindered the evacuation but mistook the withdrawal for reinforcement. They could not believe the British would give up ground that had cost so much blood. The U.S. airborne divisions securing "Hells Highway" suffered dearly. The 82nd lost 1,432 men, and the 101st 2,110. The XXX Corps advance cost an estimated 1,480 men and 70 tanks. German casualty records are incomplete and often underestimated, but likely numbered between six thousand to eight thousand men, a ratio of about one German to two Allied dead.

Germany's last victory in the west was won by hastily assembled ad-hoc units, flexibly led by innovative veteran commanders. German fighting power rather than Allied mistakes decided the outcome. Key to success was Model's instant recognition that his center of gravity hinged on the Waal at Nijmegen. A still-functioning German General Staff system enabled the rapid assembly and deployment of ad-hoc units despite the defeat of its field army in the west. MARKET, the Allied airborne landings were broadly successful; failure came with the inability of GARDEN, the ground operation, to link up in time. Arnhem was not to be captured until March 1945, after a grim winter of forced civilian evacuations for the Dutch people and a static front line.

Robert Kershaw

See also: Bittrich, Willi; Model, Walther; Student, Kurt

Additional Reading

Kershaw, Robert. *It Never Snows in September: The German View of* MARKET-GARDEN *and the Battle of Arnhem, September 1944.* Hersham, Surrey, UK: Ian Allen, 1990.

Ryan, Cornelius. *A Bridge Too Far.* New York: Simon & Shuster, 1974.

Marschall, Wilhelm (1886–1976)

Kriegsmarine general admiral.

Born in Augsburg, Germany, on September 30, 1886, Wilhelm Marschall was a submarine commander during World War I. Between 1937 and 1938, he commanded German naval forces off Spain during the Spanish Civil War. Appointed fleet commander in October 1939, he was relieved from his post by the commander of the navy, Grand Admiral Erich Raeder, for not strictly following the operational plan in the German campaign against Norway from April to June 1940. Marschall held that a commander at sea had to have freedom of action. Given command of Navy Group West in the summer of 1942, which he considered vindication of his earlier ideas, Marschall was promoted to general admiral in February 1943. Raeder's successor, Grand Admiral Karl Dönitz, preferred others in command positions, and Marschall then held posts ashore. He died in Munich on March 20, 1976.

Spencer C. Tucker

See also: Norway Campaign

Additional Reading

Bekker, Cajus. *Hitler's Naval War.* Garden City, NY: Doubleday, 1974.

Marseille, Hans-Joachim (1919–1942)

Luftwaffe captain.

Hans-Joachim Marseille was a fighter pilot and the leading German ace in North Africa. Born in Berlin on December 13, 1919, he joined the Luftwaffe in 1938. Though a gifted flyer, he chafed at military discipline. Sometimes called the "Star of North Africa," he was noted for his uncanny ability at deflection shooting and running up multiple kills in a single day. His best day was September 1, 1942, when he was credited with shooting down seventeen British aircraft during three sorties. He died shortly thereafter, in a flying accident over Alam Halfa, on September 30. His final tally was 158 victories. Just before his death, he was promoted to captain and was awarded the Diamonds to the Knight's Cross of the Iron Cross.

Marlyn R. Pierce

See also: Luftwaffe (German Air Force)

Additional Reading

Musciano, Walter. *Messerschmitt Aces.* New York: Arco Publishing, 1982.

Mellenthin, Friedrich-Wilhelm von (1904–1997)

Wehrmacht major general.

Born in Breslau, Germany, on August 30, 1904, Friedrich-Wilhelm von Mellenthin joined the Reichswehr in 1924 and qualified as a General Staff officer in 1937. Mellenthin served for fifteen months on General Erwin Rommel's staff in North Africa. After he was medically evacuated to Germany for amoebic dysentery, he was posted to the eastern front. As the chief of staff of XLVIII Panzer Corps, Mellenthin worked for the first time with Major General Hermann Balck, who was the commander of the subordinate 11th Panzer Division. Balck later assumed command of the corps, and the Balck-Mellenthin partnership lasted for almost the rest of the war. In August 1944, Balck and Mellenthin moved to the Fourth Panzer Army, which halted the Soviet Offensive at the great bend in the Vistula. Just four weeks later, Mellenthin and Balck transferred to the western front to take command of Army Group G in Lorraine. In December 1944, Mellenthin was assigned as commander of the 9th Panzer Division, fighting in the Ardennes. He was captured on May 3, 1945 while serving as the chief of staff of the Fifth Panzer Army. Released from U.S. captivity in 1947, Mellenthin wrote two significant books after the war, *Panzer Battles* and *German Generals of World War II as I Knew Them.* He died in Johannesburg, South Africa, on June 28, 1997.

David T. Zabecki

See also: Balck, Hermann; Rommel, Erwin

Additional Reading

Zabecki, David T. "Friedrich-Wilhelm von Mellenthin." In *Chief of Staff: The Principal Officers behind History's Great Commanders. Vol 2, World War II to Korea and Vietnam*, edited by David T. Zabecki. Annapolis, MD: U.S. Naval Institute Press, 2008.

Mersa Matrûh, Battle of (June 26–29, 1942). *See* North Africa Campaign

Messerschmitt Bf 109 Fighter. *See* Aircraft, Military

Messerschmidt Me 262 Jet Fighter. *See* Aircraft, Military

Messerschmitt, Wilhelm (1898–1978)

Aircraft designer and developer of the most widely produced World War II aircraft.

Born in Frankfurt-am-Main, Germany, on June 26, 1898, Messerschmitt served briefly during World War I and then completed his engineering studies in Munich. In 1927, he became a partner in Bayerische Flugzeugwerke (BFW). In 1934, Messerschmitt's low-wing monoplane design won a competition that resulted in the Bf 109, the most widely produced fighter plane of World War II. Between 1939 and 1945, more than thirty-three thousand were built. Messerschmitt's company also pioneered developments in jet- and rocket-propelled aircraft, including the rocket-powered Me 163 Komet and the Me 262 jet fighter. After the war, Messerschmitt was arrested and imprisoned for employing slave labor. In 1958, he resumed work in aviation, combining with two other manufacturers to form Messerschmitt-Bolkow-Blohm. He died in Munich, Germany, on September 15, 1978.

Marlyn R. Pierce

See also: Aircraft, Military

Additional Reading

Van Ishoven, Armand. *Messerschmitt: Aircraft Designer.* New York: Doubleday, 1975.

Metz, Battle of (September 27–November 22, 1944)

Metz was one of the few siege-warfare battles of the western front in Europe during World War II. The heavily fortified city in the Moselle River Valley in Lorraine lay in the path of Lieutenant General George S. Patton's U.S. Third Army in its drive to reach the Rhine. Bypassing Metz would lengthen the Third Army supply lines by some one hundred miles. Furthermore, Metz lay astride one of the principal invasion routes between Germany and France and would be an important staging point for an Allied drive into Germany through Trier and the Kaiserslauten Corridor.

Metz had long been a key fortress, and its defenses faced in both directions. The strongest defenses actually faced west. As part of the prewar French Maginot Line fortress system, Metz had an inner circle of fifteen forts and a perimeter defense of twenty-eight ferro-concrete bastions. Following the defeat of France in 1940, the Germans had annexed Metz. They subsequently added to its fortifications a number of 210 mm and 105 mm guns in revolving armored turrets, which could withstand direct fire. General of Panzer Troops Otto von Knobelsdorff commanded the Metz sector. He had the equivalent of some four and a half divisions. The defense of Metz itself fell to the fourteen-thousand-man 462nd Volksgrenadier Division.

The U.S. assault of the outer ring of the German defenses began on September 27. Without major preparations, the U.S. XX Corps mounted a frontal assault into the area of greatest German strength and was repulsed. The battle then disintegrated into a protracted siege, similar to the static warfare of World War I. Fall rains worsened conditions, turning the ground into a sea of mud. All attempts in September and early October to take the fortress failed, and the rains continued amid mounting U.S. casualties. U.S. efforts were also handicapped by the shift in logistics support to the north for

Operation MARKET-GARDEN, the failed Allied effort to secure a crossing over the Rhine at Arnhem.

During October 3 to 15, the main U.S. effort was directed against Fort Driant, the newest and most powerful of the Metz forts. The assaulting infantry took 50 percent casualties before the attack was aborted. The Americans attacked again on November 9, taking Fort Königsmacker, and then Forts Valstrofe and Distroff. The Americans then closed in on Metz from three directions. This time, they abandoned costly frontal assaults in favor of bypassing strong points and then reducing them with demolition charges. On November 14, meanwhile, Lieutenant General Heinrich Kittel assumed command of the German forces at Metz.

The first U.S. troops entered Metz on November 17. The Germans withdrew some of their defenders from the city, in defiance of Hitler's orders that it be held to the last. Although Metz finally surrendered on November 22, some German troops chose to obey Hitler and fight on. The last Metz fort, Jeanne d'Arc, did not surrender until December 13. Although the battle ended in a German defeat, it held up the advance of the U.S. Third Army for three months, permitting German forces to withdraw to the Sarre River and securing time for them to establish a solid line of defense. Metz was the most-costly single battle of the war for the U.S. Third Army.

Gene Mueller and Spencer C. Tucker

See also: MARKET-GARDEN, Allied Operation

Additional Reading

Kemp, Anthony. *The Unknown Battle: Metz, 1944.* Briarcliff Manor, NY: Stein and Day, 1981.

MG 42 Machine Gun. See Infantry Weapons

Milch, Erhard (1892–1972)

Luftwaffe field marshal who was instrumental in developing the Luftwaffe.

Born on March 30, 1892 in Wilhelmshaven, Germany, Erhard Milch served as an aerial artillery observer during World War I. Following the war, he pursued a career in civil aviation and rose to be the chief executive of Lufthansa, the German national airline. He became close friends with Hermann Göring in the process, and when the latter was appointed Reich commissar for air, Milch followed as his state secretary. In many ways, Milch was the man who built the Luftwaffe into the world's most powerful air force by 1939, but he also shared responsibilities for its shortcomings during the war. He was named inspector general of the Luftwaffe in 1939, and his lone field command of the war came in 1940 when he commanded Fifth Air Fleet in Norway. Following the suicide of Ernst Udet in 1941, Milch took over his position as director of air armament. He tripled aircraft production and improved aircraft maintenance procedures, but Milch found himself increasingly estranged from both Göring and Hitler, who disliked his realistic assessments. Göring removed him from his posts in July 1944. Taken prisoner by the British in May 1945, Milch was sentenced to life imprisonment for war crimes, chiefly the use of forced labor in production. He was released from prison in 1954 and died on January 25, 1972 in Wuppertal-Barmen, Germany.

Matthew Alan McNiece

See also: Göring, Hermann

Additional Reading

Murray, Williamson. *Luftwaffe*. Mount Pleasant, SC: Nautical and Aviation Publishing Company of America, 1985.

Minsk-Bialystok, Battle of (June 22–July 9, 1941). *See* Soviet Union, Invasion of (Operation BARBAROSSA)

Model, Walther (1891–1945)

Wehrmacht field marshal.

Born in Genthin, Germany, on January 24, 1891, Walther Model served during World War I as a captain. In May 1940, he commanded the 3rd Panzer Division in the invasion of France and the Low Countries. In October 1941, he assumed command of the XLI Panzer Corps in Russia, and, three months later, he took over Ninth Army. Although he was one of Germany's most capable commanders, he nonetheless helped convince Hitler to delay plans for Operation CITADEL, leading to the German defeat in the Battle of Kursk. As the commander of Army Group North Ukraine in January 1944, he proved a master of defensive warfare, earning the nickname "Hitler's Fireman." In August 1944, he was transferred to the western front as OB West and simultaneously the commander of Army Group B. In early September, Model relinquished command of OB West to Field Marshal Gerd von Rundstedt but retained command of Army Group B. In September, Model blunted the Allied drive to take Arnhem during Operation MARKET-GARDEN. He also stopped the U.S. First Army cold during the Hürtgen Forest campaign. In December 1944, Model commanded Army Group B during the Ardennes Offensive (the Battle of the Bulge). In 1945, Model was tasked with defending the Ruhr. He clashed with Hitler when the latter refused to allow him to retreat. Model committed suicide on April 21, 1945, in Lintorf near Duisburg, Germany, on the destruction of his encircled army group. Model was one of few German generals who did not hesitate to contest Hitler's orders when he believed them wrong. Preoccupied with the immediate military situation, he was not interested in politics or overall national strategy.

Martin Moll

See also: Ardennes Offensive (Battle of the Bulge); Hürtgen Forest Campaign, Allied; Kursk, Battle of; MARKET-GARDEN, Allied Operation; Ruhr Ground Campaign, Allied

Additional Reading

D'Este, Carlo. "Field-Marshal Walter Model." In *Hitler's Generals*, edited by Correlli Barnet, 319–334. New York: Grove Weidenfeld, 1989.

Mölders, Werner (1913–1941)

Luftwaffe colonel.

Born on March 18, 1913 in Gelsenkirchen, Germany, Werner Mölders qualified as a Luftwaffe pilot in 1936. Two years later, he replaced Adolf Galland as the leader of the fighter squadron of the Kondor Legion in Spain. Mölders realized that the tactics of World War I were obsolete and ineffective with high-speed modern aircraft. Rather than keeping his planes in a tight, three-plane "V" formation, he experimented with flying them widely spaced and paired in four-plane flights. This formation has been called the "Finger Four." The formation allowed the wingman to cover the lead pilot as he made his attack, without trying to maintain formation. This tactical innovation was eventually adopted by every air force. Mölders emerged from the Spanish Civil War as its leading ace, with fourteen victories. Mölders was appointed Luftwaffe general of fighters in September 1941. He had a total of 115 victories when he was killed in a plane crash at Breslau-Hundsfeld Airfield in Germany on November 22, 1941.

Marlyn R. Pierce

See also: Galland, Adolf; Kondor Legion

Additional Reading

Musciano, Walter. *Messerschmitt Aces.* New York: Arco Publishing, 1982.

Moscow, Battle of (September 30, 1941–April 1942)

The battle for Moscow was the centerpiece of Operation TAIFUN (TYPHOON). The operation breaks generally into three phases: the first German offensive encompassed the period from September 30 to nearly the end of October, the second German offensive took place between November 17 and December 5, and the Soviet counteroffensive lasted from December 6 to spring 1942. General Heinz Guderian's Second Panzer Group of Army Group Center spearheaded the offensive. The Germans took Orel on October 3, and, by October 21, around Vyazma and Bryansk, they captured six hundred and sixty-five thousand Soviet prisoners. On October 6, the Germans broke through the Rzhev-Vyazma Line and advanced toward the Mozhaisk Line, an improvised line of fortifications thrown up by the Soviets, fifty miles west of Moscow during summer 1941. The Germans bypassed the Mozhaisk Line on the south and captured Kaluga on October 12, and Kalinin two days later. On October 18, the Soviets abandoned Mozhaisk itself after heavy fighting. However, fall rains and mud, increasing Soviet resistance as the Germans neared the capital, and an early drop in temperature to well below zero ground the German advance to a halt.

On October 10, Marshal Georgy Zhukov took command of Moscow's defense. With the help of the weather and with the defenders' backs pressed against the capital, Soviet resistance solidified as the Germans advanced. For the first time in the war, the Soviets were able to confront the Germans head on and force them to fight for every mile. By the beginning of November, the Germans had made very little progress. The German failure to capture Moscow with the October offensive raised Soviet civilian and military morale and gave the Soviet STAVKA (High Command) time to assemble large strategic reserves to the east.

The second German offensive opened on November 16 in the Kalinin-Volokolamsk sector, and, in two days, the Germans entered Klin, north of Moscow, and Istr, only fifteen miles west—the closest the Germans were able to get to Moscow in force. On December 4, temperatures fell to well below freezing and remained there, stalling the German offensive. Complicating the situation further, on December 1, Hitler threw the German Army High Command into greater disarray by relieving Field Marshal Gerd von Rundtstedt as commander of Army Group South, replacing him with Field Marshal Walther von Reichenau.

On December 6, the Soviets launched their winter counteroffensive along the Moscow Front, from Kalinin in the north to Yelets in the south. The Soviet plan had been to encircle the Germans west of the capital, but Hitler, after personally assuming supreme

German tanks and infantry advancing into a village in the district of Volokolamsk/Klin, during the Battle of Moscow, December 1941. (Arthur Grimm/ullstein bild via Getty Images)

command of the German Army, ordered a stiffening of the defense east of the Rzhev-Vyazma-Gzhatsk-Yukhnovo Line. The Soviets recaptured Kalinin on December 15 and Kaluga on December 30. By the end of January 1942, the Red Army counteroffensive came to a virtual standstill. Fierce combat in the Moscow area continued from January until the end of April 1942, by which point the German Army had been driven back 160 miles from the Soviet capital. Apart from being a substantial propaganda blow to Germany, the Battle of Moscow proved that there were definite limits to German military power and marked the end of the German Blitzkrieg on the eastern front.

Arthur T. Frame

See also: Guderian, Heinz; Reichenau, Walther von; Rundstedt, Karl Rudolf Gerd von; Soviet Union, Invasion of (Operation BARBAROSSA)

Additional Reading

Erickson, John. *The Road to Stalingrad: Stalin's War with Germany.* New York: Harper and Row, 1975.

Ziemke, Earl F., and Magna E. Bauer. *Moscow to Stalingrad: Decision in the East.* Washington, DC: U.S. Government Printing Office, 1987.

Munich Conference and Agreement (September 29–30, 1938)

The international conference at which the major powers agreed to the territorial dismemberment of Czechoslovakia yielded the Sudetenland to Germany. Hitler's expansion of power both domestically and internationally in the late 1930s was predicated on a mixture of belligerence, bluff, bullying, and inspired political insight. His theme of incorporating all Germans into a

"Greater Germany" focused him toward the east, where he astutely estimated that the Western democracies would not make a stand. In March 1938, he assimilated Austria, claiming at the time to have no interest in Czechoslovakia. This situation did not sit well with the largely German population of the Sudetenland, in western Bohemia. A Nazi movement emerged in the Sudetenland, and its leader, Konrad Henlein, met with Hitler in late March 1938 and called for immediate "justice" for his people. Disturbances and clashes between German Czechs and the police followed. The French government openly said that France would fight if Germany intervened. British Prime Minister Neville Chamberlain had previously warned that such a conflict would draw in other nations. Chamberlain did not, however, believe that the Czech situation justified war. He convinced French Premier Édouard Daladier to join in pressing Prague to make a deal, while, at the same time, hinting to Berlin that intervention could lead to war.

With tension growing, French Foreign Minister Georges Bonnet told Chamberlain that he was prepared to force concessions from Prague, although, officially, France stood by its commitments to defend Czechoslovakia. For his part, Chamberlain was more than ever determined to avoid war, although he remained committed to supporting France. On September 13, Chamberlain requested a meeting with Hitler, which took place three days later at Berchtesgaden. Hitler posed as a moderate, calling only for self-determination for the Sudeten Germans. Although he could secure no specifics, Chamberlain decided that annexation of areas with populations that were 50 percent or more German would satisfy the Führer. Hitler then agreed not to act unless there was a major incident. Once the French agreed to the 50 percent plan, Czech President Edvard Beneš was told to accept it or face German invasion.

On September 22, Chamberlain again met Hitler, this time at Godesberg, only to find that the Führer had now upped the ante. He had a map showing areas that Germany would occupy by October 1, and he demanded that all Czech officials be withdrawn from them by that date and that all military, economic, and political establishments be removed. U.S. President Franklin D. Roosevelt made a direct appeal to Hitler, urging an international conference. On September 28, Italian dictator Benito Mussolini talked to Hitler and secured his agreement for such a meeting. Chamberlain, Daladier, and Mussolini met with Hitler in Munich on September 29. The Soviet Union was not invited, and Czechoslovakia itself was not officially represented—because the objective was to give Hitler the Sudetenland and avoid war. The Munich Agreement, dated September 30 but actually signed just after midnight on October 1, gave Hitler everything he demanded. Early on the morning of October 1, 1938, German troops marched across the frontier, and, two days later, Hitler made a triumphal entry into Eger, the unofficial capital of the Sudeten Germans.

The Munich Agreement had far-reaching international influence. Chamberlain and Daladier were warmly received by welcoming crowds when they returned home, especially the British prime minister, when he reported that he believed he had achieved "peace in our time." The Munich Agreement, however, effectively ended the French security system. Poland, Romania, and Yugoslavia now all doubted French commitments to defend them, and Stalin was further alienated from the West. On March 15, 1940, Nazi troops occupied what remained of Czechoslovakia. The Czech lands became the Protectorate of Bohemia and Moravia.

Fred R. van Hartesveldt and
Spencer C. Tucker

See also: Austria, Annexation of (*Anschluss*)

Additional Reading

Taylor, Telford. *Munich: The Price of Peace.* Garden City, NY: Doubleday, 1979.

N

Netherlands Campaign (May 10–15, 1940)

In May 1940, the Germans launched Case YELLOW (Fall GELB), their attack against France and the neutral Low Countries. The Netherlands was overrun in five days and suffered heavy losses. General Henry G. Winkelman's Netherlands Army of ten infantry divisions faced Colonel General Fedor von Bock's Army Group B, consisting of General of Artillery Georg von Küchler's Eighteenth Army of eleven divisions and Colonel General Walther von Reichenau's Sixth Army with seventeen infantry and two panzer divisions. The Dutch forces were basically militia, with little training and no fighting experience. They had no tanks and hardly any antitank weapons. Although some Dutch units fought well, the army as a whole broke down rapidly.

The attack against Fortress Holland began in the early hours of May 10, 1940. As in the previous month's offensive against Norway, an air assault spearheaded Germany's operation. On May 10 alone, however, the Luftwaffe lost some 170 aircraft and had about the same number damaged. Most key defensive installations were in German hands by the middle of the first day, however. Of the crucial bridges over the Juliana Canal, the Germans captured all but one completely intact. Although by May 12 Allied bombers began to target key bridges in the Netherlands, most bridges had already been secured by the Germans, allowing their forces to advance rapidly.

On May 13, Lieutenant General Alfred Ritter von Hubicki's 9th Panzer Division broke through toward the bridges at Moordijk, fifteen miles south of Rotterdam. On May 14, the Germans demanded the surrender of Rotterdam. The Dutch, at first, refused. In one of the most controversial decisions of the war, Reich Marshal Hermann Göring, commander of the Luftwaffe, then decided to employ Ju 87 Stuka dive-bombers of *Fliegerkorps* IV against the city to hasten Dutch capitulation. The city center was virtually destroyed. Recognizing that further resistance would be futile, the Netherlands government capitulated. On May 15, Queen Wilhelmina and the government fled to Britain, where a government-in-exile was quickly established. In the five-day campaign, the Netherlands lost 2,890 dead and 6,900 wounded. There are no separate German casualty figures for the Netherlands fighting. The Netherlands remained under German occupation for the next four years.

Thomas J. Weiler

See also: Bock, Fedor von; Göring, Hermann; Küchler, Georg von; Reichenau, Walther von

Additional Reading

Deighton, Len. *Blitzkrieg: From the Rise of Hitler to the Fall of Dunkirk.* New York: Alfred A. Knopf, 1980.

NEULAND, U-Boat Operation (February 1942–September 1943)

Operation NEULAND (NEW LAND) was the extension of the German submarine campaign into the Caribbean, following Operation PAUKENSCHLAG (DRUMBEAT). This new operation was aimed at Allied oil and gasoline shipments in and from the Caribbean Sea. On February 16, 1942, the *U-67* and *U-156* entered the two most important oil ports of the western hemisphere, Saint Nicholas on Aruba and Willemstad on Curaçao. Although the Caribbean had been formally integrated into the U.S. seaward defense organization in July 1941, the initial response to the German threat was completely uncoordinated and ineffective. Between February 1 and June 1, 1942, German and Italian submarines sank fifty-two tankers (out of a total of 114 Allied tankers sunk in that period).

The introduction of convoys in the Caribbean did not bring instant relief. The largely U.S. escort forces in the Caribbean were inadequately equipped and too inexperienced to take on the battle-hardened U-boat veterans. Nevertheless, by September 1942, the convoy system had forced the U-boats to concentrate around Trinidad. Since February, the Allied antisubmarine forces had accounted for six U-boats sunk and had damaged several more. For the Germans, however, this was still a favorable exchange rate, given the destruction of 187 Allied merchant ships in the Caribbean to that point. By the end of the offensive, the U-boats, in 319 days, had sunk a total of nearly 1.9 million tons of Allied shipping in the Caribbean, or 36 percent of all Allied merchant ship losses in 1942 worldwide.

When U-boat Command attempted to revive operations in the Caribbean following the collapse of the main U-boat campaign in the North Atlantic in May 1943, the offensive ended in failure before it could begin in earnest.

Dirk Steffen

See also: DRUMBEAT, U-Boat Operation

Additional Reading

Kelshall, Gaylord. *The U-Boat War in the Caribbean.* Annapolis, MD: Naval Institute Press, 1994.

Night of the Long Knives (June 30, 1934)

The Night of the Long Knives (*Nacht der langen Messer*) on June 30, 1934, was one of the final steps in Hitler's consolidation of power over the Nazi Party and Germany itself. The brown-shirted Sturmabteilung (SA) had been the paramilitary force of street thugs of the National Socialist German Workers' Party (Nazis). Ernst Röhm, a former Germany army officer, who immediately after the war had been Hitler's company commander, was the chief of staff of the SA. The four million SA members who helped Hitler come to power were true believers in National Socialism. When they became Nazis, they thought they were joining a revolution. Instead, once they had served their purpose, they started making themselves pests within the party. Hitler was also weary of Röhm, who had a potential power base large enough to challenge him for leadership. Besides, as a homosexual, Röhm was beginning to be a political embarrassment. Röhm had a special grudge against the German Army. He was forced to resign his commission following his conviction for supporting Hitler's Beer Hall Putsch in Munich in 1923. After the Nazis came to power in 1933, Röhm aggressively pushed an agenda of subordinating the army to the SA, under his control, of course. Thus, the senior leaders of the Reichswehr were ready to support almost any action that would suppress the SA.

Hitler's main agency to suppress the SA was Heinrich Himmler's black-shirted Schutzstaffel (SS), which, officially, was a very elite and fanatical component of the SA. On the night of June 30, 1934, Röhm was arrested, along with hundreds of others. Over a period of three days, between 150 and 300 people, including Röhm, were murdered. When it was over, the SA was broken, and the Schutzstaffel (SS), blindly loyal to Hitler, was now the dominant force in the Nazi Party. The Riechwehr, which had provided arms and transportation for the SS murder squads, was happy with the elimination of the SA as a shadow army. Ironically, over the course of the next eleven years, the Schutzstaffel's armed branch, the Waffen-SS, eventually grew into the parallel and competitor army that the German generals had feared most.

John H. Barnhill and David T. Zabecki

See also: Himmler, Heinrich; Röhm, Ernst; Sturmabteilungen (SA); Waffen-SS

Additional Reading

Maracin, Paul. *The Night of the Long Knives: 48 Hours that Changed the History of the World.* New York: The Lyons Press, 2004.

NORDWIND, Operation (December 31, 1944–January 25 1945)

Operation NORDWIND was the last major offensive mounted in the west by the German Army. The main objective was Lieutenant General Alexander Patch's U.S. Seventh Army of Allied 6th Army Group, which was closing to the Rhine River in Alsace, France. One hour before midnight on December 31, 1944, without artillery preparation, SS-Obergurppenführer Max Simon's XIII SS Corps of Colonel General Johannes Blaskowitz's Army Group G, led by the 17th SS Panzergrenadier Division commanded by SS-Standartenführer Hans Linger, struck the U.S. 44th Infantry Division in the center of Major General Wade H. Haislip's U.S. XV Corps, between Sarreguemines and Rimling. The Germans then headed for the Rohrbach road junction, which had been contested previously.

South and southeast from Bitche, a much less powerful German thrust by the 256th and 361st Volksgrenadier Divisions of General of Infantry Gustav Höhhe's LXXXIX Army Corps' made deeper gains, because that area of the Low Vosges mountain range was only lightly held by a cavalry task force of U.S. VI Corps. By dawn on January 1, 1945, the U.S. task force was in a hasty retreat. By January 4, General of Aviation Erich Petersen's XC Infantry Corps of Lieutenant General Hans von Obstfelder's First Army had punched a hole some six miles deep into the Seventh Army front, reaching to the town of Wingen on the Moder River. The two German corps hoped to reach the Saverne gap, severing the Seventh Army's line of communication on the Rhine. If they could accomplish this, they would also envelop the U.S. 100th Infantry Division.

On January 4, General of Division Jacques Philippe Leclerc's French 2nd Armored Division moved into position to support the U.S. XV Corps. Supreme Allied Commander General Dwight D. Eisenhower believed that Patch's extended line was dangerous and had so informed 6th Army Group commander Lieutenant General Jacob Devers. When the Germans attacked Patch, Eisenhower ordered Devers to pull VI Corps back and hold the forward areas with reconnaissance units. He believed that the German offensive in the area would slow down and that light troops might stop a German reoccupation of Alsace. But when Devers announced the withdrawal, which would expose Strasbourg to recapture, French head of state General Charles de Gaulle vowed to withdraw all French forces from his command. Faced with an immovable de Gaulle, Eisenhower relented.

On January 5, the Nineteenth Army's XIV SS Corps under General Otto von dem Bach attacked across the Rhine at Gambsheim and into U.S. VI Corps' eastern flank. The Germans established the bridgehead with the 553rd Volksgrenadier Division and the 405th Infantry Division. Elements of the 553rd Volksgrenadier Division and the 10th SS Panzer Division under SS-Brigadeführer Heinz Harmel occupied the town of Herrlisheim. On January 7, the German LXIV Corps crossed the Rhine south of Rheinau, threatening the VI Corps' rear. That same day, the XXXIX Panzer Corps started shifting elements of the 21st Panzer Division under Lieutenant General Edgar Feuchtinger and the 25th Panzergrenadier Division under Lieutenant General Paul Schürmann from west of Bitche to the Lauterbourg area in preparation for a major push down the west bank of the Rhine. Near the end of the day, the U.S. 12th Armored Division's Combat Command B arrived in the area and was ordered to prepare immediately to attack the Germans in Herrlisheim.

On January 9, the General of Panzer Troops Karl Decker's XXXIX Panzer Corps penetrated the VI Corps' center, driving the U.S. line back into the Haguenau Forest. The VI Corps was now fighting for its life on three sides. VI Corps committed its remaining reserve, the 14th Armored Division, to the fierce fighting that followed in the towns of Hatten and Rittershoffen. On January 17, the 12th Armored Division's 23rd Tank Battalion and 66th Armored Infantry Battalion attacked Herrlisheim in freezing fog. Both units immediately lost contact with the divisional headquarters, and by January 19, both battalions had been wiped out.

The Germans progressively forced both U.S. VI and XV Corps back to positions on or near the Moder River. The two corps formed a new line on the night of January 20 to 21. The Germans launched a six-division drive on January 24, but the German attack culminated the following day. NORDWIND had run its course, and the German forces began to withdraw across the Rhine soon afterward. Operation NORDWIND cost the Americans some twenty-nine thousand total casualties, and the French about two thousand. German casualties totaled about twenty-three thousand.

Uzal W. Ent and David T. Zabecki

See also: Blaskowitz, Johannes Albrecht

Additional Reading

Bonn, Keith E. *When the Odds Were Even: The Vosges Mountains Campaign, October 1944–January 1945*. Novalto, CA: Presidio Press, 1994.

Normandy Invasion and Campaign (June 6–July 31, 1944)

German leaders had long anticipated an Allied effort to land on the European mainland. Fortress Europe and its coasts of the Netherlands, Belgium, and France bristled with German fortifications. Organization Todt had begun erecting defenses there in mid-1942. Field Marshal Erwin Rommel, who commanded Army Group B and the coastal defenses, disagreed with German commander in chief West Field Marshal Gerd von Rundstedt. Rommel told Adolf

Normandy Invasion, 1944

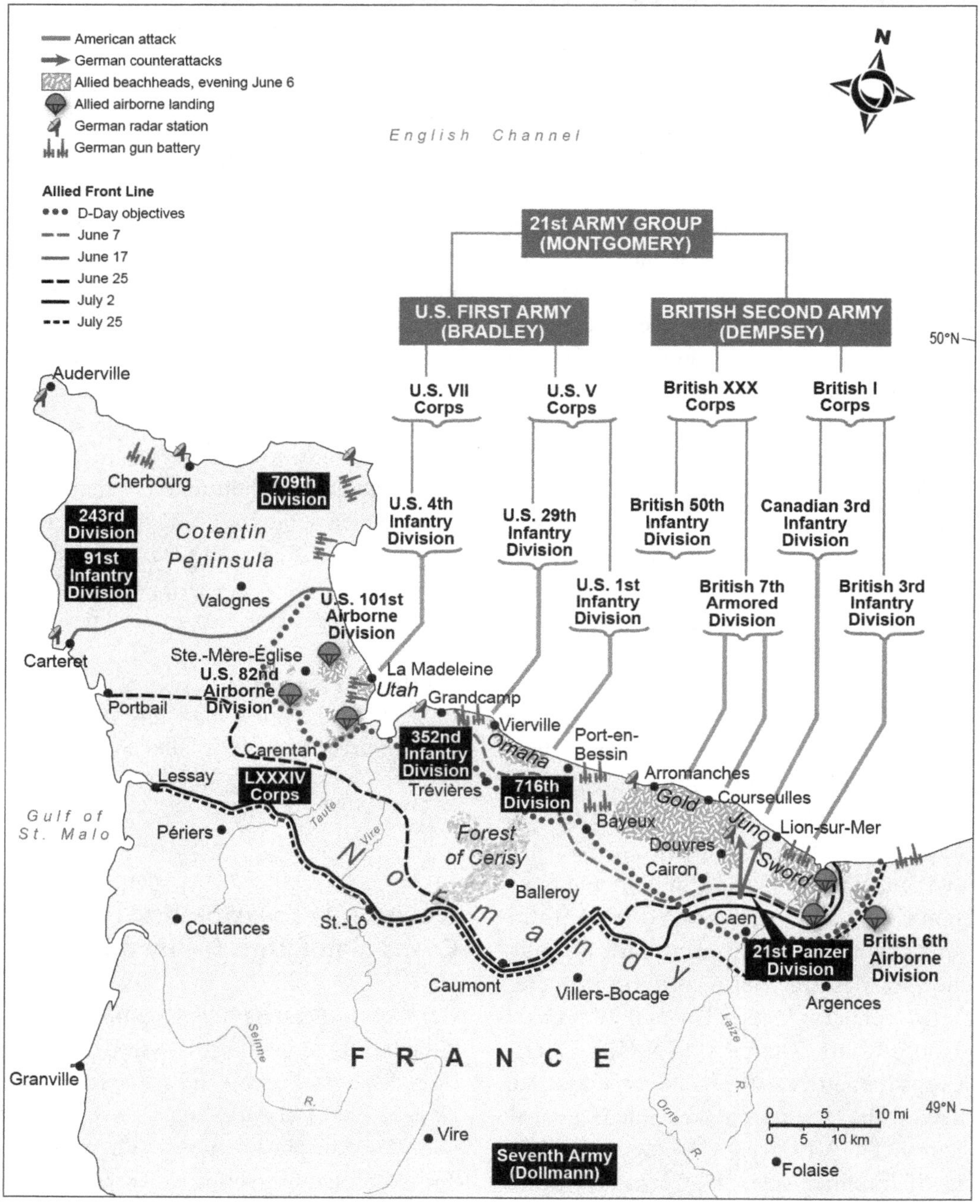

Hitler, "If we don't manage to throw them back at once, the invasion will succeed in spite of the Atlantic Wall." Rundstedt argued that Allied naval and air supremacy made a forward defense impossible, and, therefore, a large mobile reserve should be used to defeat the Allied forces once they were ashore. Hitler opted for the worst possible plan, which was a combination of Rommel's and Rundstedt's. Indeed, Hitler seems to have welcomed the invasion as a chance to engage and destroy the British and U.S. forces.

Rommel had under his command the Fifteenth Army in northern France and the Seventh Army in Normandy, a total of twenty-five static coastal divisions, sixteen infantry and parachute divisions, twenty armored and mechanized divisions, and seven reserve divisions. The Germans were hopelessly overmatched in the air and on the water, however. The Luftwaffe's Third Air Fleet in France deployed only 329 aircraft on D-Day, and German naval forces in the area consisted of four destroyers and thirty-nine E-boats. Germany also deployed several dozen U-boats during the campaign, most from French ports.

Meanwhile, U.S. and British aircraft worked to soften the German defenses and isolate the beachheads. Between April 1 and June 5, 1944, Allied aircraft flew two hundred thousand sorties in support of the coming invasion and dropped one hundred and ninety-five thousand tons of bombs. The Allies lost two thousand of their own aircraft in the process, but, by D-Day, they had largely isolated the landing areas and had achieved virtually total air supremacy. In one of the greatest military engineering achievements in history, thousands of men labored in Britain for months to build two large artificial harbors known as "Mulberries." Plans called for these, after the initial Allied landings, to be hauled across the Channel from Britain and sunk in place. By the end of October, 25 percent of stores, 20 percent of personnel, and 15 percent of vehicles had passed through Mulberry B.

The Allies worked out precise and elaborate plans for the mammoth cross-Channel invasion, code-named OVERLORD, to occur on the Cotentin Peninsula in Normandy. British Admiral Bertram H. Ramsay had overall command of the naval operation, code-named NEPTUNE, and British General Sir Bernard Montgomery exercised overall command of the land forces. The overall Allied commander was U.S. General Dwight D. Eisenhower. The object of the operation was "to secure a lodgment on the continent, from which further offensive operations can be developed."

The German 21st Panzer and 12th SS Panzer Divisions were stationed just outside Caen. If they were permitted to reach the beaches, they could strike the amphibious forces from the flank and roll them up. To combat these, the invaders relied on a night drop of paratroops, to occur before the landing itself. Three Allied airborne divisions took part: the British 6th and the U.S. 82nd and 101st. The lightly armed paratroopers, operating in conjunction with the French Resistance, had the vital task of securing the flanks of the lodgment and destroying key transportation choke points to prevent the Germans from reinforcing their beach defenses.

The amphibious assault took place early on the morning of June 6, with five infantry divisions landing along the fifty-mile stretch of coast, divided into five sectors. The designated beaches were, from west to east, the U.S. 4th Infantry Division (Utah), the U.S. 1st Infantry (Omaha), the British 50th Infantry (Gold), the Canadian 3rd Infantry (Juno), and the British 3rd Infantry

(Sword). Operation OVERLORD proved a vast undertaking. The airborne forces alone required 1,340 C-47 transports and 2,500 gliders. Ten thousand aircraft secured the skies. Naval support for the invasion came from 138 bombardment warships, 221 destroyers and other convoy escorts, 287 minesweepers, 495 light craft, and 441 auxiliaries. In addition, there were four thousand landing ships and other craft of various sizes.

The airborne operation involving twenty-three thousand, four hundred U.S. and British paratroops occurred on schedule on the night of June 5 to 6, but thick cloud banks over Normandy caused pilots to veer off-course to avoid midair collisions. German antiaircraft fire, jumpy Allied flight crews, and Allied Pathfinders who were immediately engaged in firefights on the ground and unable to set up their beacons led to premature drops and to paratroopers being scattered all over the peninsula and some into the English Channel. Nonetheless, improvised Allied units were soon moving on the objectives and, despite tough German resistance, most of these were secured.

Success was likely if the Allies could establish a bridgehead large enough to allow them to build up their strength and overcome the German defenders. Once they broke out, the Allies would have the whole of France for maneuver, because their armies were fully mechanized and the bulk of the defending German forces were not. The only possibility of German success was for the defenders to commit their panzer reserves rapidly, but this step was fatally delayed by two factors. The first was naval gunfire support and air superiority of thirty to one over Normandy itself. The second was Hitler's failure to immediately commit resources available elsewhere. Hitler was convinced that the invasion at Normandy was a feint and that the main thrust would come in the Pas de Calais sector.

Allied deception plans played a key role in deluding him. Not until late July did Hitler authorize the movement of the panzer forces from the Pas de Calais to Normandy. In effect, the deception totally immobilized nineteen German divisions east of the Seine. Although units of the Fifteenth Army were moved west to Normandy before that date, this was done piecemeal and, hence, they were much easier for the Allies to defeat.

The landing was in jeopardy only on Omaha Beach. Troops of the U.S. 1st Infantry Division were pinned down by a withering German fire. U.S. First Army commander, Lieutenant General Omar N. Bradley, even considered withdrawal. Gunfire support ships opened up against the German shore batteries, and destroyer captains repeatedly risked running their ships aground to provide close-in fire support to the troops ashore. Still, German resistance was fierce, and it was nearly noon before the defenders began to give way. The invaders overcame stubborn German opposition, with sheer determination reinforced by the knowledge that there was no place to retreat. The landings on the other beaches were easier. Overall, for the first day, the Allies sustained some ten thousand, three hundred casualties—forty-three hundred British and Canadian and six thousand U.S. Still, the losses were comparatively light. The Allies put ashore 75,215 British and Canadian troops and 57,500 U.S. forces on D-Day and one million men within a month.

The Allied ground offensive, meanwhile, proceeded more slowly than expected. Hitler ordered his armies to fight for every inch of ground rather than withdraw along phase lines, as his generals wanted. This decision by Hitler at first delayed the Allied timetable. However, it also greatly accelerated the ultimate defeat and ensured that it would be costly. Complete Allied air superiority devastated the Germans by day and forced them to move largely at night. The Norman countryside, however, proved ideal defensive terrain. Over the centuries, the dividing lines between individual fields had been allowed to grow up into tangled hedgerows. This *bocage* resisted passage and slowed the Allied advance to a crawl. On June 17 and 18, the Germans blocked Montgomery's efforts to take the city of Caen. U.S. VII Corps had more success on the Allied right, gradually pushing across the base of the Cotentin Peninsula. On June 18, it turned north to liberate the important port of Cherbourg, held by eighteen thousand German defenders under Lieutenant General Karl-Wilhelm von Schlieben, while the remainder of Bradley's army maintained an aggressive defense. Cherbourg fell on June 27, but its defenders destroyed the harbor facilities, and it would take U.S. engineers six weeks to get them back in operation.

Not until Operation COBRA on July 25 to 31 were the Allies able to break out. Bradley's U.S. First Army forced the German line west of Saint-Lô, and Collins's VII Corps made the main effort. All northern France was open for the highly mechanized Allied units to maneuver. On August 15, a large Allied force came ashore on the French Mediterranean coast in Operation DRAGOON. The German defenders were now in full retreat, but it remained to be seen if the Allies could maintain their fast-lengthening supply lines and end the war in the west before the Germans had a chance to recover.

Spencer C. Tucker

See also: COBRA, Allied Breakout Operation; FORTITUDE, Allied Deception Operation; Organization Todt (OT); Rommel, Erwin; Rundstedt, Karl Rudolf Gerd von; Southern France, Allied Invasion and Campaign (Operation DRAGOON)

Additional Reading

D'Este, Carlo. *Decision in Normandy.* New York: E. P. Dutton, 1983.

Hastings, Max. *Overlord: D-Day, June 6, 1944.* New York: Simon and Schuster, 1984.

Isby, David C. *The German Army at D-Day: Fighting the Invasion.* London: Greenhill, 2004.

North Africa Campaign (June 10, 1940–May 13, 1943)

The campaign in North Africa was fought over control of the Suez Canal and access to the Mediterranean. The Suez Canal and the Mediterranean were Britain's primary lifelines to its overseas dominions and access to Middle Eastern oil and raw materials from Asia. The ground campaign in North Africa and the naval campaign for the Mediterranean, therefore, were two sides of the same strategic coin. For Germany, however, North Africa was never a decisive theater of war. Germany committed forces to North Africa to shore up its unreliable and overextended ally, Italy. The primary mission of German forces was one of economy of force, a key point that Field Marshal Erwin Rommel never seemed to have understood.

The war in North Africa started between the British and Italians across the Libyan-Egyptian border in an area known as the Western Desert. Italian Marshal Rodolfo Graziani cautiously moved into Egypt on September 13, 1940, halting at Sidi Barrani, just short of the British main positions at Mersa Matrûh. On December 9, the Western Desert Force, commanded by General Sir Richard O'Connor, attacked at Sidi

North African Operations, 1940–1942

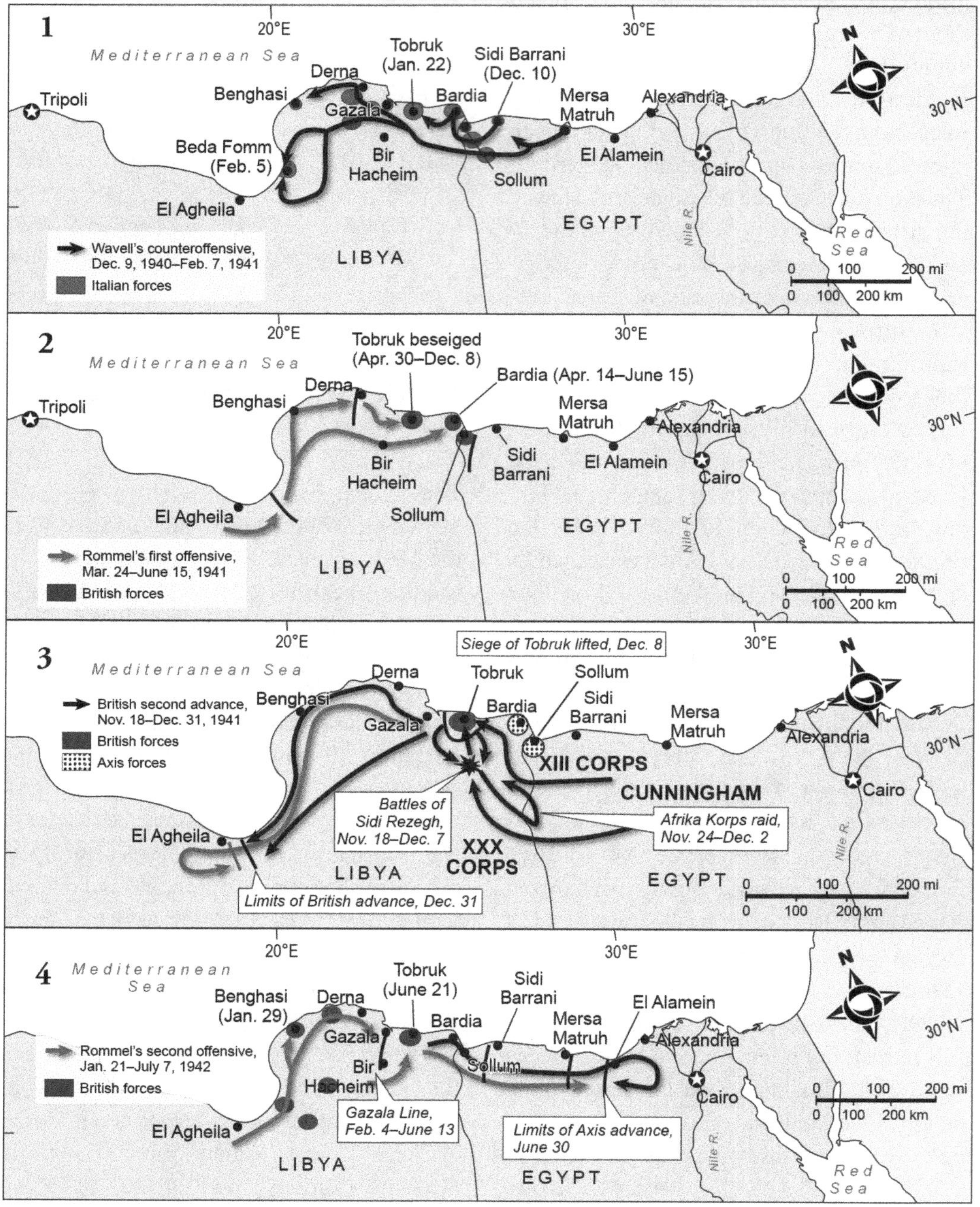

Barrani, drove the Italian Tenth Army from Egypt and achieved a major victory on January 3, 1941 at Bardia, just inside Libya. Driving deeper into Cyrenaica (eastern Libya), the British captured the vital port of Tobruk on January 22. Continuing forward, O'Connor trapped the Italian Tenth Army at Beda Fomm on February 7, 1941.

Adolf Hitler decided to reinforce the Italians in North Africa, and by the end of February, Lieutenant General Erwin Rommel arrived in command of the three-division-strong Deutsches Afrika Korps, consisting of the 15th and 21st Panzer Divisions, and the 90th Light Afrika Division. Rommel probed El Agheila on March 4 and continued driving rapidly to the east despite Hitler's orders to maintain an overall defensive posture. The Germans surrounded Tobruk on April 10 but were unable to take the fortress by a coup de main. Rommel left a siege force of mostly Italian units and continued his drive toward the Egyptian border. But the Tobruk garrison held out for 240 days and tied down vital Axis manpower in Rommel's rear area. Rommel's main force, meanwhile, reached Sollum on the Egyptian border on April 14, and the Germans occupied the key terrain of the Halfaya Pass. The British came to call the heavily fortified and fiercely defended pass "Hellfire Pass."

Churchill pressured British Middle East Commander General Sir Archibald for action. Operation BATTLEAXE began on June 15, with a frontal attack through the Halfaya Pass toward Sollum. The German 88 mm antiaircraft guns stopped the British armor, and the Germans then counterattacked. The British lost ninety-one tanks, and Operation BATTLEAXE was over by June 17. Churchill relieved Wavell four days later and replaced him the following month with General Sir Claude Auchinleck. General Sir Alan Cunningham took command of the Western Desert Force, which had been redesignated the British Eighth Army.

Rommel's force in North Africa slipped to near-bottom priority for logistical sustainment after Germany attacked the Soviet Union in June 1941. By November 1941, Rommel had 414 tanks, 320 aircraft, and nine divisions (three German), four of which were tied down in the siege of Tobruk. The British had some seven hundred tanks, one thousand aircraft, and eight (larger) divisions. The British launched Operation CRUSADER on November 18 and finally broke through to Tobruk on November 29. Overwhelmed by attrition to his forces, Rommel began to withdraw on December 7. The Germans retreated across Cyrenaica, reaching El Agheila on January 6, 1942. Operation CRUSADER was a victory for the British, but they were unable to exploit it because of a lack of reinforcements.

Rommel launched his second offensive on January 21, 1942. Within days, he drove the British back almost three hundred miles, halting on February 4 between Gazala and Bir Hacheim. Both sides then concentrated on building up their strength for the next four months. Rommel resumed operations on May 26, with Operation VENEZIA (VENICE), his attack against the Gazala Line. Rommel swept his armor around the Free French Brigade at Bir Hacheim on the southern end of the line and turned north, cutting across the Allied rear.

By May 28, the Axis armored units behind the Allied lines were in trouble. Rommel had lost more than one-third of his tanks, and the rest were short of fuel and ammunition. On May 29, the Italian Trieste Division managed to clear a path through the center of the Gazala Line, and that opening became a lifeline to Rommel's Panzers.

On May 30, Rommel consolidated his remaining armor in a defensive position that came to be called "The Cauldron."

On June 5 to 6, Rommel successfully beat back a series of piecemeal British counterattacks against the Cauldron. On June 10 to 11, the Axis finally drove the Free French from Bir Hacheim, and on June 11, Rommel's Panzers broke out of the Cauldron. The Eighth Army once more started falling back to the Egyptian border. On June 15, German tanks reached the coast, and Rommel shifted his attention to Tobruk, which fell on June 21.

The British fell back to Mersa Matrûh, about one hundred miles inside Egypt. Rommel, now promoted to field marshal for his victory at Gazala, pursued. Rommel had only sixty operational tanks, but he still attacked at Mersa Matrûh on June 26 and routed four British divisions in three days of fighting. The British fell back again another 120 miles to the east to the vicinity of El Alamein, less than 100 miles from Alexandria.

General Auchinleck was determined to hold near El Alamein. Although under constant pressure from Rommel's forces, Auchinleck improvised a fluid defensive line anchored on Ruweisat Ridge, a few miles south of the El Alamein perimeter. Rommel attacked on July 1, intending to sweep around El Alamein, but Auchinleck skillfully battled Rommel to a standstill over the course of three weeks of fighting. Auchinleck then launched a major counterattack on July 21–22 but made no progress. Exhausted, both sides paused to regroup.

Despite the fact that the British had finally halted Rommel's advance, British Prime Minister Winston Churchill relieved Auchinleck in early August and replaced him with General Sir Harold Alexander as commander in chief of the Middle East. Lieutenant General Sir Bernard L. Montgomery assumed command of the British Eighth Army.

On August 31, 1942, Rommel launched what he believed would be the final attack to carry the Axis forces to the Nile. Montgomery, however, had made extensive preparations around El Alamein, based on a plan developed by Auchinleck. Rommel intended to sweep around to the south of Ruweisat Ridge and cut off El Alamein from the rear. However, the British had laid extensive minefields and had heavily fortified Alam Halfa Ridge behind and southeast of El Alamein. Rommel's attack ran short of fuel and stalled by September 3. Montgomery counterattacked immediately but halted as soon as the Axis forces were pushed back to their starting positions. Taken together, the battles of Ruweisat Ridge and Alam Halfa were the real operational turning point of the war in North Africa.

Montgomery used the time after Alam Halfa to plan carefully a set-piece counterattack from El Alamein. The battle started on October 23, 1942, and the British tried for five days to break through the Axis positions. On October 31, Montgomery renewed the attack with strong support from the Royal Air Force. Critically short of fuel and ammunition, Rommel was forced to disengage on November 3. The following day, the fourteen-hundred-mile Axis withdrawal to Tunisia began. For the next three months, Montgomery followed, rather than aggressively pursued, Rommel and the Axis forces across the northern coast of Africa. Rommel reached the Tunisian border at the end of January 1943. By the time he got there, however, another Allied force was waiting for him.

On November 8, 1942, four days after Rommel began his long withdrawal, the British and Americans initiated Operation

TORCH, the invasion of Northwest Africa. U.S. Lieutenant General Dwight D. Eisenhower was in overall command. In a coordinated series of landings, the Western Task Force, under Major General George S. Patton Jr., landed on the Atlantic coast near Casablanca; the Center Task Force, under Major General Lloyd Fredendall, landed just inside the Mediterranean around Oran; and the Eastern Task Force, under Major General Charles Ryder, landed near Algiers. Although all the landing sites were in Vichy French territory, the ultimate objectives of the operation were the Tunisian city of Tunis and the port and airfield complex at Bizerte.

The Germans reacted by sending troops from Sicily to Tunisia on November 9. From the moment the Allies landed, the campaign in Northwest Africa and the race for Tunis was a logistical battle. The side that could mass forces more quickly would win. For the Germans, control of the Tunis complex was critical to prevent Rommel from being trapped between Montgomery in the east and the newly formed British First Army in the west. On November 28, the Allies reached Tebourba, only twelve miles from Tunis, but an Axis counterattack drove them back twenty miles in seven days. In January 1943, the winter rains and resulting mud brought mechanized operations to a halt in northern Tunisia. The Axis side had temporarily won the race.

Waiting for better weather in the spring, the Allies continued to build up their forces. Lieutenant General Sir Kenneth Anderson's British First Army was organized into three corps—the British V Corps, the U.S. II Corps, and the French XIX Corps. The Axis forces in northern Tunisia now consisted of Colonel General Jürgen von Arnim's Fifth Panzer Army. Once Rommel's Panzerarmee Afrika crossed into southern Tunisia, it occupied positions in the old French fortifications of the Mareth Line. Rommel's ten divisions were well below half strength, with a total of only 78,000 troops and 129 tanks. Before he had to face Montgomery, rapidly closing from the rear, Rommel intended to eliminate the threat of the British First Army to his north. On February 14, the Germans launched the first leg of a two-pronged offensive, with von Arnim's forces attacking through the Faid Pass for Sidi Bou Zid. The following day, Rommel in the south attacked toward Gafsa. The bulk of Rommel's forces, however, remained along the Mareth Line. By February 18, the Kasserine Pass, held by U.S., II Corps, was in Axis hands. The U.S. Army had suffered its first major defeat at the hands of the Germans. Rommel tried to advance north through the Kasserine Pass on February 19, but he did not get the support he expected from Arnim. Hampered by a divided German command structure and the rapidly massing Allied reinforcements, the attack stalled.

The Allies recaptured Kasserine Pass on February 25. Rommel returned to the Mareth Line and prepared to face Montgomery. On February 24, the Axis powers realigned their command structure, with Rommel becoming the commander of Armeegruppe Afrika, which included the Afrika Korps, von Arnim's Fifth Panzer Army, and the Italian First Army under General Giovanni Messe. For the first time, the Axis powers had a unified command structure in Africa.

Montgomery's units crossed into Tunisia on February 4, reaching Medenine on February 16. Hoping to catch the British off balance, on March 6, Rommel attacked south from the Mareth Line. Warned by Allied intelligence ULTRA intercepts, Montgomery was ready. Immediately following the failure of the Medenine attack, Rommel returned to Germany on sick leave. Arnim assumed overall Axis command, and Messe took command in south Tunisia. By March 26, the British broke through the Mareth Line at the Tebaga gap, forcing the Italian First Army and the remainder of the Afrika Korps back to the north. Under continuous pressure from the British Eighth Army on one side and U.S. II Corps on the other, the Axis forces withdrew north to Enfidaville.

On April 7, 1942, the Allied First and Eighth Armies linked up, squeezing the Axis forces into a tight pocket. On the east coast, the Eighth Army took Gabes on April 6, Sfax on April 10, Sousse on April 12, and Enfidaville on April 21. In the north, the U.S. II Corps, now under Lieutenant General Omar N. Bradley, took Mateur on May 3 and Bizerte on May 7. Montgomery's 7th Armoured Division also captured Tunis on May 7. The remaining Axis forces in Tunisia were caught in two pockets, one between Bizerte and Tunis, and the other on isolated Cape Bon.

Arnim surrendered his forces on May 12, and Meese surrendered his on May 13. The Royal Navy, waiting in strength offshore, made sure that few Germans or Italians escaped to Sicily by sea. Axis losses in Tunisia alone totaled 40,000 dead or wounded, 240,000 prisoners, 250 tanks, 2,330 aircraft, and 232 vessels. British and American casualties were 33,000 and 18,558, respectively. For the entire North African Campaign, the British suffered 220,000 casualties. Total Axis losses came to 620,000, which included the loss of three field armies. The losses were large for what amounted to a secondary theater for both sides.

David T. Zabecki

See also: Rommel, Erwin

Additional Reading

Barnett, Correlli. *The Desert Generals.* New York: Viking Press, 1961.

Mellenthin, Friedrich Wilhelm von. *Panzer Battles: A Study of the Employment of Armor in the Second World War.* Norman: University of Oklahoma Press, 1956.

Pitt, Barrie. *The Crucible of War: Western Desert 1941.* New York: Paragon House, 1989.

Pitt, Barrie. *The Crucible of War: The Year of Alamein, 1942.* New York: Paragon House, 1990.

North Cape, Battle of (December 26, 1943)

In the autumn of 1943, the western Allies agreed to send forty merchant ships a month to the Soviet Union via the Arctic to Murmansk. The chief German resistance was likely to come from two German submarine flotillas in Norway, but German Navy commander Grand Admiral Karl Dönitz intended to commit German surface units as well. Dönitz had planned to use the battleship *Tirpitz* for this purpose, but it had been damaged during a British midget submarine raid in September. Gaining permission from Hitler also proved difficult, but Dönitz persevered, and, in December 1943, he was ready to attack. On December 19, he informed Hitler that he would attack the next eastbound convoy. Allied intelligence ULTRA intercepts and increased German air, surface, and submarine activity provided advance warning to British Home Fleet commander, Admiral Sir Bruce Fraser of the German plans.

On December 20, convoy JW 55B of nineteen merchant ships sailed eastbound, and two days later, the corresponding homebound convoy RA 55A of twenty-two merchant ships departed Kola Inlet. Each convoy had a close escort of about a dozen destroyers. Long-range protection of both convoys fell to Vice Admiral Robert Burnett's Force 1, with the cruisers HMS *Norfolk*, *Belfast*, and *Sheffield.*

On December 22, Luftwaffe reconnaissance aircraft spotted the eastbound JW 55B. The British deciphered the German sighting report and the order to all U-boats in the area to close with the convoy. Fraser assessed that German surface units in Norway, led by the battleship *Scharnhorst,* would join the hunt, and he departed Iceland on December 23 with the battleship *Duke of York* (flag), light cruiser *Jamaica*, and four destroyers. Fraser's intention was to position his own surface forces between the Germans and their base at Altenfjord.

German Rear Admiral Erich Bey led the *Scharnhorst* and five large fleet destroyers to sea on December 25 from Altenfjord. The *Scharnhorst* was commanded by Captain Fritz Hintze. At 0900 hours on September 26, the *Belfast* secured a radar contact on *Scharnhorst.* At 0930 hours, the *Norfolk* opened fire and probably hit the *Scharnhorst* with its second or third eight-inch salvo, which may have knocked out the battle cruiser's radar and convinced Bey to break off the action without replying. Shortly after noon, the *Belfast* reported a radar contact. A second action involved all three British cruisers and lasted about twenty minutes. Again, the British observed hits on the *Scharnhorst.*

Bey headed south, and Burnett pursued. The *Duke of York* picked up *Scharnhorst* on radar and opened fire at 25,800 yards. The *Scharnhorst* was hit with the first salvo. Bey responded with a burst of speed and tried to open the range. He almost succeeded, but a British salvo disabled one of the *Scharnhorst*'s boiler rooms at a critical juncture, and Fraser's cruisers and destroyers fired from both flanks a total of fifty-five torpedoes. The *Scharnhorst* went down at 1945 hours. The British ships searched for survivors, but only thirty-six of the *Scharnhorst*'s three-thousand-man crew were recovered. Admiral Bey was not among them. British losses were eleven killed, eleven wounded, and three ships damaged, but the last capital-ship duel in European waters ended in a British victory.

James Levy

See also: Dönitz, Karl; Warships, Surface

Additional Reading

Watts, A. J. *The Loss of the Scharnhorst.* London: Allan, 1972.

Northwest Africa Landings, Allied (Operation TORCH) (November 8–16, 1942). *See* North Africa Campaign

Norway Campaign (April 9–June 8, 1940)

Convinced that the Allies were planning a Norwegian intervention, Hitler began in February 1940 to prepare for the German occupation of Denmark and Norway, Operation WESSERÜBUNG (WESSER EXERCISE). The invasion was scheduled for March 20, but ice in the Baltic delayed it until April 9. Meanwhile, the British began mine-laying operations in Norwegian territorial waters early on April 8.

Germany committed five infantry divisions, two regiments of mountain troops, and a battalion of light tanks. To seize six Norwegian coastal cities, the German navy transported 8,850 soldiers. The remaining 54,500 troops would be sent in once the initial objectives were secure. General of Infantry Nikolaus von Falkenhorst, commander of the XXI Army Corps, was the overall ground forces commander. The Luftwaffe assembled more than one thousand aircraft for the operation. The most daring feature of German air operations was the first large-scale use of transport aircraft to deploy troops, support units, and supplies into the attack. More than five hundred aircraft took part. Lieutenant General Hans Ferdinand Geisler, commander of the X Air Corps, was the overall air commander. The Kriegsmarine committed to the operation the battleships *Gneisenau* and *Scharnhorst* and the pre-Dreadnaught *Schleswig-Holstein*; ten warship groups totaling three heavy cruisers, four light cruisers, and fourteen destroyers; and eight U-boat groups totaling thirty-five submarines. The overall commander of Naval Group Command West was General Admiral Alfred Saalwächter.

The Germans secured most of their immediate objectives. German paratroopers seized Sola, the largest Norwegian air base, and by April 11, two hundred German warplanes were flying from the captured airfield. In the water approaches to Oslo, the Norwegians managed to sink the heavy cruiser *Blücher*. The British Navy struck swiftly at the German fleet. On April 10, British destroyers attacked German destroyers at Narvik. Backed by the old battleship HMS *Warspite*, the British attacked again on April 13, sinking the last of the ten German destroyers. But British warships operating off the central Norwegian coast without fighter protection came under attack from approximately ninety Luftwaffe bombers. The Royal Navy quickly decided not to risk major warships within range of German air power.

The Allies committed twelve thousand, five hundred soldiers to central Norway. By April 20, five British and three French battalions were ashore, intending to recapture Trondheim. The operation failed, and the Allies abandoned central Norway by May 3. In the north, meanwhile, a British brigade and three French battalions besieged three German battalions at Narvik. On May 28, French, British, Polish, and Norwegian troops ousted the Germans from Narvik and drove them to the Swedish border. But with the Germans now overrunning France, the Allies finally withdrew their twenty-five thousand troops from Norway by June 8.

During the fighting on land, the Germans lost 3,692 men killed and missing, the Norwegians 1,335, and the French and Poles 530. The British lost 1,896 dead, missing, and severely wounded. The Luftwaffe lost 242 aircraft, and the British lost 112 aircraft. In fighting at sea, the British lost an aircraft carrier, two light cruisers, and seven destroyers. The French and Poles each lost a destroyer. The Norwegian Campaign badly damaged the German surface navy; its losses included the *Blücher*, the light cruisers *Königsberg* and *Karlsruhe*, and ten destroyers. The Germans now had only three cruisers and four destroyers undamaged, although other damaged ships could be repaired. After repairs at Narvik, the flow of Swedish iron ore—the main reason Germany had conquered Norway—continued without interruption to the end of the war.

Sherwood S. Cordier

See also: Raeder, Erich

Additional Reading

Kersaudy, François. *Norway, 1940.* London: Collins, 1990.

Moulton, J. L. *The Norwegian Campaign of 1940: A Study of Warfare in Three Dimensions.* London: Camelot Press, 1966.

O

Oberkommando der Luftwaffe (OKL) (1935–1945)

The *Oberkommando der Luftwaffe* (OKL) was the operational high command of the German Air Force during World War II. Reich Minister of Aviation Hermann Göring controlled all aspects of German aviation, civilian and military. Although the *Oberkommando der Luftwaffe* was supposed to command all aspects of military aviation, Göring purposely kept functions fragmented as a way of maintaining his personal control. The focus and coherence of Germany's aviation programs suffered accordingly. The OKL was far less operationally effective than its two service counterparts, the Army's *Oberkommando des Heeres* (OKH) and the Navy's *Oberkommando der Marine* (OKM). In theory, all three service high commands were operationally subordinate to the *Oberkommando der Wehrmacht* (OKW), the supreme command of the armed forces. In practice, like much else in the organization of the Third Reich, they functioned like so many competing feudal fiefdoms, with OKL being the most fragmented and inefficient.

David T. Zabecki

See also: Göring, Hermann; *Oberkommando der Marine* (OKM); *Oberkommando der Wehrmacht* (OKW); *Oberkommando des Heeres* (OKH)

Additional Reading

Murray, Williamson. *Luftwaffe*. Mount Pleasant, SC: Nautical and Aviation Publishing Company, 1985.

Oberkommando der Marine (OKM) (1936–1945)

The *Oberkommando der Marine* (OKM) was the operational high command of the German Navy of World War II. The OKM was established on January 11, 1936 from the Reichswehr's *Marineleiting* (Naval Command). It was the navy's equivalent of the Army's *Oberkommando des Heeres* (OKH) and the air force's *Oberkommando der Luftwaffe* (OKL). From 1938 on, all three service commands were in theory operationally subordinate to the *Oberkommando der Wehrmacht* (OKW), the supreme command of the armed forces. In practice, like much else in the organization of the Third Reich, all four command organs functioned like so many competing feudal fiefdoms. Within OKM, the *Seekriegsleitung* (SKL) (Naval Warfare Command) was established in 1937. The commander in chief of the navy was dual-hatted as the commander of SKL, assisted by the chief of the admiralty staff.

David T. Zabecki

See also: *Oberkommando der Luftwaffe* (OKL); *Oberkommando der Wehrmacht* (OKW); *Oberkommando des Heeres* (OKH)

Additional Reading

Ruge, Friedrich. *Der Seekrieg: The German Navy's Story 1939–1945*. Annapolis, MD: U.S. Naval Institute Press, 1957.

Oberkommando der Wehrmacht (OKW) (1938–1945)

In 1933, the Nazi regime appointed as defense minister a professional soldier, General Werner von Blomberg. The National Defense Law of May 21, 1935 redesignated the defense minister as war minister and commander in chief of the Wehrmacht. In January 1938, Blomberg resigned, following defamation by rivals within the regime. On February 4, 1938, Hitler dissolved the War Ministry, personally assumed the duties of war minister and commander in chief, and elevated the ministry's interservice office to a command headquarters, *Oberkommando der Wehrmacht* (OKW).

Hitler marginalized the traditional General Staff and elevated inferior, but compliant, officers. The most senior were Wilhelm Keitel as chief of the OKW and Alfred Jodl as chief of the Military Operations Office (Wehrmachtführungsamt). Hitler preferred to communicate directly with the military services rather than through OKW. Nominally, OKW was the superior command headquarters, but it lacked comprehensive interservice authorities. The capacities of the OKW operations staff remained limited—its total complement, including clerical staff, numbered about twenty-five in 1942 and reached about fifty in 1944.

After Hitler took direct command of the army in December 1941, he transferred to OKW many of the army's administrative authorities. For most of the war, Hitler was located in forward field headquarters, while most OKW staff were in Berlin. OKW's authority increased after the assassination attempt of July 1944, for which Hitler blamed the army most. As a result, army leaders lost Hitler's confidence. OKW's authority peaked days before Hitler committed suicide in April 1945, when OKW took command of OKH and after Hitler's suicide, when it supported the regime's new leader in its dying days.

Bruce Newsome

See also: Blomberg, Werner von; Blomberg-Fritsch Crisis; Jodl, Alfred; Keitel, Wilhelm; *Oberkommando des Heeres* (OKH)

Additional Reading

Megargee, Geoffrey P. *Inside Hitler's High Command.* Lawrence: University of Kansas Press, 2000.

Oberkommando des Heeres (OKH) (1935–1945)

In May 1935, the Nazi regime established an army high command (*Oberkommando des Heeres*—OKH) between the army General Staff and the new war minister and commander in chief of the military (Wehrmacht). The regime appointed Werner von Fritsch to command the army and Ludwig Beck to lead the army general staff. In 1936, the commander of the army was granted equal rank with cabinet members. In January 1938, Fritsch resigned, following defamation by members of the regime. On February 4, 1938, Hitler absorbed the duties of war minister and commander in chief, elevated the War Ministry's interservice office to a new command (*Oberkommando der Wehrmacht*—OKW), and appointed Walther von Brauchitsch as commander of the army. Beck opposed the structural changes, opposed the expansion of Nazi paramilitary forces, and curbed the regime's belligerence, but he failed to mobilize opposition and resigned in August, almost immediately taking an ultimately fatal part in a revolutionary conspiracy. In September, Hitler appointed Franz Halder as chief of the army's General Staff.

Through 1940, OKH led Germany's invasions of its neighbors, while OKW led planning for operations overseas, with increasing intervention from Hitler. The army was responsible for the eastern front that emerged in 1941, but OKW took authority for all other fronts. Consequently, the army's operations department contained sections for only Russia, the Balkans, and (from 1943) counterinsurgency. Disagreements intensified after the invasion of the Soviet Union, particularly from October onwards, when the army became overstretched. Brauchitsch repeatedly urged withdrawal to shorter lines. Brauchitsch resigned when he felt incapacitated by cardiac illness, perhaps hoping that the break would be temporary. On December 10, 1941, Hitler assumed the title of commander in chief of the army.

In September 1942, Hitler replaced Halder with Kurt Zeitzler, who, in turn, was replaced on July 1, 1944 by Heinz Guderian. By 1945, Guderian lacked any real dialogue with Hitler, although Hitler refused to accept his resignation until he abruptly dismissed Guderian on March 28, 1945. Hitler did not replace Guderian, although General Hans Krebs acted as chief. Within one month, Hitler transferred all OKH's remaining activities to OKW's direct or indirect command.

Bruce Newsome

See also: Beck, Ludwig; Brauchitsch, Walther von; Fritsch, Werner von; German General Staff of World War II; Guderian, Heinz; Halder, Franz; Krebs, Hans; *Oberkommando der Wehrmacht* (OKW); Zeitzler, Kurt

Additional Reading

Wheeler-Bennett, John W. *The Nemesis of Power: The German Army in Politics, 1918–1945*. New York: Macmillan, 1964.

Opposition to Hitler, German Military (1938–1945)

Various members of the German military opposed to Hitler and the Nazi regime engaged in numerous forms of resistance, from passive disobedience to several assassination attempts. Their efforts culminated with the July Bomb Plot of 1944. When President Paul von Hindenburg died in August 1934, the German military swore an oath of loyalty to Hitler himself, thus committing itself to unquestioned loyalty to the new Nazi regime. Along with promises to restore the military to its former greatness and reasserting Germany's power on the world stage, many were convinced to support the Nazi regime. Yet there still remained those who harbored grave concerns over the direction Hitler was leading Germany, and such concerns would drive many into the opposition.

Hitler's intention to invade Czechoslovakia in 1938 sparked the first major stirrings of opposition. Many generals were opposed to going to war and openly voiced their concerns. Among them was General Ludwig Beck, chief of the General Staff, who became the principle figure of the military opposition in the subsequent years. Beck was convinced that Hitler had to be removed from power, but he failed to gather enough support from the military high command to take action. Beck's successor as chief of the General Staff, General Franz Halder, was also convinced Hitler needed to be removed in the advent of war with Britain and France. Halder collaborated with Admiral Wilhelm Canaris, head of the Abwehr, and Major General Hans Oster, head of Military Counterintelligence, in organizing plans for a military coup known as the September Plot. The success for such a coup depended heavily upon the firm determination of the British to stand up to Hitler. Such plans failed because Prime Minister Neville Chamberlain preferred a policy of appeasement, and thus rejected any offers to cooperate with the military opposition.

It was not until the military setbacks after the defeat at Moscow in 1941, combined with horror at war crimes being committed behind the front lines, that the opposition began to gather support again. A new breed of leaders emerged, consisting more of lower-ranking officers. Among this new breed was General Henning von Treskow, chief of staff of Army Group Center, who lead a major opposition circle on the eastern front from 1942 to 1943. His circle made an attempt to assassinate Hitler during a visit to the eastern front on March 13, 1943. A bomb was secretly smuggled onto Hitler's plane, but because of technical malfunctions, it failed to explode. Along with that and other assassination plots, Treskow's circle also engaged in activities ranging from falsifying reports to the prevention of war crimes whenever possible. Attempts were made at contacting the Allies to request support, but they were ignored because of the Allied commitment to the unconditional surrender of Germany.

With the Allied invasion of France in June 1944, the opposition grew more desperate in order to save Germany from final defeat, which resulted in the ill-fated July Bomb Plot, or Operation VALKYRIE. On July 20, 1944, Colonel Claus Schenk von Stauffenberg, chief of staff of the Replacement Army, planted a bomb in Hitler's headquarters in East Prussia, but Hitler survived the explosion. Meanwhile, waiting for confirmation that the Führer was dead, Stauffenberg's coconspirators lost cohesion. When news came that Hitler was still alive, SS chief Heinrich Himmler and the head of the *Oberkommando der Wehrmacht* (Armed Forces High Command), Field Marshal Wilhelm Keitel, moved quickly to crush the plot. By that night, Stauffenberg, Beck, and other leading conspirators were executed. The failure of the July Bomb Plot was followed by a wave of repressions throughout Germany, and many more were tried before the dreaded People's Court (*Volksgericht*) for their connections to the failed coup. The opposition to Hitler within the military was effectively crushed as a result.

Stephen T. Satkiewicz

See also: Beck, Ludwig; Canaris, Wilhelm; Halder, Franz; Himmler, Heinrich; Keitel, Wilhelm; *Oberkommando der Wehrmacht* (OKW); Stauffenberg, Claus Schenk von

Additional Reading

Fest, Joachim. *Plotting Hitler's Death: The Story of the German Resistance.* Translated by Bruce Little. New York: Metropolitan Books, 1994.

Thomsett, Michael C. *The German Opposition to Hitler: The Resistance, the Underground, and Assassination Plots, 1938–1945.* Jefferson, NC: McFarland & Company, Inc., Publishers, 1997.

Oradour-sur-Glane Massacre (June 10, 1944)

Oradour-sur-Glane was the site of a German atrocity against French civilians. Located fifteen miles northwest of Limoges in central France, the small village of Oradour, was sacked on June 10, 1944 by troops from Sturmbannführer Otto Dickmann's 1st Battalion, 4th SS Panzergrenadier Regiment of the 2nd SS Panzer Division (Das Reich). In the immediate aftermath of the Allied Normandy Invasion of June 6, the 2nd SS Panzer Division, commanded by Obersturmbannführer Heinz Lammerding, received orders to redeploy to the Normandy front. As it made its way north, the division came under attack from French Resistance forces and engaged in several firefights. On June 9, the Resistance captured one of the division's officers, Sturmbannführer Helmut Kampfe. Possibly, the massacre at Oradour was in reprisal for this act.

On entering the village, the Panzergrenadiers of Dickmann's battalion forced the startled residents to assemble in the central square. Separating the men from the women and children, the Germans herded the former into barns and the latter into the village church. They then burned both the barns and church, tossing in grenades for good measure and gunning down those who tried to flee. After plundering and setting fire to other buildings, the Waffen-SS troops withdrew. A total of 642 victims, including 207 children, lay dead. Only seven villagers (five men, one woman, and a child) managed to escape. The 2nd SS Panzer Division proceeded to the Normandy front without encountering further Resistance activity.

In 1953, seven Germans and fourteen Alsatians were tried by a French military court at Bordeaux. The court found twenty of the defendants guilty and sentenced two to death and eighteen to imprisonment at hard labor for terms ranging from five to twenty years. Amnesties and pardons, however, led to all twenty being freed within five years.

Bruce J. DeHart

See also: Normandy Invasion and Campaign; Waffen-SS

Additional Reading

Hastings, Max. *Das Reich: Resistance and the March of the 2nd S.S. Panzer Division through France, June 1944.* New York: Holt, Rinehart, and Winston, 1981.

Organization Todt (OT) (1933–1945)

Organization Todt (OT), named for German Minister of Arms and Munitions Fritz Todt, handled construction projects throughout territory occupied by the German Army during World War II. Formed in 1933 by Todt, then head of technology and road construction, the OT was, at first, chiefly identified with construction of the great autobahn road system in Germany that was the pride of the Third Reich. In 1938, Hitler assigned OT the task of quickly completing the Westwall, defenses in western Germany that were designed to hold back a French Army attack in order to allow Germany to concentrate its military resources in the east. With the beginning of World War II, the OT provided the German Army with engineers and construction specialists for the building and repair of bridges, dams, airfields, and fortifications, as well as factories. OT's most ambitious task was the construction of the Atlantic Wall, the

German defenses against an invasion of Europe by the Western Allies; it ran from Norway to the Bay of Biscay. In autumn 1944, the organization was renamed the Front-OT, when it was armed and enlisted in the defense of German territory.

Spencer C. Tucker

See also: Atlantic Wall; Todt, Fritz; Westwall

Additional Reading

Seidler, Franz Wilhelm. *Die Organisation Todt: Bauen für Staat und Wehrmacht, 1938–1945*. Koblenz, Germany: Bernard and Graefe, 1987.

P

Palatinate Campaign, Allied (March 17–25, 1945)

The Allied Palatinate Campaign of March 1945 defeated the German forces west of the Rhine River and south of Worms. When German forces retreated from the Westwall in February and March 1945, they had insufficient fortified positions between them and the Rhine. Despite this, German commander in chief west, Field Marshal Albert Kesselring, insisted on the principle of no retreat unless absolutely necessary. Thus, the Germans were driven back to the river by the advancing Allied armies at a considerable cost to both the attacking and defending forces.

In early March, Allied commanders carefully studied the area known as the Palatinate (*Pfalz*), as they consolidated their victories in the adjoining Rhineland to the north and pummeled the Westwall in and around the Saarland. The Palatinate is the southern-most area of Germany, west of the Rhine River. In March 1945, it was in the sector of responsibility of SS-Oberstgruppenführer Paul Hausser's Army Group G and was defended by the First Army, commanded by General of Infantry Hermann Foertsch. General of Infantry Erich Brandenberger's Seventh Army was deployed to the north of the First Army.

On March 17, Supreme Allied Commander, General Dwight D. Eisenhower, decided to release Lieutenant General George S. Patton's U.S. Third Army to attack southeastward toward Kaiserslautern and the Rhine from the direction of Trier. Patton's line of advance was to go deep and cut across the axis of attack of Lieutenant General Alexander Patch's Seventh U.S. Army, which was on Patton's right and was still slugging its way through the Westwall but headed northeastward, also toward Kaiserslautern. Patton was to cut off the Germans being driven backward by Patch before they could flee across the Rhine. The French First Army, under General Jean de Lattre de Tassigny, yet farther south, was on Patch's right flank and likewise was attacking northeastward toward Speyer and the Rhine from the Saar and Strasbourg regions.

From March 17 to 24, the Germans fought a desperate delaying action. Foertsch's First Army, along with elements of Brandenberger's Seventh Army, bore the brunt of the Allied two-pronged attack. Large numbers of retreating German soldiers discarded their uniforms and donned whatever civilian clothing they could find in an effort to escape. German officials directed the evacuation of the civilian population to the degree possible. Policemen and firemen disappeared too, as did the civilian officials themselves, along with their incriminating Nazi files. German cities fell in rapid succession. Bad Kreuznach and Bingen capitulated on March 18. Worms fell to the Americans on March 19, and the same fate befell Zweibrücken, Mainz, Idar-Oberstein, and Kaiserslautern on March 20.

As the situation developed, the only possible escape route for the Germans was through the heavily forested Haardt Mountains of Pfälzer Forest, south of Kaiserslautern. That route, however, had limited roads and trails, which were soon either blocked or covered by the pursuing U.S. ground and air forces. Landau, Neustadt, Germersheim, and Doerrenbach surrendered on March 22. Bergzabern surrendered on March 23, and Speyer and Leimersheim did likewise on March 24. Only mopping-up operations remained by March 25. Many German cities were badly damaged in the fighting. Bad Kreuznach, Kaiserslautern, and Ludwigshafen were more than 25 percent destroyed. Pirmasens and Worms lost at least 50 percent of their structures, and in Mainz and Zweibrücken, more than 75 percent of the buildings were reduced to rubble.

In the combined Rhineland and Palatinate Campaigns, there were twenty thousand U.S. and sixty thousand German military dead and wounded. Additionally, the Americans captured two hundred and fifty thousand German prisoners. By the end of March, the victorious combat forces were headed eastward at high speed, and U.S. Military Government detachments were left in charge throughout the Palatinate.

Dewey A. Browder

See also: Brandenberger, Erich; Hausser, Paul; Kesselring, Albert; Remagen Bridge, U.S. Capture of; Rhineland Offensive, Allied

Additional Reading

Whitaker, W. Denis, and Shelagh Whitaker. *Rhineland: The Battle to End the War.* New York: St. Martin's Press, 1989.

Panther Pz.Kpfw.V Tank. *See* Tanks and Self-Propelled Guns

Panzer Division (1935–1945)

Panzer Divisions were armored divisions fielded by the German Wehrmacht and Waffen-SS during World War II. German field commanders, most notably Heinz Guderian, used massed formations of panzer divisions to defeat swiftly the Allied forces in France in May and June 1940 and to fight mobile campaigns in North Africa in 1941 to 1942. The panzer division, thereafter, became associated with the "Blitzkrieg" style of warfare. An expanded panzer force fought in the 1941 BARBAROSSA campaign in Russia. Despite their fame, panzer divisions were only a small proportion of the total combat forces of the Wehrmacht during the war. At their height, the Wehrmacht fielded twenty-nine panzer divisions out of a total force of almost three hundred divisions. Later in the war, when the Germans were almost exclusively on the defensive, panzer divisions were usually employed as "fire brigades" in mobile defensive operations. The divisions typically counterattacked to repulse Soviet and Western allied breakthroughs. The first three panzer divisions were established in 1935, with an additional two divisions available at the outbreak of war in 1939. By 1944, a full-strength panzer division typically fielded about 150 to 200 tanks. The Waffen-SS fielded eight panzer divisions. These divisions were similar in organization to those of the Wehrmacht.

John J. McGrath

See also: Guderian, Heinz; Panzergrenadier; Waffen-SS

Additional Reading

Rosado, Jorge. *Wehrmacht Panzer Divisions: 1939–45.* London: Amber Books, 2005.

Panzergrenadier

Panzergrenadier is the military German term for armored or mechanized infantry. In World War II, the term was adopted in 1942 to refer to both motorized and armored infantry elements found in panzer and panzergrenadier divisions. Prior to 1942, infantry in panzer divisions had been known as rifle (*Schützen*) troops. In 1943, the Wehrmacht adopted the traditional Prussian term "grenadier" to designate infantry elements and all the motorized and armored infantry became panzergrenadiers. Throughout the war the Wehrmacht fielded only a total of sixteen panzergrenadier divisions. One of these, the elite Grossdeutschland Panzergrenadier Division was, in fact, organized as a panzer division with a full panzer regiment. The Waffen-SS also deployed several panzergrenadier divisions.

In theory the panzergrenadiers, whether assigned to panzer or panzergrenadier divisions, were supposed to be true armored infantry, riding into battle on the half-tracked Sd.Kfz. (*Sonderkraftfahrzeug*) 251, also called the SPW (*Schützenpanzerwagen* or armored personnel carrier). The Sd.Kfz. 251, first fielded in 1939, came in numerous variants, based on armament and armored plating. Although planned to be the basic battlefield transportation for the panzergrenadiers, in practice there were never enough of the SPWs available. Most panzergrenadiers, accordingly, rode into battle in trucks. A typical panzer division in 1944 had only one or two of its four panzergrenadier battalions equipped with the Sd.Kfz. 251 or

Panzergrenadiers mounted in a Sd.Kfz. 251 half-track approach a settlement in Russia in early 1942. (ullstein bild via Getty Images)

other SPWs. A typical panzergrenadier division was similarly equipped. Roughly only 10 percent of Wehrmacht, Waffen-SS, and Luftwaffe panzergrenadier battalions were transported in armored vehicles.

John J. McGrath

See also: Panzer Division; Waffen-SS

Additional Reading

Zetterling, Niklas. *Normandy 1944: German Military Organization, Combat Power and Organizational Effectiveness.* Winnipeg: J. J. Fedorowicz, 2000.

Paris, Allied Liberation of (August 19–26, 1944)

The Germans occupied the French capital of Paris on June 14, 1940. On August 7, 1944, German General of Infantry Dietrich von Choltitz assumed command of the greater Paris area. In a personal meeting with Hitler, Choltitz was instructed to destroy Paris before allowing it to fall into Allied hands. Initially, the Western Allies had intended to bypass Paris on the assumption that once German forces had been isolated there, they would surrender. Supreme Allied Commander General Dwight D. Eisenhower issued orders to commander of French Forces of the Interior General Pierre Joseph Koenig that there be no uprising in the city, with consequent diversion of Allied troops, but political events dictated otherwise. The French Resistance was determined to liberate Paris, and the two rival factions of the Resistance, the Gaullists and the Communists, vied for the credit of liberating the capital.

On August 19, therefore, when Allied forces were still more than fifty miles from the city to the north and south, Gaullist elements in Paris preempted their Communist rivals by seizing the Paris prefecture of police. General von Choltitz immediately deployed infantry, backed by tanks, around the city, and the fighting spread. German tanks opened fire on the prefecture of police. By August 23, more than four hundred street barricades were in place, and localized intense fighting was occurring in many areas of the city. As the number of German casualties steadily mounted, Choltitz was faced with a dilemma. Swedish consul general in Paris Raoul Nordling pleaded with Choltitz to save the city and attempted, on his own initiative, to arrange a cease-fire. However, commander of Communist forces, Henri Tanguy (alias Colonel Rol), refused.

Choltitz could not cede the city to the insurgent civilians without resistance, because his family was in Germany. His not-unreasonable fear of reprisals against them apparently had some bearing on his decisions. Choltitz, however, minimized the combat in various ways, especially by his decision to move the bulk of German combat forces outside the city and into formal tactical defensive positions, oriented toward the approaching Allied armies in areas beyond the city limits. During the fighting, he also withheld the use of heavy artillery.

On August 21, Major General Philippe Leclerc, against Allied orders, turned his Free French 2nd Armored Division north toward Paris. Meanwhile, within the city, Resistance leaders met and decided to continue fighting. Choltitz, now determined to spare the city, sent Nordling to the Allies to ask that they enter Paris. Choltitz pledged to hold off destroying the city until they arrived. Eisenhower then agreed that Leclerc's division should move into Paris. At the same time, Choltitz ignored repeated orders from Berlin to begin the destruction of the French capital.

By early August 24, Leclerc's tanks reached Rambouillet, twenty miles south of Paris. The leader of the French government-in-exile, General Charles de Gaulle, arrived at the Chateau of Rambouillet that same day. Fighting was now raging in virtually every section of the city. By 1330 hours on August 24, Leclerc's tanks were in front of the Hôtel de Ville (city hall) in the center of Paris. On August 25, French and U.S. forces eliminated pockets of German resistance, and, at 1500 hours, Choltitz and his staff surrendered to French officers. Many of the German troops, unaware of the surrender, continued to fight. De Gaulle arrived in the city that evening.

Robert Bateman and Spencer C. Tucker

See also: Choltitz, Dietrich von

Additional Reading

Collins, Larry, and Dominique Lapierre. *Is Paris Burning?* New York: Simon and Schuster, 1965.

Ludewig, Joachim. *Rückzug: The German Retreat from France, 1944.* Lexington: University Press of Kentucky, 2012.

Paulus, Friedrich (1890–1957)

Wehrmacht field marshal.

Born on September 23, 1890 in Breitenau, Friedrich Paulus served on both fronts during World War I. He participated in the conquest of Poland and the 1940 offensive into Belgium and France. When the invasion of Britain, Operation SEA LION, was canceled, Paulus became deputy chief of staff of the Army Supreme Command and helped plan Operation BARBAROSSA, the invasion of the Soviet Union. In January 1942, Paulus assumed command of the Sixth Army in Russia. Later that year the Sixth Army was encircled at Stalingrad. Although relief efforts failed, Hitler refused Paulus permission to break out, ordering him instead to hold all ground. On January 24, 1943, Hitler denied Paulus's request for permission to surrender and promoted him to field marshal. Paulus surrendered nonetheless on January 31. Paulus was the first German field marshal to be captured in battle. Paulus remained in a Soviet prison until 1953. On his release, he became an inspector in the East German Volkspolizei (People's Police) in Dresden. He died in that city on February 1, 1957.

Timothy C. Dowling

See also: Stalingrad, Battle of

Additional Reading

Middlebrook, Martin. "Paulus." In *Hitler's Generals*, edited by Correlli Barnett, 223–240. New York: Grove Weidenfeld, 1989.

PEDESTAL, Convoy Battle (August 10–15, 1942)

In mid-1942, Malta was the center of gravity of the war in the Mediterranean. The tiny but strategically situated island lay south of Sicily and astride the main supply route of the Axis forces in North Africa, under the command of Field Marshal Erwin Rommel. Operating from bases on Malta, the British Royal Air Force and Royal Navy wrought havoc with Rommel's supply convoys from Italy. Being an island, however, Malta was entirely dependent on supply convoys by sea, which came under fierce sustained attacks as the Axis tried to strangle the island. In June 1942, three of five freighters had been lost from the Allied HARPOON convoy, as Malta faced a growing shortage of supplies, particularly of fuel. Therefore, despite the very real risks of heavy losses among the merchant vessels and their escorting warships, the Allies had no choice but to mount another convoy operation.

The convoy designated PEDESTAL numbered fourteen ships, including the tanker *Ohio.* Close escort to Malta was provided by the Royal Navy's Force X of four cruisers and eleven destroyers. Additional cover, as far as the Skerki Channel, came from Force Z of two battleships, three aircraft carriers with one hundred aircraft, three cruisers, and thirteen destroyers. The carrier HMS *Furious* launched forty Spitfire fighters to reinforce Malta's airfields before returning to Gibraltar. Nine submarines were deployed to counter possible movements by Italian surface forces.

On August 10, 1942, Axis forces received immediate confirmation that the convoy had passed through the Straits of Gibraltar. Eighteen Italian and two German submarines were deployed to intercept, and the convoy was shadowed from the air. At 1350 hours on August 11, German submarine *U-73* torpedoed and sank the carrier HMS *Eagle.* Major air attacks from Sardinia and from Sicily continued for the next four days. As the convoy entered the Skerki Channel, Italian submarines struck, torpedoing the cruisers *Cairo* and *Nigeria* and the tanker *Ohio.* The *Ohio* continued, but the *Cairo* was scuttled, and the *Nigeria* turned back to Gibraltar. By 1100 hours on August 15, Spitfire fighter cover from Malta effectively prevented further successful attacks. Four merchantmen and the *Ohio,* barely afloat, entered Valetta's Grand Harbor, bringing thirty-two thousand tons of supplies and eleven thousand, five hundred tons of fuel to the garrison, sufficient for two months of operations.

Operation PEDESTAL was an Axis tactical victory but a strategic victory for the Allies. The British lost eight freighters, a carrier, two cruisers, and a destroyer. The Italians lost two submarines and several light craft, with two cruisers and two submarines heavily damaged. Most significantly, however, the British, despite heavy merchant ship losses, had succeeded in resupplying Malta, which had an immediate serious impact on Rommel's supply lines to North Africa at a critical juncture in the war. In September, Allied forces managed to sink one hundred thousand tons of Axis shipping, including twenty-four thousand tons of fuel destined for Rommel, who was thus left desperately short of supplies for his attack at El Alamein in October 1942.

Paul E. Fontenoy

See also: Malta Air and Naval Campaign; North Africa Campaign; Rommel, Erwin

Additional Reading

Bradford, Ernle. *Siege: Malta 1940–1943.* London: Pen and Sword, 2003.

Peiper, Joachim (1915–1976)

Waffen-SS Obersturmbannführer.

Born in Berlin on January 30, 1915, Joachim Peiper was commissioned in the SS in 1936. He was a company commander in the SS Liebestandarte Adolf Hitler (LAH) during the invasion of the France and the Low Countries in May 1940. He served in the LAH in the invasion of the Soviet Union in June 1941. During the Ardennes Offensive (the Battle of the Bulge) in December 1944, Peiper commanded *Kampfgruppe* (battle group) Peiper, which was the lead element for the 1st SS Panzer Division, itself the spearhead of the entire Sixth Panzer Army. Peiper's mission was to race ahead of the main body, bypass all resistance, and capture the bridges across the Meuse River at the small Belgian village of Huy. But *Kampfgruppe* Peiper never achieved its objective, being thwarted on December 20, long before reaching Huy, by a determined defense by U.S. Army combat engineers, Along the way, Peiper's unit committed one of the most infamous massacres of the war, at Malmédy. On July 16, 1946, a U.S. military court at Dachau condemned Peiper and forty-three others to death, although the sentences were subsequently reduced to life in prison. Peiper was later released. On July 14, 1976, Peiper's house in the small village of Traves, France, burned in mysterious circumstances, reputedly firebombed. Although Peiper's body was never completely identified, he was declared dead.

Robert Bateman and Spencer C. Tucker

See also: Ardennes Offensive (Battle of the Bulge); Malmédy Massacre

Additional Reading

Reynolds, Michael. *The Devil's Adjutant: Joachim Peiper, Panzer Leader.* New York: Sarpedon, 1995.

Plan Z (1939–1943)

German naval construction program initiated prior to World War II.

Plan Z was based on Hitler's projection that no major military undertakings would be initiated until 1944 or 1945. Plan Z, which clearly violated the Treaty of Versailles, called for a powerful balanced fleet, and it was eagerly supported by the commander of the German navy, Grand Admiral Erich Raeder. Hitler approved Plan Z on January 27, 1939, three months before he revoked the Anglo-German Naval Agreement of 1935. Plan Z called for a powerful fleet of surface ships and submarines, centered on six superbattleships of fifty-six thousand tons, twelve small battleships of twenty-thousand tons, four aircraft carriers, forty-four light cruisers, sixty-eight destroyers, ninety torpedo boats, and 240 U-boats. Four battleships of the *Bismarck* and *Scharnhorst* classes and five heavy cruisers, as well as the three *Deutschland*-class pocket battleships, were already completed or under construction. The total program would include eight hundred vessels of all types and was scheduled to be completed in 1948. Later, the completion date was advanced to 1944.

Contrary to this unrealistic plan, little construction was actually undertaken because of the lack of human and industrial resources. After the German defeat at Stalingrad in January 1943, the Kriegsmarine suspended all construction of heavy surface warships in favor of submarines. The plan remains one of the most striking examples of the lack of realism in German military strategy. From its inception, the program wasted enormous resources, and, up to 1943, it worked against a buildup of submarines, the major threat to British and U.S. mastery of the Atlantic.

Martin Moll

See also: Anglo-German Naval Agreement; Kriegsmarine (German Navy); Raeder, Erich

Additional Reading

Thomas, Charles S. *The German Navy in the Nazi Era.* London: Unwin Hyman, 1990.

Plate River, Battle of (December 13, 1939)

The battle of the Plate River was the first major naval surface engagement of World War II and the only one to take place in South American waters. Grand Admiral

The German armored cruiser *Admiral Graf Spee* was scuttled by its crew off Montevideo, Uruguay, following the Battle of the Plate River on December 13, 1939. (Popperfoto via Getty Images)

Erich Raeder, commander of the German Navy, envisioned using his capital ships as commerce raiders and ordered his captains to avoid engaging enemy warships, even inferior forces, because even light damage could be fatal, given Germany's lack of foreign bases. On September 1, 1939, the German pocket battleship *Graf Spee* was already at sea, commanded by Captain Hans Langsdorff. Over the course of three months, the *Admiral Graf Spee* sank ten British merchantmen totaling fifty thousand gross tons. By early December, Langsdorff decided to return to Germany after one final victory. Intelligence indicated a valuable convoy sailing from Argentina's Plate River under escort. Despite standing orders, he decided to attack.

On December 13, 1939, lookouts aboard the *Graf Spee* spotted masts on the horizon. They were the heavy cruiser and two light cruisers of Commodore Henry Harwood's Royal Navy Force G. Langsdorff ordered his ship to close with the British ships and fired the first salvo at 0617 hours. During the engagement, the *Graf Spee* inflicted heavy damage on the HMS *Exeter*, HMS *Ajax*, and HMNZS *Achilles*, but the *Graf Spee* also took its share of punishment. At least eighteen shells caused damage that included a large hole in the ship's bow, as well as destruction of the ship's galley and freshwater plant. At 0740 hours, Langsdorff disengaged and made for the neutral port of Montevideo, Uruguay.

Langsdorff hoped to make repairs at Montevideo, but Uruguayan officials only allowed the belligerent seventy-two hours in port. After discussions with Berlin, on December 17, 1939, Langsdorff had the *Graf Spee* weigh anchor and sailed to just beyond Uruguay's territorial limit. There, in the Río de la Plata estuary, Langsdorff scuttled his ship rather than waste the lives of his crew. Tugs transported the Germans to Argentina, where most spent the war in internment. Total human casualties in the Battle of the Río de la Plata were thirty-seven German and seventy-three British dead. On December 20, Captain Langsdorff took a hotel room in Buenos Aires. There he wrapped himself in his ship's ensign and committed suicide with a pistol. The battle was the first important victory won by the British in World War II.

Rodney Madison

See also: Langsdorff, Hans Wilhelm

Additional Reading

Grove, Eric. *The Price of Disobedience: The Battle of the River Plate Reconsidered.* Annapolis, MD: Naval Institute Press, 2000.

Ploesti Air Raids, Allied (August 1, 1943–August 18, 1944)

Operation TIDAL WAVE, the U.S. aerial attack on the Ploesti Oil Fields in Romania, was part of the "Oil Plan" of the Combined Bomber Offensive against Germany and its allies' economies. Ploesti provided approximately 60 percent of Germany's crude oil supply, and the majority of the output went to the German military. The Ploesti oil fields consisted of some forty oil refineries and produced some four hundred thousand tons of refined petrol annually. The Soviet Air Force had attacked Ploesti on June 23, 1941 and U.S. bombers had attacked on June 12, 1942. Ploesti was defended by a Luftwaffe control center at Lipesk, under the command of General Alfred Gerstenberg. The layered defense system consisted of heavy and light Flak guns, fifty-two Messerschmitt Bf 109 fighters, and some Romanian IAR 80 fighters.

On August 1, 177, B-24s of the U.S. Ninth Air Force's IX Bomber Command took off from North Africa and approached over Albania and Yugoslavia, with an attack height of approximately three hundred feet. Effective flak and fighter defense produced confusion among the bombers, which missed their primary target, the Romanian's Americana refinery. Overall, the Ninth Air Force lost fifty-three bombers, a loss rate of 30 percent. While initial estimates concluded that the raid had destroyed 42 percent of Ploesti's total capacity, the Allies soon realized that it had been operating at only 60 percent capacity. Ploesti was soon back to production and operating at a higher capacity by the end of 1943. Between April 5 and August 19, 1944, the U. S. Fifteenth Air Force made nineteen high-level raids against Ploesti, losing 223 aircraft, for a total loss rate of 4.1 percent. Some 2,829 U.S. airmen were killed or captured during the entire campaign. Eventually, Ploesti's capability to supply the German war machine was severely reduced, as the German Army was retreating in the face of the Red Army's advance.

Ross Mahoney

See also: Combined Bomber Offensive, Allied (Operation POINTBLANK)

Additional Reading

Wolff, Leon. *Low Level Mission.* New York: Berkley Publishing, 1958.

Poland Campaign (September 1–October 6, 1939)

World War II began with the German invasion of Poland on September 1, 1939. The subsequent thirty-six-day campaign triggered a global war that lasted six years. The

Poland Campaign was soon overshadowed by the campaigns and battles that followed. As a result, it is best remembered today in a series of myths and legends, almost all of them untrue. Contrary to the most popularly cherished beliefs about World War II, Polish horse cavalry units never mounted suicidal charges against German panzers, the Polish air force was not destroyed on the ground on the first day of the war, and the Polish Army was far from being a pushover for the German Army.

Under the command of Marshal Edward Rydz-Śmigły, the Polish Army in the summer of 1939 had roughly five hundred thousand men, organized into thirty regular and nine reserve infantry divisions, eleven cavalry brigades, and two mechanized brigades. The Polish Army had 887 tanks, less than a third of the almost 2,500 tanks fielded by the Germans. When it became obvious that they would be attacked by Germany, the Poles opted for a forward defense, which was designed to withdraw slowly to the east to buy more time for mobilization. Plan ZACHOD (West), issued on March 23, 1939, was based on a fighting withdrawal. The Polish Army by itself could have never beaten the Germans, regardless of its strategic plan. Plan ZACHOD assumed a strong attack by Britain and France against Germany in the west. Unfortunately for the Poles, that promised attack never came.

In August 1939, the Wehrmacht had fifty-one active divisions, fifty-one reserve divisions, and one active cavalry brigade. All the reserve divisions were infantry units, and the active force included six panzer and four motorized divisions. The average panzer division had 310 tanks, most of which were the lightly armed Pz.Kpfw.I and Pz.Kpfw.II models. The Germans had a total of about five hundred of the heavier Pz.Kpfw.III and Pz.Kpfw.IV tanks. The Wehrmacht's active strength was roughly seven hundred and thirty thousand men, and its reserve strength was about 1.1 million men.

On April 3, 1939, Hitler's headquarters responded to British Prime Minister Neville Chamberlain's declaration of support for Poland by issuing Fall WEISS (Case WHITE), the plan for the invasion. The success of Fall WEISS hinged on a calculated political risk that made most of Hitler's generals nervous. The Germans had to secure a quick victory in Poland in order to shift their forces rapidly back to the west to fend off any attack from the French and British. The Wehrmacht of 1939 was neither large nor strong enough to simultaneously mount a massive attack in the east and a strong defense in the west. Thus, the attack in the east could only be strengthened at the risk of weakening the defense in the west. Willing to gamble that the French and British would not act in time to save Poland, Hitler took that risk. Fall WEISS then called for Germany's border with France to be guarded by the relatively weak Army Group C, which consisted of twenty-one active and fourteen reserve divisions.

A total of fifty-two divisions, including all the panzer and motorized divisions, were allocated for the attack on Poland. They were organized into Army Group North and Army Group South under Colonel Generals Fedor von Bock and Gerd von Rundstedt, respectively. The original plan did not include military operations east of the Vistula, on the assumption that Soviet forces would move rapidly into that area. The campaign would end with the Tenth Army linking up with Army Group North at Warsaw, sealing off the Polish units in western Poland and preventing them from escaping east to the Narew–Vistula–San River line.

Hitler initially set August 26 as the start of the attack. But then Hitler himself blinked, when Britain and France on August 24 responded to the German-Soviet Nonaggression Pact announced the day before, by giving Poland written guarantees of military support. Late on August 25, Hitler canceled the attack orders. But on August 31, Hitler signed "Führer Directive No. 1 for the Conduct of the War." On August 30, Rydz-Śmigły ordered a general mobilization, but that move brought an immediate and sharp reaction from Poland's erstwhile allies, Britain and France, which were afraid of provoking Germany. Within hours, the French government pressured Rydz-Śmigły into revoking the mobilization order.

With the German forces in position and ready to move, Hitler needed only an incident of provocation to provide him with a fig leaf of respectability. Leaving nothing to chance, the German Sicherheitsdienst (Security Service, SD), dressed in Polish uniforms, "raided" the German Silesian border town of Gleiwitz on the night of August 31. They seized the local radio station and played a prerecorded anti-German message in Polish. The SD unit then withdrew, leaving behind several "Polish casualties" as evidence. The bodies were actually prisoners from the Sachsenhausen concentration camp, dressed in Polish uniforms and murdered specially for Hitler's ghastly charade.

At 0445 hours on September 1, the Luftwaffe attacked Polish airfields and rail centers. For the most part, the attacks on the Polish airfields were failures. Anticipating the strikes, the Polish Air Force on August 31 dispersed its front-line aircraft to secret secondary bases to avoid having them caught and destroyed on the ground. The Luftwaffe, nonetheless, dwarfed the Polish Air Force, which had only 392 first-line combat aircraft. The Luftwaffe in March 1939 had a strength of 4,303 aircraft, including 1,180 bombers, 336 dive bombers, and 1,179 fighters. In support of the German invasion, Army Group North was allocated Luftflotte 1 (First Air Fleet) under General Albert Kesselring; Army Group South was supported by General Alexander Löhr's Luftflotte 4. The combined force totaled thirty-six groups and included all of Germany's dive bombers, 70 percent of its bombers, and 50 percent of its fighters.

Vastly outnumbered and technically outclassed, the Polish pilots put up a stiff resistance. By September 6, Polish fighter units were down to 50 percent of their original strength. A few days later, the surviving fighters began withdrawing toward Romania with the rest of the Polish Army. The Poles lost almost three hundred of their combat aircraft, but the Germans suffered heavy losses as well, with 285 aircraft destroyed and another 279 severely damaged. Despite the great technological disparity in aircraft, Polish fighter pilots claimed at least 121 confirmed air-to-air kills for the campaign. German records indicate that the true number may have been closer to 160.

At 0443 hours on September 1, the obsolescent German battleship *Schleswig-Holstein* opened fire on the Polish military supply base on Westerplatte Island in Danzig Harbor. The ground war started within minutes after that. The Third Army, under General Georg von Küchler, attacked south toward Warsaw, and General Günther von Kluge's Fourth Army sliced into the Polish Corridor, which divided East Prussia from the rest of Germany. The Fourth Army's objective was to clear a path for the one panzer and two motorized divisions of General Heinz Guderian's XIX Corps to drive a pincer arm southwest toward Warsaw.

Poland and Eastern Europe, 1939–1940

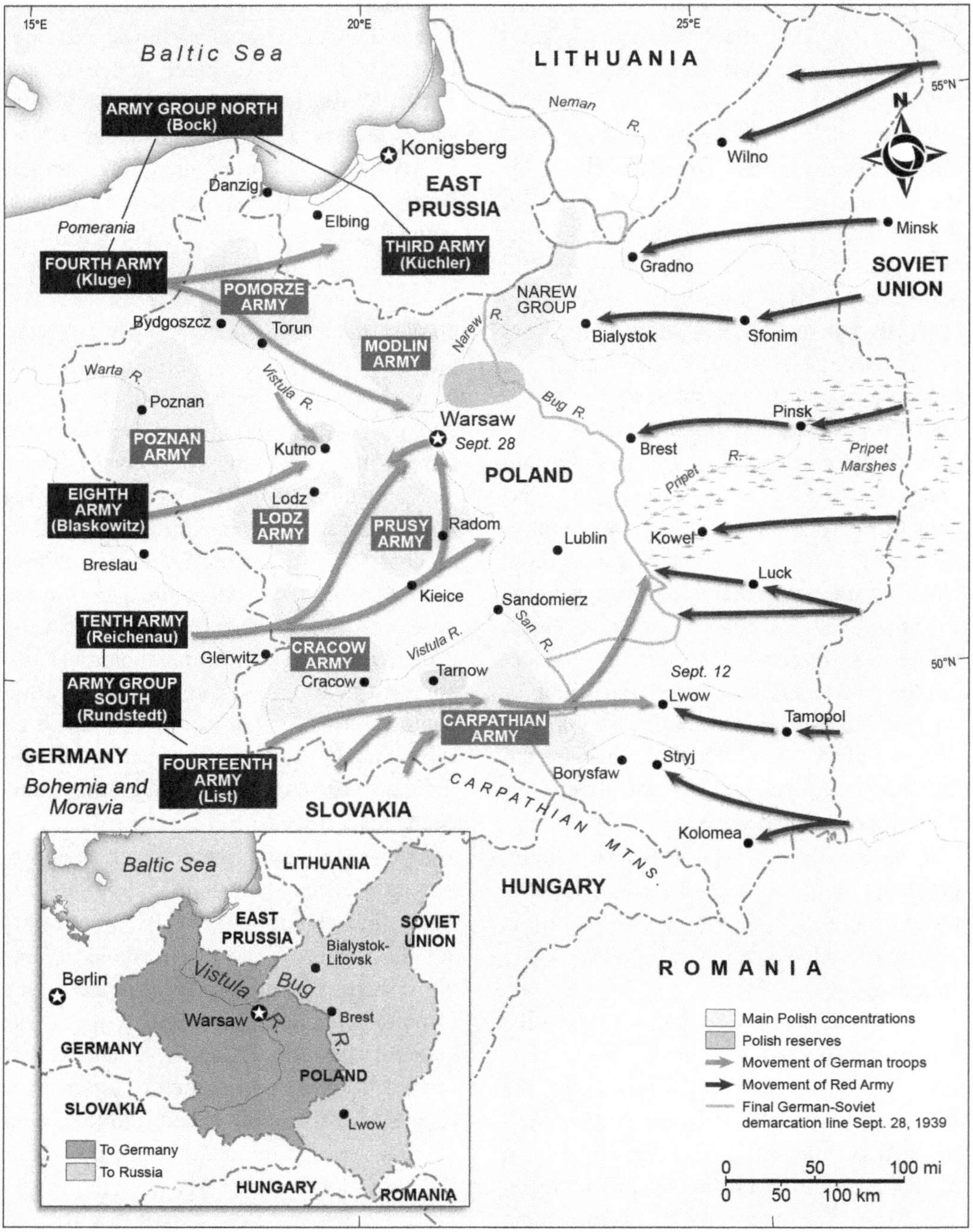

In the south, Army Group South crossed into Poland. General Johannes Blaskowitz's Eighth Army drove toward the Polish industrial city of Lodz. In Rundstedt's center, his Tenth Army, under General Walther von Reichenau, struck from Oppeln to encircle Warsaw from the south. The Fourteenth Army, under Colonel General Wilhelm List, attacked from German Silesia and Slovakia to cut off Krakow.

By September 4, the Germans had managed to drive a deep wedge into the Polish defenses. On September 5, the first major clash between German and Polish tanks occurred at Piotrkow, with the Germans penetrating the Polish defenses and securing the key road links to Warsaw. The breakthrough at Piotrkow marked the end of the first phase of the Poland Campaign. By the evening of September 5, the Polish armies were retreating all along the line. Rydz-Śmigły believed he had no alternative but to order a withdrawal to the line of the Vistula.

Warsaw was now directly threatened. On September 8, the 4th Panzer Division attempted but failed to take the Polish capital by storm. In their rush to reach Warsaw, the Germans lost track of General Tadeusz Kutrzeba's bypassed Army Poznan, which was entrenched behind a bend in the Bzura River, about thirty miles west of Warsaw. Kutrzeba's Bzura River Offensive was the only major Polish counterattack of the campaign. On September 9, the Poles caught the German 24th and 30th Infantry Divisions by surprise, capturing more than fifteen hundred prisoners. But the Germans, with their far greater mobility and firepower, were able to shift other forces rapidly to contain this Polish offensive. Army Poznan surrendered on September 21. On September 1, Rydz-Śmigły ordered the surviving Polish units to withdraw toward the southeast, to the so-called Romanian Bridgehead.

With the Buzra Offensive under control, the Germans were then able to turn their attention back to Warsaw to conduct a set-piece siege. By September 23, Warsaw's food and water were running out, and the city was completely ringed by thirteen German divisions and more than one thousand guns. On September 25, a day the Poles still call "Black Monday," Hitler personally ordered an armada of 420 German bombers to savage the capital with repeated sorties. Warsaw finally surrendered on September 27, after suffering some two thousand military and forty thousand civilians dead.

Plan ZACHOD had been based on holding until the French and British could attack Germany from the west. The Poles were promised that attack no later than September 16. It did not occur. On September 17, Soviet leader Josef Stalin drove the final nail into the Polish coffin by invading Poland from the east. Hiding behind the excuse of occupying eastern Poland "to protect its fraternal Byelorussian and Ukrainian populations," the Soviets marched in with two fronts (army groups). The Byelorussian Front, under General M. P. Kovalev, and the Ukranian Front, under General Semen Timoshenko, had a combined strength of twenty-four infantry divisions, fifteen cavalry divisions, and two tank corps. The Soviets reached the Bug River on September 23.

The last Polish forces surrendered on October 6. Poland suffered staggering losses in the campaign, amounting to 66,300 killed, 133,700 wounded, 587,000 taken prisoner by the Germans, and another 200,000 taken prisoner by the Soviets. Polish civilian deaths were close to one hundred thousand. Virtually all of Poland's military hardware was destroyed or captured, with the exception of the handful of obsolete fighter aircraft that escaped to Romania.

Despite the claims of German Minister of Propaganda Josef Goebbels, the Germans paid a high price for such a short campaign. The Wehrmacht suffered sixteen thousand dead and thirty-two thousand wounded. It lost 217 tanks totally destroyed and another 457 so heavily damaged that most never returned to service. Thus, the Germans lost one-quarter of the tanks as well as one-fifth of the combat aircraft they committed to the campaign. On top of that, they expended eight months' worth of fuel, ammunition, and repair parts in an operation that lasted a little more than one month.

The Anglo-French failure to deliver their promised attack on Germany in September 1939 remains one of the great "what-ifs" of the twentieth century. Strong Allied intervention in the west might not have saved Poland in the end. On the other hand, it certainly would have forced Germany into a two-front war two years earlier than the German invasion of the Soviet Union. The German war machine of 1939 was nowhere near as large and strong as it would be by June 1941. In September 1939, French and British forces were capable of throwing ninety-eight divisions and some thirty-five hundred combat aircraft against Army Group C's thirty-five infantry divisions supported by about one thousand aircraft. Behind them lay the vulnerable industrial base of the Rhineland. But in the end, the French made only a feeble effort into the Saarland; the British record was worse and largely confined to debate over the legality of using the Royal Air Force to bomb private property in Germany.

David T. Zabecki

See also: Blaskowitz, Johannes Albrecht; Bock, Fedor von; German-Soviet Nonaggression Pact; Guderian, Heinz; Hitler, Adolf; Kesselring, Albert; Kluge, Günther von; Küchler, Georg von; List, Siegmund Wilhelm Walter; Löhr, Alexander; Reichenau, Walther von; Rundstedt, Karl Rudolf Gerd von

Additional Reading

Kennedy, Robert M. *The Campaign in Poland (1939).* U.S. Department of the Army Pamphlet 20–255, April 1956.

Rossino, Alexander B. *Hitler Strikes Poland: Blitzkrieg, Ideology, and Atrocity.* Lawrence: University Press of Kansas, 2003.

Zagola, Steven, and Victor Madej. *The Polish Campaign, 1939.* New York: Hippocrene Books, 1985.

Poland-East Prussia Campaign, Soviet (July 20, 1944–April 9, 1945)

On June 22, 1944, the third anniversary of the German invasion of the Soviet Union, the Red Army launched Operation BAGRATION, a massive offensive to drive German forces from western Belorussia. Continuing the offensive into Poland, on July 20, 1944, units of the 1st Byelorussian Front crossed the Bug River in three places and captured Lublin. There, the Soviets established their own Polish government and army and declared open season on the London-based Polish government-in-exile's anti-Communist Polish Home Army. On July 25, the Red Army reached the Vistula. German Colonel General Joseph Harpe, commander of Army Group A (the redesignated Army Group North), could do little more than delay the inevitable. At the end of July, *Stavka* ordered the 1st and 2nd Byelorussian Fronts to drive to the Narew River and Warsaw. In that drive, the Soviets destroyed twenty-eight German divisions, inflicting three hundred and fifty thousand casualties, but logistical problems, in consequence of the rapid advance and two months of solid fighting, forced a pause.

On August 29, Stalin ordered that all Red Army fronts were to dig in, generally along the line of the Vistula and Narew Rivers. During the Warsaw Rising of August 1 to October 2, 1944, the Soviets not only refused to help the Poles in any meaningful way, but they also obstructed efforts by the Western Allies to airdrop supplies to the Polish fighters. *Stavka*, meanwhile, laid plans for the final control of Poland in an offensive that would carry from the Vistula to the Oder. Stalin's orders were to destroy German Army Group A, with the secondary objective of drawing off German reserves in response to western appeals during the German Ardennes Offensive. The Soviet offensive was massive. The 1st Ukrainian and 1st Byelorussian Fronts together contained 2.2 million ground troops (a six-to-one advantage over the defending Germans) in 163 divisions, supported by more than 32,000 artillery pieces and almost 4,800 aircraft.

The second half of the offensive to clear Poland began on January 12, 1945. The defending forces included the Wehrmacht's severely weakened Army Group Center and Army Group A, with a total strength of only four hundred thousand soldiers and three hundred tanks. Zhukov's 1st Belorussian Front and Konev's 1st Ukrainian Front together fielded 2.2 million troops with seven thousand tanks and armored vehicles. By January 17, the 1st Byelorussian Front and the Soviet-controlled Polish First Army had liberated Warsaw. Within the next week, the 1st Byelorussian and 1st Ukrainian Fronts had punched a 310-mile hole in the German lines and driven 100 miles. There was little Harpe and the German forces could do to arrest the Soviet advance. On January 28, forces of the 1st Byelorussian Front entered German Pomerania, where they were met by the hastily formed Army Group Vistula, commanded by the inept head of the SS, Heinrich Himmler. On January 29, the Soviets encircled the East Prussian capital of Königsberg.

Hitler sacked General Heinz Guderian as chief of the German Army General Staff on March 28, 1945. Königsberg fell on April 9, as the 1st Ukrainian Front eliminated isolated pockets of German forces in southwestern Poland. The Soviet forces had once again outrun their logistical support and were forced to halt. Nevertheless, the Red Army was now poised to begin its final offensive: the drive on Berlin to end the war.

Michael Share, Spencer C. Tucker, and Erica R. Fagen

See also: Belorussia Offensive, Soviet; Berlin, Land Battle for; Guderian, Heinz; Himmler, Heinrich; Warsaw Rising

Additional Reading

Erickson, John. *The Road to Berlin.* Boulder, CO: Westview Press, 1983.

Hastings, Max. *Armageddon: The Battle for Germany, 1944–1945.* New York: A.A. Knopf, 2004.

Prien, Günther (1908–1941)

Kriegsmarine officer and U-boat captain.

Born on January 16, 1908 in Lübeck on the Baltic coast, Günther Prien joined the German Navy and volunteered for submarine school in 1935. During the Spanish Civil War, he served on *U-26* off the coast of Spain. In October 1939, commander of German submarines, Admiral Karl Dönitz, selected Prien for a daring mission to penetrate the principal anchorage of the British Home Fleet at Scapa Flow in the Orkney

Islands. On October 13, Prien was able to pass his *U-47* into the harbor. At about 0100 hours on October 14, Prien fired four torpedoes at the battleship HMS *Royal Oak*, sinking it. Prien's exploit was a major propaganda coup for the German Navy. Prien went on to sink thirty-one Allied ships and assisted in sinking four others, for a total of 213,283 tons. On March 8, 1941, British destroyers HMS *Verity* and *Wolverine* surprised Prien's *U-47* on the surface. The *U-47* dived, but it was never heard from again.

Matthew Alan McNiece

See also: Atlantic, Battle of the; Submarines

Additional Reading

Blair, Clay. *Hitler's U-Boat War: The Hunters, 1939–1942.* New York: Random House, 1996.

R

Raeder, Erich (1876–1960)

Kriegsmarine grand admiral.

The second of three grand admirals in German history was born in Hamberg-Wandsbek on April 24, 1876. Raeder spent most of World War I as Admiral Franz von Hipper's chief of staff. In 1928, he replaced Admiral Hans Zenker as commander in chief of the German Navy. In 1933, Raeder gained approval from Hitler to build a navy beyond the Treaty of Versailles limits, two years before Hitler formally declared the treaty void. Raeder remained a strong battleship advocate, hoping eventually to build a fleet that could challenge British naval supremacy. Plan Z was to have provided that by 1948, but the war started four years earlier than anticipated, forcing Raeder to fight with less than 20 percent of his planned surface force. Still, he favored surface forces, de-emphasizing U-boat construction, research, and development until pressed by Hitler. Even then, he expended resources on battleships, hoping to resume construction

Grand Admiral Erich Raeder, commander in chief of the German Navy (1935–1943), visits the crew of the battle cruiser *Scharnhorst* in April 1942 to express his appreciation after its escape from Brest, France, through the English Channel. Operation CERBERUS, also known as the "Channel Dash," took place during February 11–13, 1942. (Library of Congress)

once Germany's strategic situation allowed. Prior to January 1943, Hitler deferred to Raeder's judgment in naval matters. That changed, however, with the surface fleet's failures against British naval forces in the winter of 1942. Raeder resigned rather than obey Hitler's order to decommission the surviving surface combatants. Raeder was replaced by Admiral Karl Dönitz on January 31, 1943.

Tried after the war before the International Military Tribunal at Nuremberg, Raeder was convicted of conspiracy against peace, conspiracy to wage a war of aggression, and war crimes for his enforcement of the Commando Order. He was sentenced to life in prison; but he was released because of poor health on September 25, 1955. Raeder died in Kiel on November 6, 1960.

Carl O. Schuster

See also: Dönitz, Karl; Kriegsmarine (German Navy); Plan Z

Additional Reading

Bird, Keith W. *Erich Raeder: Admiral of the Third Reich*. Annapolis, MD: U.S. Naval Institute Press, 2006.

Rall, Günther (1918–2009)

Luftwaffe major and ace, Bundesluftwaffe lieutenant general.

Günther Rall was the third-highest scoring ace of World War II with 275 victories. Born in Gaggenau, Baden, on March 10, 1918, Rall joined the Luftwaffe in March. During World War II, Rall served primarily with *Jagdgeschwader* 52 (JG-52) on the eastern front, achieving all but three of his 275 victories against the Red Air Force. Rall himself was shot down eight times out of approximately eight hundred combat missions. He was awarded the Knights Cross of the Iron Cross with Oak Leaves and Swords. Rall joined the *Bundesluftwaffe* in 1956 as a major, and rose to the rank of lieutenant general, serving as chief of staff of the *Bundesluftwaffe* from 1971 to 1973. Rall died on October 4, 2009 at his home in Bad Reichenhall, Germany.

Marlyn R. Pierce

See also: Luftwaffe (German Air Force); Appendix A

Additional Reading

Rall, Günther. *My Logbook: Reminiscences 1938–2006*. Edited by Kurt Braatz. Translated by John Weal. Moosburg, Germany: Neunundzwanzigsechs Verlag, 2006.

Reichenau, Walther von (1884–1942)

Wehrmacht field marshal.

Born in Karlsruhe, Germany, on October 8, 1884, Walther von Reichenau served as General Staff officer during World War I. He was one of the few aristocratic officers to support Adolf Hitler actively during the Nazi rise to power. He also played a key role in convincing senior Nazi Party leaders of the necessity of suppressing Ernst Röhm and the Strumabteilungen (SA), which led directly to the Night of the Long Knives Blood Purge. Reichenau commanded the Tenth Army during the invasion of Poland in September 1939 and the Sixth Army during the invasion of France and the Low Countries, although his vocal protests over German atrocities in Poland and his opposition to the violation of the neutrality of Belgian and the Netherlands permanently alienated him from Hitler. Reichenau commanded the Sixth Army in Operation BARBAROSSA, the invasion of the Soviet Union. On January 15, 1942, Reichenau collapsed from a cerebral hemorrhage and died two days later.

Gene Mueller and Spencer C. Tucker

See also: Night of the Long Knives

Additional Reading

Görlitz, Walter. "Reichenau: Field-Marshal Walther von Reichenau." In *Hitler's Generals*, edited by Corelli Barnett, 209–219. London: Weidenfeld and Nicolson, 1989.

Reichsarbeitsdienst (Reich Labor Service) (1934–1945)

The Reich Labor Service (*Reichsarbeitsdienst*—RAD) was the state-run labor organization that directed the mandatory labor of German citizens working on civil and military projects. It operated within Germany, its war fronts, and newly acquired territories. The RAD was established in 1934. The organization's goals were both practical and ideological. The RAD was essential to Hitler's concepts of German rearmament. Young Germans who served in the RAD lived and worked under conditions of strict military discipline and received premilitary training. They marched and drilled with shovels in the place of rifles. As soon as they were conscripted into the expanding Wehrmacht, they replaced those shovels with rifles. During World War II, the RAD also was directly instrumental to the German war effort. The organization provided the German military with the necessary manpower to maintain strategic roads, shelters, and fortifications. Workers also engaged in agricultural projects related to Hitler's vision of reoccupying and Germanizing Eastern Europe, known as *Lebensraum* (living space). Even though RAD members performed practical labor service, their presence in the East was part of an ideologically driven campaign intended to reinforce racial hierarchies. RAD members were integrated into the armed forces during World War II, primarily through Organization Todt (OT). Beginning in 1938, RAD labor was used in building and maintaining the defensive Westwall. RAD laborers also worked as road builders, contributing to the construction of the autobahn, the world's first superhighway system.

Natalie R. Spagnuolo

See also: Organization Todt (OT); Westwall

Additional Reading

Patel, Kiran Klaus. *Soldiers of Labor. Labor Service in Nazi Germany and New Deal America, 1933–1945.* New York: Cambridge University Press, 2005.

Reichsheer (German Army) (1919–1945)

At the tactical level of warfare, the German Army—the Reichsheer—of World War II may well have been the best ground force in the history of warfare to that time. On the strategic level, the Germans had major blind spots that go a long way toward explaining why they lost two world wars despite having the best army in the field. The Reichsheer of World War II (the Wehrmacht was the entire German military, not just the army) grew out of the one-hundred-thousand-man Reichswehr that was allowed to Germany following World War I under the terms of the Treaty of Versailles. On October 1, 1934, Hitler ordered the threefold secret expansion of the Reichswehr. Conscription was reintroduced in March 1935. By 1939, the two main components of the German Army were the Field Army

(*Feldheer*) and the Replacement Army (*Ersatzheer*). The Field Army had more than two million soldiers and was organized into 120 divisions—ninety-nine infantry, nine panzer, six motorized, one cavalry, three mountain, and two parachute. The Replacement Army consisted of a force of approximately one hundred thousand men in training or transit. From 1942 on, the numbers of replacements became progressively insufficient to keep front-line units up to authorized strength levels.

The infantry division was the primary tactical element of the German Army. By 1944, there were 226 infantry divisions, typically consisting of 12,352 troops, 615 motor vehicles, and 4,656 horses. Despite its reputation as the master of mechanized and mobile warfare, the German Army relied heavily on horses, right up until the end of the war. Almost all field artillery in the infantry divisions was horse-drawn. The Germans did field various forms of motorized or mechanized units. By 1941, they had a total of ten motorized infantry divisions and light infantry divisions. Later in the war, these units were redesignated as panzergrenadier divisions. Germany ultimately fielded twenty-two of these units. They were organized along the general lines of the infantry divisions, but they had more motor vehicles and an organic tank regiment. The 1944 panzergrenadier division had 13,833 soldiers, 2,637 motor vehicles, 48 tanks, and more than 1,400 horses.

Organizationally, all German parachute divisions were part of the Luftwaffe, but operationally they fought under army command. The Germans had eleven parachute divisions in 1944. After the near-disaster on Crete, German parachute divisions never again jumped in combat. They spent the remainder of the war fighting as light infantry, but their traditional paratrooper élan remained, and they were fierce opponents, especially in Italy. The Luftwaffe also fielded ground divisions that operated under army command. The formation of these air force field units was another desperate measure. As attrition ground down the Luftwaffe's aircraft, especially on the eastern front, excess personnel were hastily grouped into these field divisions. Often, the new ground soldiers had little or no infantry training. Germany had nineteen Luftwaffe field divisions in 1944.

The panzer division was the mailed striking fist of the German Army. The first three panzer divisions were raised as completely new units in the fall of 1935, but they were not fully operational until September 1937. Thereafter, new panzer divisions were established by converting infantry or other divisions. There were twenty-six panzer divisions by 1944, with the typical division having 13,700 troops and 150 tanks. During the last year of the war, however, many panzer divisions could only field a handful of tanks.

The Waffen-Schutzstaffel (Waffen-SS) was separate from the army and even from the Wehrmacht. It was essentially the Nazi Party's army, and it fielded combat divisions that fought under army command and control, much like the Luftwaffe's field and parachute divisions. By 1944, there were seven SS panzer divisions and eleven panzergrenadier divisions. The organization of the Waffen-SS divisions was similar to the organization of their Wehrmacht counterparts, but because of their unquestioning loyalty to Hitler, they were often better equipped.

Contrary to the popular stereotypes, reinforced by countless Hollywood movies and television programs, the common German soldier of World War II was anything but stupid and unimaginative, and his officers and noncommissioned officers (NCOs) were neither machinelike nor inflexible martinets. Rather, the German Army encouraged initiative among its subordinate leaders and stressed flexibility and creativity to a degree far greater than any other army prior to 1945. This was the key to its tactical excellence. German combat orders, rather than dictating detailed and rigid timelines and specific instructions on how to accomplish missions, tended to be short and as broad as possible. The principle under which the German command system operated was called *Auftragstaktik*, which can only very loosely be translated into English as "mission orders." Such a practice was virtually unheard of in almost all the other armies of World War II.

Command and control in the German Army suffered from a confused structure at the very top, which only compounded the German weaknesses at the strategic and operational levels. Three different high-command headquarters were seldom in agreement and were often in competition. The *Oberkommando das Heeres* (Army High Command, OKH), the *Oberkommando der Wehrmacht* (Armed Forces High Command, OKW), and the supreme commander (Hitler) and his staff often issued conflicting orders to the same units. In theory, OKH ran the war in the Soviet Union, and the OKW ran the war everywhere else. Hitler's *Führerhauptquartier* (Führer Headquarters) issued all the key strategic orders.

David T. Zabecki

See also: Waffen-SS; Wehrmacht (German Armed Forces)

Additional Reading

Rosinski, Herbert. *The German Army.* New York: Praeger, 1966.

U.S. War Department. *TM-E 30–451 Handbook on German Military Forces.* Baton Rouge: Louisiana State University Press, 1990.

Zabecki, David T., and Bruce Condell, eds. *On the German Art of War: Truppenführung.* Boulder, CO: Lynne Rienner, 2001.

Reichssicherheitshauptamt (Reich Main Security Office) (1939–1945)

The Reichssicherheitshauptamt (RSHA), Reich Security Main Office, was an administrative branch of the Schutzstaffel (SS) that combined the Sicherheitsdienst (SD—the Office of Reich Security) and the Sicherheitspolizei (Sipo—or the Reich Security Police). It was established by a decree issued by Reichsführer-SS Heinrich Himmler on September 27, 1939. SS-Gruppenführer Reinhard Heydrich was chief of the RSHA until his death on June 4, 1942. After the brief interim period following Heydrich's death, when Himmler took over his duties, SS-Obergruppenführer Ernst Kaltenbrunner replaced him in January 1943 until the end of the war.

The RSHA was divided into seven *Amter* (offices) that oversaw all security issues. Each office was further divided and subdivided into various departments focusing on specific tasks and duties. The most notorious was Amt IV, *Gegner-Erforschung und—Bekämpfung—Geheimes Saatspolizei*, which was the Gestapo, Secret State Police, headquarters. It was central to the development, organization, and implementation of the "Final Solution to the Jewish Problem"—that is, the extermination of the Jews. Its *Referat*, or subdivision, B-4, headed by SS-Obersturmbannführer Adolf Eichmann, was the department charged with the deportations of Jews and other undesirables to concentration, labor, and death camps.

The head of the RSHA was also responsible for coordinating the operations of the Einsatzgruppen, the "special task groups." During the invasion of the Soviet Union, the Einsatzgruppen followed the advances of the Wehrmacht, with the objective of pacifying the areas conquered by the German military. Such pacification often meant the direct shootings of perceived enemies of the state. The Einsatizgruppen were, in effect, little more than mobile killing units.

Emmanuel Hogg

See also: Einsatzgruppen; Himmler, Heinrich; Holocaust, German Military Complicity in

Additional Reading

Höhne, Heinz. *The Order of the Death's Head: The Story of Hitler's SS*. New York: Coward-McCann, 1969.

Reichswald, Battle of the (February 8–March 10, 1945)

In early 1945, German forces in the West defended the Westwall (known to the Allies as the Siegfried Line) against Allied attack. General of Parachute Troops Alfred Schlemm's First Parachute Army of Army Group H held the line between the Rhine and Maas rivers. The Allied attack here marked the opening phase of Operation VERITABLE, the advance of Lieutenant General Henry Crerar's Canadian First Army to the Rhine River. This Allied offensive saw Canadian First Army push across the German-Dutch border, secure Cleve, and then turn south between the Rhine and the Maas to meet Lieutenant General William H. Simpson's U.S. Ninth Army as it was driving northeast across the Roer River and toward the Rhine in Operation GRENADE. The Allies hoped to surround and destroy defending German units and secure crossing points over the Rhine. To accomplish this, Canadian forces, reinforced by the British army's XXX Corps, would have to cross the heavily wooded Reichswald State Forest and eliminate the German pillboxes and bunkers of the Westwall. To this operation, the Allies eventually committed some two hundred thousand men. General Schlemm commanded only ninety thousand men.

The assault commenced on February 9, 1945 with a five-hour artillery barrage by one thousand Allied guns against the German fortifications. British Lieutenant General Sir Brian Horrocks's XXX Corps led the attack. Delays in the advance, however, enabled Schlemm to bring up reserves, as well as Pz.Kpfw.IV tanks and assault guns of the Panzer Lehr Division. The Germans fought with great tenacity in what was some of the most bitterly contested combat of the war. By opening the gates of the Roer River dams, Schlemm forced Simpson to postpone Ninth Army's attack for almost two weeks. By the time the Ninth Army launched what was to have been a supporting attack on February 23, the Canadian and British troops had already achieved almost all their objectives.

Supported by massive artillery barrages and air support, the Commonwealth forces slowly pushed the Germans from their defensive positions. The Germans fought particularly hard in and around the critical towns of Cleve, Goch, and Calcar. Schlemm was able to get his paratroops and most of his heavy equipment across the Rhine before blowing its bridges. The last *Fallschirmjäger* (paratroops) crossed the Rhine at Bruedrich in boats on March 10, 1945.

British and Canadian forces took 15,634 casualties. The operation cost the Germans heavier losses, however. The eleven German divisions involved in the fighting lost between twenty-two thousand and seventy-five thousand men; some sixteen thousand Germans were taken prisoner. The commitment of so many German reserves to the fighting in the Reichswald helped open the way for U.S. advances farther south.

Terry Shoptaugh and Spencer C. Tucker

See also: Rhine Crossings, Allied; Westwall

Additional Reading

Elstob, Peter. *Battle of the Reichswald.* New York: Ballantine Books, 1970.

Reitsch, Hanna (1912–1979)

Test pilot who worked with the Luftwaffe during World War II.

Born in Hirschberg, Silesia, on March 29, 1912, Hanna Reitsch mastered glider aviation as a young woman. She also mastered powered aircraft and became a valued test pilot, with the rating of flight captain, testing experimental aircraft for the Luftwaffe. In 1937, she became the first woman to pilot a helicopter. During World War II, Reitsch tested a variety of aircraft, including fighter planes, dive bombers, and the Messerschmitt Me 163 rocket aircraft. Reitsch was one of just two women to be awarded the Iron Cross First Class and the only civilian so honored. Reitsch piloted the final German flight into Berlin, carrying Luftwaffe Colonel General Robert von Greim to a meeting with Hitler and landing on a shell-pocked Berlin avenue on April 26, 1945. Reitsch offered to stay with Hitler and share his fate, but she was ordered to fly Greim from the city several days later. Many aviation historians consider her to have been the twentieth century's outstanding female pilot. Reitsch died at Frankfurt, Germany, on August 24, 1979.

Elizabeth D. Schafer

See also: Greim, Robert Ritter von; Luftwaffe (German Air Force)

Additional Reading

Piszkiewicz, Dennis. *From Nazi Test Pilot to Hitler's Bunker: The Fantastic Flights of Hanna Reitsch.* Westport, CT: Praeger, 1997.

Remagen Bridge, U.S. Capture of (March 7, 1945)

As the Allied armies advanced toward the Rhine River in early 1945, their senior commanders were not counting on capturing a bridge intact. As the Wehrmacht reeled back toward the Reich in disarray, the Ludendorff Railway Bridge at Remagen was one of the last remaining bridges over the Rhine that was still standing. The defense of the bridge was disorganized at best. Army Group B commander, Field Marshal Walter Model, had ordered reinforcements sent to the area, but by the morning of March 7, there were fewer than one thousand Volkstrum militiamen in the Remagen sector. Captain Wilhelm Bratge, the commandant at Remagen, had only thirty-six soldiers under his direct command at the bridge itself.

Adding to the German command and control confusion, an order issued late on March 6 transferred the command responsibility at Remagen to Major Hans Scheller, the adjutant of the sector between Remagen and Schleiden. Bratge did not learn of the transfer of authority until Scheller arrived in Remagen at 1115 hours on March 7. Bratge wanted to blow the bridge as soon as possible; Scheller wanted to keep it open until the last minute to give more German troops the chance to get to the east bank. Meanwhile, Captain Karl Friesenhahn, the engineer officer responsible for the demolition, started putting the charges in place at about 1100 hours, as reports from Army Group B indicated U.S. advanced elements approaching the western bluffs above Remagen.

Under the command of German-born Lieutenant Karl Heinz Timmermann, Company A, 27th Armored Infantry Battalion, U.S. 9th Armored Division reached the western approaches to the bridge at 1300 hours. When U.S. tanks approached the Rhine at about 1600 hours, Major Scheller finally gave the order to blow the bridge. Friesenhahn hit the electric firing switch, but nothing happened. He had to ignite the backup primer cord system by hand. When the charges finally blew, the bridge shuddered and seemed to lift into the air slightly, but then it settled back down into its foundations. When the smoke cleared, the Ludendorff Bridge was still standing. With Staff Sergeant Joseph S. Petrencsik and Sergeant Alexander A. Drabik in the lead, Timmermann leapfrogged his men across the span under heavy fire, dodging from girder to girder. As soon as they reached the east bank, more U.S. forces poured across the bridge behind them. Drabik was the first U.S. soldier to fight his way across the Rhine and into the heart of Germany.

The Germans reacted spasmodically. On the evening of March 7, they were only able to mount a weak counterattack of about one hundred engineers and flak gunners. On the morning of March 8, Model ordered the 11th Panzer Division to counterattack from their assembly areas near Düsseldorf. But with only four thousand troops, twenty-five tanks, eighteen artillery pieces, and almost no gas left, it took the division's lead elements two days to reach the Remagen sector. Meanwhile, every German artillery piece within range opened up on the bridge. Three shells hit the bridge on March 9, further weakening the span and tearing more holes in the deck.

In a typical rage of fury, Hitler fired (for the last time) Field Marshal Gerd von Rundstedt as OB-West on March 10 and replaced him with Field Marshal Albert Kesselring. He also ordered Lieutenant General Rudolf Hübner to convene a three-man drumhead court-martial to punish those directly responsible for the disaster. Four officers were tried, convicted, and executed all on the same day. Major Scheller, engineer officers Major Herbert Strobel and Major August Kraft, and Flak artillery Lieutenant Karl Heinz Peters were shot in the back of the neck and buried in shallow graves. The letters they were allowed to write to their families before being shot were then burned. Their families also were stripped of their military pensions, but the German government restored them after the war. Captains Bratge and Friesenhahn were tried in absentia. Bratge was convicted and condemned; Friesenhahn was acquitted. Both, however, were by then safely in an Allied POW pen.

More than eight thousand GIs managed to get across the river by the evening of March 8. With two tactical floating bridges in the water, U.S. engineers closed the Ludendorff Bridge for repairs on March 13. Just before 1500 hours on March 17, as some two hundred welders, carpenters, and other engineers swarmed over the bridge, it suddenly collapsed into the Rhine. Twenty-three American GIs were killed, and another ninety-three were injured in the wreck.

Within a week of seizing the Ludendorff Bridge, the Americans had eight tactical bridges across the Rhine. Although Model was convinced that the Americans intended to exploit north to the Ruhr, U.S. First Army commander General Courtney Hodges actually had orders to be prepared to break out on or about March 23 to the southeast, to link up with General George Patton's U.S. Third Army, which started crossing the Rhine that day. When the German counterattack finally came on March 24, it was poorly coordinated and understrength. Between March 6 and 24, U.S. forces took seventy-four hundred casualties in the fight for the Remagen Bridgehead, including 863 killed. There is no accurate count of the German casualties, but they lost eleven thousand, seven hundred as prisoners alone.

David T. Zabecki

See also: Kesselring, Albert; Model, Walther; Rhine Crossings, Allied; Rundstedt, Karl Rudolf Gerd von

Additional Reading

Hechler, Kenneth. *The Bridge at Remagen.* New York: Ballantine Books, 1957.

Rhine Crossings, Allied (March 7–24, 1945)

The Rhine River was a formidable defensive advantage for the German Army and the greatest natural obstacle in the path of the advancing Western Allies after their crossing of the English Channel. Ranging in width from seven hundred to twelve hundred feet and at no point fordable, the river was at flood levels in early March 1945, thanks to spring rains and melting snow. The Rhine was also in German territory and, thus, would be defended at great cost. Allied plans called for British Field Marshal Sir Bernard Montgomery's 21st Army Group to cross the Rhine in the north, while U.S. General Omar N. Bradley's 12th Army Group would cross in the south. The majority of resources were to be assigned to Montgomery, whose forces were then to secure Germany's industrial heartland of the Ruhr Valley.

German defenders had already blown most of the bridges across the Rhine that were accessible to the advancing Allies when, on the afternoon of March 7, lead elements of the 9th Armored Division of Bradley's army group were able to secure the Ludendorff Railroad Bridge at Remagen. U.S. Lieutenant General George S. Patton, meanwhile, sought to secure a crossing for his Third Army. Late on the night of March 21, elements of the U.S. 5th Infantry Division crossed the river at Oppenheim without resistance. By evening, the bridgehead was five miles deep. Patton's army made two other assault crossings of the Rhine, on March 25 at Boppard, and the next day at Saint Goar.

The Allied plan still called for the northern crossings, code-named Operation PLUNDER, to be the main attack. Montgomery massed nearly one million men along the lower Rhine: 21st Army Group units in the crossing included the nine divisions of the British Second Army and the twelve divisions of the U.S. Ninth Army. Operation PLUNDER began late on March 23, with Allied units getting across the Rhine between Wesel and Emmerich. Opposing PLUNDER was General of Parachutists Alfred Schlemm's First Parachute Army of Army Group H. This formation had suffered heavy losses in the Battle of the Reichswald and had only some eighty-five thousand men and thirty-five tanks. There was little artillery and no air support to speak of. Within one week of the start of the operation, the Allies had taken thirty thousand prisoners. On March 27, when Schlemm was wounded, command passed to General of Infantry Günther Blumentritt. Although under strict orders to stand and fight, the First Parachute Army, under heavy Allied pressure, began on April 1 to withdraw to the northeast, behind the Dortmund-Ems Canal to the Teutoburg Forest, opening a gap between it and the German Fifteenth Army in the Ruhr.

To support Operation PLUNDER at Wesel and impede any German reinforcement, the Allies planned a massive airborne assault. Operation VARSITY, mounted on March 24, involved 21,692 Allied paratroopers and glider troops of the British 6th Airborne and U.S. 17th Airborne Divisions of Major General Matthew B. Ridgway's XVIII Airborne Corps. The drop zones for VARSITY were east of the Rhine in the Wesel area, close enough to the advancing ground forces to provide for a quick linkup, but not deep enough to give any real additional depth to the operation. By March 25, the airborne forces had secured most of their objectives. The defending German 84th Infantry Division was virtually destroyed, with thirty-five hundred Germans taken prisoner. Although VARSITY was a success, it was a costly one; casualties were higher for the airborne forces in this operation than for the Allied ground units in their crossings.

Meanwhile, the U.S. Ninth Army's 90th Infantry Division crossed all three of its regiments near Wallach shortly after midnight on March 24. The 15th (Scottish) Infantry Division of Lieutenant General Neil Ritchie's British XII Corps got across the river west of Xanten, opposed only by sporadic artillery, mortar, and machine-gun fire. Then, early on March 24, the 79th Infantry Division conducted the last amphibious crossing of the river, at points east and southeast of Rheinberg. For generations, the Germans had considered the Rhine a natural barrier that would protect them from invasion, but superior resources at the points of attack and military engineering gave the Allies access to the German heartland.

Troy D. Morgan and Spencer C. Tucker

See also: Blumentritt, Günther; Reichswald, Battle of the; Remagen Bridge, U.S. Capture of

Additional Reading

Breuer, William B. *Storming Hitler's Rhine: The Allied Assault—February–March 1945*. New York: St. Martin's Press, 1985.

Rhineland, Remilitarization of (March 7, 1936)

The Rhineland remilitarization was one of the seminal events on the road to World War II in Europe. The 1919 Treaty of Versailles, imposed on Germany by the victorious Allies after World War I, demilitarized the entire Rhineland (the German territory west of the Rhine River), as well as a belt thirty miles east of the Rhine. In 1925, the German government voluntarily negotiated and signed the Locarno Pacts. Among their provisions was one guaranteeing continuation of the Rhineland demilitarization. On coming to power, Hitler chose to violate those treaties. Timed to occur in the midst of France's most bitterly contested election campaign after World War I, his move was hastily mounted with the preliminary directive issued on March 2, 1936. On March 7, Operation WINTER EXERCISE sent across the Rhine bridges into the Rhineland just nineteen battalions of infantry and thirteen artillery groups, supported by two antiaircraft battalions and two squadrons of twenty-seven single-seater fighter planes without reserves, a total strength of twenty-two thousand men, as well as fourteen thousand local police. The troops were armed with little more than rifles and machine guns.

Astonishingly, France had no contingency plans for such an eventuality. The most that France did was to mobilize thirteen divisions and reinforce the Maginot Line. In a vain cover for its own inaction, Paris appealed to Britain for support, but Foreign Secretary Anthony Eden made it clear that Britain would not fight for the Rhineland, which was, after all, German territory. Had the French acted by themselves, their forces would have defeated the Germans. Hitler later recalled, "We had no army worth mentioning. If the French had taken any action, we would have been defeated; our resistance would have been over in a few days." A French military move probably would have been the end of the Nazi regime. As Hitler noted, "Retreat on our part would have spelled collapse." Acquisition of the Rhineland fortified Hitler's popularity in Germany. It also assured his ascendancy over his generals. Hitler had effectively destroyed the post–World War I security system.

Spencer C. Tucker

Additional Reading

Shirer, William L. *The Rise and Fall of the Third Reich: A History of Nazi Germany.* New York: Simon and Schuster, 1960.

Rhineland Offensive, Allied (February 8–March 21, 1945)

The Ardennes Offensive ended in a German defeat. Although delaying the Allied timetable by five weeks, it bled Germany of manpower and materiel resources. By February 1945, Allied forces in the west were moving to reach and cross the Rhine River. A series of offensives—Operations VERITABLE, GRENADE, LUMBERJACK, and UNDERTONE—in February to March 1945 was designed to drive German forces from the area north of the Mosel River in preparation for the main Allied invasion of Germany by Field Marshal Sir Bernard L. Montgomery's 21st Army Group in the north, across the Rhine north of the Ruhr. General Dwight D. Eisenhower, the supreme Allied commander, also wanted to occupy the Rhineland (the area of Germany west of the Rhine River) south of the Mosel River in order to secure Montgomery's right flank and provide territory for a secondary invasion of Germany through the Kaiserslautern-Frankfurt corridor.

At the start of the campaign, the area between the Ruhr Mosel Rivers was defended by Field Marshal Walther Model's Army Group B. General of Infantry Gustav-Adolf von Zangen's Fifteenth Army was in the north, General of Panzer Troops Hasso von Manteuffel's Fifth Panzer Army was in the center, and General of Infantry Erich Brandenburger's Seventh Army was in the south. Below the Mosel, Germany west of the Rhine was defended by General of Infantry Hans von Obstfelder's First Army of SS-Oberstgruppenführer Paul Hausser's Army Group G. Below Karlsruhe Hauser's Nineteenth Army, under General of Infantry Siegfried Rasp, defended along the east bank of the Rhine.

Montgomery's attack in the north, Operation VERITABLE, began on February 8 with an assault on the German Westwall entrenchments in and around the Reichswald State Forest. Despite the attackers' greater numbers and air superiority, stubborn German resistance and poor weather slowed the advance. When the Germans breached the Roer River dams before the Allies could seize them, the flooding of that river postponed Operation GRENADE, a supporting attack by the U.S. Ninth Army, and allowed the Germans to concentrate their reserves against the British and Canadians.

Having committed almost all their reserves against VERITABLE, the Germans could not hold back the Americans, as the First and Third Armies launched Operation LUMBERJACK to penetrate the Westwall defenses. Patton, ignoring orders to halt his offensive, sent his forces forward, reaching the Prum River by the end of February. The U.S. First Army north of Patton likewise pressed the defenders ever closer to the Rhine. Launching Operation GRENADE on February 23, after the Roer River flooding had receded, the U.S. Ninth Army broke through the thinned defenses and advanced toward the Rhine. Operation UNDERTONE was the final stage of clearing the Rhineland, with the goal of removing German forces from the Saar and Palatinate. Mounted by Lieutenant General Alexander M. Patch's Seventh Army, it began on March 13.

Hitler's stubborn refusal to permit his armies to retreat or even maneuver contributed greatly to the subsequent German debacle. Standing in place, the German defenders were destroyed in detail or cut off and forced to surrender. Only a relative handful escaped east across the river. By March 24, German forces had been forced back across the Rhine. British and Canadian casualties in these battles approached sixteen thousand men, and U.S. losses among all the armies engaged were almost twice that number. The collapse of the German defenses west of the Rhine began when pressure was applied at several points simultaneously. Lacking the reserves to meet so many attacks and forbidden by Hitler to fall back, the German armies suffered severely. In the Rhineland Campaign, the Allies took more than two hundred thousand German prisoners.

Terry Shoptaugh and Spencer C. Tucker

See also: Ardennes Offensive (Battle of the Bulge); Brandenberger, Erich; Hausser, Paul; Manteuffel, Hasso Eccard von; Model, Walther; Palatinate Campaign, Allied; Reichswald, Battle of the

Additional Reading

Ford, Ken. *The Rhineland Campaign 1945: The Last Killing Ground in the West.* Oxford: Osprey Military, 2000.

Richthofen, Wolfram von (1895–1945)

Luftwaffe field marshal.

Born in Barzdorf, Germany, on October 10, 1895, Wolfram von Richthofen was the cousin of Manfred von Richthofen, the "Red Baron" of World War I. Like his famous cousin, he served as a pilot during World War I. In 1936, Richthofen went to Spain as chief of the Luftwaffe's Development and Testing Branch. He eventually became the commander of the Kondor Legion. In Spain, Richthofen pioneered such close-air support techniques as having air force officers serve with ground troops. Richthofen departed Spain convinced that ground support should be the primary Luftwaffe role. He commanded VIII Air Corps in the invasion of Poland in September 1939, and he directed the aerial destruction of Warsaw. During the invasion of France and the Low Countries in 1940, Richthofen commanded three squadrons of Ju 87 Stuka dive bombers that provided effective flying artillery support to the advancing German Sixth Army.

In July 1940, Richthofen commanded the VIII Air Corps during the Battle of Britain and in the German invasions of Greece and Crete. In 1942, he assumed command of

Luftflotte 4 (Fourth Air Fleet), supporting German forces in the southern Soviet Union and at Stalingrad. Promoted to field marshal in February 1943 (the youngest in the German military), he took command of Luftflotte 2 in Italy. In November 1944, Richthofen was diagnosed with a brain tumor and medically retired. After Germany surrendered, he was held by the Americans in Austria. He died of his brain tumor on July 12, 1945 in Ischl, Austria.

Marlyn R. Pierce

See also: Britain, Battle of; Crete, German Invasion of; Kondor Legion; Stalingrad, Battle of

Additional Reading

Mitcham, Samuel W. *Eagles of the Third Reich: The Men Who Made the Luftwaffe.* Novato, CA: Presidio, 1997.

Rockets, Guided Bombs, and Guided Missiles (1931–1945)

All three of the German military services established rocket and missile development programs during the 1930s. In 1932, the army established a rocket research facility at Kummersdorf-West, which was responsible for coordinating all German rocket research. The head of the program, Captain (later Major General) Walter Dornberger, led a team of brilliant scientists, including Wernher von Braun, Walter Thiel, Heinrich Grünow, and Walter Riedel. During the 1930s, they worked on the development of solid-fuel artillery rockets and long-range, liquid-fuel rockets. In 1936, both the army and Luftwaffe consolidated their research efforts at an elaborate new complex at Peenemünde, on the Baltic coast.

Adopted by the German army on 1940, the 150 mm Wurfgranate 41 was an artillery rocket capable of carrying a high-explosive (HE), smoke, or chemical warhead. The Wgr 41 rocket was spin-stabilized, weighed 75.3 pounds, and had a maximum range of seven thousand meters. It was fired electrically in a ripple-volley from the six-barrel Nebelwerfur 41 (NbW 41) rocket launcher, mounted on a simple two-wheel towed carriage. Initially intended to establish tactical smoke screens—and hence the name Nebelwerfur (Smoke Launcher)—it was more often used to fire HE. The German Army first used the NbW 41 in Russia in 1941 and in North Africa in 1942. In 1942, the German Army adopted NbW 42, identical to the NbW 41 but firing a 248-pound, 210 mm rocket to a maximum range of eighty-two hundred meters.

In 1940, 280 mm and 320 mm rockets also entered service, which used the same engine but mounted different warheads. The 28 cm Wurfkörper Sprengstoff weighed 184.5 pounds, carried an HE warhead, and had a maximum range of two thousand meters. The 32 cm Wurfkörper Flamme carried an incendiary warhead, weighed 173 pounds, and had a range of twenty-two hundred meters. Both rocket types could be fired directly from their shipping crates or from a Wurfgerät 41, a steel-tube frame that mounted four crates. Late in 1940, six of either the 280 mm or 320 mm rockets were mounted on a Sd.Kfz. 251/1 half-track to support the panzer divisions. The resulting Wurfrahmen 40 system was dubbed the *Stuka-zu-Fuss* (Foot Stuka) by the German troops, because of its effectiveness similar to the Ju 87 Stuka dive bomber.

German rockets were spin-stabilized, while Allied rockets generally were fin-stabilized. Spin-stabilization was more effective but technically more difficult to achieve. In 1941, the Germans examined captured Soviet rockets, which were easy to produce, fin-stabilized, and launched from rails. The Germans concluded that they probably had not pursued the best design option, but at that point their production lines were in full operation. The Waffen-SS, however, decided that the Soviet designs were better, and established its own factories in Germany to produce such rockets separately from the army. In March 1944, Hitler had to intervene personally on the side of the army to prevent chaos in the armaments supply system.

The Raketen-Sprenggranate 4831 was Germany's most advanced solid-fuel rocket. Also called the *Rheinbote* (Rhine Messenger), it was a four-stage, unguided ballistic rocket with a range of more than 120 miles and a speed approaching Mach 5.5. More than two hundred were fired against Antwerp in 1944, but with a warhead of only about 90 pounds, it had limited military effect. Despite advice to the contrary from Dornberger, Hitler personally insisted on continual development of the *Rheinbote* until the very end of the war.

The Germans developed a number of aircraft-launched rockets. Introduced in mid-1943, the 210 mm Bordrakete 21 was the first air-to-air rocket carried by Luftwaffe aircraft. Single-engine fighters mounted two, and twin-engine fighters mounted four. The rocket had a maximum range of twelve hundred meters and was detonated by a time fuze set for six hundred to twelve hundred meters from the point of launch. In 1944, the Rakete 4-Kilogramm Minenkopf (R4M) air-to-air rocket entered Luftwaffe service. Nicknamed the *Orkan* (Hurricane) because of its distinctive smoke trail, the R4M had a 55 mm warhead, weighed 8.5 pounds, and had a maximum effective range of one thousand meters.

Germany developed the world's first operational wire-guided missiles. The Ruhrstahl X-4 was an air-to-air missile that carried control wire bobbins in its wing tips. As the missile flew, the wire unwound and carried guidance signals to the spoiler tabs on the missile's wing surfaces. The 44-pound warhead was triggered by a proximity fuze. Testing conducted in 1944 indicated that the wire link between the missile and the launch aircraft was too restricting, leading to design modifications based on radio guidance and acoustic homing systems. No version of the X-4 ever entered operational service.

The X-4's wire guidance system was more successful in the X-7 ground-launched antimissile. Carrying a shaped-charge warhead detonated by an impact fuze, the 22-pound X-7 could penetrate 200 mm of armor at ranges up to one thousand meters. Like the X-4, the X-7 never entered operational service, but the X-7 became the prototype of all the wire-guided antitank missiles that have been standard in most of the world's armies since the late 1960s.

Developed between 1939 and 1942, the Fritz X (also known as the FX 400 and the SD 1400), was one of history's first operational guided bombs. It was a 3,000-pound armor-piercing glide bomb with wings and a small tail unit. Radio signals from the dropping aircraft moved spoilers on the bomb's tail surfaces to direct its trajectory to the target. The most significant operational use of the Fritz X occurred on September 9, 1943, when three of the devices were used to sink the Italian battleship *Roma*.

Germany's infamous *Vergeltung* (Retribution) weapons were the world's first operational guided surface-to-surface missiles. The Flakzielgerät 76 (FZG 76), also known as the Fieseler Fi 103 and as the V-1, was the forerunner of the modern cruise missile. The V-2 was the forerunner of the modern intercontinental ballistic missile. Both weapons were designed to attack cities.

The first long-range missile produced by Dornberger's Kummersdorf-West team was the Aggregat 1 (A-1), powered by a liquid oxygen and alcohol engine. The follow-up A-2 had a better weight distribution and was successfully fired from Borkum on the Baltic Coast in 1934. In 1937, testing began on the A-3, which used advanced graphite rudders to direct the engine exhaust and improve stability during takeoff. The results of the A-3 testing convinced Dornberger and his team that a military missile was feasible.

The resulting A-4 (later designated the V-2) had a guidance system, a 2,200-pound warhead, and a range of 190 miles. The first tests of the A-4 engine began in 1940, but, by that time, it seemed to many in Germany that the war was already won. The A-4 flew successfully for the first time in October 1942. With Germany's strategic situation now changing for the worse, in December of that year, Dornberger received the support of Hitler and Armaments Minister Albert Speer to start mass production.

Typical of the bureaucratic infighting of the Third Reich, the Luftwaffe felt threatened by the long-range strike capability that the A-4 would give the army. The Luftwaffe, in reaction, intensified the development of its own jet-propelled missile. The V-1 flying bomb was originally designated the FZG 76 Flakzielgerät (Air Defense Aiming Device), a purposely misleading name. The Allies called it the "Buzz Bomb" and the "Doodlebug," names that referred to the high-pitched whine of its jet engine. Simpler and cheaper to build than the A-4, the V-1 carried a slightly smaller warhead of 1,870 pounds to a range of 140 miles.

The initial testing of the V-1 began at Peenemünde in December 1941. It was essentially a pilotless, mono-wing aircraft, powered by a pulse-jet engine. The V-1 was 25.4 feet in length and weighed a total of 4,858 pounds. It carried 150 gallons of fuel and had an operational range of 140 miles. Its Asksania autopilot system was set prior to launch, making it secure from electronic jamming during flight. Launched from a fixed ramp, roughly forty-five meters long, its cruising speed once airborne was 350 miles per hour at the relatively low altitude of thirty-five hundred to four thousand feet. The V-1, however, was anything but a precision weapon, with 80 percent of the missiles landing within an eight-mile radius of their intended targets.

The V-1 entered full-scale production in September 1943. By January 1944, the production rate was fourteen hundred per month, increasing to three thousand per month by that September. The intended start date for the V-1 attacks against Britain was February 15 1944, when about twelve thousand were ready for launch, but the campaign did not start until June 1944. The resulting high number of civilian casualties forced the Allies to devote extensive resources to locating and attacking the V-1 launch sites and production facilities.

On August 17 to 18, 1943, the Allies' Operation HYDRA dealt the German missile program a major setback when the Royal Air Force bombed Peenemünde. Further Allied bombing forced the Germans to disperse both V-1 and V-2 production to underground factories, such as those at Nordhausen in Thurungia. The Allies' Operation CROSSBOW, which started on December 5, 1943, targeted both the V-1 launch sites and intercepted the missiles in flight. By June 1944, almost 40 percent of the Allied air effort was directed against the V-1 threat. The attacks on Britain only ended, however, when Allied ground forces overran the launch sites in France. The Germans then turned the V-1s on Antwerp. By the end of the war, 9,251 V-1s had been launched against Britain, and another twelve thousand against other Allied targets on the Continent, including 2,448 against the port of Antwerp and other targets in Belgium. V-1 casualties totaled 7,810 killed and 44,435 injured, mostly civilians.

Although a V-1 could be produced for only about 5 percent the cost of a V-2, it had some significant tactical shortcomings. The V-1's slow 350 miles per hour air speed made it vulnerable to antiaircraft fire and Allied fighter interception. A total of 4,621 of the V-1s launched against Britain and 2,455 launched against Antwerp were destroyed before they reached their targets. The V-1 also had serious reliability problems. The requirement for greater operational range to hit Britain gave a new impetus to the V-2 program. In May 1943, Hitler personally gave the V-2 project his highest priority for the allocation of resources. Late that spring, the Germans started constructing V-2 launching-bunkers in northern France, targeted against Britain.

The V-2 was 46 feet long, weighed 27,000 pounds, and had a range of 190 miles. Its bi-fuel engine burned alcohol and liquid oxygen. Its 2,200-pound warhead carried a TNT and ammonium nitrate mixture called Amatol, and it was detonated by a simple impact fuze. Amatol, however, was a relatively weak explosive. Experiments with more powerful explosives were unsuccessful because the heating of the missile body

V-2 guided missiles at a launching site somewhere in Germany, ca. 1944. The weapons were developed by Dr. Wernher von Braun, who, after the war, became one of the leaders of the American space program. (Roger Viollet/Getty Images)

from air friction often caused premature explosions. When full manufacture of the V-2 started, the schedule called for an initial production rate of three hundred in October 1943, increasing to nine hundred a month by December. The Germans produced more than ten thousand V-2s before the end of the war, largely by using concentration camp prisoners as forced laborers.

Although much more expensive to make, the V-2 had several significant tactical advantages over the V-1. Because the V-2 launched vertically, it could be fired from any location, with only a couple hundred square meters of clearance. The V-1 was somewhat more accurate, but the V-2 was far more deadly and almost impossible to defend against after it was launched. The V-1 was slow enough to be tracked visually, and its loud engine noise gave significant warning to the target area. The V-2 was deadly silent and gave no warning. It dropped from about sixty miles up at speeds approaching 2,200 miles per hour.

The first V-2 that landed hit Britain on September 8, 1944. By the time the last two V-2s were fired on March 27, 1945, the Germans had fired at least 3,172. Thirteen British cities had been hit with 1,402, of which 1,358 hit London. Belgium was hit with 1,664 of the missiles, of which 1,610 hit Antwerp. Twenty-two were fired against Paris, and twenty-five against Lille. When Allied forces captured, intact, the Remagen Bridge over the Rhine in March 1945, the Germans fired eleven V-2s in a desperate attempt to destroy the bridge. One actually hit close. The Allies lost 4,148 killed and 8,477 wounded from V-2 strikes. As with the V-1 strikes, most of the V-2 casualties were civilians.

Germans development work on the Aggregate series of ballistic missiles extended through the A-12. Most of those designs never got off the drawing board. The potentially most threatening to the Allies was the A-9/10, a two-stage missile, with the A-10 as the booster and the A-9 as the second stage delivery vehicle. Conceived as a trans-Atlantic weapon, initial design work started in 1940. It was later cancelled but then resurrected in 1944 under the code name *Projekt Amerika*. The projected range was three thousand miles. When the war ended, the A-12 was being designed as a four-stage system capable of putting a ten-ton payload into a low-Earth orbit.

The V-2 was one of the most technologically advanced weapons systems of World War II, but it was an expensive and resource-intensive program that diverted many of Germany's scarce resources to the production of a weapon that could deliver a warhead weighing only about one ton. The justification for the program was more the result of the irrational expectations of Germany's political leadership than of objective military analysis. Ironically, while the V-1 and V-2 programs did little to help the Germans, the Allies during the immediate postwar period were the real beneficiaries of the resulting technologies.

David T. Zabecki and Jonathan B. A. Bailey

See also: Artillery; Braun, Wernher von; CROSSBOW, Anglo-American Air Operation; Dornberger, Walter; Speer, Albert

Additional Reading

Holsken, Dieter. *V-Missiles of the Third Reich: The V-1 and V-2*. Boylston, MA: Monogram Aviation Publications, 1994.

Miranda, Justo, and Paula Mercado. *Secret Wonder Weapons of the Third Reich: German Missiles 1934–1945*. Atglen: PA: Schiffer Publishing, Ltd., 2000.

Rogge, Bernhard (1899–1982)

Kriegsmarine vice admiral, Bundesmarine vice admiral.

Born in Schleswig, Germany, on November 4, 1899, Bernhard Rogge served in the merchant marines during World War I. Although he had a Jewish grandparent, he was exempted from Nazi racial laws and accepted as an officer in the German Navy. As the commander of the armed merchant cruiser *Atlantis* between March 1940 and November 1941, he sank twenty-two ships, weighing an aggregate 145,697 tons, the most of any commerce raider during the war. On November 22, 1941, the *Atlantis* was sunk by the British heavy cruiser HMS *Devonshire*. Rogge and most of his crew survived, and their lifeboats were taken in tow by the *U-126*. In 1945, Rogge was promoted to vice admiral and commanded the 3rd Battle Group in the Baltic. In 1955, Rogge joined the new West German Bundesmarine as a vice admiral. He died in Reinbek bei Hamburg, Germany, on June 29, 1982.

Frank Toomey

See also: Kriegsmarine (German Navy)

Additional Reading

Ruge, Friedrich. *Der Seekrieg: The German Navy's Story, 1939–1945*. Annapolis, MD: Naval Institute Press, 1957.

Röhm, Ernst (1887–1934)

Reichswehr captain and chief of staff of the Sturmabteilungen (SA).

Röhm was born in Munich on October 27, 1887. He was a career officer in the Bavarian Army. As an officer in the post–World War I Reichswehr from 1919 to 1923, he helped Germany evade the disarmament provisions of the Treaty of Versailles, supporting paramilitary units with money and weapons. Röhm was an early patron and supporter of Adolf Hitler and the National Socialist German Workers' Party (NSDAP). In 1923, he led a paramilitary unit Reichsflagge (Reich Flag) in the Beer Hall Putsch, an unsuccessful attempt by Hitler to seize power in Munich. On January 5, 1931, Hitler appointed him chief of staff of the Sturmabteilungen (Storm Troops, or SA). SA violence aided the Nazi consolidation of power after January 30, 1933. In mid-1934, Hitler, with army support, moved against Röhm and the SA during the "Night of the Long Knives Blood Purge. On July 2, Röhm was killed in Munich's Stadelheim Prison on Hitler's orders.

Eleanor Hancock

See also: Night of the Long Knives; Sturmabteilungen (SA)

Additional Reading

Hancock, Eleanor. *Ernst Röhm: Hitler's SA Chief of Staff.* New York: Palgrave MacMillan, 2008.

Romania Campaign, Soviet (August 20–31, 1944)

With 1.2 million men under arms in 1944, Romania was the third-largest Axis military force in Europe. The Soviet invasion that started on August 20, 1944 led to the overthrow of Romania's Fascist government, but the restored monarchy was soon replaced by a communist state. At the start of the Soviet invasion, most of Romania was in the sector of German Army Group South Ukraine, commanded by Colonel General Johannes Friessner. The opposing Soviet forces came under the 2nd Ukrainian

Front, commanded by General Rodion Malinovsky, and the 3rd Ukrainian Front, commanded by Marshal Fyodor Tolbukhin. On August 20, a ten-hour artillery barrage from eleven thousand Soviet guns opened the Jassy–Kishinev Offensive. Waves of Soviet planes also broke through heavy antiaircraft defenses protecting Romania's harbor at Constanta, sinking and damaging Romanian warships. Romania capitulated three days later. German forces tried to restore control by seizing the capital of Bucharest, but they were repulsed by Romanian units. Soviet and Romanian forces then enveloped the remaining Germans outside Bucharest on August 27, taking seven thousand prisoners. The Red Army entered Bucharest on August 31. The Jassy–Kishinev Offensive cost the Germans some one hundred thousand killed and one hundred and fifteen thousand captured. Total Soviet casualties were some sixty-seven thousand. In September 1944, the remnants of Army Group South Ukraine were absorbed into Army Group South.

Gerald D. Swick and David T. Zabecki

Additional Reading

Tarnstrom, Ronald L. *Balkan Battles.* Lindsborg, KS: Trogen Books, 1998.

Rome, Allied Liberation of (June 4, 1944). *See* Italy Campaign, Allied

Rommel, Erwin (1891–1944)

Wehrmacht field marshal.

Erwin Rommel earned enduring fame as a panzer commander during World War II, and his success was built upon a distinguished record of service during World War I as an infantry officer. The incongruity of an infantryman transitioning to armor underscores the question that still dogs his legacy—just how successful was this man, and what did it mean in terms of understanding Germany at war?

Rommel was born on November 15, 1892 in Ulm, the son of a middle-class schoolteacher. During World War I, when he was assigned to a mountain infantry unit in the Italian Alps, he exploited repeated Italian failures with such success that he earned *Pour le Mérite* for his role in the battle of Caporetto. After the war, Rommel retained a thirst for the adulation that had come his way for military service. During World War II, he said little about the justification of Germany waging the war, but his actions suggest he sided with the Nazi regime. When the Germans attacked Poland in 1939, Rommel commanded Hitler's personal bodyguard. In the summer of 1940, he commanded 7th Panzer Division across France, although many suspected that his supplication with Hitler enabled him to get this command. While leading this division across the Meuse River during the Ardennes breakout, his onsite presence blunted a near disaster as the unit sought a bridgehead. Contemporary critics, however, branded him meddlesome with lower ranks, reckless with the men under his command, and self-serving in terms of promoting his own exploits but minimizing those of others.

This combination of acclaim and resentment followed him to North Africa when Hitler selected him to lead the Afrika Korps, a weak complement of two German divisions tasked with stabilizing the collapsing Italian empire in Libya. Rommel soon exceeded this mandate and ushered in a desert war that committed Germany to the Mediterranean theater to a greater extent than desired. Here, an ambiguity of accomplishment came into view: success in the tactical application of Blitzkrieg but an apparent ignorance of strategic realities. His ability to bait British forces into futile armor attacks at battles such as Battleaxe, Crusader, and Gazala, all the while preserving his inferior tank forces, meant that by early fall 1942, he had pushed the British back to a last stand defense of Cairo at El Alamein. His defeat there came at the hands of superior numbers, and so even retreat did not diminish his fame. But the end of his offensive operations underscored his liability as a senior commander, that he overextended his small army and, with it, Germany's stake in the desert.

While having done little to earn distinction as an army group commander, Hitler ordered him to defend France against the impending Allied invasion. Rommel readied a great deal of the coastline, even Normandy where the invasion came, but he believed the invasion had to be stopped at the shore. When it was not, he urged Hitler to make peace. This stand hastened his death when implicated in the attempted assassination of Hitler on July 20, 1944. Rommel had been wounded in Normandy only three days earlier. While at home near Stuttgart on convalescent leave, Rommel took his own life on October 14, 1943 to shield his family from torture at the hands of the Gestapo. With this end, his life came full circle, a tribute to German military excellence but rendering that service at the behest of a criminal regime. Ambiguity plagues his legacy still.

Matthew J. Flynn

See also: Afrika Korps; Blitzkrieg

Additional Reading

Fraser, David. *Knight's Cross: A Life of Field Marshal Erwin Rommel*. New York: HarperCollins, 1993.

Mellenthin, F. W. *German Generals of World War II: As I Saw Them*. Norman: University of Oklahoma Press, 1977.

Roslavl, Battle of (August 1–8, 1941). *See* Soviet Union, Invasion of (Operation BARBAROSSA)

Rostov, Battle of (November 17–30, 1941)

After clearing Ukraine during the summer of 1941, Field Marshal Gerd von Rundstedt's Army Group South continued its advance east and south. Barring its way was the Soviet city of Rostov on the Sea of Azov, at the mouth of the Don River. Rostov was the gateway to the Caucasus Mountains, the Soviet oil fields to the south, and the road to Persia, through which Britain and the United States were to supply the Red Army.

Between September 29 and October 13, 1941, Rundstedt's armies overran the coal- and iron-rich Donets Basin region, where 20 percent of Soviet steel was produced. They also forced the Mius River and captured Taganrog on the Sea of Azov. On November 17, the Soviet Southern Front, under General Yakov Cherevichenko, attacked the Germans near Rostov. General Eberhard von Mackensen's III Panzer Corps counterattacked, and the 1st SS Panzer Division captured Rostov on November 21. The Soviets counterattacked and drove the Germans out of the city by November 29. The following day, the Germans withdrew behind the Mius River. On December 1, Hitler fired Rundstedt and replaced him with Field Marshal Walther von Reichenau.

The battle for Rostov was the first serious setback for the Germans since the start of Operation BARBAROSSA. The Germans suffered an estimated twenty thousand casualties and the Soviets thirty-three thousand. The failure at Rostov also triggered the relief of all four of the German army's top commanders.

Claude R. Sasso and Spencer C. Tucker

See also: Mackensen, Eberhard von; Reichenau, Walther von; Rundstedt, Karl Rudolf Gerd von

Additional Reading

Erickson, John. *The Road to Stalingrad.* Boulder, CO: Westview Press, 1984.

Rudel, Hans-Ulrich (1916–1982)

Luftwaffe colonel and the most highly decorated German soldier of World War II.

Born at Seiferdaj, Silesia, Germany, on July 2, 1916, Rudel joined the Luftwaffe in 1936 and qualified as a dive-bomber pilot in May 1940. On February 9, 1945, after destroying a Soviet tank, his Ju 87 was hit by antiaircraft fire. He returned to action six weeks later despite the amputation of his right leg and orders that he not fly. Rudel ended the war commanding *Schlachtgeschwader* 2 (Ground-Attack Wing 2). His final tally was 2,530 sorties. He was credited with the destruction of the Soviet battleship *Marat*, 1 cruiser, 1 destroyer, 70 landing craft, 150 gun emplacements, 519 tanks and 800 other combat vehicles, and 7 aircraft. For his exceptional service, Hitler instituted the Gold Oak Leaves to the Knight's Cross of the Iron Cross. Rudel was the only recipient of this award. At the end of the war, Rudel surrendered to the Americans and was held prisoner until March 1946. An unrepentant Nazi, he wrote several books supporting the regime and condemning the German General Staff for failing Hitler. His extreme right-wing views made him unwelcome in the Federal Republic of Germany's armed forces and aviation industry. Rudel died in Rosenheim, Germany, on December 18, 1982.

Marlyn R. Pierce

See also: Luftwaffe (German Air Force)

Additional Reading

Rudel, Hans-Ulrich. *Stuka Pilot.* New York: Ballantine Books, 1958.

Ruge, Friedrich (1894–1985)

Kriegsmarine vice admiral Bundesmarine vice admiral.

Friedrich Oskar Ruge was born in Leipzig on Christmas Eve, 1894. He served in the Kaiserliche Marine during World War I. Following Germany's surrender in 1918, Ruge was interned with fellow German naval personnel and the High Seas Fleet at the British Royal Navy's base at Scapa Flow, Scotland. On June 21, 1919, Ruge played a key role when the High Seas Fleet scuttled itself, sinking fifty-two battleships, cruisers, and destroyers. During World War II, Ruge was the senior German naval officer in Italy. In November 1943, he transferred to France, where he became the naval adviser to Field Marshal Erwin Rommel. With the establishment of the Bundeswehr in 1955, Ruge came out of retirement in 1956 and was appointed a vice admiral and first inspector of the Bundesmarine, the equivalent of the U.S. Navy's chief of naval operations. Ruge died in Tübingen on July 3, 1985.

Fred L. Borch III

See also: Kriegsmarine (German Navy)

Additional Reading

Ruge, Friedrich. *Rommel in Normandy: Reminiscences.* San Rafael, CA: Presidio Press, 1979.

Ruhr Air Campaign, Allied (March 5–July 31, 1943)

The Ruhr Air Campaign was a British-directed strategic bombing effort aimed at the heart of the German industrial region. The campaign was designed to destroy the coke plants, steel manufacturing, and synthetic oil facilities concentrated in the Northern Rhine Westphalia area of western Germany. Royal Air Force (RAF) Bomber Command chose urban city centers as their objectives, since those areas were easier to locate and target by air—hitting the industrial complexes were "regarded as a bonus." The result was terror bombing designed to force Germany into submission. German defenses consisted of an integrated network of radars, searchlights, antiaircraft flak artillery, and night fighters. The Kammhuber Line was an effective defense inflicting considerable losses on Allied aircraft. An estimated 75 percent of Allied bomber losses were attributed to the Kammhuber Line defenses. As the Ruhr Air Campaign continued, RAF losses exceeded 5 percent, and with a few exceptions, bomb damage was not significant. Still, the bombings inflicted heavy losses on the German populace.

The Ruhr Air Campaign began on the night of March 5 to 6 when 442 aircraft attacked the Krupp works at Essen. On March 26 to 27, Bomber Command launched 393 aircraft against the Thyssen Steel Works at Duisburg. Essen was hit again on the night of April 3 to 4, this time with 348 aircraft. On April 30 to May 1, the Krupp factory at Essen was targeted by 345 aircraft. The raid brought to a total ten thousand tons dropped on Essen, making it the most bombed city in history to that date. On May 4 to 5, Dortmund was hit for the first time, with 596 aircraft severely damaging the Hoesch and Dortmunder steel factories.

On May 17, the RAF launched on a daring raid: Operation CHASTISE, the destruction of the Mohne and Eder Dams. The effects, however, did little to disrupt the Ruhr's electricity or water supplies, and, within a month, both were back to full capacities. More than sixteen hundred people died from the flooding, some half of whom were POWs or forced laborers from Eastern Europe. On May 29 to 30, a particularly accurate bombing raid on Wuppertal resulted in a firestorm on the ground, leaving 2,450 dead and 120,000 homeless. Back-to-back raids on Cologne started in July. The one on July 3 to 4 hit the industrial area along the Rhein, and the raid on July 8 to 9 hit the city's western sectors. Essen was hit on July 25 to 26 by a force of six hundred bombers in less than an hour, resulting in a complete stoppage of the Krupp Works. The last raid of the Ruhr air campaign was the July 30 to 31 attack on Remscheid, which caused a firestorm that nearly completely destroyed the city.

Despite massive bombings during the Ruhr air campaign and into 1944, Armaments Minister Albert Speer was able to increase military production. Historian Max Hastings pointed out that "morale of the German people remained unbroken until the end," and Bomber Command "destroyed centuries of construction and culture." Thousands of acres were burned and thousands of people killed, yet war production increased.

William H. Van Husen

See also: Combined Bomber Offensive, Allied (Operation POINTBLANK); Kammhuber Line; Speer, Albert

Additional Reading

Hastings, Max. *Bomber Command.* New York: Dial Press, 1979.

Ruhr Ground Campaign, Allied (March 25–April 18, 1945)

By March 1945, the Western Allies had defeated all German opposition west of the Rhine River and had crossed Germany's last defensive barrier at several points. The Ruhr Valley was Germany's industrial heartland, and the most important Allied military objective after Berlin. Concentrated within a two-thousand-square-mile area were eighteen manufacturing cities and coal deposits supplying 69 percent of Germany's requirements. Between 1942 and 1945, the Allied air campaign had diminished the Ruhr's productive capacity and forced a 25 to 30 percent drop in steel production. Sixty-five German divisions defended the Ruhr. These units were largely concentrated in the west to defend against a direct assault from the Rhine. Although understrength, these divisions presented a formidable obstacle to any direct U.S. offensive. General Omar N. Bradley, the commander of the Allied 12th Army Group, chose to envelop the Ruhr in a classic pincer movement. Lieutenant General Courtney H. Hodges's First Army would advance along the Ruhr's southern boundary while Lieutenant General William H. Simpson's Ninth Army enveloped the Ruhr from the north. The two armies planned to link up at Paderborn.

The Ruhr Campaign began on March 25, when the First Army broke out of the Remagen bridgehead over the Rhine and advanced eastward, encountering stiff German resistance on the approach to Paderborn. Students and instructors from a local Waffen-SS Panzer training camp blocked the U.S. advance with their Pz.Kpfw.VI Tiger and Pz.Kpfw.V Panther tanks. At noon on Easter Sunday, April 1, forward armored elements of the First and Ninth Armies linked up in the Lippstadt area west of Paderborn, completing the Ruhr envelopment.

The Ruhr Pocket (*Ruhr Kessel*) measured some thirty by eighty miles. Trapped within were Field Marshal Walther Model's Army Group B headquarters, Colonel General Josef Harpe's Fifth Panzer Army, most of General of Infantry Gustav von Zangen's Fifteenth Army, and two corps of the First Parachute Army. In all, German forces caught in the pocket included remnants of eighteen divisions and seven corps commands. The encircled German forces were unable to muster sufficient strength to break through the U.S. ring and could not count on a relief from outside the pocket. Characteristically, Hitler ordered Model to defend "Fortress Ruhr" to the last man.

Initially, the Americans deployed thirteen divisions for the Ruhr battle. Later, with progress slower than expected, four additional divisions were committed. German resistance proved spotty and unpredictable. Essen, home of the Krupp industrial combine, was taken on April 11, and, by April 14, the Americans had effectively cut the area in two when troops from the U.S. First and Ninth Armies met up along the Ruhr River. Major General Matthew B. Ridgway, XVIII Airborne Corps commander, wrote to Model and demanded his surrender, but the German commander refused to disobey Hitler's order. Instead, he disbanded his army and issued all his troops discharge papers. On April 21, Model committed suicide. All organized resistance in the Ruhr Pocket ceased on April 18. During the two-week campaign, the Americans captured three hundred and seventeen thousand German soldiers, including thirty generals and an admiral—more than the Allies had captured in Tunisia or the Soviets had at Stalingrad. The Western Allies also liberated two hundred thousand forced laborers and 5,639 prisoners of war.

Thomas G. Nester

See also: Model, Walther; Remagen Bridge, U.S. Capture of; Ruhr Air Campaign, Allied

Additional Reading

Kessler, Leo. *The Battle of the Ruhr Pocket, April 1945.* Chelsea, MI: Scarborough House, 1990.

MacDonald, Charles B. *The Last Offensive.* New York: Barnes and Noble, 1973.

Rundstedt, Karl Rudolf Gerd von (1875–1953)

Wehrmacht field marshal.

Born at Aschersleben, Germany, on December 12, 1875, Karl Gerd von Rundstedt joined the army in 1893 and served throughout World War I. Following the war, he rose steadily in the new Reichswehr. Unhappy with Hitler's growing power, Rundstedt retired on October 31, 1938. He was recalled to duty at the age of sixty-four, and, in September 1939, he led Army Group South into Poland. In May 1940, Rundstedt commanded Army Group A during the invasion of France. In June 1941, Rundstedt participated in the invasion of the Soviet Union, Operation BARBAROSSA, as commander of Army Group South. His forces made slow progress during the first weeks, but in September 1941, he took part in the capture of Kiev and six hundred and sixty-five thousand Soviet troops. Rundstedt strongly opposed continuing the advance into the Soviet Union during the winter and advised Hitler to call a halt, but his views were rejected. Hitler replaced Rundstedt with General Walther von Reichenau. In March 1942, Hitler again recalled Rundstedt to active duty, sending him to France as OB West (commander in chief, West). After the Allied Normandy landings, he urged Hitler to make peace. The Führer responded by replacing him with Field Marshal Günther von Kluge, but, in September, Rundstedt returned to his former post. In December 1944, he had overall command of the Ardennes Offensive. After that attack failed, Rundstedt again was sacked as OB West in March 1945.

Rundstedt was the prototype of the old-style Prussian officer, deeply attached to Germany's imperial traditions. He never failed to contradict Hitler on military matters when he felt it necessary to do so, but he also never questioned the political leadership and goal of the regime. Captured by the Western Allies on May 1, 1945, Rundstedt was released in May 1949 and lived near Celle, Germany, until his death on February 24, 1953.

Martin Moll

See also: Ardennes Offensive (Battle of the Bulge); France, Battle of; Normandy Invasion and Campaign; Poland Campaign; Soviet Union, Invasion of (Operation BARBAROSSA)

Additional Reading

Messenger, Charles. *The Last Prussian: Biography of Field Marshal Gerd von Rundstedt, 1875–1953.* Washington, DC: Brassey's Defence Publishers, 1991.

Ruweisat Ridge, Battle of (July 21–27, 1942). *See* North Africa Campaign

S

Saarland, French Invasion of the (September 7–16, 1939)

The abortive French invasion of the German Saarland at the very start of World War II was one of the lost opportunities of the war. On May 19, 1939, French and Polish military officials agreed that their armies would attack Germany if Germany moved against either state. Supreme commander of French land forces, General Maurice Gamelin, pledged that he would invade Germany with the majority of his troops no more than fifteen days after mobilization. Britain and France also promised that in the event of a German attack, they would move against Germany immediately from the air.

Despite the Allied pledge, the French military strategy for war with Germany was to remain on the defensive, wearing down the enemy until France's own army was strong enough to seize the initiative. On September 1, Germany invaded Poland. Six days later, the Polish General Staff radioed an appeal for Gamelin to act quickly, in hopes that Germany would divert units from the invasion to the west. The French mobilization had just begun, and most heavy artillery was still in storage. Regardless, honor demanded some action on behalf of the Poles. Thus, Gamelin mounted an attack within a ninety-mile-wide sector between the Rhine and Moselle Rivers in the Saarland. The invasion force was designated 2nd Army Group, commanded by General André Prételat.

With five field armies totaling fifty-five divisions committed against Poland, the Germans had only twenty-two divisions deployed along their western border. Most of those units were inadequately trained and poorly equipped reserves. The mechanized and motorized troops had all been committed to the fighting in Poland, and artillery had been stripped from the Westwall. German forces in the west had no tanks, little artillery, and virtually no aircraft. Army Group A in the north was commanded by Colonel General Kurt von Hammerstein-Equord, recalled to active duty from retirement. Army Group C in the south was commanded by Colonel General Wilhelm von Leeb. Defending the Palatinate and the Saarland was the First Army, commanded by Colonel General Erwin von Witzleben.

On the night of September 7 to 8, a few light French units entered German territory along a fifteen-mile front southeast of Saarbrücken. On September 9, stronger forces from the French Fourth and Fifth Armies followed, while the Third Army advanced into the Wendt Forest, slightly to the west. Despite Gamelin's earlier pledge to use the majority of his troops, no more than fifteen divisions crossed the frontier.

The French 2nd Army Group advanced a mere five miles by September 12, capturing twenty deserted German villages. Gamelin then ordered Prételat to halt short of the Westwall and prepare for retreat should the Germans counterattack through Belgium. As it became clear that the Poles were collapsing under the German hammer blows, Prételat was ordered on September 30 to start withdrawing his troops. By mid-October, Germany had seventy divisions in the west. On October 16, a small German infantry force attacked the remaining French troops, and, in two days, Germany reoccupied all the territory the 2nd Army Group had required two weeks to capture. Casualties on both sides in the ineffectual campaign were light. Most French losses resulted from a thick belt of German mines and booby traps.

Gerald D. Swick

See also: Leeb, Wilhelm Ritter von; Poland Campaign; Westwall; Witzleben, Erwin von

Additional Reading

Horne, Alistair. *To Lose a Battle: France 1940.* Boston, MA: Little, Brown, 1969.

Saint-Lô, Battle for (July 11–19, 1944)

Saint-Lô was a strategically important crossroad that was vital to the development of the Normandy campaign. The Germans had first occupied the town on June 19, 1940. Allied operational planners expected that St-Lô would fall by D-Day+17. But St-Lô was not captured on time for various reasons, including intense resistance by German forces and the nature of the geography between the invasion beaches and St-Lô. Known as the *bocage*, it provided a tactical advantage to the German defenders. Finally, supply problems, exacerbated by the English Channel storm of June 19 to 20, slowed offensive action.

During June, U.S. forces attempted to advance on St-Lô but became bogged down in what became known as the "Battle of the Hedgerows." German forces near St-Lô consisted of the Seventh Army, commanded by SS-Oberstgruppenführer Paul Hausser, that included the LXXXIV Corps commanded by General Dietrich von Choltitz, and the II Parachute Corps commanded by Lieutenant General Eugen Meindl.

The 30th Infantry Division of U.S. XIX Corps attacked across the Vire-et-Taute canal on July 7. The initial movement led to the outflanking of German units defending against U.S.VIII and VII Corps. The 17th SS Panzergrenadier Division, 2nd SS Panzer Division, and II Parachute Corps reinforced the sector, and the Panzer Lehr Division under General Fritz Bayerlein was ordered west for a counterattack. However, confusion in the U.S. command caused delays. By July 11, the U.S. 2nd Infantry Division had taken the key position of Hill 192 in preparation for their advance toward St-Lô.

By July 11, the Panzer Lehr Division, reinforced by the 17th SS Panzergrenadier Division, counterattacked the positions of U.S. XIX Corps, but the Germans ran into the newly arrived U.S. 9th Infantry Division, which had moved in to cut the Perriers-St-Lô road. Bayerlein had expected to hit the flank of 30th Infantry Division, but he was repulsed by both U.S. divisions. After repulsing the attack of the Panzer Lehr Division, U.S. XIX and VII Corps continued to advance. From July 15, on, the persistent pressure applied by both U.S. XIX and now V Corps forced the Germans back toward St-Lô, with the city defended by II Parachute Corps and three reinforced battle groups. When advances by XIX Corps east of the River Vire made the German position untenable, Hausser ordered the II Parachute Corps to evacuate St-Lô. U.S. units entered on July 18. By that point, the German 352nd Infantry Division was down to only two hundred effectives.

Ross Mahoney

See also: Bayerlein, Fritz; Choltitz, Dietrich von; COBRA, Allied Breakout Operation; Hausser, Paul

Additional Reading

Carafano, James Jay. *After D-Day: Operation Cobra and the Normandy Breakout*. Boulder, CO: Lynne Rienner Publishers, 2000.

Salerno Landings, Allied (September 9–15, 1943)

The main Allied invasion of the Italian mainland, Operation AVALANCHE, took place in the Bay of Salerno, near Naples, on September 9, 1943. It was the follow-up of the Sicily campaign and took place on the day after Italy announced its surrender to the Allies. After the fall of Sicily, the German forces in Italy, under the command of Field Marshal Albert Kesselring, prepared for the defense of the Italian mainland. Kesselring placed the defense of Southern Italy in the hands of the Tenth Army, with two corps and six divisions commanded by Colonel General Heinrich von Vietinghoff. The German Army was supported by the Luftwaffe's Second Air Fleet, under the command of Field Marshal Wolfram von Richthofen. Three of the German divisions in southern Italy were located near Salerno, with the 16th Panzer Division covering Salerno itself and the Luftwaffe's Hermann Göring Panzer Division and the 15th Panzer Grenadier Division stationed nearby.

The Allied landing was poorly planned and executed. Because of a limited number of landing craft available, the Allies could only land three divisions in the initial assault, and those three divisions covered a front of thirty-five miles. Kesselring reacted immediately and decisively by ordering the Hermann Göring Division and the 15th Panzer Grenadier Division to Salerno. The 26th Panzer Division was immediately transferred from Calabria to the Salerno front. As the Allies only slowly developed the beachhead, the Germans prepared a strong counterattack that began on September 12. The attack by the four German divisions drove back the U.S. 36th Infantry Division. Finally, the deployment of the U.S. 82nd Airborne Division, dropped as reinforcements at threatened points, and the powerful naval gunfire support from the U.S. and British fleets slowed the momentum of the German counterattack of September 13 and 14. By September 15, Kesselring knew that the beachhead could not be overrun, and he ordered the Tenth Army to assume defensive positions. The long battle for the beachhead and the higher-than-expected Allied casualties enabled the Germans to form a coherent defense line across southern Italy, well south of Rome. Kesselring and the German leaders demonstrated an impressive ability to react quickly and decisively.

James S. Corum

See also: Kesselring, Albert; Richthofen, Wolfram von; Sicily, Allied Invasion of; Vietinghoff genannt Scheel, Heinrich von

Additional Reading

Blumenson, Martin. *Salerno to Cassino: The United States Army in World War II*. Washington, DC: Center of Military History, 1969.

Scharnhorst Battle Cruiser. *See* Warships, Surface

Scheldt Estuary, Battles for (October 8–November 2, 1944)

Advancing British liberated Antwerp on October 4, 1944. The Allies, however, were unable to use the vital port until they also secured the Scheldt River estuary, which remained under German control for almost two more months. After the German Fifteenth Army escaped on September 4 from the Breskens pocket (formed on the mainland north of the Leopold Canal and west of Antwerp), it was deployed to hold the Scheldt estuary and prevent the Allies from opening Antwerp. German commander Colonel General Gustav von Zagen left only a rearguard on the mainland and concentrated his strength on the South Beveland and Walcheren Island, both of which formed the northern boundary of the estuary. Zagen, however, only had four depleted divisions and assorted support troops.

In late September, British Field Marshal Sir Bernard Montgomery, commander of the Allied 21st Army Group, assigned clearing the Scheldt to the Canadian First Army, which was already assigned to capturing the channel ports, including Boulogne and Calais. The British attacks to clear the Scheldt began on October 8. Canadian Lieutenant General Guy Simonds, commanding the Canadian First Army, designed the plan. A key element in Simonds's plan was the destruction of dikes that protected Walcheren from the North Sea. This action flooded most of the island and restricted German movement and communications. Also important to the plan was the use of special equipment, including flamethrower "Wasps" (converted universal carriers) and "Buffaloes" (amphibious vehicles).

The Canadian 3rd Infantry Division cleared the Breskens pocket after nearly a month of tough fighting. Then the Canadian 2nd Infantry Division and the Scottish 52nd Lowland Division took South Beveland, reaching the causeway to Walcheren at the end of October. The island was defended by the 70th Infantry Division, commanded by Lieutenant General Wilhelm Daser. Three attempts by the Canadians to cross the causeway ended in failure. On November 1, commandos amphibiously assaulted the south and west ends of Walcheren, supported by the 52nd Division in the south. It took a week to clear all pockets of German resistance, but the parts of the island that commanded the Scheldt were taken on November 3.

The battles to clear the Scheldt estuary cost the Allies thirteen thousand casualties. The Germans suffered roughly the same number of casualties, and lost more than forty-one thousand troops as prisoners. The remnants of the Fifteenth Army withdrew north, into Holland. The first oceangoing ships arrived on November 29. Denying the Allies use of the port for nearly three months delayed the defeat of Germany considerably. The Germans also harassed Antwerp with V-1 buzz bombs and V-2 rockets, which, however, had little effect on port operations, beyond the decision to transfer ammunition resupply to other ports.

Britton W. MacDonald

See also: Antwerp, Allied Liberation of

Additional Reading

Levine, Alan J. *From the Normandy Beaches to the Baltic Sea: The Northwest Europe Campaign, 1944–1945.* Westport, CT: Praeger, 2000.

Schörner, Ferdinand (1892–1973)

Wehrmacht field marshal.

Born in Munich on May 12, 1892, Schörner served in the Bavarian Army during World War I, specializing in mountain warfare. He commanded the 6th Mountain Division during the invasion of France in May 1940, and the invasion of Greece in April 1941. Transferred to south Russia in October 1943, Schörner commanded Army Group South Ukraine from March to July 1944, and Army Group North from July 1944 to January 1945. Schörner commanded Army Group Center from January to May 1945, which he managed to keep largely intact until Germany's surrender. Promoted to field marshal in April 1945, he was named in Adolf Hitler's testament to succeed Hitler as commander in chief of the German Army (Oberbefehlshaber des Heeres). Schörner was released from Russian captivity in 1955, but, in Munich in 1957, a German court sentenced him to four and a half years in prison for ordering the execution without trial of a soldier found drunk in duty. Following his release, Schörner lived in Munich, where he died on July 2, 1973.

Spencer C. Tucker and John P. Vanzo

See also: France, Battle of

Additional Reading

Mellenthin, Friedrich. *German Generals of World War II: As I Saw Them.* Norman: University of Oklahoma Press, 1977.

Schweinfurt and Regensburg Air Raids, Allied (August 17, 1943)

Operation JUGGLER was a joint raid, deep into Germany against key industrial targets. Launched on August 17, 1943, the U.S. 1st Bombardment Wing attacked the ball-bearing industry at Schweinfurt, while the U.S. 4th Bombardment Wing launched a simultaneous raid against the Messerschmitt factories at Regensburg and then continued on to Allied bases in North Africa. The total U.S. bomber force consisted of 376 B-17s. A delay caused by fog, however, resulted in the Regensburg force launching three hours before the Schweinfurt force. This delay caused havoc for the Schweinfurt force. The decision to attack a target deep in Germany meant that the bombers would attack their targets without constant fighter cover. As German fighters, under the command of General Adolf Galland, had been expecting the Regensburg force to return to Britain, they scrambled and were ready when the delayed Schweinfurt force arrived. The Schweinfurt force suffered three hours of attacks. The total Luftwaffe force consisted of some four hundred Bf 109, Bf 110, and FW 190 fighters, launching head-on attacks against the U.S. bomber stream.

German armaments minister Albert Speer later reported that ball-bearing production had been reduced by only 34 percent. The Eighth Air Force suffered heavy and unacceptable losses in the raid, with 60 out of 376 bombers lost, a rate of approximately 15 percent. The Germans lost only about twenty-seven fighters, with some two hundred civilians killed on the ground. A follow-up raid on Schweinfurt on October 14 had marginally greater success, but of the 291 B-17s committed to the mission, 77 were lost, and 121 were damaged. The Eighth Air Force then curtailed deep-penetration raids until deep fighter escort became available.

Ross Mahoney

See also: Combined Bomber Offensive, Allied (Operation POINTBLANK); Galland, Adolf

Additional Reading

Coffey, Thomas M. *Decision over Schweinfurt.* Philadelphia, PA: David McKay Company, Inc, 1977.

Seeckt, Hans von (1866–1936)

Reichswehr colonel general.

Hans von Seeckt was one of the most influential military leaders and thinkers of the twentieth century. In the aftermath of World War I, he led the German Army through a process of reform and doctrine and equipment development that served as the foundation for the rapid expansion of the Wehrmacht from 1933 to 1939. Seeckt was born in Schleswig on April 22, 1866. During World War I, he was the chief of staff to Field Marshal August von Mackensen on the eastern front. They were one of the most successful commander/chief of staff teams of all times. Appointed chief of the German General Staff in 1919, Seeckt led the army through a comprehensive examination of the lessons of the world war. He organized more than five hundred officers and specialists into committees to examine the doctrinal and technological lessons of the war. From this foundation, Seeckt drew up a series of new army doctrine manuals that were not geared to the small one-hundred-thousand-man force allowed by Versailles, but for a modern army equipped with aircraft and tanks and the full range of modern weapons.

In 1920, in the aftermath of the Kapp-Lüttwitz Putsch, Seeckt was made commander in chief of the German Army—the Reichswehr. Seeckt's overriding goal was to restore Germany military power, and, during his seven years as chief of staff and army commander, he built an elite, superbly trained army that was ready to employ advanced concepts of combined arms maneuver warfare that served as the foundation of what was popularly known as Blitzkrieg in World War II. To evade the Allied restrictions, Seeckt established a program of cooperation with the Soviet Union that allowed the Germans to conduct pilot and tank training at Russian bases. German tanks and aircraft were secretly developed and tested in Russia. After retiring from the German military, in 1934 and 1935, Seeckt served in China as a military adviser to Chiang Kai-shek. Seeckt died in Berlin on December 27, 1936.

James S. Corum

See also: Blitzkrieg

Additional Reading

Citino, Robert. *The German Way of War.* Lawrence: University Press of Kansas, 2005.

Corum, James S. *The Roots of Blitzkrieg: Hans von Seeckt and German Military Reform.* Lawrence: University Press of Kansas, 1992.

Seelow Heights, Battle of (April 16–19, 1945)

On April 15, 1945, Soviet Marshal Georgy Zhukov's 1st Belorussian Front reached the forward positions of German General Theodor Busse's Ninth Army. Busse's one hundred thousand men were responsible for defending the high ground around the Seelow Heights that dominated the Oder River's flood plain and a key approach route to Berlin. With the Soviet Air Force commanding the skies over the battlefield and more than one million men, three thousand tanks, and sixteen thousand artillery pieces and mortars under his command, Zhukov had overwhelming superiority. Busse controlled the high ground and had spent four weeks preparing defensive positions, building bunkers, laying obstacles, and establishing "kill zones." Busse's superior, General Gotthard Heinrici, Commander of Army Group Vistula, had decided not to resist the Soviet crossing at the Oder's riverbank but, rather, to fortify the Seelow Heights and the surrounding terrain, building three lines of resistance. The spring thaw had softened the ground, making it difficult terrain for armored vehicles, and Heinrici had his engineers release water from the upstream reservoir, reducing the already soggy Oder floodplain to a morass.

Zhukov opened his attack with a massive artillery barrage during the early predawn hours of April 16 but inflicted little initial damage on German forces. Heinrici had anticipated the Soviet's timing and withdrew the bulk of his screen, starting just hours earlier. German artillery had preregistered major areas of the battlefield, inflicting heavy casualties on the Soviet forces. Zhukov redoubled his efforts, brining up his artillery. The Soviets made a four to eight kilometer advance on April 17, with Zhukov putting his Forty-Seventh Army and Third Shock Army deep into the German second defensive line. The Germans had committed their final reserves on April 18, but by then the Seelow Heights had been bypassed from the north by Marshal Ivan Konev's 1st Ukrainian Front. By nightfall, the Soviets had advanced another three to eight kilometers in the German center and three to five kilometers along the right flank, reaching Busse's third line of defense.

Zhukov finally broke through Busse's final line and drove past Seelow Heights by midday on April 19. The gateway to Berlin was open, with only broken German formations and rear echelons lying between Zhukov and the capital. Zhukov enveloped the Fourth Panzer Army and the Ninth Army. The bulk of Konev's 1st Ukrainian Front rushed north to Berlin, while other elements drove west toward the approaching Americans. Germany's eastern front had dissolved. Berlin was encircled by April 23, and fell nine days later. Seelow Heights was a key component of the Oder-Neisse defense line that constituted Berlin's last line of defense. The Germans lost about twelve thousand, three hundred people, killed in the battle. Some estimates put Soviet battle deaths as high as thirty-three thousand.

Carl O. Schuster

See also: Berlin, Land Battle for; Heinrici, Gotthard

Additional Reading

Beevor, Anthony. *The Fall of Berlin.* New York: Viking Press, 2002.

SEELÖWE (SEA LION), Operation (Planned 1940)

Operation SEA LION was the abortive German preparations for an invasion of Britain. Following the defeat of France in June 1940, Hitler still believed that the British would see reason and be forced to the peace table. The failure of London to respond to Hitler's peace feelers led him to issue a directive on July 2 to initiate immediate preparations for an invasion. On July 16, Hitler issued Führer Directive 16, "On Preparation for a Landing Operation against England," which placed the navy primarily in a transport role. Projected for September 15, 1940, the key precondition for Operation SEA LION, as the invasion of Britain was to be known, was German air superiority.

The German Army's demand for a broad-front landing caused an intense debate with naval leaders, who preferred a narrow-front approach. Both services vigorously sought to persuade Hitler to support their proposals. Initially, the army won support for its plans, but a compromise was reached eventually on August 26. The army also had no real enthusiasm for an enterprise. In its planning, the navy estimated that convoying thirteen divisions in the initial assault wave against Britain would require 155 transports and more than 3,000 smaller craft: 1,720 barges, 470 tugs, and 1,160 motorboats. Conflicting interests and rivalries prevented any real collaboration among the army, navy, and air force. On August 1, 1940, a Hitler directive ordered the Luftwaffe to switch its preinvasion tactics to a strategic air offensive and to be prepared to switch targets at any time if a new invasion date was set. The failure of the Luftwaffe to gain control of the skies during the Battle of Britain and the approach of bad weather resulted in the decision to indefinitely postpone the invasion. On October 12, SEA LION was deferred until the spring of 1941. Until 1942, it continued to serve as a deception.

Keith W. Bird

See also: Britain, Battle of

Additional Reading

Kiesler, Egbert. *Hitler on the Doorstep: Operation "Sea Lion": The German Plan to Invade Britain, 1940.* Annapolis, MD: Naval Institute Press, 1997.

Senger und Etterlin, Fridolin Rudolf von (1891–1963)

Wehrmach general of panzer troops.

Born in Waldshut on September 4, Fridolin von Senger und Etterlin attended Eton College and was a Rhodes Scholar from 1912 to 1914. During World War I, he served as a cavalry officer. During the interwar years, he was a critic of the "all-tank" theorists, and he supported the development of mechanized infantry (panzergrenadiers). Senger commanded the 17th Panzer Division in Operation BARBAROSSA and Field Marshal Erich von Manstein's subsequent offensive in the Ukraine. In 1943, doubts about the capability of Italian troops led to Senger's reassignment to coordinate Axis strategy in Sicily. He stayed in Italy for the remainder of the war and led German troops in several significant battles, including the withdrawal from Sardinia and Corsica and the Battle of Monte Cassino. He was held as a prisoner of war from 1946 to 1948. Senger, during the 1950s, advised Federal Republic of Germany Chancellor Konrad Adenauer on rearmament and the formation of the new German Army, the Bundeswehr. Senger died in Freiburg on January 4, 1963.

Thomas Lansford

See also: Cassino/Rapido River, Battles of; Panzergrenadier

Additional Reading

Senger und Etterlin, Ferdinand von, and Stefan Senger und Etterlin. "General Frido von Senger und Etterlin." In *Hitler's Generals*, edited by Correlli Barnett, 375–392. New York: Grove Weidenfeld, 1989.

Sevastopol, Siege of (October 30, 1941–July 4, 1942). *See* Crimea Campaign, Soviet

SICHELSCHNITT (SICKLE CUT) (1940). *See* France, Battle of; Manstein, Erich von

Sicily, Allied Invasion of (July 9–August 17, 1943)

The German defense of Sicily in July 1943 sought to keep Benito Mussolini's Italy in the war. After the Allies landed, the Germans fought a masterful delaying action that took advantage of favorable terrain and serious Allied errors and tied down two Allied armies long enough for Germany to occupy mainland Italy. The Germans also evacuated almost all their forces from the island and used them to defend Italy.

Field Marshal Albert Kesselring was the overall German commander in the Mediterranean. The Italian Sixth Army nominally commanded German units, but, soon after the Allied invasion, General of Panzer Troops Hans Hube took command of German forces in Sicily under the XIV Panzer Corps. The major German ground units at the time of the invasion were the 15th Panzergrenadier Division and the Luftwaffe's Hermann Göring Panzer Division. Allied air forces relentlessly attacked German airpower on Sicily, and, by July, only a few dozen German aircraft remained to face thousands of Allied aircraft. Thus, about thirty thousand Germans (later increased to sixty thousand) faced some four hundred and sixty thousand Allies, who enjoyed near-total air and naval superiority. Roughly two hundred thousand Italian troops in Sicily had little combat value, due to poor training, equipment, leadership, and morale.

Germany counterattacked the landing beaches immediately. Once the beachheads were secure, the British, under General Sir Bernard Montgomery, advanced north along Sicily's east coast and tried to encircle German troops in central Sicily. U.S. forces under Lieutenant General George Patton advanced rapidly into western Sicily. On July 26, Mussolini was overthrown. The Germans in Sicily then needed to tie down Allied forces in order to allow other German troops to secure Italy without interference.

On August 11, the Germans began evacuating Sicily using barges and ferries, with hundreds of flak guns for protection. When Messina fell on August 17, the Germans had evacuated some fifty-two thousand men; fourteen thousand, one hundred vehicles; and forty-seven tanks. About seventy thousand Italian troops also were evacuated. Germany took perhaps twenty thousand casualties—killed, wounded, and captured—in Sicily but inflicted a similar number of casualties on the Allies. Hube delayed the Allies long enough for German forces to occupy Italy, and then escaped with a combat-ready panzer corps.

James D. Perry

See also: Kesselring, Albert

Additional Reading

D'Este, Carlo. *Bitter Victory: The Battle for Sicily, 1943.* London: Collins, 1988.

Garland, Albert N., and Howard Smyth. *Sicily and the Surrender of Italy.* Washington, DC: US Government Printing Office, 1965.

Siegfried Line Campaign, Allied (September 11–December 16, 1944)

Allied forces first crossed the German border on September 11, 1944 and then spent the next three months trying to penetrate the defenses of the Westwall, which the Allies called the "Siegfried Line." At the start of September, the Allied forces were opposed by six field armies in the west, under the overall command of the commander in chief west (OB West) Field Marshal Gerd von Rundstedt. Directly under Rundstedt, two army groups defended their respective sectors, with the Mosel River as the boundary. Army Group B in the north was commanded by Field Marshal Walter Model. The Fifteenth Army, commanded by General of Infantry Gustav von Zangen, was in the

Netherlands. The First Parachute Army, commanded by Colonel General Kurt Student, held the central sector, down to Cologne, and Army Group B's southern sector was held by the Seventh Army, commanded by General of Infantry Erich Brandenburger. Army Group G in the south was commanded by Colonel General Johannes Blaskowitz until September 20, and then by General of Panzer Troops Hermann Balck. The German Saarland and the sector of western France down to about Metz was held by the First Army, commanded by General of Panzer Troops Otto von Knobelsdorff. The southern sector in Alsace was defended by the Nineteenth Army, commanded by General of Infantry Friedrich Wiese. Army Group G's center, in the sector opposite Nancy, was held by General of Panzer Troops Hasso von Manteuffel's Fifth Panzer Army. On October 23, the Fifth Panzer Army was withdrawn from Army Group G and redeployed north to Army Group B, entering the line between the First Parachute Army and the Seventh Army.

By September 11, 1944, the Allied forces were advancing on the German frontier in a relatively continuous front from Switzerland to Antwerp, with Field Marshal Sir Bernard Montgomery's 21st Army Group in the north, General Omar N. Bradley's 12th Army Group in the center, and Lieutenant General Jacob L. Devers's Allied 6th Army Group in the south. After extensive high-level debate, Allied theater commander General Dwight D. Eisenhower shifted logistical priority to the 21st Army Group and authorized Montgomery to conduct Operation MARKET-GARDEN, an effort to flank the German northern defenses, cross the Rhine River at Arnhem, and rapidly penetrate and capture the industrial heart of Germany. When the MARKET-GARDEN operation, which began on September 17, failed to achieve the final objective of crossing the Rhine at Arnhem, Eisenhower returned to the broad-advance concept to maintain pressure on the German forces and penetrate the Siegfried Line defenses.

Initial contact with the Westwall was made by elements of Lieutenant General Courtney H. Hodges's First Army, as it advanced to the German frontier in early September in the area north of Luxemburg. On September 29, the First Army began a major offensive against Westwall positions around Aachen, a key defensive stronghold in the Siegfried Line, with the objective of opening a route to the Rhine River. After a vicious urban battle, the Aachen garrison surrendered on October 21. In October and again in early November, the First Army also attempted to clear the Hürtgen Forest in an effort to open a route to the Rhine and secure the Roer River dams, which potentially allowed the German military to flood crossing areas downstream in the Roer River valley. After initial successes, aggressive German counterattacks pushed back the attackers, and the battle for the Hürtgen Forest became a bloody contest that held up the First Army. At the same time, Lieutenant General William Simpson's U.S. Ninth Army cleared the German defenses to the north and secured the west bank of the Roer River by December 9, but it did not attempt to cross the river due to the flooding threat posed by the dams.

During September, Lieutenant General George S. Patton's U.S. Third Army fought through the Lorraine border region south of Luxembourg toward the Westwall, battling German forces that used old French defensive positions of the Maginot Line and pre–World War I fortifications (especially those around Metz) to strengthen resistance to the U.S. advance. Patton's offensive then

Following a path blasted by U.S. Army engineers, an American M-4 Sherman tank passes through a belt of steel and concrete "Dragon's Teeth" obstacles in the Siegfried Line, September 16, 1944. (Popperfoto via Getty Images)

bogged down from a combination of the German Army Group G defensive effort and logistical shortages. After resupplying and refitting in late October, the Third Army reinitiated the assault on Metz on November 8, and the city's garrison finally surrendered on November 22. After cleaning out the remaining German positions in Lorraine, the Third Army reached the Siegfried Line on December 15 and quickly seized several river crossings. Patton then paused the advance to resupply his forces before pushing through the Westwall and breaking out toward the Rhine in an attack planned for December 19. The Germans, however, struck first, launching their Ardennes Offensive on December 16.

During the three months of the Siegfried Line Campaign, the U.S. First and Ninth Armies lost fifty thousand casualties killed or wounded, sixty-nine hundred taken prisoner, and some 650 tanks. German casualties were high, although the exact numbers are unknown. At least ninety-five thousand German soldiers were taken prisoners by the Americans.

Jerome V. Martin and David T. Zabecki

See also: Ardennes Offensive (Battle of the Bulge); Balck, Hermann; Blaskowitz, Johannes Albrecht; Brandenberger, Erich; Hürtgen Forest Campaign, Allied; Lorraine Campaign, Allied; Manteuffel, Hasso Eccard von; MARKET-GARDEN, Allied Operation; Model, Walther; Rundstedt, Karl Rudolf Gerd von; Student, Kurt; Westwall

Additional Reading

Adams, John A. *The Battle for Western Europe, Fall 1944: An Operational*

Assessment. Bloomington: Indiana University Press, 2010.

MacDonald, Charles B. *U.S. Army in World War II: European Theater of Operations: The Siegfried Line Campaign*. Washington, DC: U.S. Government Printing Office, 1963.

Skorzeny, Otto (1908–1975)

Waffen-SS Obersturmbannführer and commando leader.

Born in Vienna, Austria, on June 12, 1908, Skorzeny studied engineering at Vienna Technical College. After the 1938 *Anschluss* (union) of Austria with Germany, Skorzeny joined the SS Leibstandarte Adolf Hitler Division (later the 1st SS Panzer Division), and fought in France, the Balkans, and the Soviet Union. In April 1943, Skorzeny was placed in charge of German Special Troops. He studied British commando operations and set up a training facility where volunteers were trained in special operations techniques. On September 9, 1943, Skorzeny and his commandos gained international attention when they rescued former Italian dictator Benito Mussolini in a daring assault on Gran Sasso, where Mussolini was being held. During the 1944 to 1945 Ardennes Offensive, Skorzeny commanded the 10th Panzer Brigade, a collection of twenty-five hundred men from different units, some speaking English and dressed in U.S. uniforms. The unit's mission was to carry out sabotage and create havoc behind Allied lines. In Operation GRIEF, during the offensive, the brigade had only limited success creating confusion among U.S. troops. Charged with war crimes following Germany's surrender, Skorzeny was acquitted for lack of evidence. In the postwar years, Skorzeny raised funds to enable ex-SS men find refuge in Latin America. He died in Madrid on July 7, 1975.

Cullen Monk

See also: Ardennes Offensive (Battle of the Bulge)

Additional Reading

Whiting, Charles. *Skorzeny: The Most Dangerous Man in Europe*. Conshohocken, PA: Combined Publishing, 1998.

Smolensk, Battle of (July 8–31, 1941). *See* Soviet Union, Invasion of (Operation BARBAROSSA)

Southern France, Allied Invasion and Campaign (Operation DRAGOON) (August 15–September 15, 1944)

Operation DRAGOON was the Allied amphibious landing in southern France. It originally was intended to coincide with the June 1944 invasion of northern France, Operation OVERLORD. Because of limited available landing craft, Operation DRAGOON could not be mounted until August 15, 1944. By August 1944, the German coastal defenses in southern France were extremely weak. Army Task Group G, commanded by General Johannes Blaskowitz, was responsible for the defense of central and southern France to the Italian border. The Nineteenth Army, commanded by General Friedrich Wiese, was responsible for the southern coast, where the Allies landed. As late as June 1944, the Nineteenth Army had fourteen divisions, but it lost four, including two of its three panzer divisions after the Allied landings in Normandy. On August 15, Wiese's forces consisted of the 11th Panzer Division and seven infantry divisions, responsible for defending four hundred miles of coastline. Blaskowitz's air and naval forces were also hopelessly weak.

At dawn on August 15, the lead elements of the U.S. 3rd, 45th, and 36th Infantry Divisions and a French armored task force came ashore on beaches between Saint-Tropez and Cannes on the French Riviera. A combined British and U.S. airborne task force also dropped inland to seize bridges and cut roads inland. U.S. Seventh Army commander Lieutenant General Alexander M. Patch Jr. led the Allied force. Major General Lucian Truscott Jr., VI Corps commander, was the landing ground force commander. Seven Free French divisions, under General Jean de Lattre de Tassigny, came ashore during the following days and moved west to seize the ports of Toulon and Marseille.

By August 17, the Allied advance had reached twenty miles inland. Facing the possibility of substantial German army units being trapped in France, Hitler ordered Blaskowitz to withdraw, leaving sufficient troops behind to deny the major ports to the Allies. The most serious fighting took place at the ports of Toulon and Marseille, but within two weeks, both fell on August 28 to the French divisions of General de Lattre's newly designated French Army B. The Germans lost thirty-seven thousand troops taken prisoner.

The heaviest fighting of the campaign for southern France took place between August 21 and 28, in the vicinity of Montélimar. As the Nineteenth Army was retreating north on the east side of the Rhône River, U.S. VI Corps attempted to prevent them from escaping. Elements of the U.S. 36th Infantry Division tried to block the main road north of Montélimar. By spreading out to the west side of the Rhône and forcing the gaps in the thinly held U.S. roadblock, five German divisions and two corps headquarters were able to break through the trap. By the time the gaps were closed on August 28, many of the Germans had managed to escape north, minus most of their equipment and leaving fifty-seven thousand POWs behind.

After escaping the trap at Montélimar, German forces only stopped to fight to keep their evacuation routes open. The result was a race for the Belfort Gap in eastern France. If the Allies got there first, the remaining elements of Army Task Group G would be cut off in southern France. If the Germans reached Belfort first, Army Task Group G would link up with Army Group B, now commanded by Field Marshal Walther Model. The result would be a cohesive German defensive line along the Vosges Mountains in Alsace. Allied advanced units got to within thirty miles of Belfort by early September, but they were halted by a stiff German defense, led by the 11th Panzer Division commanded by Major General Wend von Wietersheim. The bulk of the Nineteenth Army managed to get through the Belfort Gap and into Alsace after having conducted a grueling twenty-eight-day and four-hundred-mile-long fighting retreat.

On September 11 at Sombernon, France, the French I Corps on Seventh Army's western flank linked up with General George S. Patton's U.S. Third Army. At midnight on September 14 to 15, Operation DRAGOON officially ended when the Seventh Army was transferred from the Allied Mediterranean Theater of Operations to the European Theater of Operations. Operation DRAGOON cost the Allies more than thirteen thousand casualties (more than half of them American) but resulted in a four-hundred-mile advance that liberated virtually all of southern France. It also hurried the introduction of Free French troops into combat and opened additional ports for supporting the drive across France into Germany. German casualties included seven thousand killed, twenty thousand wounded, and some one hundred and thirty thousand captured either during the main operation or later during mopping up.

Arthur T. Frame and David T. Zabecki

See also: Blaskowitz, Johannes Albrecht; Model, Walther; Normandy Invasion and Campaign

Additional Reading

Clarke, Jeffrey J., and Robert Ross Smith. *Riviera to the Rhine. United States Army in World War II.* Washington, DC: Center of Military History, 1993.

Ludewig, Joachim. *Rückzug: The German Retreat from France, 1944.* Lexington: University Press of Kentucky, 2012.

Soviet Union, Invasion of (Operation BARBAROSSA) (June 22, 1941–September 26, 1941)

The German invasion of the Soviet Union opened World War II on the eastern front, commencing the largest, most bitterly contested, and bloodiest land campaign of the war. Hitler's objective for Operation BARBAROSSA was simple: he sought to crush the Soviet Union in one swift blow. With the Soviet Union defeated and its vast resources at his disposal, surely Britain would have to sue for peace. Hitler predicted a quick victory in a campaign of, at most, three months.

German success hinged on the speed of advance of 154 German and Axis divisions deployed in three army groups: Army Group North in East Prussia, under Field Marshal Wilhelm von Leeb; Army Group Center in northern Poland, commanded by Field Marshal Fedor von Bock; and Army Group South in southern Poland and Romania under Field Marshal Karl Gerd von Rundstedt. Army Group North consisted of three panzer, three motorized, and twenty-four infantry divisions supported by the Luftflotte 1 (Air Fleet 1) and joined by Finnish forces. Farther north, German General Nikolaus von Falkenhorst's Norway Army would carry out an offensive against Murmansk in order to sever its supply route to Leningrad. Bock's Army Group Center had nine panzer, seven motorized, and thirty-four infantry divisions, with the Luftflotte 2 in support. Rundstedt's Army Group South consisted of five panzer, three motorized, and thirty-five infantry divisions, along with three Italian divisions, two Romanian armies, and Hungarian and Slovak units. Luftflotte 4 provided the air support.

Facing this onslaught were 170 Soviet divisions organized into three "strategic axes" (commanding multiple fronts, the equivalent of army groups)—northern, central, and southern (or Ukrainian), commanded by Marshals Kliment E. Voroshilov, Semen K. Timoshenko, and Semen M. Budenny, respectively. Voroshilov's units were responsible for the defense of Leningrad, Karelia, and the recently acquired Baltic states. Timoshenko's units protected the approaches to Smolensk and Moscow. And those of Budenny guarded the Ukraine. For the most part, these forces were largely nonmechanized and were arrayed in three linear defensive echelons, the first as far as thirty miles from the border, and the last as much as 180 miles back.

Eastern Front, July 16, 1941–December 5, 1941

The German plan had three phases, in which they hoped to achieve three broad objectives: the destruction of Soviet armed forces; the capture of political and industrial centers; and the occupation of coal, iron, and agricultural centers in the Ukraine and Caucasus. Phase one called for German ground forces, supported by air, to drive deep into Soviet territory and encircle and destroy Soviet forces west of the Dvina-Dnieper Line, while disrupting supply lines and creating maximum chaos. Phase two objectives were the seizure of Leningrad, Moscow, and the Ukraine to prevent political-military direction and economic support to the Red Army. In Phase three, the Wehrmacht was to advance to and hold the Volga-Archangel Line.

Stalin refused to believe Soviet intelligence reports that German forces were massing on the western approaches to the Soviet Union. He also received a reported one hundred Western warnings, but he dismissed them all as efforts by the Western powers to involve the Soviet Union in the war. Although Stalin had used the respite of the Soviet-German Nonaggression Pact period to improve war stocks and develop military industries, he ultimately resisted fully mobilizing the Red Army, for fear that doing so would provoke Hitler. These factors, plus the self-inflicted decapitation of the Soviet armed forces during the 1937 Purges that liquidated 40 to 50 percent of the senior officer corps, left the Red Army unable to prevent the Wehrmacht from achieving tremendous initial victories.

Despite all the German preparations, there was a great disparity in military hardware. The Luftwaffe, still waging operations against Britain and also supporting the Afrika Korps in North Africa, was forced to keep 1,150 combat aircraft in these theaters. Thus, only 2,770 combat aircraft were available against the Soviet Union. Arrayed against them were 18,570 Soviet aircraft, 8,154 of which were initially in the west and the bulk of them tactical aircraft of sturdy basic designs, including the excellent Ilyushin Il-2 Shturmovik ground-attack aircraft.

Germany deployed some 6,000 tanks, the Soviets 23,140 (10,394 in the west)—and even in 1941, the Soviets possessed some of the best tanks of the war. Their BT-series and T-26 were superior in armor, firepower, and maneuverability to the German light Pz.Kpfw.I and II and could destroy any German tank. Similarly, the Soviet T-34 medium tank and KV-1 heavy tank were superior to the Pz.Kpfw.III and IV and, indeed, any German tank in June 1941.

The German attack started at 0300 hours on June 22, 1941. Soviet forces were taken completely by surprise. German panzer divisions easily broke through the defenses and were deep into Soviet territory by nightfall. Striking Soviet air forces within range, the Luftwaffe in one day's operation gained air superiority over the operational area. Army Group North took Kaunas in one day and reached the Dvina River after four days, and then rolled into Riga on June 29. Not until they reached new Soviet defensive positions south of Pskov on July 8 did the Germans encounter stiff resistance.

The progress of Army Group South was slowed by numerous natural obstacles, which allowed Soviet forces to withdraw in a more orderly manner and even to counterattack occasionally. Soviet forces avoided German encirclement attempts in this southern zone until Uman, where, in early August, over one hundred thousand men were encircled and surrendered, along with three hundred tanks and eight hundred pieces of heavy artillery.

The most spectacular results were achieved by Army Group Center. It reached the Dnieper River by July 6, where it encountered increased Soviet resistance. Before arriving there, however, one column took Vilnius on June 24, and then headed for Minsk, where it joined the second column that had come from Brest-Litovsk. On June 27, the two columns met to surround a large number of Soviet troops in the Minsk area, resulting in the surrender of three hundred and twenty thousand men, three thousand tanks, and two thousand pieces of heavy artillery. Even with stiffening resistance, Soviet forces could not prevent the Germans from crossing the Dnieper on July 9 and seizing Smolensk on July 16, where they captured another three hundred thousand prisoners by July 31.

Phase one of BARBAROSSA seemed a success. Despite increased resistance, Wehrmacht forces appeared to have open roads to Leningrad, Moscow, and Kiev after capturing nearly a million Soviet troops and killing countless others. Phase two of the German plan, however, proved more difficult for several reasons. Soviet defenses were stiffening because the initial shock of invasion had worn off and an additional five million men in reserve forces had been mobilized and thrown into the breach. In addition, Hitler and his generals had been debating the best course of action for Phase two, and the objectives continued to change. The generals believed the army should concentrate on securing Moscow because it was the Soviet capital and a vital communication and industrial center. Hitler, however, at first thought the priority should be the seizure of Leningrad and a linkup with the Finns and then the Germans and Finns together should clear the Baltic and open a sea line of communications.

Colonel General Heinz Guderian, commander of the Second Panzer Group, was one of the main advocates for continuing to Moscow. Immediately after the fall of Smolensk, Guderian pushed for permission to move immediately to eliminate a large concentration of Soviet stragglers from some twenty-one divisions that were clustered in the vicinity of Roslavl, on the Second Panzer Group's right. Roslavl was also an important communications and road center that would give the Germans control of the transportation network southwest of Moscow. Guderian launched the attack on Roslavl on August 1. The battle ended on August 8, with the Germans capturing thirty-eight thousand prisoners, two hundred tanks, and an equal number of artillery pieces.

The road toward the northeast and Moscow was now wide open. On August 12, however, Hitler issued Führer Directive 34, ordering Army Group North to continue its push toward Leningrad and Army Group South to move into the Crimea and the Donets basin. Army Group Center was ordered to halt temporarily and provide support to the efforts on both of its flanks. The advance toward for Moscow lost its momentum, and the Germans would never again recover it sufficiently.

Phase two finally began with an assault on Kiev, which fell to the Germans on September 26 and netted six hundred and fifty thousand additional prisoners. Then fall rain and mud slowed the German advance in the south. Movement toward Leningrad also slowed, partly because of increased Soviet resistance but also because Hitler concocted a new plan, which called for Leningrad to be encircled, put under siege, and starved into submission. The Crimea, the Don Baisin, and the Caucasus were to be taken for their coal and oil resources.

The new plan, Operation TAIFUN (TYPHOON), accorded the highest priority to the encirclement and capture of Moscow. Previously transferred panzer forces were now to revert to Army Group Center, and operations were to commence on September 30. Because the strategic objective did not change, it can be argued that Operation BARBAROSSA continued for the entire period of Germany's strategic advance, from the surprise attack on June 22, 1941 until the assault that stalled before Moscow in November. However, the commencement of Operation TAIFUN, with its change of operational focus and main objectives, technically ended Operation BARBAROSSA.

Arthur T. Frame

See also: Bock, Fedor von; German-Soviet Nonaggression Pact; Guderian, Heinz; Leeb, Wilhelm Ritter von; Rundstedt, Karl Rudolf Gerd von

Additional Reading

Erickson, John. *The Road to Stalingrad: Stalin's War with Germany.* New York: Harper and Row, 1975.

Glantz, David M., and Jonathan House. *When Titans Clashed: How the Red Army Stopped Hitler.* Lawrence: University Press of Kansas, 1995.

Ziemke, Earl F., and Magna E. Bauer. *Moscow to Stalingrad: Decision in the East.* Washington, DC: U.S. Government Printing Office, 1987.

Spanish Civil War (1936–1939)

In 1936, the Spanish Republic was divided almost equally between the political extremes. On the left stood a coalition of socialist and poor peasants, supported by an urban working class, largely organized by anarchist and communist union organizations. On the right stood a coalition of landowners and businessmen, committed Catholics, monarchists and the members of Spain's new fascist party, the Falange.

In July 1936, the nation exploded into civil war when a leading Falange politician was killed by government police. A group of senior Spanish army leaders had long planned a coup, and the descent into open violence offered the generals the opportunity. The coup was repressed in days of bloody battles in Madrid and Barcelona, but elsewhere the generals seized power. In North Africa, the best of Spain's military forces rallied to the coup to support their former commander General Francesco Franco. The main problem was that the Spanish Navy stayed loyal to the Republic, and the thirty-thousand-man strong North African Army therefore could not get across the straits of Gibraltar. Without reinforcements from the African Army, the Nationalist forces in southern Spain could not hope to march on Madrid.

The Nationalists, ideologically friendly to the Nazi regime in Germany, requested support from Hitler. The Wehrmacht's senior leaders, then in the midst of a massive rearmament program, were unanimous in wanting to avoid any commitment. Hitler, however, overruled his generals. Within days, a group of Ju 52 transports was on its way to Spanish Morocco to provide an airlift for Franco's forces to the Spanish mainland. Joined by Italian planes, the Nationalists carried out the world's first major airlift, bringing more than twenty thousand troops and a considerable amount of equipment to join the Nationalist forces on the mainland. By late 1936, however, the war had bogged down. The Soviet Union announced its support for the Republic, and large shipments of weapons and war supplies, accompanied by a small corps of Soviet advisors, arrived in Republican ports. In November, Hitler decided to expand the German support to the Nationalists. But he decided initially that the German support would remain limited to some weapons, German trainers, one small tank battalion, and a Luftwaffe task force later called the Kondor Legion.

In the spring of 1937, the Kondor Legion was ready to support a major Nationalist offensive to destroy the Basque state in northern Spain. The most infamous incident of the war occurred on April 26, 1937, when the Luftwaffe bombed and strafed the Basque town of Guernica with more than 100,000 pounds of high explosives and incendiaries. The civilian casualty count remains uncertain to this day, with estimates ranging from 150 to 1,650.

Spain proved to be very important for the development of the Wehrmacht. The German Army and Luftwaffe trained its forces and tested its equipment and doctrines in a modern campaign facing a formidable enemy. In Spain, the Germans first used the 88 mm antiaircraft gun in ground-fire roles, where it proved an exceptionally effective weapon. The German Army was also able to conduct tank operations. Most importantly, the Luftwaffe developed the ability to support the ground forces effectively in a major campaign. By the end of the Spanish War, the Luftwaffe not only had the most current combat experience of any of the major powers, but it had the most effective doctrine. The success of the Wehrmacht in the 1939 and 1940 campaigns had their foundation in the Spanish experience. In addition, the Luftwaffe developed a cadre of senior and mid-level air commanders, who were highly experienced and proven in battle.

James S. Corum

See also: Kondor Legion; Richthofen, Wolfram von; Sperrle, Hugo

Additional Reading

Corum, James. *The Luftwaffe: Creating the Operational Air War 1918–1940.* Lawrence: University Press of Kansas, 1997.

Whealey, Robert H. *Hitler and Spain: The Nazi Role in the Spanish Civil War, 1936–1939.* Lexington: University Press of Kentucky, 1989.

Speer, Albert (1905–1981)

Third Reich minister for armaments.

Born on March 19, 1905 in Mannheim, Albert Speer was educated at the Munich Institute of Technology and the Institute of Technology in Berlin-Charlottenburg. He received his architect's license in 1927. Speer joined the Nazi Party in March 1931. He also joined the Nazi organization for professional architects and soon began receiving party commissions. In 1933, Speer designed the party's celebrations at Templehof Airport, introducing the "cathedral of light" concept that became a hallmark of party rallies. This brought him to the attention of Joseph Goebbels, the minister of propaganda, who put Speer in contact with Hitler. The Führer soon commissioned Speer to design his official apartments. In 1941, Speer offered his services to the army reserve and became chief of defense construction. When Fritz Todt died in a plane crash in February 1942, Hitler again turned to Speer. On February 15, Speer was sworn in as the new minister for armament and munitions. His brief also covered most aspects of construction and transportation, including control of the paramilitary Organization Todt. Between 1942 and 1944, Speer tripled overall German armament output. Ammunition production increased 300 percent, and tank output rose 600 percent. By 1943, he was in charge of naval armaments, as well as German rocket and atomic programs.

Speer's name appeared on the list of putative ministers during the attempted coup of July 20, 1944; his friendship with Hitler and the fact that he was listed as someone to be approached after the attempted coup saved him. Speer remained at his posts and was made responsible for the construction of Germany's western defenses. Yet Speer was now less than committed to the Nazi cause. He spoke publicly of final victory and promised miracle weapons, but, privately, he doubted both. When Hitler adopted a scorched-earth policy, Speer sought to undermine it, and he involved himself in several wild schemes to assassinate or eliminate the top Nazi leadership. Speer was arrested by the British on May 23, 1945. He then became one of the main defendants at the International Military Tribunal at Nuremburg. Speer adopted the strategy of accepting collective responsibility while simultaneously denying personal culpability. Found guilty, he received twenty years' imprisonment and served the full sentence. While he was in prison, Speer wrote the accounts of his work and experiences in Nazi Germany that would make him both famous and infamous. He remained a significant literary and historical figure until his death in Paddington, England, on September 1, 1981.

Timothy C. Dowling

See also: Organization Todt (OT); Todt, Fritz

Additional Reading

Fest, Joachim. *Speer: The Final Verdict.* Translated by Ewald Osers and Alexandra Dring. New York: Harcourt, 2002.

Speidel, Hans (1897–1984)

Wehrmacht lieutenant general, Bundeswehr general.

Born in Metzingen, Germany, on October 28, 1897, Hans Speidel served in World War I as an infantry officer. Remaining in the postwar Reichswehr, he graduated from the University of Tübingen with a doctorate in political science and history in 1925, and then qualified as a General Staff officer. During World War II, he served in Russia for two years, and, during that time, he became convinced that the war could not be won and that Hitler's regime had to be overthrown. In April 1944, Speidel was appointed chief of staff of Field Marshal Erwin Rommel's Army Group B in France. Speidel tried to convince Rommel to back the coup against Hitler. However, Speidel was not part of the inner circle of officers who carried out the July 20, 1944 assassination attempt. Speidel helped ensure that Paris was not demolished as Hitler had ordered, and he was arrested by the Gestapo on September 7. He was held prisoner for seven months, and then managed to escape and go into hiding. French troops captured him on April 29, 1945.

After the war, Speidel was appointed a lieutenant general in the new German military force, the Bundeswehr. In April 1957, Speidel became commander in chief of NATO Land Forces in central Europe and was promoted to full general. He died at Bad Honnef, Germany, on November 28, 1984.

Thomas Lansford

See also: Opposition to Hitler, German Military; Rommel, Erwin

Additional Reading

Hart, Russell. "Hans Speidel." In *Chief of Staff: The Principal Officers behind History's Great Commanders*, vol. II, *World War II to Korea and Vietnam*, edited by

David T. Zabecki, 50–61. Annapolis, MD: U.S. Naval Institute Press, 2008.

Sperrle, Hugo (1885–1953)

Luftwaffe field marshal.

Born at Ludwigsburg on February 2, 1885, Sperrle served as an aerial observer during World War I. During the 1920s, he underwent pilot training at the secret German base in Lipetsk, Russia. In 1936, he was ordered to organize and command the Kondor Legion to support the Nationalists in the Spanish Civil War. He commanded Luftflotte (Air Fleet) 3 during the attack on France and the Low Countries in 1940. Sperrle's Luftflotte 3 and Field Marshal Albert Kesselring's Luftflotte 2 bore the brunt of the fighting during the air campaign against Britain. Following the Battle of Britain, Sperrle and his command stayed in France when the rest of the Luftwaffe transferred to the east for Operation BARBAROSSA. Following the Allied breakout from Normandy, Sperrle was blamed for the Luftwaffe's failures and relieved of his command in August 1944. He was captured by the British in May 1945 and tried for war crimes at the American Military Tribunal at Nuremberg but was acquitted in 1948. Sperrle died in Munich on April 2, 1953.

Marlyn R. Pierce

See also: Britain, Battle of; Kondor Legion

Additional Reading

Mitcham, Samuel W. *Eagles of the Third Reich: The Men Who Made the Luftwaffe.* Novato, CA: Presidio Press, 1997.

Stab-in-the-Back Legend (*Dolchstosslegende*)

This is a seductive but misleading and mendacious myth advanced by German generals Paul von Hindenburg and Erich Ludendorff and other World War I senior officers that socialist conspirators, malingerers, and defeatists at home had betrayed a German Army that remained unbeaten and unbroken in the field throughout the summer and fall of 1918. Hindenburg and Ludendorff in their self-serving postwar memoirs claimed that soldiers had seen lions consumed by jackals at home. Eagerly adopted by the German *völkisch* right, the *Dolchstosslegende* consoled German soldiers, including most notably Adolf Hitler, who had seen their authority and status within society plummet after November 1918.

By 1928, the *Dolchstosslegende* was a leading theme of National Socialist propaganda, with Jews joining the list of "criminals" who had reputedly betrayed and dishonored the sacrifice of soldiers at the front. As soldiers attempted to regain the authority and respect they believed was their due, they supported demagogues such as Hitler who told them what they wanted to hear. The ultimate tragedy of the *Dolchstosslegende* was that it encouraged a new generation of German soldiers to serve a criminal Nazi regime that ended calamitously in an even greater military and moral *Götterdämmerung.*

William J. Astore

See also: Hindenburg, Paul von; Ludendorff, Erich

Additional Reading

Bessel, Richard. *Germany after the First World War.* New York: Oxford University Press, 1993.

Stalingrad, Battle of (August 24, 1942–February 2, 1943)

The Battle of Stalingrad was the first large encirclement of a German Army in World

Battle of Stalingrad, 1942–1943

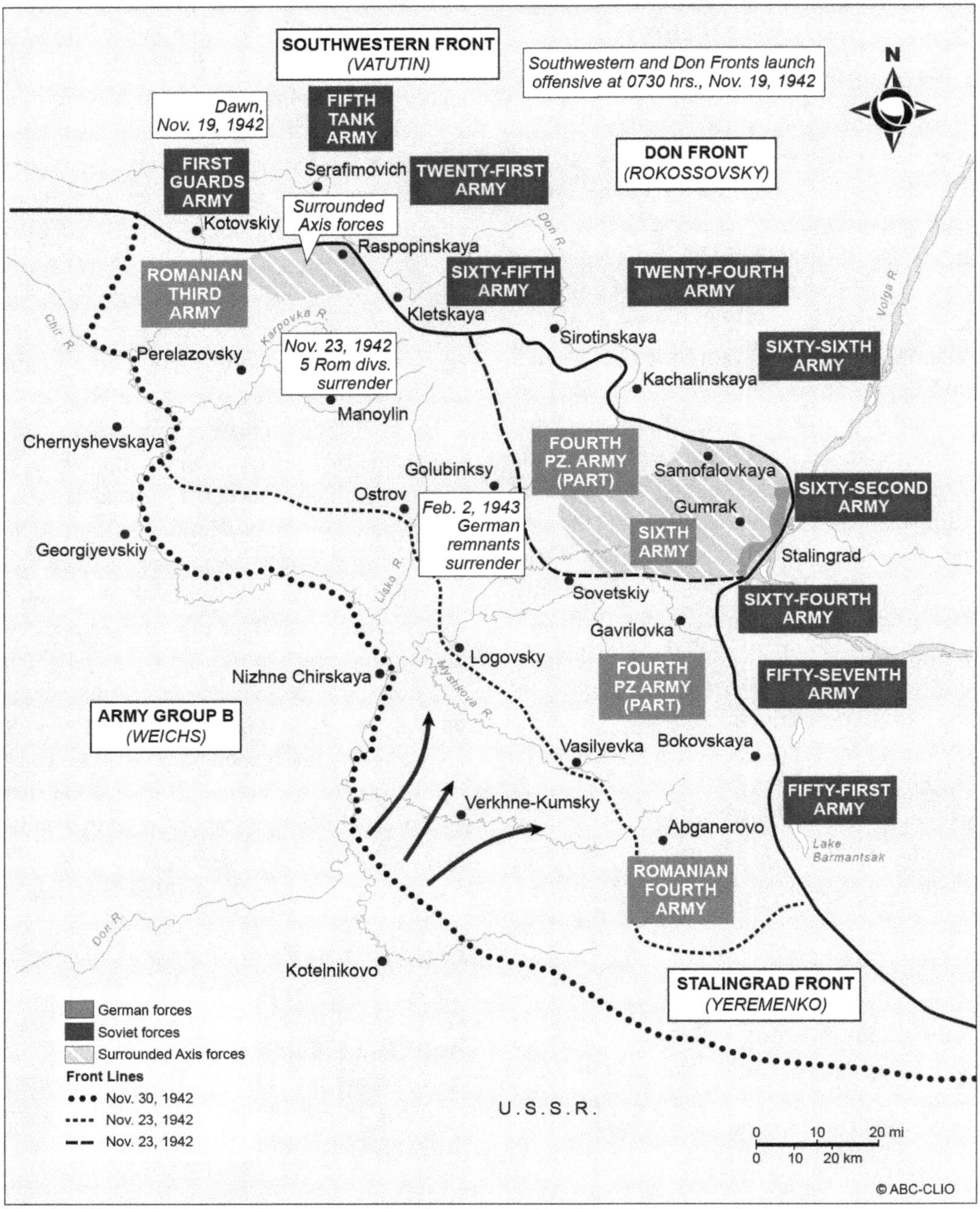

War II. Between the battles of Stalingrad and Kursk, the strategic initiative shifted to the Soviets. In spring 1942, Hitler placed major emphasis in the summer campaign on the southern portion of the German-Soviet Front in Operation BLAU (BLUE). Hitler's original plan called for Army Groups A and B to coordinate in a great effort to secure the Don and Donets Valleys and capture the cities of Rostov and Stalingrad. The two army groups could then move southeast to capture the oil fields that were so important to the Red Army. On July 13, however, Hitler ordered a change of plans, demanding the simultaneous capture of both Stalingrad—a major industrial center and key crossing point on the Volga River—and the Caucasus. Dividing the effort placed further strains on already inadequate German resources, especially on logistical support. To meet the German threat toward Stalingrad, on July 12, 1942, the Soviet General Staff formed the Stalingrad Front.

Angry over the slow progress of General Friedrich Paulus's Sixth Army into Stalingrad, Hitler, on August 11, ordered General Hermann Hoth's Fourth Panzer Army to move north toward the city from the Caucasus, leaving a badly depleted Army Group A holding a five-hundred-mile front and stalling the southernmost drive. Hitler also ordered his sole strategic reserve in the area, Field Marshal Erich von Manstein's Eleventh Army, north to Leningrad.

Beginning on August 24, a costly battle of attrition raged for Stalingrad. Luftwaffe carpet bombing at the end of August killed some forty thousand people, but it also turned the city into defensive bastions of ruined buildings and rubble. The ruined city posed a formidable obstacle. Germany's strength lay in maneuver warfare, but Hitler compelled the Sixth Army to engage the Soviet strength of static defense. On August 29, Marshal Georgy Zhukov arrived at Stalingrad to assume overall command of operations.

Zhukov assembled one million men into four fronts (army groups) for a great double envelopment. This deep movement, Operation URANUS, began on November 19 and was timed to coincide with the frosts that would make Soviet cross-country tank maneuvers possible against the Axis infantry. By November 23, Operation URANUS had encircled the Sixth Army and had driven some units of the Fourth Panzer Army into the pocket. Hitler now ordered Manstein back from the Leningrad Front and gave him the newly organized Army Group Don, drawn from Army Group A—with the mission of saving the situation.

Manstein prepared to attack to relieve the encircled Sixth Army, but the Soviets struck first. Attacking just to the north of Stalingrad on December 7, elements of the Fifth Tank Army stormed across the Chir River north of Stalingrad and hit the XLVIII Panzer Corps. The 11th Panzer Division under General Hermann Balck counterattacked. Between December 8 and 22, Balck's single division counterattacked sequentially in three separate directions, defeated three different Soviet tank corps, and, in the process, virtually destroyed the Soviet Fifth Tank Army. Tactically, it was one of the most brilliantly fought divisional battles of the war, but operationally Manstein's relief offensive was completely disrupted when another Soviet drive threatened to take Rostov, at the mouth of the Don on the Azov Sea. That would have cut off Field Marshal Ewald von Kleist's Army Group A in the Caucasus. Manstein was forced to commit heavy forces to defend Rostov, and that sealed the fate of the Sixth Army in Stalingrad.

Hitler, meanwhile, forbade any withdrawal, convinced by guarantees from

Reich Marshal Hermann Göring that the Sixth Army could be resupplied from the air. But the Soviets at that point had achieved air superiority. By November 20, the second day of URANUS, the Soviets committed between 1,350 and 1,414 combat aircraft to Stalingrad. Meanwhile, Colonel General Wolfram von Richtofen's Fourth Air Fleet, flying in support of the Sixth Army, had 732 combat aircraft, of which only 402 were operational.

Hitler still refused to authorize any attempt by the Sixth Army to break out. He allowed only a linking up with a relief force. Paulus favored a breakout, but he was not prepared to gamble either his army or his career. Manstein's reduced force had managed to reach within thirty-five miles of the Sixth Army's positions, but the Germans had insufficient fuel, their horses had mostly been eaten, and any link-up operation would take weeks to prepare.

In mid-December, the Volga froze, allowing the Soviets to use vehicles to cross the ice. During the next seven weeks, Zhukov sent thirty-five thousand vehicles across the river, along with 122 mm howitzers to blast the German defensive works. By then, seven Soviet armies surrounded the Sixth Army. Even in this hopeless situation, Paulus refused to disobey Hitler by ordering a breakout. Paulus himself surrendered on January 31 (he maintained he had been "taken by surprise"), but he refused to order his men to do the same. The last German units capitulated on February 2.

The Stalingrad Campaign may have cost the Soviets 1.1 million casualties, more than 485,000 dead. Of the ninety-one thousand Germans (including twenty-two generals) taken prisoner by the Soviets, fewer than five thousand survived the war and Soviet captivity. The last Germans taken prisoner at Stalingrad were not released until 1955.

Eva-Maria Stolberg, Spencer C. Tucker, and David T. Zabecki

See also: Balck, Hermann; Caucasus Campaign; Göring, Hermann; Hoth, Hermann; Kleist, Paul Ewald von; Manstein, Erich von; Paulus, Friedrich; Richthofen, Wolfram von; Rostov, Battle of

Additional Reading

Beevor, Antony. *Stalingrad: The Fateful Siege, 1942–1943.* New York: Viking, 1998.

Melvin, Mungo. *Manstein: Hitler's Greatest General.* London: Weidenfeld & Nicolson, 2010.

Stauffenberg, Claus Schenk von (1907–1944)

Wehrmacht colonel.

Born on November 15, 1907 at Greifenstein Castle, Jettingen, into a staunchly Roman Catholic Prussian noble family, Claus von Stauffenberg joined the 17th Cavalry Regiment in 1926 as an officer candidate, and he was commissioned in 1930. Stauffenberg seriously questioned National Socialism after the virulent anti-Jewish *Kristallnacht* of November 9, 1938. Service with German forces in the Soviet Union exacerbated his disillusionment with Hitler's inhumane policies. Stauffenberg was badly wounded by the explosion of a mine in April 1943, losing his left eye, right hand, and two fingers of his left hand. In July 1944, Stauffenberg was appointed chief of staff to General Friedrich Fromm, commander of the Reserve Army. This position gave him access to Hitler. As a severely disabled war hero, he was spared the searches of persons who were admitted to see Hitler. On July 20, 1944, Stauffenberg placed a bomb hidden in a briefcase beside Hitler at his

Colonel Claus Schenk Graf von Stauffenberg, photographed in 1934. On July 20, 1944, he planted the bomb in the failed attempt to assassinate Hitler. Stauffenberg was executed by firing squad early the following day. Today he is considered one of the greatest heroes of the modern German Bundeswehr. (Stiftung/ullstein bild via Getty Images)

headquarters, the Wolf's Lair, in Rastenberg, East Prussia, and quickly left the scene to fly to Berlin. The briefcase was moved, and the explosion only slightly injured Hitler. However, Stauffenberg was convinced the Führer was dead. The subsequent coup in Berlin failed because of delays, poor coordination, and simple bad luck. Stauffenberg and several others were arrested on the night of July 20, court-martialed, and shot in the courtyard of the War Ministry in Berlin. Several thousand others who were also opposed to the regime also subsequently perished. Stauffenberg today is considered one of the heroes and ethical role models of the Bundeswehr.

Annette E. Richardson

See also: Fromm, Friedrich; Opposition to Hitler, German Military

Additional Reading

Fest, Joachim. *Plotting Hitler's Death.* New York: Metropolitan Books, 1996.

Steinhoff, Johannes (1913–1994)

Luftwaffe colonel and ace, Bundesluftwaffe general.

Born in Bottendorf on September 15, 1913, Johannes "Macky" Steinhoff joined the German Navy in 1934. His interest in aviation led him to transfer to the Luftwaffe in 1936, and, by the beginning of World War II, he was a squadron commander in *Jagdgeschwader* (Fighter Wing) 26. Steinhoff served in every theater of war to which the Luftwaffe was deployed, and he ran up the impressive tally of 176 victories. He was one of the leading members of the "Fighter Pilots' Revolt" against Hermann Göring. Steinhoff's final assignment was a posting to *Jagdverband* (Fighter Group) 44, Adolf Galland's "Squadron of Experts." On April 18, 1945, Steinhoff crashed his Me 262 on takeoff. The resulting fire left him scarred for the rest of his life, and he ended the war recovering in a hospital. Steinhoff joined the air force of the Federal Republic of Germany in 1955, rising to the rank of full general. He served as Inspector of the *Bundesluftwaffe* from 1966 to 1970, and chairman of the Military Committee of the North Atlantic Treaty Organization from 1971 until his retirement in 1974. Steinhoff died at Bottendorf, Germany, on February 21, 1994.

Marlyn R. Pierce

Lieutenant General Johannes "Macky" Steinhoff, pictured in 1966 as chief of the *Bundesluftwaffe*. During World War II, he became history's twenty-third highest-scoring ace, with 176 victories. In this picture, he is also wearing U.S. Air Force Senior Pilot wings. (Keystone/Hulton Archive/Getty Images)

See also: Appendix A

Additional Reading

Steinhoff, Johannes. *The Final Hours: A German Jet Pilot Plots against Göring.* Baltimore, MD: Nautical and Aviation Publishing, 1977.

STRANGLE, Allied Air Operation (March 15–May 11, 1944)

Operation STRANGLE was an interdiction campaign by Allied air forces during the spring of 1944, directed against German supply lines in central Italy that supported the Gustav Line. STRANGLE was intended to force a German withdrawal through airpower alone. The Germans established the Gustav Line centered on Monte Cassino to block an Allied northward advance on Rome. By spring 1944, three major ground assaults had failed to breach this line, and even the amphibious landing at Anzio in January 1944 had stalled. U.S. Lieutenant General Ira C. Eaker, commander of the Allied Mediterranean Allied Air Forces, decided to launch a supply interdiction operation to break the stalemate and force a German withdrawal.

Operation STRANGLE was directed mainly against the Italian rail system, Germany's primary means of supply transportation, but it also targeted ports and bridges. The campaign involved an interdiction belt running across Italy from east to west, as far north of the Gustav Line as possible, to force the Germans to use alternate transport means to the front. The attacks started on March 19, 1944 and continued until May 11. The Luftwaffe's Second Air Fleet in Italy, commanded by Field Marshal Wolfram von Richthofen, had no more than 250 operational bombers and fighter-bombers, 200 fighters, and 75 reconnaissance aircraft. Nonetheless, Operation STRANGLE failed to force the Germans to withdraw from the Gustav Line in order to shorten their supply lines.

By the end of April, the Allies concluded that airpower alone would not force a German withdrawal from the Gustav Line, and they launched Operation DIADEM on May 11. The operation combined an aerial interdiction campaign against supply lines with a ground offensive. This air offensive was focused closer to the immediate German rear areas and also targeted their operational reserves and major command-and-control facilities. Within less than a month, Allied ground forces penetrated the Gustav Line, linked up with the Anzio beachhead, and captured Rome on June 4.

Paul E. Fontenoy

See also: Anzio, Battle of; Italy Campaign, Allied; Richthofen, Wolfram von

Additional Reading

Brookes, Andrew. *Air War over Italy, 1943–1945*. Shepperton, UK: Ian Allen, 2000.

Stroop, Jürgen (1895–1952)

Waffen-SS Gruppenführer and lieutenant general of the Waffen-SS and Police.

Born on September 26, 1895 in Detmold, Stroop served in a Bavarian infantry regiment in World War I. A fanatic anti-Semite, Stoop joined the SS in 1932. Between April 19 and May 16, 1943, Stroop commanded the forces that crushed the uprising by Jews in the Warsaw Ghetto. He was responsible for the deaths of more than seventy-one thousand people, including those who likely perished at Treblinka and other concentration camps. He surrendered to the Americans at the end of the war and was tried and convicted for the execution of U.S. fliers in Greece. He was then extradited to Poland, where he was tried for his crimes in Poland. Sentenced to death on charges related to the Warsaw Ghetto Uprising, Stroop was convicted and hanged in Warsaw on March 6, 1952.

Matthew Alan McNiece

See also: Warsaw Ghetto Uprising

Additional Reading

Moczarski, Kazimierz. *Conversations with an Executioner.* Edited by Mariana Fitzpatrick. Englewood Cliffs, NJ: Prentice-Hall, 1981.

Student, Kurt (1890–1978)

Luftwaffe colonel general.

Born at Birkholtz, Brandenburg, on May 12, 1890, Student commanded a fighter squadron on the Western Front during World War I. In August 1933, he headed the test center for aviation equipment and organized Germany's first airborne forces. As commander of the 7th Air Division of paratroops and glider-borne infantry, Student played a key role in the May 1940 invasion of France and the Benelux, directing his elite forces in reducing key strong points, most notably Fortress Eben Emael in Belgium. In May 1941, he commanded the airborne assault on Crete. The heavy casualties in this operation, the consequence of Allied ULTRA intercepts, convinced Hitler that the days of parachute troops were over. From that point, the German airborne forces were employed as elite infantry. In 1944, Student commanded the First Parachute Army in France during the Allied Normandy Invasion. In November 1944, he assumed command of Army Group H in defense of the Rhine. In late April 1945, he commanded Army Group Vistula. Taken prisoner by the British in Schleswig-Holstein, he was charged and convicted of war crimes by a British court, but he was released in 1948. Student died in Lemgo, Federal Republic of Germany, on July 1, 1978.

Spencer C. Tucker

See also: Crete, German Invasion of

Additional Reading

Hackett, Sir John. "Colonel-General Kurt Student." In *Hitler's Generals*, edited by Correlli Barnett, 463–479. New York: George Weidenfeld, 1989.

Stuka Ju 87 Dive Bomber. *See* Aircraft, Military

Stülpnagel, Joachim von (1880–1968)

Reichswehr lieutenant general.

Joachim von Stülpnagel was one of Germany's most radical and revolutionary military thinkers. Born on March 5, 1880 in Glogau, Stülpnagel served as a General Staff Officer during World War I. Chief of the T1 (operations) section of the Truppenamt, Stülpnagel wrote a monograph that advocated that Germany adopt a ruthless and extreme method of warfare. In his view, nothing should be off-limits or too extreme—all persons and all things could become weapons. Such a deliberately brutal and fanatical method of war of attrition—conducted both by soldiers and civilians—would allow Germany to blunt the enemy's initial attack; deprive him of operational assets; and, consequently, make it possible for a well-equipped and superbly trained Reichswehr to launch a decisive battle that ultimately would destroy the enemy. Although Stülpnagel left the army in December 1931, his two-part strategy of attrition and annihilation greatly influenced German operational planning in the run-up to World War II. He died in Oberaudorf on May 17, 1968.

Fred L. Borch III

See also: Reichsheer (German Army)

Additional Reading

Citino, Robert M. *The German Way of War.* Lawrence: University Press of Kansas, 2005.

Stülpnagel, Karl von (1886–1944)

Wehrmacht general of infantry.

Born in Darmstadt on January 2, 1886, Karl von Stülpnagel served on the General Staff during World War I. In 1938, he was appointed head of the Operations Section of the Army General Staff. Stülpnagel's personal opposition to war against Britain led him to join his close associates, Generals Ludwig Beck and Franz Halder, in the conspiracy against Adolf Hitler. Stülpnagel commanded the Seventeenth Army in Operation BARBAROSSA, the invasion of the Soviet Union. In March 1942, Stülpnagel took over from his cousin Otto von Stülpnagel the post of military governor of Paris. A key member of the coup plot of July 1944, Stülpnagel ordered the arrest of some one thousand German security personnel in Paris when he first thought that the bomb had killed Hitler. Stülpnagel was arrested by the Gestapo and taken to Berlin. He was tried by the Nazi People's Court, convicted, and sentenced to death. Stülpnagel was hanged at Ploetzensee Prison on August 30, 1944.

Gene Mueller and Spencer C. Tucker

See also: Beck, Ludwig; Halder, Franz; Opposition to Hitler, German Military

Additional Reading

Hamerow, Theodore S. *On the Road to the Wolf's Lair: German Resistance to Hitler.* Cambridge, MA: Harvard University Press, 1997.

Stülpnagel, Otto von (1878–1948)

Wehrmacht general of infantry.

Born in Berlin on June 16, 1878, Otto von Stülpnagel served on the western front in World War I. After the war, he became an avid Nazi. During the 1930s, he frequently clashed with Colonel Heinz Guderian over the utility of tanks and armor. Stülpnagel retired in 1939, but, in 1940, he was recalled to active duty and assigned as military governor of the German-occupied portion of

France. He endorsed harsh measures against the Resistance, and he even advocated for the death sentence for those caught listening to the British Broadcasting Corporation. Stülpnagel resigned his post and was succeeded in March 1942 by his cousin, General Karl von Stülpnagel. Charged after the war with crimes in France, Otto von Stülpnagel hanged himself in Paris on February 6, 1948 rather than stand trial.

Thomas Lansford

See also: Guderian, Heinz; Stülpnagel, Karl von

Additional Reading

Mitchell, Allan. *Nazi Paris: The History of an Occupation*. New York: Berghahn, 2008.

Sturmabteilungen (SA) (1921–1945)

The SA "Brownshirts" (after the color of their uniforms), or Stormtroopers, were a paramilitary organization instrumental in the Nazi Party's success and Hitler's ascension to power during the Weimar Republic. In order to defend themselves better against the Communists and other political rivals, the Nazis established the Sturmabteilungen (Storm Detachment) in August 1921. World War I veterans, chiefly Ernst Röhm, commanded the SA from its inception. Initially headquartered in Munich, the SA spread throughout Bavaria by bolstering its numbers with former Freikorps soldiers, while older, educated World War I veterans and militarily experienced officers composed the senior leadership. The majority of SA membership, however, consisted of fervent, young unemployed men, many of whom had lost their fathers during the Great War and found solace within the ranks of the Brownshirts. Street violence between paramilitary organizations became omnipresent throughout Germany.

In 1923, Röhm enabled the SA to obtain weapons, vehicles, and military matériel through his ties with the Reichswehr, which supported the Nazis because they counteracted their mutual enemy—the Communists. In November of that year, Hitler and Nazi leaders felt confident enough with the support of the well-armed SA to stage a coup against the Weimar government during the Munich Beer Hall Putsch. The coup failed, Hitler went to prison, and the government banned the SA. Röhm, however, continued to strengthen his Stormtroopers in secret. When Hitler finished his prison term, he and Röhm disagreed over the role of the SA. The latter wanted to militarize the Brownshirts to an even greater degree, but Hitler had learned a great lesson from the failed Beer Hall Putsch. The SA could remain a useful tool but would never be the army of Röhm's vision. Hitler would have to win political power through legal means.

When the Great Depression hit Germany, SA enrollment soared. By 1932, the Brownshirts roamed the streets of Germany with an estimated force of almost three hundred thousand men, and the Weimar government began to see the Nazi Party and the SA as a major threat. Nonetheless, the Reichswehr still supported Hitler and the Brownshirts because they opposed the Communists. Hitler used the SA as a menacing alternate army against Weimar, but after he became chancellor on January 30, 1933, he needed the full support of the Reichswehr, and he, therefore, refused to support Röhm's dream of a revolutionary new army with the SA at its core. Hitler implored Röhm to desist with his plans to amalgamate the SA into the Reichswehr, but the SA commander refused. At around 4.5 million members in June 1934, the Brownshirts became disobedient to Hitler, still wanting a violent revolt to dismantle the government and create a German revolution. Thus, on June 30, 1934, Hitler carried out the Night of the Long Knives Blood Purge, which ended with the death of Röhm and at least 120 other supposed conspirators against the Nazi Party.

The death of Röhm also marked a turning point in the prestige of the SA. After the Night of the Long Knives, the power of the Stormtroopers collapsed, and the Schutzstaffel (SS) superseded the SA's powers. In the years that followed, SA membership remained voluntary, and Stormtrooper numbers continued to grow, but Hitler limited their role to duties such as physical and military training, without the use of weapons. The SA never regained its former power, but their role as Hitler's secondary brute squad would continue throughout World War II. The postwar International Military Tribunal at Nuremberg did not condemn the SA as a criminal organization. Thus, the crimes and violence of the SA went unpunished, overshadowed by the SS and the Holocaust.

Edward Gutiérrez

See also: Freikorps (Free Corps); Night of the Long Knives; Röhm, Ernst; Waffen-SS

Additional Reading

Campbell, Bruce. *The SA Generals and the Rise of Nazism*. Lexington: University of Kentucky Press, 1998.

Fischer, Conan. *Stormtroopers: A Social, Economic and Ideological Analysis, 1929–1935*. London: Allen and Unwin, 1983.

Submarines

One of the ironies of the two world wars is that Germany, the nation whose submarines constituted its primary naval striking arm, entered those wars with its most senior naval leaders, believing submarines would have only a supporting role in their naval operations. Called *Unterseebooten* (U-boats) in German, their rise to prominence in Germany's naval operations was the result of the circumstances of those wars, not the senior leadership's vision.

Commander of the German Navy, Admiral Erich Raeder, envisioned a large but nonetheless supporting role for the submarine force. He believed that surface raiding groups would be the primary arm attacking enemy commerce and that U-boats would restrict the enemy's employment of their major combatants against those raiding groups. World War II's outbreak five years before he expected was what prevented him from employing that doctrine. However, he retained his faith in surface raiding against Allied maritime commerce almost to the end of his tenure as Kriegsmarine commander, limiting research and development of U-boat technologies. All the later developments in U-boat hull design, propulsion, and sensor systems were launched upon Grand Admiral Karl Dönitz's assumption of command. Fortunately for the Allies, they came too late to affect the war.

The Treaty of Versailles prohibited Germany from building or possessing submarines. To preserve the capability, German leaders dispersed their designers and engineers to foreign countries. Some went to Finland, some to Spain, but most moved to Holland where the Reichmarine established a submarine design office. Torpedo research was conducted in Sweden. The greatest technological advances were in sensors, fire-control systems, and weaponry. Hydrophones and submarine-silencing technology improved. Germany developed test ranges for accurately measuring U-boat machinery noise, leading them to identify the noisiest equipment and modify either the installation or design to reduce the acoustic signatures.

The simple hydrophones of World War I were replaced by groupings of acoustic sensors mounted along the hull. The system was called *Gruppen Horch-Geraete Anlange* (Group Listening Devices Equipment, or GHG). It was more sensitive than early systems and gave an accurate bearing of the sound source and identified the signal strength. Large ships and convoys could be detected dozens of miles away. The new analog computer fire-control systems converted range, bearing, and target angle information into enemy course and speed and produced both a predicted launch azimuth for the torpedoes and projected "best spread" to ensure a hit. Commanders no longer needed to aim their entire U-boat toward the firing azimuth or calculate that azimuth based on personal judgment. They entered the target information into the fire control system and followed its recommendations once they were confident that they had a firing solution. That development, coupled with the introduction of more lethal torpedoes, made the new U-boats far more effective weapons platforms.

Diesel engine technology also advanced. Jumbo turbochargers developed for aircraft engines increased engine power and efficiency and, therefore, U-boat surface speed. Improvements in metallurgy and the introduction of welding in hull construction produced a stronger hull at a reduced displacement. Diving depths increased to two hundred meters, nearly three times that of 1918. In contrast to the World War I U-boats, the majority of those built during World War II were single-hull designs, providing more internal space for equipment and weapons.

Berlin brought the cadre of engineers and scientists involved in the covert naval programs home after 1933. With the lessons of World War I firmly in mind, the new Kriegsmarine wanted to concentrate on two types of U-boats, long-range boats to attack enemy commerce and coastal boats to control the North and Baltic Seas. However, the Anglo-German Naval Agreement awarded Germany 45 percent of Britain's submarine tonnage, and, with France now the main enemy, the need for long-range U-boats gave way to the requirement for a large-number of U-boats that could be committed either in the North Sea or off the French ports. The 500- to 750-ton medium U-boats met that requirement, and three could be built for every two long-range boats. Germany, however, first had to build a corps of trained submariners to man the force.

Thus, the first six boats were Type IIA coastal boats, which differed little from the UB-II boats of World War I. The three torpedo tubes on the Type IIAs were all located in the bow, and a 20 mm antiaircraft gun was the only surface armament. They were followed by twenty Type IIB boats, eight Type IIC boats, and sixteen Type IID boats. Each new model was slightly larger and had greater range than the previous model. Intended primarily as training or mine-laying boats, many were used operationally during the war's early months. The Type IIDs, which entered service in 1941, carried a quadruple 20 mm antiaircraft gun mount.

Two oceangoing Type IA boats were started just before the first Type IIAs entered service in 1935 and were commissioned one year later. It was not a successful design. However, the lessons learned from the Type IA boats were applied to good effect in the development of the later Type VII, Type IX, and Type X U-boats. The first eight Type IX boats, laid down in 1938, were similarly armed and equipped, except with an antiaircraft battery of one 20 mm and one 37 mm cannon. Their maneuverability and diving stability were markedly better that the previous classes. They had a sixty-five to seventy-eight nautical mile submerged range at four knots. Diving depth exceeded two hundred meters. Later U-boat models were larger and had even greater range, but crew size never changed from the four officers and forty-four men of the first models. Some 204 were built during the war.

Construction of the Type VII, which was the dominant U-boat of the war, began in March 1934. The Type VII was based on a 550-ton design surface displacement, intended to provide an operational range of sixty-five hundred nautical miles. The installation of saddle tanks outside the VIIB's pressure hull extended the range another twenty-five hundred nautical miles, but damaged tanks often leaked oil, giving away the submarine's position. All U-boats had a passive electronic detection system installed before the war's start. The early system monitored only communications frequencies from 70 to 1200 Hz and 1.5 to 25 MHz, but Allied radar developments stayed ahead of U-boat passive detection systems for most of the war. Poor ventilation also affected all but the final U-boat models built during the war, making undersea service an uncomfortable experience.

Germany was also unique in World War II in that it built specifically designed supply U-boats to defeat the Allied blockade and transport weapons and equipment to deployed U-boats. Called *Milchkuhe* (Milk Cows), these logistic support boats had limited machinery repair capabilities, carried an additional 430 tons of diesel oil

German Navy submarine U-255, a Type-VIIC U-boat, approaches its berth in Bergen, Norway. Based in Norway during 1942–1943, U-255 was one of the most successful German submarines to operate in the Arctic during the war. It survived the war, having sunk a U.S. destroyer escort and ten merchant ships. (Naval Historical Center)

for transfer to other U-boats, and had a range of 12,350 nautical miles surfaced at ten knots. In their early years, 1941 to 1942, they enabled Germany's Type VII boats to operate as far away as the U.S. East Coast and extend their patrols for up to three additional weeks. Eight Milk Cows were built between 1941 and 1943. All were sunk during the war. Germany also built four Type VIIF models for the logistics role, losing three.

The Type VII boats conducted most of the fighting during the Battle of the Atlantic and in the Mediterranean. Twin rudders made them exceptionally maneuverable, and no submarine of World War II could exceed their diving speed of fifty seconds from surface running to twenty meters of depth. They had four torpedo tubes forward and one aft, carrying fifteen torpedoes or a mix of torpedoes and up to thirty-nine mines. Each successive variant had incremental improvements and greater displacement. Snorkels and increasingly capable radar-detection systems were introduced in 1942. Radar was installed after March 1943, and anechoic coatings were added to the hull to reduce sonar signatures. Nonetheless, advances in Allied radars and magnetic anomaly detection (MAD) systems turned the tide in the U-boat war after May 1943.

When Dönitz replaced Raeder as head of the German Navy in January 1943, he reoriented German naval research priorities and gathered a team of experts to design a new type of U-boat to operate in the new warfare environment. They pursued two paths. The first was to use available technology and systems to develop a more survivable U-boat as rapidly as possible. The second was to develop a new, revolutionary design to gain a qualitative advantage ahead of Allied developments.

The first path led to the Type XXI "*Elektrik* U-boat." Optimized for operations submerged, it had twice the battery capacity of earlier U-boats and a streamlined sail and hull to reduce underwater resistance. The double hull gave it a greater diving depth of 250 meters and enabled designers to sound-dampen much of the internal equipment. Outer hull openings were shaped to reduce water-flow noises. The anechoic covering reduced sonar detectability, and the Type XXI had a special silenced electric motor that allowed it to creep away at two to three knots without emitting a noise that the Allied hydrophones could detect. Its surface armament was reduced to two antiaircraft cannons mounted in a conical turret in the rear of the sail. Its speed submerged exceeded its speed on the surface (17.2 knots versus 15 knots), and its underwater endurance was ten times that of earlier models (30 nautical miles at 15 knots, or 110 nautical miles at 10 knots). It could outrun the Allies' Mark 8 antisubmarine torpedo and its six 533 mm bow torpedo tubes made it the most powerful U-boat of the war. It also had an automated torpedo loading system that enabled a trained crew to reload all six tubes in twenty minutes, less than half the time required on a Type VII boat.

The Type XXI also was designed for near-mass production, with sections built in separate facilities and transported to shipyards for final assembly. The design was ready by May 1943, and construction began shortly thereafter. Its fifteen thousand, five hundred nautical mile range gave it the capacity to strike in the Atlantic from bases inside Germany. It also carried a new radar, new communications equipment, and revamped encryption system that the Allies never penetrated. The first units were completed in December 1944 and began sea trials in January 1945, far too late to see action or to affect the outcome of the Battle of the Atlantic.

The second option was to develop the "Walter" boat, which used a revolutionary propulsion system that had been in testing since April 1940. Walter boats used highly concentrated hydrogen peroxide as an oxidizing agent to burn diesel fuel in a special combustion chamber that exhausted through a steam turbine. The power densities achieved far exceeded that of the traditional diesel-electric drive, and, more importantly, the Walter plant was self-contained and could be used underwater. The design never had a high priority during Raeder's tenure. Another problem was the instability of the highly concentrated hydrogen peroxide, which could break down into pure oxygen and water almost upon contact with dust or lint. It had to be stored in specially designed and maintained ceramic tanks.

Four experimental three-hundred-ton boats built in late 1944 tested successfully, and production of the new Type XVIIB coastal "Walter" boats began in October 1944. They used conventional diesel-electric propulsion for surface and most submerged operations. The Walter engines were employed only for high-speed dashes, at speeds up to twenty-five knots, to escape Allied attacks. Intended for operations in the North Sea, they carried only two torpedoes. Three were built, but none saw combat. Both were scuttled at Cuxhaven on May 7, 1945.

In the interim, Dönitz had large numbers of short-range, conventionally powered single-hull Type XXIII coastal U-boats built to attack Allied shipping in the North and Baltic Seas. The sixty-two Type XXIII's were mass produced. They displaced less than 260 tons; had a streamlined hull; 12.6 knots maximum submerged speed; and carried only two torpedoes, both mounted outside the hull. Germany also produced a range of small one- and two-man submarines for special operations, including the *Biber*, *Marder*, *Neger*, and *SeeHund*, but their thirty-nautical-mile range limited their operations to coastal areas. They achieved little more than create false alarms in Allied-controlled harbors.

Of the 1,117 U-boats Germany built in World War II, 783 were lost. They sunk thirty-five hundred merchant ships, totaling 14.5 million Gross Registered Tons (GRT), and 175 warships. German U-boats, particularly the Type XXI and Type XVII, were highly sought after as reparations, especially for their propulsion technology. Britain raised and commissioned the Type XVII *U-1407* as *HMS Meteorite* for use as a test platform to examine the utility of the Walter system. The United States examined the system as well. The Soviet Union adapted the German Type XXI as its *Whiskey*-class submarines and the German closed-cycle diesel AIP system for the Soviet's *Quebec*-class diesel boats. The United States' early postwar conventional and nuclear submarine hulls reflected the influence of Germany's Type XXI's, but the advent of nuclear power eventually relegated German U-boat advances to the history books.

Carl O. Schuster

See also: Anglo-German Naval Agreement; Atlantic, Battle of the; Dönitz, Karl; Raeder, Erich

Additional Reading

Lenton, H. T. *German Submarines of World War II.* Vols. I & II. New York: Doubleday, 1967.

Moeller, Eberhard, and Werner Brack. *The Encyclopedia of U-Boats from 1904 to the Present.* London: Greenhill Books, 2004.

T

Tanks and Self-Propelled Guns

German Tanks Between the World Wars

The first German tank after World War I was a large thinly armored, fast, two-turreted heavy tank (code named *Grosstraktor*). In 1932, a four-turreted medium tank was procured (code named *mittlerer Traktor*, later the *Neubaufahrzeug*, and finally the *Neubaupanzer IV*). The tank had been specified at fifteen tons (like the *Grosstraktor*), but would weigh twenty-three tons due to increased armor and armament. The main turret mounted coaxial 75 mm and 37 mm guns; smaller front and rear turrets mounted machine guns. This type saw combat during the invasion of Norway in 1940.

Pz.Kpfw.I

In 1932, the Germans specified a light tank. Krupp imported secretly two Carden-Lloyd Mk IV tankettes and delivered six derivatives (codenamed *Kleintraktor*) between 1932 and 1933. The Krupp hull was accepted, but the turret was taken from the Daimler-Benz submission. Designated the Panzerkampfwagen I (Pz.Kpfw.I), production began in July 1934, and deployment in 1935. In 1936, 180 Pz.Kpfw.Is were sent to Spain to support Nationalist forces. They proved inferior to the better-armed and armored Soviet T-26 tanks used by the Republicans. The German Army started World War II with more Pz.Kpfw.I tanks than any other panzer model. When Germany invaded the Soviet Union in June 1941, German tank divisions still deployed 180 Pz.Kpfw.Is—6 percent of all their tanks. The Pz.Kpfw.I was lightly armed and armored. The first model (Ausführung or Ausf. A) of the Pz.Kpfw.I was powered by an engine generating 60 horsepower and the second model (Ausf. B) by an engine generating 100 horsepower. The larger engine necessitated a slightly longer hull and a fifth road wheel on each side. Two wartime models followed: a reconnaissance tank with armor up to 30 mms thick, a 20 mm cannon, and torsion-bar suspension, and a well-armored (80 mm) infantry support tank, with a 150-horsepower engine.

Pz.Kpfw.II

In July 1934, the Armaments Office specified a new tank, armed with a 20 mm cannon. In October 1935, the MAN corporation produced a mild-steel prototype. Large, individually suspended road wheels and a reasonably powerful engine helped the tank reach 25 miles per hour. With torsion-bar suspension (Ausf. D of 1938 and subsequent models), it could reach 34 miles per hour. In early 1944, a reconnaissance version (the Ausf. L, Luchs) was introduced, with interleaved road wheels, torsion-bar suspension, and a more powerful engine. The pilot Ausf. M mounted a 50 mm gun. Frontal armor increased from 14.5 mm to 35 mm for the Ausf. F.

The Pz.Kpfw.II was outnumbered by the Pz.Kpfw.I at the time of the invasion of Poland, but it was the most numerous in German service during the invasion of France. By the invasion of the Soviet Union

Tanks and Self-Propelled Guns

Model	Pz.Kpfw. I	Pz.Kpfw. II	Pz.Kpfw. III	StG and StH	Pz.Kpfw. IV	Pz.Kpfw. 35(t)	Pz.Kpfw. 38(t)	Pz.Kpfw. VI Tiger I	Pz.Kpfw. V Panther	Pz.Kpfw. VIB Tiger II
Year of Introduction	1935	1936	1937	1940	1938	1936	1939	1942	1943	1943
Number Built	1,500	1,856	6,157	9,236 (StG III); 1,141 (StG IV); 1,299 (StH)	8,523	434	1,414	1,347	6,042	484
Combat Weight (metric tons)	5.5	7.2, later 11.8	15, later 23	20, later 24	20, later 26	10.5	10	56	43	70
Engine Power (hp)	60, later 150	140, later 180	250, later 300	250	300	125, later 150	125	650, later 700	650, later 700	700
Maximum Speed (km/hr; mph)	40; 25	40; 25	40; 25	40; 25	40; 25	40; 25	40; 25	40; 25	55; 35	42; 26
Cruising Range (km; miles)	200; 120	200; 120	155; 96	155; 96	200; 120	120, later 190; 75, later	250; 180	110; 70	250; 160	170; 110
Main Gun Caliber (mm)	7.92, later 20	20	37, later 50 or 75	75 or 105	75	37	37	88	75	88
Machine Guns	2	1	2	1	2	2	2	2	2	2
Maximum Armor thickness (mm)	13, later 80	14.5, later 30	15, later 70	50, later 80	15, later 80	26	30, later 80	100, later 110	100, later 110	180
Crew	2	3	5	4	5	4	4	5	5	5

in June 1941, the panzer divisions deployed 106 Pz.Kpfw.II tanks, less than any other type, and just 3 percent of all tanks in German service. Soon the Pz.Kpfw.II was limited to reconnaissance missions, and then converted into self-propelled guns or tractors or carriers. Variants included the Sturmpanzer II Bison self-propelled 150 mm infantry gun and a flamethrower model. Conversions included the Marder I and II tank hunters (armed with captured Soviet 76.2 mm and German 75 mm L40 guns) and the Wespe self-propelled 105 mm howitzer. Some eight hundred Ausf. L Leopard tanks were ordered, but just over one hundred were produced between September 1943 and January 1944.

Pz.Kpfw.III

In 1935, the Armaments Office specified two new tanks: a fifteen-ton tank (eventually the Pz.Kpfw.III) armed with an antitank gun, and a twenty-ton tank (eventually the Pz.Kpfw.IV) armed with a close-support gun/howitzer. The Daimler Benz design was selected. The inspector for motorized troops specified a 50 mm gun, but the Ordnance Department argued that the infantry's 37 mm antitank gun would be sufficient and cheaper to acquire, although they specified room for upgrade. Up-gunning with a 50 mm L42 cannon began in August 1940. Introduction of the L60 was ordered as early as August 1940, although production of the new vehicle (Ausf. J) did not begin until December 1941, and some Ausf. J vehicles were armed with the shorter gun. The final model (Ausf. N) was armed with 75 mm L24 gun/howitzers. The Pz.Kpfw.III had been specified at fifteen metric tons. The final Ausf. L model in June 1942 weighed twenty-three tons, maximum armor thickness had increased from 15 mm to 70 mm, and the main armament had increased from 37 mm to 75 mm. The final vehicles were 50 percent heavier than the first models, but they reached 40 kilometers per hour (25 miles per hour), thanks to a 250-horsepower engine—300 horsepower in newer vehicles. The first Pz.Kpfw.IIIs were delivered in May 1937. When the Germans invaded the Soviet Union in June 1941, the panzer divisions deployed 965 Pz.Kpfw.IIIs—more than any other type, or 30 percent of all their tanks. Production of the Pz.Kpfw.III ended in August 1943 after 6,157 vehicles.

The most numerous variant and the most numerous German turret-less self-propelled gun of World War II was the assault gun Sturmgeschütz III (StuG III). In 1936, it was required as an infantry support weapon and specified with the 75 mm L24 gun, but after 550 vehicles, the StuG III in September 1941 was fitted with the 75 mm L43 gun. From September 1942 onward, most vehicles (8,054) mounted the L48 gun. The StuH III variant mounted a 105 mm howitzer. Early models (Ausf. A through Ausf. D) of the StuG III had 50 mm thick armor at the front and 30 mm on the sides and rear before receiving an extra 9 mm. In June 1942, frontal armor was increased to 80 mm. From January through the end of the war, 9,236 StuG IIIs were built. From October 1942 onward, 1,299 StuH IIIs were built.

Pz.Kpfw.IV

The Pz.Kpfw.IV was specified in 1935 at the same time as the Pz.Kpfw.III. MAN's hull was accepted but with a running gear that was adapted from the Pz.Kpfw.III. Krupp's turret was accepted, and Krupp became the lead developer. The Pz.Kpfw.IV started with the 75 mm L24 gun. The up-gunned Pz.Kpfw.IV mounting an L48 gun went into production in March 1942 and arrived at the front in May 1942. The maximum armor thickness of the Pz.Kpfw.IV rose from 15 mm (Ausf. A, October 1937) to 80 mm (Ausf. H, April 1943). The heaviest model, the Ausf. H, weighed twenty-six metric tons. All models of the Pz.Kpfw.IV were powered by the Maybach HL 120 TRM engine.

Production of the Pz.Kpfw.IV began in October 1937. The first vehicles were delivered in January 1938. The Pz.Kpfw.IV accounted for 6 percent of all turreted German tanks deployed at the beginning of the war, 8 percent upon the invasion of France, and 9 percent upon the invasion of the Soviet Union in June 1941. The Pz.Kpfw.IV was the only panzer to be produced throughout the war and accounted for 35 percent of all turreted tanks produced by Nazi Germany.

Counting only series-production vehicles (excluding the conversions), 13,415 vehicles were built on the Pz.Kpfw.IV or the hybrid Pz.Kpfw.III/IV platforms, equivalent to 29 percent of all German tanks and self-propelled guns produced during the war. The models included eighteen deployed variants, including the turreted tank. In early 1943, field units received the first of the Sturmpanzer IV Brummbär—eventually 306 were produced (including sixty conversions), each armed with a 150 mm L12 howitzer within a superstructure 100 mm thick at the front and 60 mm on the sides. Some 724 Hummel self-propelled artillery pieces mounting 150 mm howitzers were built. From May 1943 through 1944, 494 Horniss/Nashorn vehicles were built, each with the 88 mm L71 gun in an open-topped superstructure on a hybrid Pz.Kpfw.IV/III platform. In November 1943, the primary StuG III assembly plant was damaged by Allied bombs, and the Krupp-Gruson factory at Magdeburg was ordered to switch production from the Pz.Kpfw.IV to a StuG IV—a slightly modified StuG III superstructure on the Pz.Kpfw.IV platform. A total of 1,141 StuG IVs were delivered from December 1943 to March 1945. Starting in January 1944, 780 Jagdpanzer IVs mounting L48 guns were produced, and from August 1944, 1,218 Jagdpanzer IVs mounting L70 guns were delivered.

In 1944, the Germans produced several Pz.Kpfw.IV variants, including 240 of the Möbelwagen, which mounted a 37 mm cannon inside a hinged superstructure; 105 of the Wirbelwind, mounting a quad 20 mm cannon in a turret; and 43 of the Ostwind, with a 37 mm cannon in a turret. Probably most of the latter two types were conversions. Another thirty-six Pz.Kpfw.IV tanks were converted into Bergepanzer IV recovery vehicles.

Pz.Kpfw.35(t)

In 1935, Skoda of Czechoslovakia developed the LT35. When Germany occupied Czechoslovakia in March 1939, the Germans adopted the tank as the Pz.Kpfw.35(t) and ordered another 219. The LT35 was well-armed, armored, and mobile for its small size and weight, although its pneumatic transmission and steering proved fragile in colder temperatures. After 1940, most were converted into tractors or maintenance vehicles, although Romania continued to use the LT35.

Pz.Kpfw.38(t)

The Czechoslovakian Army accepted the LT38 on July 1, 1938. In 1939, German occupiers received the deliveries. In September 1939, about 11 percent (301) of the tanks in German service were Pz.Kpfw.35(t) or 38(t). The LT38 carried the same armament and engine as the LT35 but superior running gear (four large road wheels resisted by semielliptic leaf springs), transmission, and armor. Some Pz.Kpfw.38(t) tanks were fitted with turrets (with 20 mm cannon) from the Sd.Kfz.222 armored car and fielded in 1944 as a reconnaissance tank. A captured Soviet 76.2 mm gun was mounted behind a three-sided superstructure to form the Marder. A German 75 mm gun was mounted within a lower and enclosed superstructure to form the Hetzer (2,584 vehicles).

Pz.Kpfw.VI Tiger I

Design of the Tiger 1 (initially Pz.Kpfw.VI Tiger Ausf. H) dates back to 1937, when a 30- to 33-ton replacement for the Pz.Kpfw. IV was first required. By 1939, the replacement was redefined as a "breakthrough vehicle." The Henschel hull was accepted for production, along with a turret designed by Krupp. Ninety Porsche hulls had been laid down already when Henschel won the contract. Some were delivered as tanks to Panzer Battalion 503, before that unit was reequipped with Henschel-made Tigers. The Porsche hulls were then converted into Ferdinand self-propelled 88 mm L71 guns. The most novel feature of all the Porsche designs was their hybrid gasoline-electric drive, but the technology was risky and required excessive amounts of precious copper.

Allied propagandists pointed to the Tiger I's weight as evidence of its poor mobility, but its large interleaved road wheels, torsion-bar suspension, powerful engine, power steering, wide tracks, and square shape made for an easy drive, agility, and the exceptional speed of 28 miles per hour for a heavy tank of its time. From December 1943, Tigers were equipped with a 700-horsepower Maybach HL230—the most powerful engine installed in any World War II tank. Twin HL 120 TRM engines, producing a combined 520 horsepower, were used to power the Ferdinand self-propelled gun.

The Tiger's weight and size did lead to strategic mobility risks. Probably more Tigers were lost after the Germans failed to recover disabled tanks before enemy capture than to enemy antitank weapons. At the time of introduction, the Tiger was practically invulnerable. The front turret mantelet started at 100 mm thick and increased to 110 mm. The front hull of the Ferdinand was 100 mm thick, and its front superstructure was 200 mm. The 75 mm gun carried by most U.S. and British tanks and the 76 mm gun carried by most Soviet tanks could penetrate about 85 mm of frontal armor. The later Soviet 85 mm tank gun could penetrate 110 mm. Only the British 17-pounder's discarding sabot rounds could penetrate the Tiger at all angles of attack. The Tiger's survivability was enhanced by armored fuel tanks and ammunition bins. Meanwhile, the Tiger's 88 mm gun was lethal to Allied tanks at longer ranges. The Ferdinand's gun was most powerful. The Henschel-built Tiger was the platform for only one deployed variant, the Sturmtiger, a self-propelled 380 mm mortar/rocket launcher for use in urban battles.

Production of the Tiger I ran from August 1942 to August 1944. It first operated in action against the Soviets in November 1942. Some operated in Tunisia from November to May 1943, and then in Sicily that July. The first massed use of all available Tigers on the eastern front was in July 1943, during the offensive around Kursk and Orel.

Pz.Kpfw.V Panther

Development of a new medium tank to replace the Pz.Kpfw.IV dated back to a

1937 requirement. The Pz.Kpfw.V was specified on November 25, 1941. The Panther Development Board required a tank that was easier to produce but capable enough to compensate for the enemy's numerical tank superiority. The Panther Board accepted the MAN design on May 11, 1942.

The Panther's 75 mm L70 gun had penetrative capabilities superior to the gun on the Tiger I. The sloped front armor offered similar protection, although the sides were thinner. The Panther could outrange almost all Allied tanks and survive almost all shots it received, but it was likely to be caught in the flank during offensive maneuvers. Despite the lethality, protection, and weight of a heavy tank, the Panther was fast and agile. The Panther had the same engine and transmission as the Tiger I, but at about fourteen tons lighter, it could reach 35 miles per hour and outpace lighter western and Soviet medium tanks, particularly off-road. The Panther benefited from the largest and most numerous road wheels of any tank of the period, tracks almost as wide as the Tiger's, and a lower ground pressure.

The appearance of the Soviet T-34 tank and political pressure for the Panther's use during the German summer offensive of 1943 contributed to its early deployment and unreliability. The drive was the most serious of the problems recognized in June 1943, at which point only one-third of the Panthers produced thus far had been accepted. Nevertheless, the entire stock was accepted, especially for Operation CITADEL in July 1943. Many broke down on their way to the battlefield. The Panther was first deployed against the Western Allies in February 1944 around Anzio, Italy. The Panther was the most produced German tank of 1944 and 1945. When production ended in April 1945, 6,042 Panthers had been built.

The Ausf. F, or Panther II, was planned in February 1943 and passed running trials in 1944 but never deployed due to the risk of interrupting existing production lines. The main change was a new, small-profile turret, with a pig's head (*Saukopf*) mantelet capable of mounting the same gun as the Tiger II, as well as a stereoscopic rangefinder and gyrostabilizer. The hull side and roof plates also were increased in thickness.

An antitank gun version, the Jagdpanther, was based on an Ausf. G chassis, with the superstructure extended in place of the turret, mounting an L71 main gun with a rangefinder and periscope-telescope sight in a limited traverse mounting. A total of 382 Jagdpanthers were produced by the end of the war. The first deployed to France in spring 1944.

Pz.Kpfw.VIB Tiger II

The requirements for the Tiger II were issued in August 1942, just as the Tiger I was entering production. The Henschel design was accepted in October 1943, and assembly began in December 1943. The Pz.Kpfw.VIB Tiger II mounted the 88 mm L71 gun. The Jagdtiger antitank variant mounted a 128 mm L61 gun in a limited traverse mounting. These weapons could destroy all Allied tanks at all practical ranges, until the last Soviet heavy tank appeared at the end of the war. The turret front of the Tiger II was 180 mm thick, and its upper hull front was 150 mm thick. Even ignoring the effects of the armor's slope, the Tiger II was practically invulnerable to Allied threats, except the British 76 mm discarding-sabot rounds; the U.S. 90 mm composite rigid projectile; and the Soviet

100 mm and 122 mm guns, whose best penetration was about 240 mm at point-blank range. The Jagdtiger mounted 250 mm thick armor on the front of its fighting compartment. Automotively identical to the latest versions of the Tiger I and Panther, except for even wider tracks and staggered, rather than interleaved, road wheels, the Tiger II was about as agile and fast as the Tiger I. At 70 metric tons, it was more difficult to hide, recover, and transport. These risks were compounded by the collapse of the German air force and logistics, just as the Tiger II was fielded. A few were deployed to France and Poland in summer 1944. Some fifty-two were used during the Ardennes offensive in December 1944. Peak usage occurred in February 1945, when 219 were in use. All together, 484 Tiger IIs were delivered before the end of the war.

Bruce Newsome

See also: Blitzkrieg; Panzer Division

Additional Reading

Senger und Etterlin, Frido von. *German Tanks of World War II. The Complete Illustrated History of German Armored Fighting Vehicles 1926–1945.* Translated by J. Lucas. London: Arms and Armour, 1969.

Thoma, Wilhelm von (1891–1948)

Wehrmacht general of panzer troops.

Born on September 11, 1891 at Dachau, Germany, Thoma served as an infantry officer during World War I. During the interwar years, he became a leading theorist of armored warfare, second in the German Army only to General Heinz Guderian. In 1934, Major Thoma took command of Germany's only tank battalion. He then had command of all German ground troops in the Spanish Civil War, from 1936 to 1939. In July 1941, Thoma replaced Lieutenant General Hans Jürgen von Arnim as commander of the 17th Panzer Division in the Soviet Union. In September 1942, Thoma was ordered to North Africa in command of the Afrika Korps. He arrived there in time to participate in the October Battle of El Alamein, when British General Sir Bernard Montgomery's Eighth Army took the offensive against Axis forces. On the death of General Georg Stumme, Thoma briefly commanded Panzerarmee Afrika. Hitler then ordered Field Marshal Erwin Rommel to return to Africa from sick leave and resume command. On his arrival on October 25, Rommel criticized Thoma for his tactics.

On November 4, 1942, complaining of Hitler's "unparalleled madness," Thoma climbed into a tank and raced from one point to another on the front lines in the thick of the battle. His tank was hit several times and caught fire, and Thoma was taken prisoner. Released from prison in early 1948, Thoma died in Söcking, Germany, on April 30, 1948.

Gene Mueller and Spencer C. Tucker

See also: Afrika Korps; Guderian, Heinz; Rommel, Erwin

Additional Reading

Liddell Hart, Basil H. *The German Generals Talk.* New York: William Morrow, 1948.

Tirpitz, Allied Attacks on (1941–1944)

The German battleship *Tirpitz*, sister ship to the *Bismarck*, was named for Admiral

Alfred von Tirpitz, father of the German High Seas Fleet. Built at Wilhelmshaven Navy Yard, it was commissioned on February 25, 1941. The *Tirpitz* displaced 52,600 tons fully loaded, mounted 8×15-inch guns, and had a crew of 2,340 men. British Royal Air Force (RAF) Bomber Command flew 269 sorties in five separate attacks against Willhelmshaven in January 1941, the objective being to destroy the German battleship. On February 28, Bomber Command flew another 116 sorties with the same intent.

The *Tirpitz*, was based in Norway beginning in January 1942. On the night of March 30 to 31 and again on April 27, 1942, the RAF attacked the *Tirpitz* at Föttenfjord, near Trondheim, but no bombs hit the battleship. On September 6, 1943, the *Tirpitz* was involved in its only real offensive action of the war, when it sortied to shell Spitsbergen. On September 22, the British midget submarines *X-6* and *X-7* slipped through German defenses at Kaa Fjord, Norway, and their crews managed to plant mines on the battleship's hull. The explosions severely damaged the *Tirpitz*, but the Germans were able to effect repairs. Then, on April 3, 1944, forty Barracuda aircraft flying from the Royal Navy carriers *Victorious* and *Furious* attacked. The *Tirpitz* took fourteen hits. Though disabled, it remained afloat, and, again, the Germans made repairs.

On September 11, 1944, thirty-eight Lancaster bombers left Scotland for airfields in the northern Soviet Union, from which they staged to attack the *Tirpitz*. On September 15, twenty-seven bombers of RAF Number 9 and Number 617 Squadrons, carrying twenty 12,000-pound armor-piercing Tallboy bombs, took off from Yagodnik, near Archangel, for Kaa Fjord. One Tallboy went through the *Tirpitz*'s forecastle, exploding in its hull. Several other near misses severely damaged the ship's engines. The Germans then decided not to repair the *Tirpitz,* and, on October 15, they moved it to Tromso to serve as a floating heavy artillery battery. On November 12, 1944, RAF Wing Commander Willis Tait led thirty-two Lancasters in an attack that scored three direct hits. One tore a one-hundred-foot hole in the *Tirpitz*'s hull, detonating the magazines and capsizing the battleship. A total of 917 men in its crew died.

William P. Head

See also: *Bismarck*, Sortie and Sinking of

Additional Reading

Zetterling, Niklas, and Michael Tamelander. *Tirpitz: The Life and Death of Germany's Last Super Battleship.* Havertown, PA: Casemate, 2009.

Tobruk, Second Battle of (April 10–November 27, 1941). *See* North Africa Campaign

Tobruk, Third Battle of (June 20–21, 1942). *See* North Africa Campaign

Todt, Fritz (1891–1942)

Third Reich minister for arms and munitions.

Born on September 4, 1891 in Pforzheim, Germany, Todt fought in the German Army during World War I. He subsequently studied engineering. When Hitler came to power in 1933, he appointed Todt head of technology and roadway construction, as chief of what became known as the Organization Todt (OT), a paramilitary construction organization. Todt was involved in every aspect of autobahn construction. With the outbreak of war, the OT provided German forces with a highly skilled corps of engineers to fill Germany's expanding imperium with new roads, bridges, aircraft fields, and fortifications. When Todt was appointed as the Reich's minister for arms and munitions in March 1940 (in addition to his other positions), he controlled all the major technical tasks of the German war effort. Over the next several years, the OT had large numbers of conscript laborers at its disposal. Todt also supervised construction of the Atlantic Wall, intended to repel an anticipated Anglo-American seaborne invasion launched from Britain. Todt died when his plane crashed shortly after takeoff from Rastenburg on the morning of February 9, 1942. Sabotage was suspected but could not be proven. Todt was succeeded by his assistant, Albert Speer.

Peter Overlack

See also: Atlantic Wall; Organization Todt (OT); Speer, Albert

Additional Reading

Speer, Albert. *Inside the Third Reich: Memoirs.* Translated by Richard and Clara Winston. New York: Touchstone, 1997.

Tresckow, Henning von (1901–1944)

Wehrmacht major general and key member of the opposition to Hitler.

Henning von Tresckow was born on January 10, 1901 in Magdeburg. He served as an infantry officer during World War I. After the war, he had no great love for the Weimar Republic and thus sympathized at first with the Nationalist Socialist Party. He welcomed the takeover of the Nazis in 1933. By 1938, however, the Nazi luster had worn off as a result of the November pogroms against the Jews, particularly *Kristallnacht* (the Night of Broken Glass). In December 1940, Tresckow was a staff officer in Army Group B, serving under his uncle, General Fedor von Bock. Nazi brutalities in the Soviet occupied territories, especially the killing of captured Red Army soldiers, further increased Tresckow's resolve to oppose the Nazi regime.

On March 14, 1943, Tresckow and his adjutant, Lieutenant Fabian von Schlabrendorff, planted a bomb on Hitler's plane in Smolensk in the Soviet Union. The bomb failed to go off because of a defective detonator, yet Tresckow and Schlabrendorff remained undetected in the plot. Tresckow's resolve was unshaken: "Hitler is not only the enemy of Germany; he is the enemy of the whole world." In September 1943, Tresckow was chief of staff of the Second Army. By January 1944, he had recruited Colonel Claus von Stauffenberg and engaged former Leipzig mayor Carl Friedrich Goerdeler, a key political opposition leader, to plan what became the July Plot, Operation VALKYRIE. On July 20, 1944, Stauffenberg planted a bomb in the vicinity of Hitler at the *Wolfschanse* bunker. The next day, upon hearing of the failed coup d'état, Tresckow headed toward Krolowy Most, Poland, on the eastern front and committed suicide. His body was cremated at the Sachsenhausen concentration camp.

William H. Van Husen

See also: Bock, Fedor von; Opposition to Hitler, German Military; Stauffenberg, Claus Schenk von

Additional Reading

Galante, Pierre. *Operation Valkyrie: The German Generals' Plot against Hitler.* New York: Harper and Row, 1981.

Tunis-Bizerte, Battle of (May 3–13, 1943). *See* North Africa Campaign

U

Udet, Ernst (1896–1941)

Luftwaffe colonel general.

Born on April 26, 1896 at Frankfurt am Main, Germany, Udet served as a pilot during World War I in Manfred von Richthofen's *Jagdgeschwader* 1 (JG 1), popularly known as the Flying Circus. After Richthofen's death, Udet temporarily commanded JG 1 until Hermann Göring assumed command. Udet ended the war with sixty-two victories, the second highest-scoring German ace. In 1935, Udet became the Luftwaffe's first inspector of fighters. He later became director of armaments, overseeing technical development. Udet was a brilliant flyer and technically proficient, but ill-suited for administration. Consequently, German industry continually failed to meet production goals. The situation was so serious by the spring of 1941 that Herman Göring replaced Udet with Erhard Milch. After having become the scapegoat for the Luftwaffe's failures over Britain and elsewhere, a despondent Udet committed suicide in Berlin on November 17, 1941.

Rodney Madison

See also: Göring, Hermann; Jeschonnek, Hans; Milch, Erhard

Additional Reading

Ishoven, Armand van. *The Fall of an Eagle: The Life of Fighter Ace Ernst Udet.* London: W. Kimber, 1979.

Ukraine Campaign, Soviet (November 6, 1943–July 27, 1944)

In late 1943, German forces in the Ukraine were on the defensive. During August to November 1943, the Soviet 1st, 2nd, 3rd, and 4th Ukrainian Fronts pushed back German Field Marshal Erich von Manstein's Army Group South from the Donets River to the Dnieper River. On November 6, General Nikolai Vatutin's 1st Ukrainian Front took the Ukrainian capital of Kiev, and, by the beginning of December, Soviet forces crossed the Dnieper. The Soviets then committed massive forces to liberate the remainder of Ukraine.

On November 11, 1943, German units launched a counterattack toward Kiev, but the drive died out by December 31. Manstein feared that Army Group South would be cut off, and he requested permission from Hitler to withdraw from the Dnieper bend, but Hitler refused. On January 5, 1944, Army General Ivan Konev's 2nd Ukrainian Front drove southwest from the vicinity of Cherkassy. Simultaneous with Konev's attack, the 1st Ukrainian Front on January 27, 1944 began the Rovno-Lutsk operation to separate Army Group South from Army Group Center. On February 29, Vatutin was fatally wounded by Ukrainian partisans. Marshal Georgii Zhukov took command of the 1st Ukrainian Front, and, on March 4, he began an offensive from Shepetovka toward the juncture between the First and Fourth Panzer Armies. The 1st

Ukrainian Front entered Tarnopol on March 9, outflanking German forces on the Bug River, which Konev's 2nd Ukrainian Front forces reached three days later. Zhukov's 1st Ukrainian Front reached the Dniester River at the end of March. Farther south, the 3rd Ukrainian Front drove back the reconstituted German Sixth Army to the Bug, sealing off the Crimean Peninsula.

On March 30, Hitler relieved Manstein and replaced him with Field Marshal Walther Model. Hitler also redesignated the two army groups in the south. Army Group South became Army Group North Ukraine, and Army Group A became Army Group South Ukraine. When Zhukov's armor reached the Carpathian Mountains, it effectively cut the German front in two. General Rodion Malinovsky's 3rd Ukrainian Front retook the Black Sea port of Odessa on April 10. Hitler then relieved Field Marshal Ewald von Kleist of command of Army Group South Ukraine, replacing him with General Ferdinand Schröder.

Stavka (the Soviet High Command) had committed all six of its tank armies in the Ukrainian operation, but now began to transfer units, including four tank armies, to Operation BAGRATION—the destruction of Army Group Center in Belorussia, which began on June 22, 1944. The Soviets retook the remainder of the Ukraine from the Germans following the Battle of Brody-Lwów on July 13 to 27, 1944.

Claude R. Sasso and Spencer C. Tucker

See also: Belorussia Offensive, Soviet; Crimea Campaign, Soviet; Kleist, Paul Ewald von; Manstein, Erich von; Model, Walther; Schörner, Ferdinand

Additional Reading

Glantz, David M., and Jonathan House. *When Titans Clashed: How the Red Army Stopped Hitler*. Lawrence: University Press of Kansas, 1995.

Melvin, Mungo. *Manstein: Hitler's Greatest General*. London: Weidenfeld & Nicolson, 2010.

Undeclared Naval War with the United States (September 1939–December 1941)

The Undeclared Naval War was a series of provocative political actions, diplomatic decisions, and naval engagements between the German Kriegsmarine and the United States Navy prior to the formal declaration of war. This state of quasibelligerency resulted from the dilemmas faced by German Chancellor Adolf Hitler and President Franklin Delano Roosevelt. Hitler wanted to keep the United States out of the war, at least until achieving victory over the Soviet Union, while preventing or limiting the support the United States was giving to Great Britain and its allies. President Roosevelt had campaigned on the promise to keep the United States out of the war, but he was under pressure from interventionists and Winston Churchill to render ever greater support to the Allies.

On September 3, 1939, the *U-30* sunk the British passenger liner *Athenia*, killing twenty-eight Americans. Two days later, Roosevelt authorized "Plain English" naval patrols (neutrality patrols), in which U.S. Navy ships shadowed German ships and radioed updates of their locations to headquarters in English, facilitating interception by British and Canadian patrols. On October 3, the Declaration of Panama established a "security zone" of three hundred to one thousand miles around the Americas, south of Canada, which had a negative impact on Germany.

On April 11, 1941, in what is often called the first shot in the undeclared naval war, though it was most likely a false contact, U.S.S. *Niblack* (DD-424) while picking up survivors of a freighter that had been sunk several hours earlier made sonar contact with what it thought was a U-boat, five hundred miles southwest of Iceland. It made a depth charge run, hit nothing, and returned to port. A week later, U.S. Admiral Ernest King extended the security zone to longitude 26 degrees west, encompassing Greenland.

On May 21, 1941, the *U-69* sunk the U.S.-flagged freighter *Robin Moor* in the South Atlantic on its way to Cape Town. U.S. public response to this first attack and sinking of a U.S. ship by Germany was muted. The incident, however, marked the first German provocation in the face of numerous episodes of U.S. goading. Subsequently, Roosevelt's June 6, 1941 congressional authorization to commandeer about eighty German merchant vessels stranded by the war in U.S. ports stipulated no restriction against handing them over to Great Britain.

Executing a June 16, 1941 directive to expand the security zone, thereby overlapping the German blockade zone, U.S. Marines occupied Iceland on July 7 under an agreement concluded between the two countries. Less than two weeks later, Admiral King ordered the U. S. Navy to escort convoys during the United States–Iceland stretch of the North Atlantic and to attack U-boats even two hundred or three hundred miles away.

On September 4, 1941, the *U-652* fired three torpedoes at the U.S.S. *Greer* (*DD-145*), after the destroyer had been shadowing the submarine all day and reposting its position to the British. The *Greer* responded by dropping eight depth charges, inflicting minor damage on the U-boat. On September 11, 1941, Roosevelt ordered escorts to "shoot on sight" all German and Italian ships that entered the security zone.

On October 16, 1941, four hundred miles south of Iceland, the U.S.S. *Kearny* (*DD-432*) was torpedoed by the *U-568*. Eleven sailors were killed, and twenty-four were injured. Though damaged, the ship made it back to port under its own power. Coming to the scene of a fifty-merchant ship convoy under attack by a wolf pack, the *Kearny* had attempted to sink the U-boats or drive them off. The U.S. government made no official protest. On October 31, six hundred miles west of Ireland, the *U-552* sank the destroyer U.S.S. *Reuben James* (*DD-245*), killing 115 out of 160 sailors. While escorting a convoy, the *Reuben James* had been investigating a suspected direction finder bearing when it was hit. Because the U-boat was being tracked, its attack was self-defense.

On November 24, in what turned out to be the final act before declared war, and based on an agreement between the Netherlands government-in-exile and the United States, Roosevelt announced that U.S. forces would be sent to Dutch Guiana to prevent Germany from gaining access to bauxite, from which aluminum used in manufacturing aircraft is made. The German press, which asserted that the Netherlands government established under the German occupation was the legitimate "owner" of the Dutch colonies, labeled the occupation as U.S. aggression in South America. On December 11, 1941, Germany finally declared war on the United States in support of Japan, which had attacked the United States at Pearl Harbor, Hawaii, four days earlier.

Kevin S. Bemel

See also: Atlantic, Battle of the; Submarines

Additional Reading

Bailey, Thomas A., and Paul B. Ryan. *Hitler vs. Roosevelt: The Undeclared Naval War.* New York: Free Press, 1979.

Morison, Samuel Eliot. *The Battle of the Atlantic, 1939–1943.* Edison, NJ: Castle Books, 2001.

V

V-1 Buzz Bomb. *See* Rockets, Guided Bombs, and Guided Missiles

V-2 Guided Missile. *See* Rockets, Guided Bombs, and Guided Missiles

Vietinghoff genannt Scheel, Heinrich von (1887–1952)

Wehrmacht colonel general.

Born on December 6, 1887 at Mainz, Germany, Heinrich Vietinghoff genannt Scheel served on both the eastern and western fronts during World War I. In September 1939, he commanded the 5th Panzer Division during the invasion of Poland. During Operation BARBAROSSA, the invasion of Russia, he commanded the XLVI Panzer Corps under Army Group Center. From December 1941 to August 1943, Vietinghoff commanded the Fifteenth Army on the Channel coast in France.

In August 1943, he assumed command of the Tenth Army in Italy, and, in October 1944, he temporarily replaced Field Marshal Albert Kesselring as commander of Army Group C when the latter was injured in a car crash. In January 1945, Vietinghoff assumed command of Army Group Kurland in East Prussia. In early March 1945, he returned to Italy as German supreme commander, after Kesselring became supreme commander west. Vietinghoff and SS General Karl Wolff met in secret talks with Allied representatives in Switzerland regarding a separate surrender of German forces in Italy, which went into effect on May 2, 1945. Taken prisoner by the Allies, Vietinghoff was held until 1948. Following the war, he served as an advisor to the Adenauer government on the issues of German rearmament. Vietinghoff died at Pfronten-Ried, Germany on February 25, 1952.

Alessandro Massignani

See also: Kesselring, Albert; Wolff, Karl

Additional Reading

Graham, Dominick, and Shelford Bidwell. *Tug of War: The Battle for Italy, 1943–45.* New York: St. Martin's Press, 1986.

Volksgrenadier (1944–1945)

Volksgrenadiers were Wehrmacht light divisions established in the autumn of 1944 based on the older tradition of the grenadier division. The prefix "Volk" was added to appeal to German nationalism in the waning months of World War II and to show that "the people" were actively involved in the defense of the Fatherland. A Volksgrenadier division had less manpower and weaponry than a regular infantry division, as the Wehrmacht assumed a more defensive role on its long retreat back to Germany on both the western and eastern fronts.

Not to be confused with the Volkssturm, militia units in which all German men age sixteen to sixty were required to join in late 1944, the Volksgrenadier divisions also drew their manpower from these same ranks. Much of their manpower, however, came from the *Ersatzheer* (Replacement Army) and the remnants of weakened or destroyed divisions. These units were subsequently fleshed out with convalescing soldiers unfit for combat, as well as personnel seconded from the Luftwaffe and the Kriegsmarine and ethnic Germans living in the conquered territories. These Volksgrenadier troops were armed mostly with short-range light automatic and semi-automatic weapons, mortars, shoulder-fired rocket launchers, and handheld antitank weapons. The Volksgrenadier divisions were mostly deployed along Germany's western border.

Steven B. Rogers

See also: *Volkssturm*

Additional Reading

Thomas, Nigel. *The German Army, 1939–45: Western Front, 1944–45*. Vol. 5. London: Osprey, 2000.

Volkssturm (1944–1945)

The mobilization of all German civilian males ages sixteen to sixty to defend the Third Reich during the final months of World War II.

Hitler established the *Volkssturm* (People's Storm) on September 25, 1944 in a desperate attempt to strengthen German resistance to the Allied forces engulfing Germany. The Nazi leadership believed that the Volkssturm would act as a national militia and could augment the Wehrmacht to defend every city and village across the Fatherland. While an eclectic range of men did answer their Führer's call, the average *Volkssturmmann* was a laborer in his forties who was unprepared and untrained for combat. While the Volkssturm used whatever weapons they could find, which included foreign and captured arms, one of the most iconic weapons they employed was the *Panzerfaust* antitank rocket launcher. Many Volkssturm units surrendered to U.S. or British troops on the western front. The eastern front was a different story, where the average Volkssturmmann fought with greater tenacity against the Russians, especially in the Battle of Berlin.

Edward Gutiérrez

See also: Berlin, Land Battle for

Additional Reading

Yeltin, David K. *Hitler's Volkssturm: The Nazi Militia and the Fall of Germany 1944–1945*. Lawrence: University Press of Kansas, 2002.

Vyazma-Bryansk, Battle of (October 2–21, 1941). *See* Moscow, Battle of

W

Waffen-SS (1939–1945)

The Waffen-SS was the military component of the German Schutzstaffel (SS) that fought alongside the Wehrmacht as a separate and elite National Socialist force. Originally a branch of the paramilitary Nazi *Sturmabteilungen* (Storm Detachments, SA), the SS initially functioned as a bodyguard unit for the Nazi hierarchy. Party leader Adolf Hitler appointed Heinrich Himmler as the Reichsführer-SS in 1929, and Himmler increased SS membership from 280 to 50,000 and put its members into a distinctive black uniform, characterized by the skull and crossed-bones and double runic *S* insignia. Himmler's aim was to transform the SS from its security function within the Nazi Party into a separate and powerful bureaucratic organ of the German state.

Between 1933 and 1936, Himmler combined all state police functions to establish the Reichssicherheitshauptamt (Reich Main Security Office, RSHA). Himmler had much higher ambitions for the SS than mere police functions. He wanted it to be a professional military body that might one day subsume the German Army itself. As its political and bureaucratic functions expanded, the SS formed illegal military units, originally known as Verfügungstruppe, or special assignment troops. On March 17, 1933, Josef "Sepp" Dietrich established, on Hitler's direct order, a personal armed guard, the Leibstandarte. Early on, members of the unit served, among other things, as honor guards and color guards at parades and other events. The 1934 Nuremberg Rally involved Dietrich's SS Leibstandarte Adolf Hitler (LAH) composed of twenty-six hundred men. But Himmler also used such units for liquidating the leadership of the SA during the "Night of the Long Knives" Blood Purge of June 1934. Early armed SS personnel also included concentration camp guards, the SS-Totenkopfverbände (Death's Head Formations), organized by Theodor Eicke. After Germany introduced conscription in 1935, the SS organized two five-thousand-man Verfügungstruppe regiments, "Deutschland" and "Germania."

On August 17, 1938, a decree by Hitler set up a separate headquarters for the military training of the SS units and established their military character as armed SS units. For obvious reasons, the leaders of the Army High Command (OKH) rejected the idea of another military establishment independent of its authority and had some success in limiting its size. By the eve of the war, there were only about twenty-three thousand men in the armed SS formations, including the Death's Head groups. But with the coming of the war, the size and scope of SS activities increased dramatically. During the Poland Campaign of September 1939, Waffen-SS regiments were integrated within regular Wehrmacht divisions. In October, the first three SS divisions were formed, one each from the Verfügungstruppe (later known as SS Das Reich Division), the Death's Head units (SS Totenkopf Division), and the police (Polizedivision). Hitler's Leibstandarte, initially a motorized regiment, became a fourth Waffen-SS division (SS Leibstandarte Adolf Hitler). In November 1939, the various SS branches were united under the name Waffen-SS.

Waffen-SS divisions were fully integrated into the regular army command structure, but that did not lessen the tension between regular army and SS commanders. The SS divisions were highly politicized and supported the National Socialist racial policies, especially in Eastern Europe. During the war, they were guilty of numerous atrocities and war crimes. There was also anger in the army over the fact that the SS units had claim on the best weaponry. Sharp tensions and inefficiencies also existed within SS headquarters, where Himmler mirrored his master in practicing a divide-and-rule style of leadership.

The Waffen-SS role was greatly expanded after the German invasion of the Soviet Union began in June 1941, where the Waffen-SS played a paramount role during this ideological war of annihilation. Waffen-SS units fought on all battlefronts in which Germany was engaged, with the exception of the Western Desert campaigns in North Africa. By the end of the war, when the total number in the SS mounted to more than eight hundred thousand men in thirty-eight divisions, some two hundred thousand were foreign volunteers (*Freiwilligen*). This practice of recruitment was accepted,

Dutch volunteer of the Waffen-SS trained as a sniper, 1941. Note the SS lightning-bolt rune insignia on the left side of the helmet. A very large percentage of the Waffen-SS troops were not ethnic Germans. (ullstein bild via Getty Images)

despite the SS pretense of representing only the most racially pure Germanic elements.

In all, as many as three hundred and fourteen thousand Waffen-SS soldiers may have been killed during the course of the war. During the International Military Tribunal at Nuremberg, the Waffen-SS was convicted of being a criminal organization. Conscripts from 1943 onward, who had not volunteered to join the Waffen-SS, were exempted from that judgment.

Neville Panthaki

See also: Dietrich, Josef "Sepp"; Einsatzgruppen; Himmler, Heinrich; Night of the Long Knives; Reichssicherheitshauptamt (Reich Main Security Office); Sturmabteilungen (SA)

Additional Reading

Gilbert, Adrian. *Waffen-SS: Hitler's Army at War*. New York: Da Capo Press, 2019.

Höhne, Heinz. *The Order of the Death's Head: The Story of Hitler's SS*. New York: Coward-McCann, 1970.

Reitlinger, Gerald. *The SS: Alibi of a Nation, 1922–1945*. Cambridge, MA: Da Capo Press, 1989.

Warlimont, Walter (1894–1976)

Wehrmacht general of artillery.

Born in Osnabrück, Germany, on October 3, 1894, Warlimont served as a battery commander during World War I. In 1927, he was the second adjutant to General Werner von Blomberg, chief of the Truppenamt, the covert General Staff. In 1929, he served as an exchange officer with the U.S. Army, while studying U.S. methods of industrial mobilization. He also married an American. In September 1938, Warlimont was appointed to head the National Defense Section (L Section) while also serving as deputy chief of the Operations Staff of the recently established *Oberkommando der Wehrmacht* (OKW—Armed Forces High Command). During World War II, Warlimont's significance lay in the fact that he attended most of the major command conferences and drafted the bulk of the principal operational plans and directives. The latter included the infamous Commissar Order. Warlimont was injured in the July 20, 1944 bomb plot against Hitler. Warlimont was not trusted by Hitler, and he was held in low esteem by certain field commanders because of his lack of combat experience in World War II. Warlimont was arrested by the Americans in 1945 and tried at the American Military Tribunals in Nuremberg for war crimes and crimes against humanity. Convicted, he was sentenced to life imprisonment. His sentence was reduced in 1951, and he was released six years later. He died on October 9, 1976 in Kreuth, Germany.

Jon D. Berlin

See also: Blomberg, Werner von; Commissar Order

Additional Reading

Megargee, Geoffrey P. *Inside Hitler's High Command*. Lawrence: University Press of Kansas, 2000.

Warlimont, Walter. *Inside Hitler's Headquarters, 1939–1945*. Translated by R. H. Barry. Novato, CA: Presidio, 1990.

Warsaw, Battle and Siege of (September 8–28, 1939). *See* Poland Campaign

Warsaw Ghetto Uprising (April 19–May 16, 1943)

Known in German as the *Aufstand im Warschauer Ghetto*, the Warsaw Ghetto

Uprising was an armed attempt by the Jews of Polish capital to block deportations to the concentration camps. Through the summer of 1942, the Germans deported or executed more than three hundred thousand Warsaw Jews, leaving between fifty-five thousand to sixty thousand people in the Ghetto. Resolved to fight back, the remaining inhabitants of the ghetto formed the Jewish Fighting Organization (Żobydska Organizacja Bojowa—ŻOB). The ŻOB's commander was Mordechai Anielewicz. The Jews in the ghetto never had more than one thousand fighters.

Lightly armed and poorly trained for combat, the ŻOB conducted its first attack against a small German *Aktion* (the German euphemism for an operation to round up and deport those destined for concentration camps) on January 18, 1943. The Germans returned in force in April to liquidate the Ghetto completely. On April 19, 1943, Waffen-SS, police, and Wehrmacht units moved into the Ghetto to complete the January operation. Ultimately, the German task force consisted of 2,090 troops armed with tanks, armored cars, artillery, mortars, and machine guns. The main element of the German force consisted of 821 panzergrenadier troops from six Waffen-SS reserve and training battalions.

As the brutal fighting continued, the Germans finally destroyed the ŻOB command post at Miła Street 18 on May 8. The last Jewish resistance was crushed on May 16. SS-Brigadeführer Jürgen Stroop, the police chief of Warsaw, acknowledged in his final report that sixteen of his troops were killed and eighty-five wounded; deaths among the Ghetto's remaining inhabitants ran into the thousands, with roughly fifty thousand taken into custody and either shot outright or deported. Although some members of the underground Polish Home Army (*Armia Krajowa*—AK) assisted the ŻOB during the ghetto uprising, the majority did not participate in the fighting, waiting instead for their own revolt, which would come in August 1944.

David M. Toczek

See also: Himmler, Heinrich; Stroop, Jürgen; Waffen-SS; Warsaw Rising

Additional Reading

Gutman, Israel. *Resistance: The Warsaw Ghetto Uprising.* Boston: Houghton Mifflin, 1994.

Warsaw Rising (August 1–October 2, 1944)

By the summer of 1944, the Red Army had pushed the German Army almost completely out of the Soviet Union and continued moving west across German-occupied Poland. The Soviets, however, had split with the London-based Polish government-in-exile and established their own Communist provisional government. As the Soviet troops advanced, they disarmed the Polish Home Army (*Armia Krajowa*—AK), a branch of the London-based government. On July 26, the London Poles ordered AK commander General Tadeusz Bór-Komorowski to capture Warsaw from the Germans before the Soviets arrived. The AK had around forty thousand fighters in Warsaw, and they were desperately short of arms and ammunition. The German garrison in Warsaw numbered more than twenty-six thousand well-equipped, combat-experienced troops, which, during the course of the battel grew to fifty thousand, including three Waffen-SS divisions and two Wehrmacht panzer divisions. The overall German commander was SS Obergruppenführer Erich von dem

Bach-Zelewski. The AK's Operation BURZA (TEMPEST) began on August 1, 1944. The lead units of the Red Army were only some twelve miles away, closing in on the east bank of the Vistula River. The savage street fighting ground on for weeks. SS chief Heinrich Himmler ordered that the entire city be "razed to the ground" and all its inhabitants killed as an object lesson to all other cities under German occupation.

On September 10, Red Army units under General Konstantin Rokossovsky finally moved into Warsaw's Praga district on the east bank of the Vistula. After five days of heavy fighting, the Soviets consolidated their positions on the east bank and ceased to advance. Not only did the Soviets provide no further support to the AK forces fighting desperately on the other side of the river, they also refused permission for Western Allied aircraft to land on Soviet airfields after making supply drops to the beleaguered insurgents. Bór-Komorowski and his surviving fighters finally surrendered to Bach-Zelewski on October 2, after sixty-three days of fierce resistance. Some fifteen thousand insurgents and one hundred and fifty thousand Polish civilians died during the rising. Another seven hundred thousand of Warsaw's inhabitants were sent to concentration or slave labor camps, where two hundred and forty-five thousand later died. Approximately 93 percent of the city was a featureless pile of rubble.

The Germans lost about ten thousand killed during the fighting. Shortly after suppressing the rising, the German army withdrew from Warsaw at its own pace, and the Red Army followed it into the city. Soviet commanders later claimed that stiff German resistance and the lack of supplies had prevented them from giving the AK any more support. Many historians, however, have suggested that the Soviet commanders were following specific orders from their leader, Josef Stalin, who wanted the German Army to eliminate any Polish opposition to the establishment of a postwar government under Moscow's control.

David T. Zabecki

See also: Bach-Zelewski, Erich von dem; Himmler, Heinrich; Waffen-SS

Additional Reading

Ciechanowski, Jan M. *The Warsaw Rising of 1944.* Cambridge, MA: Cambridge University Press, 2002.

Warships, Surface (1938–1945)

Germany's surface warships in the twentieth century had a reputation for robust construction, heavy armor, and damage-limiting internal compartmentalization. During the interwar period, Germany developed innovative propulsion systems and new shipbuilding techniques. Much of the innovation was driven by navy commander Admiral Erich Raeder, who, upon taking over in 1928, initiated a two-pole strategy based on long-range ships to attack enemy commerce and shorter-ranged but powerful combatants to protect Germany's coastal waters and shoreline. Widespread use of welding, as opposed to riveting, reduced labor hours and hull weight, accelerating ship construction and allowing warship designs to incorporate more capability within the same displacement. The introduction of diesel-engine propulsion in warships and commercial shipping extended the ships' ranges and reduced operating costs. The Deutschland-class armored ships, often called pocket battleships, employed diesel engines and welded construction, giving them an operating range exceeding ten thousand nautical

Table 1: Battleships and Battle Cruisers

Ship Type	Class	First Launched	# Built	Main Battery Armament	Max. Armor	Propulsion	Top Speed	Max. Range
Battle Cruiser	Scharnhorst	1936	2	9x280 mm	350 mm	Steam Turbine 3 shafts	31 kts	7,100 nm
Battleship	Bismarck	1939	2	9x380 mm	380 mm	Steam Turbine 3 shafts	30.1 kts	8,870 nm

Table 2: Armored, Heavy, and Light Cruisers

Type of Cruiser	Class	First Launched	# Built	Main Battery	Max. Armor	Propulsion	Top Speed	Max. Range
Light	Emden	1925	1	8 × 150 mm	55 mm	Steam 2 shafts	29 kts	5,300 nm
Light	Karlsruhe	1927	3	9 × 150 mm	77 mm	Combined Diesel & Steam 3 shafts	32 kts	5,200 nm
Light	Leipzig	1929	1	9 × 150 mm	55 mm	Combined Diesel & Steam 3 shafts	32 kts	5,700 nm
Armored	Deutschland	1931	1	6 × 280 mm	100 mm	Diesel 2 shafts	26 kts	10,000 nm
Light	Nürnberg	1934	1	9 × 150 mm	55 mm	Combined Diesel & Steam 3 shafts	32 kts	5,700 nm
Armored	Admiral Graf Spee	1934	2	6 × 280 mm	130 mm	Diesel 2-shafts	26 kts	9,000 nm
Heavy	Admiral Hipper	1937	3	8 × 03 mm	170 mm	Steam 3 shafts	32.5 kts	6,800 nm
Heavy	Prinz Eugen	1938	1	8 × 203 mm	180 mm	Steam 3 shafts	32.5 kts	6,800 nm

Table 3: Destroyers

Class	First Launched	# Built	Main Gun Armament	AAW Weapons	ASW Weapons	Propulsion	Top Speed	Max. Range
1934 Destroyer	1935	16	5 × 128 mm	4 × 37 mm	Depth Charges	Steam 2-shafts	38.5 kts	4,400 nm
1936 Destroyer	1937	6	5 × 128 mm	3 × 37 mm	Depth Charges	Steam 2-shafts	38 kts	4,450 nm
1935 Torpedo Boat	1938	12	1 × 105 mm	3 × 20 mm	Depth Charges	Steam 2-shafts	35.5 kts	2,680 nm
1936A Destroyer	1939	8	4-5 × 150 mm	6 × 37 mm 6–8 × 20 mm	Depth Charges	Steam 2-shafts	38.5 kts	5,000 nm
1937 Torpedo Boat	1939	9	1 × 105 mm	2 × 37 mm	Depth Charges	Steam 2-shafts	35.5 kts	3,000 nm
1936A (Mob) Destroyer	1941	7	5 × 150 mm	6 × 37 mm 8 × 20 mm	Depth Charges	Steam 2-shafts	38.5kts	5,000 nm
1939 Torpedo Boat	1941	15	4 × 105 mm	7–9 × 20 mm	Depth Charges	Steam 2-shafts	33.5 kts	5,000 nm
1936B Destroyer	1942	8	5 × 128 mm	6 × 37 mm 13 × 20 mm	Depth Charges	Steam 2-shafts	38 kts	5,000 nm

miles on a fuel load that would take a steam-powered ship slightly more than half that distance. The Königsberg and later classes of light cruisers were the first modern warships to have combined diesel-steam propulsion. The resulting cruisers had greater range and better armor protection than their counterparts but later suffered hull cracks in heavy seas when their antiaircraft armament was reinforced after 1941.

Raeder also initiated development of exceptionally high-pressured steam plants for warships, rushing them into construction before the testing was complete. Using steam pressures exceeding one thousand pounds per square inch provided exceptionally high power densities, resulting in destroyers with top speeds exceeding thirty-eight knots. Remembering how German destroyers were outgunned in World War I, he directed the installation of 150 mm guns on the destroyers built in the 1930s. Although that gave them far superior firepower over their British and Soviet opponents, it came at the expense of sea handling, since the excess weight forward made them poor gun platforms in any kind of seaway. The experiment was abandoned in all destroyers built after 1938. The steam plants also proved troublesome and difficult to maintain, and they often failed under arduous wartime conditions. Destroyer operational ready rates fell by 40 percent by 1941 because of propulsion system problems and remained a major problem until a special committee, formed that year, developed a set of solutions that eventually corrected the problems with new construction and maintenance procedures introduced in late 1942.

Germany was unique among the major powers in World War II in building a class of small destroyers (less than one thousand tons standard displacement) designed as torpedo boats, which sacrificed gun armament for torpedoes and high speed. Intended to engage enemy ships in the North and Baltic Seas, they were comparatively inexpensive but often fought at a tactical disadvantage, due to their inadequate gun armament and Germany's faulty torpedo problems, which were not solved until 1942. The ships also handled poorly in heavy seaways, but with speeds approaching forty knots, they should have proven dangerous opponents in preradar nighttime engagements.

Admiral Raeder planned to build a force of super battleships with the necessary range to lead surface raiding groups against enemy commerce across the globe. However, the war's early outbreak precluded their construction. Instead, Germany fought the war with the two battleships and two battle cruisers whose construction had started in the 1930s. The armament, armor, and hull subdivisions of the two Bismarck-class ships made them very robust, and their main and secondary batteries made them among the most powerful ships of their day. Unlike other countries' battleships, the Bismarck-class units had an extensive hydrophone array and active sonars to warn of incoming torpedoes and submarines, respectively. But their armor distribution and reliance on three propellers for propulsion made them vulnerable to underwater damage. The propulsion system's design streamlined the hull, giving the ships an additional one to two knots of speed, but could not produce the "twisting motion" that enabled twin- and quadruple-propeller designs to reduce turning radius or, when necessary, compensate for rudder damage.

The two battle cruisers had a similar propulsion system design, armor distribution, and antiaircraft armament as the battleships. Their main battery and secondary armament were simply an expansion on those of the Deutschland-class, since the design to

German battleship *Bismarck* seen from the German heavy cruiser *Prinz Eugen*, May 1941. The Royal Navy sunk the *Bismarck* on May 27. (ullstein bild via Getty Images)

build them came after the weapons had already been ordered for a fourth pocket battleship. Range and speed were exceptional, and the ships' hydrophone arrays saved them from torpedo attack more than once. They had comparatively successful careers as surface raiders, but they suffered from Germany's failure to update their electronic sensor systems continuously. That left them at a severe disadvantage in both surface-to-surface and air-defense engagements after 1942.

Germany built only four heavy cruisers before and during World War II, but the three that actually served in combat operations had better protection, slightly more surface firepower, and a more extensive antiaircraft armament than their British opponents, primarily because of their welded construction and the fact they exceeded the 1921 Washington Naval Treaty limits of ten thousand tons standard displacement. Those advantages, however, came at the expense of range, because they were built for engaging French naval units in the North Sea or English Channel. That mission never arose, and their range proved inadequate for the surface-raiding role they ultimately had to perform.

One area in which Germany dominated in the war's early years was in the design and employment of fast attack craft. Called Schnellbooten (Fast Boats), these small (less than 150 tons) units were powered by turbocharged diesel engines, heavily armed for their size and exceptionally fast. After 1940, they had armor protection around the pilothouse, making them very robust and dangerous platforms.

Although Germany built a vast array of radar warning devices during the war, Admiral Raeder's belief that radar would not have a significant impact on naval operations led the Kriegsmarine to suspend radar research from 1940 to 1942. Grand Admiral Karl Dönitz reversed that decision in March 1943, but the resulting new radars did not enter service until late 1944. By then, Germany's maritime and strategic situation was such that "sensor-equality" made little difference.

Carl O. Schuster

See also: *Bismarck*, Sortie and Sinking of; Dönitz, Karl; Plan Z; Raeder, Erich

Additional Reading

Groener, Erich, et al. *German Warships 1915–1945.* Vols. I & II. Annapolis, MD: U.S. Naval Institute Press, 1991.

Wehrmacht (German Armed Forces) (1935–1945)

The Wehrmacht was the official name of the German armed forces during the National Socialist regime. It was formed as the successor to the interwar Reichswehr on March 16, 1935 and was formally dissolved by the Allied Control Council Law No 34 on August 20, 1946, more than one year after Third Reich's unconditional surrender. The Wehrmacht consisted of three primary branches: the army (*Heer*), air force (*Luftwaffe*) and navy (*Kriegsmarine*). Initially, the Reich defense minister, Field Marshal Werner von Blomberg, was the commander in chief of the Wehrmacht.

With the Blomberg-Fritsch Crisis in January 1938, Hitler consolidated his personal control over the Wehrmacht by dismissing Blomberg and assuming his military and political functions. As a result, the Wehrmacht lost relative autonomy in the National Socialist system. At the same time, Hitler replaced the commander in chief of the army, General Werner von Fritsch, who was falsely accused of homosexual activities, with Colonel General Walther von Brauchitsch, a man much more willing than Fritsch to accept Hitler's leadership. The Reichs Defense Ministry was changed to *Oberkommando der Wehrmacht* (OKW), General Wilhelm Keitel, was appointed the chief of OKW, but he had no direct command authority. He was responsible for ensuring that soldiers and material were available for intelligence, prisoners of war, and general administration. With this splitting of command powers, no single military leader was responsible either for an overview of the strategic situation or for the armed forces as a whole.

At the start of World War II the SS-Verfügungstruppe (redesignated the Waffen-SS on December 1, 1939) was subordinated operationally to the commander in chief of the army, becoming a constant source of tension and controversy between the different Wehrmacht and SS organizations. The next great change in command structure was a consequence of the failed campaign against the Soviet Union. During the 1941 winter crisis, Hitler forced Brauchitsch to retire and assumed the direct position of commander in chief of the army. This move was widely welcomed in the officer corps initially. From that point on, the chief of staff of the army, Colonel General Franz Halder, and the chief of the replacement army, Colonel General Friedrich Fromm, were directly subordinated to Hitler. A further separation of responsibilities had an important effect on German strategic effectiveness. The eastern front was placed under the High Command of the Army (*Oberkommando des Heeres*—OKH), while OKW's operations staff, under General Alfred Jodl, assumed control of all other theatres.

The last change in the Wehrmacht's command structure occurred in July 1944. Following the successful Allied landings in

Normandy and the Soviet crushing of Army Group Center, Hitler started to transfer powers from the Wehrmacht to his most loyal followers. On July 13, Hitler cut the powers of military commanders in the rear areas when fighting on Reich soil, passing them to the Nazi Party's regional political leaders, the gauleiters. Two days later, Reichsführer-SS Heinrich Himmler received responsibility for fifteen newly raised army divisions, giving him control over these units comparable to that he exercised over his Waffen-SS. This change proved decisive in motivating the officers linked to the July 20 assassination plot to act against Hitler. Furthermore, it makes clear that the last change in command structure was already in motion before the July 20 assassination attempt, though it certainly gained momentum with the plotters' failure. Hitler replaced Fromm with Himmler, who now commanded 2.5 million soldiers, including six hundred thousand in the Waffen-SS and 1.9 million in the Ersatzheer. Propaganda Minister Josef Goebbels became *Generalbevollmächtigter für den totalen Kriegseinsatz* (Plenipotentiary for the Total War) on July 25, 1944. With the establishment of the Volkssturm on September 25, 1944, another army was created, although regular officers were used only for training. The gauleiters were responsible for deployment and command, frequently relying on the cadre of local party organizations such as the Strurmabteilungen (SA), the SS, or the Hitler Youth (Hitler-Jugend—HJ) in these roles. As chief of the replacement army, Himmler was responsible for training and equipment, while head of the Nazi Party Chancellery, Martin Bormann, received the power to issue political and organizational ordinances. The organizational chaos of the German armed forces in this last stage of the war limited the effective use of its resources.

During the war, some 17.3 million soldiers went through the ranks of the Wehrmacht. Of those, 13.6 million served in the army, 2.5 million in the Luftwaffe and 1.2 million in the navy. This number does not include personnel who did not achieve the status of soldier, such as men of auxiliary organizations (Wehrmachtsgefolge) like the Reich Labor Service (*Reichsarbeitsdienst*), Organization Todt, the Air Protection Warning Service, the German Red Cross, police serving in their specialized units, members of the Volkssturm, and most of the non-German manpower. The most important group of non-Germans was captured Soviet soldiers who became *Hiwis* ("voluntary helpers") or who joined the Eastern volunteer units (*Osteinheiten*). Also not formally part of the Wehrmacht were the nine hundred thousand men who fought in the Waffen-SS. According to the latest research, 5.3 million soldiers (including Waffen-SS) died—nearly half of them after July 1944.

Adrian E. Wettstein

See also: Blomberg, Werner von; Blomberg-Fritsch Crisis; Brauchitsch, Walther von; Fritsch, Werner von; Fromm, Friedrich; Halder, Franz; Jodl, Alfred; Keitel, Wilhelm; *Oberkommando der Wehrmacht* (OKW); *Oberkommando des Heeres* (OKH); Waffen-SS

Additional Reading

Megargee, Geoffrey P. *Inside Hitler's High Command*. Lawrence: University Press of Kansas, 2000.

U.S. War Department Handbook on German Military Forces (reprint of Technical Manual 30–451. Washington, DC: Government

Printing Office, 1945). Baton Rouge: Louisiana State University Press, 1990.

Weichs zur Glon, Maximilian von (1881–1954)

Wehrmacht field marshal.

Born in Dessau, Germany, on November 12, Maximilian von Weichs zur Glon served as a General Staff officer during World War I. In 1938, his career suffered a temporary setback when he and fifteen other generals were forced into retirement by Hitler following the Fritsch Affair. Weichs was recalled to active duty in 1939. He commanded the XIII Corps during the Poland Campaign and the Second Army during the France campaign in 1940 and in 1941 during Operation BARBAROSSA, the invasion of the Soviet Union. Weichs assumed command of Army Group B when Hitler divided Army Group South in July 1942. In November, when the Soviets launched their encirclement Army Group B's Sixth Army at Stalingrad, Weichs had no reserves, and Hitler refused his request to withdraw the Sixth Army westward. Although restoring the situation was beyond the means Weichs had available, Hitler showed his lack of confidence in him by assigning most of Army Group B's forces in late November to the newly established Army Group Don, commanded by Field Marshal Erich von Manstein. Weichs was promoted to field marshal in February 1943, but his remaining forces were distributed between Army Group Center and Army Group Don. He was transferred to the Führer Reserve on July 10.

Weichs's retirement was short-lived. He was recalled on July 26 and designated both commander in chief, southeast, and commander of Army Group F, with responsibility for all Axis forces in the Balkans. With the collapse of Romania and the defection of Bulgaria in August and September 1944, Weichs successfully extricated German forces in the Balkans with minimal losses. By January 1945, the remnants of Army Group F were fighting in Hungary. Hitler forced him into retirement again in March. Weichs was held as a prisoner after the war and was one of the defendants at the American Military Tribunals in Nuremberg. Due to ill health, he was released in 1948 before the trial took place. He died at Burg Rösberg near Bonn on September 27, 1954.

Jon D. Berlin

See also: American Military Tribunals; Blomberg-Fritsch Crisis

Additional Reading

Mitcham, Samuel W., Jr. *Hitler's Field Marshals and Their Battles*. Chelsea, MI: Scarborough House, 1990.

Westphal, Siegfried (1902–1982)

Wehrmacht general of cavalry.

Born in Leipzig, Germany, on March 28, 1902, Westphal served as an officer candidate at the end of World War I. In June 1941, he was assigned as the operations officer of General Erwin Rommel's *Panzergruppe Afrika*. He was badly wounded by artillery fire in June 1942. In October 1942, he was assigned as the chief of staff of the German-Italian Panzer Army. In June 1943, Westphal was assigned as chief of staff to Field Marshal Albert Kesselring, commander in chief, south, and, in that position, he played important roles in the Sicily and Italy campaigns. In September 1944, Westphal became chief of staff to the commander in chief, west, Field Marshal Gerd von Rundstedt. Westphal helped plan the German

Ardennes Offensive that led to the December 1944 to January 1945 Battle of the Bulge. Westphal rejected all involvement with National Socialism and firmly believed in the separation of politics from the military. Westphal died at Celle, Germany, on July 2, 1982.

Spencer C. Tucker

See also: Ardennes Offensive (Battle of the Bulge); Kesselring, Albert; Rommel, Erwin; Rundstedt, Karl Rudolf Gerd von

Additional Reading

Megargee, Geoffrey P. "Siegfreid Westphal." In *Chief of Staff: The Principal Officers behind History's Great Commanders*, vol. II, *World War II to Korea and Vietnam*, edited by David T. Zabecki, 37–49. Annapolis, MD: U.S. Naval Institute Press, 2008.

Westwall (1937–1945)

Defensive system along Germany's western border.

In 1937, Hitler authorized a line of fortifications—known to the Germans as the Westwall and to the Western Allies as the Siegfried Line—along Germany's western borders. From June 1938 to May 1940, the Westwall received, in total, about 8.8 million cubic meters of reinforced concrete, including about 280 kilometers of antivehicle obstacles and 17,229 structures. The German government presented the Westwall as a terrifying deterrent. That image encouraged France and Britain to settle at Munich in September 1938. France, after declaring war on Germany on September 3, 1939, occupied parts of the Saar without contesting the Westwall, even though the inferior border forces could have been overrun within weeks.

When Western Allied forces advanced on Germany in September 1944, the Westwall had been inactive for years. U.S. forces penetrated the Westwall through Luxemburg, near Wallendorf, and then Aachen, but failed to exploit their opportunities. Instead, the Western Allies launched a larger attempt to cross the Rhine through Arnhem in the Netherlands. Failure here forced the Western Allies to focus south, but, in the meantime, the Germans had manned and adapted the Westwall. In October, U.S. forces captured Aachen, but the U.S. success was contained. Western Allied forces continued to attack parts of the Westwall through 1944, into 1945, and secured parts, but often at great cost, infamously in a forested area around Hürtgen to the south of Aachen. During the final months of the war, Hitler insisted that the Westwall be defended to the last man, but the defenders gradually withdrew in March.

Bruce Newsome

See also: Hürtgen Forest Campaign, Allied; Siegfried Line Campaign, Allied

Additional Reading

Zaloga, Steven J. *The Siegfried Line, 1944–45: Battles on the German Frontier.* Oxford: Osprey, 2007.

Westwall, Allied Advance to (August 17–September 10, 1944)

After Allied forces crossed the Seine River in France, they spent the next twenty-four days pursuing the rapidly retreating German forces to the German border. On August 19, Allied supreme commander, General Dwight D. Eisenhower, decided to continue the advance east of the Seine River despite growing logistical difficulties. Allied plans called for the main effort to be made northeast of the Ardennes Forest by British General Sir Bernard Montgomery's 21st Army Group, supported on his left by the U.S. First Army of U.S. Lieutenant General Omar Bradley's 12th Army Group. Montgomery's forces were to move northeast from the lower Seine through Liège to cross the Rhine and seize the Ruhr industrial area. Meanwhile, Lieutenant General George S. Patton Jr.'s U.S. Third Army of 12th Army Group was to make a secondary effort south of the Ardennes and east from the upper Seine across the Moselle between Metz and Nancy and into the Saarland. Intermediate Allied objectives were to clear the Channel ports; seize the German V-weapon sites in the Pas de Calais area; liberate northwestern France, Belgium, and the Netherlands; and destroy German forces between the Seine and Germany. But the ultimate Allied objectives were a quick crossing of the Rhine and seizure of the Ruhr. Speed was essential for the Allied forces to reach the Rhine before the Germans could organize an effective defense of the Westwall, a fortified line on Germany's western border running some three hundred miles from Cleves on the Dutch-German border to Basel, Switzerland.

The German general retreat in the west began on August 17. Leaving behind the garrisons in the Channel ports, Field Marshal Walther Model's Army Group B, consisting of elements of forty-six divisions under the First, Seventh, Fifth Panzer, and Fifteenth Armies, withdrew to the northeast. Closely pursued by the Allies, the retreating German forces conducted an orderly withdrawal but were unable to reestablish a continuous line of defense until they reached the Westwall. By September 10, Army Group B and the remnants of the seven divisions of the Nineteenth Army, under Colonel General Johannes Blaskowitz's Army Group G, withdrawing from southern France, linked up and established a continuous front with some sixty-three understrength divisions spread from the North Sea to Switzerland. With the Mosel River as the boundary, Model's Army Group B held the north, and Blaskowitz's Army Group G held the south. The overall commander was Field Marshal Gerd von Rundstedt, Oberbefehlshaber West (commander in chief, west, or OB West).

Paris was liberated on August 25, and the Allied pursuit east of the Seine advanced rapidly. General Henry Crerar's Canadian First Army advanced up the Channel coast, overrunning the German V-weapon sites in the Pas de Calais on September 6. Farther east, General Sir Miles Dempsey's Second British Army rapidly advanced to the Albert Canal between Antwerp and Hasselt, taking Brussels on September 3, and Antwerp on September 4. However, the Germans still held the Scheldt estuary, thus preventing Allied use of the vital port of Antwerp.

On the British right, U.S. Lieutenant General Courtney Hodges's First Army captured Mons on September 3, taking some twenty-five thousand German prisoners in the "Mons pocket." By September 10, First Army was deployed from Hasselt on the Albert Canal through Liège, Verviers, and Malmédy to Luxembourg. Despite logistical restrictions, Patton's Third Army also made good progress, and, by September 1, it had crossed the Meuse between Verdun and Commercy and was in position to attack toward the Moselle and the Westwall between Metz and Nancy, when its advance ground to a halt for lack of gasoline and other supplies. On September 2, Alexander Patch's Seventh U.S. Army, advancing northward from southern France, linked up with Allied forces near Lyon, thereby completing the Allied line from the channel to the Swiss border and ending the great pursuit.

The Normandy invasion and breakout and the subsequent pursuit to the Westwall was costly for both sides. From June 6 to September 11, 1944, the Germans lost about five hundred thousand men. During the same period, the Allies suffered some two hundred and twenty-four thousand casualties. The continuation of the Allied drive into Germany would be much slower and even more costly.

Charles R. Schrader

See also: Antwerp, Allied Liberation of; Blaskowitz, Johannes Albrecht; Model, Walther; Paris, Allied Liberation of; Rundstedt, Karl Rudolf Gerd von; Scheldt Estuary, Battles for; Westwall

Additional Reading

Blumenson, Martin. *United States Army in World War II: The European Theater of Operations—Breakout and Pursuit.* Washington, DC: Office of the Chief of Military History, Department of the Army, 1961.

Ludewig, Joachim. *Rückzug: The German Retreat from France, 1944.* Lexington: University Press of Kentucky, 2012.

Wever, Walther (1887–1936)

Luftwaffe lieutenant general.

Born in Posen, Prussia (today's Poznan, Poland), on November 11, 1887, Wever served as a General Staff officer during World War I. In 1933, he was selected as the chief of Air Command Office, essentially the chief of the clandestine Luftwaffe General Staff. Wever became one the key architects of the Luftwaffe. An ardent Nazi, he used Adolf Hitler's book, *Mein Kampf*, as the basis for planning the air force. He deduced that the Soviet Union was the real enemy and believed the Luftwaffe would need a long-range bomber to strike Soviet bases and factories. Wever remained the chief advocate of a four-engine, strategic "Ural" bomber. He believed that the other central tasks for the Luftwaffe were achieving air superiority and providing ground support. Toward this end, he set about developing and organizing a balanced air force. On June 3, 1936, during a visit to Dresden, Wever failed to release the aileron lock on his aircraft and crashed at the end of the runway. With his death, the Luftwaffe lost one of its leading strategic visionaries. His death also brought a shift in Luftwaffe priorities, from strategic to tactical airpower.

Marlyn R. Pierce

See also: Luftwaffe (German Air Force)

Additional Reading

Mitcham, Samuel W. *Eagles of the Third Reich: The Men Who Made the Luftwaffe.* Novato, CA: Presidio, 1997.

Wilhelm Gustloff Sinking (January 30, 1945)

The sinking of the liner *Wilhelm Gustloff* was history's worst maritime disaster. The twenty-five-thousand-ton *Wilhelm Gustloff* was launched in 1937 as the flagship of Hitler's "Strength through Joy" movement, which provided low-cost vacations for German workers. The *Wilhelm Gustloff* was a cruise ship until World War II, when it became a floating barracks for German submariners training in the Baltic.

With the westward advance of the Soviet Army, the *Wilhelm Gustloff* was used in evacuating German personnel from the

Baltic. On the night of January 30, 1945, it was sunk by the Soviet submarine *S-13*, commanded by Captain Third Grade Alexander Marinseko. When it went down, the ship was carrying nearly one thousand submariners and other military personnel, but just before it sailed, it had taken on a large number of refugees, so there were probably more than eight thousand people on board. The ship sank quickly, and only 964 survivors were picked from the sea. Some of those died of their wounds or exposure, so the total number of people who perished in the tragedy probably exceeds seven thousand.

The *Wilhelm Gustloff* was the largest German vessel ever sunk by a Soviet submarine. Many Germans erroneously believed that the *Wilhelm Gustloff* was marked with red crosses and was a noncombatant. In reality, the ship mounted antiaircraft guns and was transporting naval personnel as well as refugees. The submarine command should never have allowed it to sail unescorted.

Spencer C. Tucker

See also: Submarines

Additional Reading

Sellwood, Arthur V. *The Damned Don't Drown: The Sinking of the "Wilhelm Gustloff."* Annapolis, MD: Naval Institute Press, 1996.

Witzleben, Erwin von (1881–1944)

Wehrmacht field marshal.

Born in Breslau, Silesia (now Wroclaw, Poland), on December 4, 1881, Witzleben served as a General Staff officer during World War I. He became an opponent of Hitler as early as 1934, when he was one of the general officers who demanded a formal inquiry into the killing of General Kurt von Schleicher during the Night of the Long Knives Purge. Following the Blomberg-Fritsch Crisis of 1938, Witzleben became a core member of the military opposition. Witzleben commanded the First Army in the 1940 campaign in France. He then became Oberbefehlshaber West (commander in chief, west) in France, but his attitude toward Hitler became known, and, in March 1942, Hitler forced him into retirement. If the July 20, 1944 plot to assassinate Hitler had succeeded, Witzleben was slated to become the commander in chief of the Wehrmacht. He was tried for treason by the Nazi People's Court. He was condemned to death on August 8, 1944 and strangled by piano wire that same day.

Robert T. Kaczowka

See also: Blomberg-Fritsch Crisis; Night of the Long Knives; Opposition to Hitler, German Military

Additional Reading

Mitcham, Samuel W., Jr. *Hitler's Field Marshals.* Chelsea, MI: Scarborough House, 1988.

Wolf Pack Tactics (*Rudeltaktik*) (1941–1943)

German submarine tactics involving coordinated night surface attacks against Allied convoys.

Early in the war, the U-boats operated mostly as lone raiders, partly because of the small numbers available for operations. To counter the U-boats, the Allies turned to convoys with armed escorts for protection, thereby causing the U-boats to focus on evasive tactics to survive rather than sinking merchant tonnage. Admiral Karl Dönitz, commander of the German submarine force, recognized that unless the

U-boats could overcome the defenses of Allied merchant convoys, the tonnage war would inevitably be lost. His solution was a concept that came to be called *Rudeltaktik*, or wolf pack attack—a method for U-boats to penetrate a convoy's antisubmarine defenses and destroy the merchant ships. Once a U-boat located an Allied convoy, other submarines would be vectored to that location. Groups of U-boats would then attack on the surface at night at relatively high speeds, maximizing the effect. U-boats would operate in a "hit-and-run" manner, launching their attack, and then fleeing on the surface before the convoy's surface escorts could react.

A wolf pack generally consisted of six to nine U-boats, but some deployed as many as twenty to thirty. Each pack deployed into a concave patrol line with about ten miles between each pack member. Using darkness, the U-boats operated on the surface to lessen the effectiveness of Allied ASDIC (early sonar), and the compact silhouette of the U-boat helped provide natural protection. The patrol line combed the Atlantic in an east or west direction, maintaining radio listening silence while under control by radio from Dönitz's command post at Lorient, France.

The Achilles heel of the wolf packs, however, was the radio communication between the U-boats and Dönitz's headquarters. The Allies introduced high-frequency direction finding (HF/DF) equipment in faster Allied escort vessels to drive away the shadowing U-boat, thereby forcing it to submerge or destroying it with depth charges or air attack. Allied technical superiority, the use of long-range aircraft, and code breaking culminated in May 1943, when the Allies destroyed more than forty German submarines. "Black May" signaled the defeat of the wolf packs, as the ratio of Allied tonnage produced to tonnage sunk by the U-boats tipped against the Germans.

During World War II, more than 130 wolf packs operated against Allied shipping, sinking more than 2,759 Allied merchant ships and 138 warships and killing almost sixty thousand seamen. Of the 1,170 U-boats Dönitz deployed throughout the war, 753 were lost, along with some twenty-nine thousand crewmen.

Steven J. Rauch

See also: Atlantic, Battle of the; Dönitz, Karl

Additional Reading

Edwards, Bernard. *Dönitz and the Wolf Packs.* London: Cassell, 1999.

Wolff, Karl (1900–1984)

SS-Obergruppenführer and general of the Waffen-SS.

Born in Darmstadt, Germany, on May 13, 1900, Wolff joined the army in 1917. Not retained in the postwar, he joined the Nazi Party and the SS in 1925. In June 1933, SS Chief Heinrich Himmler appointed Wolff as his adjutant. Three years later, he became chief of Himmler's personal staff, a position of immense influence that controlled access to Himmler. In summer 1939, Wolff began working at Hitler's headquarters as Himmler's representative. Managing the administrative friction caused by the *Endlösung*, the "Final Solution to the Jewish Problem," Wolff coordinated the transportation for the deportations of Jews to the death camps. In September 1943, Wolff became the highest SS and police official in Italy. By early 1945, Wolff became convinced that Germany would lose the war, and he made contact with the Allies. He signed a treaty of unconditional surrender at the Italian front on May 2, 1945, one week before the general capitulation. Arrested after the war and charged with minor crimes, he was sentenced to four years but spent only a week in prison. In 1962, he was arrested by the West German government and charged with genocide. Found guilty in 1964, he was sentenced to fifteen years in prison but was released in 1971. Wolff died in Rosenheim, Bavaria, Germany, on July 15, 1984.

Martin Moll

See also: Himmler, Heinrich; Holocaust, German Military Complicity in

Additional Reading

Koehl, Robert Lewis. *The Black Corps: The Structure and Power Struggles of the Nazi SS.* Madison: University of Wisconsin Press, 1983.

Y

Yugoslavia Campaign (April 6–18, 1941)

Hitler pressured Yugoslavia to join the Tripartite Pact on March 25, 1941. This move precipitated a bloodless military coup in Belgrade on March 26 to 27. Hitler was enraged by the coup, and on March 27, he issued Führer Directive No. 25, ordering the conquest of Yugoslavia. The weak Yugoslav army was no match for the Germans. Mobilized on March 29, it totaled fewer than one million men in thirty-one divisions under seven field armies. The Yugoslavs had few modern tanks and little artillery and relied on animal transport. After only ten days for planning and preparations, the Germans began their assault on April 6, 1941 with a massive air attack on Belgrade that killed some seventeen thousand civilians, destroyed much of the Yugoslav Air Force, and cut communications between the Yugoslav Supreme Command and its units in the field.

The First Panzer Group under General Paul von Kleist attacked from Bulgaria on April 8. At the same time, General Georg-Hans Reinhardt's XLI Panzer Corps attacked from Romania. Using bridges over the Danube, Drava, and Sava Rivers seized by General Maximilian von Weich's German Second Army between April 1 and 7, XLVI Panzer Corps attacked toward Belgrade on April 10. On the evening of April 12, the three converging German corps surrounded Belgrade, and, the next morning, German forces entered Belgrade unopposed. Yugoslavia surrendered unconditionally on April 17, ending a twelve-day campaign. The Germans sustained only 558 casualties, including 151 killed. Yugoslavia was then annexed or occupied by the victorious Axis powers, except for Croatia and Bosnia-Herzegovina, which formed the pro-Axis Independent State of Croatia.

Charles R. Schrader

See also: Kleist, Paul Ewald von; List, Siegmund Wilhelm Walter; Löhr, Alexander; Weichs zur Glon, Maximilian von

Additional Reading

Littlefield, Frank. *Germany and Yugoslavia, 1933–1941: The German Conquest of Yugoslavia.* New York: Columbia University Press, 1988.

Z

Zeitzler, Kurt (1895–1963)

Wehrmacht colonel general.

Born in Cossmar-Luckau, Germany, on June 9, 1895, Zeitzler commanded a battalion during World War I. Zeitzler was an early supporter of Hitler in the officer corps. In 1934, he was one of the first officers assigned to the emerging panzer forces. Zeitzler briefly commanded a regiment before becoming chief of staff of General Ewald von Kleist's XXII Army Corps in the September 1939 invasion of Poland and of Panzer Group Kleist (later First Panzer Army) in the invasion of France in 1940. Zeitzler continued as chief of staff of First Panzer Army during the invasions of Greece and Yugoslavia and for Operation BARBAROSSA, the invasion of the Soviet Union, in June 1941. In April 1942, Zeitzler was assigned as chief of staff to OB West, Field Marshal Gerd von Rundstedt. Zeitzler played a major role in defeating the disastrous British raid at Dieppe that August. In September, Hitler promoted Zeitzler to replace General Franz Halder as chief of the *Oberkommando des Heeres* (OKH). An aggressive officer with the nickname "*Kugelblitz*" (Thunderball), Zeitzler seemed to be the type of officer who would fit in well with Hitler.

The Battle of Stalingrad drove a wedge between Hitler and Zeitzler. Once the Sixth Army was cut off, Zeitzler urged that it be allowed to break out, whereas Hitler demanded it remain in place. Zeitzler went so far as to predict that a Luftwaffe airlift of supplies to the beleaguered army would not be successful, angering Hitler further. Following the collapse of Operation CITADEL, the Battle of Kursk, which he had largely planned, Zeitzler fell out completely with Hitler. He had offered his resignation four times, but each time, Hitler refused to accept it. On June 30, Zeitzler simply walked off the job, citing "reasons of health." Imprisoned after the war, Zeitzler was released in 1947. He died at Hohenassachau, Germany, on September 25, 1963.

Gene Mueller and Spencer C. Tucker

See also: Kleist, Paul Ewald von; Rundstedt, Karl Rudolf Gerd von

Additional Reading

Liddell Hart, Basil H. *The German Generals Talk.* New York: William Morrow, 1948.

Epilogue: Why Germany Lost World War II

Germany lost World War II through weaknesses in its national leadership, alliance strategy, command structure, economic power, occupation policy, and intelligence, as well as the flawed conduct of military campaigns. German defeat was not preordained, but the material odds against Germany were highly unfavorable. With better decisions, Germany would more likely have protracted the process of defeat rather than gaining outright victory.

Adolf Hitler made Germany's strategic decisions and many operational decisions as well. Hitler's strategy failed, and the ultimate responsibility for Germany's defeat clearly rests with him. His leadership style, inability to accept information or opinions that conflicted with his preconceptions, and tolerance of bureaucratic inefficiency and infighting, reduced German strategic effectiveness. However, Hitler was not *solely* responsible for Germany's defeat. His decisions were not uniformly bad, and Germany would not have won had Hitler simply deferred to his generals. Hitler's generals supported his strategy because they largely shared his values and goals. They, too, wanted to make Germany supreme in Europe, and like Hitler, they underestimated Germany's enemies, especially the Soviet Union. Hitler's intervention into operational matters was often negative, but sometimes positive, such as his decision to make the main effort in the Ardennes in 1940. Other times, he made the "least-worst" choice, such as sacrificing the Sixth Army at Stalingrad to enable other German forces to escape destruction.

Hitler's decisions for war with Britain, the Soviet Union, and the United States ultimately led to Germany's defeat. These decisions were not necessarily inherently unsound, because Germany fought first Britain and France alone, and then, essentially, fought the Soviet Union alone until late 1942. By the time Anglo-American pressure became truly serious, the outcome of the decisive campaign of the war—the eastern front—was already decided. The decision to fight Britain and France in 1939 was viable, even though Germany had no great quantitative advantages. If Germany had waited longer, however, its situation would not have improved. Similarly, Germany attacked the Soviet Union at a time of maximum relative advantage. The "window of opportunity" to defeat the Soviets was widest in 1941. If Germany had waited until 1942, Soviet and U.S. power would have greatly increased, and Britain would remain undefeated. The most dubious decision was to declare war on the United States. The assumption that Germany could beat the Soviets before the United States could invade Europe proved false, as did the hope that Germany's declaration of war on the United States would elicit a Japanese attack on the Soviet Union. Instead, Germany gained a powerful new enemy for the sake of a weak and uncooperative friend.

Germany failed to develop and execute an effective alliance grand strategy. The Axis powers were intrinsically much weaker than the Allies and needed to coordinate closely in order to win. However, the Axis never conducted any meaningful combined military or political planning. A major reason the Axis lost the war was the failure to unite against Britain in 1939 to 1941 or against the Soviet Union in 1941 to 1942. Germany, Italy, and Japan signed an anti-Soviet agreement in 1936, but Germany did not consult Italy or Japan before signing the German-Soviet Nonaggression Pact in 1939. Italy did not consult Germany before attacking Greece, causing a costly diversion of German forces before Operation BARBAROSSA. In turn, Germany did not consult Italy or Japan—or even Romania, Hungary, or Finland—before attacking the Soviet Union in June 1941. Japan signed a nonaggression pact with the Soviets in April 1941 and rejected German requests that it attack the Soviets after June 1941. The Japanese, for their part, did not consult Germany before attacking China in 1937 nor did they coordinate closely with Germany when planning for war with Britain and the United States in late 1941. After the Japanese attack at Pearl Harbor, the Allies concentrated on attacking Germany until it fell, while Axis efforts remained divided.

The German command structure was ineffective on many levels. At the highest level, Germany lacked a war cabinet to formulate strategy and coordinate the military, domestic, political, diplomatic, and economic functions. Nor did Germany establish a combined chiefs of staff to coordinate military operations with Italy and Japan. Within the German military, the planning and execution of joint operations was weak. In theory, *Oberkommando der Wehrmacht* (OKW) coordinated the army, navy, and Luftwaffe, but, in practice, the high command of the Army (*Oberkommando des Heeres*, OKH) and the Luftwaffe rejected OKW authority, and, meanwhile, the navy fought its own war in the Atlantic. For much of the war, OKH managed the eastern front, while OKW managed all other theaters. This engendered constant squabbles over resources and precluded unified strategic planning. Within important theaters, German command was sometimes disastrously divided. For example, in June 1944, the German theater commander in the West did not control Luftwaffe or navy forces, and neither he nor the local commander in Normandy controlled the mobile divisions held in "OKW reserve." As a result, the Germans did not counterattack the Allied landings as promptly or effectively as possible.

Collectively, the Allies had a vastly larger population and geographic area than the Axis, of which Germany was the strongest partner. The major Allies—the British and French Empires, the United States, and the Soviet Union—were twelve times larger than Germany in population and 137 times larger in land area. The large population and vast geographic extent of the Soviet Union permitted the Soviets to absorb horrendous losses and to recover from mistakes, while Siberia provided a secure area in which to reconstitute war industry. Meanwhile, North American industry was totally inaccessible to German power.

Economically, the 1939 Gross Domestic Product (GDP) of Britain and France was only slightly greater than that of Germany.

In 1941, the GDP of Germany, its European allies, and its conquests was almost twice that of the Soviet Union, whose economy nearly collapsed under the weight of the German attack. Thus, Germany had the economic potential to fight the Soviets at least to a standstill if Britain and the United States stood aside. However, the entry of the United States into the war increased the economic odds against the Axis; the combined GDP of the Allies in 1942 more than twice that of the Axis. As the war progressed, this imbalance increased as the U.S. GDP soared. From 1943 to 1945, the total Allied GDP was well over three times that of the Axis GDP.

GDP does not indicate how efficiently or extensively an economy is mobilized for war. Germany had a higher GDP per capita than the USSR but was less productive than Britain or the United States. Germany spent about 40 percent of its national income on defense in 1940, rising to 70 percent in 1943 to 1944. The British spent 44 percent of national income on defense in 1940, rising to about 53 percent from 1941 to 1945, while the United States barely exceeded 40 percent after 1943, and the Soviets peaked at 60 percent in 1942 to 1943. However, the U.S. economy alone was three times the size of Germany's, and the total Anglo-American-Soviet economy was five times larger than Germany's. German productivity and its high level of mobilization in 1943 to 1944 could not offset the absolute Allied economic advantage.

The Axis and Allies had about the same number of troops under arms until 1942, mainly because the United States was neutral. In contrast, by 1944 the British, Soviet and U.S. armed forces had over twenty-eight million troops compared to 9.4 million German and 5.4 million Japanese troops. The German disadvantage was even greater in equipment. During the war, Britain, the United States, and the Soviet Union produced 3.5 times as many infantry weapons as Germany, five times as many tanks, and 4.5 times as many combat aircraft. The Germans were not oblivious to the dire economic and demographic odds against them. Awareness of the United States' growing power and willingness to intervene made the Germans anxious to gain European hegemony before the United States' latent power could be mobilized. This strategy failed, as did the subsequent effort to defeat Allied quantitative superiority with high-quality weapons.

Some historians argue that Germany was defeated because she operated a "peacetime economy" until early 1942 and did not maximize armaments production from June 1940 until June 1941. In fact, Germany was already highly mobilized in 1939; it had operated a quasiwartime economy in peacetime since 1936. When war came, it further reduced civilian consumption and redirected labor to war work. Many "consumer goods" were actually produced for the Wehrmacht. Throughout the war, Germany mobilized a much higher proportion of women for war work than Britain, and many German women ran farms after their men were drafted. Between June 1940 and June 1941, almost every man fit for service and not doing vital war work was in the Wehrmacht. After conquering Poland and France, Germany used a million French prisoners and a million Poles as forced labor. German armaments production was relatively low from 1939 to 1942, not because Germany was on a peacetime footing, but because Germany was investing massively in armaments factories at the expense of immediate production. This investment, and Armaments Minister Albert Speer's economic rationalization measures, resulted in greatly increased production later in the war. Thus, Germany did not lose because it "relaxed" economically before attacking the Soviet Union.

Failure to organize conquered territories effectively contributed importantly to German defeat. In 1942, Germany controlled half of Europe and more than three hundred million people. However, no more than ninety million were Germans, while eighty million were German allies—chiefly Italians, Romanians, and Hungarians. The rest were conquered subjects treated in accordance with Nazi racial ideology. In Eastern Europe, the Nazis slated "inferior" peoples for enslavement and extermination. Better Nazi treatment of the Soviet people and encouragement of independence for Ukrainians and others might have facilitated the collapse of the multinational Soviet dictatorship. Germany conscripted millions of forced laborers in the east. Many people joined partisan groups to avoid this. The Germans killed millions of Soviet prisoners who might have worked—or even fought—for Germany. In the Soviet Union, Germany was an enemy rather than a liberator, and this made the task of conquest and occupation immeasurably more difficult.

Western Europeans were treated less brutally but still had little reason to embrace the German cause. War disrupted the European economy, cutting off normal overseas trade, and net importers of food and energy required German assistance or did without. As a result, the economy of German-controlled Europe was smaller than the prewar GDPs of the conquered nations might have suggested. Germany exacerbated the economic strain by plundering Western Europe of food, raw materials, finished goods, and laborers with increasing ruthlessness as the war progressed. German exploitation was not even efficiently administered. Within each occupied area, various economic, political, and military organizations competed with each other and worked at cross-purposes.

Intelligence failures significantly contributed to German defeat. Broadly speaking, German intelligence failed to determine the enemy's capabilities and intentions and to conceal Germany's capabilities and intentions. German intelligence was poorly organized and uncoordinated. The numerous German foreign intelligence services hated each other and guarded their products jealously. The military disdained the intelligence branches and assigned them low-quality personnel, whose products were often seriously flawed. The net result was to reduce Germany's operational advantages relative to its enemies.

Before attacking the Soviet Union, Germany greatly underestimated the size of the Red Army, the quality of Soviet equipment (especially tanks and combat aircraft), and Soviet ability to generate new forces and produce new equipment. German intelligence failed to detect the buildup of Soviet forces before the Soviet counteroffensives at Moscow, Leningrad, and Rostov in 1941; at Stalingrad in 1942; and at Kursk in 1943. Anglo-American landings in North Africa and Sicily in 1942 to 1943 surprised Germany. In June 1944, Germany was completely deceived on two fronts. In the East, Germany believed the Soviets would strike in the Ukraine, and, thus, the Soviet attack in Belorussia shattered Army Group Center. In the West, Germany expected an Allied assault in the Pas de Calais, and, thus, the Normandy landings achieved surprise. Had Germany known what the Allies intended, or had the Allies not known what Germany intended, Germany might have avoided many defeats or made the Allies pay a much higher price for victory.

German counterintelligence failed catastrophically. Significantly, Admiral Wilhelm Canaris, the head of the Abwehr, cooperated with enemy intelligence, and protected people such as his deputy, Hans Oster, who plotted to overthrow or kill Hitler. However, his actions do not fully explain the ineffectiveness of German counterintelligence. Poor German security discipline facilitated British efforts to decrypt German messages sent via the Enigma cipher machine. This gave the British a clear picture of German forces and plans and contributed to Anglo-American victories on land and in the Battle of the Atlantic. The British captured every German agent sent to infiltrate Britain and forced them to provide deceptive information to German intelligence, which never realized its agents were enemy-controlled. On the eastern front, Soviet intelligence lured thousands of German agents to their doom, often forcing them to transmit deceptive information, and ran a massive partisan campaign behind German lines that gathered intelligence and conducted sabotage attacks. German counterintelligence was never able to suppress the partisans or turn Soviet agents against Moscow.

The principal military reason for German defeat was the failure of Operation BARBAROSSA. The majority of German ground forces fought in the East after 1941 and suffered most of their casualties there. Soviet survival gave the United States time to mobilize and enabled Anglo-American land operations to succeed with relatively low casualties. German defeat in the East resulted from faulty planning, great underestimation of Soviet capabilities, and mismanaged conduct of the campaign itself. Operational studies in 1940 assumed Germany would crush Soviet forces west of the Dnepr in a few months and would meet little resistance afterward. Logistical studies underestimated the difficulty of operating tanks, trucks, and wheeled vehicles in Russia; of keeping horses alive in Russia; and of converting Soviet-gauge railroads for German use. Intelligence studies failed to anticipate Soviet capability to mobilize new forces and produce new equipment and wrongly believed that the Red Army's leadership, training, and equipment were grossly inferior to Germany's.

The July 1941 frontier battles achieved less success at a far higher cost than expected. German mobile spearheads broke through Soviet lines and drove deep into the rear, but German infantry had great difficulty sealing and liquidating the pockets. Enough Soviets escaped, and enough new units were raised to continue organized resistance. In August, Hitler diverted troops from Army Group Center to support attacks on Leningrad and Kiev. This decision remains controversial. Some German generals wanted to capture Moscow instead, which they thought would cause a Soviet collapse. However, driving on Moscow without securing Army Group Center's flanks would have been highly risky. Ultimately, the Germans had insufficient forces to secure all their objectives simultaneously, and, in attempting to capture Leningrad and Moscow sequentially, the Germans captured neither. The Soviet counterattack at Moscow, using forces brought from the Soviet Far East, sealed the fate of Operation BARBAROSSA.

The 1942 campaign sought to seize the Caucasus oil fields. The Germans divided their force and advanced simultaneously on divergent axes towards Stalingrad and the Caucasus. Germany should have first secured Stalingrad, and then attacked the Caucasus; simultaneous drives dissipated German strength and increased logistical difficulties. Germany captured much terrain in the Don Bend and the North Caucasus but took relatively few prisoners, before both advances bogged down. Constant, vigorous Soviet counterattacks eroded German strength before Sixth Army even reached Stalingrad. The prolonged frontal assault on Stalingrad forfeited Germany's advantage in mobile warfare. The Soviets employed just enough troops to keep the city from falling while they prepared their winter counteroffensive against the weak German flanks. The Germans frustrated Soviet efforts to reach Rostov, thus cutting off German forces in the Caucasus, and to destroy the Rzhev salient, but the destruction of Sixth Army was a heavy blow to the Wehrmacht.

With the defeats at Stalingrad and Tunisia, Germany lost the strategic initiative. Many argue that it should have adopted a mobile defense, especially in the East. However, Germany lacked sufficient trucks and fuel supplies to mount a mobile defense, and thus static defense was the only real option for much of the German Army. Moreover, Germany faced opponents whose armies were much more mobile than its; the United States provided the Soviets with over four hundred thousand trucks, significantly increasing the Red Army's mobility. When Germany took the offensive later in the war, it only hastened its defeat. For example, the Germans delayed excessively before launching their offensive at Kursk in 1943; this permitted the Soviets to fortify the salient and inflict crippling attrition on the German spearheads. German attacks in the West in 1944 were even more ill-advised, resulting in the loss of irreplaceable reserves for no commensurate result.

The loss of air superiority decisively contributed to Germany's defeat. Allied air superiority secured the British and Soviet homelands from effective German strategic air attack, permitted Allied strategic bombing of Germany, ensured the success of Allied amphibious invasions, and severely limited German tactical mobility. The Allies gained air superiority by outproducing the Luftwaffe and by deliberately attacking targets in Germany that were important enough to force the Luftwaffe to fight. Air defense of the Reich enjoyed a low priority until relatively late in the war, and Germany was slow to develop effective organizations and tactics for air defense. Germany produced more than seven thousand bombers and crews in 1943 and 1944, when it should have focused entirely on fighters and fighter pilots. Germany hoped to counter Allied numerical superiority with technological superiority. But late-war German fighters were mostly older designs like the Bf 109 that were not superior to U.S. fighters. Me 262 jet fighters never entered service in sufficient numbers to make a difference. The German pilot training system failed to generate sufficient numbers of well-trained replacements, partly because of fuel shortages. Relentless combat forced Germany to commit its pilots to replace losses, yet losses only accelerated as poorly trained pilots fought well-trained, numerically superior opponents.

Controversy surrounds the role of strategic bombing in Germany's defeat. Allied bombing tied down an enormous defensive force, forced the Germans into a disruptive and inefficient dispersal of industry, decimated the Luftwaffe fighter force, and crippled Germany's oil industry and transportation system. But bombing did not fatally weaken German morale or paralyze war production. New research shows that German wartime industrial investment was much larger than previously understood. Therefore, without strategic bombing,

German production would have been far greater than it was.

German failure to deny the Atlantic to the Allies ensured its defeat. British survival, the buildup of U.S. forces in Britain, and amphibious assaults on Europe required Allied command of the sea. The Allies won because they built huge numbers of merchant ships and convoy escorts, improved their antisubmarine tactics and technologies, and developed intelligence advantages. The Allies were relatively slow to employ airpower against the U-boats, but, ultimately, long-range aircraft with maritime-search radars proved highly effective. Decryption of German Enigma messages enabled the Allies to locate and avoid enemy submarines. Shipborne radar allowed escorts to sink submarines or keep them away from the convoys. Germany developed "snorkels" that allowed submarines to use diesel engines underwater, radar detectors, acoustic torpedoes, and advanced Type XXI submarines. However, even with new weapons, by mid-1943, Germany lacked enough experienced submarine crews to overcome the huge, highly effective Allied antisubmarine force.

Despite Germany's reputation, it was not very efficient or militarily effective in World War II. The Reich had many competing fiefdoms that impaired efficient conduct of the war. The Wehrmacht excelled at combined arms warfare at the tactical level, but woefully inadequate intelligence and logistical support undercut the conduct of operations. Germany was ineffective strategically because it tried to achieve objectives that were well beyond its means, and its industrial and demographic base was far too small to win a protracted conflict with the Allies. Unlike the Allies, Germany had no margin for error and could not survive its mistakes.

James D. Perry

See also: Abwehr; Atlantic, Battle of the; Canaris, Wilhelm; Combined Bomber Offensive, Allied (Operation POINTBLANK); German-Soviet Nonaggression Pact; Normandy Invasion and Campaign; North Africa Campaign; Soviet Union, Invasion of (Operation BARBAROSSA); Speer, Albert; Stalingrad, Battle of

Additional Reading

Harrison, Mark, ed. *The Economics of World War II.* Cambridge: Cambridge University Press, 1998.

Megargee, Geoffrey. *Inside Hitler's High Command.* Lawrence: University Press of Kansas, 2000.

Shirer, William L. *The Rise and Fall of the Third Reich: A History of Nazi Germany.* New York: Simon and Schuster, 1960.

Primary Source Documents

1. Wehrmacht Principal Operations Manual, HDv 300 *Truppenführung*: Introduction

Heeresdienstvorschrift 300, Truppenführung *(Unit Command) was the German Army principal operations manual of World War II. Published as Part I in 1933 and Part II in 1934, it remained in force through May 1945. It was an updated version of the previous operations manual,* HDv 487, Führung und Gefecht der verbundenen Waffen *(Command and Combat of the Combined Arms, published as Part I in 1921 and Part II in 1923).* HDv 487 *had been one of the most significant products of the post-World War I reforms carried out by General Hans von Seeckt. Those two manuals continue to influence modern combat operations to this day. The Introduction section of* Truppenführung *sets forth the Wehrmacht's basic philosophy of war fighting.*

Berlin 1933

This is a classified publication as defined in Paragraph 1 of the law against the disclosure of military secrets of 3 June 1914. Illegal use will be subject to penalties in accordance with this law, where no other disciplinary measures apply.

Chief of the Army High Command

Reference: TA Nr. 3000/33 T 4.

17 October 1933

Truppenführung contains the basic principles for command, field service, and joint operations in war.

This manual assumes strength, arms, and equipment in an army with unlimited resources.

As far as this doctrine is applied to the training and deployment of units, consideration must be given to the limits set by peacetime conditions, by law, and by international treaty.

Any amendment of or addition to this manual must be authorized by me.

Freiherr von Hammerstein-Equord.

Introduction

1. War is an art, a free and creative activity founded on scientific principles. It makes the very highest demands on the human personality.
2. The conduct of war is subject to continual development. New weapons dictate ever-changing forms. Their appearance must be anticipated and their influence evaluated. Then they must be placed into service quickly.

3. Combat situations are of an unlimited variety. They change frequently and suddenly and can seldom be assessed in advance. Incalculable elements often have a decisive influence. One's own will is pitted against the independent will of the enemy. Friction and errors are daily occurrences.
4. Lessons in the conduct of war cannot be exhaustively compiled in the form of regulations. The principles enunciated must be applied in accordance with the situation.

   Simple actions, logically carried out, will lead most surely to the objective.
5. War subjects the individual to the most severe tests of his spiritual and physical endurance. For this reason, character counts more in war than intellect. Many who distinguish themselves on the battlefield remain unnoticed in peacetime.
6. The command of an Army and its subordinate units requires leaders capable of judgment, with clear vision and foresight, and the ability to make independent and decisive decisions and carry them out unwaveringly and positively. Such leaders must be impervious to the changes in the fortunes of war and possess full awareness of the high degree of responsibility placed on their shoulders.
7. An officer is in every sense a leader and a teacher. In addition to his knowledge of men and his sense of justice, he must be distinguished by superior knowledge and experience, by moral excellence, by self-discipline, and by high courage.
8. The example and personal bearing of officers and other soldiers who are responsible for leadership has a decisive effect on the troops. The officer, who in the face of the enemy displays coolness, decisiveness, and courage, carries his troops with him. He also must win their affections and earn their trust through his understanding of their feelings, their way of thinking, and through his selfless care for them.

   Mutual trust is the surest foundation for discipline in times of need and danger.
9. Every leader in every situation must exert himself totally and not avoid responsibility. Willingness to accept responsibility is the most important quality of a leader. It should not, however, be based upon individualism without consideration of the whole, nor used as a justification for failure to carry out orders where seeming to know better may affect obedience. Independence of spirit must not become arbitrariness. By contrast, independence of action within acceptable boundaries is the key to great success.
10. The decisive factor, despite technology and weaponry, is the value of the individual. The wider his experience in combat, the greater his importance.

    The emptiness of the battlefield requires soldiers who can think and act independently, who can make calculated, decisive, and daring use of every situation, and who understand that victory depends on each individual.

    Training, physical fitness, selflessness, determination, self-confidence and daring equip a man to master the most difficult situations.
11. The caliber of a leader and of the men determines the combat power of a unit, which is augmented by the quantity, care, and maintenance of their weapons and equipment.

    Superior combat power can compensate for inferior numbers. The greater this quality, the greater the force and mobility in war.

Superior leadership and superior unit readiness are guaranteed conditions for victory.

12. Leaders must live with their troops and share in their dangers and deprivations, their joys and sorrows. Only thus can they acquire a first-hand knowledge of the combat capabilities and needs of their soldiers.

The individual is a part of the whole and is not only responsible for himself alone, but also for his comrades. He who is capable of more than the others, who can achieve more, must guide and lead the inexperienced and the weak.

Out of such a foundation grows genuine comradeship, which is as important between the leaders and the men as it is among the men themselves.

13. Units that are only superficially held together, not bonded by long training and discipline, easily fail in moments of grave danger and under the pressure of unexpected events. From the very beginning of a war, therefore, great importance must be attached to creating and maintaining inner strength and to the discipline and training of units.

It is the duty of every officer to act immediately and with any means at his disposal—even the most severe—against a breakdown in discipline or acts of mutiny, looting, panic, or other negative influences.

Discipline is the backbone of an Army, and its maintenance is in the best interests of all.

14. The readiness and strength of units must be capable of meeting the highest demands in decisive moments. The commander who needlessly tires his unit jeopardizes success and is responsible for the consequences.

The forces deployed in battle must be committed in proportion to the objective. Orders that are impossible to execute will reduce confidence in the leadership and damage morale.

15. Every man, from the youngest soldier upward, must be required at all times and in all situations to commit his whole mental, spiritual, and physical strength. Only in this way will the full force of a unit be brought to bear in decisive action. Only thus will men develop, who will in the hour of danger maintain their courage and decisiveness and carry their weaker comrades with them to achieve deeds of daring.

The first criterion in war remains decisive action. Everyone, from the highest commander down to the youngest soldier, must constantly be aware that inaction and neglect incriminate him more severely than any error in the choice of means. [Emphasis in the original.]

Source: *On the German Art of War: Truppenführung*, edited and translated by Bruce Condell and David T. Zabecki. Copyright © 2001 by Lynne Rienner Publishers, Inc. Used with permission of the publisher.

2. Hitler's Directive for Fall Weiss, the Attack on Poland

April 11, 1939

In response to Adolf Hitler's pressure on Poland to cede the Danzig corridor to Germany, in 1939, Great Britain and France gave Poland a guarantee that should Poland be attacked, both nations would respond by declaring war on its aggressor.

Believing that this action meant that Poland would not yield without war, in April, an infuriated Hitler issued a military directive that the Wehrmacht should prepare to attack Poland any time after September 1, 1939. Hitler's order came just eight days after General Wilhelm Keitel's warning order of April 3 to the Wehrmacht.

The present attitude of Poland requires, over and above the plan "Frontier Security East," the initiation of military preparations, to remove if necessary any threat from this direction forever.

1) Political Requirements and Aims

German relations with Poland continue to be based on the principles of avoiding any disturbances. Should Poland, however, change her policy towards Germany, which so far has been based on the same principles as our own, and adopt a threatening attitude towards Germany, a final settlement might become necessary in spite of the Treaty in force with Poland.

The aim will then be to destroy Polish military strength, and create in the East a situation which will satisfy the requirements of national defense. The Free State of Danzig will be proclaimed a part of the Reich territory at the outbreak of hostilities, at the latest.

The political leaders consider it their task in this case to isolate Poland if possible, that is to say, to limit the war to Poland only.

The development of increasing internal crises in France and resulting British restraint might produce such a situation in the not too distant future.

Intervention by Russia, if she were in a position to intervene, cannot be expected to be of any use to Poland, because this would mean Poland's destruction by Bolshevism.

The attitude of the Baltic States will be determined wholly by German military superiority. (In the course of further developments, it may become necessary to occupy the Baltic states up to the border of the former Courland and to incorporate them in the Reich.)

Germany cannot count on Hungary as a certain ally. Italy's attitude is determined by the Rome-Berlin Axis.

2) Military Conclusions

The great objections in the reconstruction of the German Wehrmacht will continue to be determined by the antagonism of the Western Democracies. "Operation white" constitutes only a precautionary complement to these preparations. It is not to be looked upon in any way, however, as the necessary prerequisite for a military conflict with the Western opponents.

The isolation of Poland will be all the more easily maintained, even after the outbreak of hostilities, if we succeed in starting the war with sudden, heavy blows and in gaining rapid successes.

The overall situation will require, however, that in all cases, precautions be taken to safeguard the western frontier and the German North Sea coast, as well as the air above them.

Against the Baltic States—Lithuania in particular—security measures are to be carried out in case of a Polish march through this country.

3) Tasks of the Wehrmacht

The task of the Wehrmacht is to destroy the Polish Armed Forces. To this end a surprise attack is to be aimed at and prepared. Camouflaged or open general mobilization will not be ordered earlier than the day before the attack and at the latest possible moment.

The forces provided for "Frontier Security West" (section I, "Frontier Security") must not be employed for the time being for any other purpose.

All other frontiers are to be kept under observation only; the Lithuanian frontier is to be covered.

Source: Bundesarchiv/Militärarchiv RM 7/269. Translated by Dr. Marcus O. Jones and David T. Zabecki.

3. Declaration of the Government of the German Reich and the Government of the U.S.S.R.

September 28, 1939

After defeating Poland and dividing its territory between them, the German and Soviet governments appealed to Britain and France to end the war, a course that would have left those governments in undisturbed enjoyment of their new acquisitions.

After the Government of the German Reich and the Government of the U.S.S.R. have, by means of the treaty signed today, definitively settled the problems arising from the collapse of the Polish state and have thereby created a sure foundation for a lasting peace in Eastern Europe, they mutually express their conviction that it would serve the true interest of all peoples to put an end to the state of war existing at present between Germany on the one side and England and France on the other. Both Governments will therefore direct their common efforts, jointly with other friendly powers if occasion arises, toward attaining this goal as soon as possible.

Should, however, the efforts of the two Governments remain fruitless, this would demonstrate the fact that England and France are responsible for the continuation of the war, whereupon, in case of the continuation of the war, the Governments of Germany and of the U.S.S.R. shall engage in mutual consultations with regard to necessary measures.

Source: *Nazi-Soviet Relations, 1939–1941: Documents from the Archives of the German Foreign Office as Released by the Department of State.* Raymond James Sontag and James Stuart Beddie, eds. Washington, DC: Department of State, publication 3023, 1948. The Avalon Project at the Yale Law School. Available at http://www.yale.edu/lawweb/avalon/nazsov/dec939.htm.

4. Three-Power (Tripartite) Pact between Germany, Italy, and Japan, Signed in Berlin

September 27, 1940

In September 1940, the governments of Germany, Italy, and Japan formally allied themselves with each other, to establish a "new order" in both Europe and Asia. This alignment effectively linked all the various opponents of the Western democracies, intensifying the ideological aspects of the international conflict.

The governments of Germany, Italy and Japan, considering it as a condition precedent of any lasting peace that all nations of the world be given each its own proper place, have decided to stand by and co-operate with one another in regard to their efforts in greater East Asia and regions of Europe respectively wherein it is their prime purpose to establish and maintain a new order of things calculated to promote the mutual prosperity and welfare of the peoples concerned.

Furthermore, it is the desire of the three governments to extend co-operation to such nations in other spheres of the world as may be inclined to put forth endeavours along lines similar to their own, in order that their ultimate aspirations for world peace may thus be realized.

Accordingly, the governments of Germany, Italy and Japan have agreed as follows:

Article One

Japan recognizes and respects the leadership of Germany and Italy in establishment of a new order in Europe.

Article Two

Germany and Italy recognize and respect the leadership of Japan in the establishment of a new order in greater East Asia.

Article Three

Germany, Italy and Japan agree to co-operate in their efforts on aforesaid lines. They further undertake to assist one another with all political, economic and military means when one of the three contracting powers is attacked by a power at present not involved in the European war or in the Chinese-Japanese conflict.

Article Four

With the view to implementing the present pact, joint technical commissions, members which are to be appointed by the respective governments of Germany, Italy and Japan will meet without delay.

Article Five

Germany, Italy and Japan affirm that the aforesaid terms do not in any way affect the political status which exists at present as between each of the three contracting powers and Soviet Russia.

Article Six

The present pact shall come into effect immediately upon signature and shall remain in force 10 years from the date of its coming into force. At the proper time before expiration of said term, the high contracting parties shall at the request of any of them enter into negotiations for its renewal.

Source: United States Department of State. *Peace and War: United States Foreign Policy, 1931–1941*, Publication 1983. Washington, D.C.: U.S. Government Printing Office, 1943, 571–72.

5. Wehrmacht Compliance with the Commissar Order

Issued on June 6, 1941

Issued by Adolf Hitler on June 6, 1941, two weeks before the start of Operation BARBAROSSA, the commissar order required the German military to execute any captured Soviet commissars, the Communist Party officials assigned to military units. The order contravened all international conventions governing the treatment of prisoners of war. Hitler nonetheless ordered that German soldiers guilty of violating international law by carrying out the order would be "excused." The following three documents are evidence of Wehrmacht compliance with the Commissar Order.

A. Daily Intelligence Report from I Army Corps to Eighteenth Army Headquarters, June 27, 1941

K.Gef.St, 27 June 1941

To
AOK 18, Ic
Ic—Daily Report

a) Enemy attack in the early morning with two battalions against the defensive positions around Schaulen, and against the city multiple times with tanks. In the counterattack, two of our own infantry regiments repulsed the enemy. Altogether 34 were killed by 11th and 21st Divisions during the tank attacks. Enemy was hit hard and demoralized; counterattacks must nevertheless be expected.

In the forest northeast of Zauniai (10 kilometers northeast of Schaulen) even stronger enemy forces. On the left flank of the corps only scattered opposition. Dispersed remnants still in forests in the area around Kurtuvėnai—Saukenai—Palentrinai.

A prisoner, shot because of resistance, was seized as a political commissar.

b) 1535 hours friendly troops in Kursenai. 1544 hours 14 enemy tanks on the Papil-Kruopinai road.
c) Interrogation of Schaulen residents revealed that some 7,000 men were transported by train toward Riga on 25 June. Larger prey is anticipated.

I AK-Ic

Transmitted to AOK18,
Lieutenant von Lüders, through Senior Lieutenant Dulier
at 1630 Hours

Source: *Bundesarchiv/Militärarchiv RH 24 1/260.* Translated by Dr. Marcus O. Jones.

B. Evening Report from V Army Corps to Ninth Army Headquarters, June 30, 1941

K.Gef.St, 30 June 1941
Evening Report
Submitted: Lt. Reppert
To AOK 9.

1) Advance elements of the 5th and 35 Infantry Divisions had contact on 30 June with only scattered groups of the enemy.

   No contact as of yet with those enemy forces deployed forward earlier on 30 June between Wola-Krupica and Dworek over the Szczara River.

   No enemy contact for the bulk of the 5th, 35th, and 161st Divisions.
2) Prisoners from the Russian 55th Rifle Regiment stated that, by order of their superiors, they were to remove their rank and unit insignia and wear civilian clothing.
3) Military commissars shot [struck from text "while fighting or fleeing"] number seven by the 5th Div; three by the 35th Div; five by the 161st Div; and twenty-two by the Corps Artillery Command.

   A Red party secretary from Wasiliski was shot by the administrative section of the corps command headquarters staff, as he remained in contact with Russian troops even after the arrival of German troops in Wasiliski.

Source: *Bundesarchiv/Militärarchiv RH 24 5/104.* Translated by Dr. Marcus O. Jones.

C. Daily Intelligence Report from I Army Corps to Fourth Panzer Group Headquarters, July 20, 1941

K.Gef.St, 20 July 1941
To Panzer Group 4, Ic
Ic—Daily Report

Entrenched enemy units north of the Nikolskaya bridgehead. Otherwise the enemy fights delaying actions. In this connection the enemy has mounted some tough resistance ("bush war"). Coherent leadership of large formations appears to exist no longer. Basically, resistance seems to consist of infantry and modest artillery units brought up by truck.

Advance reconnaissance pushed southeasterly of Dno against strong opposition with first-class and medium armor, which fled to the east.

The new position of the 202nd Motor Rifle Division was detected by I Army Corps. Breakdown: Rifle Regiments 252nd, 28th (deception designation 4023), 645th (deception designation 3849). Additionally from the 11th Division, prisoners from the 183rd Rifle Division (Rifle Regiments 227th, 285th, Reconnaissance Battalion 350).

Today 310 prisoners. Yesterday and today only one political commissar captured and shot.

I AK-Ic

Submitted to Panzer Group 4,
Lt. von Sternburg, at 1630 hours,
by Lt. Kleykamp

Source: *Bundesarchiv/Militärarchiv RH 24 1/260.* Translated by Dr. Marcus O. Jones.

6. Radio Message to Hitler from Sixth Army Commander General Friedrich Paulus, Requesting Permission to Break Out from Stalingrad

November 23, 1941

On November 19, 1941 the Red Army launched Operation URANUS, the double envelopment of the German Sixth Army at Stalingrad. By November 23, the encirclement was complete. That same day, General Paulus requested permission from Hitler to break out of the encirclement and withdraw from Stalingrad. Hitler forbade any withdrawal, convinced that the Sixth Army could be resupplied from the air.

Radio Communication

Secret Military Correspondence
To Army High Command
My Führer!

Matters have come to a head since receipt of your radio communication of 22 November.

The closure of the pocket in the southwest and west has not succeeded. Enemy breakthroughs there are imminent. Munitions and fuel are diminishing. Many batteries and anti-armor weapons are expended. Timely and adequate replenishment is impossible.

Should all forces not concentrate to crush the oncoming enemy in the southwest and west, the annihilation of the [Sixth] Army is at hand. To that end, the withdrawal of all divisions in Stalingrad and strong reinforcement from the northern front are essential. Breakthrough to the southwest is then unavoidable, as the weakening of the eastern and northern flanks will make them indefensible.

Although much equipment will indeed be lost, the great bulk of valuable personnel and at least some amount [of] equipment will be saved.

I bear full responsibility for this difficult message, even as the [corps] commanding generals Heitz, von Seydlitz, Strecker, Hube and Jennecke share the same opinion on the situation.

On account of the situation, once again, please permit freedom of action.

Heil my Führer!
Paulus
23 Nov. 1941

Source: *Bundesarchiv/Militärarchiv RH 20/6/2.* Translated by Dr. Marcus O. Jones.

7. Adolf Hitler, Secret "Night-and-Fog Decree" on the Punishment of Offenders in Occupied Territory

December 7, 1941

Resistance efforts were launched in all territories occupied by the German military.

Guerrilla and partisan activities were particularly widespread in the Soviet Union. Even when they were not so effective, at the very least, such undertakings had considerable nuisance value, and they were also a propaganda liability. In December 1941, Adolf Hitler ordered that, in principle, the German military should employ the death penalty to punish all such offenses.

The Führer and Supreme Commander of the Armed Forces

Directives for the prosecution of offences committed within the occupied territories against the German State or the occupying power, of December 7th, 1941.

Within the occupied territories, communistic elements and other circles hostile to Germany have increased their efforts against the German State and the occupying powers since the Russian campaign started. The amount and the danger of these machinations oblige us to take severe measures as a deterrent. First of all, the following directives are to be applied:

I. Within the occupied territories, the adequate punishment for offences committed against the German State or the occupying power which endanger their security or a state of readiness is on principle the death penalty.

II. The offences listed in paragraph I as a rule are to be dealt with in the occupied countries only if it is probable that sentence of death will be passed upon the offender, at least the principal offender, and if the trial and the execution can be completed in a very short time. Otherwise the offenders, at least the principal offenders, are to be taken to Germany.

III. Prisoners taken to Germany are subjected to military procedure only if particular military interests require this. In case German or foreign authorities inquire about such prisoners, they are to be told that they were arrested, but that the proceedings do not allow any further information.

IV. The Commanders in the occupied territories and the Court authorities within the framework of their jurisdiction, are personally responsible for the observance of this decree.

V. The Chief of the High Command of the Armed Forces determines in which occupied territories this decree is to be applied. He is authorized to explain and to issue executive orders and supplements. The Reich Minister of Justice will issue executive orders within his own jurisdiction.

Source: *United States,* Office of United States Chief of Counsel for Prosecution of Axis Criminality, Nazi Conspiracy and Aggression, *8 vols. and 2 suppl. vols.* Washington, DC: U.S. Government Printing Office, 1946–1948. *VII: 873–874 (Doc. No. L-90).*

8. Luftwaffe Report of the Effects of Operation GOMORRAH, the Allied Fire Bombing of Hamburg

July 24–August 3, 1943

Over the course of ten days from July 24 to August 3, 1943, the major German port city of Hamburg was attacked repeatedly by British and U.S. strategic bombers, often dropping incendiary bombs. The resulting explosions and firestorm from Operation GOMORRAH killed 42,600 people, injured 37,000, and forced some one million German civilians to flee the city.

Regional Air Command XI

Hamburg Blankenese, 4 August 1943

Ia op 3 (LS) 4a Nr. 17057/43
Re: Effects of the Fire Storm

Regional Air Command XI reports on the firestorm that resulted from the large-scale air raid on Hamburg and its effects:

The deployment of civil fire brigades and fire-fighting units was hindered in some districts by the large amounts of explosive and incendiary bombs.

As a result of the rapid spread of large-area fires and the lack of oxygen, the population was forced to flee the increasing temperatures of air raid shelters for the streets, which were bordered on both sides by burning buildings. Because extreme heat and a lack of oxygen also prevailed here owing to the extreme scale of the fires, many were rendered unconscious and burned to death by collapsing buildings. In the narrow streets especially, people were trapped by the fire-storm and consumed by burning buildings.

The effects of the firestorm are as follows.

The air streams vertically upward from the burning buildings. As every fire requires oxygen from the air to sustain itself, the air in the streets and open areas is drawn with powerful suction to feed the source with more oxygen. With the expansion of the core fire, any fresh air remaining in the streets becomes extraordinarily hot (no longer breathable); last of all, the fire pushes into the streets. Those who do not flee the air raid shelters early enough and wait out the fires underground, must suffocate from the lack of oxygen.

It must be made clear to the population that in the event of row and area fires which civil fire brigades have no prospect of fighting successfully, air raid shelters are to be evacuated *immediately*. Water reserves are to be kept at the ready in the air raid shelters to wet cloths, which are to be held over the mouth and nose against heat to facilitate evacuation from burning buildings. Woolen blankets soaked in water and wrapped around the head and body have proven themselves to be very effective protection against heat.

All units are to be immediately aware of the occurrence of the firestorm and its effects. and appropriately advised on the avoidance of large human losses.

Commanding General Regional
Air Command XI
/signed/ Wolf
General of Aviation

Source: *Bundesarchiv/Militärarchiv RL 19/593.* Translated by Dr. Marcus O. Jones.

9. Field Marshal Erwin Rommel, Normandy Situation Report to Hitler

July 15, 1944

Six weeks after the Normandy Invasion began, Field Marshal Erwin Rommel, commander of German Army Group B in Normandy, sent Hitler a teletype message warning that Germany faced defeat by the Allies and should withdraw from France. Ignoring this advice, Hitler ordered what became a disastrous German counterattack against advancing Allied units around Caen. On July 17, Rommel was severely injured when British fighter planes strafed his car. In company with other like-minded German generals, Rommel had intended that, if Hitler ignored his advice, he would open negotiations with Allied commanders in France for an armistice and a separate peace in the West, a move he hoped would spare Germany from invasion by Russian forces from the east.

Commander-in-Chief, Army Group B
Headquarters, 15 July 1944

Estimate of the Situation

The situation on the Normandy front grows more difficult each day and is approaching the proportions of a major crisis.

The combat power of our divisions is declining very rapidly as a result of high losses from the intensity of the fighting, the enemy's extraordinarily superiority in matériel, especially artillery and armor, and the effects of the enemy air force, which completely dominates the battle space. Replacements from home arrive only sparsely and reach the front only after weeks because of the difficult transport situation. Currently, some 10,000 men (of whom 6,000 have arrived) are supposed to replace losses of approximately 97,000 men (including 2,360 officers)—that is, a daily average of 2,500–3,000 men.

The losses in materiel by troops in action have been extraordinarily high and have been replaced only to a slight extent; for example, 17 tanks to replace around 225.

The newly arrived divisions are unaccustomed to combat and—with their shortage of artillery, antitank weapons, and weapons for close-range tank warfare—are incapable of successfully defending against large-scale enemy attacks after heavy shelling and bombing lasting several hours. As combat has shown, even the most valiant troops are ground up by the enemy's material superiority. The destruction of the rail network, as well as the strong threat by the enemy air force to roads and highways up to 150 kilometers behind the front, has endangered supply conditions such that only the most critical supplies can be brought up, and artillery and mortar ammunition above all must be rationed tightly. These circumstances will not likely improve, as maneuvering space diminishes continually as a result of enemy action and because enemy air activity will likely become more intensive as numerous air bases on the beachheads become active.

Significant new forces cannot be moved to the Normandy front without weakening the Fifteenth Army's front on the Channel or the Mediterranean Front of the Seventh Army in southern France. The Seventh Army front alone urgently requires two fresh divisions, as the forces there are exhausted.

New forces and large amounts of war matériel flow daily into [the] front on the enemy side. Our air force does nothing to disrupt enemy reinforcement. Enemy pressure grows continually stronger.

Under these circumstances we can expect that the enemy will break through our own thin front in the foreseeable future, above all the Seventh Army sector, and push into the open expanse of France. I refer to the current reports of the Seventh Army and II Parachute Corps. Apart from the local reserves of Panzer Group West, which are tied down in combat for the time being on the group's front, and which can only move at night because of enemy air supremacy. There are no mobile reserves to counter such a break-through on the Seventh Army front. As before, our own air force factors only slightly into the balance.

Our troops everywhere are fighting heroically, but the unequal contest is drawing to a close. It is necessary, in my view, to admit the consequences from this situation. I feel bound as commander-in-chief of the army group to express this clearly.

/signed/ Rommel
General Field Marshal

Source: *Bundesarchiv/Militärarchiv RH 19-IX/8, Bl. 105-08.* Translated by Dr. Marcus O. Jones.

10. Final Coordinating Order from Hitler to Field Marshal Walther Model for the Ardennes Offensive

December 15, 1944

The day before the Germans launched their Ardennes Offensive (Battle of the Bulge) on December 16, 1944, Hitler sent a final message to Army Group B commander, Field Marshal Walther Model, typically trying to micromanage the deployment of the forces, and thereby restricting the options of his commanders in the field. The Fifth Panzer Army attacked in the center, the Sixth Panzer Army on the right, and the Seventh Army on the left. The Fifteenth Army, on the right of Sixth Panzer Army, did not attack but was tasked with providing flanking support.

The Führer 15 December 1944
Via Officer only
98/44 Secret Military Correspondence

To General Field Marshal Model

I have made my final decisions.

All the preconditions for the success of the operation are present. The scale and scope of success now depends solely on the conduct of the operation.

I oblige you again to carry out all orders from the highest command unconditionally and to enforce obedience down to the level of the lowest unit.

I forbid any redirection of Panzer units eastward of the Maas towards the north. I order that the armored units of the Sixth Panzer Army be placed far enough from the covering front of LXVII Army Corps that they not become involved in the latter's fighting, and that the entire road network in the right area of the Fifth Panzer Army, if necessary to Namur, immediately be made available to the Sixth Panzer Army should a smooth transition in and around Lüttich not be possible.

I hold you personally responsible for ensuring that no massing of the Panzer units arises in the area around Lüttich such as to make necessary their deployment east of the Maas.

The natural cover of the eastern flank of the advance to Antwerp is the Maas Canal itself and is not to be formed farther to the west.

The left wing of the Fifteenth Army is to be made so strong that it will not be necessary to deploy infantry divisions of the Sixth Panzer Army in the fighting around Simmerath, which would weaken the defensive flank between Monschau and Lüttich.

If these principles for the conduct of the operation are followed, then great success is assured.

/signed/ Adolf Hitler

Source: *Bundesarchiv/Militärarchiv RH 19 IV/244 S.29-39.* Translated by Dr. Marcus O. Jones.

11. Message from Reichsführer-SS Heinrich Himmler to the Officers of Army Group Vistula for the Defense of Berlin

February 14, 1945

As the Soviet Army closed in on Berlin from the east, the head of the SS, Heinrich Himmler, was appointed commander of both Army Group Weichsel (Vistula), responsible for defending the capital, and Germany's entire Replacement Army (Ersatzheer). A man with absolutely no military training or experience, Himmler's assignment was based solely on his fanaticism and political reliability. The "traitor Seydlitz" mentioned *in the third paragraph was General of Artillery Walther Kurt von Seydlitz-Kurzbach, a corps commander captured by the Soviets at Stalingrad.(See Document Number 52.) In captivity, Seydlitz became the leader of the League of German Officers (*Bund deutscher Offiziere*), an anti-Nazi association of officer POWs.*

High Command of the Army
14 February 1945
National Socialist Command Staff of the Army
Az.: I/I Nr. 1410/45

The Reichsführer-SS requests that the officers of his army group note and appropriately evaluate the following appeal.

To all officers of Army Group Weichsel!

A few days ago I announced that former SS-Standartenführer and Bromberg police chief von Salisch was court-martialed and shot for having left his city like a coward. Likewise shot after a court-martial which I confirmed was Colonel von Hassenstein, who vacated a post entrusted to him against orders and without apparent urgency.

I expect from every officer that he serve as a model of courage and staunchness and that he precede our brave soldiers in every way. When an officer leads the way, his men stand by him. In those instances, however, in which human weakness, cowardice, or momentary panic beset one, the officer shows himself worthy of the rank and epaulettes conferred upon him.

As has always been customary in the Prusso-German army, I expect a harsh crackdown through the military courts. It is better that one or another coward dies than the notion takes hold in an otherwise brave unit that one can head for the rear. These officers will be the example to the thousands of violated German women and girls, murdered elderly and children, and burned villages, farms, and goods that there is but one thing to do at this decisive phase of the war: to stand and fight, in order to be able again to attack and crush the enemy. Since 1918 this Jewish-Bolshevik threat has menaced us at home and abroad. Although it changes its appearance, it remains the same in its essence. Had fate not granted us the Führer, Germany and all of Europe as well would long ago have drowned in the Red Swamp. Stalin and his Bolshevism have never changed. The hopes that the traitor Seydlitz and his committee have awakened through their appeal are belied most terribly by the fate of the German population here in the East, for whose welfare he is allegedly so concerned.

For Stalin, prisoners, deserters and defectors are tools which he unscrupulously exploits to his advantage, employed as agents under the supervision of commissars or used as canon-fodder.

We would be unworthy of our great traditions if we descendants were weaker than the officers of Frederick the Great, those of the Wars of Liberation, or our fathers in the World War.

It cannot be doubted that we have had much misfortune and suffered some setbacks. But it cannot be any less doubted that our power is great enough to resist our enemies on the other fronts and crush the Bolshevik hordes and drive them from the country, if everyone, especially each officer, does his duty. Our ambition is to be the truest supporters and followers to the Führer in rescuing the people and the Reich. We want to blot out any notion of the individual who can bring us shame. We want to be followed unswervingly and not surpassed by the officer corps which served Old Fritz [Frederick] in times even more taxing than the present. Officers of the great German people's army—who may sometimes be exhausted by efforts and stresses of a physical and mental nature; who, from general to lieutenant, have given so much blood for the nation; who have absorbed so many wounds; who have been and are the leaders in this mighty struggle to unparalleled victories—lead the brave soldiers of the German people better, valiantly, and more dutifully than ever! Plant the fanatical will to victory and the blazing hatred for these Bolshevik beasts in your hearts and theirs. School our men to awaken such a holy German rage against this consuming Bolshevik menace that the individual Bolshevik is left with but two choices: either to cross over and be taken prisoner, or be struck down as a beast and destroyer of the whole human institution.

And now, my comrades, let us do our duty with the old courage and strong hearts. God has never forsaken our people and has of late stood by us in our hours of greatest need.

Long live the Führer!
Himmler
Reichsführer-SS
Commander in Chief,
Army Group Weichsel
Commander in Chief,
Replacement Army

Source: *Bundesarchiv/Militärarchiv RH 19/ XV/10.* Translated by Dr. Marcus O. Jones.

12. German Army Group Vistula Intelligence Assessment of the Soviet 1st Belorussian Front, Battle of Seelow Heights

April 19, 1945

Soviet Forces started crossing the Oder River on April 16, 1945. Although they crossed in several places, Seelow Heights, on the west bank of the Oder, was a major German strongpoint between the river and Berlin. On April 19, the same day German Army Group Vistula Intelligence issued this estimate of the enemy situation, the 1st Belorussian Front broke through the final line of the Seelow Heights. Nothing but shattered German units and remnants lay between the Soviets and Berlin.

Ic/AO

Army Group [Vistula] Enemy Assessment, 19 April 1945

The concentration of forces perceived yesterday on both sides of the Seelow-Müncheberg road and north thereof to the area south of Wriezen has been clearly verified today. Its importance derives alone from the identification of an armored corps, a mechanized corps, and the Guard Cavalry Corps in the area near Neu-Hardenberg—Wriezen.

Particularly in light of the assembled armored forces, the enemy's intention finally to demolish those of our forces most heavily engaged in prior engagements and force an operational breakthrough toward Berlin must be considered demonstrated. A comparatively quiet disposition of enemy forces on both sides of Frankfurt [am Oder] and on the front north of Wriezen also indicates this intent.

According to the latest assessments, it must be supposed that the enemy is taking advantage of gaps in our front and ruthlessly driving farther to the west and southwest with strong numbers of available armored forces, and seeks to wipe out our remaining force concentrations with the artillery detected in the most recent movements.

The breakthrough of powerful packs of armored forces east of Müncheberg toward the south represents a particular threat. Should they not be destroyed or cut-off, a threat to the rearward connections of all forces along the Frankfurt-Libbenichen line must be anticipated. That this most recent southward thrust is occurring in the large and contiguous forests is an advantage that should be pointed out.

In front of the Third Panzer Army there are indications that the enemy intends a further occupation of the ground between the rivers, especially along the Schwedt-Fiddichow line, west of Greifenhagen, and on both sides of the Autobahn. Reinforcement of the infantry units there with heavy weapons is apparent. Indications of an imminent major attack are not yet in evidence. However, the available forces and the emplaced artillery are already sufficient to establish a bridgehead on the West-Oder-Arm in the short term.

Source: *Bundesarchiv/Militärarchiv RH 19/XV/9b.* Translated by Dr. Marcus O. Jones.

13. Grand Admiral Karl Dönitz, Broadcast Informing the German People of Their Unconditional Surrender

May 8, 1945

One week after telling the German people of Hitler's death, Grand Admiral Karl Dönitz, his successor as president of the Reich, spoke again on the radio to give them the news that Germany had signed an unconditional surrender, which would come into effect at 2300 hours on May 8, 1945. He appealed to his countrymen to conduct themselves with dignity and to hope that, ultimately, they would be able to find a respected place in Europe.

GERMAN MEN AND WOMEN:

When I addressed the German nation on May 1 telling it that the Fuehrer had appointed me his successor, I said that my foremost task was to save the lives of the German people. In order to achieve this goal, I ordered the German High Command during the night of 6–7 May to sign the unconditional surrender for all fronts.

On May 8 at 2300 hours the arms will be silent.

German soldiers, veterans of countless battles, are now treading the bitter path of captivity, and thereby making the last sacrifice for the life of our women and children, and for the future of our nation.

We bow to all who have fallen. I have pledged myself to the German people that in the coming times of want I will help courageous women and children, as far as I humanly can, to alleviate their conditions. Whether this will be possible I do not know.

We must face facts squarely. The unity of state and party does not exist any more. The party has left the scene of its activities.

With the occupation of Germany, the power has been transferred to the occupying authorities. It is up to them to confirm me in my function and the Government I have appointed or decide whether to appoint a different one.

Should I be required to help our Fatherland, I will remain at my post.

Should the will of the German people express itself in the appointment of a head of state, or should the powers of occupation make it impossible for me to continue in my office remains to be seen.

Duty keeps me in my difficult post for the sake of Germany. I will not remain one hour more than can be reconciled with the dignity of the Reich. I will disregard my person in this matter.

All of us have to face a difficult path. We have to walk it with dignity, courage and discipline which those demand of us who sacrificed their all for us. We must walk it by making the greatest efforts to create a firm basis for our future lives.

We will walk it in unity. Without this unity we shall not be able to overcome the misery of the times to come. We will walk it in the hope that one day our children may lead a free and secure existence in a peaceful Europe. On this thorny path, which we all will have to tread, I will try to help you as much as is possible, should I remain at my post. Should we succeed in going this way together, this step will be a service to the nation and to the Reich.

Source: *New York Times*, May 9, 1945. From *United States Congressional Serial Set: Surrender of Italy, Germany and Japan, World War II* (United States Congressional Serial Set, Volume 10949, Report no. 93). U.S. G.P.O., 1946, pp. 52–54. http://digital.library.wisc.edu/1711.dl/History.v10949n0093.

14. German Surrender at Reims, France

May 7, 1945

The Germans surrendered to the Allied forces in the west at Reims, France, on May 7, 1945. Colonel General Alfred Jodl signed for the German High Command. General of the Army Dwight D. Eisenhower's chief of staff, Lieutenant General Walter Bedell Smith, signed for the Western Allies. General Ivan Alexeyevich Susloparov signed for the Soviet High Command, although he did not have specific authorization from Moscow to do so.

Only this text in English is authoritative

Act of Military Surrender

1. We the undersigned, acting by authority of the German High Command, hereby surrender unconditionally to the Supreme Commander, Allied Expeditionary Force and simultaneously to the Soviet High Command all forces on land, sea, and in the air who are at this date under German control.
2. The German High Command will at once issue orders to all German military, naval, and air authorities and to all forces under German control to cease active operations at 2301 hours Central European time on 8 May and to remain in the positions occupied at that time. No ship, vessel, or aircraft is to be scuttled, or any damage dome to their hull, machinery or equipment.
3. The German High Command will at once issue to the appropriate commanders, and ensure the carrying out of any further orders issued by the Supreme Commander, Allied Expeditionary Force and by the Soviet High Command.
4. This act of military surrender is without prejudice to, and will be superseded by any general instrument of surrender imposed by, or on behalf of the United Nations and applicable to GERMANY and the German armed forces as a whole.
5. In the event of the German High Command or any of the forces under their control failing to act in accordance with this Act of Surrender, the Supreme Commander, Allied Expeditionary Force and the Soviet High Command will take such punitive or other action as they deem appropriate.

Signed at Rheims, France at 0241 on the 7th day of May, 1945.
On behalf of the German High Command.
/signed/ Jodl

In The Presence of

On behalf of the Supreme Commander
On behalf of the Soviet
Allied Expeditionary Force.
High Command.
/signed/ W. B. Smith
/signed/ Susloparov

Source: *Bundesarchiv/Militärarchiv RW 44 I/37.* Translated by Dr. Marcus O. Jones.

15. German Surrender at Berlin

May 8, 1945

At the insistence of the Kremlin, the Germans were required to sign a second instrument of surrender in Berlin, the day after they signed in Reims. In Reims, only Colonel General Alfred Jodl had signed for the Wehrmacht High Command. In Berlin, Field Marshal Wilhelm Keitel signed for both the Wehrmacht High Command and the German Army. General-Admiral Hans-Georg von Friedeburg signed for the German Navy. Colonel General Hans-Jürgen Stumpff signed for the Luftwaffe.

Declaration of Surrender

1. We the undersigned, acting in the authority and name of the High Command of the German Armed Forces, hereby declare the unconditional surrender of all forces presently under German control or under German orders on land, at sea, or in the air to the Supreme Commander of Allied Expeditionary Forces and the High Command of the Red Army simultaneously.
2. The Supreme Command of the German Armed Forces will immediately issue the order to all authorities of the German land, sea, and air forces to cease combat operations at 2301 hours Central European Time on 8 May and to remain in the positions occupied at that time and disarm themselves completely, while they surrender weapons and equipment to the local Allied commanders or to those officers designated to receive them by Allied representatives. No ship, boat, or aircraft of any sort is to be scuttled, nor are ship hulls, mechanical apparatus, weapons, machines of any sort, optics, or technical equipment that serve any military purpose to be damaged.
3. The Supreme Command of the German Armed Forces will immediately forward to the responsible authorities and carry out any additional orders of the Supreme Commander of Allied Expeditionary Forces and the High Command of the Red Army.
4. This act of surrender is without prejudice to and will be superseded by any general instrument of surrender imposed by the United Nations and in its name on Germany and the German armed forces.
5. In the event of the failure of the High Command of the German Armed Forces or any of the forces subordinate to or under its control to act in accordance with the stipulations of this act of surrender, the High Command of the Red Army and Supreme Commander of Allied Expeditionary Forces will

take such punitive measures as they deem appropriate.

6. This act is recorded in the English, Russian, and German languages. The English and Russian versions are alone authoritative.

Signed at Berlin on the 8 May 1945

/*signed*/ von Friedeburg   /*signed*/ Keitel   /*signed*/ Stumpff

For the Supreme Command of the German Wehrmacht

In the presence of:

For the High Command of the Red Army

/*signed*/ Zhukov

For the Supreme Commander, Allied Expeditionary Forces

/*signed*/ AWTedder

Also present signing as witnesses:

General, Commander in Chief French First Army
/*signed*/ J. de Lattre-Tassigny

/*signed*/ Carl Spaatz
Commanding General, United States Strategic Air Forces

Source: *Bundesarchiv/Militärarchiv RW 44 I/37.* Translated by Dr. Marcus O. Jones.

Appendix A: German Aces (1936–1945)

Ace is a designation used by many countries to designate a fighter pilot with five of more aerial victories. The term originated during World War I, and the United States, France, Belgium, and Italy were probably the only countries to use the term during that conflict. Nonetheless, pilots in other countries that did not acknowledge it (like Austria-Hungary and Russia) or tried not to recognize it (like Britain), did so on an unofficial level. By World War II, the term was being used, officially or unofficially, by all countries except Germany and Japan, which spent most of the war taking heroism for granted as something to be expected of all its servicemen.

During World War I, the Germans began using the term *Kanone* (cannon) for pilots who scored more than ten victories, starting with Oswald Boelcke. Some aviators were honored for fewer, but the term "ace" for five victories was never officially recognized by the Germans in either world war. The *Orden Pour le Mérite*, awarded to officers for consistent valor over an extended period of service, could be awarded to fighter pilots, initially with eight victories. That level was later increased to twenty, as the state-of-the-art of fighter planes advanced.

During World War II, the Luftwaffe began using the term *Experte* (expert), but not really for anything specific. As a general rule of thumb, a fighter pilot could be regarded as an *Experte* for about forty victories on the western front and, later, for one hundred over the East, although the general criterion was twenty for night fighters. Any of those numerical yardsticks could be waived somewhat if other factors, such as leadership, were added to one's accomplishments. The Germans produced the highest scoring combat pilots of both wars, and of all times. The highest-scoring U.S. pilot was Major Richard I. Bong, with forty victories in World War II. The highest-scoring Royal Air Force pilot was Canadian Major William A. Bishop with seventy-two victories in World War I. The highest-scoring French pilot was Captain René Fonck with seventy-five victories in World War I. The highest-scoring Japanese pilot was Chief Petty Officer Hiroyoshi Nishizawa with eighty-seven victories during World War II. The highest-scoring Finnish pilot was Warrant Officer Eino Ilmari Juutilainen with ninety-four victories during World War II. And the highest-scoring Russian pilot was Major Ivan N. Kozhedub with sixty-two victories during World War II. By contrast, the highest-scoring German pilot of World War I was Capt. Manfred von Richtoffen with eighty victories, and the highest-scoring German pilot of World War II was Captain Erich

Hartmann with 352 victories, a record not likely to ever be equaled. During World War II, 105 Luftwaffe pilots scored one hundred or more aerial victories.

Major Heinz-Wolfgang Schnaufer, with a total of 121 kills, was the world's leading night-fighter ace. Senior Lieutenant Heinz Schmidt, with 173 total kills, scored a single-day record of eighteen victories in four missions on November 3, 1943. Lieutenant Günther Scheel had the highest kill-to-mission ratio, with seventy-one victories in seventy missions. Senior Lieutenant Kurt Welter, with sixty-three total kills, was (and still is) the world's leading jet ace with twenty-six kills in the Me 262.

The first table lists the German pilots with ten or more victories during the relatively short Spanish Civil War. The second table lists the German pilots with one hundred or more victories during World War II, including any Spanish Civil War totals.

Jon Guttman

Highest Scoring German Fighter Pilots of the Spanish Civil War

			Confirmed Victories		
Final Rank	**First Name**	**Last Name**	**Spain**	**WWII Total**	**Wartime Fate**
Maj.	Werner	Mölders	14	115	Kac Nov. 22, 1941
Capt.	Wolfgang	Schellmann	12	25	KIA June 22, 1941
Capt.	Harro	Harder	11	22	KIA Aug. 12, 1940
Lt.	Peter	Boddem	10	10	KAc Mar. 20, 1939

Leading *Experten* of World War II

(Includes Spanish Civil War Totals)

Final Rank	First Name	Last Name	Confirmed Victories	Wartime Fate
Major	Erich	Hartmann	352	
Major	Gerhard	Barkhorn	301	
Major	Günther	Rall	275	
Sr. Lt.	Otto	Kittel	267	KIA Feb. 16, 1945
Major	Walter	Nowotny	258	KIA Oct. 8, 1944
Major	Wilhelm	Batz	237	
Major	Erich	Rudorffer	224	
Lt. Col.	Heinz	Bär	221	
Col.	Hermann	Graf	212	
Major	Heinrich	Ehrler	208	KIA Apr. 4, 1945
Major	Theodor	Weissenberger	208	
Major	Hans	Philipp	206	KIA Oct 8, 1943
Sr. Lt.	Walter	Schuck	206	WIA Apr. 10, 1945
Sr. Lt.	Anton	Hafner	204	KIA Oct. 17, 1944

Final Rank	First Name	Last Name	Confirmed Victories	Wartime Fate
Capt.	Helmut	Lipfert	203	
Capt.	Walter	Krupinski	197	
Major	Anton	Hackl	192	
Capt.	Joachim	Brendel	189	
Sr. Lt.	Maximilian	Stotz	189	KIA Aug. 19, 1943
Capt.	Joachim	Kirschner	188	KIA Dec. 17, 1943
Major	Kurt Hans	Brändle	180	KIA Nov. 3, 1943
Sr. Lt.	Günther	Josten	178	
Col.	Johannes	Steinhoff	176	WAc Apr. 18, 1945
Capt.	Ernst-Wilhelm	Reinert	174	
Capt.	Günther	Schack	174	
Capt.	Emil	Lang	173	KIA Sept. 3, 1944
Sr. Lt.	Heinz	Schmidt	173	KIA Sept. 5, 1943
Capt.	Horst	Adameit	166	KIA Aug, 7, 1944
Col.	Wolf-Dietrich	Wilcke	162	KIA Mar. 23, 1944
Capt.	Hans-Joachim	Marseille	158	KAc Sept. 30, 1942
Capt.	Heinrich	Sturm	158	KAc Dec. 22, 1944
Sr. Lt.	Gerhard	Thyben	157	
Sr. Lt.	Heinz	Beisswenger	152	KIA Mar. 6, 1943
Lt.	Peter	Düttmann	152	
Col.	Gordon	Gollob	150	
Sr. Lt.	Fritz	Tegtmeier	146	
Sr. Lt.	Albin	Wolf	144	KIA Apr. 2, 1944
Lt.	Kurt	Tanzer	143	
Major	Friedrich-Karl	Müller	140	KAc May 29, 1944
Lt.	Friedrich	Wachowiak	140	KIA June 16, 1944
Sr. Lt.	Karl	Gratz	138	
Capt.	Rudolf	Trenkel	138	
Capt.	Heinrich	Setz	138	
Sr. Lt.	Walter	Wolfrum	137	
Col.	Adolf	Dickfeld	136	
Sr. Lt.	Otto	Fönnekeld	136	KIA Aug. 30, 1944
Capt.	Karl-Heinz	Weber	136	KIA June 7, 1944
Major	Joachim	Müncheberg	135	KIA Mar. 23, 1943
Sr. Lt.	Hans	Waldmann	134	KAc Mar. 18, 1945
Capt.	Franz	Schall	133	KAc Apr. 10, 1945
Major	Johannes	Wiese	133	
Major	Adolf	Borchers	132	

(*continued*)

Final Rank	First Name	Last Name	Confirmed Victories	Wartime Fate
Major	Erwin	Clausen	132	KIA Oct. 4, 1943
Capt.	Alfred	Grislawski	132	
Capt.	Wilhelm	Lemke	131	KIA Nov. 30, 1943
Sr. Lt.	Gerhard	Hoffmann	130	KAc Apr. 11, 1945
Col.	Walter	Dahl	129	
Major	Franz	Eisenach	129	
Sr. Lt.	Heinrich	Sterr	129	KIA Nov. 26, 1944
Capt.	Franz	Dörr	128	
Col.	Walter	Oesau	127	KIA May 11, 1944
Sr. Lt.	Josef	Zwernemann	126	KIA Apr. 8, 1944
Col.	Dietrich	Hrabak	125	
Sr. Lt.	Wolf-Udo	Ettel	124	KIA July 17, 1943
Col.	Herbert	Ihlefeld	123	
Capt.	Wolfgang	Tonne	122	KAc Apr. 20, 1943
Off. Candidate	Heinz	Marquardt	121	
Major	Heinz-Wolfgang	Schnaufer	121	
Capt.	Robert	Weiss	121	KIA Dec. 29, 1944
Sr. Lt.	Friedrich	Obleser	120	
Major	Erich	Leie	118	KIA Mar. 7, 1945
Lt.	Franz-Josef	Beerenbrock	117	POW Nov. 9, 1942
Lt.	Hans-Joachim	Birkner	117	KAc Dec. 14, 1944
Lt.	Jakob	Norz	117	KAc Sept. 16, 1944
Lt.	Heinz	Wernicke	117	KIA Dec. 27, 1944
Sr. Lt.	August	Lambert	116	KIA Apr. 15, 1945
Major	Werner	Mölders	115	Kac Nov. 22, 1941
Lt.	Wilhelm	Crinius	114	POW Jan. 13, 1943
Major	Werner	Schroer	114	
Sr. Lt.	Hans	Dammers	113	
Sr. Lt.	Berthold	Korts	113	KIA Aug. 29, 1943
Lt. Col.	Kurt	Bühligen	112	
Major	Kurt	Ubben	111	KIA Apr. 27, 1944
Sr. Lt.	Franz	Woidich	110	
Col.	Günther	Lützow	110	KIA Apr. 21, 1945
Capt.	Emil	Bitsch	108	KIA Mar. 15, 1944
Major	Hans	Hahn	108	POW Feb. 21, 1943
Sr. Lt.	Berhard	Vechtel	108	
Sr. Lt.	Viktor	Bauer	106	
Capt.	Werner	Lucas	106	KIA Oct. 24, 1943

Final Rank	First Name	Last Name	Confirmed Victories	Wartime Fate
Capt.	Eberhard	von Boremski	104	
Maj. Gen.	Adolf	Galland	104	WIA Apr. 26, 1945
Sr. Lt.	Heinz	Sachsenberg	104	
Major	Hartmann	Grasser	103	
Major	Siegfried	Freytag	102	
Capt.	Friedrich	Geisshardt	102	DOW Apr. 6, 1943
Col.	Helmut	Lent	102	
Lt. Col.	Egon	Mayer	102	KIA Mar. 2, 1944
Sr. Lt.	Max-Hellmuth	Ostermann	102	KIA Aug. 9, 1942
Capt.	Josef	Wurmheller	102	KIA June 22, 1944
Col.	Josef	Priller	101	
Sr. Lt.	Rudolf	Meitig	101	KIA June 12, 1943
Lt.	Ulrich	Wernitz	101	
Capt.	Paul-Heinrich	Dähne	100	KIA Apr. 24, 1945
Maj.	Reinhard	Seiler	100	WIA July 6, 1943

KIA: Killed in action
WIA: Wounded in action
DOW: Died of wounds
POW: Prisoner of War
KAc: Killed in an accident
WAc: Wounded or injured in accident

See also: Barkhorn, Gerhard; Göring, Hermann; Hartmann, Erich Alfred; Mölders, Werner; Rall, Günther; Steinhoff, Johannes; Udet, Ernst

Additional Reading

Toliver, Raymond F., and Trevor J. Constable. *Fighter Aces of the Luftwaffe.* Atglen, PA: Schiffer Publishing, 1996.

Appendix B: Chiefs of the General and Admiralty Staffs (1919–1945)

Since the days of Generals Gerhard von Scharnhorst and August Neidhardt von Gneisenau, during the Napoleonic Wars, the General Staff has been the central institution of the Prussian/German Armies. In the late nineteenth century, British military historian Spencer Wilkinson called it "the Brain" of the German Army. The institution developed a worldwide reputation for competence and precision in centralized military planning. By World War II, however, Germany had four general (or admiralty, in the case of the navy) staffs. These staffs operated as the cores of the High Command of the German Armed Forces (*Oberkommando der Wehrmacht*—OKW), the High Command of the Army (*Oberkommando des Heeres*—OKH), the High Command of the Air Force (*Oberkommando der Luftwaffe*—OKL), and the High Command of the Navy (*Oberkommando der Marine*—OKM). As explained in the entries for these four organizations and for the German General Staff in this encyclopedia, the resulting overall command structure was chaotic and often dysfunctional. The four High Commands frequently competed with and maneuvered around each other, which was exactly the way Hitler, as commander in chief of the Wehrmacht wanted it.

Field Marshal Paul von Hindenburg was chief of the German General Staff during the last two-and-a-half years of World War I. When he retired in 1919, he was replaced by Lieutenant General Wilhelm Groener, who held the position for only four days. Groener, in turn, was succeeded by Major General Hans von Seeckt, who held the position for only eight days because the German General Staff was abolished by the Treaty of Versailles. In October 1919, however, the General Staff was resurrected clandestinely as the Troop Office (Truppenamt) of Germany's new one-hundred-thousand-man Reichswehr. Seeckt remained as the chief of the Truppenamt until March 1920, when he became the chief of the Army Command (Heeresleitung), the defacto commander of the Reichswehr. He was replaced as the chief of the Troop Office by Major General Wilhelm Heye.

The last chief of the Troop Office was Major General Ludwig Beck, who became the first chief of the reborn General Staff on July 1, 1935. In 1938, Hitler dismissed the minister of war and commander in chief of the Wehrmacht, Field Marshal Werner von Blomberg, and assumed direct command of the Wehrmacht personally. Hitler established the Wehrmacht High Command as

Chief of the German General Staff

- Lieutenant General Wilhelm Groener — July 3, 1919 to July 7, 1919
- Major General Hans von Seeckt — July 7, 1919 to July 15, 1919

Chief of the Troop Office

- Major General Hans von Seeckt — October 11, 1919 to March 26, 1920
- Major General Wilhelm Heye — March 26, 1920 to February 1, 1923
- Major General Otto Hasse — February 1, 1923 to October 31, 1925
- Major General Georg Wetzell — October 31, 1925 to January 27, 1927
- Major General Werner von Blomberg — January 27, 1927 to September 30, 1929
- Major General Kurt von Hammerstein-Equord — September 30, 1929 to October 31, 1930
- Major General Wilhelm Adam — October 31, 1930 to September 30, 1933
- Major General Ludwig Beck — October 1, 1933 to July 1, 1935

Chief of the Army High Command General Staff

- Colonel General Ludwig Beck — July 1, 1935 to August 31, 1938
- Colonel General Franz Halder — September 1, 1938 to September 24, 1942
- Colonel General Kurt Zeitzler — September 24, 1942 to June 10, 1944
- Lieutenant General Adolf Heusinger — June 10, 1944 to July 21, 1944
- Colonel General Heinz Guderian — July 21, 1944 to March 28, 1945
- General of Infantry Hans Krebs — April 1, 1945 to May 1, 1945

Chief of the Luftwaffe High Command General Staff

- General of Aviation Walther Wever — March 1, 1935 to June 3, 1936
- General of Aviation Albert Kesselring — June 5, 1936 to May 31, 1937
- General of Aviation Hans-Jürgen Stumpff — June 1, 1937 to January 31, 1939
- Colonel General Hans Jeschonnek — February 1, 1939 to August 18, 1943
- General of Aviation Günther Korten — August 25, 1943 to July 22, 1944
- General of Aviation Werner Kreipe — August 2, 1944 to October 28, 1944
- General of Aviation Karl Koller — November 12, 1944 to May 8, 1945
- General of Aviation Hans-Jürgen Stumpff — May 8, 1945 to May 23, 1945

Chief of the Naval Warfare Command Admiralty Staff

- Vice Admiral Günther Guse — October 1, 1937 to October 31, 1938
- Admiral Otto Schniewind — October 31, 1938 to June 12, 1941
- Admiral Kurt Fricke — June 13, 1941 to February 21, 1943
- Admiral Wilhelm Meisel — February 21, 1943 to July 22. 1945

Chief of Staff of the Armed Forces High Command (OKW)

- Field Marshal Wilhelm Keitel — February 4, 1938 to May 8, 1945

Chief of the Armed Forces High Command Operations Staff

- Colonel General Alfred Jodl — September 1, 1939 to May 8, 1945 his personal staff, with the compliant General Wilhelm Keitel as its chief. In 1939, the Wehrmacht High Command assumed an operational role with the establishment of the OKW Operations Staff (*Wehrmachtführungsstabes*), and General Alfred Jodl as its chief. On operational matters, Hitler normally dealt directly with Jodl, bypassing Keitel.

The high command of the Luftwaffe was established in March 1935. The first chief of the OKL General Staff was General of Aviation Walther Wever. The high command of the navy was established in January 1936. Within OKM, the Naval Warfare Command (*Seekriegsleitung*—SKL) was established the following year. The Admiralty Staff was the core of the SKL.

David T. Zabecki

See also: German General Staff of World War II; *Oberkommando der Luftwaffe* (OKL); *Oberkommando der Marine* (OKM); *Oberkommando der Wehrmacht* (OKW); *Oberkommando des Heeres* (OKH)

Additional Reading

Megargee, Geoffrey P. *Inside Hitler's High Command.* Lawrence: University of Kansas Press, 2000.

Wheeler-Bennett, John W. *The Nemesis of Power: The German Army in Politics, 1918–1945.* New York: Macmillan, 1964.

Appendix C: Field Marshals and Grand Admirals (1933–1945)

Generalfeldmarschall (general field marshal) was the highest military rank in several of the preunification German states, the Holy Roman Empire, the Kaiserreich, and the Third Reich. Commonly written in English as simply field marshal, it was the highest of the general officer ranks. The British equivalent was also called field marshal; the French equivalent was marshal of France; and, in the twentieth century, the U.S. equivalent was general of the army. In addition to their unique insignias of rank, British, French, and German marshals were authorized to carry a marshal's baton (*Marschallstab*). German field marshals generally had two versions. The formal baton was short, thick, relatively heavy, and ornately decorated. While in the field, German field marshals generally carried a service baton (*Interimstab*) that was much lighter and thinner and looked somewhat like a swagger stick, except much longer.

Traditionally, the rank of field marshal was only conferred upon a senior general officer in recognition for a major battlefield victory. Prior to 1918, the rank almost always included a patent of nobility (for those officers who were not already noblemen) and the right of direct access to the king or the Kaiser (*Immediatrecht*). During the Third Reich period, the right of direct access to the Führer was retained. When Erwin Rommel was promoted to field marshal following the battle of Gazala in 1942, he immediately used that right to go over the head of his theater commander, Field Marshal Albert Kesselring, and convince Hitler that he could win in North Africa without Germany having to eliminate the key British base of Malta in the middle of the Mediterranean. It was one of the major German strategic blunders of the war.

Another firm tradition held that a German field marshal never surrendered or allowed himself to be captured alive. When the German Sixth Army was on the verge of being crushed at Stalingrad, Hitler promoted Colonel General Friedrich Paulus to field marshal, anticipating that he would shoot himself rather than become the first German field marshal ever captured. Paulus, however, refused to kill himself and was captured. Afterward, Hitler was more outraged at Paulus's violation of that tradition than he was with the destruction of the German Sixth Army.

Adolf Hitler reestablished the rank of field marshal in the Wehrmacht on February 4, 1938, when Luftwaffe head Hermann Göring was promoted to that rank. On July 19, 1940, following the German victory in the Battle of France, Hitler promoted twelve more officers to field marshal. That same day, he also promoted Göring to the newly established rank of Reich marshal. Between 1938 and 1945, a total of twenty-five officers were promoted to the rank of Generalfeldmarschall in the Wehrmacht.

- Hermann Göring—February 4, 1938
- Fedor von Bock—July 19, 1940
- Walther von Brauchitsch—July 19, 1940
- Albert Kesselring—July 19, 1940
- Wilhelm Keitel—July 19, 1940
- Günther von Kluge—July 19, 1940
- Wilhelm Ritter von Leeb—July 19, 1940
- Siegmund Wilhelm Walter List—July 19, 1940
- Erhard Milch—July 19, 1940
- Walther von Reichenau—July 19, 1940
- Karl Rudolf Gerd von Rundstedt—July 19, 1940
- Hugo Sperrle—July 19, 1940
- Erwin von Witzleben—July 19, 1940
- Eduard von Böhm-Ermolli—October 31, 1940
- Erwin Rommel—June 22, 1942
- Georg von Küchler—June 30, 1942
- Erich von Manstein—July 1, 1942
- Friedrich Paulus—January 31, 1943
- Ernst Busch—February 1, 1943
- Paul von Kleist—February 1, 1943
- Maximilian von Weichs—February 1, 1943
- Wolfram von Richthofen—February 16, 1943
- Walter Model—March 1, 1944
- Ferdinand Schörner—April 5, 1945
- Robert Ritter von Greim—April 25, 1945

On July 19, 1940, Hitler established the unique rank of Reichsmarschall (marshal of the Reich) for the head of the Luftwaffe, Hermann Göring. Technically superior to field marshal, the rank of Reich marshal was based on a military rank established by the Holy Roman Empire in 1664. Göring was the only man ever to hold that rank since the Holy Roman Empire, making him, theoretically, the most senior-ranking German officer of all time.

Established in 1901, the rank of Grossadmiral (grand admiral) was the German Navy's equivalent of field marshal. Grand admirals also were authorized to carry batons. The rank was conferred only twice during the period of the Third Reich.

- Erich Raeder—April 1, 1939
- Karl Dönitz—January 30, 1943

The ranks of field marshal and grand admiral were not revived by the post-World War II Bundeswehr. Currently general and admiral are the most senior German military ranks. On March 25, 1982, the German Democratic Republic established the rank of Marschall der DDR for the Nationale Volksarmee (NVA), specifically for wartime service, No one ever served in the rank.

David T. Zabecki

See also: Appendix D

Additional Reading

Rosinski, Herbert. *The German Army.* Praeger, New York: 1966.

Appendix D: German Military Ranks (1919–1945)

At the start of World War II, officers comprised only 2.86 percent of the German military, and that percentage actually declined as the war progressed and the Wehrmacht grew. In contrast, officers made up 7 percent of the U.S. Army. The German armies of World Wars I and II were especially noted for conferring promotions very sparingly. In most of the world's armies, command authority is tied rigidly to rank. The senior officer is always in command. The German Army, however, was always different in this respect. The principle in the German Army was always that function overrode rank. An officer in a command position, even if his actual rank was below that authorized for the position, always exercised command authority over lower-level commanders, even if they happened to outrank him. Such a situation would have been unthinkable in the British Army or U.S. Army, but it was common in the German Army.

The basic German rank for the common soldier has always been *Soldat* or *Schütze* (Rifleman). The exact rank titles, however, have traditionally been a function of the soldier's branch. Infantrymen were generally called *Grenadier*; light infantrymen, *Jäger* (Hunter); artillerymen, *Kannonier*; combat engineers, *Pionier*; and so forth. When the Luftwaffe was established in 1935, the basic enlisted rank was designated *Flieger*. The basic naval rank is *Matrose* (seaman).

Dating from at least the sixteenth century, the rank of *Gefreiter*, derived from "the exempted," denoted an older soldier who was exempted from guard duty. The usual English translations for *Gefreiter* include lance corporal and private first class. In the navy of World War II, the second enlisted rank was called *Matrosengefreiter*. While the World War II army and air force had three distinct *Gefretier* ranks, the navy had five. Arguably, the most famous *Gefreiter* of all time was Adolf Hitler, who served in that rank during World War I.

Unteroffizier is both a specific rank title as well as a collective term for army and air force noncommissioned officers (NCOs) and navy petty officers. As the lowest NCO rank, *Unteroffizier* existed as early as the seventeenth century. The rank is roughly equivalent to a U.S. sergeant in World War II. The equivalent navy rank was *Bootsmannmatt* (boatswain's mate).

The group of *Feldwebel* ranks are the senior-most German NCOs. The rank title dates to the Middle Ages and the Landsknecht regiments. In cavalry and artillery units, however, the rank title was *Wachtmeister* (watch master). During World War II, the army and air force had three distinct senior NCO ranks: *Feldwebel*, *Oberfeldwebel*, and

American and German Military Ranks in World War II

	U.S. Army and Army Air Force WWII	Wehrmacht Heer and Luftwaffe	Waffen-SS	U.S. Navy WWII	Keiegsmarine
Officers		Reischmarschall			
	General of the Army	Generalfeldmarschall	Reichsführer-SS	Fleet Admiral	Grossadmiral
	General	Generaloberst	Oberstgruppenführer	Admiral	Generaladmiral
	Lieutenant General	General der Infantrie General der Artillerie General der Kavallerie General der Flieger General der Panzer Truppen	Obergruppenführer	Vice Admiral	Admiral
	Major General	Generalleutnant	Gruppenführer	Rear Admiral	Vizeadmiral
	Brigadier General	Generalmajor	Brigadeführer	Commodore	Konteradmiral
			Oberführer		Kommodore
	Colonel	Oberst	Standartenführer	Captain	Kapitän zur See
	Lieutanant Colonel	Oberstleutnant	Obersturmbannführer	Commander	Frigattenkapitän
	Major	Major	Sturmbannführer	Lieutenant Commander	Korvettenkapitän
	Captain	Hauptmann	Hauptsturmführer	Lieutanant	Kapitänleutnant
	First Lieutanant	Oberleutnant	Obersturmführer	Lieutenant (Junior Grade)	Oberleutnant zur See
	Second Lieutanant	Leutnant	Untersturmführer	Ensign	Leutnant zur See

Enlisted	Master Sergeant First Sergeant	Stabsfeldwebel	Sturmscharführer	Chief Petty Officer	Stabsoberbootsmann
					Oberbootsmann
	Technical Sergeant	Oberfeldwebel	Hauptscharführer	Petty Officer First Class	Stabsbootsmann
		Feldwebel Wachtmeister	Oberscharführer		Bootsmann
	Staff Sergeant	Unterfeldwebel	Scharführer	Petty Officer Second Class	Oberbootsmannmaat
	Sergeant	Unteroffizier	Unterführer	Petty Officer Third Class	Bootsmannmaat
		Stabsgefreiter			Matrosenoberstabsgefreiter
	Corporal	Obergefreiter		Seaman First Class	Matrosenstabsgefreiter
		Gefreiter	Rottenführer		Matrosenhauptgrfreiter
	Private First Class	Oberchütze	Sturmmann	Seaman Second Class	Matrosenobergefreiter
					Matrosengefreiter
	Private	Schütze	SS-Mann	Seaman Third Class	Matrose

Stabsfeldwebel. The navy had four with *Bootsmann*, *Stabsbootsmann*, *Oberbootsmann*, and *Stabsoberbootsmann*.

Through the end of World War II, *Fahnenjunker* (officer cadet) and *Fähnrich* (officer candidate) were the two levels of training ranks prior to an officer's commissioning. Although *Fähnrich* translates literally to ensign, the rank was in no way equivalent to the U.S. Navy rank of Ensign, which is a fully commissioned officer. The *Fähnrich* served in the ranks, initially in a junior NCO position, and then at increasingly higher levels of responsibility, but always for the purpose of developing a future commissioned officer.

By the early eighteenth century, three distinct classes of officers had emerged in most of the world's armies. Known as company grade officers in the U.S. Army and as *Hauptleute* (head men) in the German military, lieutenants and captains were responsible for the leadership of platoons and companies. Field-grade officers in the U.S. Army and *Stabsoffiziere* (staff officers) in the German military included majors and colonels who lead battalions and regiments. General officers, or *Herren* (gentlemen), command the higher military echelons and also coordinate the overall direction of the military forces.

Since the nineteenth century and continuing in today's Bundeswehr, certain initials immediately following an officer's rank title are used to indicate a special status. All qualified General Staff officers at the rank of colonel and below add the letters "i.G." for *im Generalstabsdienst*. All reserve officers add "d.R." for *der Reserve*. And all retired officers add "a.D." for *ausser Dienst*.

The basic German officer rank is *Leutnant* (lieutenant), or *Leutnant zur See* (naval lieutenant) for the navy. The origins of the rank date to the Middle Ages. During late eighteenth century, the rank of *Oberleutnant* (senior lieutenant) and *Oberleutnant zur See* evolved. *Hauptmann* (captain) is the usual rank held by company and battery commanders in most of the world's armies. The navy equivalent was *Kapitänleutnant* (captain lieutenant).

Major and *Korvettenkapitän* (corvette captain) are the lowest of the senior officer ranks. The rank of *Oberst* (colonel) originated in the Middle Ages as a designation for the senior knight on a battlefield. As professional standing armies began to emerge during the sixteenth and seventeenth centuries, an Oberst became the commander of a regiment. During the eighteenth century, *Oberstleutnant* (lieutenant colonel) became the rank of the principal deputy to an *Oberst* and also the rank of the commander of a battalion. The naval equivalents to lieutenant colonel and colonel are *Frigattenkapitän* (frigate captain) and *Kapitän zur See* (naval captain), respectively.

The rank of general in Germany can be traced back at least to the various religious orders of the Holy Roman Empire. By the nineteenth century, the standard rank structure of German generals started with *Generalmajor* (major general), followed by *Generalleutnant* (lieutenant general), *General Generaloberst* (colonel general), and *Generalfeldmarschall* (general field marshal). At the third level, generals were always generals of a specific arm or branch of service: *General der Infanterie* (general of infantry), *General der Kavallerie* (general of cavalry), *General der Artillerie* (general of artillery), *General der Panzer Truppen* (general of panzer troops). When the Luftwaffe was established, the rank of *General der Flieger* (general of aviation) was also added.

The rank of *Generalfeldmarschall* originated in the Holy Roman Empire. In 1940,

Hitler established the unique rank of *Reichsmarschall* (marshal of the Reich) for the head of the Luftwaffe. Hermann Göring was the only man ever to hold that rank since the Holy Roman Empire.

Through the end of World War II, a German *Generalmajor* typically commanded a brigade, and a *Generalleutnant* commanded a division. In the U.S. Army, brigades were commanded by brigadier generals, and divisions by major generals. Thus, a pre-1945 *Generalmajor* was really the same rank as U.S. brigadier general, and a *Generalleutnant* the equivalent of a U.S. major general.

During World War II, the German Navy admiral ranks were *Konteradmiral* (rear admiral), *Vizeadmiral* (vice admiral), Admiral (admiral), *Generaladmiral* (general admiral), and *Grossadmiral* (grand admiral). A *Konteradmiral* was the equivalent of an army *Generalmajor.* A German *Vizeadmiral* and *Admiral* were actually one rank level below their U.S. and British counterparts with the same rank titles. The navy also had the rank of *Kommodore,* above *Kapitän zur See* but below *Konteradmiral.* The army and Luftwaffe did not have a rank at that level, but the Waffen-SS did.

The Waffen-SS of World War II was a special case. Like many of the paramilitary organizations of the Third Reich, the Schutzstaffel (SS) had its own uniforms and its unique insignias of rank, but its rank structure was clearly along military lines. The two basic enlisted SS ranks were *SS-Mann* and *Sturmmann* (assault man), which were the equivalent of the army's *Schütze* and *Oberschütze.* All SS rank titles above that level ended in *-Führer* (-leader). The highest rank in the SS was *Reichsführer-SS,* equivalent to *Generalfeldmarschall* and held only by Heinrich Himmler. Once the Waffen-SS branch of the SS became a full-fledged military armed force, it retained its own unique ranks titles but appended the army rank equivalent "of the Waffen-SS." Thus, a senior Waffen-SS officer like Josef "Sepp" Dietrich held the rather cumbersome full rank title of *SS-Oberstgruppenführer und Generaloberst der Waffen-SS* (SS supreme group leader and colonel general of the Waffen-SS).

For the ease of reading, all German rank titles in this encyclopedia are rendered in English. They are given as direct translations, rather than rank equivalents. Thus, a World War II Wehrmacht *Generalmajor* is translated as a major general, although the World War II rank was equivalent to a U.S. Brigadier General. There are a few exceptions to this basic rule. The ranks of *Gefreiter* and *Feldwebel* are almost impossible to translate directly into English and are best left in the German original. All Waffen-SS ranks titles likewise are given in their original German because of the cumbersome and unfamiliar English translations. This also is an easy way for readers to identify the Waffen-SS soldiers.

David T. Zabecki

***See also*:** Dietrich, Josef "Sepp"; Göring, Hermann; Himmler, Heinrich; Appendix C; Appendix E

Additional Reading

Davis, Brian L. *Badges & Insignia of the Third Reich, 1933–1945.* Poole, Dorset, UK: Blandford Press, 1983.

Davis, Brian L. *German Army Uniforms and Insignia, 1933–1945.* New York: Arco Publishing, 1977.

Appendix E: German Military Medals and Decorations (1933–1945)

When the Third Reich was established in 1933, some, but not all, of the military decorations from the Kaiserreich were carried forward. Not used during World War II period was Prussia's premier combat decoration, the *Orden Pour le Merite* (Order of Merit), established in 1740 by King Friedrich II (Frederick the Great). It was widely known as "The Blue Max," in reference to World War I ace Max Immelmann. Only officers were eligible, and 687 were awarded during World War I, and another 122 awarded the higher level *Pour le Merite mit Eichenlaub* (with Oak Leaves). Still serving officers who had won the *Orden Pour le Merite*, such as Erwin Rommel and Hermann Göring, continued to wear it on their Wehrmacht uniforms.

Prussia's Iron Cross, established in 1813, and the most famous of all German military decorations, was carried forward into World War II. Through the end of World War I, there were only three levels of the Iron Cross, Second Class, First Class, and the Grand Cross, awarded only five times during World War I. The Iron Cross was revived by Hitler on September 1, 1939 in four classes: Grand Cross, Knight's Cross (a grade that had not previously existed), First Class, and Second Class. Four other grades of the Iron Cross were added by Hitler during the war so that there were a total of eight grades by 1945. Both officers and enlisted men were eligible for all classes of the Iron Cross, but only thirty-five awards above the level of the Knight's Cross were made to noncommissioned officers, many of whom were pilots. The award of the Iron Cross was progressive. A soldier received the Iron Cross Second Class for his first act of valor, regardless of the circumstances. The Iron Cross First Class recognized the second act of valor, and so on up the line.

The design of the Third Reich's Iron Cross adhered closely to the original Prussian decoration, an iron cross pattée set in a frame of silver. The obverse of the World War II version a raised swastika in the center, and the date 1939 at the base of the lower arm. The reverse was plain except for the date 1813, the year in which the Prussian decoration was first instituted. The ribbon of each grade of the Iron Cross had a red center stripe and was edged with white and black stripes. The Iron Cross, Second Class (*Eiserne Kreuz II klasse*) had a suspension ribbon, but the full medal was worn only on special occasions. For normal daily wear, the ribbon alone was tucked diagonally into the second button of the uniform tunic. Between 2.3 million and 5 million were awarded between 1939 and 1945. The Iron Cross, First Class (*Eiserne Kreuz I klasse*) was a breast badge. There was no ribbon. Between three hundred thousand and seven hundred thousand were awarded in World War II. The Knight's Cross of the Iron Cross (*Ritterkreuz*), and all the higher levels were neck orders. A total of 7,318 Knight's Crosses were awarded. It was roughly equivalent to the U.S. Army's Distinguished Service Cross.

The Knight's Cross with Oak Leaves (*mit dem Eichenlaub*) was instituted by Hitler on June 3, 1940. A total of 882 were awarded between 1940 and 1945. A silver cluster of three oak leaves was attached to the suspension loop of the cross. This was not the same thing as the "Oak Leaf Cluster" used by the U.S. Army to indicate a second award of the same decoration. The recipients of the Oak Leaves received a different and higher grade of the Order of the Iron Cross. The Knight's Cross with Oak Leaves and Swords (*mit dem Eichenlaub und Schwertern*) was instituted on June 21, 1941. By 1945, 159 had been awarded. The Knight's Cross with Oak Leaves, Swords, and Diamonds (*mit dem Eichenlaub, mit Schwertern und Billanten*) was authorized by Hitler on July 15, 1941. Only twenty-seven were awarded between 1941 and 1945.

Hitler established the highest grade of the Knight's Cross, Knight's Cross with Golden Oak Leaves, Swords and Diamonds (*mit dem Goldenen Eichlaub, Schwertern und Brillanten*), on December 29, 1944. Only one was awarded, to Luftwaffe Stuka pilot Hans-Ulrich Rudel. The Grand Cross (*Grosskreuz*) was a neck order, similar to the Knight's Cross, except the cross badge itself was larger. The Grand Cross was awarded only once during World War II, to Reich Marshall Hermann Göring.

Other Third Reich military decorations of note were the War Order of the German Cross (in Gold and Silver), and the War Merit Cross. Established by Hitler on September 28, 1941, the German Cross in Gold or Silver (*Kriegsorden des Deutsche Kreuz*) recognized outstanding achievement in combat (gold) or honorable service in execution of the war (silver) above that required for the Iron Cross First Class but not sufficient for the award of the Knight's Cross. One could not be awarded the German Cross unless he had previously been awarded the Iron Cross First Class or War Merit Cross 1st Class with swords. But, while this meant that the German Cross was a "bridge" between the Iron Cross 1st Class and the Knight's Cross, it was not in the line of succession with the Iron Cross series.

The central feature of the German Cross was a black enamel swastika in the center of the eight-pointed breast star. The gold version had a gold wreath, while the silver German Cross had a silver wreath. Both wreaths had the numeral 1941 at the bottom, reflecting the date of the awards' establishment. About thirty thousand German Crosses in gold were awarded. Only twelve hundred silver versions were awarded, of which about nine hundred went to soldiers and Waffen-SS personnel.

In October 1939, Hitler announced that a new War Merit Cross (*Kriegsverdienstkreuz*) would be awarded to those military and civilian personnel who performed brave acts or wartime meritorious service falling short of that required for the award of the Iron Cross. The *Kriegsverdienstkreuz*, or KVK, was a cross-shaped medal of eight points, with narrow, straight widening arms. A swastika surrounded by a circular oak wreath was centered in the middle of the obverse and the numerals 1939 were centered on the reverse. The KVK came in two classes, both of which could be awarded with or without swords. The award for swords was restricted to those who had served bravely in combat. The decoration without swords was for outstanding service not in direct combat. The KVK with swords had a pair of crossed swords set in the angles of the cross. The decoration without swords was simply the plain cross. The First Class was a breast badge. The Second Class suspended from a red, white, and black ribbon. Like the Iron Cross Second Class, the ribbon of the War Merit Cross Second Class was normally worn in the second button of the uniform tunic.

On August 19, 1940, Hitler authorized a higher class of the KVK. This new decoration, called the Knight's Cross of the War Merit Cross (*Ritterkreuz des Kriegsverdienstkreuzes*), with or without swords, was a neck order. The Knight's Cross version was for award to Wehrmacht personnel, including civilians, who made significant contributions to the war effort but falling short of the level required for the award of the Knight's Cross of the Iron Cross. By the end of the war, a total of 118 awards with swords and 137 awards without swords had been made. About five hundred thousand awards of the KVK First Class with swords and one hundred thousand without swords were made during World War II. Some six million KVKs Second Class with swords were awarded between 1940 and 1945, and 1.6 million without swords.

While technically considered badges rather than medals, various combat badges had a level of prestige equal to decorations. The Infantry Assault Badge *(Infanterie Sturmabzeichen)* was established on December 30, 1939. It consisted of a wreath with a rifle and bayonet, surmounted by an eagle and swastika. It was awarded only to infantry and mountain infantry soldiers for participation in infantry assaults on at least three different days. The badge came in silver, but, in 1940, a bronze version was authorized for motorized infantrymen.

The Tank Combat Badge (*Panzerkampfabzeichen*) was established on the same date as the Infantry Assault Badge and was roughly the same size, the Tank Combat Badge was an oval wreath surrounding a tank moving forward at an angle and surmounted by an eagle and swastika. Originally it was awarded in silver to tank crews, only for participation in three engagements on different days. In 1940, a bronze version was authorized for all other armored vehicle crewmen. In June 1943, the badge was further modified with the addition of numerals at the base of the wreath indication participation in twenty-five, fifty, seventy-five, or one hundred tank battles.

The General Assault Badge (*Allgemaines Sturmabzeichen*), authorized on June 1, 1940, was initially awarded to combat engineers who participated in direct assaults. The badge was an oval wreath with an eagle and swastika in the center, and beneath the swastika were a crossed bayonet and stick hand grenade. Later, eligibility for the General Assault Badge was extended to all soldiers not otherwise qualified for the Infantry Assault Badge or the Tank Combat Badge.

After three years of war, Hitler realized that Germans serving as infantrymen in the army and Waffen-SS deserved recognition for their combat bravery—and that the Iron Cross Second Class could not be awarded to all of them. Consequently, in November 1942, Hitler announced that all officers and men of the army and Waffen-SS who participated in hand-to-hand combat, unsupported by armor, would be awarded the Close Combat Bar (*Nahkampfspange*). The bar (or badge) was awarded in bronze, silver, and gold for fifteen days, thirty days, and fifty days, respectively, of hand-to-hand combat. If, however, the soldier was wounded in combat, the qualifying period was reduced to ten days, twenty days, and forty days, respectively. The bar featured at its center an eagle and swastika atop a crossed bayonet and stick hand grenade, flanked on both sides by oak leaves and acorns. The badge was worn one centimeter above the upper left pocket of the uniform. Of the eighteen to twenty million men who served in the Wehrmacht and Waffen-SS, about thirty-five thousand received the bronze version. Fewer than ten thousand were awarded the silver Close Combat Bar. Only 631 men were awarded the gold badge, which was regarded by Hitler as akin to the German Cross in gold and the highest award that an infantryman could receive short of the Knight's Cross.

In May 1939, Hitler revived the World War I era Wound Badge (*Verwundetenabzeichen*) in three classes. The black badge was awarded for up to two wounds, the silver badge for three and four wounds, and the gold badge for five or more wounds. This formula, however, was waived for more serious wounds. For example, a soldier who lost a leg, arm, or eyesight was immediately awarded the silver Wound Badge. In the case of death or total disability, the gold badge was awarded. The design of these Third Reich wound badges was very similar to the World War I badge established in March 1918. It was an oval badge consisting of a steel helmet in the center, with two crossed swords in the background. The two major changes were that the helmet on the Third Reich badge was the 1935 pattern steel helmet rather than the World War I version and the addition of the swastika to the helmet in the center of the badge.

Fred L. Borch III and David T. Zabecki

See also: Göring, Hermann; Hitler, Adolf; Rommel, Erwin; Rudel, Hans-Ulrich

Additional Reading

Angolia, John. *For Führer and Fatherland.* San Jose, CA: R. J. Bender Publishing, 1987.

Williamson, Gordon. *The Iron Cross: A History 1813–1957.* Poole, Dorset, UK: Blandford Press, 1984.

Appendix F: Wehrmacht Officers in the Bundeswehr (1955–1990)

The Wehrmacht was formally dissolved by the Allied Control Council on August 20, 1946. But only nine years later, the world looked considerably different. At the onset of the Cold War, the Western Allies had formed the North Atlantic Treaty Organization (NATO) with a unified military command structure. NATO's mission was to deter an increasingly belligerent Soviet Union, which first had liberated the countries of Eastern Europe, then occupied them, and finally enslaved them as Communist satellite states. By the mid-1950s, NATO forces were vastly outnumbered on the ground in the heart of Europe. Begrudgingly, the United States, France, and Britain concluded that the only way they could restore the military balance even partially was to rearm their former German enemy, albeit under firm NATO operational control. Thus, the Paris Accords of May 5, 1955 authorized the establishment of the Bundeswehr, the new armed forces of the Federal Republic of Germany.

Armies cannot be created overnight. The rank-and-file soldiers can be brought in off the streets and trained to a minimum level of effectiveness in about six months. But what about the leadership? Where do you find the people with the background and experience to train, organize, and lead a new army built from scratch, especially the general officers? How many years does it take to "grow" a general? In West Germany's case, the answer was obvious, but far from simple. Just ten years earlier Germany, even in defeat, had what had been one of the best armies in history. But that army had been corrupted into the servant of the odious and criminal Third Reich. Germany produced many great generals between 1933 and 1945, but by 1955, many of them were dead; some were now too old; and many more were, for all time, compromised by their complicity in the Third Reich's war crimes or by their unquestioning subservience to Hitler and the Nazis. The challenge, then, was one of finding enough former Wehrmacht generals and senior officers who had relatively unblemished records and who were willing to go back into uniform late in their lives. Especially challenging was the finding of qualified General Staff officers who had served the Wehrmacht in the most senior positions, and therefore had the background and experience to become the Bundeswehr's senior command echelon.

All former Wehrmacht soldiers who volunteered for the Bundeswehr were subjected to the West German government's rigorous Personal Screening Board.

	Wehrmacht Rank	Bundeswehr Rank
Federal Army (*Bundesheer*)		
• Baudissin, Wolf von	Major	Lt. General
• Bennecke, Jürgen	Major	General
• Brandt, Jürgen	Lieutenant	General
• Deckert, Gerhard	SS- *Untersturmführer*	Major General
• de Maizière, Ulrich	Lt. Colonel	General
• Foertsch, Friedrich	Lt. General	General
• Freytag von Loringhoven, Bernd	Major	Lt. General
• Gehlen, Reinhard	Lt. General	Lt. General
• Guderian, Heinz-Günther	Major	Major General
• Heusinger, Adolf	Lt. General	General
• Kendziora, Alfred	SS- *Untersturmführer*	Brig. General
• Kielmansegg, Johan von	Colonel	General
• Kiessling, Günter	Lieutenant	General
• Mack, Hans-Joachim	Flak Helper	General
• Model, Hansgeorg	Officer Candidate	Brig. General
• Senger und Etterlin, Ferdinand von	Sr. Lieutenant	General
• Schnell, Karl	Major	General
• Schmückle, Gerd	Major	General
• Schulze, Franz-Josef	Sr. Lieutenant	General
• Speidel, Hans	Lt. General	General
• Trettner, Heinz	Lt. General	General
Federal Air Force (*Bundesluftwaffe*)		
• Barkhorn, Gerhard	Major	Major General
• Eimler, Eberhard	*Volkssturm*	General
• Hartmann, Erich	Major	Colonel
• Kammhuber, Josef	General of Aviation	General
• Obleser, Friedrich	Captain	Lt. General
• Panitzki, Werner	Colonel	Lt. General
• Rall, Günther	Major	Lt. General
• Steinhoff, Johannes	Colonel	General
• Wust, Harald	Sr. Lieutenant	General
Federal Navy (*Bundesmarine*)		
• Kretschmer, Otto	Frigate Captain	Flotilla Admiral
• Luther, Günter	Sr. Lieutenant	Admiral
• Rogge, Bernhard	Vice Admiral	Vice Admiral
• Rugge, Friedrich	Vice Admiral	Vice Admiral
• Zimmermann, Armin	Corvette Captain	Admiral

Ultimately, sixty-one Wehrmacht generals and admirals were given clean bills of health, but, in the end, only forty-two of them joined the Bundeswehr by the autumn of 1957. Out of 237 colonels in the new Bundeswehr, one hundred were former Wehrmacht officers. Initially, only Waffen-SS soldiers at the rank of *Hauptsturmführer* (captain) and below were allowed to serve. Later, officers up to *Obersturmbannführer* (lieutenant colonel) were allowed to join, provided they passed the rigorous screening process.

Among that group, the senior-most were Hans Speidel and Adolf Heusinger, who, on October 10 and November 12, 1955, respectively, were sworn in as the Bundeswehr's first two lieutenant generals. Speidel and Heusinger were promoted to be the Bundeswehr's first four-star generals in April and June 1957, respectively. From 1957 to 1961, Heusinger served as the first general inspector (chief of staff) of the Bundeswehr and then from 1961 to 1964 as the first German officer to be chairman of NATO's Military Committee. From 1957 to 1963, Speidel served as the commander in chief of NATO Land Forces, Central Europe. The Bundeswehr's last four-star general who was also a Wehrmacht veteran retired in 1990. At the age of fourteen, Eberhard Eimler was drafted into the Volkssturm in East Prussia. He was inspector (chief of staff) of the *Bundesluftwaffe* from 1983 to 1987, and from 1987 to 1990, he was deputy supreme allied commander Europe. Listed in the table are some of the most prominent Bundeswehr officers who were Wehrmacht veterans.

David T. Zabecki

See also: Barkhorn, Gerhard; Hartmann, Erich Alfred; Heusinger, Adolf; Kammhuber, Josef; Kretschmer, Otto; Rall, Günther; Rogge, Bernhard; Ruge, Friedrich; Speidel, Hans; Steinhoff, Johannes

Additional Reading

Range, Clemens. *Die Generale un Admirale der Bundeswehr*. Bonn: Mittler, 1990.

Searle, Alaric. *Wehrmacht Generals, West German Society, and the Debate on Rearmament, 1949–1959*. Westport, CT: Praeger, 2003.

Chronology of the Wehrmacht

November 1918

9 Abdication of German Kaiser Wilhelm II and German Republic proclaimed.

11 Armistice with Germany on the western front goes into effect at 11:00 hours.

December 1918

1 Allied troops occupy the Rhineland.

January 1919

4–15 German troops and Freikorps units crush the Spartacist Rebellion.

March 1919

3–18 German Freikorps units battle Russian Bolshevik forces in Latvia.

6 The Weimar Republic establishes the *Vorläufige Reichswehr* (Provisional National Defense), consisting of a *Vorläufige Reichsheer* (Provisional National Army) and a *Vorläufige Reichsmarine* (Provisional National Navy).

May 1919

3 Freikorps units crush the Soviet Republic in Bavaria.

June 1919

21 German fleet scuttled at Scapa Flow.

28 Treaty of Versailles is signed between Allied powers and Germany.

July 1919

7–15 Hans von Seeckt serves as the last chief of the German General Staff.

September 1919

12 Adolf Hitler attends his first meeting of the German Workers' Party.

October 1919

11 Seeckt becomes chief of the Truppenamt, the clandestine General Staff.

February 1920

4 Allied governments present the "blacklist" of accused German war criminals to the German

Foreign Ministry, requesting extradition to try them in Allied military tribunals.

23 The Allies accept a compromise: a German civil court in Leipzig will try the "war criminals." Only 113 are tried; most are acquitted.

March 1920

13–17 Kapp-Lüttwiz *Putsch* fails in Berlin.

17 Seeckt becomes chief of the *Heeresleitung* (Army Command).

January 1921

1 The Reichswehr is officially established.

April 1921

11 The Reichsmarine (German Navy) is activated.

August 1921

3 The Nazi Party establishes the Sturmabteilungen (Storm Detachments—SA) its paramilitary force of street thugs.

April 1922

16 Germany and the Soviet Union sign the Treaty of Rapallo, leading to clandestine military cooperation.

January 1923

24 Last U.S. occupation troops leave Germany.

June 1923

23 The Reichswehr issues its capstone operational manual, *H.Dv. 487 Führung und Gefecht der Verbundenen Waffen* (Command and Combat of the Combined Arms).

November 1923

8–9 Hitler's Beer Hall *Putsch* in Munich fails.

February 1924

26 Hitler, Ludendorff, and Röhm go on trial for the Beer Hall *Putsch*.

April 1924

1 Hitler sentenced to five years in Landsberg Prison.

December 1924

20 Hitler released from prison after serving only eight months.

April 1925

26 Hindenburg elected president of Germany.

May 1925

28 The first group of German aviators depart from Stettin to establish a Russo-German flight training and test center at Lipetsk in the Soviet Union.

June 1925

8 Inter-Allied Military Control Commission reports that Germany is in major violation of the disarmament provisions of the Treaty of Versailles.

July 1926

4 Various National Socialist paramilitary youth organizations are consolidated as the Hitler Youth.

October 1926

9 Seeckt resigns as chief of the German Army.

September 1927

18 Speaking at the dedication of a monument to the 1914 Battle of Tannenberg, German President Hindenburg repudiates the German War Guilt clause of the Treaty of Versailles.

April 1932

10 Hindenburg reelected president of Germany, having defeated Hitler in a runoff.

13 German chancellor Heinrich Brüning bans the Nazi paramilitary SA.

November 1932

6 The Nazis win 33.1 percent of the vote in German elections.

January 1933

30 Hindenburg appoints National Socialist Party leader Adolf Hitler chancellor.

February 1933

27 The Reichstag building is destroyed by fire, set by an anarchist but blamed on the Communists and exploited by Hitler and the National Socialists.

28 Hindenburg signs an emergency decree suspending constitutional guarantees of free speech, free press, and privacy.

March 1933

24 The German Reichstag passes the Enabling Act, conferring dictatorial powers on Chancellor Adolf Hitler.

May 1933

15 The Luftwaffe is established clandestinely.

October 1933

14 The Germany government announces its intention to resign from the League of Nations.

17 The Germany Army issues its capstone operational manual, *H.Dv. 300 Truppenführung* (Unit Command).

November 1933

9 In a staged ceremony, most of the surviving Freikorps leaders surrendered their old battle standards to the SA and SS as a demonstration of allegiance to the Nazi regime.

April 1934

13 The Leibstandarte SS Adolf Hitler Regiment is established as Hitler's personal bodyguard.

June 1934

30 Hitler conducts the "Night of the Long Knives" purge to suppress his own SA and gain support from the leadership of the *Reichswehr.*

August 1934

2 Following the death of President Paul von Hindenburg, Hitler assumes the position of head of state as well as chancellor, with the combined title of Führer.

20 German Army officers are required to swear a personal oath of loyalty to Hitler.

October 1934

1 Hitler secretly orders the establishment of a German air force and the expansion of the army and navy.

February 1935

26 The Luftwaffe High Command (*Oberkommando der Luftwaffe*—OKL) is established.

March 1935

9 Germany publicly acknowledges the existence of the Luftwaffe.

16 Germany introduces military conscription in violation of the Treaty of Versailles. The Reichswehr is officially redesignated the Wehrmacht.

May 1935

21 The High Command of the Army (*Oberkommando des Heeres*—OKH) is established.

21 Reichsmarine is renamed the Kriegsmarine.

June 1935

18 Germany and the United Kingdom sign the Anglo-German Naval Agreement, which permits Germany to build up to 35 percent of the size of the Royal Navy and parity in submarines.

26 The Reich Labor Service (*Reichsarbeitsdienst*—RAD) is established to reduce

unemployment, but also to provide premilitary training for young men.

28 Germany commissions its first U-boat since 1918.

July 1935

1 The Truppenamt is redesignated the General Staff.

September 1935

15 The German Reichstag passes the anti-Jewish Nuremberg Laws.

October 1935

15 The Kriegsakademie is reopened in Berlin.

Germany forms its first Panzer division.

January 1936

11 The High Command of the Navy (*Oberkommando der Marine*—OKM) is established.

February 1936

10 Himmler and the Gestapo assume absolute control over German internal security.

March 1936

7 German forces move into and remilitarize the Rhineland, violating both the Treaty of Versailles and the Locarno Pacts.

16 Germany reintroduces conscription and announces its intention to expand the army to thirty-six divisions.

July 1936

18 The Spanish Civil War starts when Spanish Army units rebel against the legitimately elected republican government.

26 Hitler agrees to Franco's request for airlift support.

October 1936

27 Formation of the Rome-Berlin Axis.

29 Soviet advisors and equipment begin operating in Spain.

November 1936

6 The Kondor Legion arrives in Spain.

25 Germany and Japan sign the Anti-Comintern Pact.

April 1937

26 Luftwaffe aircraft destroy Guernica.

September 1937

7 Hitler delivers his *Lebensraum* speech and declares the Treaty of Versailles dead.

November 1937

5 Hitler holds the "Hossbach Meeting" at the Reich Chancellery.

6 Italy joins Germany and Japan in the Anti-Comintern Pact.

February 1938

4 After sacking Werner von Blomberg and Werner von Fritsch and thirteen other generals, Hitler assumes direct control of the German military and establishes the Armed Forces High Command (*Oberkommando der Wehrmacht*—OKW).

March 1938

12–13 The German Army moves into Austria.

A Nazi government in Vienna declares Austria a province of the German Reich.

April 1938

10 An Austrian plebiscite approves the Anschluss by 99.73 percent.

May 1938

28 Organization Todt becomes the paramilitary construction organization of the Third Reich.

29 Hitler orders completion of the West Wall.

August 1938

17 Hitler issues a decree establishing a separate headquarters for the military

training of SS units and establishes their military character as Waffen—SS units.

September 1938

30 Munich Agreement signed, forcing Czechoslovakia to cede the Sudetenland to Germany.

October 1938

1 German forces begin the occupation of the Sudetenland.

November 1938

9–10 Nazi mobs in Germany sack and loot Jewish shops during what becomes known as *Kristallnacht*, the Night of Broken Glass.

January 1939

29 Hitler approves Plan Z.

March 1939

15 German forces invade Czechoslovakia in violation of the Munich Agreement and establish the Czech region as the Protectorate of Bohemia and Moravia.
Hitler demands that Poland return the free city of Danzig to Germany.

31 The United Kingdom and France extend a "guarantee" to Poland to protect it from attack.

April 1939

1 Nationalist leader General Francisco Franco declares his forces victorious and the Spanish Civil War at an end.

3 Hitler orders the German military to begin planning for the attack German attack on Poland, planned for August 25, 1939.

28 Hitler renounces the Anglo-German Naval Agreement and the German-Polish Nonaggression Pact.

May 1939

6 Carl Friedrich Goerdeler, a leader of the German opposition to Adolf Hitler, informs the British government that the German and Soviet governments are secretly bargaining to divide Eastern Europe between them.

22 Conclusion of the Pact of Friendship and Alliance between Germany and Italy, informally known as the Pact of Steel.

31 Germany and Denmark sign a ten-year nonaggression pact.

July 1939

10 British Prime Minister Neville Chamberlain reaffirms that Britain will defend Poland if Germany invades that country.

August 1939

23 Germany and the Soviet Union sign the Molotov-Ribbentrop Pact in Moscow.

25 Hitler postpones Fall WEISS, the German invasion of Poland from August 25 to September 1.

27 A German He 178 makes history's first flight powered by a jet engine.

31 Nazi SS troops conduct the Gleiwitz Raid into Poland.

September 1939

1 Germany invades Poland, starting World War II.

1–7 German forces defeat Polish forces at the Battle of Westerplatte, in Danzig.

2 Great Britain and France issue an ultimatum to Germany, calling on that country to withdraw its forces from Poland.

3 Great Britain and France declare war on Germany.

A German U-boat torpedoes and sinks the British passenger liner *Athenia*.

7 French forces cross into German territory near Saarbrücken.

8–27 German forces besiege and capture Warsaw.

9–15 Polish forces launch an unsuccessful counteroffensive along the Bzura River.

10 The lead elements of the British Expeditionary Force land in France.

17 Soviet forces invade Poland from the east.

The German submarine *U-29* torpedoes and sinks the British aircraft carries HMS *Courageous.*

19 German and Soviet forces link up in Poland, near Brest Litovsk.

27 Himmler establishes the Reich Security Main Office (*Reichssicherheitshauptamt*—RSHA).

28 Polish resistance in Warsaw against the Germans comes to an end.

29 Germany and the Soviet Union formalize the Fourth Partition of Poland.

October 1939

4 French forces that had invaded western Germany withdraw to the Maginot Line.

5 Polish organized resistance ends at Kock.

6 Hitler offers peace to the Western Powers on a forgive-and-forget basis.

9 Hitler orders preparations for a German offensive in the west.

14 German submarine *U-47* penetrates the British naval base a Scapa Flow in the Orkney Islands, sinking the battleship HMS *Royal Oak.*

November 1939

1 Germany annexes western Poland.

December 1939

1 SS-Verfügungstruppe (Service Troops) is redesignated the Waffen-SS.

13–17 Battle of the Platte River, ending with the scuttling of the *Admiral Graf Spee* in Montevideo harbor.

February 1940

16 Royal Navy forces rescue British POWs from the German supply ship *Altmark.*

April 1940

Katyn Massacre of Polish officers by the Soviets takes place throughout April and into early May 1940. The Soviets later try to pin the blame on Germany.

9 German forces invade Denmark and Norway.

10&13 The Royal Navy inflicts a major defeat on the German Navy during two naval battles off Narvik, Norway.

14 British forces start landing north of Narvik.

27 Himmler issues orders for the construction of a concentration camp at Auschwitz.

May 1940

10 German forces invade The Netherlands, Belgium, Luxembourg, and France.

Luftwaffe bombers accidently bomb Freiburg, thinking they were hitting Dijon.

10–11 German forces capture Fort Eben Emael.

13–14 German forces break through at Sedan and cross the Meuse River.

14 The Luftwaffe bombs Rotterdam.

15 Netherlands armed forces surrender to Germany.

19 British bombers strike the German ports of Hamburg and Bremen.

26 Operation DYNAMO, the evacuation of British and French forces at Dunkirk, France, starts.

26–29 Hitler prohibits the extended German Panzers from closing on Dunkirk, to allow the German infantry to close up.

28 Allied forces push German forces out of Narvik.

June 1940

4 Operation DYNAMO, the Dunkirk evacuation, ends.

8 Allied forces complete their evacuation from Norway.

German forces reach the Seine.

German forces breach the Maginot Line south of Saarbrücken.

14 German troops enter Paris.

22 France signs an armistice with Germany.

30 German forces occupy Guernsey.

July 1940

1 German submarines attack merchant ships in the Atlantic Ocean.

10 The Battle of Britain starts, the first major air campaign in history.

16 Hitler orders planning begun for Operation SEA LION, a naval invasion of Great Britain.

August 1940

13 *Adlertag* (Eagle Day); the Luftwaffe launches its main assault during the Battle of Britain.

17 Hitler declares a blockade of Great Britain.

25–26 The Royal Air Force (RAF) conducts its first air raid on Berlin.

September 1940

13 Italian forces invade Egypt.

15 The Luftwaffe mounts a major air attack on London, marking the turning point in the Battle of Britain.

23 Hitler meets Spanish leader Franco at Hendaye and urges him to join the war on the Axis side; Franco is noncommittal, infuriating Hitler.

27 The Axis Tripartite Pact is signed between Germany, Italy, and Japan.

29 Germany annexes Luxembourg.

October 1940

7 German forces enter Romania.

10 Operation SEA LION is shelved, following the German defeat in the Battle of Britain.

16–20 German U-boats sink eighteen British merchant ships during the Convoy Battle in the North Channel.

28 Italian forces invade Greece from Italian-occupied Albania.

31 The Battle of Britain ends; the Germans go over to night bombing (the "Blitz").

November 1940

3 British forces start arriving in Greece.

14–15 German air forces attack Coventry, England, destroying much of the city.

19–20 German air forces attack on Birmingham, England.

20 Pressured by Germany, Hungary joins the Axis.

22 The Greeks turn back the Italian invasion of their country and mount a counteroffensive, capturing Koritsá, Albania.

23 Pressured by Germany, Romania joins the Axis.

26 German occupation forces establish the Warsaw Ghetto.

December 1940

9 British forces begin an offensive to drive the Italians from Egypt.

29–30 Luftwaffe firebomb raids gut large sections of London.

January 1941

3 British forces drive Italian forces out of Egypt.

8 Luftwaffe forces based in Sicily start operating against Allied shipping, supplying Allied forces in North Africa.

22 British and Australian forces capture the key port of Tobruk.

February 1941

5–7 British forces severely defeat Italian forces at the Battle of Beda Fomm.

8 British forces take Benghazi, Libya.

12 General Erwin Rommel arrives in North Africa to assume command of the Afrika Korps.

March 1941

11 U.S. President Franklin Roosevelt signs Lend-Lease legislation.

24 Rommel starts an offensive against British forces in Libya.

25 The Yugoslav government agrees to join the Axis.

26 The Yugoslav government is overthrown.

April 1941

6 Germany invades Yugoslavia and Greece, coming to the rescue of its Axis partner Italy.

Luftwaffe aircraft bomb Belgrade.

9 Axis forces under Rommel capture Bardia.

10 Axis forces encircle Tobruk.

13 German forces capture Belgrade.

17 The Yugoslav Army surrenders to the Germans.

18 Chief of naval operations, Admiral Ernest King orders U.S. ships in the Atlantic to attack any Axis ship within twenty-five miles of the Western Hemisphere.

23 Greece signs an armistice with Germany.

24–30 British Expeditionary Force evacuates Greece for Crete.

May 1941

1 The British repulse an Axis attack on Tobruk.

4 Hitler delivers his "Thousand Year Reich" speech.

6 The first of some eventual 425,000 German POWs arrive in United States for internment.

10 German Deputy Führer Rudolf Hess flies to Scotland and is taken prisoner by the British.

20 Operation MERCUR, German forces launch, the airborne assault against Crete,

21 German submarine *U-69* sinks the American-flagged freighter SS *Robin Moor* in the South Atlantic.

21–22 Royal Navy ships intercept and sink twelve ships of the German invasion convoy headed for Crete.

24 The German battleship *Bismarck* sinks the British battle cruiser HMS *Hood*.

25 Axis forces under Rommel take the Halfaya Pass.

27 Royal Navy forces sink the German battleship *Bismarck*.

28 Axis forces under Rommel capture Sollum.

28–31 Allied forces evacuate Crete.

June 1941

1 Remaining Allied troops on Crete surrender to German forces.

6 Hitler issues the Commissar Order.

8 German troops arrive in Finland in preparation for the attack on the Soviet Union.

14 In response to the *Robin Moor* sinking, Roosevelt freezes the funds in the United States of Axis countries.

15–17 German and Italian forces under Rommel defeat the British BATTLEAXE counteroffensive at the Battle of Halfaya Pass.

16 Roosevelt orders all German consulates closed and their staffs to leave the United States.

22 Operation BARBAROSSA, German forces launch the invasion of the Soviet Union. Germany, Italy, and Romania declare war on the Soviet Union.

26–29 German forces capture Minsk.

27 Hungary declares war on the Soviet Union.

30 German forces take Lwów.

July 1941

3 Stalin orders a scorched earth policy in response to the German invasion.

7 U.S. Marines arrive in Iceland to assume the defense of that country.

16 German forces capture Smolensk.

19 U.S. naval forces start escorting convoys to and from Iceland.

31 Germans start preparations for the "Final Solution," the plan to exterminate the Jews of Europe.

August 1941

1–8 German forces defeat Soviet forces at the Battle of Roslavl.

12 British Prime Minister Winston Churchill and U.S. President Franklin Roosevelt meet and draw up the Atlantic Charter.

September 1941

1 U.S. naval escorts for convoys extended to the midpoint in the Atlantic.

4 The German submarine *U-652* fires three torpedoes at, but fails to hit the destroyer USS *Greer.*

8 German forces begin the siege of Leningrad.

11 U.S. Navy forces in the Atlantic given "shoot on sight" orders.

16–19 German forces encircle and capture Kiev.

24 German forces cut off the Crimean Peninsula.

29–30 German *Einsatzgruppen* murder nearly 34,000 Jews at Babi Yar near Kiev.

October 1941

2 Operation TIAFUN, German forces start the drive on Moscow.

2–10 German forces defeat Soviet forces at the Battle of Vyazma-Bryansk.

15 German forces reach the Don River.

16 German and Romanian forces capture Odessa in the Soviet Union.

17 The German submarine *U-568* torpedoes the destroyer USS *Kearny,* killing eleven American sailors.

20–24 German forces take Kharkov.

23 The U.S. Lend-Lease Act is extended to the Soviet Union.

25 German forces break through the Soviet lines in the Crimea.

30 German forces in the Crimea encircle Sevastopol.

31 The German submarine *U-552* torpedoes and sinks the destroyer USS *Reuben James,* killing 115 American sailors.

November 1941

13 The British carrier HMS *Ark Royal* is sunk by a German submarine.

15 German forces resume Operation TIAFUN after it bogged down in mid-October.

16 German forces penetrate to within fifteen miles of Moscow.

17–18 The British Keyes Raid to assassinate Rommel fails.

18 Operation CRUSADER, British forces launch the counteroffensive against Italian and German forces in Libya.

21 German forces take Rostov.

22 German commerce raider *Atlantis* is sunk.

23 *Totensonntag*—Sunday of the Dead; Rommel counterattacks against the British and loses 70 of his 160 remaining tanks.

27 British forces relieve the Tobruk garrison.

29 Soviet forces retake Rostov.

December 1941

1 Hitler relieves Field Marshal Gerd von Rundstedt as commander of Army Group South.

6 Soviet forces counterattack in front of Moscow.

7 Japanese carrier aircraft attack Pearl Harbor.

The British Operation CRUSADER counteroffensive forces Rommel to withdraw.

9 Hitler issues the "Night and Fog" decree providing for the death of all those thought to endanger security in German-occupied territory.

11 Italy and Germany declare war on the United States.

16 Axis forces in North Africa retreat to El Agheila.

19 Hitler relieves Walther von Brauchitsch as chief of the German army and assumes personal command.

24 British forces recapture Benghazi, Libya.

26 Soviet forces land on the Kerch Peninsula.

January 1942

13 Operation PAUKENSCHLAG, Germany U-boats start the offensive along the eastern U.S. coast.

Soviet forces recapture Kiev.

20 The Wannsee Conference outside of Berlin discusses the procedures for the "Final Solution" (*Die Endlösung*), the extermination of the Jews in Europe.

21 Axis forces under Rommel launch a major offensive against British forces in Libya.

26 The first U.S. troops committed to the war effort in the European Theater arrive in Northern Ireland.

28 German forces recapture Benghazi, Libya.

February 1942

4 Rommel's offensive advances almost three hundred miles, reaching between Gazala and Bir Hacheim.

8 Albert Speer takes control of Organization Todt after Fritz Todt dies in a plane crash in Russia.

9 Speer succeeds Todt as German armaments minister.

11–13 The "Channel Dash," the German battleships *Scharnhorst* and *Gneisenau* and the heavy cruiser *Prinz Eugen* escape through the English Channel from Brest, France, to Wilhelmshaven.

16 Operation NEULAND, the German navy sends U-boats into the Caribbean.

March 1942

10 Rundstedt is brought back from retirement as commander in chief, west.

28 British commandos raid the French port of Saint-Nazaire and destroy the Normandy Dry Dock, the only such facility on the French coast capable of accommodating the German battleship *Tirpitz*.

May 1942

12–22 German forces defeat Soviet forces at the Second Battle of Kharkov.

26 Axis forces under Rommel attack the Allies' Gazala Line.

27 British-trained Czech commandos ambush and mortally wound Reichsprotektor of Bohemia and Moravia Reinhard Heydrich in Prague.

30–31 The RAF conducts a one-thousand-bomber raid on Cologne.

June 1942

4 Heydrich dies in Prague.

5 German forces besiege Sevastopol.

5–6 Axis forces under Rommel successfully beat back British attacks at the Battle of the Cauldron.

9–10 The Germans wipe out the village of Lidice in Bohemia in retaliation for Heydrich's death.

10–11 Axis forces under Rommel drive Free French forces from Bir Hacheim.

12 Axis forces under Rommel destroy 120 British tanks at the "Knightsbridge" position.

13 British forces abandon Gazala.

20–21 Axis forces under Rommel capture Tobruk.

23 Axis forces under Rommel cross into Egypt.

24 Eisenhower is named commander of U.S. forces in Europe.

25 German forces defeat Soviet forces at Kharkov.

28 German forces launch Operation BLAU, the great summer offensive in Russia.

28–29 Axis forces under Rommel route British forces at the First Battle of Mersa Matrûh.

July 1942

1–27 British forces halt Rommel's advance in North Africa at the Battle of Ruweisat Ridge.

4 German forces secure Sevastopol in the Crimea.

U.S. Army Air Forces (USAAF) bombers fly their first mission in Europe.

4–7 German U-boats sink 21 Allied merchant ships during the Battle of Convoy PQ-17.

6 German forces capture Voronezh.

13 Hitler orders an abrupt change in German strategy, demanding the simultaneous capture of Stalingrad and the Caucasus.

19 Dönitz withdraws the last U-boats from U.S. East Coast waters.

22 The Warsaw Ghetto deportations to the German death camps start.

23 German forces capture Rostov-on-Don.

25 Operation EDELWEISS, German forces launch, the Caucasus Campaign.

29 German forces enter the Caucasus.

August 1942

9 German forces capture the Caucasus oilfields.

13 Montgomery assumes command of the British Eighth Army in Egypt.

15 Allied Convoy PEDESTAL reaches Malta, lifting the siege of the island fortress.

19 British and Canadian forces carry out a costly raid on German installations at Dieppe, France.

23 German forces reach the Volga, north of Stalingrad.

31 Axis forces under Rommel fail to outflank the British at the Battle of Alam el Halfa.

September 1942

2 Axis forces pull back westward following Battle of Alam el Halfa.

12 The British transport RMS *Laconia* is sunk by a German U-boat; German vessels attempting to rescue *Laconia* survivors are then attacked by a U.S. aircraft.

12–21 German forces sink 13 Allied merchant ships during the Battle of Convoy PQ-18.

17 Dönitz issues the Laconia Order, forbidding U-boats to pick up survivors after attacks.

24 Hitler dismisses General Franz Halder as chief of staff of the German Army.

October 1942

14 German forces suspend operations in the Caucasus.

18 Hitler issues the Commando Order, requiring all captured commandos to be shot summarily.

23 British forces open the Battle of El Alamein against Axis forces under Rommel

November 1942

1 British forces break through at El Alamein.

4 Axis forces at El Alamein begin their 1,400-mile withdrawal to Tunisia.

7–8 Axis forces under Rommel withdrawing after the Battle of El Alamein escape from the pursuing British forces at the Second Battle of Mersa Matrûh.

8 Operation TORCH, British and American forces land in Morocco and Algeria.

9 Germany deploys additional forces to Tunisia from Sicily.

11 Axis forces occupy Vichy-administered France.

13 British forces retake Tobruk.

19–22 German forces under Nehring consolidate control of Tunisia.

19–23 Operation URANUS, Soviet forces encircle German forces in Stalingrad.

24 Field Marshal Erich von Manstein assumes command of Army Group Don.

27 The French scuttle some seventy-seven warships at Toulon rather than see them fall into German hands.

28 Axis forces in Tunisia counterattack and drive Allied forces back from Tunis.

December 1942

2 U.S. scientists in Chicago achieve the first nuclear chain reaction.

7–22 A single German Panzer division under General Hermann Balck defeats three Soviet tank corps during a series or running battles on the Chir River, north of Stalingrad.

12–23 German Operation WINTERGEWITTER (WINTER STORM) under Manstein fails to relieve Stalingrad.

13 Axis forces withdraw from El Agheila.

22 German forces began a withdrawal from positions along the Terek River in the Caucasus.

28 Hitler approves the withdrawal of Army Group A from the Caucasus.

30–31 The Royal Navy wins an operational victory over German surface raiders at the Battle of Barents Sea.

Axis forces terminate the Malta Air Campaign.

January 1943

12–18 Soviet forces open a narrow land corridor to Leningrad.

16 Soviet forces capture Pitomnik, the principal German airfield within the Stalingrad pocket.

18 German forces in Tunisia under General Hans-Jürgen von Arnim launch a counteroffensive against the Allies.

23 British forces take Tripoli, Libya.

24–27 Soviet forces attack across the Don.

25 Soviet forces retake Voronezh.

27 USAAF bomb Wilhelmshaven, Germany.

28 Germany finally shifts its economy to a full wartime footing.

30 Dönitz succeeds Admiral Erich Raeder as commander of the German Navy.

Ernst Kaltenbrunner is appointed to succeed Heydrich as head of the RSHA.

31 Field Marshal Friedrich Paulus surrenders at Stalingrad.

February 1943

1 German forces complete the withdrawal from the Caucasus to the Taman Peninsula.

2 Remaining German forces surrender at Stalingrad.

3 Soviet forces start series of attacks against the Germans along the Donets River line.

6 Soviet Forces cross the Donets River.

8 Soviet forces recapture Kursk.

14 Soviet forces retake Rostov.

German forces under Arnim attack at Sidi Bou Zid and Sbeitla.

German forces under Rommel occupy Gafsa and then capture the American airfield at Thelepte.

19 Soviet forces retake Kharkov.

19–25 German forces defeat American forces at the Battle of Kasserine Pass in Tunisia.

22 German forces counterattack in the Donets area.

March 1943

5–6 The RAF initiates the bombing campaign against the Ruhr industrial region.

6 Axis forces under Rommel attack south from the Mareth Line to block British forces under Montgomery from entering Tunisia.

9 Rommel leaves North Africa for Germany.

Arnim replaces Rommel as commander of Axis forces in North Africa.

14–15 German forces recapture Kharkov.

16–20 German U-boats sink twenty-one Allied merchant ships during the Battle of Convoys HX-229 and SC-122.

17–25 U.S. forces win a tactical victory over German forces at the Battle of El Guettar.

20–31 Following a series of savage convoy battles, the introduction of new anti-submarine tactics brings about the turning point in the Battle of the Atlantic.

26 British forces under Montgomery break the Axis Mareth Line at the Tebaga Gap.

April 1943

3–4 Allied aircraft bomb Essen in the Ruhr.

12 Germany announces the discovery of mass graves of Polish officers in the Katyn Forest.

19 Polish Jews start the Warsaw Ghetto Uprising.

22 U.S. and British forces start the offensive to take Tunis.

30 Allied aircraft bomb the Krupp armaments factory in Essen.

May 1943

4–5 Allied aircraft bomb Dortmund in the Ruhr.

7 British and American forces capture Bizerte and Tunis.

12–13 Some 275,000 German and Italian troops surrender in North Africa.

15–20 German Navy loses five U-boats during the Battle of Allied Convoy SC-130.

16 German forces crush the Warsaw Ghetto Uprising.

17 RAF aircraft destroy the Möhne and Eder Dams in the Ruhr.

23–24 Allied aircraft bomb Dortmund in the Ruhr.

24 Dönitz suspends U-boat operations in the North Atlantic.

June 1943

10 Operation POINTBLANK, Allied air forces start the Combined Bomber Offensive against Germany.

11–12 Allied aircraft bomb Düsseldorf in the Ruhr.

28–28 Allied aircraft bomb Cologne.

July 1943

3–4 Allied aircraft bomb Cologne, targeting industrial facilities along the Rhine.

5 Operation ZITADELLE, German forces launch a failed attack to cut off the Kursk salient.

9 Operation HUSKY, U.S. and British forces invade Sicily.

12 Soviet forces counterattack at Kursk.

13 Hitler calls off the Kursk offensive to be able to shift forces to Sicily.

22 U.S. forces capture Palermo, Sicily.

24 Allied bombers use "window" chaff to confuse German radar for the first time.

24–29 Operation GOMORRAH, RAF aircraft conduct a thousand bomber raid against Hamburg.

25–26 Allied aircraft bomb Essen, causing a complete stoppage of the Krupp Works.

26 King Victor Emmanuel III of Italy dismisses Mussolini; Marshal Pietro
Badoglio succeeds Mussolini as the Italian leader.

31 U.S. forces attack at Troina, a linchpin in the German "Etna Line" in Sicily.

August 1943

1 USAAF bombers conduct a low-level attack on the Romanian oil fields at Ploieşti.

5 Soviet forces recapture Belgorod and Orel.

6 German forces withdraw from Troina.

11 German forces start the evacuation of Sicily from Messina

17 British and U.S. forces capture Messina, concluding the conquest of Sicily.

USAAF conduct daylight raids against Regensburg and Schweinfurt.

17–18 RAF bombers strike the German missile research and development center at Peenemünde.

23 Soviet forces end their Kursk counteroffensive and also recapture Kharkov.

September 1943

1 Dönitz sends U-boats back into the North Atlantic.

3 Operation BAYTOWN, British forces land at Calabria, Italy.

6 German battleship *Tirpitz* sorties to shell Spitsbergen.

8 The Italian government signs an armistice with the Allies.

8–23 German forces seize control of the Dodecanese Islands.

9 Operation AVALANCHE, Allied forces land at Salerno and Taranto, Italy.

10–11 German forces occupy Rome.

12 Former Italian leader Mussolini is rescued by German commandos led by Otto Skorzeny.

14 British forces occupy the islands of Kos and Leros in the Dodecanese.

German forces start withdrawing to the Dnieper River line.

17 German forces in Italy start withdrawing to the Gustav Line.

18 Allied forces capture Sardinia.

22 Soviet forces secure a bridgehead on Dnieper River.

Royal Navy midget submarines attack and damage the German battleship *Tirpitz.*

23 Supported by the Germans, Mussolini establishes a new fascist government in northern Italy.

25 Soviet forces retake Smolensk and Roslavl.

27 P-47s fighters with extended-range belly tanks start escorting U.S. bombers over Europe.

October 1943

1 Allied forces capture Naples.

Soviet forces cross the Dnieper River.

3 German forces recapture the Greek island of Kos from British forces.

5 Free French forces liberate Corsica.

9 Soviet forces reoccupy the Taman Peninsula.

12–15 U.S. forces attack across the Volturno River.

13 Italy declares war on Germany.

USAAF conducts a second raid against Schweinfurt.

14 Soviets forces capture Zaporozhe, Ukraine.

25 Soviets take Dnepropetrovsk, Ukraine.

31 German forces in the Crimea are cut off.

November 1943

3 Soviet forces break out of their Dnieper bridgeheads.

6 Soviet forces liberate Kiev.

15 German forces in Italy halt the Allied advance at the Winter Line.

18 RAF Bomber Command initiates a sustained bombing campaign against Berlin.

28 Roosevelt, Churchill, and Stalin confer at Teheran until December 1.

28–30 British forces in Italy attack across the Sangro River.

December 1943

5 Allies initiate Operation CROSSBOW to attack German V-1 and V-2 sites.

13 P-51s fighters start escorting U.S. bombers on raids over Europe.

20–28 Canadian forces defeat German forces at the Battle of Ortona, securing the Adriatic coast of Italy.

24 Eisenhower is appointed supreme commander, Allied Expeditionary Force for Operation OVERLORD.

26 Royal Navy forces sink the *Scharnhorst* at the Battle of North Cape.

January 1944

5 Soviet forces attack in the Ukraine.

20–22 German forces repulse the U.S. attempt to cross the Rapido River.

21 German air forces launch the "Baby Blitz" air campaign against London.

22 Allied forces establish a beachhead at Anzio.

27 Soviet forces lift the nine-hundred-day siege of Leningrad.

Soviet forces in the Ukraine attack with the intention of splitting German Army Group South and Army Group Center.

28 Soviet forces cut off sixty thousand German troops in the Korsun-Cherkassy Pocket.

February 1944

3 The Allied offensive in Italy stalls at Cassino.

7 Soviet forces reach the Dnieper, and then turn south into the Crimean Peninsula.

15 Allied heavy bombers bomb Monte Cassino.

20–26 Allied air forces launch Operation ARGUMENT, coordinated air strikes, known as "Big Week," against German factories.

March 1944

6 USAAF bombers attack Berlin for the first time.

9 Soviet forces take Tarnopol and outflank German forces on the Bug River.

19 Operation STRANGLE, Allied air forces launch a major interdiction campaign against German supply lines in Italy.

22 Dönitz orders U-boats to disperse from wolf packs and start operating singly.

30 Hitler relieves Manstein and replaces him with Field Marshal Walther Model as commander of Army Group South.

April 1944

2 Soviet troops enter Romania.

3 Royal Navy aircraft bomb and damage the German battleship *Tirpitz*.

8 Soviet forces enter the Crimea.

10 Soviet forces retake Odessa in the Ukraine.

15 Soviets troops take Tarnopol in the Ukraine.

May 1944

9 Soviet Forces liberate Sevastopol.

11 Operation DAIDEM, Allied forces attack to break the Winter Line.

13 Remaining German forces in the Crimea surrender.

17–18 Allied forces break the Gustav Line.

18 Free Polish forces take Monte Cassino.

23 Allied forces break out from the Anzio beachhead.

25 Allied forces from Anzio and the Gustav Line link up.

June 1944

1 German forces start conducting a fighting withdrawal from the Gustav Line, north to the Gothic Line.

4–5 Allied troops enter Rome.

6 Operation OVERLORD, Allied troops land in Normandy, France.

9 Soviet forces attack into Finland.

10 German forces moving toward the Normandy landing zones destroy the town of Oradour-sur-Glane, France.

12–13 First German V-1 "Buzz Bombs" hit Britain.

18 Soviet forces breach the Mannerheim Line.

22 Operation BAGRATION, Soviet forces begin their great Belorussian offensive.

26–30 Operation EPSOM, British forces fail to take Caen.

July 1944

3 Soviet forces liberate Minsk.

8–10 Operation CHARNWOOD, British and Canadian forces capture Caen.

18 U.S. forces liberate St-Lô, France.

18–20 Operation GOODWOOD, British and Canadian forces attempt but fail to break out from Caen.

20 An assassination attempt on German leader Adolf Hitler fails, as does the associated effort by the German opposition to seize power.

Soviet forces cross the Bug River.

21 General Kurt Zeitzler resigns as chief of staff of the German Army and is replaced by General Heinz Guderian.

25 Soviet forces liberate the Majdanek concentration camp.

Soviet forces reach the Vistula.

25–31 Operation COBRA, Allied forces break out from Normandy.

28 Soviet forces retake Brest-Litovsk, Belorussia.

Model replaces Field Marshal Ernst Busch as commander of Army Group Center.

29 The first operational combat jet aircraft, the German Me 262 enters action.

August 1944

1 Polish resistance forces start the Warsaw Uprising against the German occupation.

American troops reach Avranches in northwestern France.

4 The last Jews taken by the Germans, are sent from The Netherlands, among them young Anne Frank.

7–12 German Panzer forces launch a failed counteroffensive to cut Allied forces off at Avranches.

13–14 Allied forces attempt to enclose German forces in the pocket at Falaise-Argentan.

15 Operation DRAGOON, Allied forces land in southern France.

17 German forces in France begin a general retreat.

Model replaces Field Marshal Günther von Kluge as German commander in chief, west.

19 The French resistance mounts an uprising in Paris.

Hitler orders General Dietrich von Choltitz to destroy Paris.

20 U.S. forces cross the Seine.

20–31 Soviet forces clear Romania.

21 Allied forces close the Falaise-Argentan pocket, trapping 60,000 German troops.

21–28 U.S. forces defeat and outflank German forces at the Battle of Montélimar in southern France.

23 Romania surrenders.

24 Romania declares war on Germany.

25 American and Free French forces liberate Paris.

Allied forces launch an attack on the German Gothic Line in Italy.

28 Allied forces secure Toulon and Marseilles.

29 Stalin orders Soviet forces to dig in along the line of the Vistula and Narew Rivers.

30 German forces withdraw from Bulgaria.

Soviet forces take Ploiești.

31 Soviet forces take Bucharest, Romania.

September 1944

2 British forces break through the eastern end of the Gothic Line.

Allied forces liberate Saint-Malo.

3 German forces withdraw from Finland.

British forces liberate Brussels.

4 The Soviet Union and Finland reach a cease-fire agreement.

British forces liberate Antwerp.

5 Rundstedt is reinstated as German commander in chief, west.

6 Allied forces liberate the southern Netherlands.

8 Bulgaria declares war on Germany.

First German V-2 missiles hit Britain.

8–9 A general uprising in Greece hastens the German withdrawal from the country.

10 Soviet forces at Warsaw halt their advance on the east bank of the Vistula River.

12 U.S. forces attack into the Hürtgen Forest.

14 Allied Operation DRAGOON forces coming north from southern France link up with the main Allied forces that landed in Normandy.

American forces liberate Nancy.

15 RAF aircraft bomb and damage the German battleship *Tirpitz.*

17–26 Operation MARKET-GARDEN, the Allied attempt to secure a crossing over the Rhine River at Arnhem, ends in failure.

19 Allied forces take the port of Brest.

25 Allied forces break through the German Gothic Line in Italy.

Germany establishes the Volkssturm, as Hitler calls up remaining sixteen- to sixty-year-old German males for military service.

26 The remaining Allied MARKET-GARDEN forces surrender at Arnhem.

27 U.S. forces start assaulting the outer ring of fortresses at Metz.

October 1944

2 The Warsaw Uprising ends with the surrender of the Polish Home Army to the Germans.

3 Hitler approves the withdrawal of German forces from Finnish Lapland.

13 The first V-1s and V-2s land on Antwerp.

14 British forces liberate Athens.

Rommel is forced to commit suicide for suspected complicity in the plot to assassinate Hitler.

16 Montgomery finally orders British forces to clear the Scheldt Estuary approaches to Antwerp.

18 Soviet forces enter Czechoslovakia.

Soviet forces cross the Norwegian border.

20 Yugoslav partisans and Soviet forces enter Belgrade.

21 U.S. forces capture Aachen, the first major German city.

23 Soviet forces enter East Prussia.

November 1944

2 Last German forces leave Greece.

3 Soviet forces reach Budapest on the east bank of the Danube.

3–8 U.S. forces capture Schmidt in the Hürtgen Forest, but German forces counterattack immediately and retake the town.

12 RAF aircraft bomb and capsize the German battleship *Tirpitz*.

14 Allied forces advancing from southern France start operations to break through the Vosges Mountains.

17 U.S. forces enter Metz.

19 French forces reach the Rhine via the Belfort Gap.

22 U.S. forces cross the Saar River.

23 The first U.S. forces reach the Rhine River.

French forces liberate Strasbourg.

26 The Belgian port of Antwerp is opened to Allied supply ships.

27 RAF bombers devastate the medieval university town of the city of Freiburg.

December 1944

16 German forces start the Ardennes Offensive, the Battle of the Bulge.

17 Waffen SS troops murder U.S. Army POWs at Malmèdy, Belgium.

21 German forces encircle U.S. forces at Bastogne.

22 U.S. forces under General George S. Patton counterattack into the south shoulder of the Bulge.

24–27 U.S. forces defeat German forces at Celles, the point of maximum penetration in the Battle of the Bulge.

26 U.S. forces relieve the siege of Bastogne.

27 Soviet forces besiege Budapest.

31 Operation NORDWIND, German forces launch their last major offensive in the west.

January 1945

1 Operation BODENPLATTE, the last major effort by the Luftwaffe to check Allied airpower in the west.

1–17 German forces begin to withdraw from the Ardennes.

5 German forces attack in force across the upper Rhine.

12 Soviet forces resume the Vistula-Oder Offensive to clear the rest of Poland.

16 Allied forces attacking from the north and south shoulders of the Bulge link up at Houffalize, Belgium.

17 Soviet troops occupy Warsaw.

19 Germans forces retreat in large numbers across the Baltic.

Soviet forces take Kraków.

20 Hungary concludes an armistice with the Soviet Union.

French and American forces attack German forces in the Colmar Pocket.

22 Soviet forces cross the Oder River.

24 Hitler establishes Army Group Vistula to defend Berlin.

25 Last German forces in the Bulge are pushed back to their December 16 starting lines.

German NORDWIND forces start to withdraw back across the Rhine.

26 Soviet forces liberate Auschwitz.

29 Soviet forces encircle the East Prussian capital of Königsberg.

30 Soviet submarine *S-13* sinks the German refugee ship MS *Wilhelm Gustloff*, in the Baltic.

February 1945

3 USAAF attacks Berlin with sixteen hundred aircraft.

4–11 Churchill, Roosevelt, and Stalin meet at Yalta in the Crimea.

7 U.S. forces resume offensive operations in the Hürtgen Forest, and finally take Schmidt.

Operation veritable, British and Canadian forces launch an attack to clear the Reichswald.

9 French and American forces eliminate the Colmar Pocket.

10 Last German NORDWIND forces retreat across the Rhine.

Soviet submarine *S-13* sinks the German refugee and medical evacuation ship SS *General von Steuben* in the Baltic.

13 The remaining German forces in Budapest surrender to Soviet forces.

13–15 RAF and USAAF bombers destroy much of Dresden.

20 Soviet forces take Danzig.

23 Operation GRENADE, U.S. forces cross the Roer River.

March 1945

1 Saudi Arabia and Turkey declare war on Germany and Japan.

3 Finland declares war on Germany.

7 Allied forces take Cologne.

U.S. forces seize intact the Remagen Bridge over the Rhine.

6–10 German forces launch the Lake Balaton counterattack in Hungary.

8–9 German forces from the Channel Islands conduct the Granville Raid.

10 British and Canadian forces clear the Reichswald as the last German forces cross over to the east bank of the Rhine.

Rundstedt is replaced by Kesselring as German commander in chief, west.

17–25 U.S. forces in the Palatinate attack in force and push to the Rhine at Mannheim.

19 U.S. forces capture Saarbrücken and Zweibrücken.

Hitler orders a scorched earth policy for Germany.

20 U.S. forces capture Kaiserslautern.

22–23 Operation PLUNDER, British and Canadian forces cross the lower Rhine in force.

24 Operation VARSITY, British and U.S. airborne forces drop on the easy bank of the Rhine.

27 Last German V-2 missiles hit Britain.

U.S. forces capture Frankfurt.

28 Last V-1 Buzz Bomb hits Britain.

Eisenhower orders all Western Allied forces to halt at the Elbe River.

Hitler dismisses Guderian as German Army chief of staff.

31 Soviet forces start the drive for Berlin.

April 1945

1 U.S. forces cut off German forces in the Ruhr Pocket.

7 Soviet forces enter Vienna.

9 RAF bombers sink the cruisers *Admiral Scheer* and *Admiral Hipper* at Kiel.

Soviet forces capture Königsberg.

12 U.S. President Franklin Roosevelt dies in Warm Springs, Georgia, and Vice-President Harry S. Truman becomes U.S. president.

13 Soviet forces secure Vienna.

Allied forces take Arnhem.

15 British forces liberate Bergen-Belsen concentration camp.

16 U.S. forces enter Nuremberg.

16–19 Soviet forces defeat German forces at the Battle of Seelow Heights, which dominate the main axis of advance to Berlin.

18 German forces in the Ruhr Pocket surrender.

Allied aircraft mount a huge raid on the island of Helgoland.

U.S. forces enter Czechoslovakia.

20 German forces in Italy withdraw to the Po River.

21 Allied air forces conduct their last attack on Berlin.

22 U.S. forces cross the Danube.

23 Soviet forces reach Berlin.

Allied forces in Italy reach the Po River.

Hitler assumes personal command of the defense of Berlin.

23–24 Himmler offers to surrender German forces to the United States and Britain.

25 U.S. and Soviet forces meet at Torgau on the Elbe River in north Germany.

The United Nations conference in San Francisco begins.

26 British forces capture Bremen.

U.S. forces enter Austria.

28 Italian partisans execute Mussolini at Lake Como, Italy.

Allied forces take Venice.

29 American forces liberate Dachau concentration camp.

German forces in Italy surrender.

30 Hitler commits suicide in Berlin.

Dönitz becomes acting president of Germany.

Soviet forces take the Reichstag building in Berlin.

May 1945

1 Dönitz establishes the "Flensburg Government."

2 German forces in Italy surrender.

German forces in Berlin surrender.

5 Allied forces liberate Denmark.

6 U.S. Fifth and Seventh Armies link up at the Brenner Pass.

U.S. forces take Pilsen, Czechoslovakia, and are ordered to halt their advance.

7 Jodl signs the German unconditional surrender at Reims.

The end of the Battle of the Atlantic, the longest battle of the war.

8 V-E Day (Victory in Europe).

9 Keitel signs Germany's unconditional surrender in Berlin.

11 German Army Group Center surrenders to the Soviets.

23 Allied forces arrest Dönitz and members of the Flensburg Government.

June 1945

5 The four Allied commanders in chief meet in Berlin and sign the Four Power Declaration on the Assumption of Supreme Authority in Germany.

9 Soviet Occupation Forces in Germany are established.

July 1945

1 Western Allied forces move into Berlin.

17 Churchill (later replaced by Atlee), Truman, and Stalin meet at Potsdam. The conference ends on August 2.

August 1945

30 The Allied Control Council begins functioning in Germany.

October 1945

16 Allies convene the International Military Tribunal at Nuremberg.

November 1945

30 The Allied Control Council establishes three air corridors between Berlin and the British and U.S. zones.

January 1946

10 The United States Constabulary is organized as the main U.S. military occupation force in Germany.

June 1946

3 Under the auspices of U.S. Occupation forces, former Wehrmacht General Reinhard Gehlen establishes the Gehlen Organization, West Germany's protointelligence agency.

August 1946

20 The Allied Control Council formally dissolves the Wehrmacht.

September 1946

6 U.S. Secretary of State James F. Byrnes declares in speech delivered in Stuttgart the U.S. intention to restore the German economy and vows that U.S. forces will remain in Europe as long as other powers retain occupying forces there.

9 Truman approves Operation PAPERCLIP, the plan to bring German V-1 rocket and V-2 missile scientists and technicians, including Wernher von Braun, to the United States.

October 1946

1 The International Military Tribunal at Nuremburg condemns twelve of the major war criminals to death, sentences seven to prison terms, and acquits three; the Tribunal also found that "no declaration of criminality should be made in respect of the General Staff and High Command."

16 Keitel, Jodl, Ribbentrop and eight other Nuremberg defendants are executed at Nuremberg;

Göring commits suicide in his jail cell a few hours earlier.

April 1947

18 The British Royal Navy detonates 6,700 tons of high explosives on the island of Heligoland to destroy completely the remnants of the U-boat facilities.

November 1947

15 U.S. Army, Europe is established.

December 1947

30 The High Command Trial opens at the U.S. Military tribunal at Nuremberg.

March 1948

17 Treaty of Brussels is signed by France, Britain, Belgium, the Netherlands, and Luxembourg—forerunner to the North Atlantic Treaty Organization (NATO).

April 1948

1 Soviet authorities in Germany impose restrictions on road and rail traffic from the Western zones of Germany into Berlin.

31 The Soviet Group of Forces in Germany replaces Soviet Occupation Forces in Germany.

June 1948

24 The Berlin Blockade begins when the Soviet Union halts all land and water traffic

between the western zones of Germany and West Berlin.

26 American and British air forces start the Berlin Airlift.

October 1948

28 The High Command Trial concludes at the American Military Tribunal at Nuremberg, convicting eleven of the generals tried, and acquitting three.

April 1949

4 NATO is established by twelve nations, including the United States.

May 1949

12 The Soviet Union ends the Berlin Blockade.

August 1949

24 North Atlantic Treaty goes into effect.

September 1949

30 The Berlin Airlift ends.

October 1950

9 The Himmerod Memorandum becomes the blueprint for the future *Bundeswehr*.

26 Adenauer appoints Theodor Blank as Plenipotentiary of the Federal Chancellor for Coordination of Issues Concerning the Increase of the Allied Forces.

November 1950

3 Theodor Blank establishes Amt Blank, the forerunner of the German Ministry of Defense.

24 United States Constabulary inactivated.

U.S. Seventh Army activated in Germany.

December 1950

18–19 NATO foreign ministers agree to plans for the defense of Western Europe, including the use of American nuclear weapons.

19 Eisenhower is appointed NATO Supreme Allied Commander, Europe (SACEUR).

March 1951

16 The Bundesgrenzschutz, the paramilitary border security force of Federal Republic of Germany is established.

April 1951

2 NATO establishes the Supreme Headquarters Allied Powers Europe (SHAPE) at Rocquencourt, France.

October 1951

24 The U.S. Congress officially ends the war with Germany.

February 1952

23 NATO authorities announce a plan to establish an army of fifty divisions within a year's time.

August 1952

1 U.S. European Command headquarters established in Frankfurt.

March 1954

26 The Soviet Union declares East Germany a sovereign state.

31 The Soviet Union petitions for NATO membership; Britain, France, and the United States veto the request.

October 1954

3 In London, the Western Allies sign an agreement that will allow the rearmament of West Germany within NATO.

23 The Allied occupation ends in West Germany, but not Berlin.

May 1955

5 West Germany regains full sovereignty.

9 West Germany joins NATO as a full member.

14 The Soviet Union and its satellites establish the Warsaw Treaty Organization to counter NATO.

June 1955

7 Amt Blank is redesignated the German Ministry of Defense.

September 1955

26 Raeder is released from Spandau prison.

November 1955

12 The new German military is officially established, as the first 101 volunteers take the oath of allegiance.

December 1955

1 The Western Allies declare that despite Soviet contentions to the contrary, Berlin remains an occupied city.

January 1956

18 The East German parliament establishes the National People's Army (Nationale Volksarmee—NVA).

February 1956

22 The Bundestag officially adopts the name *Bundeswehr* for the new German armed forces.

Selected Bibliography

German Official History of World War II

Blank, Ralf, Jörg Echternkamp, Karola Fings, Jürgen Förster, Winfried Heinemann, Tobias Jersak, Armin Nolzen, and Christoph Rass. *German Wartime Society 1939–1945: Politicization, Disintegration, and the Struggle for Survival.* Vol. IX, Part 1. *Germany and the Second World War.* Oxford: Clarendon Press, 2008.

Boog, Horst, Gerhard Krebs, and Detlef Vogel. *The Strategic Air War in Europe and the War in the West and East Asia 1943–1944/5.* Vol. VII. *Germany and the Second World War.* Oxford: Clarendon Press, 2006.

Boog, Horst, Jürgen Förster, Joachim Hoffmann, Ernst Klink, Rolf-Dieter Müller, and Gerd R. Ueberschär. *The Attack on the Soviet Union.* Vol. IV, Part 1. *Germany and the Second World War.* Oxford: Clarendon Press, 1998.

Boog, Horst, Jürgen Förster, Joachim Hoffmann, Ernst Klink, Rolf-Dieter Müller, and Gerd R. Ueberschär. *The Attack on the Soviet Union.* Vol. IV, Part 2. *Germany and the Second World War.* Oxford: Clarendon Press, 1998.

Boog, Horst, Werner Rahn, Reinhard Stumpf, and Bernd Wegner. *The Global War.* Vol. VI. *Germany and the Second World War.* Oxford: Clarendon Press, 2001.

Das Deutsche Reich und der Zweite Weltkrieg (Germany and the Second World War) [Volumes 1 through 9 published in English as of 2018.]:

Deist, Wilhelm, Manfred Messerschmidt, Hans-Erich Volkmann, and Wolfram Wette. *The Build-Up of German Aggression.* Vol. I. *Germany and the Second World War.* Oxford: Clarendon Press, 1990.

Echternkamp, Jörg. *German Wartime Society 1939–1945: Exploitation, Interpretations, Exclusion, Ration, and the Struggle for Survival.* Vol. IX, Part 2. *Germany and the Second World War.* Oxford: Clarendon Press, 2014.

Frieser, Karl-Heinz, Klaus Schmider, Klaus Schönherr, Gerhard Schreiber, Krisztián Ungváry, and Bernd Wegner. *The Eastern Front 1943–1944: The War in the East and on the Neighboring Fronts.* Vol. VIII. *Germany and the Second World War.* Oxford: Clarendon Press, 2017.

Kroener, Bernhard R., Rolf-Dieter Müller, and Hans Umbreit. *Organization and Mobilization of the German Sphere of Power: Wartime Administration, Economy, and Manpower Resources 1939–1941.* Vol. V, Part 1. *Germany and the Second World War.* Oxford: Clarendon Press, 2000.

Kroener, Bernhard R., Rolf-Dieter Müller, and Hans Umbreit. *Organization and Mobilization of the German Sphere of Power: Wartime Administration, Economy, and Manpower Resources 1942-1944/5.* Vol. V, Part 2. *Germany and the Second World War.* Oxford: Clarendon Press, 2003.

Maier, Klaus A., Horst Rohde, Bernd Stegemann, and Hans Umbreit. *Germany's Initial Conquests in Europe*. Vol. II. *Germany and the Second World War*. Oxford: Clarendon Press, 1991.

Müller, Rolf-Dieter, hrsg. *Der Zusammenbruch des Deutschen Reiches 1945 und die Folgen des Zweiten Weltkrieges*—Teilbd 1: *Die militärische Niederwerfung der Wehrmacht*, Bd. X *Das Deutsche Reich und der Zweite Weltkrieg*. Stuttgart: Deutsche Verlags-Anstalt, 2008.

Müller, Rolf-Dieter, hrsg. *Der Zusammenbruch des Deutschen Reiches 1945 und die Folgen des Zweiten Weltkrieges*—Teilbd 2: *Die Auflösung der Wehrmacht und Die Auswirkungen des Krieges,* Bd. X *Das Deutsche Reich und der Zweite Weltkrieg*. Stuttgart: Deutsche Verlags-Anstalt, 2008.

Schreiber, Gerhard, Bernd Stegemann, and Detlef Vogel. *The Mediterranean, South-East Europe, and North Africa 1939–1942*. Vol. III. *Germany and the Second World War*. Oxford: Clarendon Press, 1995.

Books and Monographs

Adair, Paul. *Hitler's Greatest Defeat: The Collapse of Army Group Centre, June 1944*. London: Brockhampton, 2002.

Balck, Hermann. *Order in Chaos: The Memoirs of General of Panzer Troops Hermann Balck*. Edited and translated by David T. Zabecki and Dieter Biedekarken. Lexington: University Press of Kentucky, 2015.

Barnett, Correlli, ed. *Hitler's Generals*. New York: Grove Weidenfeld, 1989.

Barton, Omer. *The Eastern Front, 1941–1945: German Troops and the Barbarization of Warfare*. New York: Palgrave, 2001.

Beevor, Antony. *Berlin: The Downfall, 1945*. London: Viking, 2002.

Beevor, Antony. *Crete: The Battle and the Resistance*. London: Murray, 1991.

Beevor, Antony. *Stalingrad*. London: Viking, 1998.

Behrendt, Hans-Otto. *Rommel's Intelligence in the Desert Campaign, 1941–1943*. London: Kimber, 1985.

Bennett, Geoffrey M. *Battle of the River Plate*. Annapolis, MD: Naval Institute Press, 1972.

Bercuson, David J., and Holger H. Herwig. *Bismarck: The Story behind the Destruction of the Pride of Hitler's Navy*. London: Hutchinson, 2002.

Blair, Clay. *Hitler's U-Boat War*. 2 vols. I.: *The Hunters, 1939–1942*. II.: *The Hunted, 1942–1945*. New York: Random House, 1996–1998.

Blumenson, Martin. *Anzio: The Gamble that Failed*. Philadelphia: Lippincott, 1963.

Boelcke, Willie A., ed. *The Secret Conferences of Dr. Goebbels: The Nazi Propaganda War, 1939–1945*. New York: Dutton, 1970.

Boog, Horst, ed. *The Conduct of the Air War in the Second World War: An International Comparison*. New York: St. Martin's Press, 1992.

Boyne, Walter J. *Clash of Titans: World War II at Sea*. New York: Simon and Schuster, 1995.

Boyne, Walter J. *Clash of Wings: World War II in the Air*. New York: Simon and Schuster, 1994.

Bradford, Ernle D. *Siege: Malta, 1940–1943*. New York: Morrow, 1986.

Brown, Anthony Cave. *Bodyguard of Lies*. New York: Harper and Row, 1975.

Burdick, Charles, and Hans-Adolf Jacobsen, eds. *The Halder War Diary, 1939–1942*. Greenhill: London, 1988.

Carafano, James J. *After D-Day: Operation Cobra and the Normandy Breakout*. Boulder, CO: Lynne Rienner, 2000.

Carell, Paul. *Hitler Moves East, 1941–1943*. Boston, MA: Little, Brown, 1964.

Citino, Robert M. *The German Way of War: From the Thirty Years' War to the Third Reich*. Lawrence: University Press of Kansas, 2005.

Citino, Robert M. *The Path to Blitzkrieg: Doctrine and Training in the German Army, 1920–1939*. Boulder, CO: Lynne Rienner Publishers, 1999.

Claasen, Adam R. A. *Hitler's Northern War: The Luftwaffe's Ill-Fated Campaign, 1940–1945*. Lawrence: University Press of Kansas, 2001.

Clark, Alan. *BARBAROSSA: The Russian-German Conflict, 1941–1945*. London: Morrow, 1965, 1996.

Clark, Alan. *The Fall of Crete*. London: Blond, 1962.

Collins, Larry, and Dominique Lapierre. *Is Paris Burning*? New York: Simon and Schuster, 1965.

Corum, James S. *The Luftwaffe: Creating the Operational Air War, 1918–1940*. Lawrence: University Press of Kansas, 1997.

Corum, James S. *The Roots of Blitzkrieg: Hans von Seeckt and German Military Reform*. Lawrence: University Press of Kansas, 1992.

Cox, Sebastian, ed. *The Strategic Air War against Germany, 1939–1945: The Official Report of the British Bombing Survey Unit*. London: Frank Cass, 1998.

Craig, Gordon A. *The Politics of the Prussian Army, 1640–1945*. New York: Oxford University Press, 1955.

Crane, Conrad C. *Bombs, Cities, and Civilians: American Airpower Strategy in World War II*. Lawrence: University Press of Kansas, 1993.

Creveld, Martin van. *Fighting Power: German and U.S. Army Performance, 1939–1945*. Westport, CT: Greenwood Press, 1982.

Davidson, Eugene. *The Trial of the Germans: An Account of the 21 Defendants before the International Military Tribunal at Nuremberg*. New York: Macmillan, 1959, 1972.

Davies, Norman. *Rising '44: The Battle for Warsaw*. New York: Viking, 2004.

Deutsch, Harold C. *The Conspiracy against Hitler in the Twilight War*. Minneapolis: Minnesota University Press, 1968.

Deutsch, Harold C. *Hitler and His Generals: The Hidden Crisis, January–June 1938*. Minneapolis: Minnesota University Press, 1974.

Dönitz, Karl. *Memoirs: Ten Years and Twenty Days*. New York: DaCapo, 1959, 1990, 1997.

Dupuy, Trevor N. *A Genius for War: The German Army and General Staff, 1807–1945*. Falls Church, VA: Nova, 1984.

Erickson, John. *Stalin's War with Germany*. 2 vols. I.: *The Road to Stalingrad*. II.: *The Road to Berlin*. New Haven, CT: Yale University Press, 1983–1984, 2000.

Fraser, David. *Knight's Cross: A Life of Field Marshal Erwin Rommel*. New York: HarperCollins, 1994.

Frieser, Karl-Heinz. *The Blitzkrieg Legend: The 1940 Campaign in the West*. Annapolis, MD: U.S. Naval Institute Press, 2005.

Fritz, Stephen G. *Frontsoldat: The German Soldier in World War II*. Lexington: University of Kentucky Press, 1995.

Fritz, Stephen G. *Ostkrieg: Hitler's War of Extermination in the East*. Lexington: University of Kentucky Press, 2011.

Gannon, Michael. *Black May 1943: The Dramatic Story behind the Climatic Allied Victory over German U-Boats in the North Atlantic*. New York: HarperCollins, 1998.

Gannon, Michael. *Operation DRUMBEAT: The Dramatic True Story of Germany's First U-Boat Attacks along the American Coast in World War II*. New York: HarperCollins, 1990.

Gilbert, Adrian, *Waffen-SS: Hitler's Army at War*. New York: Da Capo Press, 2019.

Gilbert, Felix. *Hitler Directs His War: The Secret Records of His Daily Military Conferences*. New York: Oxford University Press, 1950.

Glantz, David M. *BARBAROSSA: Hitler's Invasion of Russia, 1941*. Charleston, SC: Arcadia, 2001.

Glantz, David M. *The Battle for Leningrad, 1941–1944*. Lawrence: Kansas University Press, 2002.

Glantz, David M., and Jonathan House. *When Titans Clashed: How the Red Army Stopped Hitler.* Lawrence: University Press of Kansas, 1995.

Glantz, David M., and Harold S. Orenstein, eds. *Battle for the Ukraine.* London: Cass, 2003.

Gross, Gerhard P. *The Myth and Reality of German Warfare: Operational Thinking from Moltke the Elder to Heusinger.* English translation edited by David T. Zabecki. Lexington: University Press of Kentucky, 2016.

Grove, Eric J., ed. *German Capital Ships and Raiders in World War II.* 2 vols. I.: *From Graf Spee to Bismarck, 1939–1941.* II.: *From* Scharnhorst *to* Tirpitz, *1942–1944.* London: Cass, 2002.

Grove, Eric J. *The Price of Disobedience: The Battle of the River Plate Reconsidered.* Annapolis, MD: Naval Institute Press, 2001.

Guderian, Heinz. *Achtung-Panzer! The Development of Armoured Forces: Their Tactics and Operational Potential.* Translated by Christopher Duffy. London: Arms and Armour Press, 1993.

Guderian, Heinz. *Panzer Leader.* Translated by Constantine Fitzgibbon. London: The Harborough, 1957.

Hart, Russell A. *Clash of Arms: How the Allies Won in Normandy.* Boulder, CO: Rienner, 2001.

Helber, Helmut, and David M. Glantz, eds. *Hitler and His Generals: Military Conferences, 1942–1943.* Translated by Roland Winter, Krista Smith, and Mary Beth Friedrich. New York: Enigma, 2003.

Hitler, Adolf. *Mein Kampf.* Boston, MA: Houghton Mifflin, 1925, 1939, 1962.

Hoffmann, Peter. *The History of the German Resistance, 1933–1945.* Cambridge, MA: MIT Press, 1977.

Hohne, Heinz. *The Order of the Death's Head: The Story of Hitler's SS.* New York: Coward-McCann, 1969.

Homze, Edward L. *Arming the Luftwaffe: The Reich Air Ministry and the German Aircraft Industry, 1919–1939.* Lincoln: Nebraska University Press, 1976.

Horne, Alistair. *To Lose a Battle: France 1940.* Boston, MA: Little, Brown, 1969.

Hough, Richard A., and Denis Richards. *The Battle of Britain: The Greatest Air Battle of World War II.* New York: Norton, 1989.

Isby, David C., ed. *Fighting in Normandy: The German Army from D-Day to Villers-Bocage.* Mechanicsburg, PA: Stackpole, 2001.

Jacobsen, Hans Adolf, and Jürgen Rohwer. *Decisive Battles of World War II: The German View.* New York: Putnam, 1965.

Kahn, David. *Hitler's Spies: German Military Intelligence in World War II.* New York: Macmillan, 1978.

Kahn, David. *Seizing the ENIGMA: The Race to Break the German U-boat Codes, 1939–1943.* London: Souvenir, 1991.

Kemp, Paul J. *U-Boats Destroyed: German Submarine Losses in the World Wars.* Annapolis, MD: Naval Institute Press, 1997.

Kemp, Peter K. *Escape of* Scharnhorst *and* Gneisenau. Annapolis, MD: Naval Institute Press, 1975.

Kennedy, Ludovic. *Pursuit: The Chase and Sinking of the* Bismarck. New York: Viking, 1974.

Kennedy, Robert M. *Department of the Army Pamphlet No. 20-255: The German Campaign in Poland (1939).* Washington, DC: U.S. Government Printing Office, 1956.

Kersaudy, François. *Norway 1940.* New York: St. Martin, 1990.

Kershaw, Ian. *Hitler.* 2 vols. I.: *1889–1936: Hubris.* II.: *1936–1945: Nemesis.* New York: Norton, 1998–2000.

Kershaw, Robert J. *It Never Snows in September: The German View of MARKET-GARDEN and the Battle of Arnhem, September 1944.* Hersham, Surrey: Ian Allen, 1994.

Kieser, Egbert. *Hitler on the Doorstep: Operation SEA LION, the German Plan to*

Invade Britain, 1940. Annapolis, MD: Naval Institute Press, 1997.

Koburger, Charles W. *Steel Ships, Iron Crosses, and Refugees: The German Navy in the Baltic, 1939–1945*. Westport, CT: Praeger, 1989.

Kurki, Allan W. *Operation MOONLIGHT SONATA: The German Raid on Coventry*. London: Praeger, 1995.

Langer, Walter C. *The Mind of Adolf Hitler: The Secret Wartime Report*. New York: Basic Books, 1972.

Liddell Hart, Basil H. *The German Generals Talk*. New York: William Morrow, 1948.

Littlejohn, David. *The Patriotic Traitors: The History of Collaboration in German-Occupied Europe, 1940–45*. Garden City, NY: Doubleday, 1972.

Lochner, Louis P., ed. *The Goebbels Diaries, 1942–1943*. New York: Doubleday, 1948.

Ludwig, Joachim. *Rückzug: The German Retreat from France, 1944*. English translation edited by David T. Zabecki. Lexington: University Press of Kentucky, 2012.

Macksey, Kenneth. *Guderian: Creator of the Blitzkrieg*. New York: Stein and Day, 1976.

Manchester, William. *The Arms of Krupp, 1587–1968*. London: Michael Joseph, 1969.

Mann, Chris, and Christer Jörgensen. *Hitler's Arctic War: The German Campaigns in Norway, Finland and the USSR, 1940–1945*. New York: St. Martin's Press, 2003.

Manstein, Erich von. *Lost Victories*. Edited and translated by Anthony G. Powell. Chicago, IL: Henry Regnery Co., 1958.

McDonald, Charles B. *A Time for Trumpets: The Untold Story of the Battle of the Bulge*. New York: William Morrow, 1984.

Megargee, Geoffrey P. *Inside Hitler's High Command*. Lawrence: University Press of Kansas, 2000.

Mellenthin, F. W. von. *German Generals of World War II: As I Saw Them*. Norman: University of Oklahoma Press, 1977.

Mellenthin, F. W. von. *Panzer Battles: A Study of the Employment of Armor in the Second World War*. Translated by H. Betzler. Norman: University of Oklahoma Press, 1956.

Melvin, Mungo. *Manstein: Hitler's Greatest General*. London: Weidenfeld & Nicholson, 2010.

Messenger, Charles. *The Last Prussian: A Biography of Field Marshal Gerd von Rundstedt*. Barnsley, South Yorkshire: Pen and Sword, 1991.

Millett, Allan R., and Williamson Murray, eds. *Military Effectiveness*. 3 vols. II: *The Interwar Period*. III.: *The Second World War*. Boston, MA: Unwin Hyman, 1988, 1990.

Moulton, James L. *A Study of Warfare in Three Dimensions: The Norwegian Campaign of 1940*. Athens: Ohio University Press, 1968.

Muller, Richard. *The German Air War in Russia*. Baltimore, MD: Nautical and Aviation Publishing Company of America, 1992.

Murray, Williamson. *Strategy for Defeat: The Luftwaffe, 1933–1945*. Maxwell Air Force Base, AL: Air University Press, 1983.

Muth, Jörg. *Command Culture: Officer Education in the U.S. Army and the German Armed Forces, 1901–1940, and the Consequences for World War II*. Denton, TX: University of North Texas Press, 2011.

Odgen, Michael. *The Battle of North Cape*. London: Kimber, 1962.

Paine, Lauran. *German Military Intelligence in World War II: The Abwehr*. New York: Stein and Day, 1984.

Reinhardt, Klaus. *Moscow, the Turning Point: The Failure of Hitler's Strategy in the Winter of 1941–1942*. London: Berg, 1992.

Robertson, Terence. *Channel Dash: The Drama of Twenty-Four Hours of War*. New York: Dutton, 1958.

Rommel, Erwin. *Infantry Attacks*. Novato, CA: Presidio Press, 1990.

Roseman, Mark. *The Wannsee Conference and the Final Solution*. New York: Penguin, 2002.

Rossino, Alexander B. *Hitler Strikes Poland: Blitzkrieg, Ideology, and Atrocity*. Lawrence: University Press of Kansas, 2003.

Ruge, Friedrich. *Der Seekrieg: The German Navy's Story, 1939–1945*. Annapolis, MD: Naval Institute Press, 1954, 1957.

Ryan, Cornelius. *The Longest Day: June 6, 1944*. New York: Simon and Schuster, 1959.

Salisbury, Harrison E. *The 900 Days: The Siege of Leningrad*. New York: Harper and Row, 1969, 1986.

Shirer, William L. *Berlin Diary: The Journal of a Foreign Correspondent, 1934–1941*. New York: Knopf, 1941.

Shirer, William L. *The Rise and Fall of the Third Reich: A History of Nazi Germany*. New York: Simon and Schuster, 1960.

Showell, Jak P. M. *The German Navy in World War II: Reference Guide to the Kriegsmarine, 1935–1945*. Annapolis, MD: Naval Institute Press, 1979.

Speer, Albert. *Inside the Third Reich*. New York: Macmillan, 1970.

Stein, George H. *The Waffen SS: Hitler's Elite Guard at War, 1939–1945*. Ithaca, NY: Cornell University Press, 1966.

Taylor, Telford. *The Anatomy of the Nuremberg Trials: A Personal Memoir*. New York: Knopf, 1992.

Taylor, Telford. *Sword and Swastika: Generals and Nazis in the Third Reich*. Chicago, IL: Quadrangle, 1952, 1969.

Trevelyan, Raleigh. *Rome "44": The Battle for the Eternal City*. New York: Viking Press, 1981.

Trevor-Roper, Hugh R., ed. *Blitzkrieg to Defeat: Hitler's War Directives, 1939–1945*. New York: Holt, 1965.

Trevor-Roper, Hugh R. *The Last Days* of Hitler. New York: Macmillan, 1947, 1978, 1987.

Tucker, Spencer C. *World War II: The Definitive Encyclopedia and Document Collection*. Santa Barbara, CA: ABC-CLIO, 2016.

U.S. War Department. *TM-E 30-451 Handbook on German Military Forces*. Washington, DC: Government Printing Office, 1945. (Reprint Baton Rouge, LA: Louisiana State University Press, 1990.)

Van Creveld, Martin. *Fighting Power: German and U.S. Army Performance, 1939–1945*. Westport, CT: Greenwood, 1982.

Van Der Vat, Dan. *The Atlantic Campaign: The Great Struggle at Sea, 1939–1945*. Annapolis, MD: Naval Institute Press, 1988.

Waite, Robert G. L. *Vanguard of Nazism: The Free Corps Movement in Postwar Germany, 1918–1923*. Cambridge, MA: Harvard University Press, 1952, 1969.

Warlimont, Walter. *Inside Hitler's Headquarters, 1939–1945*. New York: Praeger, 1964.

Watson, Bruce Allen. *Exit Rommel: The Tunisian Campaign, 1942–1943*. Westport, CT: Praeger, 1999.

Weinberg, Gerhard L. *The Foreign Policy of Hitler's Germany: Diplomatic Revolution in Europe, 1933–1936*. Chicago, IL: Chicago University Press, 1970.

Weinberg, Gerhard L. *The Foreign Policy of Hitler's Germany: Starting World War II, 1937–1939*. Chicago, IL: Chicago University Press, 1980.

Wheeler-Bennett, John W. *Munich: Prologue to Tragedy*. London: Macmillan, 1948, 1966.

Wheeler-Bennett, John W. *The Nemesis of Power: The German Army in Politics, 1918–1945*. New York: St. Martin, 1953, 1967.

Woodman, Richard. *Malta Convoys, 1940–1943*. London: Murray, 2000.

Zabecki, David T., ed. *Chief of Staff: The Principal Officers Behind History's Great Commanders,* Vol. II *World War II to Korea and Vietnam*. Annapolis, MD: U.S. Naval Institute Press, 2008.

Zabecki, David T., ed. *Germany at War: 400 Years of Military History*. Santa Barbara, CA: ABC-CLIO, 2014.

Zabecki, David T., and Bruce Condell, trans. and eds. *On the German Art of War: Truppenführung*. Boulder, CO: Lynne Rienner, 2001.

List of Contributors

Editor

Major General David T. Zabecki, PhD
U.S. Army, Retired

Contributors

William J. Astore, PhD
Professor of History
Pennsylvania College of Technology

Major General Jonathan B. A. Bailey, CB, MBE, PhD
British Army, Retired

Lee Baker, PhD
Associate Professor of History
University of Cincinnati

Nicholas W. Barcheski
Virginia Military Institute

John H. Barnhill, PhD
Independent Scholar

Michael B. Barrett, PhD
Department of History
The Citadel

Lieutenant Colonel Robert Bateman
U.S. Army

Rabbi Kevin S. Bemel
Lieutenant Commander, Chaplain Corps
U.S. Navy Reserve

Jon D. Berlin, PhD
Joint Military Intelligence College

Keith W. Bird, PhD
Chancellor
Kentucky Community and Technical College System

Andy Blackburn
Independent Scholar

Brigadier General Philip L. Bolté
United States Army, Retired

Fred L. Borch III
Regimental Historian and Archivist
The Judge Advocate General's Corps, U.S. Army

Anna Boros-McGee
Independent Scholar
Budapest, Hungary

Dewey A. Browder, PhD
Department of History
Austin Peay State University

Jeffrey A. Charlston, PhD
U.S. Army Center of Military History

Paul H. Collier, PhD
Independent Scholar
Adelaide, Australia

Sherwood S. Cordier, PhD
Professor Emeritus
Department of History
Western Michigan University

Lieutenant Colonel James S. Corum, PhD
U.S. Army Reserve, Retired

Conrad C. Crane, PhD
Director, U.S. Army Military History Institute

Bruce J. DeHart, PhD
Professor of History
University of North Carolina at Pembroke

Paul W. Doerr, PhD
Professor and Department Head
Department of History and Classics
Acadia University, Nova Scotia

Timothy C. Dowling, PhD
Associate Professor of History
Virginia Military Institute

Robert W. Duvall
Independent Scholar

Jason C. Engle
University of Southern Mississippi

Brigadier General Uzal W. Ent
Pennsylvania National Guard, Retired

Erica R. Fagen
PhD Candidate, Department of History
University of Massachusetts Amherst

Pamela Feltus
Independent Scholar

Matthew J. Flynn, PhD
Associate Professor of Military History
Command and Staff College
Marine Corps University

Paul E. Fontenoy
Curator for Maritime Research
North Carolina Maritime Museum

Arthur T. Frame, PhD
Professor of Operational Warfare
U.S. Army Command and General Staff College

Paul Frazier, PhD
Adjunct Professor of History
University of Cincinnati

Robert L. Glaze, PhD
University of Tennessee, Knoxville

Joseph C. Greaney
Associate Dean of Academic Affairs
Broward College

Jack Greene, PhD
Military History Workshop International

Edward Gutiérrez, PhD
University of Hartford

Jon Guttman
Research Director
The History Net

Kyle D. Haire
Virginia Military Institute

Craig S. Hamilton
Virginia Military Institute

Eleanor Hancock, PhD
Associate Professor of History
University of New South Wales, Canberra

William P. Head, PhD
Chief Historian
Warner Robins Air Logistics Center

Emmanuel Hogg
PhD Candidate
Carleton University

Lieutenant Colonel C. J. Horn
National Defense University College

Ilisa Horowitz
Independent Scholar

John A. Hutcheson Jr., PhD
Professor of History
Chair, Division of Social Sciences
Dalton State College

Lance Janda, PhD
Assistant Professor
Department of History & Humanities
Cameron University

Marcus O. Jones, PhD
Associate Professor of History
U.S. Naval Academy

Robert T. Kaczowka
Al Akhawayn University
Ifrane, Morocco

Colonel Robert Kershaw
British Army, Retired
Salisbury England

Dieter H. Kollmer, PhD
Lieutenant Colonel and Senior Historian
Zentrum für Militärgeschichte und Sozialwissenschaften der Bundeswehr
Center for Military History and Social Sciences, German Armed Forces
Potsdam, Germany

Thomas Lansford, PhD
Professor of Political Science
University of Southern Mississippi

James Levy, PhD
Assistant Professor of History
Hofstra University

Raymond D. Limbach, MA
Pritzker Military Museum and Library

Dana Lombardy
Senior Executive Director
World War One Historical Association

Britton W. MacDonald
Temple University
Saskatoon, Saskatchewan, Canada

Rodney Madison
Department of History
Oregon State University

Ross Mahoney
Aviation Historian
Royal Air Force Museum

Wendy A. Maier-Sarti, PhD
Professor of History
Oakton Community College

Jerome V. Martin, PhD
Command Historian
U.S. Strategic Command

Alessandro Massignani
Independent Scholar

John J. McGrath
U.S. Army Combat Studies Institute

Matthew Alan McNiece, PhD
Associate Professor of History and Political Science
Howard Payne University

Major General Mungo Melvin, CB OBE MA
British Army, Retired

Martin Moll, PhD
University of Graz
Graz, Austria

Cullen Monk
Virginia Military Institute

Troy D. Morgan
Independent Scholar

Gene Mueller, PhD
Texan A&M University

Michael S. Neiberg, PhD
Professor
U.S. Army War College

Thomas G. Nester, PhD
Professor of History
Bridgewater State University

Bruce Newsome, PhD
Lecturer in International Relations
University of California Berkeley

Vincent P. O'Hara
Independent Scholar

Eric W. Osborne, PhD
Adjunct Professor of History
Virginia Military Institute

Peter Overlack, PhD
Independent Scholar
Brisbane, Australia

Neville Panthaki
York University
Toronto, Ontario, Canada

James D. Perry, PhD
Independent Historian

Roy B. Perry, III
Virginia Military Institute

Marlyn R. Pierce, PhD
Assistant Professor of History
US Army Command and General Staff College

Steven J. Rauch
Command Historian
U.S. Army Signal Center

Annette E. Richardson, PhD
University of Alberta
Edmonton, Alberta, Canada

Spencer E. Robbins III
Virginia Military Institute

Priscilla Roberts, PhD
Associate Professor of History, School of Humanities
University of Hong Kong

Steven B. Rogers, PhD
Senior Historian, Retired
U.S. Department of Justice

Jürgen Rohwer, PhD
Professor of History
University of Stuttgart
Stuttgart, Germany

Stanley Sandler, PhD
Retired Historian
U.S. Army Special Operations Command

Claude R. Sasso, PhD
Adjunct Professor
William Jewell College

Stephen T. Satkiewicz
Independent Scholar

Elizabeth D. Schafer, PhD
Independent Scholar

Charles R. Schrader
Independent Scholar

Captain Carl O. Schuster, MA
U.S. Navy, Retired

T. P. Schweider
U.S. Marine Corps, Retired

Kellie Searle
Independent Scholar

Michael Share, PhD
Department of History
University of Hong Kong

Terry Shoptaugh, PhD
Archivist and Professor
Minnesota State University

Donna Sinclair
Independent Scholar

Natalie R. Spagnuolo
PhD Student, Critical Disability Studies
Faculty of Health, York University

Major Jeffrey W. Stamp
U.S. Air Force

Dirk Steffen
Director of Consultancy
Risk Intelligence

Eva-Maria Stolberg, PhD
Institute of Russian History
University of Bonn
Bonn, Germany

John A. Suprin, MA
Assistant Professor of Military History
U.S. Army Command and General Staff College

Gerald D. Swick
Senior Editor for Digital Media
Weider History Group, Inc.

Lieutenant Colonel David M. Toczek
U.S. Army

Frank Toomey
Virginia Military Institute

Spencer C. Tucker, PhD
Senior Fellow
Military History, ABC-CLIO, Inc.

Fred R. van Hartesveldt, PhD
Professor of History
Fort Valley State University

William H. Van Husen, MA

U.S. Air Force, Retired

John P. Vanzo, PhD

Associate Professor of Political Science and Geography

Bainbridge State College

Thomas J. Weiler, PhD

Department of Political Science

University of Bonn and Trier

Bonn, Germany

Adrian E. Wettstein, PhD

Department of Strategic Studies

Swiss Military Academy at ETH Zurich

Zurich, Switzerland

James H. Willbanks, PhD

Director, Department of Military History

U.S. Army Command and General Staff College

Harold Wise

Adjunct Professor of History

Elizabeth City State University

Berryman E. Woodruff IV

Virginia Military Institute

M. David Yaman

Virginia Military Institute

About the Editor

David T. Zabecki (Maj. Gen. U.S. Army, retired) is the author, editor, or translator of more than twenty military history books. His ABC-CLIO encyclopedia, *Germany at War: 400 Years of Military History*, won a Society for Military History Distinguished Book Award in 2016. His 2018 book, *The Generals' War: Operational Level Command on the Western Front in 1918*, won the Tomlinson Book Prize from the World War I Historical Association. He is editor emeritus of *Vietnam* magazine. He is a graduate of the U.S. Army Command and General Staff College, the U.S. Army War College, and the Harvard University John F. Kennedy School of Government Executive Program for Russian and American General Officers. In 2004, he received a PhD in military history from Britain's Royal Military College of Science, Cranfield University. In 2012, he was the Shifrin distinguished professor of military history at the U.S. Naval Academy, Annapolis. He is an honorary senior research fellow in the War Studies Programme at the University of Birmingham (UK). He is also a fellow of the American College of National Security Leaders.

He enlisted in the U.S. Army in 1966 and served as an infantry rifleman in Vietnam in 1967–1968, including the Tet Offensive. He spent most of his subsequent military career as a field artillery officer and an operations officer. In 2005 and 2006, he served as the commanding general of the U.S. Southern European Task Force Rear (Airborne) and simultaneously as U.S. Army Europe's senior mission commander, south of the Alps. During 2004 and the first half of 2005, he was the U.S. Department of Defense executive director for all World War II 60th anniversary observances in Europe. In June 2004, he commanded the 3,300-soldier task force that supported the 60th anniversary of the D-Day landings in Normandy, France. In late 2003 and early 2004, he was attached to the U.S. State Department as the senior security advisor on the U.S. Coordinating and Monitoring Mission in Israel, charged with advancing the Roadmap to Peace in the Middle East initiative.

Index

Note: Page numbers in **bold** refer to main entries; page numbers followed by *t* indicate tables and *f* indicate figures; page numbers followed by "Doc" refer to primary documents.

Abwehr, **1**
  abolishment of, 1
  absorbed into Reich Security Main Office, 1
  designation for German military intelligence, 1
  distrusted by Nazi leadership, 1
  subordinated to Armed Forces High Command, 1
Afrika Korps, **1–2**
  and Armeegruppe Afrika member, 2, 179
  and Battle of Battleaxe, 177, 224
  and Battle of El Alamein, 2, 29, 178, 194, 224, 269
  and Battle of Gazala, 177–178, 337
  Bayerlein, Fritz, commander of, 29
  Cramer, Hans, commander of, 2
  15th Panzer Division, 2, 177
  Messe, Giovanni, commander of, 2, 180
  90th Light Motorized Infantry Divisions, 2, 177
  164th Light Motorized Infantry Divisions, 2, 177
  and Operation SONNENBLUME (SUNFLOWER), 1–2
  and Operation VENEZIA, 177
  Ramcke Parachute Brigade, 2
  Rommel, Erwin, commander of, 1–2, 29, 177, 224
  surrender of, 2
  10th Panzer Division, 2
  Thoma, Wilhelm von, commander of, 269
  and Tunisia Campaign, 179–180
  21st Panzer Division, 2, 171, 177
Aircraft, military, **2–9**
  aircraft oddities, 8–9
  antitank planes, 7
  Arado Ar 196 floatplane scout, 3*t*, 7
  Arado Ar 234B-2 bomber, 5*t*, *8*
  and Battle of Britain, 5–6
  battlefield reconnaissance planes, 7
  Blohm und Voss BV 40 glider fighter, 8–9
  Blohm und Voss BV 138B-1 maritime reconnaissance, 3*t*, 6–7
  Blohm und Voss BV 222 Wiking flying boat, 7
  bombers, 7–8
  dive bombers, 8
  Dornier Do 17 bomber, 2, 3*t*
  Dornier Do 24 flying boats, 7
  Dornier Do 217E-2 bomber, 4*t*
  Dornier Do 335 Pfeil (Arrow) fighter, 8
  Fieseler Fi 152 fighter, 3*t*
  flying boats, 6–7
  Focke-Wulf Fw 189A-1 battlefield reconnaissance plane, 4*t*, 7

Aircraft, military (*Cont.*)
Focke-Wulf Fw 190A-8 fighter, 4*t,* 6, 8
Focke-Wulf Fw 200C Condor maritime reconnaissance plane, 6–7
fuel-injection system technology, 8
"general purpose" fighters, 5
Heinkel He 51 fighter, 2, 3*t*
Heinkel He 111 bomber, 2, 3*t,* 132
Heinkel He 115 floatplane torpedo bomber, 7
Heinkel He 162 jet bomber, 8
Heinkel He 177 bomber, 5
Heinkel He 219 twin-engine fighter, 7
Heinkel Hs 123 close support, 2, 3*t*
Henschel Hs 129B-2 close support plane, 4*t*
and invasion of Soviet Union, 6
Junkers Ju 52 transport series, 2, 3*t,* 6, 151
Junkers Ju 87 "Stuka" dive-bomber series, 2, 3*t,* 6*f,* 7, 50, 132
Junkers Ju 88 bomber series, 4*t,* 5, 154*f*
Junkers Ju 88A-4 bomber, 4*t*
Junkers Ju 90 airliner, 7
and Kondor Legion, 2, 5
limitations of Treaty of Versailles on, 2
Messerschmitt Me 109 fighter series, 2, 3*t,* 5–6
Messerschmitt Me 110 night fighter series, 4*t,* 5, 7
Messerschmitt Me 163B-1 interceptor, 4*t,* 7
Messerschmitt Me 262A-1 fighter, 4*t*
radar technology, 7–8
and Spanish Civil War, 2
transport planes, 7
Alam Halfa, Battle of. *See* North Africa Campaign
American Military Tribunals, **9–10**
acquittal of Hugo Sperrle, 249
conviction of Georg von Küchler, 139
conviction of Walter Warlimont, 281
dates of, 9
High Command Trial, 9, 63, 139, 249, 281
Judges Trial, 9
and *Judgment at Nuremberg* (film), 9, 63
Krupp Trial, 137
and Weichs zur Glon, Maximilian von (released before trial), 291
Anglo-German Naval Agreement, **10**
criticism of, 10
impetus of, 10
and Kriegsmarine (German Navy), 134, 136
and Plan Z, 10, 195
revoked by Hitler, 10, 195
signing of, 10
terms of, 10, 259
Antwerp, Allied liberation of, **10–11,** 231
Allies' failure to immediately clear Scheldt estuary, 11, 231–232, 293
casualties, 11
events of, 10–11
significance of Antwerp's port facilities, 10
Anzio, Battle of, **11–12,** 123–124
Allied attack on Monte Cassino, 12, 124
casualties, 12
events of, 11–12
German counterattack, 12, 123, 152
Lucas, John P., Allied commander, 12, 123
Mackensen, Eberhard von, German commander, 12, 123, 152
Operation SHINGLE (Allied amphibious landing at Anzio), 11–12, 53–54, 123, 152, 254
planning and preparation for, 53–54, 124
Ardennes Offensive (Battle of the Bulge), **12–15**
Battle for Bastogne, 14, 27–28, 29
Battle of France compared with, 13–14
"Big Solution," criticism by German general staff, 12–13
casualties, 15
choice of Ardennes, 12
code name Wacht am Rhein (Watch on the Rhine), 13

definition of salient ("bulge"), 13
events of, 14
final coordinating order from Hitler to Field Marshal Model, 320 (Doc. 10)
Kampfgruppe Peiper, 14, 194–195
Malmédy Massacre, 14, 152–153, 195
map, 13*f*
and Model, Walther, Army Group B commander, 13, 163, 320 (Doc. 10)
planning and preparation for, 12–13, 291–292
purpose of, 12
"Small Solution" alternative plan, 13
and use of Enigma machine, 77
weather conditions, 14

Artillery, **15–18**
air-to-ground artillery, 17–18
artillerymen, 17
calibers of field artillery, 15
failure to apply lessons of World War I, 17–18
Flak 18 air defense gun, 16–17
Flak 35 air defense gun, 16*t*
Flak air defense guns, 16–17, 16*t*, 35, 97, 102, 197, 212, 226, 237
"German 88" antiaircraft gun, 16–17
German stores and availability of, 17–18
heavy artillery, 15
Hummel (Bumblebee) SP heavy artillery, 15
infantry guns, 15–16
interwar technological developments, 15
K18 field gun, 16*t*
le FH (leichte Feldhaubitze) 18 light field howitzer, 15, 16*t*
le IG (leichtes Infantriegeschütz) 18 light infantry gun, 15–16, 16*t*
Mrs (Mörser) 18 heavy howitzer, 15, 16*t*
s FH (schweres Infantriegeschütz) 18 heavy field howitzer, 15, 16*t*, 17*f*
Sd.Kfz. (*Sonderkraftfahrzeug*) 124 Wespe SP howitzer, 15, 16*t*
Sd.Kfz. (*Sonderkraftfahrzeug*) 165 Hummel SP howitzer, 16*t*
self-propelled (SP) artillery, 15
sK (schwere Kanone) 18 heavy field gun, 15, 16*t*
Stu. H (Sturmhaubitze) 40 SP assault gun, 16*t*
Stu. H (Sturmhaubitze) 42 SP assault howitzer, 16*t*
Stu. H (Sturmhaubitze) 43 Brummbär SP assault howitzer, 16*t*
Stu. H (Sturmhaubitze) 43 SP assault howitzer, 16*t*
Stu. K (Sturmhaubitze) 40 SP assault gun, 16*t*
Wespe (Wasp) self-propelled anti-tank artillery, 15, 16*t*

Atlantic, Battle of the, **18–20**
and Allied possession of Iceland, 70–71
and Allied Submarine Detection Investigating Committee (sonar) location device, 20
battle for Convoys SC 122 and HX 229, 20, 65
casualties, 21
and Dönitz, Karl, commander, 20–21
and failures of German counterintelligence, 18–19, 261, 305
and German U-boats, 18–19, 261
longest WWII campaign, 18
map, 19*f*
and superior Allied resources and technology, 21

Atlantic Wall, **20–21**
Atlantikwall, German defense system, 20–21
and British raid on Dieppe, 71
Hitler's orders for, 20
impact of, 21
materials and munitions, 20–21, 57
and Normandy invasion, 173
and Organization Todt, 187–188
planning and construction of, 20–21, 187–188, 271

Austria, annexation of (Anschluss), **21–22**
 background to, 21
 and Bock, Fedor von, Eighth Army commander, 21–22
 events of, 21–22
 Hitler's reasons for, 21
Avranches counteroffensive, **22–23**
 American counter-moves, 22
 background to, 22
 codename Operation LÜTTICH, 22–23, 78
 damage to German tanks, 23
 events of, 22–23

Babi Yar Massacre, **24**
 Blobel, Paul, Sonderkommando 4a commander, 24
 brutality of, 24
 casualties, 24
 events of, 24
Bach-Zelewski, Erich von dem, **24–25**
 conviction for role in Night of the Long Knives blood purge, 25
 prosecution testimony at Nuremberg war crimes trials, 25
 Warsaw Rising commander, 25, 282–283
 World War I service, 24
Balck, Hermann, **25–26**
 11th Panzer Division commander, 25
 Army Group G commander, 26, 238
 and Battle of Chir River, 25, 57
 and Battle of Stalingrad, 251
 German Sixth Army commander, 26, 51
 and Lorraine Campaign, 146, 147, 148
 and Mellenthin, Friedrich-Wilhelm, 160
 military reputation of, 25*f,* 26
 and Soviet offensive, 25–26, 160
 and Soviet siege of Budapest, 51
 surrender of troops to U.S., 26
 World War I service, 25
 woundings of, 25
 XLVIII Panzer Corps commander, 25–26, 160
Barents Sea, Battle of, **26–27**
 background to, 26
 codename Operation REGENBOGEN (RAINBOW), 26
 events of, 26–27
 impact of German failure at, 26
 and Kummetz, Oskar, commander, 26
Barkhorn, Gerhard, **27**
 Experte fighter pilot, 27, 328*t*
 mission statistics, 27
 postwar career, 328*t*
 Wehrmacht officer rank, 350*t*
Bastogne, Battle for, 14, **27–28**
 background to, 27
 casualties, 28
 events of, 28
 significance of, 27
Bayerlein, Fritz, **28–29**
 Afrika Korps commander, 29
 and Allied Operation COBRA, 59
 and Battle for Bastogne, 28
 and Battle for Saint-Lô, 230
 and Battle of El Alamein, 29
 Panzer Lehr Division commander, 28, 29
 World War I service, 28
 wounding of, 29
Beck, Ludwig, **29–30**
 arrest and execution of, 29, 30*f*
 assessment of, 30
 chief of General Staff, 29, 92, 133, 184, 333
 military rank, 334*t*
 opposition to Hitler, 29, 30*f,* 185–186, 256
 primary author of *Truppenführung* (*Unit Command*), 29
 Truppenamt (Troop Office) chief, 29, 333
 World War I service, 29
Belgium and Flanders Campaign, **30–31**
 background to, 30
 Battle of Eben Emael, 31, 79
 and Bock, Fedor von, Army Group B commander, 30–31
 casualties, 31

events of, 30–31
and Küchler, Georg von, Eighteenth Army commander, 31
and Reichenau, Walther von, Sixth Army commander, 30–31
and SICHELSCHNITT (SICKEL CUT) plan, 31
surrender of King Leopold II, 31
Belorussia Offensive, Soviet, **32,** 52, 202, 274
and Allied Tehran Conference, 32
Army Group Center, 32
and Busch, Ernst, German Army Group Center commander, 32
casualties, 32
codename Operation BAGRATION, 32
events of, 32
impact of, 32
map of destruction of Army Group Center, 33*f*
Berlin, land battle for, **32–34**
Army Group Vistula commanders, 34
Army Group Vistula intelligence enemy assessment, 322–323 (Doc. 12)
background to, 32, 34
Battle of Seelow Heights, 34, 234–235
casualties, 34
Stalin's orders for, 34
Berlin air campaign, Allied, **34–35**
attack on Tempelhof Airport, 35
Berlin's significance, 34–35
destruction of, 35
and Kammhuber Line, 35
Luftwaffe's defense of Berlin, 35
RAF Bomber Command raids, 35
U.S. Army Air Force raids, 35
Bey, Eric, **35–36**
and Battle of North Cape, 36, 181
Knights Cross of the Iron Cross awarded to, 36
and Operation CERBERUS, 36
World War I service, 35–36
"Big Week" Allied air campaign, **36–37**
and Allied combined bomber offensive, 62
codename Operation ARGUMENT, 36
events of, 36
significance and impact of, 36
Bismarck, sortie and sinking of, **37**
background to, 37
impact of, 37
See also Warships, surface: *Bismarck* (battleship)
Bittrich, Willi, **37–38**
and Ardennes Offensive, 38
conviction for war crimes by the French, 38
and Operation MARKET-GARDEN, 38, 157
II SS Panzer Corps commander, 38, 157
World War I service, 37–38
Black May, Allied anti-U-Boat campaign, **38**
impact of, 38
U-boat destruction, 38
and Wolf Pack tactics (*Rudeltaktik*), 38, 73, 296
Blaskowitz, Johannes Albrecht, **39**
Army Task Group G commander, 39, 81, 146, 147, 148, 170, 238, 240–241, 293
charged with war crimes, 9, 39
and Operation DRAGOON, 39, 240–241
and Operation NORDWIND, 170
and Poland Campaign, 201
suicide of, 39
World War I service, 39
Blitz, air campaign, **39–40**
British casualties and Luftwaffe aircraft losses, 40
impact of, 40
phase 1, attacks on London, 39
phase 2, attacks on Coventry, 39–40
phase 3, attacks on British port cities, 40
Blitzkrieg, **40–43**
creation of term *Blitzkrieg,* 40
definition of military doctrine, 40
and German's lessons from World War I, 40–41

Blitzkrieg (*Cont.*)
interwar German philosophical and technological debates, 40–41
and invasion of Soviet Union, 42–43
myth of, 40, 42–43
panzer division growth after Polish Campaign, 42
and Polish Campaign of 1939, 41–42, 42*f*
and *Time* magazine articles, 40
Blomberg, Werner von, **43–44**
and Blomberg-Fritsch Crisis, 44
defense minister in Hitler's first cabinet, 43, 184
dismissal of, 44, 333
first field marshal of the Third Reich, 43
military rank, 334
Nuremberg testimony of, 44
personal oath of allegiance to Hitler, 43, 148
World War I service, 43
Blomberg-Fritsch Crisis, **44**
and Blomberg, Werner von, 43–44
and Fritsch, Werner von, 51
impact of, 44
Blumentritt, Günther, **44–45**
First Parachute Army commander, 45, 214
postwar career, 45
SS XII Corps commander, 45
World War I service, 44
Bock, Fedor von, **45**
and annexation of Austria, 21
Army Group South commander, 45
and Battle of France, 45, 85, 86
and Belgium and Flanders Campaign, 30
and invasion of Soviet Union, 45, 242
and invasions of Poland, 45, 198
monarchist views of, 45
and Netherlands Campaign, 168
promotion to rank of field marshal in the Wehrmacht, 45, 338
World War I service, 45
BODENPLATTE, air operation, **45–46**
casualties and aircraft losses, 46
events of, 45–46
impact of, 46
planning and preparation for, 45
Bohemia and Moravia, annexation of, **46**
background to, 46
brutality of German occupation, 46
Brandenberger, Erich, **46–47**
and Ardennes Offensive, 47
and invasion of Soviet Union, 46
Nineteenth Army commander, 47
Seventh Army commander, 47
surrender of, 47
World War I service, 46
Brauchitsch, Walther von, **47**
commander of the German Army, 47, 184–185, 289
dismissal of, 92, 289
International War Crimes testimony, 47
promotion to rank of field marshal in the Wehrmacht, 47, 338
relationship with Hitler, 47
Braun, Wernher von, **47–48**
education and career as physicist, 47–48
surrender to U.S. military, 48
and U.S. space program, 48
Britain, Battle of, **48–51**
aircraft, 50
background to, 48
casualties and aircraft losses, 50
events of, 50
map, 49*f*
naming of, 48
objectives, 50
RAF integrated air defense system, 50, 52
Budapest, Soviet siege of, **51**
casualties, 51
and expulsion of German troops, 51
Operation KONRAD I, 51
Operation KONRAD II, 51
Operation KONRAD III, 51
Busch, Ernst, **51–52**
Army Group Northwest commander, 52
and invasion of France, 52

and invasion of Poland, 52
and Operation BAGRATION, 32, 52
Pour le Mérite awarded to, 51
promotion to rank of field marshal in the Wehrmacht, 338
World War I service, 51

Canaris, Wilhelm, **53**
Anti-Nazi activities of, 1, 53, 186, 305
conviction and hanging for implication in implication in bomb plot against Hitler, 53
leader of Abwehr (German military intelligence), 1, 53
World War I service, 53
Case BLUE, Führer Directive 41, "The Spring Offensive in the Soviet Union, Case BLUE," 90*t*
Case WHITE (Fall WEISS), plan for the invasion of Poland, 198. *See also* Hitler, Adolf, directive for Fall Weiss, attack on Poland (Doc. 2)
Case YELLOW (Fall GELB), German attack against France and neutral Low Countries, 85, 155, 168
Führer Directive 10, "Concentration of Forces for Case YELLOW," 89*t*
Cassino/Rapido River, battles of, **53–54**
bombing of abbey, 55
casualties, 54
significance of, 53
Caucasus Campaign, **54–56**
background to, 54
events of, 55–56
German fuel shortage, 55
objectives, 54
river-crossing operation, 55*f*
Channel Dash, **56**
British caught by surprise, 56
and Operation CERBERUS, 56
Channel Islands Campaign, **56–57**
Channel Islands only British territory occupied by Germany during WWII, 57
and invasion of Normandy, 57
Chiefs of General and Admiralty Staffs, 333–335
Chief of Staff of the Armed Forces High Command, 334*t*, 335
Chief of the Armed Forces High Command Operations Staff, 334*t*, 335
Chief of the Army High Command General Staff, 333, 334
Chief of the German General Staff, 333, 334*t*
Chief of the Luftwaffe High Command General Staff, 333, 334*t*, 335
Chief of the Naval Warfare Command Admiralty Staff, 333, 334*t*, 335
Chief of the Troop Office, 333, 334*t*
Chir River, Battle of, **57–58**
events of, 57
significance of, 57–58
Choltitz, Dietrich von, **58**
LXXXIV Corps commander in France, 58
refusal to destroy Paris, 58
surrender and prisoner of war, 58
Ciliax, Otto, **58–59**
and Channel Dash, 59
COBRA, Allied breakout operation, **59–60**
background to, 59
events of, 59–60
impact of, 60
Colmar Pocket, battle for the, **60–61**
casualties, 60
and Operation NORDWIND (NORTHWIND), 60
Cologne, Allied air raid on, **61**
casualties, 61
code-named Operation Millennium, 61
Combined bomber offensive, Allied (Operation POINTBLANK), **61–63**
British plan, code-named THUNDERCLAP, 62
and Casablanca Conference, 62
casualties, 63
and Dresden fire-bombing, 62

Combined bomber (*Cont.*)
  objectives, 61
  Ploesti Air Raids, Allied, 197
  post-war assessments, 63
  U.S. plan, code-named CLARION, 62
Commando Order, **63**
  and British commando raid on Dieppe, 63
  terms of, 63
  and war crimes trials, 63, 206
Commissar Order, **64**, 139, 281
  and Operation BARBAROSSA, 64
  terms of, 64
  and war crimes trials, 128, 139
  and Warlimont, Walter, 281
  See also Wehrmacht compliance with the Commissar order (Doc. 5)
Convoy PQ 17, battle of, **64**
  significance of Allied defeat, 64
Convoys SC 122 and HX 229, battle of, **65**
  largest convoy battle in the Battle of the Atlantic, 65
Crete, German Invasion of, **65–67**
  casualties, 67
  Führer Directive 28, "Operation MERCURY: The Invasion of Crete," 89
  German paratroopers landing in Crete, 66*f*
  objectives, 65
  planning and preparation for, 65–66
Crimea Campaign, Soviet, **67**
  background to, 67
  casualties, 67
  siege of Sevastopol, 67
Crimean Campaign, **67–68**
  number of Soviet prisoners taken, 68
CROSSBOW, Anglo-American air operation, **68–69**
  casualties, 69
  German long-range weapons, 68–69
  prioritized over Operation OVERLORD, 69
CRUSADER, British operation. *See* North Africa Campaign
Declaration of the Government of the German Reich and the Government of the U.S.S.R. (Doc. 3), 313
  request to end war with England and France, 313
  on responsibility of the war's continuation being on England and France, 313
  on signing of treaty between Germany and Soviet Union, 313
Denmark Campaign, **70–71**
  and Allied occupation of Denmark, 71
  casualties, 70
  code-named Operation WESSERÜBUNG SUD (WESER EXERCISE SOUTH), 70
  German troops march into the city of Aalborg, 71*f*
Dieppe, British raid on, **71–72**
  and Atlantic Wall, 71
  casualties, 71
  lessons from, 71
  strategic significance of Dieppe, 71
Dietl, Eduard, **72**
Dietrich, Josef "Sepp," **72**
  commander of German U-boat fleet, 73
  interwar commander of torpedo-boat flotilla, 73
  World War I service, 72–73
Dönitz, Karl, **72–74**
  and Battle of the Atlantic, 20–21
  conviction Laconia Order at International Military Tribunal, 73, 142
  and Kriegsmarine, 136–137
  and Operation DRUMBEAT, 75
  rank of grand admiral, 73, 338
  and submarines, 261–262
  and surface warships, 288–289
  unconditional surrender of, 96
  and Wolf Pack tactics (*Rudeltaktik*), 20, 73, 295–296
Dönitz, Karl, broadcast informing German people of surrender (Doc. 13), 323–324

on duty to remain in his post, 323
on Germans in captivity, 323
on need for dignity, courage, and discipline, 324
on need to help the German people, 323
on order to sign unconditional surrender, 323
Dornberger, Walter, **74**
charged as a war criminal for launching the V-2s against London, 74
emigration to U.S., 74
interwar Reichswehr officer, 74
at U.S. Air Force Air Material Command, 74
World War I service, 74
Dresden, Allied air attack on, **74–75**
background to, 62, 74
casualties, 75
controversy regarding, 74–75
events of, 74
and suspension of the Allied Strategic Bombing Campaign, 74
DRUMBEAT, U-Boat Operation, **75**, 136, 169
Dunkirk, evacuation of. *See* France, Battle of

Eben Emael, Battle of. *See* Belgium and Flanders Campaign
Einsatzgruppen, **76**
and Babi Yar Massacre, 24
and German military complicity in the Holocaust, 111–112
and Heydrich, Reinhard, 76
leadership tried for crimes against humanity, 76
and Operation BARBAROSSA, 76
and Reichssicherheitshauptamt (Reich Main Security Office), 210
El Alamein, Battle of. *See* North Africa Campaign
Enigma machine, **76–77**
and Bletchley Park group, 77
and Germany's defeat, 77, 305, 307
and Polish cryptography group, 76–77
invention of, 76

Falaise-Argentan Pocket, **78–79**
background to, 78
casualties and losses, 78
impact on Operation MARKET-GARDEN, 78–79
Fall GELB (Case YELLOW), German attack against France and neutral Low Countries, 85, 155, 168
Führer Directive 10, "Concentration of Forces for Case YELLOW," 89*t*
Fall WEISS (Case WHITE), plan for the invasion of Poland, 198. *See also* Hitler, Adolf, directive for Fall Weiss, attack on Poland (Doc. 2)
Fallschirmjäger (Airborne troops), **79**
Field marshals and grand admirals, 337–338
and direct access to the Führer, 337
Generalfeldmarschall (general field marshal) in the Wehrmacht, 338
Grossadmiral (grand admiral) in the Wehrmacht, 338
history of, 337–338
Hitler's reestablishment of rank of field marshal in the Wehrmacht, 337
and refusal to surrender or be captured alive, 337
Reich marshal, 338
Flak 18 88 mm gun. *See* Artillery
FORTITUDE, Allied deception operation, **79–80**
FORTITUDE North, 80
FORTITUDE South, 80
support for Operation OVERLORD, 80–81
France, Allied liberation of, **80–83**
landing at Normandy, 81
liberation of Avranches, 82
liberation of Caen and Saint-Lô, 81
liberation of Montelimar, 83
Operation COBRA, 81

France (*Cont.*)
Operation DRAGOON, 82
Operation GOODWOOD, 81
See also Normandy invasion and campaign
France, Battle of, **83–87**
British Expeditionary Force's withdrawal to Dunkirk, 85–86
casualties and equipment losses, 86
cease-fire signed, 86
comparisons of forces and technology, 83, 85
escape of de Gaulle to Britain, 86
Fall GELB (Case YELLOW) plan, 85
German capture of Verdun, 87
map of German conquest of France, 84*f*
and SICHELSCHNITT (SICKEL CUT) plan, 85
Freikorps (Free Corps), **87**
background to and creation of, 87
and Kapp-Lüttwitz Putsch, 87
surrender to SA, 87
Friedeburg, Hans Georg von, **87–88**
commander of German naval forces, 87
commander of German submarine forces, 87
World War I service, 87
Fritsch, Werner von, **88**
and Blomberg-Fritsch crisis, 44
commander in chief of the army, 88
suicide of, 87
World War I service, 88
Fromm, Friedrich, **88**
commander of the Replacement Army and chief of army equipment, 88
and conspiracy to assassinate Hitler, 88
execution of, 88
World War I service, 88
Führer Directives, **88–90**
definition of, 89
list of Führer Directives (1939–1943), 89–91*t*
Galland, Adolf, **91**
and Battle of Britain, 91
and "Fighter Pilots Revolt," 91
Spanish Civil War service, 91
wounding of, 91
Gazala, Battle of. *See* North Africa Campaign
German aces, 327–331
definition of ace, 327
Experte (expert), 327
Hartmann, Erich (highest-scoring World War II German pilot), 103, 327, 331*t*
highest scoring German fighter pilots of Spanish Civil War, 328*t*
Kanone (cannon; World War I), 327
leading *Experten* of World War II, 328–330*t*
Orden Pour le Mérite (World War I), 327
Richtoffen, Manfred von (highest-scoring World War I German pilot), 327
Scheel, Günther (highest kill-to-mission ratio), 328
Schmidt, Heinz (single-day record), 328, 329*t*
Schnaufer, Heinz-Wolfgang (world's leading night-fighting ace), 328, 330*t*
Welter, Kurt (world's leading jet ace), 328
German General Staff of World War II, **91–93**
history and evolution of, 91–92
and Hitler's "Leader Principle," 92
and Hitler's occupation of three highest positions in army chain of command, 92
and Treaty of Versailles, 92
See also Chiefs of General and Admiralty Staffs
German Junkers Ju 88 bombers attacking port of Vallette, 154*f*
German military medals and decorations, 345–348

Close Combat Bar, 347–348
General Assault Badge, 347
German Cross, 346
Infantry Assault Badge, 347
Iron Cross, 345–346
Knight's Cross of the War Merit Cross, 347
Knight's Cross with Golden Oak Leaves, Swords and Diamonds, 346
Knight's Cross with Oak Leaves, 346
Orden Pour le Merite, 345
Tank Combat Badge, 347
War Merit Cross, 346–347
War Order of the German Cross, 346
Wound Badge, 348
German military ranks, 339–343
admirals, 343
American and German military ranks in World War II: enlisted, 341*t*
American and German military ranks in World War II: officers, 340–341*t*
army and air force noncommissioned officers (NCOs) and navy petty officers, 339
army and air force senior NCO ranks, 339, 342
basic enlisted Luftwaffe rank, 339
basic naval rank, 339
boatswain's mates, 339
brigadier generals, 343
colonels, 342
corvette captains, 342
generals, 342
historical rank for common soldier, 339
initials following rank title, 342
lieutenants and naval lieutenants, 342
marshal and field marshal, 342–343
navy senior NCO ranks, 342
older soldiers who exempted from guard duty, 339
staff officers, 342
training ranks prior to officer's commissioning, 342
Waffen-SS ranks, 343
See also Field marshals and grand admirals
German-Soviet Nonaggression Pact, **93–94**, 199, 302
division of Baltic States and Poland between Soviet Union and Germany, 93
origins of, 93
Soviet Union's agreement to provide Germany with resources, 93
German surrender at Berlin (Doc. 15), 325–326
agreement on punitive actions if act of surrender is not followed, 325
on carrying out further orders by Allies, 325
order to cease active operations, 325
unconditional surrender, 325
German surrender at Reims, France (Doc. 14), 324–325
agreement on punitive actions if act of surrender is not followed, 325–326
on carrying out further orders by Allies, 325
order to cease active operations, 325
unconditional surrender, 325
Germany, collapse and surrender of, **94–97**
casualties and displaced persons, 96
Dönitz's unconditional surrender, 96
drive to the Rhine River, 94
fall of Berlin, 96
and German V weapons, 94
map, 95*f*
Operation PLUNDER, 94
scorched earth policy of Hitler, 96
See also German surrender at Berlin (Doc. 15), 325–326; German surrender at Reims, France (Doc. 14), 324–325
Germany, reasons for defeat in World War II, 301–307
campaign to seize Caucasus oil fields (1942), 305–306

Germany, reasons (*Cont.*)
declaration of war on United States, 301–302
economic factors, 302–303
failure of Operation BARBAROSSA, 305
failure to deny Atlantic to the Allies, 307
failure to develop effective alliance grand strategy, 302
failure to organize conquered territories, 304
German command structure, 302
German counterintelligence failures, 305
Hitler's decisions and leadership, 301–302, 306
inability to mount mobile defense at war's end, 306
intelligence failures, 304
July 1941 frontier battles, 305
land area and population, 302
loss of air superiority, 306
military personnel, 303
myth of "peacetime economy," 303–304
strategic bombing, 306–307
underestimating size of Red Army, 304
GOODWOOD, British operation, **97**
casualties and equipment losses, 97
previous operations, 97
Göring, Hermann, **98–99**
advocacy of heavily armed, twin-engine, general purpose fighters, 5
and Allied invasion of Sicily, 237
and Allied Salerno landings, 231
and Battle of France, 86
commander in chief of the Luftwaffe, 98, 149, 150
conviction at International Military Tribunal, 98, 120, 121
"Fighter Pilots' Revolt" against, 253
and Galland, Adolf, 91
Grand Cross awarded to, 346
and Milch, Erhard, 162
and Netherlands Campaign, 168
and *Oberkommando der Luftwaffe* (OKL), 183
Orden Pour le Merite awarded to, 343
president of Reichstag, 98
promotion to rank of field marshal in the Wehrmacht, 98, 337, 338
promotion to rank of Reich marshal, 98, 338, 343
suicide of, 98
in uniform and wearing Grand Cross of the Iron Cross, 98*f*
World War I service, 98
Greece Campaign, **99–100**
casualties and impact of, 100
code-named Operation MARITA, 99
German infantry during Operation MARITA, 99*f*
objective, 99
Greim, Robert Ritter von, **100**
number of victories, 100
Pour le Mérite awarded to, 100
promotion to rank of field marshal in the Wehrmacht, 100, 338
suicide of, 100
World War I service, 100
Guderian, Heinz, **100–101**
chief of the General Staff, 101
XIX Panzer Corps commander in invasion of France, 100–101
Second Panzer Group in Army Group Center in invasion of Soviet Union, 101
World War I service, 100
Guernica air raid. *See* Spanish Civil War

Halder, Franz, **102**
chief of the army General Staff, 102
imprisoned in Flossenbürg concentration camp, 102
at U.S. Army Historical Division, 102
World War I service, 102
Hamburg, Allied air raids (Operation GOMORRAH), **102–103**
casualties and destruction, 102–103

events of, 102
strategic significance of Hamburg, 102
Hartmann, Erich Alfred, **103**
highest-scoring aerial ace of all time, 104, 327–328, 328*t*
imprisonment, 104
Knight's Cross of the Iron Cross with Oak Leaves, Swords and Diamonds awarded to, 103
postwar career, 104
Wehrmacht officer rank, 350*t*
Hausser, Paul, **103**
Army Group G commander, 189, 215
author of claim of Waffen-SS troops as "soldiers as any others," 103
and Battle for Saint-Lô, 59, 81, 230
I SS Panzer Corps commander, 103
Heinrici, Gotthard, **104**
Army Group Vistula commander, 104
defense of Seelow Heights, 104
and invasions of Poland and France, 104
and invasion of Soviet Union, 104
surrender to British forces, 104
World War I service, 104
Heisenberg, Werner, **104**
Knight's Cross of the Iron Cross with Oak Leaves and Swords awarded to, 105
postwar career, 105
Soviet prisoner, 105
Spanish Civil War service, 104
and *Wilde Sau* (Wild Boar) single-engine fighter unit, 105
Hermann, Hans-Joachim "Hajo," **104–105**
Heusinger, Adolf, **105**
chief of operations Staff of OKH, 105
Nuremberg Trials testimony, 105
postwar career, 105
prisoner of war, 105
Himmler, Heinrich, **105–107**
Army Group Upper Rhine commander, 107
Army Group Vistula commander, 107
and Beer Hall Putsch, 106
captured by British troops, 107
head of the Gestapo, 106
inspects a prisoner-of-war camp, 106*f*
member of National Socialist German Worker's Party, 106
and Night of the Long Knives, 103, 106, 169, 279
proponent of Nazi racial theories, 107
Reichsführer of the Schutzstaffel (SS), 106
suicide of, 107
Waffen-SS commander, 105–107, 279, 280, 290
and World War I, 105–106
Himmler, Heinrich, message to officers of Army Group Vistula for defense of Berlin (Doc. 11), 320–322
on hatred for Bolsheviks, 322
on need for harsh crackdowns in military courts, 321
on Stalin's use of prisoners, deserters, and defectors, 321
on "traitor" Seydlitz-Kurzbach, 321
Hindenburg, Paul von, **107–108**
appointment of Hitler as chancellor, 107
Austro-Prussian War service, 107
Franco-Prussian War service, 107
World War I service, 107
Hitler, Adolf, **108–110**
Anschluss (annexation) of Austria, 109
appointed chancellor, 108
and Battle of Britain, 109
and Beer Hall Putsch, 108
declaration of war on U.S., 109
invasion of Poland, 109
invasion of Soviet Union, 109
member of *Deutsche Arbeiterpartei* (German Worker's Party), 109
Nazi Germany as totalitarian state under, 108
and Nuremberg Laws, 108
occupation of Czechoslovakia, 109
requirement of loyalty oath, 109

Hitler, Adolf (*Cont.*)
responsibility for German defeat, 301, 305
restructuring of Nazi Party, 108
suicide of, 109
wounding of, 108
World War I service, 108
Hitler, Adolf, directive for Fall Weiss, attack on Poland (Doc. 2), 311–313
aims, 312
attitude of Baltic States, 312
destruction of Polish Armed Forces as task of Wehrmacht, 312–313
military considerations, 312
political considerations, 312
Hitler, Adolf, final coordinating order for Ardennes Offensive (Doc. 10), 320
call to carry out orders and enforce obedience, 320
forbiddance of redirection of Panzer units, 320
on presence of preconditions, 320
on using Maas Canal as natural cover of eastern flank, 320
Hitler, Adolf, secret "Night-and-Fog Decree" on punishment of offenders in occupied territory (Doc. 7), 316–317
on areas of responsibility and authority, 317
on death penalty within occupied territories, 317
on increase in communistic elements and hostile circles, 317
on location of trial and execution, 317
on prisoners taken to Germany, 317
Hitler Youth, **110**
ages of, 111
history of, 110
roles of, 110
Hoepner, Erich, **110–111**
conviction by People's Court and execution, 111
court-martialed and cashiered, 111
and invasion of Soviet Union, 111
support for abortive plot to remove Hitler from power, 110
World War I service, 110
Holocaust, German military complicity in, **111–112**
American Military Tribunal trial and convictions, 111
and "Guidelines for the Behavior of Troops in Russia" (OKW document), 112
and invasion of Poland, 111
and invasion of Soviet Union, 112
myth of "clean Wehrmacht," 111, 112
and treatment of prisoners, 112
Hossbach, Friedrich, **112–113**
adjutant to Adolf Hitler, 112
and "Hossbach Memorandum," 112–113
World War I service, 112
Hoth, Hermann, **113**
Battle of Kursk commander, 113
conviction by U.S. military court for crimes against humanity committed by subordinates, 113
World War I service, 113
Hürtgen Forest Campaign, Allied, **113–115**
and Ardennes Offensive, 115
casualties, 113
events of, 113–114
significance of, 113

Infantry weapons, **116–119**
hand grenades, 118
infantry fighting vehicles, 119
infantry mortars, 118
machine guns, 118
pistols, 117–118
semi-automatic and automatic weapons, 116–117
International Military Tribunal: The Nuremberg Trials, **119–121**
controversy and debate regarding, 120, 121
individuals indicted, 120

organizations indicted, 120
verdicts, 121
Italy Campaign, Allied, **121–124**
advance to Rome, 123
Allied liberation of Rome, 124
casualties, 124
closing of Brenner Pass, 124
invasion of Sicily, 123
map, 122*f*

Jeschonnek, Hans, **125**
role in secret building of Luftwaffe, 125
suicide of, 125
World War I service, 125
Jewish Fighting Organization (Żobydska Organizacja Bojowa—ŻOB), 282. *See also* Warsaw Ghetto Uprising
Jodl, Alfred, **125–126**
chief of OKW, 125
convicted for war crimes at International Military Tribunal, 125
World War I service, 125
July 1944 Bomb Plot against Hitler. *See* Opposition to Hitler, German military

Kammhuber, Josef, **127**
inspector of new *Bundesluftwaffe*, 127
and Kammhuber Line, 127
World War I service, 127
Kammhuber Line, **127**
creation of, 127
rendered ineffective by antiradar chaff countermeasures, 127
Kasserine Pass, Battle of. *See* North Africa Campaign
Keitel, Wilhelm, **128–129**
chief of OKW, 128
conviction and execution at International Military Tribunal for role in Commisar Order, 128
promotion to rank of field marshal in the Wehrmacht, 338
World War I service, 128
Kesselring, Albert, **129**
commander in chief, west, 129
conviction for role in Ardeatine Caves Massacre, 129
Luftflotte 1 and Luftflotte 2 commander, 129
promotion to rank of field marshal in the Wehrmacht, 338
World War I service, 129
Kharkov, Battles of, **129–130**
and Operation BARBAROSSA (First Battle of Kharkov), 130
and Red Army's Winter Offensive (Second Battle of Kharkov), 130
Third Battle of Kharkov), 130
Kiev Pocket, Battle of. *See* Soviet Union, invasion of (Operation BARBAROSSA)
Kleist, Paul Ewald von, **131**
First Panzer Group commander in invasion of Soviet Union, 131
promotion to rank of field marshal in the Wehrmacht, 338
World War I service, 131
Kluge, Günther von, **131**
Army Group Center commander in Soviet Union, 131
Avranches German counterattack commander, 131
promotion to rank of field marshal in the Wehrmacht, 338
suicide of, 131
World War I service, 131
Kondor Legion, **132**
bombing of Guernica, 132
creation of, 132
and Spanish Civil War, 132
Krebs, Hans, **132**
assumed suicide of, 132
German army chief of staff, 132
liaison with the Soviets after Hitler's suicide, 132
World War I service, 131

Kretschmer, Otto, **132–133**
Knight's Cross of the Iron Cross with Oak Leaves and Swords awarded to, 133
most successful German World War II U-boat commander, 132
prisoner of war, 133
wartime statistics, 133
Kriegsakademie (War Academy), **133–134**
creation of, 133
reopening after Hitler's repudiation of Treaty of Versailles, 133
replaced by Führungsakademie (Leadership Academy), 133
Kriegsmarine (German Navy), **134–137**
controversial wartime record of, 137
and Dönitz, Karl, 136–137
naval order of battles (1932, 1935, 1938, and 1939), 134*t*
and Raeder, Erich, 134
renamed from Reichsmarine when Hitler abrogated Treaty of Versailles, 134
Kristallnacht (the Night of Broken Glass), 252, 271
Krupp, Alfried Felix, **137–138**
Admiral Raeder's Z-Plan of January 1939, 135*t*
conviction at Krupp Trial of American Military Tribunal, 137
member of supporting branch of Schutzstaffel (SS), 137
minister of the war economy, 137
use of slave labor, 137
Krupp, Gustav, **138**
chairman of the board of Friedrich Krupp AG, 138
Economics Ministry's chief administrator of mines, 138
indicted by International Military Tribunal, 138
use of concentration camp labor, 138
Küchler, Georg von, **138–139**
Army North Group commander, 139
conviction for war crimes at American Military Tribunals, 139
Eighteenth Army commander, 138–139
promotion to rank of field marshal in the Wehrmacht, 338
World War I service, 138
Kursk, Battle of, **139–141**
casualties, 141
map, 140*f*
significance of, 139

Laconia Order, **142**
text of, 142
and war crimes conviction of Karl Dönitz, 73, 142
Landwehr, **142–143**
disbanded after Treaty of Versailles, 142
history and purpose of, 142
incorporation into regular army, 142
permanent disbandment after World War II, 142
revival by Hitler, 142
Langsdorff, Hans Wilhelm, **143**
Admiral Graf Spee commander, 143
and Battle of River Plate, 143
suicide of, 143
World War I service, 143
Leeb, Wilhelm Ritter von, **143–144**
Army Group C commander, 143
Army Group North commander in invasion of Soviet Union, 143–144
conviction for minor war crimes, 144
Die Abwehr (The Defense), 143
promotion to rank of field marshal in the Wehrmacht, 338
retirement after Blomberg-Fritsch Crisis, 143
World War I service, 143
Leningrad, Siege of, **144–145**
events of, 145
objectives, 144
and Operation BARBAROSSA, 144
significance and impact of, 144

Lidice Massacre, **145**
casualties and aftermath, 145
and death of Reinhard Heydrich, 145
List, Siegmund Wilhelm Walter, **145–146**
Army Group A commander in Soviet Union, 145–146
avoidance of generals' purge, 145
conviction at Nuremberg, 146
and invasions of Poland and France, 145
promotion to rank of field marshal in the Wehrmacht, 338
removal from command, 146
Löhr, Alexander, **146**
Army Group E commander, 146
conviction for war crimes in Yugoslav military court and execution, 146
and invasion of Poland, 146
prisoner of war, 146
World War I service, 146
and Yugoslavia Campaign, 146, 299
Lorraine Campaign, Allied, **146–148**
background to, 146
battle of Arracourt, 147
casualties, 148
events of, 147–148
fall of Metz, 147–148
fall of Nancy, 148
German Ardennes counteroffensive, 148
limitations of Allied and German combat power, 147
objectives, 148
Loyalty Oath to Hitler, **148**
"Herr Hitler" address replaced with "Mein Führer," 148
made into law, 148
rewriting of, 148
Ludendorff, Erich, **149**
and Beer Hall Putsch, 149
and Hindenburg, Paul von, 107, 149
and Stab-in-the-Back Legend, 249
The Total War, 149
Luftwaffe (German Air Force), **149–151**
impact of Treaty of Versailles on, 149
organization of, 150–151
organizational weaknesses, 149–150
pilot losses during Operation POINTBLANK, 151
Luftwaffe report of effects of Operation GOMORRAH, Allied fire-bombing of Hamburg (Doc. 8), 317–318
Lütjens, Günther, **151**
military weaknesses of, 151
and sinking of the *Bismarck,* 37, 151

Mackensen, Eberhard von, **152**
and Battle of Anzio, 12, 123
and Battle of Rostov, 224
conviction for role in Ardeatine Caves Massacre, 152
family of, 152
Malmédy Massacre, **152–153**
events of, 152
and U.S. military court trial and convictions, 153
Malta air and naval campaign, **153–155**
arrival of Keith Park in Malta, 155
attack on Allied convoy PEDESTAL, 155
German Junkers Ju 88 bombers attacking port of Vallette, 154*f*
Luftwaffe raids, 154–155
map of Mediterranean maritime battles, 1940–1943, 153*f*
strategic importance of Malta, 154
Manstein, Erich von, **155–156**
controversy of, 155–156
conviction for war crimes, 155
defense witness at International Military Tribunal, 155–156
promotion to rank of field marshal in the Wehrmacht, 155, 338
and SICHELSCHNITT (SICKEL CUT) plan, 155
Manteuffel, Hasso Eccard von, **156–157**
and Ardennes Offensive, 12
and Battle for Bastogne, 28, 156
and Operation BARBAROSSA, 156
prisoner of war, 156
World War I service, 156

Mareth Line, Battle of. *See* North Africa Campaign
MARKET-GARDEN, Allied operation, **157–159**
 and Allied liberation of France, 83
 and Battle of Metz, 161–162
 and Bittrich, Willi, 38
 casualties, 159
 and Falaise-Argentan Pocket, 78
 impact of, 159
 and Model, Walther, 157, 159, 163
 and Montgomery, Bernard, 238
 objectives, 157
 planning and preparation for, 157
 Polish Parachute Brigade landings at Driel, 158–159
Marschall, Wilhelm, **159–160**
 Navy Group West commander, 159
 World War I service, 159
Marseille, Hans-Joachim, **160**
 number of victories, 160
 "Star of North Africa," 160
Mellenthin, Friedrich-Wilhelm von, **160**
Mersa Matrûh, Battle of. *See* North Africa Campaign
Messerschmidt Bf 109 fighter. *See* Aircraft, military
Messerschmidt Me 262 jet fighter. *See* Aircraft, military
Messerschmitt, Wilhelm, **161**
 aircraft company of, 161
 arrest and imprisonment for employing slave labor, 161
 low-wing monoplane design, 161
 World War I service, 161
Metz, Battle of, **161–162**
 events of, 161–162
 impact of, 162
 strategic importance of Metz, 161, **161–162**
 surrender of Metz, 162
Milch, Erhard, **162**
 conviction for war crimes, 162
 prison of war, 162
 promotion to rank of field marshal in the Wehrmacht, 338
 role in development of Luftwaffe, 162
 World War I service, 162
Minsk-Bialystok, Battle of. *See* Soviet Union, invasion of (Operation BARBAROSSA)
Model, Walther, **163**
 and Ardennes Offensive, 13, 163, 320 (Doc. 10)
 nickname of "Hitler's Fireman," 163
 and Operation MARKET-GARDEN, 157, 159, 163
 promotion to rank of field marshal in the Wehrmacht, 338
 World War I service, 163
Mölders, Werner, **163–164**
 and "Finger Four" formation, 163–164
 Luftwaffe general of fighters, 164
 and Spanish Civil War, 164
Moscow, Battle of, **164–165**
 background and objective, 164
 Battle of Vyazma-Bryansk, 164–165
 centerpiece of Operation TAIFUN (TYPHOON), 164
 events of, 164–165
 German offensives, 164
 Soviet winter counteroffensive, 164–165
Munich Conference and Agreement, **165–167**
 background to, 165–166
 influence and significance of, 166–167
 provisions of, 166

Netherlands Campaign, **168**
 casualties and destruction of, 168
 and Dutch government-in-exile, 168
 German aircraft losses, 168
 and German Case YELLOW (Fall GELB), attack against France and neutral Low Countries, 85, 168
NEULAND, U-boat operation, **168–169**
 impact of, 169

number of Allied tankers and merchant ships sunk, 169
objective of Allied oil and gasoline shipments, 169
Night of the Long Knives, **169–170**
arrest and murder of Ernst Röhm, 170, 222, 258
and Bach-Zelewski, Erich von dem, 25
background to, 169–170
and Blomberg, Werner von, 43
and Dietl, Eduard, 72
and Himmler, Heinrich, 106, 169, 279
impact of, 170, 258
purge of Sturmabteilung and other opponents, 108, 170
and Reichenau, Walther von, 206
and Schutzstaffel (SS), 170
and Sturmabteilung (SA), 169–170
"Night-and-Fog Decree." *See* Hitler, Adolf, secret "Night-and-Fog Decree" on punishment of offenders in occupied territory (Doc. 7)
NORDWIND, Operation, **170–171**
and Battle for the Colmar Pocket, 60
casualties, 171
last major Germany Army offensive in the west, 170
objective, 170
Normandy invasion and campaign, **171–175**
and Atlantic Wall, 171, 173
casualties, 174
events of, 173–174
impact of, 174–175
map, 172*f*
objective, 173
Omaha beach landing, 174
Operation FORTITUDE, deception support operation, 79–80
Operation NEPTUNE, naval operation, 173
Operation OVERLORD, cross-Channel invasion, 61, 69, 173–174, 240
personnel and munitions, 174
North Africa Campaign, **175–180**
Allied Northwest Africa Landings (Operation TORCH), 178–179
Battle of Alam Halfa, 29, 178
Battle of Battleaxe, 177, 224
Battle of El Alamein, 2, 29, 178, 194, 224, 269
Battle of Gazala, 177–178, 224, 337
Battle of Kasserine Pass, 179
Battle of Mersa Matrûh, 175, 178
Battle of Ruweisat Ridge, 178
Battle of Tunis-Bizerte, 180
casualties, 180
map, 176*f*
objectives, 175
Operation CRUSADER, 177
Second Battle of Tobruk, 177
Third Battle of Tobruk, 178
North Cape, Battle of, **180–181**
background to, 180
casualties, 181
objectives, 180
Northwest Africa Landings, Allied (Operation TORCH). *See* North Africa Campaign
Norway Campaign, **181–182**
casualties and aircraft losses, 182
objectives, 182
planning and preparation for, 181–182

Oberkommando der Luftwaffe (OKL), **183**
and the Blitz, 39–40
creation of, 150
relative lack of functionality of, 183
Wever, Walther, first chief of General Staff, 335
Oberkommando der Marine (OKM), **183**
creation of, 183, 335
Naval Warfare Command, 335
Oberkommando der Wehrmacht (OKW), **184**
and Abwehr, 1
and American Military Tribunal, 111
creation of, 184, 335

Oberkommando der Wehrmacht (OKW) (*Cont.*)
"Guidelines for the Behavior of Troops in Russia," 112
and International Military Tribunal, 93
and Jodl, Alfred, chief of the Military Operations Office, 92, 120, 125, 184, 289
Keitel, Wilhelm, chief of, 92, 120, 128, 184, 334*t*
organizational weaknesses of, 184, 185, 302
Oberkommando des Heeres (OKH), **184–185**
chiefs of the General Staff, 92–93, 299
creation of, 92, 184
and invasion of Soviet Union, 185
transfer of activities to OKW command, 185
Operation GOMORRAH, Luftwaffe report on effects of (Doc. 8), 317–318
call for evacuation of air raid shelters, 318
on effects of firestorm, 318
on forced flight of population, 318
on water and protection from heat and smoke, 318
Operation SHINGLE, Operation (Allied amphibious landing of Anzio), 11–12, 53–54, 123, 152, 254. *See also* Anzio, Battle of
Opposition to Hitler, German military, **185–186**
and Beck, Ludwig, 29, 30, 185–186, 256
and Canaris, Wilhelm, 1, 53, 186, 305
and Fromm, Friedrich, 88, 289
and Halder, Franz, 102, 186, 256, 289
history of, 185–186
July 1944 Bomb Plot against Hitler (Operation VALKYRIE), 53, 105, 107, 185, 186, 252–253, 281
and Stauffenberg, Claus Schenk von, 88, 105, 186, 252–253, 253*f*, 271
and Treskow, Henning von, 186
Oradour-sur-Glane Massacre, **187**
atrocities against civilians, 187
convictions in French military court, 187
Organization Todt (OT), **187–188**
construction of Atlantic Wall, 171, 187–188
named for Fritz Todt, 187
Speer, Albert, head of, 247
Todt, Fritz, head of, 271

Palatinate Campaign, Allied, **189–190**
casualties, 190
damage to cities, 190
German insistence on principle of no retreat, 189
German surrender, 190
planning and preparation for, 189
Panther Pz.Kpfw.V tank. *See* Tanks and self-propelled guns
Panzer Division, **190**
and "Blitzkrieg" style of warfare, 190
definition of and use of the term, 190
and Operation BARBAROSSA, 190
statistics, 190
typical Panzer Division, 191–192
Panzergrenadier, **191–192**
definition of, 191
Grossdeutschland Panzergrenadier Division, 191
Sd.Kfz. (*Sonderkraftfahrzeug*) 251 half-track armored fighting vehicle, 191*f*, 191–192
typical panzergrenadier division, 191–192
and Waffen-SS, 191
Paris, Allied liberation of, **192–193**
arrival of de Gaulle, 193
German General Choltitz's refusal to destroy Paris, 192
German surrender, 193
Resistance uprising and German response, 192
Paulus, Friedrich, **193**
and Battle of Stalingrad, 193, 251, 252, 316, 337

and battles of Kharkov, 130
first German field marshal to be captured in battle, 193, 252, 337
promotion to rank of field marshal in the Wehrmacht, 338
World War I service, 193
Paulus, Friedrich, radio message to Hitler requesting permission to break out from Stalingrad (Doc. 6), 316
and capture of Paulus, 193, 252, 337
Hitler's refusal to give permission to break out, 193, 316
on need for reinforcement and to withdraw divisions, 316
PEDESTAL, convoy battle, **193–194**
Axis tactical victory and strategic Allied victory, 194
background to, 193–194
impact of, 194
Peiper, Joachim, **194–195**
and Ardennes Offensive, 14
conviction in Dachau court, 195
and *Kampfgruppe* (battle group) Peiper, 14, 194–195
and Malmédy Massacre, 152–153, 195
SS Liebestandarte Adolf Hitler (LAH) company commander, 194
Plan Z, 10, 135*t*, 136, **195**, 205
Plate River, Battle of, **195–197**
Admiral Graf Spee scuttled to Montevideo, 196*f*, 196–197
casualties, 197
first major naval surface engagement of World War II, 195
significance of, 197
and suicide of Captain Langsdorff, 197
Ploesti Air Raids, Allied, **197**
background to, 197
casualties and impact of, 197
part of "Oil Plan" of Combined Bomber Offensive, 197
Poland Campaign, **197–202**
battle and siege of Warsaw, 201
casualties, 201–202
events of, 199, 201–202
map of Poland and Eastern Europe, 1939–1940, 200*f*
significance of, 197–198
surrender of Poland, 201
myths of, 198
Poland-East Prussia Campaign, Soviet, **202–203**
casualties in drive to Narew River and Warsaw, 202–203
liberation of Warsaw and entrance to German Pomerania, 203
Warsaw Rising, 203, 282–283
Prien, Günther, **203–204**
sinking of HMS *Royal Oak*, 204
Spanish Civil War service, 203

Raeder, Erich, **205–206**
and Battle of Plate River, 195–196
convictions at International Military Tribunal, 120, 121, 206
Kriegsmarine strategy of, 134–137
rank of grand admiral, 120, 338
resignation of, 206
and sinking of *Bismarck*, 37, 151
on submarine force, 258
visit to crew of the battle cruiser *Scharnhorst*, 205*f*
and surface warships, 73, 205, 283, 287, 288
World War I service, 205
Z-Plan, 135*t*, 195, 205
Rall, Günther, **206**
Knights Cross of the Iron Cross with Oak Leaves and Swords awarded to, 206
third-highest scoring ace of World War II, 206, 328*t*
Wehrmacht officer rank, 350*t*
Reichenau, Walther von, 224, **206–207**
and Night of the Long Knives, 206
promotion to rank of field marshal in the Wehrmacht, 338

Reichenau (*Cont.*)
Sixth Army commander in invasion of Soviet Union, 206
World War I service, 206
Reichsarbeitsdienst (Reich Labor Service), **207**
creation of, 207
goals of, 207
and Organization Todt, 207
role of, 207
significance for war effort, 207
Reichsheer (German Army), **207–209**
command and control, 209
Field Army, 207–208
history of, 207–208
infantry division, 208
myths and stereotypes of, 208–209
panzer division, 208, 290
parachute divisions, 208
Replacement Army, 208
success of, 207
Waffen-Schutzstaffel (Waffen-SS), 208, 279–281
Reichssicherheitshauptamt (Reich Main Security Office), **209–210**
creation of, 209
and Einsatzgruppen, 210
Gestapo, 209
organization of, 209
Reichswald, Battle of the, **210–211**
casualties and impact of, 210–211
objectives, 210
and Operation VERITABLE, 210
Reitsch, Hanna, 100, **211**
first woman to fly a helicopter, 211
Iron Cross First Class awarded to, 211
Remagen Bridge, U.S. capture of, **211–213**
casualties and impact of, 212–213
and collapse and surrender of Germany, 94
and German V-2 missiles, 221
Hitler's response to, 212
Rhine crossings, Allied, **213–214**
and Operation PLUNDER, 213–214
and Operation VARSITY, 214
significance of Rhine River, 213, 214
Rhineland, remilitarization of, **214–215**
Locarno Pacts, 214
Operation WINTER EXERCISE, 214–215
significance of, 214, 215
Rhineland Offensive, Allied, **215–216**
and Ardennes Offensive, 215
Operation GRENADE, 216
Operation LUMBERJACK, 216
Operation VERITABLE, 215–216
significance of, 216
Richthofen, Wolfram von, **216–217**
and Allied Salerno landings, 231
Kondor Legion commander, 216
Luftflotte 2 and Luftflotte 4 commander, 217
and Operation STRANGLE, 254
promotion to rank of field marshal in the Wehrmacht, 217, 338
VIII Air Corps commander, 216
World War I service, 216
Rockets, guided bombs, and guided missiles, **217–221**
aircraft-launched rockets, 218
Dornberger, Walter, head of rocket research, 217
early rockets, 217
first operational wire-guided missiles, 218
Fritz X guided bomb, 218
Rakete 4-Kilogramm Minenkopf (R4M) air-to-air rocket, 218
Raketen-Sprenggranate 4831 solid-fuel rocket, 218
scientists, 217
spin-stabilized rockets, 217–218
V-1 buzz bomb, 218–221
V-2 guided missile, 218–221
Rogge, Bernhard, **222**
Atlantis commander, 222
World War I service, 22

Röhm, Ernst, **222**
and Beer Hall Putsch, 222
and Night of the Long Knives, 169–170, 206, 222, 258
and Sturmabteilungen (SA), 169–170, 222, 257–258
World War I service, 222
Romania Campaign, Soviet, **222–223**
background to, 222–223
casualties, 223
significance of Romania, 222
Rome, Allied liberation of. *See* Italy Campaign, Allied
Rommel, Erwin, **223–224**
and Allied liberation of France, 81
and Battle of El Alamein, 224
difficult reputation of, 223
head of Afrika Korps, 1–2, 29, 223–224, 177–178, 269
implicated in attempted assassination of Hitler, 224
on Malta, 129
and Normandy campaign, 171, 173
and North Africa Campaign, 177–180
Orden Pour le Merite awarded to, 346
and PEDESTAL convoy battle, 193–194
promotion to rank of field marshal in the Wehrmacht, 337, 338*t*
suicide of, 224
World War I service, 223
Rommel, Erwin, Normandy situation report to Hitler (Doc. 9), 318–319
on decline of combat power and loss of men, 319
on expectations for defeat, 319
on uninterrupted enemy reinforcement, 319
Roslavl, Battle of. *See* Soviet Union, invasion of (Operation BARBAROSSA)
Rostov, Battle of, **224–225**
background to, 224
casualties, 224–225
impact of setback for Germans, 224–225
military significance of Rostov, 224
Rudel, Hans-Ulrich, **225**
dive-bomber pilot statistics, 225
extreme right-wing views of, 225
sole recipient of Gold Oak Leaves to the Knight's Cross of the Iron Cross, 225
surrender to and prisoner of U.S., 225
Ruge, Friedrich, **225**
post-war career, 225
senior German naval officer in Italy, 225
World War I service, 225
Ruhr Air Campaign, Allied, **226**
attacks on Krupp Works, 226
casualties, 226
firestorms and ground destruction, 226
objectives of urban centers, 226
Operation CHASTISE, 226
Ruhr Ground Campaign, Allied, **227–228**
background to, 227
captured Germany soldiers and officers, 227
liberation of prisoners of war, 227–228
Ruhr Pocket (*Ruhr Kessel*), 227
Rundstedt, Karl Rudolf Gerd von, **228**
Ardennes Offensive commander, 228
Army Group South commander in invasion of Soviet Union, 228
captured and released by Allies, 228
promotion to rank of field marshal in the Wehrmacht, 338
World War I service, 228
Ruweisat Ridge, Battle of. *See* North Africa Campaign

Saarland, French invasion of the, **229–230**
background to, 229
casualties, 230
significance of, 229
Saint-Lô, battle for, **230–231**
and "Battle of the Hedgerows," 230
strategic importance of Saint-Lô, 230
Salerno landings, Allied, **231**
background to, 232
impact of, 231

Salerno landings (*Cont.*)
main Allied invasion of the Italian mainland, 231
and Operation AVALANCHE, 231
Scharnhorst battle cruiser. *See* Warships, surface
Scheldt Estuary, battles for, **231–232**
casualties, 232
destruction of the dikes, 232
impact of delay of Allied control after Ardennes Offensive, 233
Schörner, Ferdinand, **232–233**
Army Group Center commander, 233
and invasions of France and Greece, 232–233
named in Hitler's testament to replace Himmler, 233
promotion to rank of field marshal in the Wehrmacht, 233, 338
World War I service, 232
Schweinfurt and Regensburg air raids, Allied, **233–234**
casualties and impact, 233
code-named Operation JUGGLER, 233
objective of destroying industrial targets, 233
Seeckt, Hans von, **234**
influence of, 234
and interwar rapid expansion of Wehrmacht, 234
military adviser to Chiang Kai-shek, 234
World War I service, 234
Seelow Heights, Battle of, **234–235**
and Busse, Theodor, 234–235
casualties and impact of, 235
challenge of spring thaw for armored vehicles, 235
and fall of Berlin, 235
Germany Army Group Vistula intelligence assessment of Soviet 1st Belorussian Front (Doc. 12), 322–323
and Zhukov, Georgy, 234–235
SEELÖWE (SEA LION), Operation, **235–236**
debate between army and navy leaders on, 235–236
deferral of and use as deception, 236
Führer Directive 16, "On Preparation for a Landing Operation against England," 235
Senger und Etterlin, Fridolin Rudolf von, **236**
coordinator of Axis strategy in Sicily, 236
interwar critic of "all-tank" strategy, 236
prisoner of war, 236
17th Panzer Division commander, 236
World War I service, 236
Sevastopol, Siege of. *See* Crimea Campaign, Soviet
SICHELSCHNITT (SICKLE CUT). *See* France, Battle of; Manstein, Erich von
Sicily, Allied invasion of, **236–237**
background to, 236–237
casualties and impact of, 237
fall of Messina, 237
German counterattack, 237
German evacuation of Sicily, 237
Siegfried Line Campaign, Allied, **237–240**
Battle of Aachen, 238
Battle of Metz, 238–239
casualties, 240
initial contact with Siegfried Line, 238
Lorraine Campaign, 238–239
Operation MARKET-GARDEN, 238
steel and concrete "Dragon's Teeth" obstacles, 239*f*
Skorzeny, Otto, **240**
acquittal of war crimes, 240
Ardennes Offensive 10th Panzer Brigade commander, 240
and Operation GRIEF, 240
rescue of Benito Mussolini, 240
Smolensk, Battle of. *See* Soviet Union, invasion of (Operation BARBAROSSA)
Southern France, Allied invasion and campaign (Operation DRAGOON), **240–242**

background to, 240–241
battle at Montélimar, 241
casualties, 241–242
delay due to limited available landing craft, 240
map of Eastern Front, 243*f*
impact of, 242
objective, 242
race for Belfort Gap, 241
Soviet Union, Invasion of (Operation BARBAROSSA), **242–246**
Army Group Center, 286
Battle of Kiev Pocket, 245
Battle of Minsk-Bialystok, 245
Battle of Roslavl, 245
Battle of Smolensk, 245
events of, 244–245
munitions, 244
objectives, 244
phase one, 244–245
phase three, 244
phase two, 244, 245–246
strategic axes of Soviet divisions, 242
Wehrmacht compliance with the Commissar order (Doc. 5), 314–316
Spanish Civil War, **246–247**
background to, 246
and development of the Wehrmacht, 247
events of, 246–247
Guernica air raid, 132, 247
inciting incident, 246
and Kondor Legion, 247
Speer, Albert, **247–248**
ammunition production under, 219, 226, 233, 247–248
anti-Nazi activities, 248
and "cathedral of light" concept, 247
chief of staff of Army Group B, 248
conviction at International Military Tribunal, 120, 121, 248
education and architecture career, 247
minister for armament and munitions, 120, 150, 247
Speidel, Hans, **248–249**
arrest of and escape from Gestapo, 248
capture by French troops, 248
postwar career, 248
Wehrmacht officer rank, 350*t*, 351
Sperrle, Hugo, **249**
acquitted of war crimes, 249
captured by British, 249
Kondor Legion organizer and commander, 249
promotion to rank of field marshal in the Wehrmacht, 338
Stab-in-the-Back Legend (Dolchstosslegende), **249**
influence of, 249
origins of, 249
Stalingrad, Battle of, **249–252**
casualties, 252
Hitler's refusal to allow Sixth Army to break out, 193, 252, 299, 316
map, 250*f*
Operation BLAU (BLUE), 251
Operation URANUS, 251–252
and Paulus, Friedrich, 193, 251, 252, 316, 337
significance of, 249, 251
See also Paulus, Friedrich, radio message to Hitler requesting permission to break out from Stalingrad (Doc. 6)
Stauffenberg, Claus Schenk von, **252–253**
arrest and execution of, 253
and July 1944 Bomb Plot against Hitler, 88, 105, 186, 252–253, 253*f*, 271
wounding of, 252
Steinhoff, Johannes, **253–254**
crash and wounding of, 253
history's twenty-third highest-scoring ace, 253, 254*f*, 329*t*
postwar career, 253
squadron commander, 253
Wehrmacht officer rank, 350*t*

STRANGLE, Allied air operation, **254–255**
events of, 254
objectives, 254
and Operation DIADEM, 254–255
Stroop, Jürgen, **255**
conviction and execution of, 255
deaths attributed to, 255
surrender of, 255
and Warsaw Ghetto Uprising, 255, 282
Student, Kurt, **255**
Army Group Vistula commander, 255
conviction for war crimes, 255
First Parachute Army commander in France, 157, 238, 255
and invasion of Crete, 66, 255
and invasion of France, 255
Stuka Ju 87 dive-bomber. *See* Aircraft, military
Stülpnagel, Joachim von, **256**
two-part strategy of attrition and annihilation, 256
World War I service, 256
Stülpnagel, Karl von, **256**
conviction by Nazi People's Court and execution, 256
head of Operations Section of the Army General Staff, 256
and invasion of Soviet Union, 256
World War I service, 256
Stülpnagel, Otto von, **256–257**
suicide of, 257
World War I service, 256
Sturmabteilungen (SA), **257–258**
Great Depression era, 257
history of, 257
membership, 257
and Munich Beer Hall Putsch, 257
and Night of the Long Knives, 169–170, 258
and Röhm, Ernst, 169–170, 222, 257–258
Submarines, **258–262**
and Anglo-German Naval Agreement, 259
diesel engine technology, 259
and Dönitz, Karl, 261–262
experimental three-hundred-ton boats, 262
interwar advancements, 258–259
known as *Unterseebooten* (U-boats), 258
and Raeder, Erich, 258–261
and restrictions of Treaty of Versailles, 258–259
sensor technology, 259
Type IA boats, 259
Type VII boats, 260–261
Type IX boats, 259–260
Type XXI "*Electrik* U-boat," 261
"Walter" propulsion boat, 262
wartime destruction of, 262

Tanks and self-propelled guns, **263–269**
Pz.Kpfw.35(t), 266
Pz.Kpfw.38(t), 266–267
Pz.Kpfw.I, 263
Pz.Kpfw.II, 263–264
Pz.Kpfw.III, 265
Pz.Kpfw.IV, 265–266
Pz.Kpfw.V Panther, 267–268
Pz.Kpfw.VI Tiger I, 267
Pz.Kpfw.VIB Tiger II, 268–269
tanks and self-propelled guns, 264*t*
Thoma, Wilhelm von, **269**
and Battle of El Alamein, 269
Spanish Civil War service, 269
World War I service, 269
Three-Power (Tripartite) Pact between Germany, Italy, and Japan (Doc. 4), 313–314
on agreed cooperation of Germany, Italy, and Japan, 314
on extension of cooperation to other nations, 313–314
on Germany's and Italy's recognition of Japan of new order in greater Asia, 314
on Japan's recognition of Germany and Italy in new order in Europe, 314

on joint technical commissions, 314
on prime purpose of a new order, 313
Tirpitz, Allied attacks on, **269–270**
casualties, 270
decision not to repair *Tirpitz*, 270
naming and building of, 269–270
Tobruk, Second Battle of. *See* North Africa Campaign
Tobruk, Third Battle of. *See* North Africa Campaign
Todt, Fritz, **270–271**
and Atlantic Wall construction, 271
and autobahn construction, 271
head of technology and roadway construction, 271
World War I service, 270
See also Organization Todt
Tresckow, Henning von, **271–272**
failed assassination attempt on Hitler (March 14, 1943), 271
and July 1944 Bomb Plot on Hitler, 271
suicide of, 272
World War I service, 271
Tunis-Bizerte, Battle of. *See* North Africa Campaign

Udet, Ernst, **273**
director of armaments, 41, 149–150, 273
number of victories, 273
suicide of, 150, 162, 273
World War I service, 273
Ukraine Campaign, Soviet, **273–274**
and Battle of Brody-Lwów, 274
German counterattack, 273
objective, 273
Undeclared naval war with United States, **274–276**
sinking of *Athenia*, 274
sinking of *Robin Moor*, 275
sinking of USS *Reuben James*, 275
torpedoes fired at USS *Greer*, 275
torpedoes fired at USS *Kearny*, 275
U.S. forces in Dutch Guiana labeled as aggression by Germany, 275
U.S. occupation of Iceland, 275

V-1 buzz bomb. *See* Rockets, guided bombs, and guided missiles
V-2 guided missile. *See* Rockets, guided bombs, and guided missiles
Vietinghoff genannt Scheel, Heinrich von, **277**
and invasion of Soviet Union, 277
postwar career, 277
secret talks with Allies regarding surrender, 277
supreme commander west, 277
World War I service, 277
Volksgrenadier, **277–278**
defensive role, 277
manpower, 277–278
weapons of, 278
Volkssturm, **278**
differences on western and eastern fronts, 278
and surrender to U.S., 278
untrained labor force in forties, 278
Vyazma-Bryansk, Battle of. *See* Moscow, Battle of

Waffen-SS, **279–281**
Bittrich, Willi, lieutenant general, 37–38
conviction as criminal organization at International Military Tribunal, 281
creation of, 279–280
Dietrich, Josef "Sepp," colonel general, 72
and Einsatzgruppen, 76
expansion of role after German invasion of Soviet Union, 280
foreign volunteers, 279–280, 279*f*
formation of 12th SS-Panzer-Division (Hitlerjugend), 110
Hausser, Paul, colonel general, 103
Himmler, Heinrich, commander, 105–107, 279, 280, 290

Waffen-SS (*Cont.*)
and military medals and decorations, 346, 347–348
military ranks, 340*t,* 343, 351
and Oradour-sur-Glane Massacre, 187
origins and history of, 170, 279–280, 289, 290
and Panzer Divisions, 190
and panzergrenadier divisions, 191
Peiper, Joachim, Obersturmbannführer, 194
and regular army, 208, 280
Skorzeny, Otto, Obersturmbannführer, 240
Stroop, Jürgen, lieutenant general, 255
and Warsaw Ghetto Uprising, 282
and Warsaw Rising, 282
wartime death toll, 281, 290
Wolff, Karl, general of, 296
Warlimont, Walter, **281**
Commissar Order drafted by, 281
conviction at American Military Tribunals and imprisonment, 9, 281
head of National Defense Section (L Section), 281
World War I service, 281
Warsaw, battle and siege of. *See* Poland Campaign
Warsaw Ghetto Uprising, **281–282**
Anielewicz, Mordechai, ŻOB commander, 282
background to, 281–282
conviction of Jürgen Stroop on charges related to, 255
destruction of ŻOB command post, 282
events of, 282
formation of Jewish Fighting Organization (Żobydska Organizacja Bojowa—ŻOB), 282
known as *Aufstand im Warschauer Ghetto,* 281
Warsaw Rising, **282–283**
Bach-Zelewski, Erich von dem, German commander, 25, 282–283
background to, 282
Bór-Komorowski, Tadeusz, Polish commander, 283–284
casualties, 283
events of, 282–283
and Operation BURZA (TEMPEST), 283
Soviet lack of support for Polish Home Army, 203, 283
Warships, surface, **283–289**
armored, heavy, and light cruisers, 285*t*
battleships and battle cruisers, 283, 284*t,* 287–288
Bismarck (battleship), 37, 135*t,* 136, 151, 195, 269–270, 288*f*
Bismarck-class battleships, 287
destroyers, 286*t,* 287
Deutschland-class armored ships ("pocket battleships"), 283, 287
diesel-engine propulsion, 283
and Dönitz, Karl, 288–289
heavy cruisers, 288
high-pressured warship steam plants, 287
interwar technological advances, 283
Königsberg light cruisers, 287
Prinz Eugen (heavy cruiser), 288*f*
radar warning devices, 288–289
and Raeder, Erich, navy commander, 283, 287–288
Schnellbooten (Fast Boats), 288
small destroyers designed as torpedo boats, 287
welding, 283
Wehrmacht (German Armed Forces), **289–291**
Federal Air Force officers, 350*t*
Federal Army officers, 350*t*
Federal Navy officers, 350*t*
officers in the Bundeswehr, 349–351
Wehrmacht compliance with the Commissar order (Doc. 5), 314–316
on "bush war" enemy resistance, 315
on casualties, shooting of prisoner because of resistance, 315

daily intelligence Report from I Army Corps to Eighteenth Army Headquarters, June 27, 1941, 314–315
daily intelligence report from I Army Corps to Fourth Panzer Group Headquarters, July 20, 1941, 315–316
evening report from V Army Corps to Ninth Army Headquarters, June 30, 1941, 315
on number of prisoners and number captured and shot, 316
on orders to prisoners to remove rank and unit insignia, to wear civilian clothing, 315
on shooting of fleeing military commissars, 315
on shooting of Red party secretary who remained in contact with Russian troops, 315
Wehrmacht Principal Operations Manual, HDv 300 *Truppenführung:* Introduction (Doc. 1), 309–311
assumptions of, 309
Beck, Ludwig, primary author of, 29
and Blitzkrieg doctrine, 41
conditions for amendments or additions, 309
contents of, 309
on influence of continual development on conduct of war, 309
on leadership and officers, 310–311
on situational nature of lessons of conduct of war, 310
on superior combat power, 310–311
on value, independence, and training of the individual, 310
on value of human character over intelligence, 310
on variety of combat situations, 310
on war as art founded on scientific principles, 309
Weichs zur Glon, Maximilian von, **291**
forced into retirement by Hitler after Fritsch Affair, 291
and France Campaign, 291
and German retreat from Balkans, 291
Hitler's lack of confidence in, 291
and Operation BARBAROSSA, 291
and Poland Campaign, 291
promotion to rank of field marshal in the Wehrmacht, 291, 338
transfer to Führer Reserve, 291
withdrawn from American Military Tribunals for medical reasons, 291
World War I service, 291
Westphal, Siegfried, **291–292**
and Ardennes Offensives, 13, 291–292
early military career, 291
rejection of National Socialism, 292
roles in Sicily and Italy campaigns, 291
wounding of, 291
Westwall, **292**
and Allied Hürtgen Forest Campaign, 113–114
and Allied Lorraine Campaign, 147
and Allied Palatinate Campaign, 189
and Allied Rhineland Offensive, 215–216
also known as Siegfried Line, 292
and Ardennes Offensive, 12
and Battle of the Reichswald, 210
construction of, 187, 207, 292
and French invasion of the Saarland, 229
Hitler's authorization of, 20, 292
impact on Allied strategy, 292
See also Siegried Line Campaign, Allied; Westwall, Allied advance to
Westwall, Allied advance to, **292–294**
Bradley, Omar, 12th Army Group commander, 293
casualties, 293
and Channel ports, 293
German general retreat, 293
liberation of Antwerp, 293
liberation of Brussels, 293
liberation of Paris, 293
Montgomery, Bernard, 21st Army Group commander, 293

Westwall, Allied (*Cont.*)
objectives, 293
planning and preparation for, 292–293
See also Ardennes Offensive (Battle of the Bulge)
Wever, Walther, **294**
chief of the Luftwaffe High Command General Staff, 334*t*
first chief of the OKL General Staff, 335
impact of death on Luftwaffe priorities, 5, 294
role in formation of *Luftwaffe,* 294
Wilhelm Gustloff sinking, **294–295**
events of, 294–295
history of *Wilhelm Gustloff,* 294
use of in World War II, 294–295
Witzleben, Erwin von, **295**
and Battle of France, 295
conviction by Nazi People's Court and murder of, 295
First Army commander, 295
forced into retirement by Hitler, 295
and French invasion of the Saarland, 229
Oberbefehlshaber West in France, 295
promotion to rank of field marshal in the Wehrmacht, 338
World War I service, 295
Wolf Pack tactics (*Rudeltaktik*), **295–296**
and battle of convoys SC 122 and HX 229, 65
and Battle of the Atlantic, 20
and Black May, Allied anti-U-boat campaign, 38, 73, 296
description and details of, 296
description of, 296
and Dönitz, Karl, 20, 73, 295–296
and USS *Kearny* incident, 275
weakness of radio communication, 296
Wolff, Karl, **296–297**
chief of Himmler's personal staff, 296
conviction of war crimes in West Germany, 297
coordinator of transportation for deportation to death camps, 296
secret talks Allies and treaty of unconditional surrender, 277, 296–297
Supreme Commander of all SS forces in Italy, 296
World War I service, 296

Yugoslavia Campaign, **298**
background to, 298
casualties, 298
events of, 298
Führer Directive 25, "Plans for Invading Yugoslavia," 89*t*
and Greece Campaign, 99, 100
Hausser, Paul, 2nd SS Division commander, 103
impact of, 298
Kleist, Paul von, First Panzer Group commander, 298
Löhr, Alexander, Luftflotte 4 commander, 299
planning and preparation for, 298
Reinhardt, Georg-Hans, XLI Panzer Corps commander, 298
Zeitzler, Kurt, chief of staff of First Panzer Army, 299

Zeitzler, Kurt, **299**
and Battle of Kursk, 299
and Battle of Stalingrad, 299
chief of *Oberkommando des Heeres* (OKH), 92–93, 185, 299
chief of staff of First Panzer Army, 299
falling out with Hitler, 299
and invasion of Poland, 299
nickname "*Kugelblitz*" (Thunderball), 299
postwar imprisonment and release, 299
World War I service, 299